A Guide to Manuscript Collections

A Guide to Manuscript Collections
of the
Indiana Historical Society
and
Indiana State Library

Eric Pumroy

with
Paul Brockman

Indianapolis
Indiana Historical Society
1986

Library of Congress Cataloging-in-Publication Data

Pumroy, Eric, 1952-
   A guide to the manuscript collections of the
Indiana Historical Society and the Indiana State
Library.

   Includes index.
   1. Indiana—History—Manuscripts—Catalogs.
   2. Indiana—History—Sources—Bibliography—Catalogs.
   3. Manuscripts—Indiana—Catalogs. 4. Indiana
Historical Society—Catalogs. 5. Indiana State
Library—Catalogs. I. Brockman, Paul. II. Indiana
Historical Society. III. Indiana State Library.
IV. Title.
Z1281.P85 1986 [F526]   016.9772   86-18593
ISBN 0-87195-006-5

Copyright 1986 by the Indiana Historical Society

CONTENTS

Preface vii
History of the Collections xi
Use of the Guide xvii
Collections of the Indiana Historical Society 1
Collections of the Indiana Division, Indiana State Library 205
Notes on Index Usage 423
Index 425

PREFACE

The preparation of this volume began in 1978 when the Indiana Historical Society hired me as an assistant manuscripts librarian with the special assignment of preparing a guide to the Society's manuscript collections. At that point the project had been under consideration for almost a decade. Gayle Thornbrough, the Society's executive secretary and its director of library and publications, had seen the need for a guide to publicize the Society's collections since her appointment to the director's position in 1968. Additional impetus for the Society to undertake the project came in the mid-1970s when Society editor Lana Ruegamer became an advocate for it. Eli Lilly's generous bequest to the Society in 1977 settled the problem of funding, and so shortly thereafter the decision was made to begin.

The first few years after the Lilly bequest were transition ones for the Historical Society and its library, with major changes both in priorities and in staff. As a consequence, the guide frequently had to be shelved in favor of more pressing matters. By the summer of 1982 the greater part of the guide entries had been written, but by that point it had become evident that the guide would be of much greater value to researchers if it also contained the collections of the Indiana State Library's Indiana Division, located just a flight of stairs away from the Society. In the late 1970s the Society and the State Library had discussed preparing separate guides to their collections, with the two to be published as companion volumes. By 1982, however, the State Library had seen its staff substantially reduced as a part of the general budget-cutting within the Indiana state government and so was in no position to undertake the preparation of a guide on its own. With the support of State Library director C. Ray Ewick and manuscripts librarian Marybelle Burch, the Historical Society staff proposed to expand the guide to include the State Library's collections. Under the proposal, I was to write the State Library's guide descriptions, aided by an assistant hired specifically for the project. In the fall of 1983 the Historical Society's Board of Trustees generously approved funding for the two-year project, which was scheduled to start in January 1984. As project assistant the Society hired Paul Brockman, who had previously worked on the Historical Society's *Indiana Newspaper Bibliography* and the Indiana Guide project.

This volume is intended to serve as a guide to the major manuscript collections in the two repositories rather than as a catalog to their entire holdings. The two libraries together hold more than six thousand separate collections, but the great majority of them are small collections containing only a few items, microfilm copies or photocopies of original documents held elsewhere, or family and local histories. Although the collections included in the guide represent only about fifteen percent of the total number of collection titles, they contain more than three-quarters of the total volume of original manuscripts. The limitation on the scope of the guide has served two purposes. First, it has helped to keep the size of both the project and this volume within manageable proportions. Second, and more important, it has given the project staff the opportunity to examine and describe the major collections more thoroughly than would otherwise have been possible. It is hoped that by concentrating on the major collections this guide has highlighted the strengths of the two repositories, thereby both helping researchers locate relevant materials for their work and stimulating research ideas on Indiana and midwestern history.

Researchers who are interested in using the collections of the Indiana Historical Society and the Indiana State Library are encouraged to call or write before visiting. Given advance notice, staff members can do preliminary searching and retrieval, enabling visiting researchers to make the best use of their time. Inquiries should be addressed to the Manuscripts Department, Indiana Historical Society Library, 315 W. Ohio St., Indianapolis, IN 46202 (317-232-1879), and to the Manuscripts Section, Indiana Division, Indiana State Library, 140 N. Senate Ave., Indianapolis, IN 46204 (317-232-3671).

Acknowledgements

A number of people were directly involved in the preparation of this volume. Foremost among these is Paul Brockman, who had the lonely task of working his way through the mountain of semi-processed twentieth-century collections in the Indiana State Library. He also prepared the index and handled much of the editorial work. The State Library part of the guide also depended heavily upon the advice and assistance of manuscripts librarian Marybelle Burch and her assistants Noraleen Young and Karen Rench. Thanks also go to the Society's library secretary Susan Darnell, who helped with much of the typing and correction work, and Elizabeth Vobach, who worked as a research assistant on the project during the summer of 1980. This volume also benefited greatly from the assistance and advice of the members of the Society's editorial division, Paula Corpuz, Kent Calder, and Kathy Breen.

Support and encouragement for the project came in abundance from Society executive secretary Gayle Thornbrough, as well as from her successor, Peter T. Harstad. The director of the Indiana Historical Society Library, Robert K. O'Neill, was strongly supportive of the expansion of the guide, and advised and assisted with the writing of proposals and other administrative work connected with the project. Support also came from O'Neill's predecessor, Thomas A. Rumer; from Indiana State Library director C. Ray Ewick; and from the Indiana Division heads Robert Logsdon and Byron Swanson. The staff of the Historical Society's Manuscripts Department showed considerable forbearance with this prolonged project, especially during the State Library phase. For this, thanks go to current and former department members Leona Alig, Carolyn Autry, Sally Childs-Helton, F. Gerald Handfield, Charles Latham, Connie McBirney, Linda Carlson Sharp, and Donald West. Thanks also go to Lana Ruegamer, whose unwavering enthusiasm for the project helped to brighten some of the long days, and to my wife, Ann Koopman, who has given me advice and support throughout the duration of the project.

Finally, thanks must go to two groups of people without whose efforts this guide would not have been possible: the donors who generously contributed their collections to the Historical Society and State Library, and the staff members and volunteers who worked to acquire them and make them accessible. Of the latter group, there are five people in particular who must be singled out for special recognition for the critical roles they played in developing the two libraries' collections. For the Historical Society they are Caroline Dunn, librarian from 1939 to 1973, Leona Alig, manuscripts librarian from 1962 to 1978, and Gayle Thornbrough, director of the library and publications from 1968 to 1981 and executive secretary from 1976 to 1984. For the State Library they are Esther Uhl McNitt, Indiana Division head from 1923 to 1941, and Hazel Hopper, manuscripts librarian from the mid-1930s to 1946 and Indiana Division head from 1946 to 1975. Their lifelong devotion to the preservation of Indiana's historical records was remarkable. The people of Indiana are much in their debt.

Eric Pumroy
June 1986

HISTORY OF THE COLLECTIONS*

The private Indiana Historical Society and the public Indiana State Library had their beginnings only a few years apart in the early nineteenth century. The Indiana General Assembly created the State Library in 1827 as a legal research library for use by legislators and government officials. The library later expanded its scope to include works on history, politics, and other matters of interest to state government officials, but it acquired very little on Indiana history throughout most of the nineteenth century. By contrast, the Indiana Historical Society was organized specifically to preserve written documentation on the history of the state. Founded in Indianapolis in 1830 as a private organization, the Society had a membership which included some of the most important political and business leaders in the state. In spite of its ambitious charge and prestigious leadership, however, the Society functioned only intermittently for the following half century. Its most promising moment came in 1859, when the General Assembly appropriated five hundred dollars to the Society for the acquisition of books and documents on Indiana history. In the following two years the Society was able to build a respectable collection, but the Civil War put an end to this revival. After 1861 the Society was dormant for more than a decade, and much of its library was lost.

Both the Historical Society and the State Library changed their attitudes about collecting Indiana history in the late nineteenth century. In 1886 banker and 1880 Democratic Party vice-presidential nominee William H. English led a small group of prominent Indianapolis men in a reorganization of the Historical Society. The members of the new Society placed their emphasis on writing and publishing, in part as a matter of personal interest, but also because of their awareness of the repeated failures of their predecessors to maintain a collection. Although largely abandoning their own ambitions for a library, Society members recognized the need for someone to collect research materials on the history of the state, and they saw the State Library as the proper institution to do it. The State Library was an unpromising candidate, however, for it had never been adequately funded and its leadership changed every two years when the legislature elected a new librarian.

---

*The principal published source on the history of the two libraries is Lana Ruegamer, *A History of the Indiana Historical Society, 1830-1980* (Indianapolis: Indiana Historical Society, 1980).

In 1888 the Society's members led a successful campaign to increase substantially the State Library's funding from the legislature, and in the mid-1890s they were active in the successful effort to pry the State Library out from the direct control of the legislature and to place it under the nonpartisan State Board of Education.

The State Library flourished under the new arrangements. For the first time there was stability in the library's leadership. While twelve people had served as state librarian between 1865 and 1897, only eight have served in the ninety years since. With greater funding and stable, professional leadership, the State Library was able to expand its mission and make long-range plans. One of the first new areas of responsibility which it defined was the collection of books, newspapers, and manuscripts on the state's history. In 1906 the State Library's board approved the establishment of a Department of Archives and History to administer the collections, with a part-time head, Earlham College History professor Harlow Lindley. In 1913 the General Assembly made the department permanent and gave it the responsibility for preserving public records as well. During the first quarter of the twentieth century, the State Library acquired a number of major manuscript collections on early Indiana, including the papers of the Lasselle family, French Indian traders in Vincennes and Logansport (1908), of John Tipton, land speculator and politician (1915), of Noah Noble, early governor and internal improvements advocate (1918), and of the Ewing brothers, Indian traders in Fort Wayne (1922). Because of this active collecting program, the State Library quickly overflowed its rooms in the State Capitol. By 1910 plans began to be laid for a separate State Library building, with the Historical Society joining other interested groups in lobbying for a new facility. In spite of a number of setbacks, the effort eventually paid off in 1929 when the General Assembly approved the construction of the Indiana State Library and Historical Building.

By this time the Historical Society had also revived its plans for a research library. When *Indianapolis News* publisher Delavan Smith died in 1922, he left to the Historical Society the extensive library of Americana collected by his father, journalist and historian William Henry Smith. The younger Smith also left a bequest of $150,000 to support the collection. During the 1920s the Society considered several locations for this new library, but the most attractive one was the planned State Library Building. In 1931 the Historical Society and the State Library reached an agreement in which the State Library would house and staff the Society's library. Under this agreement, the Smith bequest would have been used exclusively for acquisitions, and the Smith Library would have functioned as the rare book room of the State Library. This administrative unification of the two libraries collapsed even before the State Library building opened, for it depended upon the state government's willingness to hire a librarian for the Smith Library. Because of the Depression the state balked at adding a new position to the payroll, and so a new agreement was drawn up late in 1933 which placed the Smith Library within the State Library Building but independent of the State Library director's authority. Now responsible for staffing its library, the Historical Society hired Florence Venn, the longtime head of the State Library's reference division.

When the Indiana State Library Building opened in 1934 it contained two repositories of books and manuscripts on Indiana history: the Historical Society's William Henry Smith Memorial Library and the State Library's newly formed Indiana Division. At that point the Historical Society's collections were limited, consisting primarily of William Henry Smith's library and a collection of manuscripts on early Indiana accumulated by William H. English which had been purchased in 1932. The Indiana Division, with a much larger staff and an established reputation, grew at a much more rapid rate than the Smith Library during the 1930s. Under the leadership of Division head Esther Uhl McNitt, the library acquired some of its most significant manuscript collections then, including the papers of patent attorney and politician Robert S. Taylor (1929), of fur trader Allen Hamilton (1938), and of politicians Daniel D. Pratt (1932), Richard W. Thompson (1937-1941), and the Embree family of Princeton, Indiana (1937).

During their first decade together the two libraries were able to work out a rough division of collecting responsibility. The Historical Society, blessed with an endowment for acquisitions, assumed responsibility for purchasing the more expensive early printed and manuscript material on Indiana and the Midwest, while the Indiana Division concentrated on collecting materials from the mid-nineteenth century on. Originally, the Historical Society expected to emphasize books rather than manuscripts, but opportunities to purchase important collections altered that plan. The foundation for the Society's manuscript collections was laid in the late 1930s and the 1940s with the purchase of a number of significant collections. The most important of these was the autograph collection of Arthur G. Mitten, purchased in 1939. In addition to documents of hundreds of American historical figures, the Mitten Collection contained an extensive collection of letters written by Indiana's first territorial governor, William Henry Harrison. These letters became the foundation for the Society's Harrison Collection, a collection which is still growing as new letters are purchased for it. Other important collections acquired at this time were the papers of Civil War general and novelist Lew Wallace (1940), the papers of army officer and land speculator Samuel Vance (1940-1943), and the papers of Vincennes fur trader Francis Vigo (1949).

In spite of the informal division of collecting responsibilities, the two libraries acquired very similar types of manuscript collections, principally nineteenth-century family papers. This overlap of collections did not lead to overt competition between the Historical Society and the State Library, partly because neither repository had an aggressive acquisitions program until the mid-1960s, and partly because of the good relations which have existed between the two governing boards and staffs. These good relationships were consciously fostered and they had the opportunity to develop because of the remarkable continuity of leadership in the two programs. For nearly thirty years the Smith Library and the Indiana Division were led by two women: Caroline Dunn, head librarian of the Smith Library from 1939 to 1973, and Hazel Hopper, Indiana Division head from 1946 to 1975. Also tying the public and private historical programs together was the unified leadership of the Society and the Indiana Historical Bureau, the state's historical agency. From 1924 to 1976 the Bureau's director also served as the Society's executive secretary. The three men who served in this dual position, Christopher Coleman (who also served as State Library director from 1936 to 1942), Howard Peckham, and Hubert Hawkins, all took a lively interest in building both libraries, steering collections to whichever one seemed most appropriate. Thus until the mid-1970s when Miss Dunn and Mrs. Hopper retired and the leadership of the Bureau and Society was split, there was little potential for the staffs of the two libraries to become competitive.

In the mid-1960s the acquisition programs for both libraries accelerated. The State Library added a field agent, Thomas Krasean, who began focusing on the collection of twentieth-century records. His initiatives were continued by his successors, John Newman, Randall Jehs, and F. Gerald Handfield (Krasean and Handfield are now director and assistant director, respectively, of the Society's Field Services Division). By the late 1970s the Indiana Division had built a strong twentieth-century collection, with particular strengths in the papers of Indiana's post-World War II politicians and in the records of women's organizations. The Society embarked on a brief expansion program in 1967, when a grant from the Lilly Endowment enabled it to hire former Indiana Superintendent of Public Instruction William E. Wilson as a field agent to collect manuscripts. Wilson stayed out of the Indiana Division's way by concentrating on nineteenth-century collections, and the program only lasted until his death in 1971. These expanded acquisition programs demonstrated the need for additional space in the State Library Building. In 1973 the state of Indiana and the Historical Society agreed to split the cost of an addition to the building, with half of the Society's two million dollar contribution coming from a personal gift from Society board member and pharmaceutical manufacturer Eli Lilly. The four-story addition opened in late 1976 with greatly expanded facilities for both the Indiana Historical Society and the manuscript collections of the Indiana Division.

Even before its move into the new building was completed, the Society saw a quadrupling of its endowment with a bequest from Eli Lilly, who died in January 1977. The effect on the Society's programs was dramatic. In 1976 the Society had a staff of eleven, with six in the library. In 1979 the Society's staff numbered forty-one, with thirteen in the library. The additional staff allowed the Society to expand its acquisitions program into the documentation of twentieth-century Indiana. Areas of particular collecting emphasis now include health and medicine, transportation, agriculture, architecture, social welfare, ethnics, and blacks. This guide includes descriptions of some of the first fruits of this new acquisition activity, such as the records of the Indianapolis Asylum for Friendless Colored Children, the Jewish Welfare Federation of Indianapolis, the Family Service Association of Indianapolis, the American Lung Association of Indiana, and the black cosmetics firm, the Madame C. J. Walker Company. In spite of this expanded activity on the part of the Historical Society, the two libraries have avoided competing for collections. In the early 1980s the staffs negotiated areas of collecting emphasis. These negotiations served as the basis for the formal collecting policy which the Historical Society adopted in 1983, in which the Society outlined both the areas it would collect and those it would leave to the State Library.

The Indiana Historical Society and the Indiana State Library have had a long and unusual history together. While it is not uncommon for states to have both private and public repositories for historical materials, Indiana is unique in having them in the same building. There certainly have been disadvantages to this arrangement, particularly for researchers who have been inconvenienced by the necessity of visiting two libraries, each of which has a distinctive method of cataloging its collections. On the positive side, though, the existence of two repositories rather than one has meant that there have been more people working for the preservation of the state's historical records, and as a consequence, that more records have been saved. Because of their combined efforts, the Indiana Historical Society and the Indiana State Library have built a rich collection, one which is invaluable for understanding not only Indiana's history, but the history of the Midwest and the nation as well.

USE OF THE GUIDE

This guide contains descriptions of more than 800 major collections of original manuscripts held by the Indiana Historical Society and the Indiana Division of the Indiana State Library. For the purpose of this guide, major collections are defined as collections containing at least 20 items, or with an extent of at least .25 linear feet. Not included in this guide are smaller collections; collections for which the libraries hold copies rather than originals; manuscript genealogies and local histories; and unprocessed collections. Both repositories have card catalogs and other in-house finding aids which will provide access to their entire holdings.

FORMAT OF THE ENTRIES

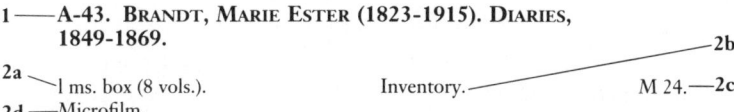

1—— A-43. BRANDT, MARIE ESTER (1823-1915). DIARIES, 1849-1869. ——2b

2a — 1 ms. box (8 vols.).   Inventory.   M 24.——2c
2d ——Microfilm.

> Brandt was a Quaker sabbath school teacher in Hanover, Jefferson Co.; and ——3
> daughter of a farmer and general store owner in Hanover.
>
> The diary entries describe daily life, social activities, and Civil War experiences ——4
> in the towns of Hanover and Madison and at Hanover College.

The collection descriptions are divided into four parts:

1. Title information, including inclusive dates of the records in the collection and life-span dates of the person for whom the collection was named. The title is preceded by a number that identifies the collection in the index. Numbers which begin with the prefix "A" are Historical Society collections; those with "B" are State Library collections.

2. Administrative information, consisting of the following:

    a. Size of collection. The size may be measured in number of items for small collections; number of manuscript or archival boxes (archival boxes = 1 linear foot; IHS ms. boxes = .25 l.f.; ISL ms. boxes = .4 l.f.); and in linear feet of shelf space when the collection contains bound volumes or more than one type of container.

xvii

b. An in-house finding aid, other than the repository's card catalog. In most cases, the finding aids will be either a calendar (an item listing of the contents of the collection arranged chronologically), or an inventory (a summary description of the collection, usually with a list of box or folder headings. The term inventory has been used loosely to accommodate the wide variety of finding aids which have been prepared over the years.)

c. Collection shelf number. For Indiana Historical Society collections the series designations are "M" for collections consisting of at least 1 ms. box; "SC" for collections of less than 1 ms. box; "BV" for bound volumes; and "OM" for oversize materials. For the Indiana State Library collections, the designations are "L" for collections of at least 1 box; "S" for collections of less than 1 box; and "V" for bound volumes. Many of the State Library's largest collections are stored in a separate stacks area and have no shelf number.

d. Additional information. If a microfilm copy of the collection exists, or if parts of the collection are restricted, such information will be indicated here.

3. Biographical sketch of the principal person or persons, or historical sketch of the organization or business.

4. Description of the collection contents.

In sections 3 and 4, town names are followed by either the county name for Indiana towns or the state or country name for non-Indiana towns. The principal exception to this rule is Indianapolis. For example, Fort Wayne, Kokomo and Indianapolis will be listed as "Fort Wayne, Allen Co., Kokomo, Howard Co., and Indianapolis."

Following the collection descriptions is a proper name/subject index, with entries keyed to the guide number. For guidelines on use of the index, see the Index Introduction (page 423).

COLLECTIONS
OF THE
INDIANA HISTORICAL SOCIETY

A-1. A. D. Cook Company. Records, 1890-1955.

11 ms. boxes, 28 vols. (6 l.f.). Inventory. M 393, BV 2048-2075.

August D. Cook (1847-1921), a German immigrant, founded the company in 1881 in Lawrenceburg, Dearborn Co., to manufacture pumps and other water well equipment. Cook was succeeded as company president by his son-in-law, Cornelius O'Brien (1883-1953). The company was sold in 1947.

The collection consists of the company's product catalogs (1890-1940); financial records (1922-1938); inventories (1929-1948); manufacturing information (1927-1938); and personal ledgers of O'Brien and his daughters (1916-1955).

A-2. Abernathy, John (b.1816). Account Books, 1853-1906.

2 vols. (.25 l.f.). BV 248-249.

Abernathy owned a general store in Melrose, Rush Co.

The collection consists of Abernathy's store account books (1853-1861). Included in the volumes are newspaper obituaries of Rush County people (1900-1906).

A-3. Adams, Marcellus M. (1834-1909). Papers, 1775-1909.

1 ms. box. Calendar. M 1.

Adams was a physician in Greenfield, Hancock Co.; and a soldier in the 45th Indiana Regiment (1862-1863).

The bulk of the papers are legal documents from the period 1863-1909 and include Adams's Civil War military papers, pension records, land records, and business papers. Also included are family land records from Hancock and Rush counties (1835-1852); and personal correspondence (1879-1909), including letters regarding his family's history.

A-4. AIKEN, OLIVER PERRY (fl.1850-1886). PAPERS, 1833-1886.

107 items. SC 7.

Aiken was a farmer in Vanderburgh and Warrick counties.

The papers consist principally of Aiken's correspondence, legal documents, and financial records relating to farming and the shipping of agricultural products from Newburgh, Warrick Co., and Evansville, Vanderburgh Co. (1850-1886). Also included are letters from merchants in Lawrenceburg, Dearborn Co., and New Orleans, La.; and Aiken family legal documents (1833-1850).

A-5. ALLEN, EDWARD B. (fl.1848-1871). PAPERS, 1854-1864.

36 items. SC 10.

Allen was a Terre Haute, Vigo Co., politician; member, Vigo County Council (1854); county auditor (1859-1864); and captain, 71st Indiana Regiment (1862).

The papers consist primarily of Allen's correspondence from the period 1860-1864 concerning the Civil War and state and local Republican Party politics.

Correspondents include Will Cumback, Henry S. Lane, Oliver P. Morton, Lazarus Noble, Caleb Smith, W. H. H. Terrell, Richard W. Thompson, David Turpie, John P. Usher, and Joseph A. Wright.

A-6. AMERICAN LUNG ASSOCIATION OF INDIANA. RECORDS, 1904-1980.

42 ms. boxes, 1 oversize box.   Inventory.   M 384, OM 129.

The association was organized as the Indiana Society for the Prevention of Tuberculosis in 1904 and became the Indiana Tuberculosis Association in

1920. In its early years the association concentrated on combating tuberculosis through lobbying on behalf of public health legislation in the state, sponsoring public health education programs, providing financial support for TB research, and testing people for TB. The association was affiliated with a number of other tuberculosis groups, including county TB associations and the Indiana Trudeau Society, organized in 1931 for physicians interested in TB research and treatments. Since the 1960s the association has shifted its emphasis from TB to lung cancer and other respiratory diseases. In 1974 the association was reorganized as the American Lung Association of Indiana, reflecting its formal relationship with the national American Lung Association.

The records are principally from the period 1930-1970 and include minutes of board of directors, executive committee, and annual meetings (1930-1970); financial statements and budgets (1930-1975); and correspondence, reports, and printed materials reflecting the activities of the state officers (1904-1980). Also included are minutes, annual reports, correspondence, and other materials from county tuberculosis associations throughout the state, particularly Grant, Howard, Madison, Miami, Spencer, Vanderburgh, Vigo, and Wayne counties (1909-1973); records of associated organizations, including the Indiana Trudeau Society (1931-1971), the Indiana Tuberculosis Council (1949-1976), the Indiana Conference of Tuberculosis Workers (1947-1970), and the Mississippi Valley Conference on Tuberculosis (1921-1965); records relating to the American Lung Association, the National Tuberculosis Association, and other national TB and lung disease organizations (1917-1980); and records relating to the Indiana State Board of Health and other state and local health agencies and organizations (1913-1974).

A-7. AMERICAN RED CROSS, INDIANAPOLIS AREA CHAPTER. RECORDS, 1916-1968.

10 archival boxes.   Inventory.

The chapter is the Indianapolis affiliate of the American Red Cross.

The records include the chapter's minutes and annual reports (1916-1951); scrapbooks of newspaper clippings about local and national Red Cross activities (1918-1919, 1941-1957); financial reports (1918-1952); and brochures, pamphlets, and Red Cross magazines, principally from the 1940s and 1950s.

A-8. ARMSTRONG, JOHN (1755-1816). PAPERS, 1775-1950.

20 ms. boxes, 1 oversize box. Calendar. M 6, OM 73.
Microfilm.

Soldier, merchant, and land speculator. Armstrong served as a soldier and officer with the 3rd and 12th Pennsylvania regiments (1776-1784) and the United States Army in the West (1784-1793); he participated in Pennsylvania's conflict with the Connecticut settlers at Wyoming (1783-1784), was commandant at Fort Pitt (1785-1786), was stationed at Fort Finney (1786-1790), explored the lower Missouri River and the Wabash River (1790), participated in the military expeditions of Col. Josiah Harmar (1790) and Gen. Arthur St. Clair (1791), and was commandant at Fort Hamilton (1791-1792). Armstrong was also owner of a general store near Cincinnati, Ohio (1793-ca.1807); Hamilton County, Ohio, justice of the peace (1796-1797); treasurer, Northwest Territory (1796-1802); officer in the Hamilton County militia (1796-ca.1807); land speculator in Pennsylvania, Ohio, and Indiana; and resident of Clark County, Ind. (1814-1817). Armstrong's family included his father-in-law, William Goforth (1731-1807), a merchant in New York, Philadelphia, and Hamilton County, Ohio (1789-1807), Hamilton County judge (1790), member of the Northwest Territory legislature (1799), and president pro tem of the Ohio constitutional convention (1802); and Armstrong's son, William G. Armstrong (1797-1858), a businessman in Bethlehem and Charlestown, Clark Co. (1816-1858), Whig member, Indiana House of Representatives (1822-1825, 1834-1837) and Indiana State Senate (1838-1841), and president of the Jeffersonville Railroad Company (1847-1858).

The collection consists principally of papers from the period 1779-1867. John Armstrong's papers include his military correspondence regarding supplies, military operations, and relations with the Indians and settlers (1782-1793), including retained copies of his letters and reports to James Wilkinson, Arthur St. Clair, Anthony Wayne, and other officers; his notebooks containing copies of orders, military correspondence, and accounts (1781-1793), including accounts for Fort Pitt and Fort Finney (1785-1790), and garrison orders for Fort Hamilton and Fort Washington (1792); bills, receipts, and accounts for army contractors (1784-1793); personal business documents, including surveys, indentures, receipts, and correspondence regarding his mercantile business and land speculation (1780s-1816); account books for his general store in Cincinnati (1793-1811) and other business ventures; a notebook for his business as Northwest Territory treasurer (1798); documents relating to his work as Hamilton County justice of the peace (1796-1797); and correspondence and papers regarding the claims of Richard McCarty as a member of George Rogers Clark's Illinois expedition (1779, 1788-1818).

William Goforth papers include daybooks for his businesses in New York City (1774-1788) and Cincinnati (1788-1816); Hamilton County court records (1790-1794, 1805); and diary of his trip from New York to Ohio (1788-1789). William G. Armstrong papers include correspondence of Armstrong and his mother, Tabitha Armstrong Lockhart (d.1848), with family members in Brookville, Franklin Co., LaPorte, LaPorte Co., Cincinnati and Madisonville, Ohio, and Georgetown, Ky. (1817-1858); indentures, receipts, correspondence, and other papers relating to his land and business dealings (1816-1858); correspondence regarding the Indiana legislature and the Whig Party in Indiana (1820s-1840s); and papers relating to the Jeffersonville Railroad Company (1847-1858). The collection also includes family correspondence of William G. Armstrong, Jr., of Jeffersonville (1858-1867); and correspondence of Charles F. Cochran regarding John Armstrong and the Armstrong family (1896-1950).

Included are papers and correspondence of John Brown, Jacob Burnet, Charles Cist, George Rogers Clark, Jonathan Clark, William Clark, Isaac Craig, Ebenezer Denny, Charles Dewey, John B. Dillon, Daniel Drake, William M. Dunn, Williamson Dunn, William G. Ewing, Paul Fearing, John S. Gano, John Francis Hamtramck, Josiah Harmar, William Henry Harrison, William Hendricks, Samuel Hodgdon, Henry Knox, James F. D. Lanier, John Law, John McLean, Joseph G. Marshall, Nathaniel Massie, George Morgan, Benjamin Parke, Joseph Francis Perrault, Arthur St. Clair, Winthrop Sargent, Benjamin Sebastian, Caleb B. Smith, Oliver H. Smith, Jeremiah Sullivan, Caleb Swan, John Cleves Symmes, Pierre Tardiveau, James Taylor, Richard W. Thompson, Anthony Wayne, William Wells, Albert S. White, James Wilkinson, and John P. Wyllys.

A-9. ARMSTRONG, JOHN H. (1809-1885). FAMILY PAPERS, 1828-1957.

3 ms. boxes.   Inventory.   M 410, OM 112.

Armstrong, son of Col. John Armstrong, was a cabinetmaker, lumber dealer, and farmer in LaPorte, LaPorte Co.; and was active in the spiritualist movement with his wife, Susannah Beggs Armstrong. Armstrong's family included Alphonso Adkins, a LaPorte railroad man, and Adkins's children, Irvin Ryan

Adkins, a Chicago, Ill., businessman, and Alta Viola Adkins, a Hammond, Lake Co., schoolteacher.

The collection consists principally of family correspondence from the period 1850-1902, including letters to Armstrong and his wife from their children and relatives in Jeffersonville, Clark Co., Centerville, Wayne Co., and Illinois, Iowa, Kansas, Nebraska, Oregon, and Minnesota (1859-1893); correspondence between Alphonso Adkins and his wife, written while he was engaged in railroad work in Nebraska (1856-1881); and letters to Adkins and his wife from their children. Also included are receipts and financial records of the Armstrong and Adkins families (1839-1909); Armstrong's account book from the 1840s and 1850s which includes writings on spiritualism; essays, poetry, and notes on religion and spiritualism; and family history information on the Armstrong and related families.

A-10. ASHTON, WILLIAM A. (fl.1839-1862). PAPERS, 1840-1869.

50 items. SC 28, BV 89.

Ashton was a physician in England, Cincinnati, Ohio, and Franklin County, Ind.

The collection consists of notebooks and papers describing disease symptoms, treatments, and recipes for medicines. Also included is a diary (1864-1869) kept by Ashton's son, Samuel H. Ashton (1839-1918), a farmer near Mt. Carmel, Ohio.

A-11. ATALANTIAN JOURNAL, 1845-1848.

3 vols. (.25 l.f.). BV 261-263.

Manuscript weekly journal written by the Terre Haute Atalantian Literati.

The journal consists of writings on Indiana and midwestern history, travel accounts, and essays on literary and social topics. Among the contributors was law student Newton Booth (1825-1892), later governor of California.

A-12. AYRES, FREDERIC MURRAY (1872-1940). PAPERS, 1916-1923.

90 items. SC 35, BV 396.

Ayres was president of L.S. Ayres & Company, an Indianapolis department store (1896-1940).

The papers consist of correspondence and legal papers relating to Ayres's work as Indiana chairman of the YMCA campaign for war work funds (1917), and as an officer of the American Red Cross in Washington, D.C., and France (1918-1919). The collection also includes a scrapbook for the Rainbow Division Parade in Indianapolis (1923).

A-13. BAILEY, ELISHA T. (b.1821). ACCOUNT BOOKS, 1857-1867.

3 vols. (.33 l.f.). BV 42-44.

Bailey was a physician and merchant in Ridgeville, Randolph Co.

The collection consists of account books for Bailey's Ridgeville general store.

A-14. BAILEY, SARAH (b.1835). PAPERS, 1820-1895.

114 items. Calendar. SC 40.

Bailey lived in Richmond, Wayne Co.; and married William Gilbert in 1865.

The bulk of the papers are letters to Bailey from the period 1853-1872 from suitors, relatives in Wayne County, and relatives and friends serving in the Union Army during the Civil War.

A-15. BAKER, CONRAD (1817-1885). PAPERS, 1858-1902.

19 ms. boxes, 30 vols. (11 l.f.). Inventory. M 8.

Attorney and politician. Baker was an attorney in Evansville, Vanderburgh Co. (1841-1865), and Indianapolis (1873-1885); Whig member, Indiana House of Representatives (1845-1846); Republican candidate for lieutenant governor of Indiana (1856); colonel, 28th Indiana Regiment (1861-1864); assistant provost marshal general for Indiana (1863-1864); lieutenant governor of Indiana (1865-1867); acting governor during illness of Gov. Oliver P. Morton (1865-1866); governor of Indiana (1867-1873); and partner in the Indianapolis law firm of Baker, Hord & Hendricks (1873-1885), firm founded by Thomas A. Hendricks.

The collection consists principally of Baker's official papers as lieutenant governor and governor (1865-1873), including correspondence relating to elections and state and national Republican Party politics; correspondence on issues before the Indiana General Assembly, including claims from Morgan's Raid, the Indiana Hospital for the Insane, Ku Klux Klan activities in the state, the creation and location of a state agricultural college (Purdue University), and prison conditions and the creation of a woman's prison; correspondence, accounts, and receipts regarding the construction of the Supreme Court and State Office Building in Indianapolis (1867-1869); his letter books regarding business during legislative sessions (1869, 1871, 1872); his letter books and correspondence on routine government business, such as appointments, claims, and invitations; a report by Gen. Alvin P. Hovey, military commander of the District of Indiana, regarding the arrests and court martials of Indiana opponents of the war (August 1865); and court opinions and calendars, circulars, fugitive requisitions, and other printed materials. Also included is Baker's correspondence with his brother, William Baker (1813-1872), regarding family matters and personal business interests in Evansville (1865-1872); scrapbooks of newspaper clippings regarding Baker's political career, Indiana politics, and family members (1865-1872); papers of the law firm of Baker, Hord & Hendricks (1863-1887), including letter books, correspondence, and notes regarding the firm's legal work; an account book for Baker's estate (1885-1896); and a register and account book for Hemlock Lodge at Pine Hills, Montgomery Co. (1896-1902).

The collection also includes correspondence and letter books of Gov. Oliver P. Morton, including letters to Morton regarding politics, the conduct of the war, and routine government business (1861-1867); and Morton's letter books

(1864-1867) containing copies of his letters on politics and government business.

Correspondents include Horace P. Biddle, Noble C. Butler, Henry B. Carrington, John Coburn, Charles F. Coffin, Schuyler Colfax, Edward T. Cox, Henry H. Crapo, Will Cumback, Jefferson C. Davis, John Defrees, Ebenezer Dumont, John Dumont, Paris C. Dunning, William H. English, John Farquhar, John Watson Foster, Walter Q. Gresham, James Harlan, Rutherford B. Hayes, Thomas A. Hendricks, Barnabas Hobbs, William R. Holloway, Alvin P. Hovey, George W. Julian, Frederick Knefler, James F. D. Lanier, William H. H. Miller, Robert H. Milroy, Oliver P. Morton, Lazarus Noble, Richard J. Oglesby, Godlove Orth, David Dale Owen, Richard Owen, Robert Dale Owen, John U. Pettit, Daniel D. Pratt, William S. Rosecrans, William H. Seward, Edwin M. Stanton, Thaddeus Stevens, Jeremiah Sullivan, William H. H. Terrell, Richard W. Thompson, Lew Wallace, Anson Wolcott, and Joseph A. Wright.

A-16. BAKER, EVAN (fl.1780-1785). PAPERS, 1780-1785.

53 items.   Calendar.   SC 43.

Baker, of Washington County, Va., was Virginia's commissary general to the Western Department during the American Revolution.

The collection consists of receipts and vouchers for supplies purchased for the state by Baker and his assistant, Nathaniel Logan; and of subpoenas and depositions relating to a subsequent court case between Baker and Logan.

A-17. BAKER, HENRY (1832-1911). DIARIES, 1875-1911.

3 ms. boxes (31 vols.).   M 29.

Baker was a farmer near Worthington, Greene Co.

The diaries include descriptions of events in Greene County, Baker's reminiscences of growing up in Indiana, and references to his work with local temperance groups.

A-18. BALL, TIMOTHY HORTON (1826-1913). PAPERS, 1826-1910.

1 ms. box.　　　　　　　　Inventory.　　　　　　　　M 309.

Ball grew up in Cedar Lake, Lake Co.; was a student at Franklin College, Franklin, Johnson Co. (1848-1851), and the Newton Theological Seminary, West Newton, Mass. (1860-1863); a Baptist minister in Lake County (1855-1913); founder of the Crown Point Institute (1865); and author of three histories of Lake County.

The papers include correspondence from family and friends in West Springfield, Mass. (1837), Valparaiso, Porter Co. (1847), and from friends attending school at North Wilbraham Academy, Mass., LaPorte University, LaPorte Co., and Wabash College, Montgomery Co. (1846-1848); Ball's diary (1839-1847); personal financial documents (1850s-1860s); papers relating to the Cedar Lake Lyceum, Lake Co.; and papers relating to Franklin College and the Newton Theological Seminary.

A-19. BANTA, ROBERT M. (fl.1860-1888). PAPERS, 1860-1865.

1 ms. box.　　　　　　　　Inventory.　　　　　　　　M 317.

Banta was a storekeeper in Franklin, Johnson Co.

The collection consists of letters written to Banta during the Civil War. Among the correspondents were relatives in Iowa and Indiana writing about farm and family matters, and soldiers serving in the 7th Indiana and 13th Iowa regiments writing about army life.

A-20. BAPTIST CHURCH. LAUGHERY ASSOCIATION. CORRESPONDENCE, 1816-1879.

1 ms. box.　　　　　　　　　　　　　　　　　　　　M 46.

The Laughery Association was founded in 1818 as an association of Baptist churches in Dearborn, Ohio, Ripley, and Switzerland counties.

The collection consists of correspondence, communications, and reports from churches affiliated with the association. Included are original letters (1818-1851) and copies of letters (1816-1879) from the collection at Franklin College, Franklin, Johnson Co.

A-21. BARKER, ISAAC (d.1898). PAPERS, 1864-1865.

27 items.   Calendar.   SC 57.

Barker, from Westfield, Hamilton Co., served in the 147th Indiana Regiment at Camp Carrington in Indianapolis, and in Virginia (1865).

The collection consists of letters from Barker to his wife while he served in the Union Army during the Civil War; and letters to Barker and his wife from William Kepner, 1st U.S. Veteran Volunteer Engineers, in Tennessee, Georgia, and Alabama (1864-1865).

A-22. BARNARD, HARRY EVERETT (1874-1946). PAPERS, 1888-1947.

18 ms. boxes.   Inventory.   M 10.

Barnard was a chemist with the U.S. Smokeless Powder Factory at the Naval Proving Ground, Indian Head, Md. (1900-1901); chemist with the New Hampshire State Board of Health (1901-1905); staff member of the Indiana State Board of Health, Indianapolis (1905-1919); member of the Indiana Food and Drug Commission (1907-1919); director of the American Institute of Baking, Chicago, Ill. (1920s); member of numerous professional and trade associations; in 1901 married Marion Harvie (1875-1969?), an English immigrant (ca.1892), a student at Brown University, R.I. (1898-1901), and an active member of woman's suffrage organizations in Indiana. The family also included Marion Barnard's sister, Dr. Alice Harvie Duden (1873-1926), a Newport, R.I., dental assistant (1895-1900), a student at the Philadelphia Dental School (1900-ca.1903), and a dentist in Concord, N.H. (ca.1903-1907), and Indianapolis (1907-1926); married Indianapolis chemist Hans Duden (1907).

The collection consists principally of family and personal correspondence from the period 1892-1926. Included are personal letters to Marion Harvie from friends and suitors in Great Britain and New England (1892-1900); correspondence between Marion Harvie at Brown University and Harry Barnard at Indian Head, Md. (1900-1901); correspondence between the Barnards and Alice Harvie Duden (1901-1926); letters to Duden from dental colleagues (ca.1900-1926); and letters of condolence to Marion Barnard on the death of her husband (1946-1947). Also included are schoolbooks of Marion Harvie; Barnard's report on meat inspection (ca.1910); and a pocket diary of Hans Duden (1910).

A-23. BARNES COLLECTION, 1833-1925.

4 ms. boxes.　　　　　　　　　Inventory.　　　　　　　　　M 11.

The collection was acquired from the Burton Historical Collection, Detroit Public Library, in 1963.

The collection includes personal correspondence, business correspondence, and legal documents of people throughout Indiana, principally from the 1850s through the 1890s. Included are warranty deeds, mortgages, estate inventories, and other legal documents from 55 Indiana counties, particularly from Cass, Jefferson, Newton, Parke, and Wayne counties (1833-1925); correspondence and business papers of D.D. Dykeman, a Logansport, Cass Co., politician and proprietor of the Lock Foundry and Machine Shop (1867-1915); letters to Frank Morris, a teacher at McGrawsville, Miami Co., from his family in Sims, Grant Co. (1888-1891); letters to W. W. Orr, a Muncie, Delaware Co., attorney, from law firms in Indiana and other states (1878-1906); letters to Charles J. Finney, a student at Crawfordsville, Montgomery Co., and Philadelphia, Pa., from his family in Attica, Fountain Co. (1877-1883); and scattered letters and documents of other Indiana people.

A-24. BARTMESS, JACOB W. (b.1836?). PAPERS, 1862-1865.

1 ms. box.　　　　　　　　　　　　　　　　　　　　　M 12.

Bartmess was a farmer and blacksmith in Jay County; and served in the 39th Indiana Regiment (1862-1865).

The collection consists of letters from Bartmess to his wife while serving in the Union Army in Tennessee, Georgia, and North Carolina.

A-25. BEARSS, DANIEL R. (1809-1884). PAPERS, 1800-1864.

82 items. SC 70.

Bearss was a storekeeper, farmer, and businessman in Peru, Miami Co. (1834-1884); Whig and Republican member, Indiana House of Representatives (1841-1844) and Indiana State Senate (1855-1857, 1861-1863, 1875-1877); owner of extensive real estate holdings in the Peru area; and director, Indianapolis, Peru and Chicago Railroad.

The bulk of the papers are letters from the period 1840-1864 and include copies of business letters written by Bearss. The correspondence relates to activities of the state legislature, Whig and Republican Party affairs, and Bearss' business interests, particularly his claims against the Potawatomi and Miami Indians. Included are letters to him from northern Indiana merchants written while he was lobbying in Washington, D.C., for the payment of the merchants' claims against the Indians (1842).

Correspondents include Schuyler Colfax, John D. Defrees, and George W. Ewing.

A-26. BEECHER, JOHN SLOANE (fl.1846-1868). PAPERS, 1832-1867.

54 items. SC 1714.

Beecher was a schoolteacher in Murfreesboro and Lebanon, Tenn.; he was the son of Truman Beecher, a merchant in Hamilton, Steuben Co. (1840s), and Albion, Noble Co. (1849-1850).

The papers consist principally of letters to Beecher in Tennessee from his father and other family members in Hamilton and Albion (1848-1850). Also included are letters of introduction for Beecher (1848); family and business letters to Truman Beecher (1832-1850); receipts; and announcements for Beecher's schools in Tennessee.

A-27. BEEM, DAVID ENOCH (1837-1923). PAPERS, 1820-1913.

3 ms. boxes. Calendar. M 15.

Beem was a student at Indiana University, Bloomington (1855-1858); an attorney in Spencer, Owen Co.; and an officer in the 14th Indiana Regiment serving in Virginia and Maryland (1861-1864).

The papers include letters from Beem to his fiancee while he served with the Union Army in Virginia and Maryland (1861-1864); Civil War documents relating to his military service and the 14th Indiana Regiment; his essays and speeches, including those written at Indiana University (1855-1858), and an incomplete history of the 14th Indiana Regiment; and family letters, court records, deeds, receipts, and other legal documents relating to Owen County (1820-1913).

A-28. BEESON, THOMAS (b.1835). PAPERS, 1849-1902.

1 ms. box, 3 vols. (.33 l.f.). Calendar. M 16, BV 938-940.

Beeson was a farmer near Hagerstown, Wayne Co. (1860s-1870s), and Losantville, Randolph Co. (1890s).

The papers include family letters to Beeson from relatives in Randolph, Henry, and Wayne counties, Ind., in Carroll County and other places in Missouri, and in Fort Scott and other places in Kansas; his farm account books (1856-1860, 1875, 1881-1884); his diaries (1858, 1861-1863); and receipts and other business papers.

A-29. BENCE, ROBERT (1836-1890). PAPERS, 1632; 1824-1890.

1 ms. box. Inventory. M 352.

Bence was a physician in Indianapolis (1860-1890); assistant surgeon and surgeon, 33rd Indiana Regiment, serving in Tennessee and Georgia (1861-1864); official in Marion County recorder's office and auditor's office after the war.

The bulk of the collection consists of Bence's Civil War letters to his wife and family in Indianapolis (1862-1864). Also included are Bence family papers from Jefferson and Livingston counties, Ky. (1824-1858); letters to Bence's father-in-law, Henry Coburn, from his sister in Dracut, Mass. (1847-1862); transcript of Allen M. Fletcher's diary of his trip to Brazil with James Cooley Fletcher (1868); letters of the Fletcher family of Indianapolis; and transcript of 1632 letter of Lydia Bates Fletcher of Concord, Mass.

A-30. BERRYMAN, NELSON (1843-1887). PAPERS, 1842-1925.

1 ms. box.   M 17.

Berryman was an attorney in Edinburg, Johnson Co. (1867-1874), and Shelbyville, Shelby Co. (1874-1887).

The papers consist of family letters, most from the period 1861-1888, including letters from Thomas Berryman in St. Louis, Mo. (1861-1862), and Nelson Berryman's letters to his wife (1860s-1880s); depositions and other legal documents relating to an 1875 land inheritance case in Shelby County; a manuscript newspaper from the Stockwell Collegiate Institute, Stockwell, Tippecanoe Co. (1864-1865); and Berryman's essays and poetry.

A-31. BERTHA BALLARD HOME ASSOCIATION. RECORDS, 1889-1975.

6 ms. boxes, 10 vols. (2.5 l.f.).   Inventory.   M 329, BV 1846-1855.

The Bertha Ballard Home was founded in 1890 by the Women Friends of Western Yearly Meeting as a Christian boarding home for young working women in Indianapolis. Originally named the Friends Boarding House for Girls, the home incorporated under the name Bertha Ballard Home Association in 1900 in response to a donation by William H. Ballard. It was operated as a nonprofit organization until it closed in 1975.

The collection consists of the minutes of the board of directors meetings for the Friends Boarding House (1889-1895) and the Bertha Ballard Home (1900-1973); financial records (1900-1975); and miscellaneous letters, legal documents, and clippings.

A-32. BERTHIER, ALEXANDRE (1753-1815). PAPERS, 1800.

26 items.   Inventory.

Berthier was an officer in the French army (1770-1814); fought in the American Revolution with Lafayette; chief of staff under Napoleon Bonaparte (1795-1814); and Ambassador Extraordinary to Spain, responsible for negotiating the retrocession of Louisiana from Spain to France (1800).

The collection consists of Berthier's papers relating to his negotiations with Spain for the return of Louisiana to France (August-October 1800). Included are retained copies of Berthier's letters to Napoleon, Prince Talleyrand, General Menou, and the Spanish Secretary of State, the Chevalier Urquijo; Berthier's copies of his instructions from Talleyrand; copy of a letter sent to Urquijo by French ambassador Alquier outlining the French argument for retrocession; preliminary drafts of a treaty written by Berthier and Urquijo; and letters of Urquijo explaining the Spanish position.

A-33. BETHELL-WARREN FAMILY. PAPERS, 1833-1931.

3 ms. boxes, 12 vols. (2 l.f.).   Inventory.   M 18, BV 945-956.

The Bethell-Warren family included Thomas F. Bethell (1816-1873), a Newburgh, Warrick Co., merchant involved in Ohio River shipping, captain in the 16th Regiment of U.S. Infantry during the Mexican War, and Democratic member of the Indiana House of Representatives (1857); Union Bethell (1826-1907), Newburgh merchant; William Warren, Sr. (d.1880), a farmer in Vanderburgh County; William Warren, Jr. (1844-ca.1937), private in the 24th Indiana Regiment (1862-1863), deputy collector of internal revenue in Vanderburgh County (1866-1869), Vanderburgh County auditor (1878-1882), and Evansville banker; and Eliza Bethell Warren (1851-ca.1950), wife of William Warren, Jr., and daughter of Thomas Bethell.

The papers include letters written by William Warren, Jr., from Evansville to his fiancee and wife, Eliza Bethell (1876-1887); account books of Thomas and Union Bethell (1857-1898) relating to the shipment of goods, particularly tobacco, on the Ohio and Mississippi rivers; Mexican War military papers of

Thomas Bethell; Civil War military papers and letters of William Warren, Jr. (1862-1863); diary of William Warren, Sr. (1849-1865); letter books of William Warren, Jr., while deputy collector of internal revenue (1866-1869); receipts and other business papers of the Bethells and William Warren, Jr.; and minutes of an 1833 meeting to erect a school and community building in Scott Township, Vanderburgh Co.

A-34. BEVAN, PHILIP (1811-1890). PAPERS, 1836-1915.

3 ms. boxes, 4 vols. (1 l.f.). M 19, BV 957-960.

Minister. Bevan was an English carpenter and sailor; immigrant to Charlestown, Clark Co. (1843); student at Lane Theological Seminary, Cincinnati (1846-1849); Presbyterian minister in Leavenworth, Crawford Co., Byrneville, Harrison Co., Martinsburg, Washington Co., and other towns in southeastern Indiana.

The papers include Bevan's letters, official documents, and financial papers, principally relating to his ministerial career (1846-1890); a diary (1836-1881); and Bevan's poems, novels, and other unpublished writings.

A-35. BLAIR, WILLIAM WYLIE (1827-1916). PAPERS, 1848-1909.

1 ms. box. Calendar. M 22.

Blair was a physician in Princeton, Gibson Co. (1850-1916); served as surgeon for the 58th Indiana Regiment (1861-1864), and as surgeon for Gen. Thomas J. Wood's division in Tennessee (1862-1864).

The collection is composed primarily of papers relating to Blair's Civil War service, including letters from Blair in Kentucky and Tennessee to his family in Princeton; and reports, lists of sick and wounded soldiers, orders, and other military documents. The collection also includes papers written by Blair on medicine in Gibson County and on his military experiences.

A-36. BLEDSOE FAMILY. COLLECTION, 1836-1863.

ca.100 items. SC 100.

The Bledsoe family, of Franklin, Johnson Co., donated this collection to the Indiana Historical Society in 1964.

The collection consists of receipts, business papers, and board of trustee reports for Franklin College, a Baptist school in Franklin (1844-1863), and for its predecessor, the Indiana Baptist Manual Labor Institute (1836-1843).

A-37. BOAZ, MIGNON (1782-1846). PAPERS, 1733-1896.

51 items.   Inventory.   SC 104, BV 92.

Boaz was a Baptist minister in Bartholomew County (1818-1846).

The bulk of the collection consists of business and tax receipts of Boaz and his son, Simeon Boaz (d.ca.1895), a farmer in Bartholomew County. The collection also includes papers relating to the settlement of Mignon Boaz's estate; a license to preach in Harrison County (1819); and a notebook of family information (1733-1814) kept by Boaz's father-in-law Elijah Pope, a Baptist minister in South Carolina and Bartholomew County.

A-38. BORDEN, WILLIAM WESLEY (1823-1906). PAPERS, 1824-1861.

49 items. SC 111.

Borden was a geologist, landowner, and farmer in New Providence, Clark Co., and New Albany, Floyd Co.

The collection consists primarily of business and tax receipts of Borden and his mother, Lydia Borden (d.1851). Also included are letters relating to family matters (1824, 1861).

A-39. BOSTON, DELBERT D. (b.1866). PAPERS, 1881-1960.

3 ms. boxes. Inventory. M 314.

Boston was a barber in Findlay, Ohio (1888-1891), and Harlan, Allen Co.; married Ella Furney of Harlan (1889).

The papers consist principally of family correspondence from the period 1888-1919, including correspondence between Boston and his fiancee and wife (1888-1915); letters from his daughter attending Indiana Normal School at Terre Haute, Vigo Co. (1908); and personal letters and postcards from relatives and friends.

A-40. BOWEN, GEORGE WASHINGTON (1838-1910). ACCOUNT BOOKS, 1859-1882.

4 vols. (.25 l.f.). BV 48-51.

Bowen was a physician in Fort Wayne, Allen Co. (1852-1910); and president of the Indiana Institute of Homeopathy (1889).

The collection consists of account books for Bowen's medical practice (1859-1882).

A-41. BOWLUS, EZRA (d.1864). PAPERS, 1862-1864.

40 items. Calendar. SC 114.

Bowlus, from Williamsport, Warren Co., was a private in the 60th Indiana Regiment (1862-1864).

The papers are composed of letters written by Bowlus to his wife while he served in the Union Army in Kentucky, Louisiana, Texas, and at Camp Morton, Indianapolis.

A-42. BOYD, LINNAES C. (b.1864). PAPERS, 1912-1913.

67 items. SC 117.

Boyd was president of the Indianapolis Water Company (1909-1912); and president of the Indiana section of the National Citizens' League for the Promotion of a Sound Banking System (1912-1913).

The papers consist of correspondence relating to the National Citizens' League, an organization lobbying for reform of the federal banking system.

A-43. BRANDT, MARIE ESTER (1823-1915). DIARIES, 1849-1869.

1 ms. box (8 vols.). Inventory. M 24.
Microfilm.

Brandt was a Quaker sabbath school teacher in Hanover, Jefferson Co.; and daughter of a farmer and general store owner in Hanover.

The diary entries describe daily life, social activities, and Civil War experiences in the towns of Hanover and Madison and at Hanover College.

A-44. BRITTON, ALEXANDER THOMPSON (1835-1899). PAPERS, 1864-1898.

1 ms. box. Inventory. M 26.

Britton was a Washington, D.C., attorney; and chairman of the Executive Committee of Inaugural Ceremonies for President Benjamin Harrison (November 1888-March 1889).

The bulk of the collection consists of letters to Britton from Washington, D.C., residents accepting his invitations to serve on committees for President Harrison's inaugural ceremonies.

A-45. BROWN, EUNICE A. (d.1870). PAPERS, 1852-1874.

34 items. SC 137.

Brown was the daughter of a tanner in Connersville, Fayette Co.

The papers consist of letters to Brown and other family members from relatives in Raysville, Henry Co., and Missouri.

A-46. BROWN, HILTON ULTIMUS (1859-1958). PAPERS, 1853-1953.

7 ms. boxes. Inventory. M 31.

Brown was a reporter, editor, and director of the *Indianapolis News* (1881-1958); member (1884-1958) and president (1903-1955) of the board of directors of Butler University, Indianapolis.

The collection consists primarily of Brown's scrapbooks, which include clippings of newspaper articles written by Brown while serving as a correspondent in the Soviet Union (1926); newspaper clippings relating to World War I and the U.S. Army in Mexico (1916-1919); and clippings and papers relating to Brown's civic and personal affairs. The collection also includes Brown's family and personal correspondence (1898-1953), including letters from his sons in the U.S. Army (1916-1918); papers relating to Butler University; correspondence and other papers relating to the operations of the *Indianapolis News* under the ownership of William Henry Smith, Delavan Smith, and Charles W. Fairbanks (1893-1922); and papers relating to the estate of William Henry Smith (1896-1898).

Correspondents include John M. Harlan, Louis Ludlow, Meredith Nicholson, J. M. Patterson, John J. Pershing, and Delavan Smith.

A-47. BRUCKER, MAGNUS (1828-1874). PAPERS, 1861-1868.

1 ms. box. Inventory. M 324.

Brucker was a German immigrant (1848); a physician in Troy, Perry Co. (1848-1874); Republican member, Indiana House of Representatives (1861, 1867); and a surgeon with the 23rd Indiana Regiment (1862-1865).

The papers consist of Brucker's letters to his wife, including letters written while he served in the Union Army in Tennessee, at Vicksburg, Miss., and in Georgia; and while he attended meetings of the Indiana legislature in Indianapolis (1867). The letters are in German.

A-48. BRUNER, ALFRED WILSON (1858-1939). PAPERS, 1875-1898.

6 vols. (.25 l.f.). Inventory. BV 7-12.

Bruner was a schoolteacher and farmer in Paoli, Orange Co.; editor of the *Paoli Republican* (ca.1897-1909); and an Indiana food and drug inspector (1907-1933).

The collection consists of notebooks with lesson plans and other writings relating to schoolteaching (1875-1879); and Bruner's farm account books (1879-1898).

A-49. BUNDY, CHESTER E. (b.1893). PAPERS, 1850-1967.

1 ms. box, 4 vols. (.5 l.f.). M 32, BV 96-99.

Bundy was a farmer in Amboy and Converse, Miami Co.; and served with the American Friends Service Committee in France (1919-1920).

The papers are composed of Bundy's diary and letters to his family, written in France where he was involved in relief operations in the war front areas after World War I; his farm account books (1909-1953); Miami County tax receipts and land deeds (1850-1900); and a Sunday school record book for the Society of Friends in Russiaville and West Middleton, Howard Co. (1880-1882).

A-50. BUTLER, AMOS W. (1860-1937). PAPERS, 1933-1937.

2 ms. boxes. Inventory. M 34.

Butler was secretary of the Indiana Board of State Charities (1898-1923); and participated in the Indiana Historical Society's archaeological program.

The papers are composed primarily of Butler's correspondence with historians and historical societies regarding midwestern Indian history.

A-51. BUTLER, FRANK (1858-1936). PAPERS, 1838-1933.

1 ms. box, 2 vols. (.5 l.f.).   Inventory.   M 347, BV 1898-1899.

Butler was an attorney in Peru, Miami Co.; and active in Democratic Party politics.

The collection includes scrapbooks of clippings relating to Butler and his son, Robert Butler, a Peru attorney; Robert Butler's correspondence as secretary of the Miami County Jefferson Club, a Democratic Party organization (1932); legal papers and divorce papers of Butler's father, Jesse Butler (1818-1874), a Miami County farmer; and other Butler family legal papers and genealogical materials.

A-52. BUTLER, NOBLE CHASE (1844-1933). PAPERS, 1809-1933.

57 ms. boxes, 25 vols. (19 l.f.).   Inventory.   M 35, BV 961-973.

Attorney and politician. Butler was a student at Hanover College, Jefferson Co. (1861-1863); private in the 93rd Indiana Regiment, detailed as chief clerk at the Headquarters, Post and Defenses of Memphis, Tenn. (1864-1865); attorney in New Albany, Floyd Co. (1866-1879), and law partner of his father and Walter Q. Gresham in firm of Butler, Gresham and Butler; register in bankruptcy in New Albany (1867-1879); clerk for the U.S. District and Circuit Courts in Indianapolis (1879-1922); active in Republican Party affairs, and was associated with Walter Q. Gresham in the reform wing of the party. He was the son of John H. Butler (1812-1900), an attorney in Salem, Washington Co. (1830s-1866), and New Albany (1866-ca.1892).

The collection consists principally of Butler's political, legal, and family correspondence from the period 1859-1920. Included is correspondence regarding Republican Party politics (1860s-1910s), particularly the political campaigns of Walter Q. Gresham for the U.S. Senate (1880) and for the Republican presidential nomination (1888); correspondence regarding Butler and Gresham's legal cases (1860s-1890s), particularly cases regarding railroads, including the Lake Erie, Evansville, and South Western Railway Co. (1877-1880), and cases involving people in New Albany and other southern Indiana towns; Butler's letter books as register of bankruptcy (1867-1879), as clerk of the U.S. Circuit Courts (1886-1904), and as a private attorney (1864-1890s); letters from his father regarding family, political, and legal matters, including letters from Salem (1861-1865), New Albany (1866-1888), and Washington, D.C. (1883-1888); and letters from family and friends in Salem (1860s), Pewee Valley and Louisville, Ky. (1850s-1860s), Indiana Asbury University, Greencastle, Putnam Co. (1859-1862), St. Charles, Mo. (1867-1869), Washington, D.C. (1880s-1910s), and West Chester, Pa. (1890s-1910s). Also included are papers relating to the New Albany Water Works (1899-1904) and Hanover College (1861-1920); financial accounts of John H. Butler (1857-1899); Noble Butler's bankruptcy and circuit court accounts (1867-1925); diary of his sister, Anne Butler, for her trip from Salem to Rhode Island (1856); Butler's speeches on legal and literary topics; and scrapbooks.

Correspondents include John H. Baker, Albert J. Beveridge, George A. Bicknell, James G. Blaine, Thomas M. Browne, William D. Bynum, Schuyler Colfax, Will Cumback, Thomas Drummond, Winfield T. Durbin, Charles E. Dyer, Charles W. Fairbanks, John Watson Foster, William Dudley Foulke, Melville W. Fuller, Horace Gray, Walter Q. Gresham, Elijah W. Halford, John M. Harlan, Benjamin Harrison, James A. Hemenway, Thomas A. Hendricks, Charles L. Henry, John H. Holliday, William R. Holloway, Louis G. Howland, Robert G. Ingersoll, Henry U. Johnson, John Worth Kern, Kenesaw Mountain Landis, Henry S. Lane, Oscar C. McCulloch, Joseph E. McDonald, Thomas R. Marshall, Claude Matthews, Louis T. Michener, Merrill Moores, Oliver P. Morton, Oliver T. Morton, James A. Mount, Meredith Nicholson, Theophilus Parvin, Stanton J. Peelle, Robert B. F. Peirce, Theodore Roosevelt, John H. Stotsenburg, William Graham Sumner, Lucius B. Swift, William Howard Taft, Robert S. Taylor, William H. H. Terrell, David Turpie, William A. Woods, Evans Woollen, and Bennett H. Young.

A-53. BUTLER, OVID (1801-1881). PAPERS, 1841-1893.

2 ms. boxes, 1 vol. (.66 l.f.).   Inventory.   M 36, BV 1011.

Butler was an Indianapolis attorney (1836-1849); owner of the *Free Soil Banner* (1848) and the *Indianapolis Journal* (1854); and president of the board of directors of Northwestern Christian University (Butler University), Indianapolis (1852-1871).

The papers include manuscript copies of Butler's antislavery and religious essays; letters and documents relating to the early history of Northwestern Christian University; letters of Butler to his family, most from 1872; his cashbook, 1867-1870; and deeds and other legal papers.

A-54. CALDWELL, JOHN (d.1835). PAPERS, 1785-1893.

1 ms. box.   Inventory.   M 320.
Microfilm.

Caldwell was the operator of a general store in Vincennes, Knox Co. (1810s), and Shawneetown, Ill. (ca.1814-1835); receiver of public monies in the U.S. land office at Shawneetown (1810s-1820s); and managed general store in Shawneetown for Frederick Rapp (1820s). His family included his son, John Caldwell (1819-1868), a Vincennes merchant; and grandson, Albert G. Caldwell (b.1846), a cadet at the U.S. Naval Academy (1862-1863), and an officer in the U.S. Navy (1860s-1880s).

The collection includes John Caldwell's bills, receipts, accounts, contracts, and correspondence for his businesses in Vincennes and Shawneetown (1810-1835), including his contracts and correspondence with Frederick Rapp (1824-1827); papers of Caldwell's wife regarding the settlement of his estate (1830s-1840s); letters of his son, John Caldwell, to his fiancee and wife, Margaret Badollet Caldwell, written while on business trips to Louisville, Ky., New York, N.Y., Philadelphia, Pa., Cincinnati, Ohio, and other places (1845-1863); and letters of Albert G. Caldwell to his mother from the U.S. Naval Academy (1862-1863), and while serving on American ships in the Mediterranean, the Atlantic, and along the South American coast (1866-1883).

A-55. CAMPBELL, LEANDER M. (1833-1890). PAPERS, 1833-1905.

1 ms. box, 7 vols. (.75 ft.).   Inventory.   M 37, BV 22-26, 975-976.

Campbell was an attorney in Danville, Hendricks Co.

The papers include Campbell's account books relating to his law practice and farming interests; his record and diary as a teacher in Kentucky and in Belleville, Hendricks Co. (1850-1853); record book and scrapbook of the Hendricks County Fremont Club (1888); copies of Campbell's speeches on patriotic topics and public education; and land deeds, receipts, and other legal papers.

A-56. CARNAHAN, JAMES R. (1840-1905). PAPERS, 1860-1904.

1 ms. box.   Inventory.   M 311.

Carnahan was a student at Wabash College, Crawfordsville, Montgomery Co. (1860-1862); an officer in the 86th Indiana Regiment (1862-1865); Tippecanoe County prosecutor (1867-1871); commander, district of Indiana, Grand Army of the Republic (1882-1883); and commissioner from Indiana, Chickamauga National Military Park (1894-ca.1905).

The papers include Carnahan's military correspondence relating to the movements of the 86th Indiana Regiment, primarily in Tennessee and Georgia (1862-1865); his war journals (1864); his reminiscence of the Battle of Chickamauga; postwar speeches and writings, most relating to the Civil War; and his essays written while a student at Wabash College.

A-57. CAUTHORN-STOUT FAMILY. PAPERS, 1780-1908.

4 ms. boxes.   Calendar.   M 4l.

The Cauthorn-Stout family included Elihu Stout (1786-1860), printer and newspaper publisher in Vincennes, Knox Co. (1804-1845), publisher of the *Indiana Gazette* (1804-1806) and the *Western Sun* (1807-1845), Indiana's first newspapers; John Francis Bayard (1786-1853), officer in the French army under Napoleon, and Vincennes businessman (1820-1853); and Henry S. Cauthorn (1828-1905), Stout's grandson and Bayard's son-in-law, student at Indiana Asbury (DePauw) University, Greencastle, Putnam Co. (1845-1848), Vincennes attorney (1851-1905), Democratic member, Indiana House of Representatives (1871, 1873, 1879, 1881), and holder of numerous city and county offices.

The collection includes Stout's receipts, accounts, and other documents relating to his publishing and personal business (1805-1851), and materials submitted to him for publication; Bayard's business documents (1819-1848), and letters from his family in Grenoble, France (1822-1833, 1849); letters from his son, Samuel Bayard in Evansville, Vanderburgh Co., to his mother in Vincennes (1856-1862); Henry S. Cauthorn's correspondence, principally from the period 1842-1880, including correspondence with friends from Indiana Asbury University (1846-1850), correspondence regarding his Vincennes business interests, and correspondence regarding state Democratic Party politics and the Indiana state legislature (1860-1880). Also included is Cauthorn's diary (1870); receipts and legal documents of French inhabitants of Vincennes (1780-1810); and an unpublished biography of Elihu Stout by Valerie Knerr (1953).

The collection includes correspondence and papers of Conrad Baker, Bishop Simon Brute de Remur, John D. Defrees, Lyman C. Draper, John Ewing, Thomas A. Hendricks, John Law, Thomas Posey, Frederick Rapp, Francis Vigo, Daniel W. Voorhees, and James D. Williams.

A-58. CAVINS, ELIJAH H. C. (1832-1910). PAPERS, 1829-1910.

3 ms. boxes.   Inventory.   M 42.

Attorney and soldier. Cavins was an attorney in Bloomfield, Greene Co. (1850s-1910); Republican member, Indiana House of Representatives (1859); officer in the 14th Indiana Regiment (1861-1864); adjutant general for the Southern Division of Indiana (1864); active member of the Grand Army of the Republic; and member of the Indiana battlefield commissions for Antietam and Gettysburg.

The papers include Cavins's Civil War letters to his wife and family, primarily written from Virginia and Maryland (1861-1864); his Civil War diary (1864); military papers for the 14th Indiana Regiment, including reports on the regiment's actions at Fredericksburg and Chancellorsville; Cavins's addresses and essays relating to the G.A.R. and the Civil War; company histories for the 14th Indiana; papers relating to the Antietam and Gettysburg battlefield memorials; personal legal and financial papers (1865-1904); financial and legal documents of his father, Samuel Cavins (1829-1863); and constitution and minutes of the Veteran Company of the Indiana Legion in Brown County (1863-1865).

A-59. CHAMBERLAIN, JOSEPH WRIGHT (1809-1867). PAPERS, 1829-1932.

5 ms. boxes.　　　　　　　　Calendar.　　　　　　　　M 44.

Chamberlain was a physician in Onondaga County, N.Y., Michigan City, LaPorte Co. (1835-1838), Berrien, Mich. (1838-1840), Leesburg, Kosciusko Co. (1840-1851), and a physician, druggist, and bookdealer in Elkhart, Elkhart Co. (1851-1867). He was the father of Orville Tryon Chamberlain (1841-1929), a student at Notre Dame University, St. Joseph Co. (1860-1861); an officer in the 74th Indiana Regiment (1862-1865); and an attorney in Elkhart specializing in pension work for Civil War veterans.

Joseph W. Chamberlain's papers consist of correspondence and business papers from the period 1829-1867, including correspondence between Chamberlain in New York and Indiana and his family in New York; correspondence regarding his medical practice in New York and Indiana, and his business interests in Indiana; and correspondence regarding Republican Party politics in Indiana (1850s-1860s). Orville T. Chamberlain's papers include his Civil War letters to his father from Kentucky, Tennessee, and Georgia (1862-1865); his Civil War diaries (1862-1864); military documents relating to the 74th Indiana; family correspondence (1869-1932), including correspondence with his brother, Tully Chamberlain, a railroad man in California, Wyoming, Nevada, and Utah (1869-1873), and letters from family members in Arizona (1928-1932); correspondence and documents relating to his winning of the Congressional Medal of Honor (1891-1929); and personal business papers (1866-1932). Also included is a Civil War diary of John D. Myers of the 74th Indiana Regiment (1864-1865).

Correspondents include Schuyler Colfax, Edward A. Hannegan, and Thomas A. Hendricks.

A-60. CHANEY, JOHN CRAWFORD (1853-1940). PAPERS, 1883-1942.

2 ms. boxes.　　　　　　　　　　　　　　　　　　　　M 45.

Chaney was an attorney in Sullivan County; assistant to the U.S. Attorney-General (1889-1893); and Republican member, U.S. House of Representatives (1905-1909).

The papers include Chaney's correspondence regarding Republican Party politics and his work in the U.S. Congress (1900-1911); Chaney's speeches on patriotic and political topics; papers and speeches of Lee Bays (d.1941), Chaney's son-in-law and town of Sullivan attorney; programs and announcements; and scrapbooks.

Correspondents include Charles W. Fairbanks, William Howard Taft, and James E. Watson.

A-61. CHEEK, WILLIAM V. (b.1796). ACCOUNT BOOKS, 1843-1849.

3 vols. (.33 l.f.). BV 114-116.

Cheek operated a general merchandise store in Lawrenceburg, Dearborn Co.

The collection consists of account books for Cheek's Lawrenceburg store.

A-62. CHENEY, JOHN J. (b.1827). ACCOUNT BOOKS, 1851-1899.

8 vols. (.50 l.f.). Inventory. BV 14-21.

Cheney was an attorney in Winchester, Randolph Co.

The collection includes cash and claim books for the law firm of Browne and Cheney (1851-1873); real estate listings for the firm of Cheney and Watson (ca.1870); and cash and fee book for the firm of Watson, Macy and Goodrich (1893-1899).

A-63. CHURCHMAN, FRANCIS MCCLINTOCK (1833-1891). PAPERS, 1868-1928.

1 ms. box. Calendar. M 53.

Churchman was an officer of the Fletcher Bank in Indianapolis (1850-1891); and owner of a farm near Beech Grove, Marion Co.

The collection includes three small account books recording Churchman's personal and farm expenses (1866-1879); correspondence of his half brother, William H. Churchman (1818-1882), relating to his position as superintendent of the Indiana Institute for the Education of the Blind, Indianapolis (1873-1882); correspondence of F. M. Churchman and his wife with their children (1888-1898); Mrs. F. M. Churchman's journals for her trips to the Chicago Columbian Exposition (1893) and to Philadelphia, Pa., and Washington, D.C. (1897); correspondence and business papers of F. M. Churchman's son, Frank F. Churchman, a real estate agent in Indianapolis and Beech Grove (1905-1928); and family bills and receipts (1868-1922).

A-64. CITIZENS FORUM. RECORDS, 1962-1985.

28 ms. boxes. Inventory. M 425.

The Citizens Forum was organized in Indianapolis in 1964 by schoolteacher Mattie Coney to lobby for an open housing ordinance in the city and to work for improved conditions in the city's black neighborhoods. It eventually became an interracial organization, with affiliated block clubs throughout the city. The forum sponsored neighborhood beautification and safety programs, provided educational programs on civic and health issues, and served as a channel for neighborhood complaints to city officials. The forum was disbanded in 1984.

The forum's records are principally from the period 1970-1984 and include minutes of board of directors meetings; correspondence of Mattie Coney and other forum officers (1962-1985); constitutions, bylaws, policies, and studies (1964-1984); financial records, principally from the period 1982-1984; grant applications and reports (1973-1984); records of block clubs, including minutes of meetings, notices, correspondence, and membership records; records of forum programs, including neighborhood safety and beautification programs, and programs with Indianapolis schools; forum newsletters, brochures, and other publications; newspaper clippings about the forum and Mattie Coney; and programs and other materials from local, state, and national organizations with which the forum was associated.

A-65. CLARKE, WILLIAM HORATIO (1840-1913). PAPERS, 1874-1882.

7 vols. (.66 l.f.). BV 27-33.

Clarke was an organist in Boston, Mass., Toronto, Canada, Rochester, N.Y., and Indianapolis; and owner of the William H. Clarke Company of Indianapolis, an organ manufacturing company (1874-1882).

The collection consists of three account books (1874-1881) and four letter books (1876-1882) of the William H. Clarke Company. The letter books contain the company's correspondence, primarily with midwestern churches regarding the purchase of organs.

A-66. CLAYPOOL HOTEL. RECORDS, 1903-1917.

2 vols. (.25 l.f.). BV 579-580.

The Claypool Hotel was constructed in downtown Indianapolis in 1902 and was razed in 1969.

The collection consists of the Claypool Hotel banquet book (1903-1909); and the minutes of the Indiana Hotel Keepers' Association (1903-1917).

A-67. COBB, DYAR (1807-1900). PAPERS, 1841-1928.

1 ms. box. Calendar. M 54.

Cobb was a farmer near Greensburg, Decatur Co.

The papers include correspondence and business papers for Cobb's Iron and Nail Company, Aurora, Dearborn Co., run by Cobb's brother, John Cobb (1881-1888); personal business papers of Cobb and his son-in-law, Oliver C. Elder (1841-1902); school notebooks and papers of Cobb's grandson, Clifford Elder (1888-1895); and Elder family correspondence (1881-1901).

A-68. COFFIN, CHARLES EMMET (1849-1934). PAPERS, 1924-1934.

27 items. Calendar. SC 259.

Coffin was an Indianapolis real estate broker and banker; and member of the Indianapolis Park Commission (1899-1922), the Indianapolis Board of Public Works, and the City Plan Commission (1922-1926).

The papers principally consist of Coffin's correspondence regarding Republican Party politics from the period 1924-1934.

Correspondents include Albert J. Beveridge, Kin Hubbard, Charles Evans Hughes, Edward L. Jackson, Frederick Landis, Louis Ludlow, Harry S. New, Meredith Nicholson, Arthur R. Robinson, Susanah Tarkington, and James E. Watson.

A-69. COLFAX, SCHUYLER (1823-1885). PAPERS, 1843-1884.

1 ms. box. M 55.

Politician. Colfax was deputy auditor of South Bend, St. Joseph Co. (1841-1849); publisher and part owner, *St. Joseph Valley Register* (1845-1863); one of the organizers of the Republican Party in Indiana; Republican member, U.S. House of Representatives (1855-1869); Speaker of the House (1863-1869); Vice-President of the United States under Ulysses S. Grant (1869-1873); involved in the Credit Mobilier scandals; and popular lecturer.

The papers are composed primarily of miscellaneous letters written by Colfax regarding politics in South Bend, Ind., and Washington, D.C.; Colfax's business interests; and his speaking engagements. The papers also include Colfax's 1865 draft of his lecture "Across the Continent," describing his trip through the American West.

Correspondents include James A. Garfield, James J. Hill, Henry S. Lane, Edwards Pierrepont, William Tecumseh Sherman, and Elihu B. Washburne.

A-70. COUPIN, CLAUDE ANTOINE GABRIEL (1767?-1802). PAPERS, 1790-1805.

1 ms. box. Inventory. M 416.

Merchant. Coupin, son of a Paris, France, businessman, purchased land in Ohio through the Compagnie du Scioto; settled at Gallipolis, on the Ohio River, as part of a group of French colonists (1790); and moved to Vincennes, Knox Co., and set up business as a merchant and silversmith (1796).

The collection includes land documents of the Compagnie du Scioto and its agent in Paris, William Playfair (1790); Coupin's correspondence and business papers, including land documents and travel papers (1790-1796), letters from his family in France regarding personal matters and French politics (1790-1796), letters from friends in Alexandria, Va., regarding settlers at Gallipolis (1791-1792), and receipts, business papers, and correspondence regarding his business affairs in Vincennes (1796-1802); and correspondence and business papers regarding the settlement of his estate by his executor, Antoine Marchal of Vincennes (1802-1805).

Correspondents include Nicholas Hingston and Manuel Lisa.

A-71. CRAIN, JACOB R. (fl.1830-1840). PAPERS, 1840.

25 items. SC 456.

Jacob R. and John A. Crain edited the *Calumet and War Club*, a Springfield, Ohio, newspaper supporting William Henry Harrison in the presidential campaign of 1840.

The papers consist of correspondence relating to the publication and distribution of the *Calumet and War Club* and a partial list of subscribers.

A-72. CRANE, ABIATHAR (1819-1856). PAPERS, 1751-1893.

1 ms. box. Calendar. M 76.
Microfilm.

Crane was a schoolteacher in Berkley, Mass. (1845-1848); and a merchant in Bainbridge, Putnam Co., specializing in the shipment of agricultural products to eastern markets (1848-1856).

The papers consist principally of Crane's correspondence for the period 1843-1856 and include letters relating to his teaching career in the Massachusetts common schools; his business interests in Putnam County; his involvement with the building of the Indianapolis and Springfield Plank Road (1850-1856); and his family in Massachusetts. The papers also include letters from Crane's relatives traveling from Massachusetts to California (1849-1850); letters from a relative teaching school in Red Wing, Minn. (1860-1863); letters of Montgomery County physician Benjamin Briggs, written from Kansas and Texas (1873-1879); and Crane family papers (1751-1819), including letters from family members in Alstead, N.H. (1807-1817).

The correspondents include John G. Davis.

A-73. CRANE, JOEL (1790-1837). PAPERS, 1818-1904.

47 items.   Calendar.   SC 457.

Crane was a farmer and mill operator near Columbus, Bartholomew Co.

The papers consist primarily of family correspondence of Crane's widow and children in Columbus (1840-1867) and include letters from relatives in New York, Michigan, and Lafayette, Tippecanoe Co. Also included are a small number of documents relating to Crane's business in New York and Indiana (1825-1833).

A-74. CRAWFORDSVILLE SEED COMPANY. CORRESPONDENCE, 1914-1918.

36 ms. boxes.   Inventory.   M 420.

The company was organized in Crawfordsville, Montgomery Co., in 1914 by Shirl Herr and Homer Flanigan to sell farm seed on a wholesale and retail basis throughout the middle west. The company was sold to Northrup King & Co. in 1966.

The collection consists of the company's correspondence with its suppliers and its customers, including farmers and retail seed dealers (1914-1918).

A-75. CROSS, GEORGE WASHINGTON (b.1816). PAPERS, 1836-1880.

1 ms. box.   Inventory.   M 433.

Cross was a businessman in Montezuma, Parke Co.; and Montezuma postmaster (1844-1847).

The papers include letters to Cross regarding family and business matters (1836-1853), including letters from Wheeling, Va. (1845-1846), and Louisiana (1836, 1851); receipts, deeds, accounts, and other papers relating to his personal business and the Montezuma post office (1837-1870); Parke County election records (1840-1846); family and business letters to Cross' son-in-law, Sharon Cross, particularly from Montezuma and Lafayette, Tippecanoe Co. (1865-1880); and letters to Nathaniel Wilson of Montezuma from his family in Lancaster, Ohio (1841-1844).

A-76. CROWE, EUGENE BURGESS (1878-1970). PAPERS, 1922-1956.

2 ms. boxes.   Inventory.   M 77.

Crowe was a furniture store owner and banker in Bedford, Lawrence Co.; Democratic member, U.S. House of Representatives (1931-1941); and member of the Indiana Democratic Central Committee.

The papers consist primarily of state and local election returns (1922-1956) and papers relating to the Indiana Democratic Party's campaign finances (1940-1944).

A-77. CURRAN, CHARLES W. (1819-ca.1868). DIARIES, 1848-1853.

5 vols.   Inventory.   SC 473.

Curran was a Methodist circuit rider in Leesville, Lawrence Co., Elizabethtown, Bartholomew Co., Leavenworth, Crawford Co., and Lexington, Scott Co. (1846-1854); and a Methodist minister in Minnesota (1854-1868).

Curran's diaries record his experiences as a circuit rider in southern Indiana (1848-1853).

A-78. DAILY, DAVID W. (1798-1878). PAPERS, 1796-1886.

2 ms. boxes.   Partial Calendar.   M 78.

Daily was a farmer and merchant in Charlestown, Clark Co.; Clark County sheriff (1828-1832); and Democratic member, Indiana State Senate (1833-1838).

The collection includes Daily's correspondence regarding business and politics; his business ledgers (1832-1841); cashbook for his business trip to New Orleans, La. (1851); receipts, legal papers, and other business documents; receipts for sheriffs' and attorneys' fees (1832-1886); and letters from his son serving in the American army in Texas and Mexico during the Mexican War (1846-1847). The collection also includes receipts and other business papers of his father, Philip Daily of Clark County (1796-1832); and an 1814 manuscript arithmetic book.

A-79. DARBY, ORANGE V. (1853-1903). PAPERS, 1860-1918.

3 ms. boxes, 9 vols. (1 l.f.).   Inventory.   M 79, BV 998-1006.

Darby owned a dry goods store in Kokomo, Howard Co.; was involved with several interurban railroad companies, including the Indiana Interurban Construction Company, of which he was president (1903).

The collection contains personal correspondence, including letters from family members in Crawfordsville, Montgomery Co., and Lafayette, Tippecanoe Co. (1877-1891), and from Darby's daughter at Wellesley, Mass. (1902-1904), and Geneva, Switzerland (1909-1910); correspondence, receipts, and other business papers regarding his dry goods store and other businesses (1860-1903); correspondence and papers relating to interurban companies in Kokomo (1901-1909); personal and business ledgers (1877-1919); invitations and announcements (1876-1892); and genealogy correspondence and notes.

A-80. DAVIS, JEFFERSON COLUMBUS (1828-1879). PAPERS, 1847-1880.

1 ms. box.   Calendar.   M 80.

Davis was a native of Clark County; officer in the U.S. Army (1848-1879); colonel, 22nd Indiana Regiment (1861); brigadier general in the Union Army (1861-1865), and division commander in Tennessee and Georgia; and army officer in the Pacific Northwest and in Alaska (1866-1879).

The collection includes official military correspondence during the Civil War (1861-1865); personal and military correspondence after the war, particularly with Civil War veterans; letters and resolutions written on Davis's death (1879-1880); and Davis's account of his military service (1866).

Correspondents include John C. Fremont, Henry W. Halleck, Thomas J. Henley, Alexander C. McClurg, John Pope, and William Tecumseh Sherman.

A-81. DAVIS, JOHN GIVAN (1810-1866). PAPERS, 1831-1865.

6 ms. boxes.   Inventory.   M 82.
Microfilm.

Politician. Davis was Parke County sheriff (1830-1833); clerk of the Parke County court (1833-1850); Democratic member, U.S. House of Representatives (1851-1855, 1857-1861); elected to Congress in 1856 as Anti-Lecompton Democrat; political ally of Indiana governor Joseph A. Wright; and owner of dry goods businesses in Montezuma, Parke Co. (1846-1863), and Terre Haute, Vigo Co. (1863-1866).

The bulk of the collection consists of Davis's political correspondence, particularly from the period 1851-1861 while he was serving in Congress. Included are letters reporting on the political climate in Indiana and in his west-central Indiana district; letters regarding railroads and the Kansas-Nebraska controversy; letters from other congressmen regarding political matters; and routine letters regarding patronage. Also included are Davis's letters from Washington to his wife and children; letters from settlers in Kansas and Nebraska (1857-1858); and letters regarding his business interests in Parke and Vigo counties.

Correspondents include Michael G. Bright, Austin H. Brown, William J. Brown, William W. Corcoran, John D. Defrees, John Dowling, Norman Eddy, Isaac C. Elston, Graham N. Fitch, Abram A. Hammond, Edward A. Hannegan, Thomas A. Hendricks, Barnabas C. Hobbs, George S. Houston, Aquilla Jones, John Law, William L. Marcy, Samuel S. Marshall, David Meriwether, William Montgomery, John Pettit, Addison Roache, James C. Robinson, Robert Smith, John J. Taylor, Richard W. Thompson, Daniel W. Voorhees, Albert S. White, William W. Wick, Henry K. Wilson, and Joseph A. Wright.

A-82. DAWSON, GOVERNOR GREENUP (1862-1916). PAPERS, 1894-1925.

2 ms. boxes, 2 vols. (.6 l.f.). Inventory. M 333, BV 1893-1894.

Dawson, known as Harry Dawson, was a medicine show performer and manager based in Mayfield, Ky., and Indianapolis (1905-1916). He performed with the Kickapoo Indian Medicine Company and other companies, managed the Dawson Concert Company, and was president of the Iceland Medicine Company of Indianapolis.

The papers consist primarily of materials from Dawson's shows, including comedy routines, original songs, advertising materials, contracts, and recipes for candies and medicines. Also included are family correspondence (1895-1925) and a diary listing the towns where his company played and the monies received on a 1916 tour of eastern Indiana.

A-83. DEAN FAMILY. PAPERS, 1799-1920.

14 ms. boxes. Inventory. M 85.

The Dean family included John Dean (1736-1824), a Quaker agent to the Indians at Brothertown, New York (1798-ca.1824); his son, Thomas Dean (1783-1843), agent to the Brothertown Indians (ca.1805-ca.1840), and postmaster at Deansville (Brothertown), N.Y. (1830s-1840s); Thomas Dean's son, John Dean (1813-1863), an attorney in Brothertown and New York City, a Democratic member of the New York state legislature (1847-1849), a clerk in the U.S. Treasury Department in Washington, D.C. (1862-1863), and a radical Republican who worked in Washington on behalf of fugitive slaves (1860-1863); and John Dean's children, Edward Dean (1843-1923), founder of Dean Brothers Pump Works in Indianapolis, and Mary Dean (1839-1917) of Brooklyn, N.Y.

The collection includes papers of the elder John and Thomas Dean regarding their work as agents to the Brothertown Indians (1799-1836), including correspondence with their Quaker sponsors regarding their work; correspondence regarding Thomas Dean's efforts to find land for the Brothertown Indians in Indiana and Wisconsin (1809-1834); minutes and accounts of the Moral Society and the Female Moral Society in Brothertown (1808-1810); Thomas Dean's journals of his trips to Indiana (1817) and Wisconsin (1826, 1833, 1836, 1839) to locate and purchase land for the Brothertown Indians; his journal from his trip to Washington, D.C., to lobby Congress on behalf of the Indians (1827); his field notes for surveys of land near Lake Winnebago, Wis. (1831, 1833); his financial accounts (1802-1844); and journal of the Marshall, N.Y., town commissioners (1840-1845). The collection also includes papers of Thomas Dean's son, John Dean, including his legal, political, and business correspondence (1836-1863); letters to his wife and family regarding his legal work in New York and Washington, D.C.; and his journals from New York (1851-1852) and Washington (1860-1863). Also included is family correspondence of John Dean's children (1860s-1910s), particularly letters from family members in New York and Indianapolis and letters describing trips to Europe (1892-1900).

Correspondents include Hendrick Aupaument, Lewis Cass, Isaac McCoy, Thomas C. McKinney, Daniel D. Pratt, and Erastus Root.

A-84. DELAPLANE, MARGARET LANDON (b.1899). SCRAPBOOKS, 1940-1965.

3 ms. boxes.   M 318.

Delaplane worked for the American Red Cross in Kokomo, Howard Co., and in Indianapolis on war relief during World War II and disaster relief in the 1940s and 1950s.

The scrapbooks contain Delaplane's letters to her daughter written while on missions for the Red Cross; letters from Red Cross headquarters; thank-you notes from World War II soldiers; photographs; and newspaper clippings relating to relief work.

A-85. DENNY, GILBERT H. (ca.1840-1864). LETTERS, 1861-1863.

45 items. Calendar. SC 498.

Denny was a farmer in Kossuth, Washington Co.; and a private and a sergeant in the 18th Indiana Regiment during the Civil War.

The collection consists of Denny's letters to his parents while he was serving with the Union Army in Missouri, Kentucky, Arkansas, and Louisiana.

A-86. DICKES, JOHN THOMAS (1858-1916). ACCOUNT BOOKS, 1886-1915.

8 vols. (1 l.f.). BV 53-60.

Dickes was a physician in Portland, Jay Co.

The collection consists of Dickes's daybooks and ledgers listing his patients' accounts.

A-87. DISABILITY INCOME INSURANCE COMPANY. RECORDS, 1935-1960.

14 vols. (1.75 l.f.). BV 769-782.

The Disability Income Insurance Company was founded in Indianapolis in 1948 by Richard A. Calkins (1898-1961), an insurance agent who had worked previously in Indianapolis for the Massachusetts Indemnity Insurance Company.

The records consist primarily of the company's financial statements, agency production books, procedure manuals, bulletins, and mailings, primarily from the period 1949-1960. The records also include material issued by the Massachusetts Indemnity Insurance Company (1935).

A-88. DOOLEY, RUFUS (1842-1927). PAPERS, 1855-1871.

3 ms. boxes.   Inventory.   M 383.

Dooley grew up on a farm near Bethany, Parke Co.; served in the 21st Indiana Regiment (reorganized as the 1st Indiana Heavy Artillery in 1863) and fought in Louisiana and at Mobile Bay, Ala. (1861-1865); and worked as a Rockville, Parke Co., hardware dealer after the war.

The collection consists primarily of Dooley's family correspondence from the period 1859-1866, including letters between Dooley and his family written while he was serving in the army; letters from relatives serving in the 31st and 72nd Indiana regiments; and letters to Dooley and his father from relatives in Iowa (1859-1864), Oxford, Ohio (1856-1866), and Waveland, Montgomery Co., and Dover, Boone Co. (1850s-1860s).

A-89. DOUGLASS, BENJAMIN PENNEBAKER (1820-1904). PAPERS, 1809-1891.

82 items.   Inventory.   SC 110.

Douglass was a merchant and attorney in Corydon, Harrison Co. (1834-1885); Democratic member, Indiana House of Representatives (1857); Harrison County auditor (1851-1859, 1867-1868); Harrison County clerk (1868-1872); and employee of the U.S. Land Office in New Mexico (1885).

The collection includes Douglass' personal and political correspondence (1856-1891); his business and legal papers; correspondence of his wife, Victoria Boone Douglass, with family in Indiana and Kentucky (1851-1884); and legal documents relating to the Boone family in Kentucky and southern Indiana (1809-1887).

A-90. DOUGLASS, SAMUEL WALTER (1832-1867). PAPERS, 1838-1894.

1 ms. box.   Calendar.   M 86.

Douglass was a Corydon, Harrison Co., merchant and farmer; and Harrison County auditor (1859) and clerk (1864).

The papers consist primarily of family correspondence from the period 1853-1861, including letters from western Virginia (1838-1868), Washington, D.C. (1857-1859), Covington, Ky. (1859-1860), Corydon (1859, 1889), and Shreveport, La. (1877-1879), and letters from Douglass' brother, Benjamin P. Douglass, written while on business trips to Louisville, Ky., and Cincinnati, Ohio (1857-1858). Also included are Douglass family legal and business documents (1858-1894).

A-91. DOWLING, JOHN (ca.1808-1878). PAPERS, 1827-1878.

2 ms. boxes. M 87.

Journalist and politician. Dowling was an Irish immigrant (1818); editor of a number of newspapers, including newspapers in Mt. Sterling and Lexington, Ky. (1829-1830), and the *Terre Haute* (Vigo Co.) *Wabash Courier* (1832-1841), the *Jackson* (Miss.) *Southerner* (1847-1850), and the *Terre Haute Journal* (1861-1873); Whig member of the Indiana House of Representatives (1846-1847); clerk for the U.S. Indian Agency in Washington, D.C. (1850-1861); Washington correspondent for the *Boston* (Mass.) *Pilot* (1873-1878); member of the Democratic Party from the 1850s. Dowling was the brother of Thomas Dowling (ca.1806-1876), co-publisher of the *Wabash Courier* (1832-1841); editor and proprietor of the *Terre Haute Express* (1842-1845); six-term Whig state representative (1836-1849); government agent responsible for transporting the Miami Indians from Indiana to their western reservation (1844); and trustee, Wabash and Erie Canal (1850).

The collection consists principally of Dowling's correspondence from the period 1830-1865, including correspondence between John and Thomas Dowling regarding politics, business interests, and family matters; letters from political and business associates in Indiana, Kentucky, and other places; correspondence regarding the work of the U.S. Indian Agency (1850-1861); and correspondence with family members, including letters from Thomas R. Palmer of Jackson, Miss. (1842-1862), letters from Dowling's daughter at St. Mary-of-the-Woods College, Vigo Co. (1842-1844), correspondence between Dowling in Washington, D.C., and his nephew, James Dowling, a student at St. Mary's College in Wilmington, Del. (1856-1858), and letters from Hiram Keeler and his wife from Logansport, Cass Co. (1842-1846), Cazenovia, N.Y. (1846-1849), and Lake County and Cleveland, Ohio (1850s). Also included are papers relating to the Wabash and Erie Canal lands in

Indiana; papers relating to the claims of the Miami Indians; and Dowling's receipts, deeds, and other legal and financial documents.

Correspondents include Chilton Allan, Thomas H. Blake, Jesse D. Bright, Charles Butler, Joseph Cable, Patrick Donahue, John Ewing, Duff Green, Edward A. Hannegan, Andrew J. Harlan, William Hendricks, William S. Holman, Richard M. Johnson, Jonathan McCarty, Joseph G. Marshall, Henry L. Pinckney, Caleb B. Smith, John P. Usher, David Wallace, and Albert S. White.

A-92. DUBLIN AND NEW CASTLE TURNPIKE COMPANY. PAPERS, 1851-1859.

28 items.　　　　　　　　　　　　　　　　　　　　SC 516.
Microfilm.

The Dublin and New Castle Turnpike Company constructed and managed a toll road between Dublin, Wayne Co., and New Castle, Henry Co.

The papers consist primarily of reports and minutes from directors and stockholders meetings.

A-93. DUBOIS COUNTY MISCELLANEOUS RECORDS, 1853-1908.

1 ms. box.　　　　　　　Inventory.　　　　　　　M 57.

The records include Dubois County deeds, receipts, contracts, payrolls, appointments, election notices, and papers concerning the county poor farm.

A-94. DUNN, GEORGE GRUNDY, SR. (1812-1857). PAPERS, 1830-1922.

3 ms. boxes, 42 vols. (5 l.f.).　　　Inventory.　　　M 90, BV 1083-1124.

Attorney and politician. Dunn was a Bedford, Lawrence Co., store clerk and teacher (1833-1835); attorney in partnership with Richard W. Thompson

(1835-1857); and Whig and Republican member, Indiana State Senate (1850-1852) and U.S. House of Representatives (1847-1849, 1855-1857). Also included are papers of his sons, Moses F. Dunn (1843-1915) and George G. Dunn, Jr. (d.1891), partners in the Bedford law firm of Dunn & Dunn.

The collection includes account books from the law firms of George Dunn, Sr., and Dunn & Dunn (1835-1922); George Dunn, Sr.'s, account books for the disposition and sale of his father-in-law's estate (1840); Bedford general store account books (1830-1834); and papers relating to Dunn & Dunn's law cases on debt collections, Civil War pensions, real estate, and railroads (1865-1911).

A-95. DUNN, JACOB PIATT (1855-1924). PAPERS, 1812-1947.

7 ms. boxes, 4 vols. (2.5 l.f.).   Inventory.   M 89, BV 1125-1128.

Historian and journalist. Dunn was an Indianapolis attorney (1876-1879, 1884-1888); prospector and journalist in Colorado (1879-1884); secretary, Indiana Historical Society (1886-1924); writer for the *Indianapolis Journal* (1888), the *Indianapolis Sentinel* (1893-1904), and other Indianapolis newspapers; Indiana State Librarian (1889-1893); Indianapolis city comptroller (1904-1906, 1914, 1916); field agent, Hispaniola Mining Company, Haiti (1921-1922); private secretary, Indiana Senator Samuel M. Ralston (1923-1924); and historian, author of *Massacres of the Mountains* (1886), *Indiana, a Redemption from Slavery* (1888), *True Indian Stories* (1908), *Greater Indianapolis* (1910), and *Indiana and Indianans* (1919).

The papers include Dunn's correspondence, business papers, essays, book manuscripts, and family papers. The correspondence includes letters relating to Democratic Party politics, Dunn's mining activities in Haiti, the publication of his books, the Indiana Historical Society, and his historical research, including letters discussing the origin of the word "Hoosier," and letters from witnesses to the Indian massacres Dunn described in his book *Massacres of the Mountains*. Dunn's writings in the collection include essays on the history of the Indianapolis Presbyterian Church, the American presence in Haiti, and miscellaneous patriotic and religious topics; and manuscripts of the book *Indiana, a Redemption from Slavery*, and parts of *Indiana and Indianans*. Also included are scrapbooks containing reviews of his books and Indiana news clippings from the 1880s.

The Dunn family papers in the collection include legal and business documents (1812-1858) of Isaac Dunn of Lawrenceburg, Dearborn Co.; papers (1838-1853) of George and Jacob Dunn, Sr., relating to their mining ventures in California; and business papers (1869-1892) of Aquilla Jones who was engaged in the wholesale shoe business in Indianapolis.

Correspondents include Theodore Roosevelt and Lew Wallace.

A-96. DUNN, WILLIAM H. (ca.1840-1863). LETTERS, 1862-1863.

46 items. Calendar. SC 521.

Dunn, from Jefferson County, was a private in the 77th Indiana Regiment (4th Indiana Cavalry) during the Civil War.

The collection consists of Dunn's letters to his wife written while he was serving with the Union Army in Kentucky and Tennessee.

A-97. EDWARDS, GEORGE (ca.1832-1864). LETTERS, 1861-1864.

114 items. Calendar. SC 532.

Edwards was a farmer in Greene County; and private in the 27th Indiana Regiment during the Civil War.

The collection consists of Edwards's letters to his wife written while he served with the Union Army in Maryland, Virginia, and Tennessee.

A-98. ELDER, JOHN (d.1851). PAPERS, 1825-1908.

4 ms. boxes, 3 vols. (1.25 l.f.). Calendar. M 93, BV 257-259.

Architect. Elder was proprietor of the Union Inn in Indianapolis (1833-1836); and an architect and builder of county courthouses and other public buildings in Indiana, based in Indianapolis (1833-1848) and Connersville, Fayette Co. (1848-1850). He was the father of John R. Elder (1820-1908), publisher of the *Indianapolis Locomotive* (1848-1860) and the *Indianapolis Sentinel* (1860-1864).

The collection consists primarily of family correspondence from the period 1825-1866 and includes letters from Elder's family in Harrisburg and Carlisle, Pa. (1820-1865); Elder's and his wife's correspondence with their son, John R. Elder, while he was a student at Dickinson College, Carlisle, Pa. (1841-1843), an apprentice printer in New York City (1843-1847), and a newspaper publisher in Indianapolis (1847-1850); letters from his son, Samuel Elder, a Chicago, Ill., businessman (1845-1849); letters of Elder and his son, Alex Elder, from Panama and California during their trip to the goldfields (1850-1851); correspondence of John R. Elder with his fiancee and wife, Amelia Line of Carlisle (1854-1856); and letters from the Line family in Carlisle (1854-1866). Also included is Elder's correspondence regarding his architectural and construction work (1833-1850); correspondence regarding John R. Elder's newspaper work (1840s-1860s); Elder's notebooks listing expenses for construction work (1836-1847); and ledgers and guest registers for the Union Inn (1833-1836).

A-99. ELY, JAMES M. (1821-1905). ACCOUNT BOOKS, 1851-1866.

2 vols. (.25 l.f.).   BV 61-62.

Ely was a physician in New Palestine, Hancock Co. (1851-1905).

The collection consists of account books for Ely's medical practice (1851-1866).

A-100. ENGLEMAN, JAMES OZRO (1873-1943). PAPERS, 1864-1943.

3 ms. boxes, 7 vols. (1.5 l.f.).   Inventory.   M 96, BV 1130-1136.

Educator. Engleman was a teacher and principal at a number of Indiana schools, including the Borden Institute, Clark Co. (1905-1906); member, principal training department, Indiana State Teachers College, Terre Haute, Vigo Co. (1907-1909); head of department of education, State Normal College, La Crosse, Wis. (1909-1913); superintendent of schools, Decatur, Ill. (1913-1921); director, division of field services, National Education Association (1922-1924); superintendent of schools, Terre Haute (1924-1927); and president, Kent State University, Kent, Ohio (1928-1938).

The collection consists of a small amount of personal papers and letters (1891-1934) of Engleman and his wife, Anna Ulen Engleman; Engleman's essays and speeches; scrapbooks containing letters and newspaper clippings relating to his career; and Anna Ulen's school notebooks and documents (1882-1898).

A-101. ENGLISH, WILLIAM HAYDEN (1822-1896). COLLECTION, 1741-1926.

119 ms. boxes, 15 vols. (38 l.f.).   Inventory.   M 98, BV 1137-1148.

Politician, businessman, and historian. English was an attorney in Lexington, Scott Co.; Lexington postmaster (1842-1845); clerk, U. S. Treasury Department, Washington, D.C. (1845-1849); secretary, Indiana Constitutional Convention (1850-1851); Democratic member, Indiana House of Representatives (1851-1852), and Speaker of the House (1852); member, U.S. House of Representatives (1853-1861); regent, Smithsonian Institute (1853-1861); founder and president, First National Bank of Indianapolis (1863-1877); treasurer and majority partner, Indianapolis Citizens Street Railway Company (1866-1876); chairman, Democratic State Central committee (1880); Democratic candidate for Vice-President (1880); owner, English Hotel and Opera House, Indianapolis (1880-1896); president, Indiana Historical Society (1886-1896); and author, *Conquest of the Country Northwest of the River Ohio, 1778-1783* (1896). English's family included his father, Elisha Gale English (1798-1874), a Scott County businessman and Democratic member of the Indiana House of Representatives and Indiana State Senate (1832-1851, 1865-1867); and his son, William E. English (1850-1926), an Indianapolis attorney and businessman, manager and owner of the English Hotel and Opera House (ca.1880-1926), Democratic member of the Indiana House of Representatives (1879) and the U.S. House of Representatives (1884-1885), Republican member of the Indiana State Senate (1917-1925), officer in the Spanish-American War and active in Spanish-American War veterans organizations.

The collection consists of English's personal papers, the papers of his father and son, and papers he collected in the course of his research on the history of Indiana. English's personal papers include correspondence relating to local, state, and national politics in the 1850s, particularly the Kansas crisis, abolitionism, and secession; the 1880 presidential election and English's work as chairman of the Democratic State Central Committee; and English's business interests, including Indianapolis banks, the Indianapolis Citizens Street Railway Company, the Fort Wayne and Southern Railroad Company, and the construction and management of the English Hotel and Opera House. Also included are English's speeches (1854-1861, 1880); bills and contracts for the construction and maintenance of the English Hotel and Opera House (1881-1886); minutes of the Indianapolis Citizens Street Railway Company (1864-1876); accounts of his business agent, Walter Rivers (1877-1886); programs from the English Opera House (1881-1885); papers relating to the Fort Wayne and Southern Railroad Company (1854-1856), the First National Bank in Indianapolis (1863-1877), and other business interests; and his bankbooks, receipts, and checks.

Elisha English papers include business papers relating to his real estate interests in Scott County; papers relating to his speculation in claims arising from Morgan's Raid in 1863; and other business and political correspondence and papers. William E. English papers include legal briefs concerning his contested election to Congress (1882); his correspondence regarding politics, his business interests, and the formation of a Spanish-American War veterans organization; business papers relating to his estate at Englishton Park, Scott Co., and to his investments in Oregon; and correspondence and personal business papers of his wife, Helen Orr English.

Correspondents of English and his family include Jesse D. Bright, Nahum Capen, Lewis Cass, Grover Cleveland, Charles E. Coffin, James A. Cravens, John Wesley Davis, W. C. DePauw, Graham N. Fitch, Walter Q. Gresham, Winfield S. Hancock, Thomas A. Hendricks, Joseph Henry, William S. Holman, Henry S. Lane, James F. D. Lanier, William C. Larrabee, Elijah B. Martindale, John C. New, Robert Dale Owen, John Pettit, William B. Phillips, John Sherman, Benjamin F. Shively, William M. Springer, Isaac Toucey, David Turpie, Daniel W. Voorhees, Henry Watterson, James Whitcomb, William W. Wick, Ashbel P. Willard, and William W. Woollen.

The largest part of the collection consists of papers collected by English relating to the history of Indiana. Included are three boxes of miscellaneous documents and letters from the period 1785-1830 relating to the Northwest Territory, the Indiana Territory, early Indiana statehood, the French at Vincennes, Indians, and the War of 1812 in the West. Included are papers of Joseph Bartholomew, Ratliff Boon, Marston G. Clark, Ninian Edwards, John Gibson, William Henry Harrison, William Hendricks, Jonathan Jennings, Pierre Menard, James Noble, Benjamin Parke, Thomas Posey, James Brown Ray, Arthur St. Clair, Waller Taylor, Isaac White, and James Wilkinson.

Also acquired by English were the papers of the Hite and Bowman families (1741-1871), who settled in western Virginia and Kentucky at the time of the American Revolution. The most prominent members of the families represented in the collection are Isaac Hite and John Bowman, early settlers in Kentucky; Joseph and Isaac Bowman, officers under George Rogers Clark during the Illinois campaign, 1777-1778; and Abraham Bowman, colonel of the 8th Virginia Regiment during the Revolutionary War. The bulk of the papers are from the period 1770-1810 and include financial and legal documents, a small amount of personal and business correspondence, and documents relating to military operations in Kentucky and the Illinois country during the American Revolution. Also included are letters of John Gwathmey regarding the early settlement of Jeffersonville and Clark County, Ind.; and letters of Gen. Jonathan Clark, Thomas Jefferson, and James Madison.

Other material collected by English includes 43 boxes of transcripts, letters, and notes compiled for a planned biographical directory of the members of the Indiana state legislature (1880s-1890s); information collected on the members of the 1850-1851 Indiana Constitutional Convention, the territorial legislators and judges, and early county officials; 12 boxes of transcripts of newspaper articles and documents relating to early Indiana history; early Indiana election returns; orderly book of Brig. Gen. Robert Todd of the Kentucky Volunteers, covering his regiment's march to Ft. Jefferson, Ohio (September 29-October 24, 1793); Todd's journal describing Anthony Wayne's 1794 campaign against the Indians; record of the proceedings of Scott Masonic Lodge, Lexington, Ind. (1823-1829); and journal of the Indianapolis Light Infantry (1877-1889).

A-102. FAIRBANKS, CHARLES WARREN (1852-1918). PAPERS, 1876-1917.

18 ms. boxes, 56 vols. (13 l.f.).   Inventory.   M 100, BV 1150-1169.

Attorney and politician. Fairbanks was agent for the Associated Press in Cleveland, Ohio, and Pittsburgh, Pa. (1872-1874); Indianapolis attorney specializing in railroad cases (1874-1897); manager, Walter Q. Gresham's presidential campaign (1888); Republican candidate for U.S. Senate (1893); U.S. Senator from Indiana (1897-1905); American chairman, U.S. and British High Command for the Adjustment of Canadian Questions (1898); Vice-President of the United States under Theodore Roosevelt (1905-1909); chairman, American Commission, Tercentenary Celebration at Quebec (1908); president, Indiana Forestry Association (ca.1910-1918); and Republican candidate for Vice-President of the United States (1916).

The collection consists principally of Fairbanks's business and political papers from the period 1876-1904. Included are his letter books (1876-1904) containing copies of his letters relating to state and national politics, the operation of his U.S. Senate office, and his legal cases involving midwestern railroad companies; correspondence, principally from the period 1894-1904, relating to the legal affairs of railroad companies, the political campaign of 1896, patronage appointments, the U.S. and British Commission on Canada which considered the question of Alaska's boundaries, the 1904 presidential election, and the Indiana Forestry Association (1910-1917); letters from his Indiana constituents giving opinions on state and national issues (1897-1904); and scrapbooks of newspaper clippings and memorabilia relating to Fairbanks's political campaigns, his official trips to Alaska and Quebec, and the work of his wife, Cornelia Cole Fairbanks (d.1913) as president-general of the Daughters of the American Revolution (1901-1905). The collection also includes Fairbanks's letters to Rev. J. Wesley Hall (1907-1917); and a diary kept by Fairbanks's daughter, Adelaide, in Vevay, Switzerland Co. (1924-1928).

Correspondents include Albert Beveridge, William Lowe Bryan, John C. Chaney, Stanley Coulter, Winfield T. Durbin, John Watson Foster, John K. Gowdy, H. C. Hansbrough, Benjamin Harrison, John Hay, James A. Hemenway, John Wesley Hill, Garret A. Hobart, Joseph B. Kealing, Charles B. Landis, William McKinley, James A. Mount, Harry S. New, Russell Sage, Delavan Smith, George W. Steele, William Howard Taft, David Turpie, Lew Wallace, James E. Watson, and Charles R. Williams.

A-103. FAMILY SERVICE ASSOCIATION OF INDIANAPOLIS. RECORDS, 1879-1970.

26 ms. boxes, 85 vols. (21.5 l.f.).   Inventory.   M 102, BV 1170-1250.
Restricted.

The Family Service Association has been a private relief and counseling agency in Indianapolis since 1835 when it was founded as the Indianapolis Benevolent

Society. In 1879 it was reorganized as a two-part agency in which one part, the new Charity Organization Society, had the responsibility for investigating families requesting assistance, and the other, the Indianapolis Benevolent Society, distributed the aid approved by the investigators. In 1922 these two societies merged with the Children's Aid Association and the Mothers Aid Association to form the Family Welfare Society, which dealt with family problems in general. In 1945 the organization became the Family Service Association, reflecting its transformation from a relief distribution agency to a family counseling one.

The records consist of minutes, correspondence, reports, financial papers, case records, and scrapbooks of the Family Service Association and its related agencies. Included are Charity Organization Society minutes (1879-1920), records of cases investigated (1880-1899), the registrar's daybooks of requests for assistance (1910-1923), a caseworker's daybook (1893-1896), scrapbooks (1886-1907), and reports, correspondence, and other papers (1882-1928); Indianapolis Benevolent Society minutes (1879-1912), order books for food, clothing, and fuel for the needy (1884-1895), and records of cases (1879-1880); and Family Welfare Society and Family Service Association minutes (1922-1952), committee meeting minutes (1925-1955), scrapbooks (1915-1971), and card files of cases (1927-1970). Also included are papers of the Children's Aid Association, including minutes (1908-1922), financial papers (1905-1922), and correspondence and reports (1905-1923); the Summer Mission for Sick Children, including correspondence, financial papers, minutes (1917-1927), and scrapbooks (1890-1899, 1913); the Society of Friendly Visitors, including minutes (1896-1901) and the secretary's book (1882-1916); the Mothers Aid Society (1917-1924); the Legal Aid Society (1919-1937); the Social Service Exchange (1928-1956); and the Dime Savings and Loan (1931-1945). The collection also includes a scrapbook of newspaper clippings and memorabilia from the 18th National Conference of Charities and Corrections in Indianapolis (1891); minute book for the Indiana Federation of Charity Organizations' Secretaries (1912-1919); and historical materials on Oscar McCulloch and other leaders in the organization.

A-104. FAUCETT, THOMAS (b.1855). DIARIES, 1873-1881.

4 vols. (.25 l.f.).   Inventory.   M 103.

Faucett was a farmer in Orange County.

The diaries record Faucett's activities and Orange County events.

A-105. FEDERATION OF ASSOCIATED CLUBS, INC. RECORDS, 1937-1978.

12 ms. boxes. Inventory. M 429.

The Federation of Associated Clubs, Inc., was formed in 1937 by Starling W. James to unite black social clubs in Indianapolis for the purpose of improving living and working conditions and providing better social opportunities for the city's blacks. The federation has sponsored American and foreign tours, provided scholarships, and campaigned for civil rights and other issues of concern to blacks.

The records consist primarily of correspondence and other papers relating to the federation's tours (1945-1978). Also included are minutes of the federation board and committees (1965-1966); general correspondence (1950-1978); and programs, newsletters, clippings, and other printed materials.

A-106. FIRST INDIANA HEAVY ARTILLERY REGIMENT. RECORDS, 1862-1865.

1 ms. box. M 403.

The 1st Indiana Heavy Artillery Regiment, also known as the 21st Indiana Regiment, served in Louisiana and Texas (1862-1864) and at the siege of Mobile, Ala. (March-April 1865).

The records include payroll and supply records; copies of company orders; reports on the regiment's battle actions at Mobile; and record of shells fired by the regiment during the siege of Mobile.

A-107. FITCH, MARY LOUISE (fl.1839-1875). PAPERS, 1839-ca.1860.

34 items. Inventory. SC 1872.

Fitch was the daughter of Mason Coggswell Fitch (1797-1848), a New Albany, Floyd Co., attorney and president of the New Albany branch of the State Bank of Indiana; and wife of Joshua Bragdon (1806-1875), a New Albany steamboat owner and captain.

The collection consists primarily of personal letters to Fitch from the period 1844-1848. Included are letters from her brother, Marshall Montgomery Fitch, written from Yale University, Conn. (1846-1848); letters from friends attending the Georgetown (Ky.) Female Collegiate Institute and Hanover College, Jefferson Co.; and letters from family and friends in Indianapolis, New Albany, Michigan City and LaPorte, LaPorte Co., and Greenland, Maine.

A-108. FITZGERALD, DESMOND (1846-1926). PAPERS, 1857-1903.

1 ms. box, 1 vol. (.33 l.f.).   Partial Calendar.   M 105, BV 1255.

Engineer. Fitzgerald was a graduate of Phillips Academy, Andover, Mass. (1864); deputy secretary of state, Rhode Island (1863-1867); resident engineer, Indianapolis and Vincennes Railroad (1867-1869); engineer, Western River Improvements Office, Osage River, Missouri (1870); engineer, Boston and Albany Railroad (1871-1873); superintendent, Western Division, Boston Water Works (1873-1903); and president, American Society of Civil Engineers (1899).

The bulk of the collection consists of Fitzgerald's letters and papers relating to the Indianapolis and Vincennes Railroad's project to extend the line from Vincennes, Knox Co., to Cairo, Ill. (1867-1869). Also included is his personal correspondence, including letters from friends in Europe (1857-1877), and from school friends at Andover and other eastern schools (1860s); correspondence and papers relating to other engineering projects; and papers relating to the American Society of Civil Engineers and the Boston Society of Civil Engineers.

Correspondents include Ambrose E. Burnside and John Carter Brown.

A-109. FLANNER, HENRY BEESON (1820-1863). PAPERS, 1803-1874.

1 ms. box.   Calendar.   M 106.

Flanner was part of a Quaker family in Jefferson County, Ohio; a schoolteacher and botanist in Raysville, Henry Co. (1842), and Mt. Pleasant, Ohio (1852-1863); and a soldier in the 113th Ohio Regiment during the Civil War.

The papers consist of correspondence of the Flanner and Beeson families in Jefferson and Columbiana counties, Ohio, and Uniontown, Pa. (1803-1842); correspondence regarding Flanner's Civil War service (1862-1863); and correspondence of Flanner's wife, Orpha Tyler Flanner, with family in Indianapolis and Raysville and with people interested in her husband's botanical specimens (1863-1874).

A-110. FLANNER, HILDEGARDE (1899-). LETTERS, 1920-1976.

1 ms. box.   Calendar.   M 107.

Flanner grew up in Indianapolis; attended the University of California at Berkeley (ca.1920-1923); married Frederick Monhoff (1926); and authored a number of poetry books and plays (1920-1942).

The collection includes letters written by Flanner in Berkeley and New York (1920-1923) and Altedena, Calif. (1927, 1942), to Martha Hawkins, an Indianapolis friend; and letters written from California to Eleanor Goodall Vonnegut of Indianapolis (1961-1976). The letters concern school, California, her writings, and her family, including her sister, writer Janet Flanner (1892-1979).

A-111. FLETCHER, CALVIN (1798-1866). PAPERS, 1817-1917.

41 ms. boxes, 16 vols. (12.5 l.f.).   Inventory.   M 108, BV 1256-1267, 1880, 1968-1970. Microfilm.

Attorney, banker, and civic leader. Fletcher was born in Ludlow, Vt.; was a teacher and attorney in Urbana, Ohio (1817-1821); attorney in Indianapolis (1821-1866); prosecuting attorney, Marion County Circuit Court (1822-1823); member, Indiana State Senate (1825-1833); member, board of directors, Indiana State Bank (1831-1841); director and president, Indianapolis branch of the Indiana State Bank (1841-1858); president, Indianapolis and Bellefontaine Railroad (1855); organizer and officer of the Indianapolis Branch Banking Company with Thomas Sharpe (1857-1866); farmer; land speculator, particularly in central and northwestern Indiana; one of the organizers of the Marion County Agricultural Society (1835); active in Whig,

Free Soil, and Republican party politics; state agent for purchasing arms in Canada for Indiana soldiers (1861); chairman, joint committee of the U.S. Sanitary Commission and Indiana Sanitary Committee (1861); worked on behalf of the Freedman's Aid Committee (1863); Methodist; teacher and superintendent of Sabbath school at Roberts Chapel; worked with William Slade and Catherine Beecher to recruit eastern-trained teachers for Indianapolis schools (1847-1848); Indianapolis school trustee (1851-1858); and active in numerous educational and charitable organizations, including the Indianapolis Benevolent Society, the Indiana Colonization Society, the Indiana Historical Society, and education and temperance societies.

The collection consists primarily of Fletcher's diaries and his family and business correspondence from the period 1817-1866. Included are his diaries (1817-1866), describing his family life, his political and business interests, daily events in Indiana and Indianapolis; diary (1821-1838) and letters of his wife, Sarah Hill Fletcher (1801-1854); Fletcher's letters to his family in Vermont from Urbana and Indianapolis (1817-1830s); his journal of his trip from Indianapolis to Vermont (1824); his correspondence with his wife during his trips to Cincinnati, Vermont, and throughout Indiana; and letters to Fletcher from his family in Vermont, Lynchburg, Va., and New York State. Also included are letters of his children, including letters written while they were attending school in Bloomington, Monroe Co. (1831-1834), Brown University, R.I. (1842-1858), and Princeton University, N.J. (1844-1848), and Lancaster, Mass. (1853-1860); letters of James Cooley Fletcher (1823-1901), written while he was working as a missionary in Brazil (1851-1854); letters of Miles Fletcher (1828-1862), written while he was teaching at Indiana Asbury (DePauw) University, Greencastle, Putnam Co. (1857-1862), and serving as Indiana Superintendent of Public Instruction (1861-1862); letters of William B. Fletcher (1837-1907), written while attending medical school in Massachusetts and New York (1858-1860) and from the Richmond, Va., prison after he was captured by Confederate troops (1861); and letters of Stephen Keyes Fletcher (1840-1897), written while he was serving in the 33rd and 115th Indiana regiments (1861-1863).

Also included is Fletcher's business correspondence, particularly regarding banking in Indianapolis and the Midwest, his legal cases, Indiana politics, his land interests in northwestern Indiana, and the Indianapolis and Bellefontaine Railroad; Fletcher's speeches on temperance, agriculture, and education; recollections of Sarah Hill Fletcher, written by her children; biographical sketches of Fletcher; Fletcher's account book of personal expenses (1843-1849); stories by Marion Wehner based upon the Fletcher papers; and typed transcripts of Fletcher's diary and much of the correspondence. Fletcher's diary and a small part of the correspondence were published as *The Diary of Calvin Fletcher* (Indianapolis: Indiana Historical Society, 1972-1983, 9v.).

Correspondents include Hervey Bates, Catherine E. Beecher, Ovid Butler, John Caven, Charles F. Coffin, Elijah Coffin, Schuyler Colfax, J. J. Cravens, W. S. Crawford, Harvey Gregg, Cyrus C. Hines, William A. Holliday, Andrew Ingram, Henry S. Lane, Nicholas McCarty, Samuel Merrill, Oliver P. Morton, James Noble, James Paxton, Albert Gallatin Porter, Daniel D. Pratt, James Rariden, James M. Ray, W. R. Revels, Thomas H. Sharpe, William Slade, Oliver H. Smith, John Tipton, George Upfold, Lew Wallace, James Whitcomb, William W. Wick, Daniel Worth, Joseph A. Wright, and Simon Yandes.

A-112. FORTUNE, WILLIAM (1863-1942). PAPERS, 1881-1942.

7 ms. boxes, 1 archival box (3 l.f.). Inventory. M 350.

Journalist and civic leader. Fortune was a newspaperman with the *Indianapolis Journal* and *News* (1886-1890); organized the Indianapolis Commercial Club with Col. Eli Lilly (1890) and served as an officer (1890-1898); executive director, G.A.R. national encampment in Indianapolis (1893); chairman, Chamber of Commerce Elevated Railroad Commission which secured the abolition of grade crossings in Indianapolis (1898-1916); organized the Indianapolis chapter of the American Red Cross (1916) and served as an officer (1916-1942); member of committee which built memorial for Nancy Hanks Lincoln at Boonville, Warrick Co. (1927); and president, American Peace Society (1928).

The collection consists primarily of papers relating to Fortune's public work, including his Commercial Club activities and his work on street paving and track elevation in Indianapolis; his work in organizing the 1893 G.A.R. encampment; and his work on the Nancy Hanks Lincoln Memorial, including his research notes and writings on Abraham Lincoln. Also included are papers relating to the Indianapolis Commercial Club and Chamber of Commerce, the Indianapolis and National Red Cross, and the American Peace Society; letters to James Whitcomb Riley and Edmund Eitel from Young Allison of Louisville, Ky. (1903-1917); testimonial letters written in appreciation of Fortune's gift of a site for a Veterans Hospital in Indianapolis (1929-1931); and Fortune's scrapbooks.

Correspondents include Louis Ludlow and Herman B Wells.

A-113. FRASER, DWIGHT (1836-1915). PAPERS, 1864-1866.

56 items. SC 591.

Fraser, from LaPorte, LaPorte Co., served as a major in the 128th Indiana Regiment during the Civil War.

The collection consists of letters from Fraser and his brother, Joshua Fraser, a lieutenant in the 128th Indiana Regiment, to their family in LaPorte, written while they served in the Union Army in Tennessee and Georgia.

A-114. FRY-RHUE FAMILY. PAPERS, 1843-1969.

3 ms. boxes. Inventory. M 111.

The Fry and Rhue families included John Fry (1809-1878), a farmer in Boone County, Ky., and Greenfield, Hancock Co.; Perry Rhue (1843-1898), a Hancock County farmer and corporal with the 29th Indiana Regiment during the Civil War; and Ward Fry Rhue (1892-1967), a soldier with the American Army in France and Germany (1918-1919).

The collection consists primarily of family papers from the period 1851-1944, including letters to John Fry from relatives and friends in Hancock County (1851-1853), Indianapolis (1856), Covington and Boone County, Ky. (1853-1859), and Pike County, Mo. (1857); Ward Rhue's World War I letters to his mother from Camp Taylor, Ky., Camp Beauregard, La., France, and Germany (1918-1919); letters to Rhue's mother, Sarah Rhue of Greenfield, from relatives throughout the country (1901-1944); and other family correspondence, legal papers, and financial papers, principally from Hancock County.

A-115. FRYBARGER, GEORGE (1796-1853). ACCOUNT BOOKS, 1831-1867.

34 vols. (5.5 l.f.). Inventory. BV 118-152.

Frybarger was the owner of a general merchandise store in Connersville, Fayette Co. (1821-1853); president of the Bank of Connersville; and prominently involved in the construction of the White Water Canal.

The collection consists of the account books for Frybarger's Connersville store and for the successor firm of W. W. Frybarger & Company.

A-116. FULLER, JOHN LOUIS HILTON (1894-). PAPERS, 1840-1962.

3 ms. boxes.   Inventory.   M 112.
Microfilm.

Banker and businessman. Fuller was a graduate of Butler University, Indianapolis (1917); a trainee with the international division of the National City Bank of New York assigned to the bank's branches in Petrograd, Russia (1917-1918), London, England (1919-1920), and New York (1920-1922); secretary-treasurer of the Western Furniture Company, Indianapolis (1923-1943); and officer with the Equitable Life Assurance Society of the United States (1930-1962).

The bulk of the papers are from the period 1917-1920 and consist of letters and diaries written by Fuller while he was working in Petrograd and London. His writings describe his work, social life in the two cities, and his experiences during the Russian Revolution. The collection also includes letters written by Fuller's father, Hector Fuller (1864-1934), a correspondent for the *Indianapolis News*, while he was serving as a correspondent in the Far East covering the Russo-Japanese War (1903-1904). Also included are miscellaneous nineteenth-century family papers; papers of the Equitable Life Assurance Society; and a letter of William Dean Howells to Hector Fuller.

A-117. GALE, WAKEFIELD (1797-1881). PAPERS, 1828-1875.

100 items.   Calendar.   SC 610.

Gale was a Presbyterian minister in Eastport, Maine (1828-1835), and Glocester (1836-1840), Rockport (1840-1859), and other towns in Massachusetts. Gale's family included his brother-in-law, Solomon Kittredge (d.1847), a Presbyterian minister in Salem, Washington Co. (1832-1834), and Bedford, Lawrence Co. (1834-1847); and his brother, Joseph W. Gale (ca.1809-1889), founder and director of Sunday schools in New Albany, Floyd Co., and in northern Kentucky (1841-1875).

The collection consists primarily of family letters to Gale from relatives in Indiana regarding family matters and religious activities in the state. Included are letters from Solomon Kittredge and his wife in Salem (1832-1833), Bedford (1834-1848), and New Albany (1849-1859); from Joseph W. Gale in New Albany (1848-1875); and from Gale's father, Joseph Gale, in Bedford (1838-1840), Pembroke, N.H. (1840-1848), and New Albany (1848-1850).

A-118. GALLION, NATHAN D. (ca.1790-1865). PAPERS, 1818-1820.

25 items.   Calendar.   SC 612.

Gallion owned general merchandise stores in Brookville, Franklin Co. (1814-1865), and Waterloo and Connersville, Fayette Co.

The collection consists of letters to Gallion from customers and business associates in Waterloo and Connersville regarding business conditions and the operations of his stores (1818-1820).

A-119. GAVIN, JAMES (1830-1873). PAPERS, 1872-1873.

31 items.   Calendar.   SC 616.

Gavin was an attorney in Greensburg, Decatur Co. (1852-1873); and law partner of John D. Miller (1840-1898).

The collection consists primarily of letters from Gavin and Miller's clients regarding collections and other legal business which the firm was handling in Greensburg, Indianapolis, and Cincinnati, Ohio. Also included is correspondence regarding the Democratic Party in Indiana (1872); and correspondence and papers regarding Gavin's personal business interests.

A-120. GEX OBUSSIER, LOUIS (1761-1845). PAPERS, 1804-1842.

26 items.   SC 620.

Gex Obussier was an emigrant from Switzerland; joined John Dufour's Swiss settlement at Vevay, Switzerland Co., where he was a farmer and winemaker

(1804-1826); moved to New Harmony, Posey Co. (1826); and was New Harmony postmaster (1829-1839).

The collection consists primarily of letters and bills from merchants in Pittsburgh, Pa., regarding supplies for Gex Obussier and the Dufour settlement (1804-1820). There are also two letters from Vevay to Obussier's daughter, Columbine Pelham, wife of William Pelham of New Harmony (1838-1840).

A-121. GIBSON, THOMAS WARE (1815-1876). ABSTRACTS, 1849.

2 vols. (.5 l.f.). BV 587-588.
Microfilm.

Gibson was an attorney in Clark County (1837-1853); and a member of the Indiana House of Representatives (1851-1852), Senate (1853), and Constitutional Convention (1850-1851).

The collection consists of title abstracts and plats for land in Clark's Grant and Jeffersonville, Clark Co., up to 1849, compiled by Thomas W. Gibson.

A-122. GILBERT, JOHN ALSOP (1799-1890). ACCOUNT BOOKS, 1833-1851.

5 vols. (.33 l.f.). Inventory. BV 664-668.

Gilbert was a farmer and a cooper associated with a pork-packing company in Muncie, Delaware Co. (1836); Delaware County justice of the peace (1838-1841); Delaware County associate judge (1839); and a partner in a Muncie grocery store (1839-1840).

The collection includes Gilbert's justice of the peace docket book (1839-1841); his accounts as a cooper (1841-1847) and grocery store owner (1839-1840); his personal accounts (1845-1851); accounts of Samuel Goodrich Benedict, a Muncie cabinetmaker (1833-1837); and record of sales of lots in New Cincinnati, Delaware Co. (1840).

A-123. GOODWIN, JOHN PEMBERTON (1880-1972). PAPERS, 1816-1969.

15 ms. boxes, 32 vols. (6.5 l.f.).   Inventory.   M 115, BV 1269-1301. Microfilm.

Banker and local historian. Goodwin was an officer in the U.S. Army (1917-1919); president, National Brookville Bank, Brookville, Franklin Co. (1925-1939); president, Brookville Telephone Company (1925-1957); member, Indiana Library and Historical Board (1945-1966); trustee, Indiana Historical Society (1953-1972); and president, Whitewater Canal Association of Indiana, Inc. (1940s). The collection also includes the papers of Goodwin's ancestors, including Samuel Goodwin (1789-1851), a farmer and tanner near Brookville (1815-1851); Joseph Goudie (1795-1879), a farmer near Brookville; John R. Goodwin (1820-1880), a Brookville physician and owner of the Brookville National Bank (1872-1880); and Charles F. Goodwin (1849-1896), partner in the Brookville National Bank (1872-1896).

The collection includes John P. Goodwin's correspondence and papers relating to DePauw University in Greencastle, Putnam Co., his World War I service, the National Brookville Bank, the Indiana State Library (1953-1967), the Indiana Historical Society (1933-1969), and the restoration of the Whitewater Canal (1941-1964); Samuel Goodwin's account books (1818-1830) and his land, legal, and financial documents relating to Franklin County (1817-1851); Joseph Goudie's account books (1837-1847), family legal papers (1820-1873), and correspondence, particularly letters to his daughter from friends and suitors (1838-1842); John R. Goodwin's diaries (1848-1861), account books (1846-1861), and miscellaneous legal and financial papers (1849-1880); Charles F. Goodwin's diaries (1878-1889), his correspondence with his fiancee and wife, Mattie Shirk, while she was a student at Western Female Seminary in Oxford, Ohio (1872-1874), his letters to his wife from Brookville (1886, 1891), letters from his daughter at the Western Female Seminary (1891), his scrapbook of papers from Brookville College and Indiana Asbury (DePauw) University (1865-1871), and papers relating to the Brookville National Bank. Also included is a record of the overseers of the poor, Brookville (1819-1927); list of subscribers to the Franklin Turnpike Company (1847); diary of Samuel Shirk of Franklin County (1855); diaries of Indianapolis businessman William O. Rockwood (1867, 1870, 1877); diary of a woman on her trip to Europe (1910); and family scrapbooks.

Correspondents include Ross Lockridge, Harry S. New, and Cornelius O'Brien.

A-124. GRAETER, CHRISTIAN (1777-1832). ACCOUNT BOOKS, 1809-1849.

6 vols. (.5 l.f.).   BV 153-157.

Graeter was a businessman and tavern owner in Vincennes, Knox Co. (1804-1832).

The collection includes Graeter's account books for his tavern (1812-1815); lists of accounts (1809-1824); and records of billiard games (1809-1815). Also included are two store account books (1839-1849) of his son, Frederick Graeter (b.1815), a grocery merchant in Vincennes.

A-125. GRAHAM, JOHN KENNEDY (1783-1841). PAPERS, 1786-1927.

5 ms. boxes, 24 vols.(4 l.f.).   Inventory.   M 116, BV 1304-1326.
Microfilm.

Surveyor and politician. Graham was a merchant and surveyor in Pennsylvania, Louisiana, and Kentucky (ca.1800-1805); merchant, farmer, and surveyor in New Albany, Floyd Co. (ca.1806-1841); laid out town of New Albany (ca.1813); delegate, Indiana Constitutional Convention (1816); member, Indiana House of Representatives (1816-1817, 1825, 1827-1828) and Indiana State Senate (1825-1826); and involved in survey of the Michigan Road (1828) and the Wabash River (1829).

The collection includes Graham's correspondence, primarily from the period 1802-1841, including letters from family members in western Pennsylvania (1802-1840); letters from business associates in Natchez, Miss., Louisville, Ky., Cincinnati, Ohio, and New Albany and other towns in southern Indiana; correspondence regarding Indiana politics and the work of the state legislature, including plans for a state prison in southeastern Indiana (1820s-1830s); and correspondence regarding his survey work on the Michigan Road in northwestern Indiana (1828) and on the Wabash River (1829). His papers also include survey drawings for New Albany, Jeffersonville, Clark Co., the Vincennes Road, and other towns and properties, primarily in southeastern Indiana (1810s-1830s); his diary (1825-1826); his notebook on the Wabash River survey (1829); transcripts of his diary (1831-1841); and the diary of his daughter, Marie Graham Grant of New Albany (1851-1921). The collection also includes papers of the Shipman family of New Albany, including the Ohio River logbooks of steamboat pilot Harry Shipman (1885, 1896), and family legal and financial documents (1827-1904); papers of the Reese family of New Albany, including letters from Dr. Alexander Reese of Hanover, Jefferson Co. (1852), and Kansas (1896-1904); family genealogical materials; and typed transcripts of many of the diaries and letters.

Correspondents include Marston G. Clark, William Clark, William Croghan, John Hay Farnham, Jonathan Jennings, Samuel Merrill, Noah Noble, Waller Taylor, Edward Tiffin, and John Tipton.

A-126. GRAND ARMY OF THE REPUBLIC. NELSON TRUSLER POST NO. 60. RECORDS, 1882-1931.

4 ms. boxes, 19 vols. (2.5 l.f.).   Inventory.   M 117, BV 1330-1348.

Nelson Trusler Post No. 60 was the Grand Army of the Republic post at Winchester, Randolph Co. It was the social and fraternal organization for Union veterans of the Civil War.

The collection consists of the post's minutes, financial records, membership books, reports, and correspondence. Also included are the records of the post's woman's relief corps (1895-1920).

A-127. GRAY, BEULAH BRAZELTON (1882-1964). PAPERS, 1813-1962.

10 ms. boxes.   Inventory.   M 391.

Gray was a reporter and columnist for the *Otwell* (Pike Co.) *Star* (1920-1945); editor of the *Otwell Star* (1929-1945); housemother, student nurses' residence, Wellborn Baptist Hospital, Evansville, Vanderburgh Co. (1945-1950); and local historian, author of *The Saga of Three Churches* (1957) and other articles, books, and pageants on southern Indiana and Pike County.

The collection includes Gray's correspondence regarding her genealogical and local history research; her correspondence with soldiers from Pike County serving in Europe and the Pacific during World War II; letters to her from

Elsie Whitehurst Lightburn in Norwich, Cheshire, England, describing conditions in England during and after World War II (1945-1949); her family and personal correspondence; and her essays, pageants, articles, and other writings. Also included are Gray and Brazelton family correspondence and legal documents (1813-1919); copybooks (1833, 1840, ca.1912); and genealogical materials.

Correspondents include Homer Capehart.

A-128. GRAY, MARION H. (1900-). COLLECTION, 1850-1935.

1 ms. box, 1 vol: (.25 l.f.).   Inventory.   M 118, BV 1367.

Gray, of Bloomington, Monroe Co., donated this collection to the Indiana Historical Society in 1977.

The collection consists of papers relating to Gray's family. Included are letters of Selma Neubacher Steele, wife of artist T. C. Steele, to Mae Hunter Weinstein, Terre Haute, Vigo Co., regarding personal matters and the work of her husband (1921-1935); constitution and minutes of the First Congregational Church Sewing Circle, Terre Haute (1881-1912); memoirs of Robert Hunter (1874-1942), who grew up in Terre Haute, worked in settlement houses in New York and Chicago, was a prominent figure in the Socialist Party in the 1910s, and authored numerous sociological and political works (photostat); memoirs of Thirza Belle Weinstein, Terre Haute (1847-1932); Weinstein family history materials; and diary of William B. Ogle, Prairieton, Vigo Co., kept on a trip to California in 1850 (photostat).

A-129. GREEN, MIRIAM WILSON (1840-1913). PAPERS, 1859-1897.

2 ms. boxes.   Inventory.   M 119.
Microfilm.

Green attended Earlham College, Richmond, Wayne Co. (1861-1862); taught school in a number of counties in eastern Indiana; married John Henley of Newport (Fountain City), Wayne Co. (1873); and was a member of the Society of Friends.

The bulk of the collection consists of letters to Green from relatives, friends, and suitors in eastern and central Indiana during the period 1859-1872, relating to school, teaching, the Civil War, the response of Quakers to the war, and family matters. The papers include letters from Green's cousin, Cyrus Green, who was involved with the Friendsville Academy, Friendsville, Tenn. (1862-1869), and letters from Daniel P. Wooton, an officer in the 41st Indiana Regiment serving in Kentucky and Tennessee (1861-1863). The papers also include postcards written to the family (1892-1897), principally correspondence between John Henley in Portland, Oreg., and his wife and children in Richmond (1892).

A-130. GREEN, REUBEN (1770-1852). PAPERS, 1831-1885.

83 items. SC 1781.

Green was a farmer in Guilford County, N.C.; and a member of the Society of Friends.

The collection consists of letters from Green and members of his family, principally to his son Robert Green (1804-1850) and family in Newport (Fountain City), Wayne Co. Included are letters from North Carolina (1831-1853), Philadelphia, Pa. (1852-1854), southeastern Kansas (1858), Springfield, Ill. (1859-1868), Washington County (1841-1854), Wayne County (1854-1868), Indianapolis (1854-1865), Crawfordsville, Montgomery Co. (1867-1868), and other Indiana places.

A-131. GRIFFITH, THORNTON (1799-1869). PAPERS, 1822-1874.

30 items. Calendar. SC 658.

Griffith moved to Indiana from Philadelphia, Pa. (1832); and was a farmer in Clinton County (1832-1850) and Montgomery County (1850-1866).

The bulk of the collection is from the period 1822-1843 and includes letters to Griffith from his father and other family members in Frederick County, Md. (1822), and Fountain County, Ind. (1827-1829); letters to the John A. Hall family in Crawfordsville, Montgomery Co., from family members in

Newberry, S.C. (1830-1832); and receipts, promissory notes, and other financial documents from Montgomery and Clinton counties (1832-1852).

A-132. GRILLS, MERTON W. (1872-1958). PAPERS, 1827-1956.

6 ms. boxes, 18 vols. (2.5 l.f.).   Inventory.   M 120, BV 1349-1366.

Grills was an insurance agent in Hagerstown, Wayne Co.; and wrote extensively about the history of Wayne and Henry counties.

The collection includes Grills's diaries (1892-1894, 1908-1912, 1931-1956); a small amount of personal and business correspondence (1908-1956); his writings on the history of Wayne and Henry counties; essays written while a student at the Richsquare Academy, Lewisville, Henry Co. (1889-1891); notes on the Christian Endeavor Convention, Fort Wayne, Allen Co. (1892); and miscellaneous poems, essays, and other writings, including a manuscript literary magazine (1897). Also included are correspondence and legal papers of the Grills family in Hagerstown (1843-1905), including letters of Grills's grandfather, Henry S. Grills, written from Hagerstown (1852-1857), and a record book of the Hagerstown and West River Turnpike Association (1854-1858); account book of Peter Schenck, a Wayne County carpenter (1827-1833); account book for a Hagerstown woolen mill (1847-1854); and account book for the Hagerstown Canal Office (1849-1851).

A-133. GRIMSLEY, JAMES (ca.1834-1899). PAPERS, 1856-1891.

1 ms. box.   Inventory.   M 121.

Grimsley was a resident of Gosport, Owen Co.; an officer in the 21st (1st Heavy Artillery) Indiana Regiment (1861-1864); active in Civil War veterans organizations; and president, Indiana State Pension Association (1890).

The collection includes orders, muster rolls, and official documents relating to Grimsley's military service and the 21st Indiana in Maryland (1861-1862) and Louisiana (1862-1863); postwar correspondence relating to Grimsley's activities in veterans organizations, including the Soldiers' and Sailors' Rights and Service Pension Alliance, the Indiana State Pension Association, and the Grand Army of the Republic (1886-1891); and his speeches on veterans affairs and patriotism.

A-134. HACK, ELIZABETH JANE MILLER (1878-1961). PAPERS, 1875-1941.

3 ms. boxes, 3 vols. (1 l.f.). Calendar. M 123, BV 1369-1371.

Hack was the author of *The Yoke* (1903), *Saul of Tarsus* (1906), and other novels written under her maiden name (Miller); wife of Indianapolis attorney Oren Hack (1876-1942). She was the sister of Ralph Miller (1874-1903), a resident of Indianapolis, a member of the Indiana Volunteer Infantry (1898-1899), and an officer in the U.S. Army in the Philippines during the Insurrection (1900-1903).

The collection consists primarily of documents and letters of Hack and her family in Indianapolis from the period 1894-1920 and includes correspondence about her writing and family matters; diaries (1894-1903) and papers (1895-1903) of Ralph Miller, including his diaries and papers from the Philippines (1900-1903); and copies of her magazine and newspaper stories.

Correspondents include Luther Burbank, Charles W. Fairbanks, Louis Ludlow, and Lew Wallace.

A-135. HACKLEMAN-TOWNER FAMILY. PAPERS, 1847-1862.

1 ms. box. Inventory. M 124.

The Hackleman-Towner family included William R. Hackleman (1821-1862), a Brookville, Franklin Co., farmer; and John H. Towner (1831-1853), a Brookville farmer and soldier in the 5th Indiana Regiment during the Mexican War.

The collection consists of Hackleman's farm diaries (1861-1862); Towner's account of his Mexican War service (1847-1848); and Towner's journal describing his trip to Panama during the California Gold Rush (1850-1853).

A-136. HALL, SAMUEL (1797-1862). PAPERS, 1810-1862.

1 ms. box. Calendar. M 315.

Businessman and politician. Hall was a Princeton, Gibson Co., attorney (1819-1862); Whig member, Indiana House of Representatives (1829-1831, 1845-

1846); judge, 4th circuit (1832-1835); member, Indiana Board of Internal Improvements (1836-1837); lieutenant governor of Indiana (1840-1843); vice-president, National Whig Convention (1840, 1844); member, Indiana Constitutional Convention (1850-1851); and president, Evansville and Illinois Railroad (1849-1859).

The collection consists primarily of correspondence and legal and financial documents relating to Hall's law practice; and correspondence regarding local and state politics, internal improvements, and the Whig and Republican parties. Also included are correspondence, notebooks, and business papers relating to the promotion, construction, and operation of the Evansville and Illinois Railroad and the Evansville and Crawfordsville Railroad (1849-1861).

Correspondents include Isaac Blackford, Schuyler Colfax, Elisha Embree, Benjamin Harrison, Henry S. Lane, John Law, John Livingston, Noah Noble, Robert Dale Owen, Benjamin Parke, John Tipton, James C. Veatch, and Joseph A. Wright.

A-137. HALL, SAMUEL (1848-1869). PAPERS, 1860-1904.

| 1 ms. box. | Calendar. | M 125. |

Hall grew up in Princeton, Gibson Co.; and moved to Omaha, Nebr., in 1865 where he worked as a store clerk (1866-1869).

The papers consist primarily of correspondence between Hall in Omaha and his mother in Princeton and letters from other family and friends in Princeton (1866-1869). Also included are letters to Hall from a soldier stationed at Fort Sedgewick, Colo., and Fort McPherson, Nebr. (1869).

A-138. HAMILTON, JOHN WATTS (fl.1853-1866). PAPERS, 1851-1899.

| 28 items. | Calendar. | SC 676. |

Hamilton was a farmer and teacher in Ripley County.

The papers include letters of Hamilton and other members of his family in Ripley County and New Castle, Henry Co., to his sister, Agnes Crandell, in

Danville, Ill. (1853-1866). The letters discuss family affairs, farming, and the Civil War. Also included are family letters to Allen Crandell from Versailles, Ripley Co. (1886-1887).

A-139. HANCOCK COUNTY MISCELLANEOUS PAPERS, 1828-1853.

67 items. SC 353-356, BV 604-605.

The collection includes Hancock County election returns (1828-1834); estray book (1828-1846); assessment list (1839); and subpoenas, court documents, and other legal papers (1828-1853).

A-140. HANNA, ROBERT BARLOW (1815-1892). PAPERS, 1859-1927.

2 ms. boxes. Calendar. M 129.

Hanna was a businessman in Attica, Fountain Co. (1860s-1870s), and Bloomington, Ill. (1880s); and captain in the 72nd Indiana Regiment serving in Kentucky and Tennessee (1862-1863).

The bulk of the collection consists of correspondence from the period 1862-1871 and includes Hanna's Civil War letters to his wife (1862-1863); letters from his son, Robert Hanna, a student at West Point Military Academy, N.Y. (1869-1871), regarding family business, Attica, and West Point; and correspondence of his son, Samuel Hanna, a student at the University of Michigan, Ann Arbor (1870-1871), with friends at Attica and Covington, Fountain Co., and Indiana University, Bloomington, Monroe Co. Also included are Hanna's letters from Bloomington, Ill., to Samuel Hanna in Howard, Kans. (1887-1888); two letters of Robert Hanna written while he was with the U.S. Army in the West (1873-1875); and letters of other Civil War soldiers in Virginia, Tennessee, and Mississippi (1862-1863).

A-141. HANNA, SAMUEL (1797-1866). PAPERS, 1830-1853.

72 items. Calendar. SC 682.

Hanna was a Fort Wayne, Allen Co., farmer, land speculator, and railroad executive; a member of the Indiana House of Representatives (1826-1827,

1831-1832, 1840-1841) and Senate (1832-1835); and a commissioner, Wabash and Erie Canal (1828-1836).

The bulk of the collection consists of Hanna's receipts, legal and financial papers, and correspondence regarding his business interests in Madison County.

A-142. HARDING, STEPHEN SELWYN (1808-1891). PAPERS, 1848-1959.

2 ms. boxes. Inventory. M 130.

Harding was an attorney in Milan and Versailles, Ripley Co. (1829-1891); Liberty Party candidate for lieutenant governor of Indiana (1843, 1846); one of the founding members of the Indiana Republican Party (1850s); abolitionist; governor of the Utah Territory (1862-1863); and chief justice, Colorado Supreme Court (1863-1866).

The bulk of the papers are from the period 1848-1891 and include Harding's letters to his family from Utah and Colorado (1862-1865); letters from his son, Attila Harding, regarding family matters and economic conditions in Utah and Idaho (1852-1904); Civil War correspondence of Attila Harding, 26th Indiana Regiment, and other Indiana soldiers (1861-1862); speeches, stories, and poems written by Harding, including a story about his experiences in the West, and an essay on the early history of Ripley County (1875); his legal and financial papers (1851-1863); and correspondence of his children (1880s-1917).

A-143. HARPER, WILLIAM (b.1834). PAPERS, 1861-1890.

1 ms. box. M 426.

Harper was a farmer in Wells County (1853-1868); a hotelkeeper in Jay and Adams counties (1868-ca.1900); and a sergeant in the 47th Indiana Regiment (1861-1865).

The papers consist primarily of Harper's letters to his wife while he was serving with the Union Army in Missouri, Arkansas, Louisiana, and Mississippi (1861-

1865); and letters of his wife's brothers, John and Joseph Watts, soldiers in the 119th (7th Cavalry) Indiana Regiment, in Tennessee, Missouri, Mississippi, Louisiana, and Texas (1863-1865). Also included are letters from family members in eastern Indiana and other places (1865-1890).

A-144. HARRAH, ALMIRA MARIA SCOTT (1817-1888). PAPERS, 1819-1903.

2 ms. boxes, 3 vols. (.75 l.f.).   Inventory.   M 131, BV 1021-1023.

Harrah was a teacher in Manhattan, Putnam Co. (1840); lived with her parents in Cloverland, Clay Co. (1840-1843); married Samuel B. Harrah (b.1816), a merchant in Point Commerce and Worthington, Greene Co.; taught school at Greencastle, Putnam Co. (1847); and active in benevolent, temperance, and women's rights organizations.

The collection includes correspondence between Harrah and her husband while she was teaching school in Greencastle; letters between her and her brother, Harvey D. Scott, while he was a student at Indiana Asbury (DePauw) University, Greencastle, and a lawyer in Terre Haute, Vigo Co., working with Richard Wigginton Thompson (1843-1847); other Harrah and Scott family correspondence, primarily from the 1840s; and family letters to Samuel B. Harrah's business partner, Carpus N. Shaw, principally from Bradford, N.Y. (1819-1850). Also included are Harrah's speeches and essays on temperance, women's rights, and humanitarianism; and scrapbooks kept by Harrah's daughter and by Harvey Scott.

A-145. HARRISON, BENJAMIN (1833-1901). COLLECTION, 1853-1940.

3 ms. boxes.   M 132.

Attorney, politician, and president of the United States. Harrison was an Indianapolis attorney (1854-1901); Indianapolis city attorney (1857); reporter, Indiana Supreme Court (1860-1862, 1864-1868); officer in the 70th Indiana Regiment (1862-1865), reaching the rank of brig. general; Republican candidate for governor of Indiana (1876); member, Mississippi River Commission (1879-1881); U.S. Senator from Indiana (1881-1887) and chairman, Senate

Committee on Territories; president of the United States (1889-1893); Republican nominee for president (1892); and writer and speaker on public affairs.

The collection consists primarily of letters written by Harrison, his first wife Caroline Scott Harrison (1832-1892), and his second wife Mary Lord Harrison (1858-1948). Included are legal documents from the early years of Harrison's law practice (1853-1866); his letters to his wife while he was serving with the Union Army in Tennessee and Georgia (1864-1865), and while he was president (1890-1891); his letters to Edward Bok regarding articles Harrison was writing for the *Ladies Home Journal* on the nature of the federal government (1895-1897); his letters to family members, including his cousin, Margaret Peltz of St. Louis, Mo. (1877-1889), and his son, Russell B. Harrison; Caroline Scott Harrison's letters to Mrs. P. C. Cheney, wife of the governor of New Hampshire (1888-1891); letters of A. S. Paddock regarding the work of the Utah Commission (1884); Civil War military correspondence and papers (1862-1865); and miscellaneous letters written by Harrison and his wives on state and national politics, Indianapolis, and family matters.

The collection includes letters to or from Edward Bok, Benjamin H. Brewster, Noble C. Butler, Person Colby Cheney, Schuyler Colfax, James A. Garfield, George W. Lasher, Louis T. Michener, Oliver P. Morton, Lazarus Noble, Godlove Orth, Robert S. Taylor, Richard W. Thompson, Harriet Taylor Upton, John Wanamaker, and William A. Woods.

A-146. HARRISON, RUSSELL B. (1854-1936). PAPERS, 1881-1893.

1 ms. box.   Inventory.   M 387.

Harrison was the son of President Benjamin Harrison (1833-1901); clerk in the U.S. Assay Office, Helena, Mont. (1878-1885); speculator in land and mines in Montana and the West; owner of the *Helena Daily Journal* (1890); and Indianapolis attorney (1900-1936).

The collection consists primarily of papers relating to Harrison's business interests, including his land dealings in Montana; his purchase of the *Helena Daily Journal*; and his plans to purchase the Austin and Northwestern Railroad and street railways in Richmond, Wayne Co., and Muncie, Delaware Co. (1890-1893). Also included are papers regarding his problems with the press during his father's administration (1889-1893); a libel suit brought against him by former Montana Territorial governor John Schuyler Crosby (1889); and letters offering papers damaging to U.S. Senator T. C. Power of Montana (1889-1890).

A-147. HARRISON, WILLIAM HENRY (1773-1841). COLLECTION, 1793-1864.

3 ms. boxes.   Calendar.   M 364.

General, politician, and president of the United States. Harrison was an officer in the U.S. Army in the Northwest Territory (1791-1798); commandant, Fort Washington, Ohio (1796-1797); secretary, Northwest Territory (1798-1799); Northwest Territory delegate to the U.S. Congress (1799-1800); governor of the Indiana Territory (1800-1813); brig. general, U.S. Army (1812-1814); commander, Army of the Northwest during the War of 1812 (1812-1813); commander of American troops at the Battle of Tippecanoe (1811) and the Battle of the Thames (1813); resident of North Bend, Ohio (1810s-1841); member, U.S. House of Representatives from Ohio (1816-1819); Ohio state senator (1819-1821); U.S. Senator from Ohio (1825-1828); U.S. Minister to Colombia (1828-1829); Whig candidate for president (1836, 1840); and president of the United States (1841).

The collection consists primarily of letters and documents written by Harrison during the period 1794-1840. Included are his letters to the U.S. secretaries of war discussing Indian relations, treaty negotiations, and military affairs during the War of 1812; his War of 1812 letters to Gov. Return Jonathan Meigs of Ohio and Gov. Isaac Shelby of Kentucky (1812-1814); other correspondence regarding military operations against the Indians (1811) and during the War of 1812; correspondence regarding Northwest Territory and Indiana Territory politics, including his letters to Thomas Worthington of Ohio (1790s-1810s); papers regarding the administration of the Indiana Territory, including appointments, petitions, and acts of the territorial legislature; receipts, provision returns, and other military documents from Greenville and Fort Washington (1794-1797); correspondence regarding Ohio and national politics (1820s-1840); correspondence regarding the 1836 and 1840 presidential elections; correspondence regarding family matters and his personal business interests; and papers relating to Harrison's illness and death (1841).

The collection includes letters to or from John Armstrong, James Barbour, Jesse Bledsoe, Jacob Burnet, John C. Calhoun, Lewis Cass, Green Clay, Henry Clay, William H. Crawford, Alexander J. Dallas, Jonathan Dayton, Henry Dearborn, Charles Delassus, William Eustis, Thomas Ewing, Albert Gallatin,

John S. Gano, John Gibson, Henry D. Gilpin, Charles Hammond, James Henry, Samuel Hodgdon, Andrew Jackson, Richard M. Johnson, Tobias Lear, Duncan McArthur, James Madison, William L. Marcy, Return Jonathan Meigs, James Monroe, Noah Noble, Benjamin Parke, Oliver Hazard Perry, John H. Piatt, Zebulon Pike, Thomas Posey, William Russell, Winthrop Sargent, Isaac Shelby, Zachary Taylor, Edward Tiffin, John Tipton, Charles S. Todd, John Tyler, Samuel C. Vance, William Wells, Charles A. Wickliffe, James Wilkinson, James Winchester, and Thomas Worthington.

A-148. HASSELMAN, OTTO H. (1847-1906). PAPERS, 1864-1905.

1 ms. box, 2 vols. (.5 l.f.).   Inventory.   M 135, BV 1024-1025.

Hasselman was an Indianapolis journalist and politician.

The collection consists of a small amount of Hasselman's correspondence and legal papers; diaries of his wife, Olive Eddy Hasselman (1879-1880, 1891-1898); diaries of her mother, Anna Eddy of Evanston, Ill. (1897, 1900); and the school diary of Hasselman's son, Lewis W. (1892).

Correspondents include Albert J. Beveridge.

A-149. HAWK, CHRISTOPHER L. (1821-1907). ACCOUNT BOOKS, 1849-1920.

6 vols. (.5 l.f.).   BV 70-75.

Hawk and his sons operated a sawmill at Findlay, Ohio (1849-1858), Orangeville, DeKalb Co. (1858-1866), and Mongo, LaGrange Co. (1866-1920).

The collection consists of Hawk's business account books, most relating to his Mongo sawmill.

A-150. HAYDEN, JOHN JAMES (1820-1901). PAPERS, 1819-1899.

5 ms. boxes.   Inventory.   M 136.

Businessman and political officeholder. Hayden was an attorney in Shawneetown, Ill., in the 1840s; an attorney, newspaper publisher, and Republican politician in Rising Sun, Ohio Co. (ca.1850-1860); Republican member, Indiana House of Representatives (1857); Indianapolis attorney, insurance agent, and dry goods merchant (1860-1875); Indianapolis draft commissioner (1862); Indiana draft commissioner (1864); clerk, U.S. Treasury Department, Washington, D.C. (1875-1886, 1889-1899).

The collection consists primarily of Hayden's family correspondence and financial papers from the period 1850-1899 and includes Hayden's letters to his family from Indianapolis (1864-1868, 1871-1875) and Washington, D.C. (1870, 1892-1899); family letters from Rising Sun and Shawneetown; and letters from his son, Henry J. Hayden, from New York, St. Louis, and Washington (1855-1886). Also included are Hayden's speeches on the early history of Indiana and the Republican Party; Hayden family genealogies; and writings of Hayden's wife, Sarah Marshall Hayden (d.1899), author of several novels, among them *Early Engagements* (1854).

Correspondents include Sarah T. Bolton, William M. Dunn, Theophilus Parvin, and W. H. H. Terrell.

A-151. HEATH, WILLIAM P. (b.1809?). LETTERS, 1855-1858.

53 items. Calendar. SC 723.

Heath was part owner of a dry goods store in Lafayette, Tippecanoe Co.

The collection consists primarily of letters from Heath to his sons, Robert Heath (d.1890) and John W. Heath, while they were students at Indiana Asbury (DePauw) University, Greencastle, Putnam Co. (1855-1858).

A-152. HEDDEN, DAVID (1802-1895). PAPERS, 1796-1944.

5 ms. boxes. Inventory. M 353.
Microfilm.

Hedden was born in Newark, N.J.; settled in New Albany, Floyd Co. (1820); owned general store in New Albany in partnership with Elias Ayres (1821-1845); and owned and operated mill in New Albany (1845-1856). Hedden's son, William J. Hedden (fl.1881-1930), owned the New Albany Hosiery Mills.

The collection includes Hedden's family and business correspondence, including letters of Hedden's partner, Elias Ayres (1825-1839); letters of business associates regarding financial conditions in eastern and midwestern cities (1825-1850s); letters of Hedden's wife during her trip to New York State (1843); letters to Hedden's wife from the Wood family of upper New York State (1837-1863); and family letters to William H. Hedden, including letters from a missionary in northern Korea (1920). Also included are Hedden's financial papers and receipts; account books for his general store, mill, and personal finances (1836-1882); account books for the New Albany Hosiery Mills (1876-1901); and family scrapbooks.

A-153. HELLER, HERBERT LYNN (1908-1983). COLLECTION, 1816-1952.

7 ms. boxes.   M 138.

Heller received an Ed.D. from Indiana University, Bloomington (1952); and taught or served in administrative positions in the New Castle, Henry Co., public schools and at Hanover College, Jefferson Co., DePauw University, Putnam Co., Alaska Methodist University, California Western University, and Baldwin-Wallace College, Ky.

The collection consists primarily of material Heller collected for his doctoral thesis, "Negro Education in Indiana from 1816 to 1869," and includes 1850 census reports, school histories, excerpts from newspapers and periodicals, miscellaneous notes, and a draft of the thesis. Also included are documents, clippings, and other miscellaneous materials which Heller collected on the history of Putnam and Henry counties.

A-154. HENDRICKS, THOMAS ANDREW (1819-1885). PAPERS, 1855-1885.

31 items.   SC 737.

Attorney and politician. Hendricks was an Indiana attorney (1843-1885); Democratic member, Indiana House of Representatives (1848) and Senate (1849); member, U.S. House of Representatives (1851-1855); commissioner,

General Land Office (1855-1859); U.S. Senator from Indiana (1863-1869); governor of Indiana (1873-1876); Democratic nominee for Vice-President of the United States (1876, 1884); and Vice-President of the United States (1885).

The collection consists of miscellaneous letters, most written by Hendricks, relating to state and national politics. The largest group contains twelve letters from Hendricks to Nahum Capen of Boston, Mass. (1869-1877).

A-155. HENDRICKS COUNTY MISCELLANEOUS PAPERS, 1830-1905.

2 ms. boxes. M 326.

The collection consists of Hendricks County records, most from the 1830s. Included are court documents, commissions, and resignations for county offices, an 1835 petition for the incorporation of the town of Danville, and an 1867 pollbook.

A-156. HENRY COUNTY MISCELLANEOUS PAPERS, 1812-1943.

17 ms. boxes, 4 vols. (4.5 l.f.).   Inventory.   M 60, BV 1013-1017.

The collection consists of official Henry County records, private papers relating to Henry County, and research notes and papers gathered by Herbert Heller for his book *Schools of New Castle, Indiana*. The bulk of the papers are from the nineteenth century and include papers relating to land, roads, churches, and the Civil War in Henry County; receipts and other papers for the Aid to Soldiers' Families organization (1860s); lawyers' papers; papers from the Henry County clerk's and auditor's offices; Henry County voting records (1853); papers relating to the history of the Presbyterian Church in the county; a student's school notebooks (ca.1900); and the 1850 diary of Catherine Taylor, a student at the Henry County Seminary. Also included are the papers of New Castle attorney and scientist Thomas B. Redding (1831-1895), including his correspondence regarding railroad and other legal business and family correspondence (1832-1895).

A-157. HERON, ALEXANDER (1827-1900). PAPERS, 1845-1943.

14 ms. boxes, 6 vols. (4.5 l.f.).　　　　　　　　M 141, BV 1382-1387.

Heron was a farmer in Brookville, Franklin Co.; and secretary of the State Board of Agriculture (1872-1891).

The collection consists primarily of family correspondence, including Heron's letters to his wife and daughter written from Connersville, Fayette Co. (1860s), and from Indianapolis while he was serving with the State Board of Agriculture (1870s-1890s). The collection also includes Heron's business correspondence regarding agricultural techniques, prices for agricultural products, and the operations of the Indiana State Fair; letters from relatives in Tipton and Fayette counties; diaries of his wife's sister, Caroline Peck, of Franklin County and Indianapolis (1875-1877, 1880, 1886, 1906-1912); Peck's personal correspondence and business papers (1890s-1912); ledger for the Whitewater Canal (1845-1848); scrapbooks of clippings and memorabilia relating to the Indiana State Fair (1871-1886); and papers relating to the Indiana Keramic Club, an organization for ceramic artists (1897-1943).

A-158. HERON, JAMES (1824-1876). PAPERS, 1844-1856.

2 ms. boxes, 58 vols. (1 l.f.).　　　Inventory.　　　M 142, BV 1388-1445.
Microfilm.

Heron was a Connersville, Fayette Co., merchant; owner of a pork packing plant (1840s); and treasurer of the White Water Valley Canal Company during the 1840s.

The collection consists of records of the White Water Valley Canal Company (1844-1849); Heron's personal business papers (1844-1851); and notebooks recording competition entries in the Fayette County Fair (1853, 1856).

A-159. HITCHCOCK, MOSES (d.1825). PAPERS, 1810-1825.

80 items.　　　　　　　　Calendar.　　　　　　　　SC 751.

Hitchcock owned a dry goods store in Lenox, N.Y. (1818), and was an attorney in Lawrenceburg, Dearborn Co. (1819-1825).

The collection consists of receipts, promissory notes, and other documents relating to Hitchcock's businesses in New York and Lawrenceburg.

A-160. HOBBS, WILLIAM P. (1821-1897). PAPERS, 1862-1886.

27 items. SC 1782.

Hobbs was a merchant and physician in Orangeville, Orange Co.; assistant surgeon in the 85th Indiana Regiment, serving in Tennessee and Georgia (1862-1864).

The collection consists primarily of correspondence between Hobbs and his wife while he was serving in the Union Army.

A-161. HODGIN, EVERETT E. (1870-1923). PAPERS, 1898-1923.

1 ms. box, 1 card file box. Inventory. M 423.

Hodgin was an Indianapolis physician (1896-1923); Indianapolis police surgeon (1907); manager for Lew Shank's mayoral campaign (1921); and president, City Board of Health (1922-1923).

The collection includes Hodgin's patient ledgers and a card file of patient records (1898-1923); records of obstetrical cases (1920-1923); notebooks containing copies of prescriptions (1921-1923); his patient ledger as police surgeon (1907); newspaper clippings regarding the 1921 mayoral campaign; and notebook for his trip to Washington, D.C. (1921).

A-162. HOLLIDAY, MARGARET YANDES (1844-1920). PAPERS, 1883-1919.

1 ms. box. Inventory. M 371.

Holliday, the daughter of Indianapolis Presbyterian minister William A. Holliday, was a missionary to Tabriz, Persia (Iran), sponsored by the First Presbyterian Church of Indianapolis (1883-1920).

The collection consists of Holliday's letters to her family in Indianapolis from Tabriz and from her trips through Europe and Russia (1883), Turkey and Constantinople (1889), and the Middle East and Egypt (1906); and her letters and annual reports to the Women's Missionary Society which oversaw her work.

A-163. HOLLOWAY, EMMA G. (1874-1962). PAPERS, 1921-1949.

1 ms. box.   Calendar.   M 144.
Restricted.

Holloway was a physician in North Manchester, Wabash Co. (ca.1900-1935); and served on the medical staff of the Indiana School for Feeble-Minded Youth, Fort Wayne, Allen Co. (1930-1935).

The collection includes material relating to the Women's Christian Temperance Union and the W.C.T.U.'s national meeting in 1921; Holloway's notes and writings on medical matters; and her notes regarding psychological testing and physical examination of patients at the Indiana School for Feeble-Minded Youth.

A-164. HOLLOWAY, WILLIAM ROBESON (1836-1911). PAPERS, 1824-1899.

13 ms. boxes, 23 vols. (5 l.f.). Inventory. M 124, BV 1478-1495, 1865-1871. Microfilm.

Journalist and politician. Holloway was a native of Richmond, Wayne Co.; assistant, *Cincinnati Times* (1852-1857); law student, office of Oliver P. Morton, Centerville, Wayne Co. (1858-1860); private secretary to Indiana governor Oliver P. Morton (1861-1862); Indiana state printer (1861-1863); owner and editor, *Indianapolis Journal* (1864-1875); Indianapolis postmaster (1869-1881); owner and founder, *Indianapolis Times* (1880-1886); involved with Indianapolis Cable Street Railway Company (1887-1889); secretary to Indianapolis mayor C. S. Denny (1894-1895); U.S. consul general at St. Petersburg, Russia (1897-1904); and U.S. consul general at Halifax, Nova Scotia (1904-1907).

The papers include Holloway's correspondence relating to national and state politics, Republican Party affairs, newspapers, the postal service, and Holloway's family; records of the *Indianapolis Times* (1881-1886); records of the Indianapolis post office (1865-1880); papers and letter book of the Indianapolis Cable Street Railway Company (1887-1888); his personal business papers, including papers relating to his investments in whiskey and farm products in New York, N.Y. (1863-1864); and letters written to presidents Ulysses S. Grant, James A. Garfield, and Benjamin Harrison recommending Holloway for positions in the federal government.

The collection also includes papers of Oliver P. Morton (1823-1877), Indiana governor (1861-1867) and U.S. Senator (1867-1877). The Morton papers include personal and political correspondence; speech notes; a scrapbook containing official proclamations issued while he was governor; letters of condolence sent to his family upon his death (1877); letters regarding William Dudley Foulke's biography of Morton (1899); and papers of Oliver T. Morton's law office regarding the Chicago and Atlantic Railroad (1887).

Correspondents include James G. Blaine, James Boyle, Henry V. Boynton, William H. Calkins, Schuyler Colfax, William Wade Dudley, Charles W. Fairbanks, Joseph B. Foraker, John Watson Foster, James A. Garfield, Ulysses S. Grant, Walter Q. Gresham, Charles Henry Grosvenor, Murat Halstead, Marcus A. Hanna, John M. Harlan, Benjamin Harrison, Rutherford B. Hayes, Robert R. Hitt, William McKinley, Joseph Medill, John C. New, Meredith Nicholson, Thomas C. Platt, Albert G. Porter, Whitelaw Reid, John Sherman, James N. Tyner, Lew Wallace, and Charles R. Williams.

A-165. HOLMAN-O'BRIEN PAPERS, 1827-1893.

1 ms. box.　　　　　　　　Inventory.　　　　　　　　M 368.

William Steele Holman (1822-1897) was a Democratic politician from Lawrenceburg, Dearborn Co.; member, Indiana House of Representatives (1851-1852); served sixteen terms in the U.S. House of Representatives between 1859 and 1897; and chaired, at various times, House committees on Appropriations, Public Buildings and Grounds, and Inquiry into Indian Affairs.

The collection consists primarily of Holman's letters on political and personal business (1854-1893) to Lawrenceburg lawyer Cornelius O'Brien (1818-1869); his son, Lawrenceburg newspaper publisher and banker William H.

O'Brien (1855-1933); and O'Brien's newspaper partner, Dr. William D. H. Hunter (1830-1898). Also included are additional Holman letters to constituents; Cornelius O'Brien's receipts for land purchased at tax sales; and other O'Brien financial papers.

A-166. HOOSIERS FOR PEACE. RECORDS, 1967-1976.

15 ms. boxes, 3 vols. (4 l.f.).   Inventory.   M 359, BV 1977-1979.

The organization was founded in Indianapolis in 1967 as Hoosiers for Peace in Vietnam to work for a prompt end to the War in Vietnam; it was reorganized as Hoosiers for Peace in 1969. The organization worked with a number of anti-war groups to sponsor speakers, rallies, and petition drives against the war. It also was involved in political campaigns for Eugene McCarthy, George McGovern, and Birch Bayh. The organization disbanded in 1973.

The records include minutes and notes of meetings (1967-1973), financial records (1967-1976), membership lists, correspondence (1967-1975), program records, clippings, literature on the war, and information on other peace groups.

A-167. HOPKINS, MARTHA ELLIS (1870-1959). PAPERS, 1914-1952.

6 ms. boxes, 8 vols. (2 l.f.).   Inventory.   M 146, BV 1446-1453.

Hopkins was a Republican Party precinct vice-committeewoman in Rensselaer, Jasper Co. (1920-ca.1952); Republican Party vice-chairman, Indiana 10th congressional district (1922-1932).

The collection includes World War I letters from members of Hopkins's family serving in army camps in the United States; correspondence regarding Republican Party activities; Jasper County voting records and pollbooks (1922-1952); and Republican Party campaign materials.

Correspondents include Harry S. New and James E. Watson.

A-168. HOUGHTON, WILLIAM (1839-1918). PAPERS, 1850-1880.

2 ms. boxes.   Calendar.   M 147.

Houghton was a Loogootee, Martin Co., farmer, businessman, and government officeholder; and an officer in the 14th Indiana Regiment during the Civil War.

The collection consists primarily of Houghton's Civil War letters to his family, written from Camp Vigo, Vigo Co. (1861), and from Virginia and Maryland (1861-1864). Also included is his war diary (1861-1862); Civil War letters from his brothers, William Houghton, 137th Indiana Regiment in Tennessee (1864), and Eugene Houghton, 18th Indiana in Virginia (1864-1865); and family letters (1865-1880), including Houghton's letters from Loogootee (1874-1880) and Eugene Houghton's letters from Iowa and Texas (1869-1875).

A-169. HOWARD, FREDERICK WILLIAM (1817-1896). PAPERS, 1806-1903.

41 items, 5 vols. (.25 l.f.).   Inventory.   SC 788, BV 820-824.

Howard was a merchant in McConnelsville, Ohio (1837-1855); and merchant and shoe salesman in Lafayette, Tippecanoe Co. (1855-1896).

The collection includes bills and receipts for Howard's Lafayette stores; five account books (1837-1900) for his stores in Ohio and Lafayette; and family correspondence, genealogies, and reminiscences.

A-170. HOWE, DANIEL WAIT (1839-1921). PAPERS, 1862-ca.1915.

6 ms. boxes.   Inventory.   M 148.

Howe was a private in the 7th Indiana Regiment (1861); an officer in the 79th Indiana Regiment (1862-1864); Indianapolis attorney (1876-1921); judge, Marion County Superior Court (1876-1890); president, Indiana Historical Society (1901-1920); and historian.

The collection consists of manuscripts of a number of Howe's writings, including an edited typescript of his Civil War diary (1862-1864); segments of the Civil War diary of Lt. William Huntzinger of the 79th Indiana (1862-1865); a draft of an unpublished work, "A History of the Army of the Cumberland"; draft revisions for his book *Puritan Republic* (1899); and other notes and writings on historical subjects.

A-171. HOWLAND, POWELL (1799-1878). PAPERS, 1831-1878.

4 ms. boxes. Inventory. M 149.

Howland was a farmer in Saratoga County, N.Y.; and farmer and businessman in Indianapolis (1839-1878).

The collection consists primarily of legal and financial documents relating to Howland's property and his money-lending business in Indianapolis. Also included are Howland's letters to his family in New York (1840-1867); receipts and other financial papers relating to the Millersville Gravel Road Company and the Indianapolis and Fall Creek Gravel Road Company (1860s-1870s); records of the Marion County Horse Company (1838-1848); Howland's memoranda books on household and farm expenses (1840-1878); and advertising circulars from agricultural implement manufacturers.

A-172. HUNTER, ROBERT (1874-1942). PAPERS, 1923-1948.

1 ms. box. Inventory and calendar. M 45.

Social worker and political writer. Hunter was a native of Terre Haute, Vigo Co.; social worker at Hull House in Chicago, Ill. (1886-1902), and at University Settlement, New York, N.Y. (1902-1903); married Caroline Stokes, daughter of financier Anson Phelps Stokes (1903); active in the Socialist Party; Socialist candidate for governor of Connecticut (1910); broke with party at outbreak of World War I; lecturer in English and economics, University of California, Santa Barbara (1918-1922); resident of Santa Barbara (1918-1942); active in Republican Party; and author of *Poverty* (1904) and *Revolution— When? Where? How?* (1940).

The papers are principally from the period 1934-1942 and include Hunter's correspondence relating to Republican Party politics, Wendell Willkie's 1940 presidential campaign, the work of the House Committee on Un-American Activities, and Hunter's book on the nature of revolutions. Also included is correspondence of Hunter and his wife regarding his early involvement in the anti-tuberculosis campaign; and their personal correspondence.

Correspondents include Jane Addams, Nicholas Murray Butler, Cass Canfield, Sidney Cockwell, Edward T. Devine, Martin Dies, Henry Ford, John Nance Garner, Herbert Hoover, Harry Hopkins, Hiram W. Johnson, H. V. Kaltenborn, Walter Lippmann, Joan London, Joseph Martin, Raymond Moley, Westbrook Pegler, Samuel B. Pettingill, Oren Root, Jr., Upton Sinclair, Irving Stone, Robert A. Taft, and Wendell Willkie.

A-173. HUNTER, WILLIAM D. H. (1830-1898). PAPERS, 1880-1885.

43 items.   Calendar.   SC 805.

Hunter was the proprietor of the *Lawrenceburg* (Dearborn Co.) *Register* (1877-1894); a member of the Indiana Democratic State Central Committee (1880-1882); appointed collector of internal revenue, Indiana 4th Congressional District (1885); and one of the organizers of the Indiana Democratic Editorial Association.

The collection consists of Hunter's correspondence relating to Democratic Party politics in southeastern Indiana, primarily from the period 1880-1882; correspondence regarding statewide politics; and correspondence regarding the Democratic Editorial Association.

Correspondents include Henry S. Cauthorn, William H. English, William S. Holman, William S. Rosecrans, John B. Stoll, and Daniel W. Voorhees.

A-174. HUTCHINGS, WILLIAM DAVIES (1825-1903). PAPERS, 1855-1970.

2 ms. boxes.   Calendar.   M 151.

Hutchings was a physician in Lexington, Scott Co. (1851-1876), and Madison, Jefferson Co. (1876-1903); and Democratic member, Indiana House of Representatives (1869).

The collection is made up primarily of personal correspondence of Hutchings, his wife Matilda Koehler (1840-1914), and his wife's family, from the period 1861-1916. Included are letters (1861-1864) of Herman Koehler, a businessman in Frederick, Md., and Alexandria, Va., supplying the U.S. Army; letters (1865-1875) of Aurora Koehler, a southeastern Indiana schoolteacher; letters of Matilda Koehler and other family members from Madison (1862-1870, 1880s-1890s) and Lexington (1865-1875); correspondence regarding Hutchings's investments in Florida real estate (1890s); Hutchings's correspondence with his son, Frederick Hutchings, an electrical engineer in Pittsburgh, Pa., Massachusetts, British Columbia, and Michigan (1885-1898); his correspondence with his son, Robert Hutchings, a medical student at Ohio Medical College, Cincinnati, and a physician in Colorado Springs, Colo. (1887-1896); and letters from his daughter, Agnes Hutchings Zulauf, on her honeymoon in Europe (1896). Also included are Hutchings's physician memorandum book (1899-1900); papers relating to King's Daughter's Hospital in Madison (1900s-1910s); and reminiscences of the Hutchings family (1969-1970).

A-175. HUTCHINGS-KOEHLER FAMILY. PAPERS, 1699, 1800-1916.

5 ms. boxes.   Calendar.   M 152.

The Hutchings and Koehler families included Herman Koehler (1805-1882), a German immigrant and apprentice confectioner in Maryland and Washington, D.C. (1819-1825), and a storekeeper and confectioner in Scott and Jefferson counties (1847-1882); his son, Herman C. Koehler (1835-1916), a Frederick, Md., businessman who unsuccessfully ran a Louisiana plantation in 1866; Herman Koehler's daughters, Aurora (1846-1928) and Septima (1848-1918) Koehler, schoolteachers in southeastern Indiana (1867-ca.1890) and mission workers with Indians in South Dakota (1896-1906), blacks in Nashville, Tenn. (1906-1908), and mill workers in LaGrange, Ga. (1908-1909); William D. Hutchings (1825-1903) and his wife, Matilda Koehler Hutchings (1840-1914), the former a physician in Lexington, Scott Co., and Madison, Jefferson Co.; and their son, Robert Hutchings (1869-1956), a student at Hanover College, Jefferson Co. (1887-1889), and Ohio Medical College in Cincinnati (1890s), and a physician in Colorado.

Herman Koehler's papers include letters from relatives in Frederick and Baltimore, Md. (1819-1869), Kleingartach, Germany (1814-1842), and Goliad, Tex. (1852-1861); his letters from his children attending school in Madison

(1860s) and from his son Robert Koehler, a Cincinnati businessman (1868-1871); his recipes for medicinal candies and remedies; and his reminiscence of his trip from Germany to Baltimore, Md., in 1818-1819. Aurora and Septima Koehler papers include Aurora's letters from her brother's plantation at Tullania, La. (1866); their correspondence as schoolteachers in southeastern Indiana (1860s-1880s); their letters from South Dakota, Tennessee, and Georgia (1896-1912); letters from teachers and students at St. Elizabeth's School, Flora, S.Dak. (1900-1908); Aurora's journal (1868-1875); Septima's journal (1863, 1867-1869); Septima's writings on South Dakota Indians; and class register books and other educational materials. Hutchings family papers include letters to Robert Hutchings at school from his parents in Madison and from school friends (1888-1890); Matilda Hutchings's poems and essays; and William Hutchings's essay on the treatment of tuberculosis.

A-176. IGLEHART, JOHN EUGENE (1848-1934). PAPERS, 1853-1935.

12 ms. boxes, 22 vols. (6.5 l.f.). Inventory and partial calendar. M 153. Microfilm.

Attorney and historian. Iglehart was an Evansville, Vanderburgh Co., attorney (1869-1934); general counsel, Evansville and Terre Haute Railroad (ca.1882-1912); district attorney, Chicago and Eastern Illinois Railroad (1912); founder, Southwestern Indiana Historical Society (1920); and historian specializing in southwestern Indiana and the Indiana years of Abraham Lincoln. Iglehart was the son of Evansville attorney Asa Iglehart (1817-1887).

The collection is composed primarily of correspondence relating to Iglehart's historical interests from the 1910s to the 1930s and includes correspondence regarding the Southwestern Indiana Historical Society, the Indiana Historical Society, the Indiana Historical Commission, the 1917 Evansville Centennial, and the Lincoln Union (1927-1932); and his correspondence with prominent historians regarding Abraham Lincoln, midwestern history, and Frederick Jackson Turner's frontier thesis. Also included are letter books from Iglehart's law firm (1870-1892) and the law firms of his father and his father's associates, John Ingle, Jr., H. Q. Wheeler, and Andrew L. Robinson (1853-1860s); Iglehart's speeches and dictations (1901-1934), most on historical matters; correspondence regarding his law practice (1871-1934); family correspondence; and depositions of persons in Warrick and Spencer counties regarding stories they had heard about Abraham Lincoln's life in southern Indiana (1915).

Correspondents include Ray Stannard Baker, William E. Barton, Albert J. Beveridge, Solon J. Buck, Christopher B. Coleman, Merle Curti, William E. Dodd, Bess Ehrmann, Lucius C. Embree, Logan Esarey, Max Farrand, Worthington C. Ford, William Fortune, John Watson Foster, George P. Hambrecht, Will H. Hays, Henry Hazlitt, James A. Hemenway, Meredith Nicholson, Frederick L. Paxson, Milo M. Quaife, Carl Sandburg, Ida Tarbell, Frederick Jackson Turner, Charles G. Vannest, Louis Warren, James E. Watson, and Jesse Weik.

A-177. ILIFF, JAMES ARTHUR (1845-1908). PAPERS, 1849-1883.

1 ms. box, 2 oversize boxes (1.25 l.f.).   M 154, OM 121.

Iliff was an officer with the 109th U.S. Colored Infantry (1865-1866) and the 41st U.S. Colored Infantry stationed in Texas (1867-1869); he was later engaged in the hat business in Indianapolis.

The collection consists primarily of Iliff's official correspondence, reports, and equipage records relating to his military service and the infantry units under his command (1865-1870). The collection also includes copies of the correspondence and papers of Iliff's father-in-law, William Willard (1809-1888), a teacher and one of the founders of the Indiana School for the Deaf. Willard's papers relate primarily to the Institute for the Deaf and Dumb in Indianapolis (1849-1864).

A-178. INDIANA ARTISTS' CLUB, INC. RECORDS, 1922-1976.

11 ms. boxes. 1 vol. (3 l.f.).   Inventory.   M 330.

The Indiana Artists' Club, an organization of professional Indiana artists, was founded in 1917 for the promotion of art within the state. Its primary activity has been the organization of an annual exhibition of artwork done by the membership. The club has also sponsored traveling exhibits, made annual donations to Indiana schools and colleges, and published an *Art Program Directory*, among other projects. The club's headquarters is in Indianapolis.

The collection consists of the minutes of regular and board meetings (1922-1965); committee records and annual reports (1927-1967); annual exhibition committee records (1952-1975); and correspondence (1924-1974). Other papers include yearbooks, exhibition catalogs (1936-1975), newspaper clippings, and a scrapbook. Also included is original artwork by Paul Wehr, done for the annual exhibition.

A-179. INDIANA CENTRAL RAILWAY COMPANY. RECORDS, 1903-1966.

3 oversize boxes. (1.5 l.f.). M 336.

The Indiana Central Railway Company was organized in 1903 to operate a passenger and freight line from Muncie, Delaware Co., to Brazil, Clay Co., running through Madison, Hamilton, Boone, Montgomery, and Parke counties. In 1929 most of the line was abandoned except for the stretch between Anderson, Madison Co., and Lebanon, Boone Co.

The records consist of monthly reports of operations (1906-1927); annual reports (1903-1930); and carload business reports (1960-1966).

A-180. INDIANA COTTON MILLS. RECORDS, 1849-1948.

3 ms. boxes. M 156.

The Indiana Cotton Mills were founded in 1848 at Cannelton, Perry Co., under the name Cannelton Cotton Mills; its business involved the carding of cotton and the manufacture of cloth, particularly cotton sheeting. The mills closed in the late 1940s.

The collection consists of business correspondence (1852-1883); orders from customers (1871); deeds and mortgages (1849-1940); treasurers' reports (1886-1907); a notebook containing a record of sheeting made (1859-1862); notes, clippings, and other materials relating to the company's history (1857-1903); and miscellaneous financial records, advertising material, legal papers, and reports for the mills.

A-181. INDIANA COUNCIL OF CHURCHES. RECORDS, 1888-1980.

27 ms. boxes. Inventory. M 344.

The Indiana Council of Churches and its predecessors, the Indiana Sunday School Union (1888-1901), the Indiana Sunday School Association (1901-1922), the Indiana Council of Religious Education (1922-1934), and the Indiana Council of Christian Education (1934-1943), have worked to promote greater understanding among denominations and to provide an agency through which the denominations can cooperate in special projects. The early emphasis of the council was on providing teaching materials and training and on inspiring workers for the Indiana Sunday Schools. Since then, it has become involved in providing publications and training for church workers; conducting workshops and church conferences; providing a ministry to migrant farm workers in Indiana; and working on poverty, civil rights, and other social concerns.

The records include minutes of executive committee, board of directors, and assembly meetings (1888-1980); correspondence, financial records, and other papers from the general secretary's office (1941-1972); minutes of the Indiana Young Peoples Conferences (1923-1939); programs for county Council of Churches meetings (1925-1947); records of the Indiana State Pastors Conferences (1931-1960); *The Indiana Churchwoman*, newsletter of the Indiana Council of Church Women (1941-1955); records of the Department of Children's Work (1960-1967); records of the Division of Research and Planning (1963-1970); records of the Vacation School Leadership program and the Indiana School for Church Leadership (1965-1971); records of the Department of Youth Ministry (1959-1970); studies of individual churches and reports on the status of churches in Allen, Bartholomew, Delaware, Grant, Lake, Rush, St. Joseph, Spencer, Tippecanoe, and Wabash counties (1965-1968); and records of other conferences, workshops, and programs sponsored by the council.

A-182. INDIANA COUNTY SUPERINTENDENTS ASSOCIATION. RECORDS, 1927-1959.

1 ms. box. 1 vol. (.66 l.f.). M 157, BV 1457.

The association, also known as the Indiana County School Superintendents Association, was primarily concerned with the promotion of rural education.

The collection consists of minutes from the association's meetings (1927-1959); and treasurers' reports, summaries of legislation concerning education, newspaper clippings, and pamphlets on education, all from the 1950s.

A-183. INDIANA DIETETIC ASSOCIATION. RECORDS, 1937-1980.

4 archival boxes, 1 vol. (4.1 l.f.).   Inventory.   M 282, BV 2042.

The Indiana Dietetic Association was organized in 1921 to improve the status of hospital dieticians. Since 1928 it has been affiliated with the American Dietetic Association and has had as its general purpose the improvement of nutrition among the general populace, the advancement of the science of dietetics, and the promotion of education in the field.

The records consist of minutes (1937-1978); membership and financial records (1970-1979); correspondence with the American Dietetic Association (1970-1978); annual meeting correspondence and papers (1971-1980); annual meeting programs (1947-1980); newsletters (1948-1978); and issues of the *Community Nutrition Report* (1971-1978).

A-184. INDIANA GUARD RESERVE. PAPERS, 1966-1975.

1 ms. box, 3 vols. (.66 l.f.).   Inventory.   M 158, BV 1497-1499.

The collection includes operations manuals, regulations, publications, promotional materials, and historical materials for the Military Department of Indiana, Indiana Guard Reserve.

A-185. INDIANA SCHOOLMEN'S CLUB. RECORDS, 1922-1980.

2 archival boxes.   Inventory.   M 371.

The Indiana Schoolmen's Club was an organization of public school administrators, teachers, and college professors of education interested in promoting fellowship, professionalism, and efficiency among educators. It began informally in 1918 and adopted a constitution in 1924. It disbanded in 1980.

The records include minutes (1922-1973); programs and correspondence regarding the quarterly meetings of the club; treasurers' records (1922-1980); and scrapbooks.

A-186. INDIANA STATE NURSES ASSOCIATION. RECORDS, 1899-1980.

2 ms. boxes, 18 archival boxes. Inventory. M 380.

The Indiana State Nurses Association was founded in 1903 to work for an improvement in the status, working conditions, and training of nurses. The association has lobbied for the registration of nurses and improved educational programs; provided placement services and insurance and savings plans for its members; and worked with other organizations on a variety of public health problems. The association has been affiliated with the Nurses Associated Alumnae (1903-1911) and the American Nurses Association since 1911.

The records include minutes and reports for the association's annual meetings (1903-1973); correspondence, memoranda, membership information, financial records, and other papers from the state headquarters in Indianapolis (1904-1980); records of the professional registry and the counseling and placement programs (1927-1971); papers of association committees, including joint committees with other state health organizations (1919-1972); records of association sections, including the General Duty, Public Health, Private Duty, Occupational Health, and Educational Administrators, Consultants, and Teachers sections (1922-1979); minutes, correspondence, reports, and registry records for the association's districts (1919-1977); correspondence and reports of the American Nurses Association and nursing associations in other states (1938-1973); minutes and correspondence of the Indiana Committee on Nursing (1963-1970); and minutes of the Indianapolis Graduate Nurses Association (1899-1919).

A-187. INDIANA TERRITORY COLLECTION, 1800-1818.

40 items. Calendar.

The collection consists of miscellaneous letters and documents relating to the Indiana Territory. Included are letters to Col. Jacob Kingsbury at Detroit from Capt. James Rhea, Lt. John Whistler, and other officers and soldiers at Fort Wayne regarding the military situation at the fort (1810-1814); letters from Indiana territorial judge and Indian agent Benjamin Parke (1777-1835) to secretaries of war William H. Crawford and John C. Calhoun regarding the proposed purchase of lands from the Miami and Delaware Indians along the White River in central Indiana (1816), and regarding the negotiations with the Indians leading to the Treaty of St. Mary's, Ohio (1818); letters of Indian agent John Johnston to John C. Calhoun regarding proposed treaties for the sale of Indian lands (1818); and manuscript copies of acts of the territorial legislature, signed by Gov. William Henry Harrison (1811).

A-188. INDIANAPOLIS ASYLUM FOR FRIENDLESS COLORED CHILDREN. RECORDS, 1871-1922.

14 ms. boxes, 8 vols. (4.5 l.f.).   Inventory.   M 165, BV 1501-1509.
Restricted.

The asylum was founded in 1869 by a group of Indianapolis Quakers as an orphanage for black children from Indianapolis and central Indiana. The asylum was operated by a Board of Women Managers whose president served as director of the asylum, and a board of directors made up of male Quakers who oversaw the financial affairs of the orphanage. In 1922 control of the orphanage was given to the Marion County Board of Commissioners. The orphanage was closed in the early 1940s.

The bulk of the records consist of records of the asylum's children, including record of admissions (1871-1922); record of children from counties other than Marion (1896-1922); and case files containing admittance papers, court orders, correspondence from welfare officials and the children's families, and reports from agents of the State Board of Charities (1900-1922). Also included are minutes of the Board of Women Managers (1870-1922); and treasurers' reports (1916-1922).

A-189. INDIANAPOLIS BELT RAILROAD AND STOCK YARDS COMPANY. RECORDS, 1874-1968.

16 ms. boxes, 39 vols. (8.25 l.f.).   Inventory.   M 67, BV 672-712.

The Indianapolis Belt Railroad and Stock Yards Company was incorporated in 1873 as the Indianapolis Belt Railway Company for the purpose of constructing a railroad around the city. In 1877 the company opened as the Union Railway Transfer and Stock Yard Company, operating both a rail line and a stockyard. In 1881 it became the Indianapolis Belt Railroad and Stock Yards Company. The following year it leased the railroad to the Indianapolis Union Railway Company, and for the rest of its existence the company was primarily a stockyard. In 1964 it became the Indianapolis Stockyards Company, Inc., and in 1967 it was sold to the Eli Lilly Company. For most of its history the company was under the direction of Samuel E. Rauh (1853-1935), president from 1897 to 1929, and his son, Charles S. Rauh (1883-1956), president from 1929 to 1956.

The collection consists of scattered records from throughout the company's history, including annual reports from the president and minutes of the board of directors meetings (1879-1967); scattered financial records (1878-1963) and tax records (1917-1968); records of property purchases, sales, leases and right-of-ways (1876-1965); appraisal reports on the company's property (1920-1955); capital stock ledgers (1877-1931); records of construction and expansion (1878-1962); payroll records (1891-1901); pension plan records (1947-1967); labor and management agreements (1929-1968); records of the Stock Yards Marketing Institute, the public relations branch of the company (1954-1968); leases with the Union Railway Company (1878-1958); scrapbooks and other materials on the company's history (1904-1950s); and audiotapes of the board of directors and stockholders meetings (1964-1967). Also included are stock and audit records of the Union Reduction Company of Cincinnati, Ohio, owned by the Rauh family (1913-1921).

A-190. INDIANAPOLIS BOARD OF TRADE. RECORDS, 1882-1957.

8 vols. (2 l.f.). BV 721-722, 724-729.

The Indianapolis Board of Trade was founded in 1870 to promote business in the city.

The collection consists of minutes of directors meetings (1882-1897) and scrapbooks of newspaper clippings relating to the Board of Trade (1911-1957).

A-191. INDIANAPOLIS CASKET COMPANY. RECORDS, 1907-1984.

20 ms. boxes, 23 archival boxes (28 l.f.) Inventory. M 419.

The company was incorporated in 1907 in Indianapolis and South Dakota; it was sold and relocated to Shelbyville, Shelby Co. (1908-1910); and was moved to Indianapolis in 1910. The company manufactured caskets and specialized in custom-made caskets for funeral homes throughout the Midwest and Kentucky. The company closed in 1984.

The records include the company's ledgers and other financial records (1918-1984); correspondence with funeral directors and suppliers (1940s-1960s); property records (1911-1965); employee records (1936-1984); production statistics (1960s-1970s); stockholders records (1950-1961); minutes of board of directors meetings (1910-1918); advertising materials; funeral directors' convention materials (1948-1959); and records of the Funeral Supply Credit Association (1935, 1953-1959).

A-192. INDIANAPOLIS CHAMBER OF COMMERCE. RECORDS, 1893-1959.

16 ms. boxes, 2 archival boxes, 3 vols. (9 l.f.).   Inventory.   M 422.

The Indianapolis Chamber of Commerce began in 1890 as the Commercial Club of Indianapolis, an organization of businessmen interested in civic improvements and in attracting new business to the city. In 1912 the club joined with the Indianapolis Trade Association, the Manufacturers Association, and the Merchants Association to form the Chamber of Commerce. Among the projects supported by the club and the chamber have been the development of a city park system, the improvement of streets, the reorganization of city government, flood control planning, and the construction of improved facilities for conventions and businesses.

The collection consists principally of the records of the Commercial Club and the Chamber of Commerce from the period 1893-1932. Commercial Club records include annual reports (1893-1912); minutes of board of directors meetings (1897-1902, 1906-1909); and committee reports and minutes (1900-1913). Chamber of Commerce records include committee reports and minutes (1913-1938); a scrapbook of the chamber's printed forms, programs, and brochures (1916-1927); and newsletters (1945-1953). Also included are records of related organizations, including minutes and reports of the Indianapolis Trade Association (1910-1913); minutes of the Junior Chamber of Commerce (1920-1928); minutes of the Motion Picture Exchange Operators, an organization promoting the good of the film industry and arbitrating disputes among distributors and theater owners (1918-1920); and minutes, clippings, and other papers of the Sales Executive Council, a professional organization for sales executives in local businesses (1927-1959).

A-193. INDIANAPOLIS CITY RECORDS, 1943, 1946.

3 ms. boxes. M 69.

The collection consists of official correspondence and reports from the years 1943 and 1946 of Indianapolis mayor Robert H. Tyndall (1887-1947). Included are materials relating to civil defense, the U.S. Conference of Mayors, and numerous departments of city government.

A-194. INDIANAPOLIS FLOWER MISSION. RECORDS, 1886-1952.

7 ms. boxes.   Inventory.   M 71.

The Indianapolis Flower Mission was a women's organization started in 1876 to provide care for the sick. The mission's activities have included visiting the sick in hospitals and at their homes, providing instruction in the care of the sick, starting a training school for nurses (1883), operating a children's hospital (1895-1909), and opening hospitals for the care of tuberculosis patients (1903, 1935).

The mission's records include minutes of board of directors meetings (1901-1948), reports of visitors to the sick (1931-1933), and miscellaneous reports, correspondence, and historical materials.

A-195. INDIANAPOLIS FREE KINDERGARTEN AND CHILDREN'S AID SOCIETY. RECORDS, 1881-1950.

2 ms. boxes, 43 vols. (4.5 l.f.).   M 166, BV 1510-1552.

The society was founded in 1882 under the leadership of Rev. Oscar C. McCulloch and Eliza Blaker as a private organization to provide preschool training for young children. At various times the society also provided domestic training classes for older children; Mothers Clubs to instruct women in child care, health, and nutrition; health examinations and training for the children; and clothing for poor children. In 1901 the society began receiving public funds for its schools. The society was dissolved about 1951.

The collection includes superintendents' reports (1884-1927); directors' reports (1938-1950); board meeting minutes (1881-1888, 1910-1950); treasurers' books (1917-1938); correspondence (1927-1949); papers on the history of the society; and business papers.

A-196. INDIANAPOLIS ORPHANS ASYLUM. RECORDS, 1850-1923.

1 ms. box, 12 vols. (1.5 l.f.).   Inventory.   M 66, BV 984-995.

The Indianapolis Orphans Asylum was founded in 1850 as the Widows and Orphans Friend Society of Indianapolis. By 1866 it had become the Indianapolis Orphans Asylum, a private organization responsible for operating the city's principal orphanage. The orphans home was discontinued in 1941.

The records consist of minutes of board meetings (1850-1873); indentures of children (1870-1903); children's records (1871-1909); record of children in the foundling ward (1891-1903); and accounts (1896-1923).

A-197. INDIANAPOLIS TRANSIT SYSTEM. RECORDS, 1955-1975.

12 ms. boxes.   Inventory.   M 427.

The Indianapolis Transit System was a private company which operated the city bus service in Indianapolis. In 1955 it was purchased by the Midland Transportation Corporation of Milwaukee, Wis., which operated the system until 1974, when the city of Indianapolis purchased it. In addition to operating the Indianapolis Transit System, the corporation also operated transit systems in Louisville, Ky., and Milwaukee, and owned property in downtown Indianapolis.

The collection consists of records from the Midland Transportation Corporation in Milwaukee relating to the operations of the Indianapolis Transit System. Included are minutes of ITS board of directors meetings (1955-1974); correspondence regarding the acquisition of ITS, the company's stock, modernization of equipment, and the operation of subsidiary companies (1955-1975); financial records and annual financial and statistical reports; and labor agreements, loan agreements, and other legal papers.

A-198. INGLE, JOHN (1788-1874). PAPERS, 1813-1868.

2 ms. boxes. Calendar. M 167.

Ingle emigrated from England to America in 1818; settled near Saundersville (now Inglefield), Vanderburgh Co., where he owned a farm; and was Saundersville postmaster (1823-1869).

The collection consists primarily of correspondence of Ingle and his wife with their family in England (1813-1868). The letters discuss the differences between life in America and England, the development of southern Indiana, conditions in England, family business, and economic, religious, and political matters. Also included is Ingle's description of his trip from Philadelphia, Pa., to Indiana, and his visit to Morris Birkbeck's Illinois settlement (1818); and letters from his son, John Ingle, Jr., in Philadelphia, to his English relatives (1834-1837).

A-199. INSTITUTE ON RELIGION AND AGING. RECORDS, 1972-1982.

10 ms. boxes. Inventory. M 421.

The institute was founded in 1971 by the Indiana Council of Churches and the Indiana Catholic Conference to educate churches about the needs of the aged, to promote improved services to the aged, and to organize and coordinate services and training programs throughout the state. The institute's principal activities were providing speakers and sponsoring seminars and conferences. It was dissolved in 1981 and was replaced by a volunteer group, the Interfaith Fellowship on Religion and Aging.

The records include minutes of the steering committee and board of directors (1972-1981); correspondence and other papers regarding workshops, conferences, grant applications, and other activities (1972-1982); newsletters (1977-1981), brochures, and other printed items; financial records; papers relating to other organizations, including the National Interfaith Coalition on Aging and the Indiana Commission on Aging and Aged; and bibliographies and position papers on aging.

A-200. INTERURBANS. RIGHT OF WAY DEEDS, 1899-1917.

8 ms. boxes. M 168.

The collection consists of right of way deeds for interurban railroad companies in Blackford, Delaware, Madison, Marion, and Wells counties. The companies include the Citizens' Street Railroad Company in Muncie; the Dayton and Muncie Traction Company; the Indiana Union Traction Company; the Muncie, Anderson and Indianapolis Street Railroad Company; and the Muncie, Hartford and Fort Wayne Railway Company.

A-201. IRELAND, JAMES (1788-1864). PAPERS, 1849-1880.

2 ms. boxes.   Calendar.   M 169.

Ireland was a farmer near Brownstown, Jackson Co.

The collection consists of correspondence among members of the Ireland family and includes letters written from Brownstown, Ind., Afton and Chariton, Iowa (1851-1880), Monmouth, Antelope Valley, and Trout Creek, Oreg. (1873-1876); Toledo and Effingham Co., Ill. (1849-1874); and the Kansas Territory (1860). The letters discuss economic matters, the Civil War, and family affairs.

A-202. JACKSON, JOSEPH W. (fl. 1875-1915). ACCOUNT BOOKS, 1875-1885.

2 vols. (.33 l.f.). BV 105-106.

Jackson ran a general store in Metamora, Franklin Co.

The collection consists of account books from Jackson's general store.

A-203. JENKS, NATHAN (1800-1863). PAPERS, 1836-1884.

55 items.   SC 874.

Jenks was a merchant at Victor, Ontario Co., N.Y.; moved to LaGrange County, Ind. (1835); laid out village of Ontario, LaGrange Co. (1837); founded LaGrange Collegiate Institute (1837); and owned a gristmill (1843) and a woolen mill (1846) at Ontario.

The collection includes Jenks's correspondence with family and friends in New York, primarily from the period 1836-1860. The letters discuss the settling of LaGrange County, the development of the LaGrange Collegiate Institute, Jenks's businesses, and family matters in Indiana and New York. Also included are documents relating to the founding of the LaGrange Collegiate Institute (1837-1841).

A-204. JEWISH WELFARE FEDERATION OF INDIANAPOLIS. RECORDS, 1900-1981.

150 archival boxes.   Inventory.
Restricted.

The Jewish Welfare Federation of Indianapolis was established in 1905 as the Jewish Federation to centralize fund raising and allocate funds to support local and national Jewish organizations. Initially the federation, which consisted of existing immigrant aid societies such as the Industrial Removal Organization and the Hebrew Ladies Benevolent Society, provided social services to the poor in the Jewish immigrant community through financial support, employment opportunities, health care, and assistance in adjusting to American life. With the decline of immigration in the 1920s the organization's interests shifted to Jewish community-related projects such as the Kirshbaum Center (1926), a community center which served as a social gathering and meeting place and offered adult education programs. In addition, the federation became a member of the Indianapolis War Chest (later the Community Chest, then the Community Fund) in 1918. The Jewish Welfare Fund, an autonomous, yet constituent agency of the Jewish Federation, was established in 1926 to raise and distribute funds for areas which the Community Fund would not support. The Welfare Fund conducted annual fund raising campaigns that provided support for local and national Jewish organizations and which helped to cover federation deficits. In 1948 the Jewish Federation and the Jewish Welfare Fund were combined and reorganized to form the Jewish Welfare Federation. The federation continues to conduct annual fund raising campaigns to support national Jewish organizations such as the United Jewish Appeal and the federation's local member organizations: the Jewish Education Association, the Jewish Community Center Association, Jewish Social Services, Jewish Family and Children's Services, Park Regency retirement housing, and the Hooverwood home for the aged. Also affiliated with the federation is the Indianapolis Jewish Community Relations Council, which was started in 1947 as a joint venture of the Anti-Defamation League and the American Jewish Congress, and became an independent organization in 1954. The council originally concentrated on combating anti-Semitism, but it later became involved in working for civil rights for both Jews and non-Jews.

The collection consists of records, correspondence, and printed materials pertaining to the Jewish Welfare Federation, its member organizations, including the Jewish Community Relations Council, and the federation's predecessor organizations. Federation central office records include board of governors, directors, and executive committee meeting minutes (1905-1970); budget and policy committee reports; personnel records; records of funds allocated to local and national organizations; annual meeting minutes and reports; public relations records (1960s-1970s); campaign records (1957-1976); records of the Women's and Young Matron's divisions (1960s-1970s); and records and correspondence relating to banquets and other federation social occasions (1960s-1970s). Also included are immigrant case files and other records of the Industrial Removal Office in Indianapolis (1900-1920); the Jewish Federation's transient files (1920s-1930s); and correspondence, financial records, directives, meeting minutes, and printed materials regarding national Jewish organizations such as the United Jewish Appeal, the United Hias Service, and the Joint Defense Appeal (1950s-1970s).

The collection also includes correspondence, minutes of meetings, reports, budgets, financial records, and printed materials of the federation's member organizations, including the Jewish Education Association; the Jewish Community Center Association, including records regarding the Kirschbaum Center and the construction of a new center; the Borinstein and Hooverwood homes for the aged; the Jewish Family and Children's Services; and the Jewish Social Services (1950s-1970s). Also included are records of the Jewish Community Relations Council (1944-1981), consisting of correspondence with national, state, and local religious, human, and civil rights organizations concerning subjects such as anti-Semitism, racial discrimination, and prayer in schools; the council's committee meeting minutes; financial records; and miscellaneous printed materials regarding anti-Semitism, Zionism, and JCRC meetings and activities.

A-205. JOHNSON, ANDREW JACKSON (1841-1916). PAPERS, 1862-1917.

59 items. SC 878.

Johnson, from Franklin, Johnson Co., served with the 70th Indiana Regiment during the Civil War.

The collection is made up primarily of Johnson's letters to his family, written while he was serving in the Union Army in Kentucky, Tennessee, and Georgia (1862-1865). Also included is a transcript of his war diary (1863-1865).

A-206. JOHNSON, GEORGE S. (b.1843). PAPERS, 1862-1908.

70 items. SC 881.

Johnson, from Dearborn County, served as a sergeant and lieutenant in the 83rd Indiana Regiment during the Civil War.

The collection consists primarily of orders, muster rolls, and other official documents of the 83rd Indiana Regiment in Tennessee, Georgia, and North Carolina (1862-1865). Also included are letters of Johnson to his family and fiancee (1863-1865) and war letters from Tennessee written by his brother-in-law, Caleb Gill, of the 57th Indiana Regiment (1862-1865).

A-207. JOLLY, CHARLES (1803-1875). PAPERS, 1832-1872.

1 ms. box. Inventory. M 170.

Jolly was a carpenter and farmer at Logan, Dearborn Co. (1830-1875); and Logan postmaster (1853-1859, 1864-1873).

The collection includes Jolly's account book (1834-1837) and miscellaneous family and business letters and documents (1832-1872); and papers of Jolly's son, William Henry Jolly (1835-1863), including his diaries (1856-1859), papers relating to his military service as a hospital steward at Vicksburg, Miss. (1863), and his poetry.

A-208. JONES, JAMES H. (b.1839). PAPERS, 1862-1865.

77 items.   Calendar.   SC 889.

Jones was a Randolph County farmer; and soldier in the 57th Indiana Regiment during the Civil War.

The collection is composed of Jones's letters to his family while he served in the Union Army in Mississippi, Tennessee, and Georgia.

A-209. JONES, LUMAN (b.1821). PAPERS, 1848-1871.

25 items.   Calendar.   SC 891.

Jones was a farmer in Waynesville, Warren Co., Ohio, and Marietta, Shelby Co., Ind.; and an officer with the 79th Indiana Regiment during the Civil War.

The collection includes letters to Jones from Jacob Cook in Lafayette, Tippecanoe Co., and in California (1848-1852); and letters from Jones to his wife while he served with the Union Army in Tennessee (1862-1865).

A-210. JUDAH-BRANDON FAMILY. PAPERS, 1820-1950.

22 ms. boxes.   Partial Inventory.   M 171.

The Judah-Brandon family included John Mantle Judah (1848-1936), who was a native of Vincennes, Knox Co.; graduate of Brown University, Providence, R.I. (1867); clerk for the Indiana Supreme Court in Indianapolis (1867-1869); Indianapolis attorney (1869-1887); partner in the firm of Caldwell and Judah, investment bankers for foreign capital in Memphis, Tenn. (1887-1895); Indianapolis resident and property owner (1895-1936); and world traveler.

Other family members whose papers figure prominently in the collection are Judah's wife, Mary Jameson Judah (1851-1930), a writer of short stories and essays; their son, Henry Judah Brandon (b.1873), a student at Phillips Academy, Andover, Mass., and Yale University, Conn. (1893), a lawyer in New York, Chicago, and Indianapolis (1890s-1910s), employee of the Hispaniola Honey Company in Haiti and New York (1917-1922), and manager of the Coldstream Golf Club, Hampstead, N.Y. (1923); John M. Judah's father, Samuel Judah (1798-1869), a Vincennes attorney; and Judah's father-in-law, Patrick Henry Jameson (1824-1910), an Indianapolis physician and public official.

The collection consists primarily of family correspondence from the period 1863-1924. Included is John M. Judah's correspondence with his family in Vincennes while he was a student at Brown and a clerk and attorney in Indianapolis; his love letters to Mary Jameson (1870-1872); correspondence between Judah and his wife while he was on business trips; their correspondence with Henry J. Brandon while he was a student (1893), a lawyer (1898-1916), and in Haiti (1917-1922); and their correspondence with the Patrick Jameson family of Indianapolis (1880s-1890s). Also included is Judah's account book kept while he was a student at Brown (1865-1867); his reminiscences; manuscripts of Mary Judah's stories and essays; correspondence regarding the publication of her book *Down Our Way* (1897); and legal documents of Samuel Judah (1826, 1853-1863), including his brief written for the Vincennes case of *John Cleves Symmes Harrison* v. *Frederick Rapp* (1826).

Correspondents include Ovid Butler, William Dudley Foulke, Catherine Merrill, Harry S. New, Meredith Nicholson, Lazarus Noble, Theodore C. Steele, Ida Tarbell, Booth Tarkington, Susan Wallace, and Israel Zangwill.

A-211. KASER, MARY ETTA (fl.1889-1918). LETTERS, 1917-1918.

60 items. Inventory. SC 894.

Mary Etta Kaser was an Indianapolis widow.

The collection consists of letters from Kaser to her daughter, Merl Young of Flat Rock, Shelby Co. (1917-1918). The letters deal with women's suffrage, World War I, economic problems, and family matters.

A-212. KELLAR MILLS. RECORDS, 1854-1871.

190 items.   SC 1660.

John Kellar (b.1811) operated a flour mill and a woolen mill near North Vernon, Jennings Co.

The collection consists of business papers regarding the operation of Kellar's mills.

A-213. KELLEY, DAVID (1827-1911). PAPERS, 1862-1865.

34 items.   SC 899.

Kelley was a farmer and merchant in Lawrence County; and an officer with the 67th Indiana Regiment (1862-1864) and the 24th Indiana Regiment (1865).

The collection consists of Kelley's letters to his family, written while he was serving with the Union Army in Tennessee, Alabama, and Louisiana; and letters to Kelley and members of his family from relatives and friends in Claysville, Washington Co., and other Indiana towns (1862-1865).

A-214. KEMPER, GENERAL WILLIAM HARRISON (1839-1927). PAPERS, 1794-1949.

2 ms. boxes.   Inventory.   M 172.

Kemper was a graduate of Long Island College Hospital, New York (1865); a Muncie, Delaware Co., physician (1865-1927); and author of medical and historical works, including *A Twentieth Century History of Delaware County* (1908) and *A Medical History of the State of Indiana* (1911).

The collection includes three of Kemper's medical notebooks (1865-1866) and a number of case histories of his Muncie patients (1899-1907); miscellaneous correspondence and business papers of Kemper and his son, Dr. Arthur T. Kemper (b.1870), most relating to medical or historical matters; Arthur Kemper's scrapbooks of newspaper articles about Muncie events (1888-1897);

forty-seven land indentures and deeds, most from Montgomery County, Ohio (1806-1877); and eight items relating to the shipment of goods from Baltimore, Md. (1794-1800).

A-215. KENT, PHINEAS MARTIN (1808-1888). PAPERS, 1833-1888.

34 items. SC 904.

Attorney and politician. Kent was an attorney in Vevay, Switzerland Co. (1834-1840); a newspaper publisher in New Albany, Floyd Co. (1840-1857); Democratic member of the New Albany City Council (1847-1848), the Indiana Constitutional Convention (1850-1851), and the Indiana House of Representatives (1851-1852); lawyer and farmer, Brookston, White Co. (1857-1888); and president, Chicago and Indianapolis Air Line Railway (1882).

The collection consists of correspondence and business papers relating to Kent's law practice in Vevay, Democratic Party politics, principally in the 1850s and 1860s, and his efforts to obtain a diplomatic appointment in 1857.

Correspondents include Jesse Bright, Michael G. Bright, Daniel W. Voorhees, and Ashbel P. Willard.

A-216. KETCHAM, JOHN LEWIS (1810-1869). PAPERS, 1830-1937.

3 ms. boxes, 10 vols. (1.33 l.f.).   Calendar.   M 173, BV 1035-1046.

Ketcham was an attorney in Indianapolis (1833-1869). He was the son of John Ketcham (1782-1865), a politician and educator in Bloomington, Monroe Co.; and son-in-law of Samuel Merrill (1792-1855), Indiana state treasurer (1822-1834), president of the State Bank of Indiana (1834-1844), president of the Madison and Indianapolis Railroad (1844-1848), and Indianapolis businessman.

The papers consist primarily of family correspondence, principally from the period 1830-1869. Included is Ketcham's correspondence with his father regarding his law practice, politics, and family matters (1833-1863); Merrill family correspondence, including letters of Samuel Merrill (1830-1853) and Catherine Merrill (1834-1861), and letters from family members in Peacham, Vt. (1834-1844), and Louisiana (1845-1855); Ketcham's correspondence with his wife, Jane Merrill Ketcham, while she was working as an army nurse in Gallatin, Tenn., during the Civil War (1862-1863, 1865); letters of Ketcham's sons, written while they were traveling and studying in Austria and Germany (1860); and his correspondence with his son, William Ketcham (1846-1921), while a student at Wabash College, Crawfordsville, Montgomery Co. (1861-1863), an officer in the 13th Indiana Regiment serving in Virginia and North Carolina (1864-1865), and a student at Dartmouth College, N.H. (1865-1869). The collection also includes miscellaneous business papers and indentures of Samuel Merrill (1833-1854); reminiscences of Jane Merrill Ketcham; William Ketcham's 1910 reminiscence of the Civil War; his account of a trip to Los Angeles, Calif., to attend a Grand Army of the Republic Encampment in 1912; his speeches on literary and patriotic topics (1886-1914); and genealogical correspondence and papers (1910s-1930s).

A-217. KILLIAN, JOHN M. (1861-1931). DIARIES, 1900-1904.

1 ms. box (5 vols.). M 418.

Killian was a farmer and amateur photographer in Rockport, Spencer Co.

The collection consists of Killian's diaries describing his farm and family life, his photography work, and Rockport events.

A-218. KINDER, TRUSTIN B. (d.1847). PAPERS, 1844-1906.

29 items. Calendar. SC 913.

Kinder was an attorney in Indianapolis and Paoli, Orange Co.; and an officer in the 2nd Indiana Regiment during the Mexican War.

The collection includes two of Kinder's letters written from Paoli (1845) and 10 letters and documents relating to his service in Texas and Mexico (1846-1847). The collection also includes papers relating to the Kinder family in Indianapolis, primarily from the period 1861-1865.

A-219. KING, JOHN LYLE (1823-1892). DIARIES, 1842-1879.

11 vols. (1.66 l.f.). Inventory. BV 745-755.

King was an attorney in Madison, Jefferson Co. (1843-1856), and Chicago, Ill. (1856-1892); Whig member, Indiana House of Representatives (1851-1852); and Chicago city attorney (1860).

The collection consists of King's diaries, including the diaries he kept while he was an attorney and politician in Madison (1842-1856); diaries covering his years in Chicago as an attorney and an active member of the Republican Party (1857-1873); and a diary of his hunting and fishing trips to Winnepeg and Lake Nipigon, Canada (1879).

A-220. KING, WILLIAM F. (1824-1892). PAPERS, 1853-1865.

38 items. Calendar. SC 918.

King was a physician in Centerville, Wayne Co. (1865-1892); assistant surgeon, 124th Indiana Regiment (1864-1865); and surgeon, 147th Indiana Regiment (1865).

The papers consist primarily of King's letters to his family written while he served with the Union Army in Tennessee, Georgia, and North Carolina (1864-1865).

A-221. KINLEY, ISAAC (1822-ca.1902). PAPERS, 1847-1901.

55 items. SC 919.
Microfilm.

Publisher and educator. Kinley was an attorney and educator in Henry County (1846-1861) and Wayne County (1861-1874); editor, *Knightstown* (Henry Co.) *Citizen*; publisher, *The Beech Tree*, a Henry County literary magazine; member, Indiana Constitutional Convention (1850-1851); Republican member, Indiana State Senate (1857-1859, 1867-1869); provost marshal, 6th Congressional District, Richmond, Wayne Co. (1863); and farmer and educator in San Jose, Calif. (1874-1902).

The papers are composed primarily of letters written by Kinley to Benjamin S. Parker (1833-1911), a Henry County educator and writer. The letters discuss poetry, the publication of *The Beech Tree* (1858-1859), Kinley's service in the state legislature (1857-1859), his work as provost marshal, and his life in California. Also included are a number of Kinley's poems.

A-222. KNODE, ARCHIBALD B. (1810-1889). PAPERS, 1815-1880.

1 ms. box, 2 vols. (1.5 l.f.).   Inventory.   M 175, BV 108-109.

Knode was a clerk in a general store in Sharpsburg, Md. (1829-1834), and a farmer in Hagerstown, Wayne Co. (1840-1889).

The collection includes Knode's diaries (1833-1834); his account books (1835-1848); record book of the Hagerstown Mining Company, organized to sponsor a mining expedition from Wayne County to California (1849); notebook relating to Knode's trip to California (1849-1850); and miscellaneous family papers (1815-1880).

A-223. KNOX COUNTY MISCELLANEOUS PAPERS, 1764-1833.

1 ms. box.   M 65.

The collection consists of estate records, court depositions, orphans records, indentures, the proceedings of the Knox County Board of Commissioners (1797-1802), and other miscellaneous legal papers relating to the early history of Vincennes and Knox County. Included are papers relating to Toussaint Dubois, Gen. Washington Johnston, Hyacinth Lasselle, Benjamin Parke, William Prince, Louis St. Ange, and Francis Vigo.

A-224. KRAMER, FRANK N. (b.1868). PAPERS, 1898-1936.

1 ms. box.   Calendar.   M 176.

Kramer, from Warren County, served in the U.S. Marine Corps during the Spanish-American War and the Philippine Insurrection.

The collection consists of Kramer's letters home while he was serving with the Marines in the Philippines (1898-1900); letters regarding his military service and pensions (1901-1936); and a scrapbook of Spanish-American War items.

A-225. KU KLUX KLAN. CROWN POINT. RECORDS, 1913-1932.

4 ms. boxes.　　　　　　　　Inventory.　　　　　　　　M 409.
Restricted.

The Ku Klux Klan was formed in Georgia in 1915 and became a prominent national organization in the 1920s as an advocate for native-born, white, Protestant Americans. At its height in 1924 the Indiana Klan had more than 300,000 members, although it quickly declined after scandals in the mid-1920s. The Crown Point, Lake Co., Klan #72 was a local affiliate of the national Ku Klux Klan.

The records include membership records and applications, principally 1923-1927; dues records (1923-1931); minutes of meetings (1925-1929); letters and bulletins from J. A. Colescott, Imperial Representative for Indiana and Michigan (1920s-1930s); financial records (1923-1932); listings of political candidates for Crown Point and Lake County elections (1923, 1930); and publications and printed materials from the state and national Klans.

A-226. KU KLUX KLAN. WAYNE COUNTY. RECORDS, 1916-1933.

10 ms. boxes, 11 vols. (4.5 l.f.).　　Inventory.　　M 407, BV 1587-1596b.
Restricted. Microfilm.

Whitewater Klan #60 in Richmond, Wayne Co., was a local affiliate of the national Ku Klux Klan.

The collection consists primarily of the Wayne County Klan's membership and financial records from the period 1922-1927. Included are membership and dues records (1921-1927); correspondence and communiques from local Klan leaders (1923-1929); documents and bulletins from the state and national Klan offices (1923-1932); minutes of meetings (1927-1928); financial records (1922-1928); and flyers, pamphlets, and other printed materials (1916-1933).

Also included are minutes and financial records of the Klan in Fountain City, Wayne Co. (1924-1925).

A-227. LAFUSE, AGGIE (fl.1860-1870). DIARIES, 1860-1870.

9 vols. (.25 l.f.). SC 948.

Lafuse lived on a farm near Liberty, Union Co.

The diaries record Lafuse's life as a young woman growing up on a farm and include descriptions of social occasions, daily activities, and local events.

A-228. LAMBERT, GEORGE WASHINGTON (1836-1899). PAPERS, 1828-1951.

3 ms. boxes. Calendar. M 178.

Lambert was a schoolteacher in Clinton, Vermillion Co., and New Goshen, Vigo Co. (1858-1861); corporal, 14th Indiana Regiment (1861-1864); member of the regimental band (1862); employee of the Vigo County auditor's and treasurer's office (1864-1872); employee of the U.S. Post Office in Indianapolis (1872-1883); and resident of Clinton (1883-1899).

The papers include Lambert's Civil War letters to his family from Virginia and Maryland (1861-1864); his Civil War diaries (1861-1863); Civil War letters to members of Lambert's family from soldiers in Kentucky and Tennessee; Lambert's diary as a teacher (1858-1861); a small amount of family correspondence (1864-1923); a large number of receipts and bills, primarily from the period 1864-1898; family land and financial documents from Vermillion and Vigo counties (1828-1860); and papers relating to Lambert's involvement in the Independent Order of Good Templars (1860-1865).

A-229. LANE, HENRY SMITH (1811-1881). PAPERS, 1788-1936.

11 ms. boxes. Inventory. M 180.

Attorney and politician. Lane was a Crawfordsville, Montgomery Co., attorney and banker (1834-1881); Whig member, Indiana House of Representatives (1837-1838) and U.S. House of Representatives (1840-1843); officer in the 1st Indiana Regiment during the Mexican War (1846-1847); one of the founders of the Indiana Republican Party; chairman, Republican National Convention (1856); elected Indiana governor (1860); member, U.S. Senate (1861-1867); and member, Commission on Indian Affairs (1869-1871). Lane was the son-in-law of Isaac Compton Elston (1798-1868), a Crawfordsville merchant, banker, and businessman (1823-1868) and president of the Crawfordsville and Wabash Railroad.

The largest section of the collection consists of Lane's personal and business correspondence from the period 1846-1876 and includes papers relating to his service in the Mexican War; the founding of the Republican Party; the elections of 1856, 1858, and 1860; political conditions in Indiana, Kentucky, and Washington, D.C., during the Civil War; his work with the Commission on Indian Affairs; and his business interests, primarily in Indiana. His papers also include personal correspondence of his wives and other family members; travel notes of his wife, Joanna, on her trips to Italy and Jerusalem (1882); and family legal documents from Maysville and other Kentucky towns (1821-1830s). The collection also includes business papers (1818-1861) of Isaac C. Elston relating to the Wabash and Erie Canal (1840s-1850s), the Crawfordsville and Wabash Railroad (1850s), the Indiana State Bank, his land interests at Michigan City, LaPorte Co., and his business interests in Crawfordsville. Other materials in the collection include correspondence and legal documents (1875-1936) of the family of Harold Taylor (1862-1936), an Indianapolis attorney and husband of Isaac Elston's granddaughter; transcripts of the Civil War letters of Henry Lane Stone, a Confederate soldier under John Hunt Morgan and prisoner of war; a record book for the Crawfordsville Land Office (1830-1831); manuscript survey maps of Vermillion County (1830s); genealogical papers on the Elstons and related families; and Elston family scrapbooks.

Correspondents include Ovid Butler, Israel T. Canby, William G. Coffin, Schuyler Colfax, Jacob D. Cox, John R. Cravens, Will Cumback, John D. Defrees, John B. Dillon, Ebenezer Dumont, Jacob Piatt Dunn, William M. Dunn, Calvin Fletcher, Horace Greeley, Walter Q. Gresham, Allen Hamilton, Edward A. Hannegan, Thomas A. Hendricks, George W. Julian, Daniel Kilgore, John Lyle King, Benson J. Lossing, Solomon Meredith, Robert H. Milroy, Oliver P. Morton, Harry S. New, Godlove Orth, Robert Dale Owen, John Pettit, Daniel D. Pratt, William H. Seward, Thomas C. Slaughter, Oliver H. Smith, James A. Speed, Jonathan Speed, Richard W. Thompson, John P. Usher, Susan Elston Wallace, and James Wilson.

A-230. LANE, HENRY SMITH (1811-1881). PAPERS, 1793-1877.

54 items.   Calendar.   SC 1908.

Lane was a Crawfordsville, Montgomery Co., lawyer and politician; Whig member of the Indiana House of Representatives (1837-1838) and U.S. House of Representatives (1840-1843); chairman, Republican National Convention (1856); and member, U.S. Senate (1861-1867).

The collection consists of papers of Lane and other Crawfordsville people. Included are letters to and from Lane regarding Republican Party politics, the situation in Kansas in the 1850s, and the Civil War; documents relating to land and business transactions in Montgomery County (1834-1877); letters of E. W. Coffeen of Crawfordsville (1854); notes on the activities of the Independent Company of Rangers, Montgomery County (1843); a letter from Vincennes, Knox Co., regarding military compensation (1816); and notes on recipes and medical cures (1793-1868).

Correspondents include Isaac C. Elston, Thomas A. Hendricks, Joseph Lane, William H. Seward, Lew Wallace, and James Wilson.

A-231. LANE, OSCAR BRUCE (1881-1975). PAPERS, 1865-1971.

14 ms. boxes, 1 vol. (3.6 l.f.).   Inventory.   M 179, BV 1597.

Lane was a student at Purdue University, West Lafayette, Tippecanoe Co. (1900-1902); teacher and school administrator, Bainbridge, Putnam Co. (1902-ca.1914); Putnam County farmer (1914-1975); Republican member, Indiana State Senate (1935-1949); and member, State Commission on Interstate Cooperation (1945-1950).

The bulk of the collection consists of Lane's papers relating to politics and his work in the state legislature, including correspondence with his constituents regarding state government services and proposed legislation, particularly relating to education and agriculture (1935-1949); correspondence regarding local and state Republican Party politics (1930s-1960s); and legislative calendars, proposed legislation, reports, and other printed materials from the General Assembly. Also included are letters to Lane from his family in Bainbridge while he was attending Purdue University (1900-1902); letters from friends in Putnam County, Indianapolis, and other places, principally 1900-

1915; correspondence regarding his work as a teacher and school administrator (1902-1914); his speeches; his accounts and receipts (1907-1944); student and teacher records from Bainbridge (1902-1914); essays of his sister, Nellie Ruth Lane, written for a University of Chicago correspondence course (1903); scrapbooks and clippings; and minutes and accounts of the Bainbridge Gravel Road Company (1867-1893).

Correspondents include Ralph F. Gates and William E. Jenner.

A-232. LANMAN, CHARLES (1819-1895). COLLECTION, 1828-1869.

1 ms. box.   M 185.

Lanman was an author and painter; and compiler of the *Dictionary of the United States Congress*, published in 1859, second edition published in 1869.

The collection consists of biographical material on sixty-one Indiana congressmen collected by Lanman for the two editions of his *Dictionary of the United States Congress*. Included are autobiographical sketches written by the congressmen, biographical sketches prepared by others, and several autograph letters of Indiana congressmen for whom Lanman did not have biographical sketches.

The collection includes letters or autobiographical sketches written by Jesse D. Bright, Schuyler Colfax, Will Cumback, John Wesley Davis, John Dowling, Elisha Embree, William H. English, Graham N. Fitch, Thomas A. Hendricks, William S. Holman, Jonathan Jennings, George W. Julian, Henry S. Lane, Oliver P. Morton, Godlove Orth, Robert Dale Owen, Albert G. Porter, Daniel D. Pratt, Caleb B. Smith, Richard W. Thompson, David Turpie, and Daniel W. Voorhees.

A-233. LAUGHLIN, CLARA E. (1873-1941). LETTERS, 1898-1903.

22 items.   Inventory.   SC 1777.

Laughlin was a Chicago, Ill., writer; editor for the Chicago magazine *The Interior* (ca.1900); and author of *Reminiscences of James Whitcomb Riley* (1916), several novels, and the series of books *The Clara Laughlin Travel Study Series*.

The collection consists of Laughlin's letters to Mary Elizabeth Riley Payne (1864-1936), the youngest sister of poet James Whitcomb Riley and a resident of Indianapolis. The letters deal with Laughlin's travels, her visits with Riley and other mutual friends, clothing styles, and current affairs.

A-234. LEONARD, JOHN FINLEY THOMPSON (d.1872). PAPERS, 1861-1870.

2 ms. boxes.   Inventory.   M 182.

Leonard was an officer in the 50th Indiana Regiment serving in Kentucky, Tennessee, and Arkansas (1861-1865); and Monroe County justice of the peace (1870).

The collection consists almost entirely of Civil War documents relating to the 50th Indiana Regiment and includes muster rolls, monthly reports on supplies, inspection reports, and receipts for ordinance, clothing, and other supplies and equipment.

A-235. LEWIS, SAMUEL B. (1840-1920). PAPERS, 1860-1930.

1 ms. box, 4 vols. (.5 l.f.).   Inventory.   M 331, BV 1856-1859.

Lewis was a physician in Manville and Canaan, Jefferson Co. (1867-1910); and surgeon in the 125th Indiana (10th Cavalry) Regiment (1864-1865).

The collection includes Lewis's medical account books and receipts (1866-1910); D.A.R. applications for his wife and daughter; bylaws and yearbooks of the Madison, Jefferson Co., chapter of the D.A.R. (1911-1923); family correspondence, including two business letters of Chauncey B. Lewis, the doctor's son; and deeds, diplomas, military papers, and other legal documents of Dr. Lewis.

A-236. LEWIS, WILLIAM (d.1838). PAPERS, 1832-1837.

27 items.   Calendar.   SC 969.

Lewis was a Presbyterian minister in Rising Sun, Ohio Co. (1832-1834), and Darr Town, Ohio (1834-1835); and a promoter of religious education in southeastern Indiana, based in Rising Sun (1835-1837).

The papers consist primarily of letters from Lewis and his wife, Mary, to her sister in Connecticut, principally concerning living conditions and religious life in Indiana. Also included are several letters relating to Miami University in Oxford, Ohio, in the 1830s.

A-237. LINDLEY, HARLOW (1875-1959). COLLECTION, 1790-1913.

2 ms. boxes, 1 oversize box. Inventory and calendar. M 186.

Lindley was a professor of history at Earlham College, Richmond, Wayne Co. (1899-1928); director, Department of History and Archives, Indiana State Library (1903-1924); director, Indiana Historical Commission (1923-1924); curator of history (1929-1934) and secretary (1934-1946), Ohio State Archaeological and Historical Society, Columbus.

The collection consists of historical papers relating to the history of Indiana and the Old Northwest collected by Lindley. Included are letters (1890-1913) from U.S. Senator and Vice-President Charles W. Fairbanks (1852-1918) to newspapermen William Henry Smith and Delavan Smith regarding Republican Party politics, railroads, their interests in the *Indianapolis News* and other newspapers, and Fairbanks's world tour in 1909-1910; papers of Vincennes merchant and Whig politician, John Ewing (1798-1858), consisting of his correspondence regarding his legal and land affairs in the Vincennes area (1839, 1853-1857), his legal work on behalf of the widow of fur trader Manuel Lisa (1853-1857), and other business and political matters (1824-1858); and papers of Northwest Territory governor Arthur St. Clair (1736-1818), consisting of his letters to his sons regarding family business and territorial affairs (1794-1813). Also included is an autobiographical sketch of Joshua Bond (b.1781), a Quaker farmer in Randolph and Jay counties; political letters (1845-1849, 1876) to newspaper publisher and Democratic Party politician Samuel Covington (1819-1889) of Rising Sun, Ohio Co., and Madison, Jefferson Co., including letters from Jesse D. Bright; Fourth of July, 1817, speech of Vevay, Switzerland Co., politician John Dumont (1787-1871); letters (1823, 1841, 1849) of Ohio politician Thomas Ewing (1789-1871); account of a trip from Richmond, Wayne Co., to Baltimore, Md., in 1844 by Quaker Eli Gause; military letters (1790, 1800) of John Francis Hamtramck (d.1803), commander of U.S. troops at Vincennes (1788-1791) and Fort Wayne; political letters (1824-1825) of Indiana governor William Hendricks (1782-1850); papers (1800, 1820, 1828) of scientist and educator William Maclure (1763-1840), including a letter to Charles-Alexandre LeSueur regarding Robert Owen's community at New Harmony; letters (1909, 1912) to Indiana governor Thomas R. Marshall (1854-1925); correspondence (1823-1841) of Arthur St. Clair (1803-1841), register of the land office in Indianapolis (1829-1838); petitions from the residents of Vincennes to Northwest Territory secretary Winthrop Sargent (1790); correspondence (1839-1855) of midwestern Indian and landscape painter George Winter (1810-1876); papers (1892-1908) of Indiana historian Jacob Piatt Dunn (1855-1924); reminiscences of Quaker Daniel Worth; a letter regarding the development of the Michigan City area (1833); and other miscellaneous documents.

The collection includes letters and documents by Conrad Baker, Clara Barton, Jesse D. Bright, Michael Brouillet, Robert Buntin, Andrew Carnegie, Charles W. Cathcart, August Chouteau, William Clark, Charles B. Farwell, William Henry Harrison, William S. Hempstead, Henry S. Lane, Charles B. Lasselle, Charles Lee, Charles-Alexandre LeSueur, Noah Noble, Benjamin Parke, John Paul, Heinrich Pestalozzi, John L. Robinson, Erastus Root, Winthrop Sargent, Zachary Taylor, John Tipton, and Thomas Worthington.

A-238. LLOYD, JOHN A. (1839-1903). DIARIES, 1867-1876.

1 ms. box.   M 187.

Lloyd was a farmer in Noble Township, LaPorte Co.

The diaries describe daily events on Lloyd's farm and in LaPorte County.

A-239. LOGGIA COLONIA ITALIANA, WAYNE COUNTY NO. 933. RECORDS, 1919-1950.

4 vols. (.5 l.f.).   BV 2044-2047.

The Loggia is an Italian benevolent and social organization in Richmond, Wayne Co., affiliated with the national organization Ordine Figli d'Italia in America (Sons of Italy in America).

The records consist of the minutes of the lodge's meetings (1920-1950); dues records (1919-1934); and a printed volume of constitution and laws for the national organization. Records prior to 1942 are in Italian.

A-240. LOMAX, JOSEPH (1809-1914). PAPERS, 1837-1945.

1 ms. box.   Inventory.   M 188.

Lomax was a newspaper editor and publisher in LaPorte, LaPorte Co., Kalamazoo, Mich., and other places; organizer (1854) and president (1855-1866) of the Grand Rapids and Indiana Railroad Company.

The papers include records of the Grand Rapids and Indiana Railroad Company (1858-1914), including land documents, financial reports, and a history of the railroad; scattered personal correspondence and business papers (1849-1914); writings and articles about Lomax as a centenarian; family correspondence and business papers of his daughter, Mary Lomax of Indianapolis (1931-1945); and letters of his son, Joseph A. Lomax of Long Beach, Calif. (1940).

A-241. LOOP, URIAH J. (ca.1843-ca.1914). PAPERS, 1862-1864.

37 items.   Calendar.   M 189.

Loop was a resident of Roanoke, Huntington Co.; and served in the 75th Indiana Regiment (1862-1864).

The collection consists of Loop's Civil War letters written from Kentucky and Tennessee to his sister in Roanoke.

A-242. LOUNSBURY, GEORGE (b.1837). PAPERS, 1854-1866.

62 items.   Inventory.   SC 1789.

Lounsbury was a farmer in Flint, Steuben Co.

The collection consists of family letters to Lounsbury, including letters from George W. Spearbeck, 8th Michigan Regiment, stationed at Port Royal, S.C. (1861-1862); and letters from family members in Silver Creek, Iowa (1857-1866), Grand Rapids, Mich., Waterville, Wis., and Steuben County, Ind.

A-243. LUSE, DOUGLASS (1795-1894). PAPERS, 1819-1893.

3 ms. boxes.   Inventory.   M 397.

Luse was a tanner in Urbana, Ohio.

The bulk of the collection consists of letters to Luse from family members in Indianapolis from the period 1824-1880. Included are letters of his sister Elizabeth (d.1878) and brother-in-law James Paxton (d.1829); his sister Susan Luse (b.1810) who moved to Indianapolis by 1835; his sister Rhode Ann (d.1876) and brother-in-law William Hannaman (d.1880), an Indianapolis printer, drugstore owner (1832-1863), and broker (1871-1880); and his son, Douglass Luse, Jr. (fl.1853-1887), a medical student at Starling Medical College in Columbus, Ohio, in the 1850s, and a physician in the Indianapolis area in the 1860s. Also included are Luse's papers and correspondence relating to his tannery business; and additional family correspondence.

A-244. MABREY, BENJAMIN BENN (1839-1915). PAPERS, 1862-1865.

1 ms. box.   M 190.

Mabrey was a farmer in Jefferson, Dearborn, and Boone counties and a private in the 82nd Indiana Regiment.

The collection consists of originals, photocopies, and transcripts of Mabrey's Civil War letters to his wife, written from Tennessee and Georgia.

A-245. McCARTY, NICHOLAS (1795-1854). ACCOUNT BOOKS, 1816-1852.

35 vols. (5.5 l.f.).   Inventory.   BV 164-198.

Merchant. McCarty owned general merchandise stores in Knox County, Ohio (1816-1818), and Indianapolis (1823-1854), and branch stores in Covington, Fountain Co., Greenfield, Hancock Co., Delphi, Carroll Co., Eagle Village,

Boone Co., and Port Royal, Morgan Co. He also owned a farm near Indianapolis and promoted the cultivation of ginseng, silk, and hemp.

The collection consists of account books, ledgers, daybooks, invoices, and blotters from his stores and other enterprises in Delphi, Covington, Eagle Village, and Greenfield, Ind. (1824-1852), and Knox County, Ohio (1816-1818).

A-246. MCCORMICK, CHARLES OWEN (1886-1957). NOTEBOOKS, 1907-1948.

1 ms. box, 5 vols. (1.25 l.f.).   Inventory.   M 414, BV 2093-2097.

McCormick was a graduate of Indiana University (1911) and the Harvard University Medical School (1913); Indianapolis obstetrician and professor, Indiana University Medical School (1916-1957); and author, *Pathology of Labor, Puerperium, and the Newborn* (1944, 1947).

The collection includes McCormick's notebooks for his freshman and sophomore medical school classes at Indiana University (1909-1911); his notebook for his premedical school classes (1907-1909); his notes and lectures on the pathology of labor, puerperium, and the newborn at Indiana University (1939); and letters and reviews on his book *Pathology of Labor, Puerperium, and the Newborn* (1944-1948).

A-247. MCCREA, EDWARD T. (1836-1915). PAPERS, 1858-1922.

1 ms. box.   Calendar.   M 191.

McCrea was an officer in the 33rd Indiana Regiment (1861-1864); a farmer and stockbreeder at New Richmond, Montgomery Co. (1867-1915); and Republican member, Indiana House of Representatives (1895-1897).

The bulk of the papers are Civil War documents relating to supplies for the 33rd Regiment. There are also a small number of Civil War letters from

McCrea to family and friends; and family, business, and political correspondence from the late nineteenth century.

A-248. MCCREA AND BROWN COMPANY. ACCOUNT BOOKS, 1897-1932.

2 vols. (.5 l.f.). BV 161-162.

The McCrea and Brown Company was a hardware store in Brazil, Clay Co.

The collection consists of the store's account books (1897-1932).

A-249. MCCULLOCH, CARLETON BUEL (1871-1949). PAPERS, 1933-1946.

3 ms. boxes. Calendar. M 192.

McCulloch was an Indianapolis physician; Democratic nominee for governor of Indiana (1920, 1924); State Democratic Party chairman (1933-1934); and vice-president and medical director of the State Life Insurance Company, Indianapolis (1934-1948).

The papers consist primarily of correspondence between McCulloch and Indiana novelist Meredith Nicholson (1866-1948). The bulk of this correspondence was written while Nicholson was serving as U.S. Minister to Paraguay (1933-1934), Venezuela (1935-1938), and Nicaragua (1938-1941). The letters relate to Indiana and Indianapolis social life and politics; national politics, especially the efforts of Paul V. McNutt to secure the 1940 Democratic presidential nomination; and affairs in the countries where Nicholson was serving. Also included is McCulloch's correspondence regarding a memorial dinner for Nicholson in 1933; and his correspondence attempting to secure a diplomatic post for Nicholson in 1941.

Correspondents include Cordell Hull, William H. Larrabee, Louis Ludlow, Paul V. McNutt, Sherman Minton, Harry S. New, Booth Tarkington, and James E. Watson.

A-250. MACDONALD, DONALD (1791-1872). PAPERS, 1824-1826.

1 ms. box.   Inventory.   M 408.

Macdonald was a resident of Edinburgh, Scotland; officer in the Royal Engineers (1808-1824); and traveled to America with Robert Owen and participated in the founding of Owen's community at New Harmony, Posey Co., Ind. (1824-1825).

The collection consists of Macdonald's diary and letters written during his trips to America (1824-1826). Included are descriptions of Macdonald's trip to America with the Owen party; their meetings with American notables, including John Adams and Thomas Jefferson; their voyage down the Ohio River; the purchase of the Harmony settlement from Frederick Rapp; the beginnings of Owen's New Harmony community; and Macdonald's trip back to England by way of New Orleans, Charleston, S.C., and Havana, Cuba. The diary was published as *The Diaries of Donald Macdonald* (Indianapolis: Indiana Historical Society, 1941).

A-251. McDONALD, JAMES D. (fl.1836-1872). ACCOUNT BOOKS, 1836-1861.

7 vols. (1 l.f.).   BV 264-270.

McDonald owned a general store and a pork slaughterhouse in Attica, Fountain Co.

The collection consists of account books for McDonald's store and for his pork business.

A-252. McGARRAH, ANDREW J. (d.1864). PAPERS, 1862-1886.

37 items.   Calendar.   SC 1023.

McGarrah was a farmer from Gibson County and a private in the 63rd Indiana Regiment (1862-1864), serving in Kentucky and Tennessee.

The collection consists primarily of McGarrah's Civil War letters to his family in Gibson County. Also included are Civil War letters from other members of McGarrah's family serving in Kentucky, Tennessee, and Georgia; and family legal papers (1867-1886).

A-253. MCLEAN, CHARLES G. (1787-1860). PAPERS, 1792-1899.

6 ms. boxes, 14 vols. (3 l.f.). Inventory. M 196, BV 1599-1602, 1926-1935.

McLean was an Irish immigrant (1797); a Presbyterian minister in Gettysburg, Pa. (1813-1841), Baltimore, Md., and Fort Plain, N.Y.; and founder and head of the Indiana Female Seminary, Indianapolis (1852-1860). Also included are papers of McLean's stepfather, James Gray (1770-1824), an immigrant from Scotland (1797); pastor of the Associate Reformed Church in Philadelphia, Pa.; writer on theological subjects; and resident of Philadelphia and Baltimore.

The collection includes papers and correspondence of James Gray, principally letters on family and church matters from the period 1809-1824; papers of Charles G. McLean, primarily from the period 1815-1840, relating to church affairs and McLean's disputes with the Presbyterian authorities; correspondence of McLean's daughters and son-in-law, Charles N. Todd, regarding family matters in Indianapolis (1860-1899); journal of an unidentified young woman traveling in Baltimore and Washington, D.C. (1809); journals of McLean's daughter, Mary Ann (1843-1855); notebook of receipts for materials and work at the Indiana Seminary (1852-1854); household accounts of Charles McLean (1852-1860) and Margaret McLean Todd (1860-1899); McLean's religious notes and writings; and texts and sermons from a minister's diary of Sundays (1807-1808).

Correspondents include John M. Duncan.

A-254. MCLEAN, WILLIAM E. (1831?-1906). NOTEBOOKS, 1856-1904.

11 vols. (.75 l.f.).   M 197, BV 1603-1608.

McLean was a Terre Haute attorney; editor of the *Terre Haute Journal* (1851-1855); Democratic member, Indiana House of Representatives (1861, 1867) and Senate (1857, 1859, 1893, 1895); colonel, 43rd Indiana Regiment (1861-1865); and first deputy commissioner, U.S. Pension Office (1885-1889).

The collection consists of McLean's notebooks containing speeches and notes for speeches, most on behalf of Democratic candidates and policies. There are also notes for speeches on slavery, temperance, Reconstruction, the G.A.R., and pension laws.

A-255. MARION COUNTY LIBRARY. RECORDS, 1844-1902.

13 vols. (1.75 l.f.). BV 609-621.

The Marion County Library was a public lending library established in 1844. The library was closed in 1930 by order of the Marion County Commissioners, and the books were donated to the Indiana Historical Society.

The records consist of the minutes of the library's board of trustees meetings (1844-1898); records of loans (1855-1902); records of book purchases (1844-1864); and catalogs (1860, 1878, 1889).

A-256. MARION COUNTY MISCELLANEOUS PAPERS, 1831-1917.

1 ms. box. Calendar. M 319.

The papers consist of nineteenth-century materials relating to Marion County collected by Earle J. Keithly, a clerk with the Fletcher National Bank of Indianapolis in the 1920s. The collection is composed of summonses (1863-1866), estate papers (1831-1872), insurance policies (1866-1890), broadsides advertising land sales (1845-1883), and promissory notes.

A-257. MARKLE, FREDERICK (d.1866). PAPERS, 1822-1894.

7 vols. 50 items (.5 l.f.). SC 1090, BV 272-278.

Markle owned a flour mill at Otter Creek, Vigo Co.

The collection consists of account books for the mills (1822-1884); and letters and financial documents, primarily from the period 1851-1852, regarding the shipment of flour from the mills to New Orleans, Boston, and Cincinnati.

A-258. MAROTT, GEORGE JOSEPH (1858-1946). PAPERS, 1904-1939.

1 ms. box, 1 vol. (.33 l.f.). Inventory. M 334, BV 1872.

Marott was the owner and manager of the Marott Shoe Store (1884-1946) and the Marott Hotel (1926-1946) in Indianapolis; was involved with a number of public utility and railroad companies in central Indiana; trustee, Citizen's Gas Company (1929-1935); and philanthropist.

The collection includes Marott's scrapbooks containing clippings and other materials about Marott, his businesses, Indiana utilities, and the world economic situation; letters from congressmen responding to Marott's questions on economic matters (1933); postcards and holiday cards to Mrs. Marott (1904-1910); and Marott personal financial papers.

Correspondents include Eugene B. Crowe, William H. Larrabee, Louis Ludlow, and Burton K. Wheeler.

A-259. MARSHALL, THOMAS (1811-1901). PAPERS, 1821-1901.

5 ms. boxes, 2 vols. (1.5 l.f.). Calendar. M 199, BV 1048-1049.
Microfilm.

Marshall was a Quaker farmer in Economy, Wayne Co., and Perry Township trustee (1854-1876).

The collection consists primarily of family correspondence from the years 1851-1901, discussing farm conditions, politics, the Civil War, and family affairs. Included are letters from Marshall's relatives in Dallas County and other places in Iowa (1855-1901); letters written by Marshall and his wife from Economy (1880-1901); letters from students at the Spiceland Academy, Henry Co. (1869-1873); letters from relatives in Memphis and other places in Tennessee (1851-1860); letters from relatives in Kansas (1890s); and Civil War letters from Marshall's son, Swain Marshall of the 8th Indiana Regiment, serving in Missouri, Arkansas, Louisiana, Texas, Virginia, and Georgia (1862-1865), from his son, Alonzo Marshall of the 69th Indiana Regiment, serving in Kentucky, Tennessee, and at the military hospital in St. Louis, Mo. (1862-1865), and from other relatives serving in Indiana and Iowa regiments. Also included is a minute book from the Daughters of Temperance chapter in Economy (1852-1854).

A-260. MARTINDALE, ELIJAH BISHOP (1828-1910). PAPERS, 1878-1907.

60 items. SC 1050.

Martindale was an Indianapolis attorney; president of the Union Fire Insurance Company, the American Central Life Insurance Company, and the Franklin Life Insurance Company; and a member of the Indianapolis Board of Trade and the Commercial Club.

The papers consist of letters to Martindale regarding the Mutual Life Policyholders Association, the Indianapolis Monetary Committee, the Oliver P. Morton Monument in Indianapolis, national politics, and Cuba.

Correspondents include Charles W. Fairbanks, Hugh Hanna, Benjamin Harrison, Jesse Overstreet, Albion W. Tourgee, Elihu B. Washburne, and Leonard Wood.

A-261. MAY, GEORGE (1772-1857). PAPERS, 1799-1836.

1 ms. box. M 202.

May was a farmer and miller in Knox, Washington, Harrison, Fountain, and Bartholomew counties.

The collection consists of May's receipts, accounts, promissory notes, and other legal and financial papers.

A-262. MAYER, CHARLES (1820-1891). PAPERS, 1838-1859.

37 items. SC 1055, BV 230-237.

Mayer was a German immigrant and owner of an Indianapolis general store specializing in toys (1840-1891).

The collection consists principally of account books for Mayer's store (1840-1857). Also included are typed transcripts of Mayer's correspondence with relatives in Germany.

A-263. MEREDITH, SAMUEL CALDWELL (1807-1899). PAPERS, 1850, 1894-1898.

30 items.   Calendar.   SC 1065.

Meredith was a Centerville, Wayne Co., printer and was grandfather of author Meredith Nicholson (1866-1948).

The collection consists of letters written by Meredith to his wife while he was in San Francisco during the Gold Rush (1850); and letters written while he was living in Indianapolis with his daughter and grandson, Meredith Nicholson (1894-1898).

A-264. MEREDITH, SOLOMON (1812-1875). PAPERS, 1833-1898.

3 ms. boxes.   Calendar.   M 203.

Soldier, politician, and businessman. Meredith was a Quaker farmer, railroad promoter, and politician in Cambridge City, Wayne Co.; Wayne County sheriff (1834-1838); Whig and Know Nothing member of the Indiana House of Representatives (1846-1849, 1855); U.S. marshal for Indiana (1849-1853); director, Indiana Central Railroad (1854-1859); member, Republican National Committee (1860); colonel, 19th Indiana Regiment, serving in Virginia and Maryland (1861-1862); brigadier general, U.S. Volunteers (1862-1865); commander, military post at Cairo, Ill. (1864); commander of Western Kentucky (1864-1865); and surveyor general, Montana Territory (1867-1869). Also included are papers of Meredith's son, Henry Meredith (1843-1882), a livestock raiser in Cambridge City; publisher, *Cambridge City Tribune* (1869-1872); Republican member, Indiana House of Representatives (1881); president, State Board of Agriculture (1882); and husband of Virginia Claypool Meredith, president of the Board of Women Managers for the 1893 World Columbian Exposition in Chicago, Ill.

The collection consists of the Meredith family's correspondence, diaries, and financial and legal papers, primarily from the period 1849-1881. Included are letters to Solomon Meredith regarding the appointment of deputies while he served as U.S. marshal (1849-1853); Meredith's official and personal Civil War correspondence, including his diary (1862) and letters to his wife from Virginia (1862-1863), and papers regarding his work as commander of Western Kentucky (1864-1865); his diaries (1857, 1858, 1872); and his legal and financial papers relating to farming, canals, and railroads (1847-1860). The collection also includes Henry Meredith's diaries (1863, 1873-1881); letters to Solomon Meredith from relatives in the Minnesota Territory (1858-1859); and materials relating to the World Columbian Exposition in Chicago (1893-1898).

Correspondents include Henry Clay, Schuyler Colfax, Elisha Embree, William H. English, Allen Hamilton, Oliver P. Morton, Caleb B. Smith, and James Whitcomb.

A-265. MERRICK, JOHN (1815-1895). PAPERS, 1831-1898.

1 ms. box, 2 vols. (.5 l.f.).   M 313, BV 1629-1898.

Merrick was a farmer in Sunman, Ripley Co. (1833-1841); Brookville, Franklin Co. (1842-1846); and Middlefork, Clinton Co. (1846-1895).

The collection consists primarily of Merrick's family correspondence from the period 1835-1872 and includes family letters from the East to Merrick and his wife in Sunman, Brookville, and Middlefork; and correspondence with Merrick's children attending Shurtleff College, Alton, Ill. (1865). Also included is Merrick's account book (1844-1854); receipts (1845-1896); and an 1890 diary of Merrick's son, John A. Merrick, a Clinton County farmer.

A-266. MERRILL, SAMUEL (1792-1855). PAPERS, 1812-1908.

13 ms. boxes.   Calendar.   M 204.

Attorney, politician, and businessman. Merrill was a student at Dartmouth College, N.H. (1812-1813); attorney in Vevay, Switzerland Co. (1816-1824); member of the Indiana House of Representatives (1819-1822); state treasurer (1822-1834); president, State Bank of Indiana (1834-1844); president, Madison and Indianapolis Railroad (1844-1848); owner, Merrill Bookstore, Indianapolis (1850-1855); compiler, *The Indiana Gazeteer* (1850); president, Indiana Historical Society (1835-1848); and president, Indianapolis Temperance Society, the Indiana Colonization Society, and the Young Men's Literary Society.

The bulk of the papers are from the period 1817-1855 and consist of Merrill's family and business correspondence and legal and financial documents. The correspondence relates to Indiana and national politics; the Indiana State Bank, including dealings between the central office and the branches; Merrill's work as state treasurer; the Madison and Indianapolis Railroad; his legal practice; his business interests, particularly in Indianapolis and Madison, regarding stock purchases, collection of debts, and transactions dealing with the sale and purchase of land; his involvement with literary and philanthropic organizations; and life in Vevay and Indianapolis. The collection also includes a large body of correspondence with relatives in Peacham, Vt. (1812-1877), New Berlin, Pa. (1817-1841), Waterproof, La. (1828-1851), and Urbana, Ohio (1834-1841); letters of Merrill's daughters, Julia, Mina, and Catherine (1855-1908), from the Cleveland, Ohio, Female Seminary (1856-1857), and from Indianapolis and Vermont; and Merrill's political and literary essays.

Correspondents include Conrad Baker, John Blanchard, John Brough, Elijah Coffin, John Ewing, Barnabas C. Hobbs, John Lewis Ketcham, James F. D. Lanier, Caleb Mills, Oliver H. Smith, Richard W. Thompson, Ithiel Town, Lew Wallace, and James Whitcomb.

A-267. MERRILL, SAMUEL (1792-1855). PAPERS, 1814-1934.

5 ms. boxes.   Inventory.   M 442.

Merrill was an Indianapolis businessman; Indiana state treasurer (1822-1834); president, State Bank of Indiana (1834-1844); and president, Madison and Indianapolis Railroad (1844-1848).

The collection consists primarily of Merrill's personal and business papers from the period 1826-1855. Included are correspondence and financial papers relating to his work as Indiana state treasurer; correspondence and financial papers relating to the operations of the Indiana State Bank (1834-1844), including Merrill's report responding to legislators' inquiries about the bank (1838); papers relating to the operation and financing of the Madison and Indianapolis Railroad, including Merrill's correspondence with the New York financial house of Winslow & Perkins (1844-1848); papers relating to Merrill's land and business investments; his letters to his wife, Jane (1834-1848); and his correspondence with family members in Vermont, New Hampshire, Massachusetts, Ohio, Illinois, and Louisiana (1830s-1850s). Also included are letters of his grandson, Indianapolis attorney Charles W. Moores, regarding the family's financial interests (1891-1908).

Correspondents include Hervey Bates, Ebenezer Dumont, Julia Dumont, Edward A. Hannegan, James F. D. Lanier, John Law, Caleb Mills, Merrill Moores, James M. Ray, Thaddeus Stevens, John Tipton, Albert S. White, and Levi Woodbury.

A-268. MIDDLETON, HARVEY N. (1895-1978). PAPERS, 1928-1978.

17 ms. boxes, 3 oversize boxes.   Inventory.   M 441.

Physician and civic leader. Middleton was a graduate of Meharry Medical College, Nashville, Tenn. (1926); physician on staff of St. Joseph Hospital, Anderson, Madison Co. (1928-1936); physician and cardiologist in Indianapolis (1936-1978); on staff of Indianapolis City Hospital and St. Vincent Hospital; assistant professor, Indiana University Medical School; general secretary, Hoosier State Medical Society (1953-1958); involved in establishing the Henry G. Morgan Health Center at Flanner House, an Indianapolis black community center (1940s); co-chairman, Indiana campaign, United Negro College Fund (1950-1952); and member, board of directors, Metropolitan YMCA (1952-ca.1970).

The collection consists primarily of papers relating to Middleton's civic and medical careers. Civic papers include board minutes, financial records, and correspondence of the Indianapolis Metropolitan YMCA (1954-1968), the Senate Avenue branch of the YMCA (1947-1959), and the Fall Creek Parkway branch (1957-1975); papers relating to Flanner House and its health center (1944-1953); papers relating to Meharry Medical College and Middleton's 50th class reunion (1949-1976); and papers relating to the United Negro College Fund (1950-1967). Medical papers include Middleton's articles on cardiology; papers of the Hoosier State Medical Association (1950-1958) and other medical organizations; and bylaws and other staff materials for Indianapolis hospitals. Also included is a small amount of personal correspondence (1942-1978) and an autobiographical sketch (1966).

A-269. MILLER, STEPHEN A. (ca.1843-1864). PAPERS, 1860-1864.

69 items.   Calendar.   SC 1078.
Microfilm.

Miller was a Howard County farmer and a private in the 57th Indiana Regiment (1861-1864).

The collection consists of Miller's Civil War letters from army camps in Richmond, Wayne Co., and Indianapolis (1861), and from Kentucky, Tennessee, and Georgia (1862-1864), to his family in Tampico and Kokomo, Howard Co., and Richmond, Wayne Co.

A-270. MILLER, WILLIAM (1809-1879). PAPERS, 1833-1920.

70 items.   Calendar.   SC 1081.

Miller was a resident of Union County (1811-1833); a farmer, storekeeper, and businessman in South Bend, St. Joseph Co. (1833-1879); and Whig member of the Indiana House of Representatives (1844-1845, 1847-1849).

The collection consists primarily of letters from Miller's family in Union and Putnam counties, Chicago, Ill., and College Corner, Ohio, during the period 1833-1850. The correspondence relates to family affairs, farming and the market for produce, and politics in the state legislature.

Correspondents include Schuyler Colfax.

A-271. MILLS, CALEB (1806-1879). PAPERS, 1834-1880.

7 ms. boxes, 1 vol. (1.85 l.f.).   Inventory.   M 207, BV 1610.
Microfilm.

Mills was a professor of languages at Wabash College, Crawfordsville, Montgomery Co. (1833-1876); leader of the movement for free public schools in Indiana (1845-1852); Indiana superintendent of public instruction (1854-1857); and assisted in the founding of the Indiana State Teachers Association (1854).

The collection includes letters to Mills from missionaries in India and Persia (1834-1846); correspondence with his son, Benjamin Marshall Mills, a lieutenant in the 49th U.S. Colored Infantry stationed in Mississippi (1864-1865); and letters from former students serving in the Union Army, including letters from Gen. John P. Hawkins regarding the recruitment of officers for black regiments (1863-1864), and from James Meteer of the 70th Indiana Regiment and the 14th U.S. Colored Infantry (1862-1864). Also included are Mills's sermons and his essays and speeches on education; Benjamin M. Mills's war diaries (1864-1865), military papers, and Wabash College writings (1866-1868); and copies of Caleb Mills's letters to Edmond O. Hovey (1832-1859).

Correspondents include Justin Perkins.

A-272. MITTEN, ARTHUR G. (1866-1938). COLLECTION, 1755-1936.

8 ms. boxes. Calendar. M 211.

Mitten was an executive with the Chicago and Eastern Illinois Railroad; a Goodland, Newton Co., farmer and philanthropist (1920-1938); vice-president, Indiana Historical Society (1930-1938); and collector of books and manuscripts, particularly those relating to the Northwest Territory, William Henry Harrison, and Indiana.

The collection consists of autographs and manuscripts acquired by Mitten. Mitten's principal categories were the Northwest Territory; the War of 1812, including the Battle of the Thames, the death of Tecumseh, and William Hull's surrender of Detroit; Indiana governors, prominent men, and state banks; signers of the Declaration of Independence; presidents of the Continental Congress; presidents of the United States; members of the cabinets of presidents George Washington, Andrew Jackson, William Henry Harrison, Zachary Taylor, and Abraham Lincoln; prominent people in American history; and prominent Europeans. Also included are papers of Samuel Hodgdon, U.S. quartermaster general in the 1790s, regarding the operations of the U.S. Army in the West and his land dealings with Timothy Pickering; papers of Henry D. Gilpin, principally on political and personal matters (1829-1858); papers of Maj. James Taylor, principally regarding military operations and supplies in the West during the War of 1812; the journal of John Sibley, Indian agent in the Territory of Orleans (1807); and report of William Clark,

Ninian Edwards, and August Chouteau on surveying the territory in Missouri ceded by the Osage Indians (1808).

The collection includes letters and papers of the following individuals: John Adams, John Quincy Adams, George Ade, John Armstrong, Chester Arthur, Conrad Baker, George Bancroft, Henry Ward Beecher, John Bell, Thomas Hart Benton, John M. Berrien, Albert J. Beveridge, Nicholas Biddle, Samuel Bigger, Montgomery Blair, Harman Blennerhassett, Willie Blount, Edward Bok, Ratliff Boon, John P. Boyd, Jesse D. Bright, James Buchanan, Jacob Burnet, Aaron Burr, Benjamin Butler, John C. Calhoun, Simon Cameron, George Canning, William Carroll, Lewis Cass, George Catlin, Ira C. Chase, Salmon P. Chase, August Chouteau, William Clark, Green Clay, Henry Clay, David Clendenin, Grover Cleveland, Howell Cobb, Schuyler Colfax, Leslie Combs, Roscoe Conkling, Calvin Coolidge, James Fenimore Cooper, William H. Crawford, John J. Crittenden, Will Cumback, Caleb Cushing, Manasseh Cutler, Alexander J. Dallas, Jefferson Davis, Henry Dearborn, William Dennison, Stephen A. Douglas, Daniel Drake, Lyman C. Draper, Francis Dufour, Paris C. Dunning, Winfield T. Durbin, John H. Eaton, Ninian Edwards, Edward Eggleston, Andrew Ellicott, William H. English, William Eustis, John Ewing, Thomas Ewing, Millard Fillmore, Graham N. Fitch, Davis Floyd, Jesse Benton Fremont, Albert Gallatin, John S. Gano, James A. Garfield, Hamlin Garland, William Lloyd Garrison, Elbridge Gerry, John Gibson, Henry D. Gilpin, William Gladstone, James P. Goodrich, Francis Granger, U. S. Grant, Isaac P. Gray, Horace Greeley, Alexander Hamilton, Henry Hamilton, Hannibal Hamlin, John F. Hamtramck, J. Frank Hanly, Edward A. Hannegan, Warren G. Harding, Josiah Harmar, Benjamin Harrison (ca. 1726-1791), Benjamin Harrison (1833-1901), Caroline Scott Harrison, William Henry Harrison, Rutherford B. Hayes, John Heckenwelder, Thomas A. Hendricks, William Hendricks, Patrick Henry, Barnabas C. Hobbs, William S. Holman, Herbert Hoover, Alvin P. Hovey, Tilghman A. Howard, William Hull, Robert M. T. Hunter, Charles J. Ingersoll, William Irvine, Andrew Jackson, Edward L. Jackson, Thomas Jefferson, Jonathan Jennings, Andrew Johnson, Reverdy Johnson, Richard M. Johnson, George W. Julian, Michael C. Kerr, Rufus King, Henry Knox, Henry S. Lane, Tobias Lear, Richard Henry Lee, Abraham Lincoln, Edward Livingston, Benson J. Lossing, Charles Lyall, Isaac McCoy, Warren T. McCray, Hugh McCulloch, Joseph E. McDonald, James McHenry, Thomas L. McKenney, William McKinley, Paul V. McNutt, James Madison, William L. Marcy, Thomas R. Marshall, Claude Matthews, Return Jonathan Meigs, Thomas Mifflin, James Monroe, Oliver P. Morton, James A. Mount, Harry S. New, John C. New, James Noble, Noah Noble, Richard J. Oglesby, Godlove S. Orth, David Dale Owen, Robert Owen, Robert Dale Owen, Lord Palmerston, Sir Robert Peel,

Oliver Hazard Perry, Timothy Pickering, Franklin Pierce, James K. Polk, Albert G. Porter, David Porter, Thomas Posey, Daniel D. Pratt, Rufus Putnam, John Randolph, James Robertson, Franklin Delano Roosevelt, Theodore Roosevelt, Benjamin Rush, Richard Rush, John Russell, Arthur St. Clair, Winthrop Sargent, Charles Scott, Winfield Scott, William H. Seward, Isaac Shelby, John Sherman, Oliver H. Smith, Edwin M. Stanton, Alexander H. Stephens, John Cleves Symmes, William Howard Taft, Waller Taylor, Zachary Taylor, Richard W. Thompson, John Tipton, Charles S. Todd, David Turpie, John Tyler, Martin Van Buren, Stephen Van Rensselaer, Daniel W. Voorhees, David Wallace, Lew Wallace, Bushrod Washington, George Washington, Anthony Wayne, Daniel Webster, Thurlow Weed, Gideon Welles, John Wentworth, James Whitcomb, Albert S. White, James Wilkinson, Ashbel Willard, James D. Williams, Woodrow Wilson, James Winchester, Levi Woodbury, John E. Wool, and Joseph A. Wright.

A-273. MOBLEY, CHARLES WILLIAM (ca.1821-1912). ACCOUNT BOOKS, 1859-1914.

10 vols. (1 l.f.). BV 279-287.

Mobley owned a hardware store in Salem, Washington Co.

The collection consists of Mobley's business account books, most from the period 1859-1893.

A-274. MOORE, WILLIAM ROBY (1845-1926). PAPERS, 1861-1919.

2 ms. boxes. Calendar. M 212.

Moore was a blacksmith in Selma, Delaware Co.; a private in the 19th Indiana Regiment (1861-1864); a railroad clerk, banker, and grain trader (1864-1887); and secretary of the Delaware County Building and Loan Association in Muncie (1887-ca.1905).

The collection consists of Moore's letters to his family while he was serving with the Union Army in Virginia (1861-1864) and a reminiscence of his life and Civil War experiences written in 1919. The reminiscence includes descriptions of treatment he received for mental illness at the turn of the century.

A-275. MOORES, JULIA MERRILL (1826-1912). PAPERS, 1838-1896.

1 ms. box.   Calendar.   M 213.

Moores was the daughter of Indianapolis banker Samuel Merrill (1792-1855) and wife of Indianapolis bookseller Charles W. Moores (1828-1864).

The collection consists of Moores's correspondence, mostly from the period before she was married (1840-1854). Included are letters from family members and friends in Indianapolis, Crawfordsville, Montgomery Co., and New Berlin, Pa.; and letters written by her to her family while she was traveling East with Henry Ward Beecher (1841), teaching school in Bloomington, Monroe Co. (1844), and visiting family in Waterproof, La. (1845-1846).

Correspondents include Henry Ward Beecher, John Muir, and James M. Ray.

A-276. MORRIS, HOWARD. COLLECTION, 1872-1900.

1 ms. box.   Inventory.   M 342.

Morris is an Indianapolis collector of railroad memorabilia.

The collection consists of financial records of a number of midwestern railroads. The bulk of the records are for the Cincinnati, Hamilton, and Dayton Railway Company and include records of freight and passenger earnings, mileage reports, bills, and receipts (1891-1900). Also included are stock and bond certificates for the Baltimore and Ohio Southwestern Company and the Ohio and Mississippi Railway Company (1894-1900) and miscellaneous papers from a number of other companies.

A-277. MORRISON, JOHN IRWIN (1806-1882). PAPERS, 1830-1889.

50 items.   SC 1721, BV 1873.

Morrison was a Salem, Washington Co., educator; Democratic member, Indiana House of Representatives (1838-1840) and Senate (1847-1850); delegate, Indiana Constitutional Convention (1850-1851); Indiana state treasurer (1865-1867); and trustee, Indiana University (1846-1855, 1874-1878).

The collection includes letters written to Morrison's wife, Catherine Morris, from her family in Salem while she was a student at Westtown Boarding School, Chester Co., Pa. (1830-1833); Morrison's history of the 1851 Constitutional Convention (1880); poetry of Morrison and his family; and a biography of Morrison written by his daughter, Alice Cathcart (ca.1882).

A-278. MUNFORD, SAMUEL E. (1837-1893). PAPERS, 1861-1914.

65 items. Calendar. M 217.

Munford was a Princeton, Gibson Co., physician (1861-1893) and a surgeon with the 17th Indiana Regiment (1861-1865).

The collection is composed of Munford's Civil War correspondence with family in Gibson County; Civil War papers and a diary (June-July 1861); postwar family letters; and papers read at Indiana medical meetings in the 1870s and 1880s.

A-279. MUTUAL SERVICE ASSOCIATION, INC. RECORDS, 1907-1981.

3 ms. boxes, 2 vols. (1 l.f.). Inventory. M 374, BV 2022-2023.

The Mutual Service Association was organized in 1903 by Indianapolis businesswomen to provide respectable housing and financial assistance to young working women. Until 1927 the organization owned a residence and summer camp for women who could not afford vacations outside the city. Since 1967 the association has owned an apartment complex and retirement home for women.

The records include the association's minutes (1927, 1951, 1964-1978); treasurers' records (1926-1971); scrapbooks (1907-1970); membership lists (1913, 1926-1931, 1945-1982); meeting programs; and issues of the *Mutual Service Journal* (1907).

A-280. NEW ALBANY AND PORTLAND FERRY COMPANY. ACCOUNT BOOKS, 1867-1884.

4 vols. (.5 l.f.). BV 288-291.

The company operated a ferry across the Ohio River between New Albany, Floyd Co., and Portland, Ky.

The collection consists of the company's account books (1867-1884).

A-281. NEW CASTLE MARBLE WORKS. RECORDS, 1893-1920.

6 vols. (.5 l.f.). BV 239-244.

The New Castle Marble Works was located in New Castle, Henry Co., and built granite and marble monuments and headstones for customers in eastern Indiana and western Ohio.

The collection consists of records of the company's orders, including designs and inscriptions for the monuments.

A-282. NEW HARMONY COLLECTION, 1821-1880.

4 ms. boxes, 8 vols. (1.5 l.f.). Partial Inventory. M 219, BV 830-835, 1050-1051.

The collection consists of miscellaneous papers relating to the family of Robert Owen (1771-1858) and the Owenite community at New Harmony, Posey Co.

Major segments of the collection include the James Dorsey papers (1827-1849), consisting of letters from Robert Owen, Robert Dale Owen, and William Owen to their attorney, James Dorsey, in New Harmony; the William A. Twigg papers (1828-1864), consisting of documents and letters relating to New Harmony; Robert Dale Owen papers (1830-1873), consisting of miscellaneous letters and documents written by Owen relating to the New Harmony community, Indiana politics, and Owen's business interests; and volumes of manuscript music belonging to Robert Dale Owen (1825).

Other materials include a petition addressed to Robert Owen by several inhabitants of New Harmony criticizing his operation of the community (1825); Robert Owen's note listing the conditions under which he had made contracts with the New Communities settled on the New Harmony estate (1827); Richard Owen's manuscript on the Educational Society at New Harmony; the journal (1838) and autobiographical notes (1886) of Miner K. Kellogg of New Harmony; memorandum book of Robert Dale Owen (1852); and miscellaneous letters of Robert Owen, Richard Owen, William Owen, and David Dale Owen.

The collection includes letters from John Badollet, Charles-Alexandre LeSueur, James Maclure, Noah Noble, Thomas Say, and Frances Wright. Also included are letters from members of the Owen family to Sarah T. Bolton, Ferdinand J. Dreer, Edward Everett Hale, Thomas Wentworth Higgenson, William Dean Howells, Benjamin Tappan, and Robert J. Walker.

A-283. NIBLACK, ALBERT P. (1858-1929). PAPERS, 1843-1927.

1 ms. box.   Inventory.   M 220.

Niblack was a native of Vincennes, Knox Co.; an officer in the U.S. Navy (1880-1923), serving in the Spanish-American War in Cuba and the Philippines (1898-1901), and as naval attache to the American Legation in Buenos Aires, Argentina (1910-1911), and Berlin, Germany (1911-1913); and reached the rank of Rear Admiral (1917).

The collection is primarily composed of Niblack's orders, communications, commissions, commendations, and other papers relating to his career in the Navy (1880-1923). Also included are papers of Niblack's father, William E. Niblack, a Vincennes politician and Democratic member of Congress (1857-1861, 1865-1875), consisting of his commissions, appointments, and other official documents (1843-1882), and two letters written by Niblack to U.S. attorney general Jeremiah Black regarding the appointment of a district attorney in Indiana (1857-1858).

Correspondents include George Dewey, John Long, and W. H. Moody.

A-284. NICHOLS, WILLIAM MERRICK (b.1845). PAPERS, 1863-1866.

28 items.   Calendar.   SC 1612.

Nichols was a student at Wabash College, Crawfordsville, Montgomery Co. (1863-1865); a teacher at Linden, Montgomery Co. (1866); and a newspaper publisher in Plymouth, Marshall Co.

The papers consist of Nichols's letters to his family in Plymouth, written while he was attending Wabash College and teaching school at Linden.

A-285. NICHOLSON, MEREDITH (1866-1947). PAPERS, 1890-1947.

3 ms. boxes.   Partial Calendar.   M 221.

Nicholson was a writer for the *Indianapolis News* (1884-1897); novelist, author of *The Hoosiers* (1900), *House of a Thousand Candles* (1905), and numerous other works; active in Indiana Democratic Party politics; and U.S. minister to Paraguay (1933-1934), Venezuela (1935-1938), and Nicaragua (1938-1941).

The collection consists primarily of Nicholson's correspondence, the bulk of it from the period 1933-1940 when he was serving as a diplomat in South America. Included are letters relating to Indiana politics and South American affairs and Nicholson's letters to his wife, Dorothy (1938-1940). The collection also includes letters from Nicholson to publisher Robert Underwood Johnson (1890-1923); notebooks containing Nicholson's poems, plot ideas, political writings, and diary entries (1891-1917); and manuscript poems.

Correspondents include Edward A. Filene, Robert Underwood Johnson, Josiah K. Lilly, Carleton B. McCulloch, Sherman Minton, Robert Walton Moore, Booth Tarkington, Frederick Van Nuys, and Alexander W. Weddell.

A-286. NORTHWEST TERRITORY COLLECTION, 1721-1838.

4 ms. boxes.   Calendar.   M 367.

The Northwest Territory Collection consists of miscellaneous papers relating to the exploration, settlement, and administration of the Northwest Territory.

The bulk of the papers are from the period 1780-1801 and relate to the U.S. Army in the West; the campaigns of generals Josiah Harmar, Arthur St. Clair, and Anthony Wayne against the Indians; Indian relations; the French settlers at Vincennes and elsewhere in the territory; the Ohio Company and other American settlers; and the administration of the territorial government. Also included are papers relating to the French and British in the Northwest and the American Revolution.

Military papers include correspondence of Josiah Harmar, Henry Knox, Arthur St. Clair, Anthony Wayne, James Wilkinson, and other military leaders regarding the military situation in the West and the campaigns against the Indians; orderly books of John Mills, adjutant general of the Legion of the United States (August 1794-January 1795); journal kept by an unidentified officer during Anthony Wayne's Fallen Timbers campaign (1794); papers regarding the negotiation of the Treaty of Greenville (1794-1795); papers regarding American relations with Spain and the Spanish Conspiracy (1790s); Maj. John Francis Hamtramck's letter book containing copies of his letters from Fort Wayne to Gen. James Wilkinson (January-February 1796); journal of William Clark on his trip from Louisville to St. Louis (1797); Lt. John Lovell's books of general orders for the transport of troops from Pittsburgh, Pa., to Fort Adams, Mississippi (1798); papers relating to the 1810 investigation of James Wilkinson's conduct; drawings of Fort Finney (1785-1786), Fort Knox (1788), Fort Jefferson (1792), Fort St. Clair (1792), the arrangement of St. Clair's troops before the battle (1791), and the Greenville area (1793); and numerous receipts and documents for army supplies, especially supplies used during the Greenville negotiations (1794-1795).

Papers relating to the settlement and administration of the Territory include papers of Gov. Arthur St. Clair and Winthrop Sargent regarding territorial affairs; abstracts of St. Clair's correspondence made by his secretary (1791); papers relating to the Ohio Company, including an account book of the company's land sales (1787-1790); papers relating to other Ohio and Indiana land companies; Northwest Territory court records (1790s); correspondence regarding territorial politics; and papers relating to Vincennes, Knox Co., in the 1780s and 1790s.

Papers relating to the Northwest prior to the formation of the Territory include contracts and other documents from French fur trading expeditions to St. Josephs, Miamis, Ouiatenon, and Vincennes (1721-1758); papers regarding relations between the British and Indians in the West (1749-1771); proclamations and letters of Thomas Gage regarding British rule in the West

(1760s); a 1767 British report on the military and political situation of the western posts; papers relating to George Rogers Clark's expedition against Vincennes and Kaskaskia (1778-1780), including Patrick Henry's secret orders to Clark in 1778; and other letters regarding military actions in the West during the American Revolution.

The collection includes letters and papers of the following individuals: John Armstrong, Jonathan Blanchard, Jacob Burnet, Mann Butler, Guy Carleton, John Carroll, Jonathan Cass, George Rogers Clark, William Clark, Victor Collot, Isaac Craig, Michel Guillaume St. Jean de Crevecoeur, George Croghan, William Croghan, Manasseh Cutler, Henry Dearborn, Ephraim Douglass, Abiel Foster, Thomas Gage, Manuel de Lemos Gayoso, John Gibson, Alexander Hamilton, John Francis Hamtramck, Josiah Harmar, William Henry Harrison, Patrick Henry, Samuel Hodgdon, William Irvine, Thomas Jefferson, John Rice Jones, Henry Knox, James McHenry, Nathaniel Massie, Return Jonathan Meigs, Thomas Mifflin, John Mills, James Monroe, George Morgan, John Peter Muhlenberg, William North, James O'Hara, Timothy Pickering, Zebulon Pike, Thomas Posey, Rufus Putnam, James Robertson, Arthur St. Clair, Winthrop Sargent, Charles Scott, Isaac Shelby, John Graves Simcoe, Baron Friedrich Von Steuben, Caleb Swan, John Cleves Symmes, Henry Vanderburgh, Francis Vigo, Francois Bissot sieur de Vincennes, George Washington, Anthony Wayne, William Wells, James Wilkinson, Thomas Worthington, and David Zeisberger.

A-287. O'HARA, JAMES (1752-1819). PAPERS, 1779-1794.

4 vols. (.25 l.f.). BV 1804-1807.

O'Hara was commissary at the general hospital at Carlisle, Pa. (1779-1780), and assistant quartermaster under Gen. Nathaniel Greene (1780-1783) during the Revolutionary War; quartermaster of the U.S. Army (1792-1796); government contractor (1796-1802); and founder of glass works in Pittsburgh, Pa. (1800).

The collection consists of O'Hara's notebook of expenditures at Carlisle, Pa., and with General Greene's army (1779-1783); his orderly books containing copies of military orders issued from Philadelphia, Pittsburgh, and the Ohio country (1792-1793); and his letter book containing copies of letters received regarding military operations and supplies for the army in the West (1792-

1794), and including copies of letters to him from Isaac Craig, Alexander Hamilton, Samuel Hodgdon, Henry Knox, Anthony Wayne, and James Wilkinson.

A-288. OSTROM, SUSAN MCWHIRTER (1888-1980). PAPERS, 1843-1980.

22 ms. boxes.   Inventory.   M 337.

Civic leader and journalist. Ostrom was a women's club columnist for the *Indianapolis News* (1913-1963); member, advisory council, Indiana Federation of Clubs (1913-1963); and director, Public Relations and Information Division, Indiana Department of Public Instruction (1942-1947). The collection also includes papers of her father, Felix T. McWhirter (1853-1915), instructor at DePauw University, Greencastle (1884-1888), real estate broker in Indianapolis (1888-1900), president, People's State Bank, Indianapolis (1900-1915), Prohibitionist candidate for governor (1904); and her brother, Felix M. McWhirter (1886-1983), president of People's Bank, Indianapolis (1915-1959), and officer in the U.S. Naval Reserve (1941-1945).

The papers include Ostrom's correspondence with politicians regarding the Equal Rights Amendment, school prayer, and other political issues, primarily from the late 1960s and the 1970s; her writings, including poems, school papers, speeches, newspaper articles, and editorials on women's rights and other political issues (1897-1976); papers relating to her work for civic improvements and rights for the blind; papers relating to the Indiana Federation of Clubs, the Woman's Department Club of Indianapolis, and the Women's Christian Temperance Union; McWhirter family genealogy; and scrapbooks, clippings, publications, plaques, and awards regarding Ostrom's life and service to the community (1910-1981). Also contained are McWhirter family papers, including letters of Felix T. McWhirter (1872-1900); business and personal papers of Felix M. McWhirter, particularly World War II letters to family and postwar military items; letters from other family members serving in the armed forces during World War II; miscellaneous family letters from Tennessee, Arkansas, and Indianapolis (1843-1900); and scrapbooks of clippings, broadsides, and other material relating to the careers of family members.

Correspondents include Birch Bayh, Otis R. Bowen, Roger D. Branigin, Julia Nixon Eisenhower, M. Stanton Evans, Betty Ford, Barry Goldwater, Wayne

Guthrie, Vance Hartke, William H. Hudnut, Andrew Jacobs, Jr., Edward M. Kennedy, and Richard Lugar.

A-289. PALMER, JOHN R. (fl.1863-1905). PAPERS, 1863-1905.

50 items.   SC 1173.

Palmer was a captain in the 11th Indiana Regiment (1864-1865).

The collection consists of receipts, muster rolls, clothing lists, and other official papers related to the supplying of the 11th Indiana Regiment, primarily from the year 1865.

A-290. PARKE COUNTY. CIRCUIT COURT RECORDS, 1833-1848.

3 vols. (.33 l.f.).   BV 730-732.

The collection consists of fee books from the Parke County Circuit Court (1833-1848).

A-291. PARSONS, GEORGE W. (1843-1910). PAPERS, 1859-1914.

1 ms. box.   Inventory.   M 224.

Parsons was a soldier and officer in the 57th Indiana Regiment serving in Tennessee and Georgia (1861-1865); captured and served two months in Andersonville Prison, Ga. (July-September 1864); and grocery and meat dealer, Hagerstown, Wayne Co. (1866-1908).

The bulk of the collection consists of Parsons's Civil War letters to his family (1861-1865). Also included are letters of the Grimmessy family of Salem, Ohio, and Muncie, Delaware Co. (1903-1914).

A-292. PATRONS OF HUSBANDRY. OLIVE GRANGE #189. RECORDS, 1883-1892.

3 vols. (.25 l.f.). BV 837-839.

Olive Grange #189 was a chapter of the Patrons of Husbandry (the Grange) organized by the farmers around Harrisville, Randolph Co.

The collection consists of the chapter's minutes and membership rolls (1883-1892).

A-293. PATTERSON, AMOS (1839-1916). PAPERS, 1860-1912.

3 ms. boxes, 5 vols. (1.25 l.f.).   Inventory.   M 355, BV 1915-1919.

Patterson studied medicine under Dr. Theophilus Parvin and Dr. William B. Fletcher in Indianapolis (1863) and at the Medical College of Ohio in Cincinnati (1866); and practiced medicine in Bartholomew Co. (1867) and Indianapolis (1868-1916).

The collection includes Patterson's visitation books with notes on patient illnesses (1870-1912); account books for his practice (1868-1874); notes on medical school lectures in Cincinnati; and account books of Drs. Parvin and Fletcher (1860-1864).

A-294. PATTON, WILLIAM C. (fl.1861-1915). DIARIES, 1862-1865.

8 vols. (.25 l.f.). SC 1903.

Patton, of Greensburg, Decatur Co., was a private in the 37th Indiana Regiment, serving primarily in Tennessee and Georgia during the Civil War.

The collection consists of Patton's Civil War diaries (1862-1865).

A-295. Paugh, Ione Swan (b.1910). Collection, 1872-1971.

4 ms. boxes.   Inventory.   M 404.

Paugh, of Manitowish Waters, Wis., donated this collection to the Historical Society in 1975. Among the family members represented in the collection are her grandfather, William F. Swan (1837-1929), a farmer in Benton County (ca.1860-1907) and Crawfordsville, Montgomery Co. (1907-1929), and a soldier in the 10th Indiana Regiment during the Civil War; her great-uncle, James Swan (1833-1917), a Benton County farmer and a soldier in the 10th Indiana Regiment; and her father, Robert A. Swan (1883-1971), a title abstractor and local historian in Fowler, Benton Co.

The collection includes diaries of William and James Swan (1872-1897); correspondence between William Swan and Robert Swan regarding farming, family matters, and business opportunities (1907-1924); diaries of Robert Swan (1955-1971); Robert Swan's family correspondence (1912-1958); diaries of Ellen Mahaffy of Benton County (1873-1874); dance programs and greeting cards (1920s); and newspaper clippings regarding the family and the Civil War.

A-296. Pegg, Lydia J. (fl.1851-1925). Papers, 1882-1925.

2 ms. boxes.   Inventory.   M 223.

Pegg was the wife of John Pegg, a Bloomingsport, Randolph Co., farmer.

The collection is composed primarily of letters to Pegg from her sisters: Lizzie Roberts, wife of a Paton, Iowa, farmer; and Hulda Rees, wife of Seth Rees, an itinerant Quaker preacher. The bulk of the letters are from the period 1898-1914 and describe family matters, farm life, and Quaker camp meetings throughout the East and Midwest. Also included are two notebooks (1882, 1886) in which working hours are logged for John Pegg and several other Randolph County men.

A-297. PERKINS, SAMUEL ELLIOTT (1811-1879). PAPERS, ca.1870.

1 ms. box.   M 225.

Perkins was an Indianapolis attorney; member of the Indiana Supreme Court (1847-1864); law professor, Northwestern Christian (now Butler) University (1857) and Indiana University (1870-1873); and judge, Marion County Superior Court (1872-1876).

The collection consists of Perkins's notes and lectures on law and Indiana court cases.

A-298. PI LAMBDA THETA. INDIANAPOLIS CHAPTER. RECORDS, 1929-1983.

4 ms. boxes, 7 vols. (2.25 l.f.).   Inventory.   M 392, BV 2037-2040.

Pi Lambda Theta is a national honorary society for women in education. The Indianapolis chapter was founded in 1929 by women from Indiana University. The chapter has provided scholarships for Indianapolis area college students, honored outstanding high school students, given recognition to professional women in the field, and contributed to charitable causes.

The collection contains the chapter's minutes (1929-1964), financial records (1929-1971), membership directories (1938-1982), constitution and bylaws, scrapbooks (1929-1959), and records of the Honors Day programs for high school students (1958-1980).

A-299. PICKETT, PHINEAS (1850-1932). PAPERS, 1860-1920.

51 items.   Calendar.   SC 1203.

Pickett was a Quaker schoolteacher and a farmer in Plainfield, Hendricks Co.

The collection consists primarily of letters to Pickett from the period 1883-1903 regarding Quaker and family affairs in Indiana. There are also letters to Pickett written in 1920 by presidents of Indiana colleges responding to his offer to donate books on Quakerism.

A-300. Pleasant Run Children's Home. Records, 1867-1974.

6 ms. boxes, 12 vols. (4 l.f.). Inventory. M 227, BV 1700-1708, 1884-1885, 1920-1922.
Restricted.

The home was founded in 1867 by an Indianapolis German fraternal organization as the Deutschen Allgemeinen Protestantischen Waisenvereins. It became the General Protestant Orphan Association in 1918 and changed to its present name in 1971. The home was an orphanage for most of its history, but since the 1960s it has been a treatment center for neglected and predelinquent children.

The records consist principally of the minutes of the Board of Directors meetings (1867-1974), which include accounts, financial statements, reports, and information about children in the home. Also included are a record of children in the home (1873-1906); minutes of the meetings of the ladies auxiliary (1902-1918); and several small notebooks containing information about the children. All records were written in German until 1918.

A-301. Pogue, George (1765-1821). Papers, 1802-1852.

85 items.   Calendar.   SC 1210.

Pogue was a blacksmith in North Carolina and settled by the White River in present-day Indianapolis (1819).

The collection consists of the George Pogue family's receipts, bills, and a small amount of personal correspondence, primarily from the period 1820-1836. Also included are account books for a Cumberland, Marion Co., tavern run by Samuel Fullen, George Pogue's son-in-law (1828, 1832).

A-302. Porter, Albert Gallatin (1824-1897). Collection, 1759-1942.

6 ms. boxes.   Inventory.   M 396.

Politician, attorney, and historian. Porter was an Indianapolis attorney (1845-1897), in partnership at various times with David MacDonald, Benjamin Harrison, William P. Fishback, and Cyrus C. Hines; Indianapolis city attorney (1851-1853); reporter, Indiana Supreme Court (1853-1856); member, Indianapolis City Council (1857-1859); Republican member, U.S. House of Representatives (1859-1863); first comptroller, U.S. Treasury Department (1878-1880); governor of Indiana (1881-1885); U.S. minister to Italy (1889-1891); and collector of historical documents for proposed history of Indiana.

The collection consists of personal papers of Porter and his family and of historical papers collected by Porter. Porter's personal papers are principally from the period 1857-1891 and include correspondence regarding his legal work, including the case of J. B. Castleman, a Confederate prisoner at Camp Morton, Indianapolis (1864-1865); Republican Party politics and his work in the U.S. House of Representatives; and his work as minister to Italy. Porter family papers, principally from the period 1814-1865, include letters and business documents from Boone County, Ky. (1814-1845), and Lawrenceburg, Dearborn Co. (1817-1862); papers of Lawrenceburg businessman Omer Tousey, including bonds for loans which Tousey made to men going to California (1852), and land grants for land near Council Bluffs, Iowa, and Kickapoo, Kans., which Tousey purchased during the period 1859-1865; letters and essays of Hiram Brown of Lebanon, Ohio (1825-1836), and Indianapolis (1836-1848); and family letters of Clay Brown, a medical student and physician in Chicago (1848), Anderson, Madison Co. (1850-1853), and Jackson, Tenn. (1853-1854).

Historical papers collected by Porter include papers of Benjamin Parke (1777-1835), a Vincennes, Knox Co., attorney, Indiana territorial delegate to Congress (1805-1808), and territorial judge (1808-1817); John Dumont (1787-1871), Switzerland County attorney, five-term member of the Indiana House of Representatives between 1816 and 1831, Indiana state senator (1831-1836), and Whig candidate for governor (1837); Charles Dewey (1780-1862), a Charleston, Clark Co., attorney, U.S. district attorney for Indiana (1825-1827), and justice, Indiana Supreme Court (1836-1847); and Samuel Merrill (1792-1855), Indiana state treasurer (1822-1834), president, State Bank of Indiana (1834-1848), and president, Madison and Indianapolis Railroad (1844-1848). The Benjamin Parke papers include his correspondence (1805-1814) with James Brown of New Orleans, including Brown's letters regarding politics in Louisiana (1805-1808) and Washington, D.C. (1814), and Parke's letters from Washington (1806-1807) and Vincennes (1813-1814). The John Dumont papers include letters to Dumont from John Briggs of Williams College and Adams, Mass. (1807-1812); letters regarding temperance and Indiana and Switzerland County politics (1830-1852); and Dumont's speeches on politics, agriculture, internal improvements, temperance, slavery, education, and secession (1815-ca.1862). The Charles Dewey papers include his official correspondence as U.S. district attorney in Indiana; correspondence regarding the bankruptcies of the Bank of Vincennes and the Farmers and Merchants Bank of Madison, Jefferson Co. (1826-1827); and documents relating to court cases on slaves in Indiana (1818-1826). The Samuel Merrill papers are principally related to the Indiana State Bank and the Madison and Indianapolis Railroad (1834-1848).

The collection also includes miscellaneous papers Porter collected on the early history of Vincennes and Indiana. Included in this group are deeds, petitions, letters, and other documents relating to the ownership of land by the French and American settlers at Vincennes (1759-1823); muster rolls and other documents of the Vincennes militia (1783-1795); letters and survey maps of Vincennes lands by Samuel Baird (1792-1793); summary of speeches at a council meeting between William Henry Harrison and midwestern Indian chiefs (1802); and other papers regarding Indians, Indiana politics, and internal improvements.

The collection includes papers of William B. Allison, Samuel Baird, Morris Birkbeck, James G. Blaine, S. M. Breckenridge, Hiram Brown, James Brown, William Clarke, Schuyler Colfax, David Davis, Henry Winter Davis, Eugene V. Debs, John D. Defrees, Charles Dewey, John B. Dillon, John Dumont, J. C. Eggleston, Charles W. Fairbanks, John Hay Farnham, Calvin Fletcher, John Watson Foster, John Gibson, James Weir Graydon, Walter Q. Gresham, George Griswold, John Francis Hamtramck, Samuel S. Harding, Benjamin Harrison, William Henry Harrison, Rutherford B. Hayes, Thomas A. Hendricks, William Hendricks, William S. Holman, Jonathan Jennings, John Rice Jones, George W. Julian, James F. D. Lanier, John Law, Joseph G. Marshall, Claude Matthews, Samuel Merrill, James P. Milliken, Caleb Mills, Justin Morrill, Oliver P. Morton, John C. New, David Dale Owen, Robert Treat Paine, Benjamin Parke, Thomas Posey, Daniel D. Pratt, James B. Ray, James M. Ray, Whitelaw Reid, Franklin D. Roosevelt, Richard Rush, Louis St. Ange, Arthur St. Clair, Winthrop Sargent, Ellen B. E. Sherman, John Sherman, William Tecumseh Sherman, Oliver H. Smith, James Speed, Leland Stanford, W. W. Storey, Berry R. Sulgrove, Jeremiah Sullivan, William H. H. Terrell, John Tipton, Omer Tousey, George Upfold, Henry Vanderburgh, Francis Vigo, William Windom, Joseph A. Wright, and Andrew Wylie.

A-303. POSEY, THOMAS (1750-1818). PAPERS, 1776-1839.

46 items.   Calendar.   M 228.

Soldier and politician. Posey was an officer in the 7th Virginia Regiment during the American Revolution (1776-1783); brigadier general in the U.S. Army, serving with Anthony Wayne in the West (1793-1794); resident of Kentucky (1794-1809); lieutenant governor of Kentucky (1805-1809); U.S. senator from Louisiana (1812-1813); governor of the Indiana Territory (1813-1816); and Indian agent for the Illinois Territory (1816-1818).

The collection includes letters written to Posey regarding his service in the American Revolution, with the American army during the 1790s, and as governor of the Indiana Territory; his Revolutionary War journal (1776-1777); an autobiographical sketch; his commissions and appointments; funeral oration delivered by John Dunbar at Corydon; and letters of his sons regarding his Revolutionary War pension (1820-1839).

Correspondents include Nathaniel Greene, James Hall, Henry Knox, Henry Lee, John Marshall, James Monroe, Benjamin Parke, John M. Robinson, Charles Scott, Anthony Wayne, and James Wilkinson.

A-304. PRAIRIE TREK EXPEDITIONS. RECORDS, 1926-1978.

17 archival boxes.   Inventory.   M 390.

The Prairie Trek Expeditions were organized in 1926 by Hillis L. Howie (d.1982), an Indianapolis teacher and Boy Scout leader, as a summer wilderness program in the Southwest. In 1934 he purchased land for a summer camp called Cottonwood Gulch, near Thoreau, N.Mex. The Treks were reorganized as a nonprofit educational institution, the Cottonwood Gulch Foundation, in 1935. Howie was director until 1970 and was succeeded by Thomas M. Billings.

The collection includes board minutes, financial records, ledgers, receipts, permits, and papers on insurance, improvements, real estate purchases, and rentals of the Cottonwood Gulch Foundation; director's records, including files on the recruitment and training of campers and staff, rosters, applications, evaluations, papers on the organization of activities and procurement of supplies, and advertising materials; staff correspondence involving payrolls, manuals, and contracts; director's correspondence with individuals and institutions regarding the organization and operation of the treks; published accounts of each trek's experiences (1926-1972); and scrapbooks, songs, cookbooks, and recipe cards.

A-305. PRICKETT, THOMAS (b.1833). PAPERS, 1861-1864.

73 items. SC 1222.

Prickett was an Elkhart County farmer; and sergeant and lieutenant in the 9th Indiana Regiment (1861-1864).

The collection consists of Prickett's letters written to his wife while he was serving with the Union Army in Tennessee.

A-306. PROCTOR, JOHN (1787-1844). ACCOUNT BOOKS, 1834-1857.

9 vols. (.75 l.f.). BV 295-303.

Proctor was a Rockport, Spencer Co., merchant and grocer (1823-1844).

The collection consists of account books for Proctor's store.

A-307. RAISBECK, SAMUEL M. (fl.1846-1904). PAPERS, 1836-1904.

1 ms. box. Calendar. M 231.

Raisbeck was an officer of the Columbus, Piqua, and Indiana Railroad, later known as the Columbus and Indianapolis Railroad (1852-1862); and resident of Piqua, Ohio, and Tuckahoe, N.Y.

The bulk of the collection consists of letters to Raisbeck concerning Columbus, Piqua, and Indiana Railroad company business, including correspondence relating to the acquisition of land and materials, construction and operation of the railroad, and company finances (1852-1862). The collection also includes papers relating to Raisbeck's acquisition of property in Piqua (1836-1881).

Correspondents include Hervey Bates.

A-308. RANDOLPH, CATHERINE LAWRENCE (1789-1816). PAPERS, 1802-1824.

25 items.   Calendar.   SC 1236.

Randolph was the granddaughter of Northwest Territory governor Arthur St. Clair (1736-1818) and wife of Thomas Randolph, attorney general of the Indiana Territory at Vincennes, Knox Co. (1808-1811).

The collection consists of Randolph's letters to family members written from Cincinnati, Ohio (1808), Vincennes (1810), and Jeffersonville, Clark Co. (1814); and letters to Randolph from her mother and stepfather, Elizabeth and Gen. James Dill, written from Natchez, Miss. (1805), and Lawrenceburg, Dearborn Co. (1808-1816). The correspondence includes numerous references to Arthur St. Clair and William Henry Harrison.

A-309. RAUH, SAMUEL E. (1853-1935). PAPERS, 1900-1948.

3 ms. boxes.   Inventory.   M 406.

Businessman. Rauh's family emigrated from Germany and established a tanning and fur business in Dayton, Ohio (1864); Rauh started Indianapolis branch of the business (1874); founded E. Rauh & Sons Fertilizer Company (1880); founded Moore Packing Company (1890); named to board of directors, Indianapolis Belt Railroad and Stock Yards Company (1895); served as the company's president (1897-1929) and chairman of the board (1929-1935); served on the boards of numerous other Indianapolis companies; and was active in the Indianapolis Jewish community. The collection also includes papers of his son, Charles S. Rauh (1883-1956), president of E. Rauh & Sons Fertilizer Company (1916-1926); vice-president (1926-1929), president (1929-1956), and chairman of the board (1936-1956) of the Indianapolis Belt Railroad and Stock Yards Company.

The collection includes personal correspondence of Samuel and Charles Rauh, including retained copies of Samuel Rauh's letters to his nephews on family and business matters (1922-1935); correspondence and business documents relating to the family's principal business interests, including the Indianapolis Belt Railroad and Stock Yards Company, the Rauh Realty Company, and E. Rauh and Sons, the family's tanning and fur business in Indianapolis and Dayton; and correspondence and business documents relating to many of the Rauhs' other Indiana business interests, including Peoples Light and Heat Company (1911-1912), the Burpee-Johnson Company (1920s), the Bedford Stone and Construction Company (1920s), the Kahn Tailoring Company (1920s), and the Indianapolis Board of Trade. Also included are papers relating to the American Jewish Relief Committee in the 1920s; and estate inventories for Samuel Rauh's brothers, Leopold and Henry Rauh (1907-1923).

A-310. RAY, JOHN W. (1828-1906). PAPERS, 1822-1921.

1 ms. box.   Calendar.   M 236.

Ray was a student at Indiana Asbury University, Greencastle, Putnam Co. (1845-1848); an Indianapolis banker; and treasurer of Indiana Asbury University (1867-1894).

The collection consists primarily of Ray's essays and addresses written while he was a student at Indiana Asbury University. Also included are minutes of the Indianapolis Sunday School Auxiliary to the Sunday School Union of the Methodist Episcopal Church (1828).

A-311. REYNOLDS, JAMES MADISON (1826-1901). PAPERS, 1840-1899.

67 items.   Calendar.   SC 1259.

Reynolds attended Indiana Asbury University (1843-1844) and was a banker and railroad executive in Lafayette, Tippecanoe Co.

The collection consists primarily of letters written to Reynolds. Included are letters written to him at Indiana Asbury from his father in Lafayette and from his fellow students Albert Gallatin Porter and Newton Booth (1843-1844);

letters regarding accusations against his brother, Gen. Joseph Jones Reynolds, while serving in the Wyoming Territory (1876); and letters from Indiana political figures regarding appointments for Reynolds (1876-1896).

Correspondents include Newton Booth, Benjamin Harrison, William R. Holloway, Claude Matthews, Albert G. Porter, Joseph J. Reynolds, Matthew Simpson, Richard W. Thompson, and Albert S. White.

A-312. REYNOLDS, STEPHEN MARION (fl.1876-1930). PAPERS, 1849-1948.

1 ms. box.   Calendar.   M 235.

Socialist leader, attorney, and author. Reynolds was a Terre Haute attorney; a member of the Social Democratic Party (1899) and the Socialist Party (1901); speaker and writer on behalf of socialism; author of *Life of Eugene V. Debs* (1908) and *The Revolution of Our Day* (1909); and Socialist candidate for governor of Indiana (1912).

The collection consists primarily of letters to Reynolds and his wife, most from the period 1899-1912 and relating to socialism. Also included are numerous letters from Eugene V. Debs to Reynolds and letters to Debs from other socialists. Subjects covered by the collection included Debs's organizing activities for the Socialist Party; the 1908 presidential campaign; and the socialist newspaper *Appeal to Reason*. Also included is correspondence relating to Reynolds's college career at Lafayette College, Easton, Pa. (1876-1877); and correspondence regarding his efforts to obtain a consular appointment under President Benjamin Harrison (1889-1892).

Correspondents include Charles E. Banks, Eugene V. Debs, Theodore Debs, Hector Fuller, Elijah W. Halford, George D. Herron, William Mailly, Horace Traubel, Ryan Walker, and Fred D. Warren.

A-313. RICHARDSON, IDA FRANCES (1847-1932). PAPERS, 1828-1933.

7 ms. boxes, 11 vols. (2.5 l.f.).   Calendar.   M 237, BV 1710-1719.

Richardson was an art student at St. Mary's Institute (now St. Mary-of-the-Woods), Vigo Co. (1867-1869); an Indianapolis schoolteacher; secretary of the Marion County Agricultural and Horticultural Society; and writer and poet.

The collection includes Richardson's diaries (1894-1913); her notebooks and correspondence relating to St. Mary's Institute (1867-1892); a biography of her father, Joel F. Richardson, taken largely from his diary written when he was an officer of the Indianapolis, Cincinnati, and Lafayette Railroad and the Indianapolis Belt Railway (1873-1877); a small amount of J. F. Richardson's correspondence concerning the railroad business (1858-1880); and Ida F. Richardson's scrapbooks, notebooks, and poetry. Also included are the minutes of the Marion County Agricultural and Horticultural Society (1902-1908) and the Record of Shares for the New Bethel and Sugar Creek Gravel Road Company (1864).

A-314. RICHSQUARE ACADEMY. PAPERS, 1851-1889.

1 ms. box, 1 vol. (.25 l.f.).   M 239, BV 1720.

Richsquare Academy was a Quaker school near Lewisville, Henry Co.

The collection consists of the constitution, bylaws, and minutes of the Richsquare Literary Society (1851-1856); handwritten student newspapers, student essays, and lecture notes, most from the period 1850-1870; and an 1889 commencement program.

A-315. RILEY, JAMES WHITCOMB (1853-1916). COLLECTION, 1887-1950.

4 ms. boxes.   M 240.

Riley was a poet; writer of Hoosier dialect verse; and author of *Raggedy Man* (1907), *The Little Orphant Annie Book* (1908), *The Old Swimmin Hole and Other Poems* (1912), and numerous other books of poetry.

The collection consists of material relating to James Whitcomb Riley collected by his niece, Harriet Eitel Wells Johnson (1879-1958) of Indianapolis. Included are manuscripts of Riley poems, many written for members of Johnson's family; a small amount of Riley correspondence; clippings and memorabilia relating to Riley; material regarding the Contemporary and Fortnightly literary clubs from the 1920s and 1930s; Johnson's family correspondence from the 1940s and 1950s; correspondence with other Hoosier authors; the correspondence of Margaret M. Scott; and the journal of Cornelius H. Menger, written while he was serving as a captain in the Coast Artillery Corps of the U.S. Army (1916-1920).

Correspondents include George Ade, Marcus Dickey, and John T. McCutcheon.

A-316. ROBERTS, ELIJAH (1795-1848). PAPERS, 1832-1914.

1 ms. box.   Inventory.   M 325.

Roberts was a free black farmer who immigrated to Rush County, Ind., from North Carolina (1829); one of the founders of the Roberts Settlement, a black community in Hamilton County (1832); and Hamilton County farmer (1832-1848).

The papers are composed primarily of promissory notes, tax receipts, property assessments, and other financial papers of Roberts and his descendants.

A-317. ROBERTSON, CARRIE FRANCIS (1852-1941). JOURNALS, 1890-1924.

26 vols. (2.5 l.f.).   Inventory.   BV 311-336.

Club woman. Robertson was the wife of Alexander M. Robertson, an Indianapolis wholesale grocer; president of the Matinee Musicale; honorary vice-president of the National Federation of Music Clubs; and member of the Indianapolis Womens Club, Indianapolis Propylaeum Club, and the board of directors of Butler University, Indianapolis.

The collection consists of Robertson's travel journals describing her trips to Europe, the Caribbean, North Africa, Egypt, Hawaii, Australia, and the South Sea Islands; her tours through the United States; and the 1916 and 1920 Republican National Conventions which she attended. The journals include postcards, photographs, and clippings relating to the places she visited.

A-318. SANDERS, F. E. (fl.1900-1913). COLLECTION, 1806-1913.

1 ms. box.   Inventory.   M 312.

Sanders was a physician in Perryville, Vermillion Co.; and an investor in land in White County, Ark., Greely and Lincoln counties, Nebr., Butler and Miller counties, Mo., and Stuartburn, Manitoba, Canada.

The collection includes Sanders's correspondence and legal documents relating to his land investments (1907-1913); personal correspondence of his wife (1905-1910); and letters, receipts, and other business papers of the Charles English family of Vermillion County (1806-1853).

A-319. SCHERRER, ADOLPH (1847-1925). PAPERS, 1853-1923.

1 ms. box, 2 vols. (.75 l.f.).   Inventory.   M 245, BV 1722-1723.

Scherrer was an emigrant from St. Gallen, Switzerland (1870); a resident of Indianapolis (1872-1925); and an architect who worked on the Indiana State Capitol Building (1880), the Maennerchor Hall, City Hospital, and other buildings in the Indianapolis area.

The collection includes correspondence regarding the construction of the Indiana State Capitol Building (1879-1880), the Soldiers' and Sailors' Monument (1887), and other buildings in Indianapolis (1894-1923); Scherrer's ledger book, contracts and specifications, and card list of Indianapolis area projects (1904-1929); and book of agreements for projects in Switzerland (1853-1868).

Correspondents include Thomas Taggart.

A-320. SCHERRER, ANTON (1878-1960). PAPERS, 1936-1948.

4 ms. boxes.   Inventory.   M 346.

Scherrer was an Indianapolis architect and author of the column "Our Town" on the people and history of Indianapolis for the *Indianapolis Times*.

The collection consists of manuscripts for the "Our Town" columns (1936-1940); notebooks for ideas for columns; letters from readers; manuscripts of speeches and essays; and architectural sketches for unidentified houses.

A-321. SCHRAMM, WILHELM AUGUST (1840-1909). PAPERS, 1845-1909.

8 ms. boxes, 2 vols. (2.25 l.f.).   Inventory.   M 248, BV 1737-1738.

Schramm was a farmer in Sugar Creek Township, Hancock Co.; and an agent for the Home Mutual Fire Insurance Company in Hancock and Marion counties. He was the son of Jacob Schramm (1805-1880), a Bavarian immigrant and author of letters describing his trip to America which were published in Germany in 1837, and in an English translation as *The Schramm Letters* (Indiana Historical Society, 1935).

The collection is principally composed of August Schramm's seventy-eight diaries covering the period 1851-1908. The diaries contain extensive descriptions of Schramm's daily life, including information about his family, farming, social life, travel, the German community in central Indiana, politics, and business conditions. The volumes from 1851 to 1858 are in German; the rest are in English. Also included are two cashbooks in German (1859-1896) for the farms of Schramm and his brother, Gustave; a writing book in German kept by his sister Anna (1845); and a small number of family papers (1863-1909).

A-322. SCHUMACHER, GEORGE A. (1904-1973). COLLECTION, 1879-1975.

2 ms. boxes.   Calendar.   M 250.

Schumacher was a Butler University, Indianapolis, English teacher (1926-1951); executive vice-president, Indiana Telephone Association (1954-1967); and author, *Maurice Thompson, Archer and Author* (1968).

The collection includes letters of Indiana authors and politicians collected by Schumacher; drafts of Schumacher's articles and book on Maurice Thompson;

and correspondence with Vincennes University officials regarding his work on Thompson (1969-1973).

The collection includes letters written by George Ade, Albert J. Beveridge, Edward Eggleston, Charles W. Fairbanks, Thomas A. Hendricks, Oliver P. Morton, Meredith Nicholson, James Whitcomb Riley, Maurice Thompson, and Lew Wallace.

A-323. SCOTT, JOHN (fl.1841-1884). PAPERS, 1841-1894.

86 items. SC 1319.

Scott was a farmer near Woostertown, Scott Co.

The collection consists primarily of letters to Scott from relatives in southern Iowa, eastern Illinois, and Indiana.

A-324. SCOTT, RANSOM D. (fl.1886-1908). PAPERS, 1886-1908.

1 ms. box. Calendar. M 247.

Scott was a farmer near Anderson, Madison Co.

The collection consists of letters written to Scott from family members in Conneaut Lake and Evansburg, Pa., describing local events and family matters.

A-325. SCRIBNER, BENJAMIN FRANKLIN (1825-1900). PAPERS, 1846-1900.

88 items. SC 1322.

Businessman and soldier. Scribner was a wholesale druggist in New Albany, Floyd Co.; corporal, 2nd Indiana Regiment in the Mexican War (1846-1847); colonel, 38th Indiana Regiment in the Civil War (1861-1864); collector of

Internal Revenues, 2nd Collecting District of Indiana (1865-1871); employee in drug brokerage office, New York City (1878); and U.S. treasury agent, Alaska (1878).

The collection consists primarily of Scribner's correspondence with family, friends, and his business partner, E. A. Maginness, from the period 1846-1866. Included are letters written from New Albany and Mexico during the Mexican War; Scribner's Civil War letters to his family while he served in Kentucky and Tennessee; and postwar letters regarding Scribner's business activities. Also included are two letters written from the ship U.S.S. *Independence* while on assignment in the Mediterranean in 1850.

A-326. SEBASTIAN, BENJAMIN (1745-1834). PAPERS, 1795-1807.

28 items.   Calendar.   SC 1728, OM 84.

Attorney. Sebastian was a Kentucky attorney and judge of the Kentucky Appellate Court (1792-1806). He participated in the intrigues with Spain to break Kentucky and the western country away from the United States (1796); received a pension from Spain; and resigned his judgeship after public disclosure of his Spanish ties (1806).

The collection consists of documents and letters relating to Sebastian's involvement in the Spanish Conspiracy. Included are documents relating to the 1796 meeting between Sebastian and Francisco Luis Hector de Carondelet, Spanish Governor General of Louisiana; letters of Sebastian and his attorney, James Brown, regarding the accusations against Sebastian; and letters regarding Sebastian's efforts to have his pension from Spain continued after 1806.

Correspondents include James Brown, Francisco Luis Hector de Carondelet, and Henry Clay.

A-327. SEVITZKY, FABIEN (1893-1967). PAPERS, 1939-1971.

105 items.   Inventory.   SC 1865.

Sevitzky was a Russian-trained musician; joined the Philadelphia Orchestra (1923); began career as conductor (1928); conductor, Indianapolis Symphony

Orchestra (1937-1955); and conductor, Miami Symphony Orchestra (1955-1967).

The collection includes letters to Sevitzky from author Booth Tarkington regarding personal matters and their collaboration on a musical based on Kipling's Mowgli stories (1940-1945); letters of Sevitzky and his wife to their secretary, Farrel Wagner, while they were on tour and at their summer music camp at LaGrange, LaGrange Co., Ind. (1939-1950); Sevitzky's correspondence with the Finnish ambassador regarding the Jean Sibelius Fund (1940-1941); retained copies of his letters to Lionel Barrymore regarding film music (1944); and letters from other conductors and musicians.

Correspondents include Eugene Goossens, Ernest MacMillan, Paul V. McNutt, Artur Rodzinski, Frederick Stock, and Bruno Walter.

A-328. SHIRK, ANDREW (1816-1882). ACCOUNT BOOKS, 1832-1868.

17 vols. (2 l.f.). BV 341-357.

Shirk owned a general store in Union and Springfield, Franklin Co., and a farm near Union.

The collection consists of Shirk's account books for his stores and farm.

A-329. SHOCKLEY, DAVID (1828-1863). PAPERS, 1859-1895.

92 items. Inventory. SC 1311.

Shockley was a farmer in Delaware County; soldier in the 69th Indiana Regiment (1862-1863); and died at the Battle of Vicksburg (1863).

The collection includes Shockley's war letters to his wife from Kentucky and the Vicksburg area (1862-1863); war letters of Calvin Feasel, 17th Indiana Battery, serving in Maryland and Virginia, to his aunt and uncle, David and Susan Shockley (1862-1865); letters to Shockley's widow, Susan Shockley Curts, from relatives in northern Missouri (1864-1894); letters of Susan Shockley Curts to sons and other relatives in northern Missouri, Kansas, Iowa, and Nebraska (1864-1895); deeds for land in Delaware County (1859-1875); and receipts and miscellaneous documents pertaining to the Shockley family (1865-1892). Also included is correspondence and legal papers of the Curts family in Delaware County and Iowa (1881-1890).

A-330. SHOEMAKER, HERMAN (1844-1937). ACCOUNT BOOKS, 1889-1907.

5 vols. (.5 l.f.). BV 305-309.

Shoemaker was a German immigrant (1848) and owner of a general store in New Providence, Clark Co. (1870-1937).

The collection consists of Shoemaker's account books for his New Providence store.

A-331. SHRYER, JOHN D. (d.1872?). ACCOUNT BOOKS, 1832-1872.

4 vols. (.33 l.f.). BV 359-362.

Shryer owned a dry goods store in Jeffersonville, Clark Co.

The collection consists of account books for Shryer's dry goods store.

A-332. SIMPSON, ELIZABETH (d.1892). PAPERS, 1790-1880.

25 items. Calendar. SC 1349.

Simpson was a resident of Fayette County, Ky.

The collection consists of letters to Simpson from relatives in Eugene, Vermillion Co., Rockville, Parke Co., and Crawfordsville, Montgomery Co., Ind., most from the period 1836-1848, relating to politics, health, and economic conditions. Also included are Simpson's coverlet patterns and receipts for schooling of children (1790-1808).

A-333. SLAWSON-TARKINGTON FAMILY. PAPERS, 1804-1911.

1 ms. box.   Inventory.   M 370.

The principal figures in the collection are Simeon Slawson (1777-1858), a farmer in New York State and Switzerland County, Ind. (1819-1858); and his son-in-law, Joseph Tarkington (1800-1891), a Methodist circuit rider in southern Indiana (1821-1862), a farmer near Greensburg, Decatur Co., and grandfather of author Booth Tarkington.

The collection consists primarily of family correspondence from the period 1830-1889, including letters to Slawson from his son Delanson (1810-1845) and his wife who were farmers near Indianapolis; other Slawson family correspondence from New Orleans, New York, and Racine, Wis., principally from the period 1830-1860; letters of Joseph Tarkington, his wife, and son John S. Tarkington; and correspondence among Tarkington's children, primarily from the period 1860-1889.

A-334. SMITH, BENJAMIN WILSON (1830-1921). PAPERS, 1851-1934.

2 ms. boxes.   Calendar.   M 253.

Educator and politician. Smith was a graduate of Indiana Asbury University, Greencastle, Putnam Co. (1855, 1858); superintendent of schools, Aurora, Dearborn Co. (1858-1860); professor and president, Valparaiso Male and Female College, Porter Co. (1862-1867); manufacturer of school furniture and books for county officials, Lafayette, Tippecanoe Co.; Republican member, Indiana House of Representatives (1883, 1885, 1897); and Tippecanoe County postmaster (1889-1893).

The collection includes Smith's school essays and speeches from Indiana Asbury University (1851-1855); his class book, Iowa Conference Seminary, Mt. Vernon, Iowa (1859); notebook and papers of the Big Creek Ditching Company, White County (1870-1874); Smith's reminiscences of his trip from Virginia to White County, Ind., in 1846 (1917); and family letters.

Correspondents include Sarah T. Bolton.

A-335. SMITH, CHARLES W. (1846-1921). PAPERS, 1832-1928.

1 ms. box.   Inventory.   M 348.

Smith was a lieutenant in the 109th U.S. Colored Infantry during the Civil War; and an Indianapolis attorney.

The collection includes documents relating to Smith's Civil War service; a journal (1832-1845) of Smith's father, Morgan L. Smith, a New Jersey man who started a farm and sawmill in Hendricks County in 1834; family letters to Morgan Smith from relatives in the East (1837-1869); Charles Smith's family letters (1872-1928); and essays and addresses by Charles Smith, including accounts of the last days of the Civil War, and the experiences of his friend, Marshall Twitchell, in Louisiana during Reconstruction.

A-336. SMITH, CLARENCE H. (1875-1959). PAPERS, 1775-1959.

38 ms. boxes.   Inventory.   M 254.

Historian and genealogist. Smith was curator of the Henry County Historical Museum in New Castle (1922-1952); an amateur historian, genealogist, and naturalist; author of history column in *New Castle Courier* entitled "Happenings of Other Days"; and active member of the Indiana Historical Society, the Society of Indiana Pioneers, the Sons of the American Revolution, and the Indiana Audubon Society. The collection also includes papers of Smith's father, Robert Barclay Smith (1835-1900), a New Castle dry goods store owner; and his grandfather, Seth Smith (1787-1865), a Loudon County, Va., attorney and a resident of Richmond, Wayne Co., Ind. (1855-1867).

The collection includes early letters, documents, journals, and diaries of the Smith family, including Robert B. Smith's personal correspondence with his father in the 1850s regarding his move to Richmond and the financial problems in establishing a business (1850s-1900); correspondence of Seth Smith and his brother Jacob Smith, primarily from Virginia, Ohio, and Maryland (1775-1850); Seth Smith's journal kept while he was in Baltimore (1806); account books of a Baltimore store (1806-1815); and an account book for a Union, Va., store (1815-1823). Also included is Clarence Smith's family correspondence (1894-1919), including letters from his brother Lynn Smith, a businessman in Alaska; Smith's correspondence relating to genealogy and history (1894-1952); letters, documents, clippings, and miscellaneous information regarding local history for the New Castle-Knightstown region; local S.A.R. and D.A.R. material, including papers relating to genealogical verification and the activities of the organizations; correspondence dealing with Smith's activities as curator of the Henry County Historical Museum (1922-1952); and correspondence regarding the Indiana Historical Society, the Indiana Audubon Society, the Henry County Nature Research Club, and Wabash College, Crawfordsville, Montgomery Co.

Correspondents include Albert J. Beveridge, Christopher B. Coleman, Josiah K. Lilly, Kate Milner Rabb, and James E. Watson.

A-337. SMITH, DELAVAN (1861-1922). PAPERS, 1868-1921.

45 ms. boxes.   Inventory.   M 255.

Publisher and businessman. Smith was publisher and part owner of the *Indianapolis News* (1896-1922), much of the time in partnership with Charles W. Fairbanks; a resident of Lake Forest, Ill.; businessman involved in mining, manufacturing, and timber and land speculation in the West; and member, board of trustees, Lake Forest University. Smith was the son of William Henry Smith (1833-1896), general manager of the Western Associated Press (1869-1892), and part owner of the *Indianapolis News* (1892-1896).

The collection consists of Smith's personal and business papers, primarily from the period 1879-1913. Included are papers relating to the *Indianapolis News*, principally from the period 1900-1913, including correspondence regarding the paper's operations and policies, circulation and advertising reports, employee information, and financial records; papers relating to Smith's other business interests, including his involvement with the American Corporation for Investors (1910-1912), the Cass Cigar Manufacturing Company (1897-1900), the Cox Multi-Mailer Company (1905-1914), the Oliver Typewriter Company (1896-1921), the Refugio Syndicate (1907-1914), and the Securities Corporation Limited (1906-1912); papers relating to Lake Forest University and particularly to Smith's interest in the university's Alice Home Hospital and Ferry Hall (1878-1912); personal correspondence, including letters from his father and other family members, from his cousin Charles W. Fairbanks, and from personal friends; and Smith's investment notebooks, bankbooks, and other personal financial records. Also included are business and personal papers of William Henry Smith, including papers relating to the Western Associated Press and national Republican Party politics (1868-1891).

Correspondents include Charles A. Boynton, Hilton U. Brown, Jacob P. Dunn, Charles W. Fairbanks, John H. Hammond, John M. Harlan, James A. Hemenway, Victor F. Lawson, Cyrus McCormick, Medill McCormick, Jesse Overstreet, and Louis F. Swift.

A-338. SMITH, EDGAR (1942-). LETTERS, 1967-1968.

65 items. SC 1395.

Smith was a resident of Bloomington, Monroe Co.; a graduate of Indiana University, Bloomington (1965, 1966); and 1st lieutenant, Company A, 504th Military Police, Battalion A, U.S. Army stationed in Qui Nhan and Nha Trong, Vietnam (July 1967-June 1968).

The collection consists of letters Smith wrote to his parents in Bloomington while he was serving in the U.S. Army in Vietnam during the war.

A-339. SMITH, GEORGE R. (ca. 1831-1863). PAPERS, 1852-1863.

76 items. SC 1899.

Smith was a farmer near Rome City, Noble Co.; and a soldier with the 12th Indiana Regiment serving at Camp Morton, Indianapolis (1862), and in Tennessee and Mississippi (1862-1863).

The collection consists primarily of Smith's Civil War letters to his wife, Margaret Smith, and family in Noble and LaGrange counties (1862-1863). Also included are Margaret Smith's letters to her husband describing home life during the war; and an 1852 letter from Smith describing a trip on Lake Erie to Ashtabula County, Ohio.

A-340. SMITH, JOSEPH TAYLOR (fl.1862-1897). PAPERS, 1862-1865.

112 items. Partial Calendar. M 256.

Smith was an attorney from Quincy (now Elwood) and Anderson, Madison Co.; and captain, 75th Indiana Regiment (1862-1865).

The collection consists primarily of clothing returns and other official documents relating to the 75th Indiana Regiment. Also included are photostatic copies of letters written by Smith to his family while he served in Kentucky, Tennessee, and Georgia (1862-1865).

A-341. SMITH, WILLIAM HENRY (1833-1896). PAPERS, 1816-1913.

32 ms. boxes, 6 vols. (8.5 l.f.).   Inventory.   M 258, BV 1798-1803. Microfilm.

Journalist, businessman, politician, and historian. Smith was a reporter and editor for the Cincinnati newspapers *Type of the Times, Commercial,* and *Gazette* (1855-1863); involved in the founding of the Republican Party in Cincinnati; secretary to Ohio Governor John Brough (1863-1864); Ohio secretary of state (1864-1868); general manager of the Western Associated Press, based in Chicago, Ill. (1869-1892, merged with the Associated Press in 1883); friend and political ally of Rutherford B. Hayes, and participant in negotiations for electoral votes for Hayes after the 1876 presidential election; member of reform wing of the Republican Party; collector of customs, Port of Chicago (1877-1882); treasurer, Mergenthaler Printing Company; part owner with Charles W. Fairbanks of the *Indianapolis News* (1892-1896); and historian, editor of *The St. Clair Papers* (1882) and author of *The Political Economy of Slavery* (1903). He was the father of Delavan Smith, publisher of the *Indianapolis News* from 1896 to 1922.

The papers are composed primarily of Smith's business, political, and historical correspondence from the period 1855-1895. Included is correspondence relating to his newspaper work in Cincinnati (1850s-1860s); Republican Party politics in Cincinnati and Ohio (1850s-1860s), including Smith's work as secretary to John Brough and as Ohio secretary of state; the Western Associated Press and its relationships with its member newspapers, the New York Associated Press, the United Press, and other press associations, including Smith's correspondence as general manager, internal memos and reports, and financial information (1869-1890s); national Republican Party politics, including Smith's involvement in Rutherford B. Hayes's 1876 presidential campaign and the negotiations for electoral votes, his work as collector of customs in Chicago, and his involvement in the reform wing of the Republican Party (1870s-1880s); and his interests in the Mergenthaler Printing Company, the developer of the linotype machine (1880s). Smith's historical papers include his correspondence with bookdealers and publishers; correspondence regarding his research, particularly relating to Arthur St. Clair and Rutherford B. Hayes; correspondence regarding his efforts to obtain transcripts of historical documents in Washington, D.C.; and Europe; his research notes; drafts of articles and speeches; draft chapters of his biography of Rutherford B. Hayes; transcripts of historical documents collected by Smith for his research, including letters of Henry Bouquet, Henry Clay, James Monroe, Arthur St. Clair, and Thomas Worthington: and a transcript of Thomas C. Donaldson's journal describing life in Washington, D.C., in the 1870s. Also included is Smith's personal correspondence, including his correspondence with his wife and children, letters from friends in Lake Forest, Ill., and letters from his son-in-law, Charles R. Williams, one of the editors of the *Indianapolis News;* personal business papers and accounts; and letters from James A. Garfield to Rutherford B. Hayes (June 1880-June 1881).

Correspondents include Herbert Baxter Adams, William Aldrich, Joseph H. Barrett, James G. Blaine, Alden J. Blethen, Charles A. Boynton, Henry Van Ness Boynton, Erastus Brooks, Francis F. Browne, C. W. Butterfield, Zachariah Chandler, Robert C. Clowry, Shelby M. Cullum, Charles A. Dana, Lyman C. Draper, Frederick Driscoll, Thomas T. Eckert, Charles W. Fairbanks, Charles B. Farwell, John V. Farwell, Walter N. Haldeman, Murat Halstead, John M. Harlan, Rutherford B. Hayes, Webb Hayes, William R. Holloway, Henry Howe, William Dean Howells, William Henry Hurlbert, Richard Underwood Johnson, Andrew J. Kellar, Charles W. Knapp, Victor F. Lawson, John A. Logan, David R. McKee, William McKinley, Elijah B. Martindale, Joseph Medill, Harry S. New, John C. New, William Penn Nixon, Adolph S. Ochs, Joseph Pulitzer, Whitelaw Reid, William K. Rogers, Carl Schurz, John Sherman, James W. Simonton, Richard Smith, David M. Stone, Melville E. Stone, Margaret Frances Sullivan, Wager Swayne, Charles P. Taft, Henry Watterson, and William H. West.

A-342. SOCIETY OF FRIENDS. RECORDS, 1813-1981.

164 vols. (10 l.f.).   BV 401-554, 1973.
Microfilm.

The Society of Friends, or Quakers, is a religious sect founded by George Fox in England in 1647. The first Quaker meetings were established in America in the late seventeenth century, and the first meeting was established in Indiana in 1809. During the first half of the nineteenth century, Quakers were among the leading opponents of slavery in the United States.

The collection includes records of the Western Yearly Meeting of Friends (1858-1963), including minutes of men's and women's meetings, treasurers' reports, marriage records, minutes of ministers and elders meetings, record of epistles sent, and reports by the education committee. Also included are records of individual monthly and quarterly meetings in Indiana, including the meetings at Dover, New Garden, and White Water, Wayne Co. (1815-1924), Lick Creek, Orange Co. (1813-1870), and Sugar River, Montgomery Co. (1833-1883); records of the Indiana Anti-Slavery Society of Friends, including minutes of the women's meetings of the Indiana Yearly Meeting of the Anti-Slavery Society of Friends, and minutes of meetings in Henry, Randolph, Union, and Wayne counties, Ind., and Preble County, Ohio (1843-1857); and records of Conservative Friends in Indiana, including meetings at Beech Grove, Marion Co. (1877-1929), Mill Creek, Plainfield, and Sugar Grove, Hendricks Co. (1851-1981), Westfield, Hamilton Co. (1879-1915), West Union, Morgan Co. (1861-1907), White River, Randolph Co. (1877-1933), and Wilmington and Laura, Ohio (1879-1948).

The library also has microfilm copies of records of meetings in Grant, Hamilton, Hancock, Hendricks, Howard, Huntington, Jackson, Jay, Madison, Marion, Miami, Montgomery, Morgan, Orange, Parke, Randolph, Rush, Union, Wabash, Washington, and Wayne counties, Ind.; Clark, Clinton, Hamilton, Highland, Logan, Miami, Morrow, Preble, and Warren counties, Ohio; and Cass and Grand Traverse, Mich.

A-343. SPANN AND RASSMAN. ACCOUNT BOOKS, 1865-1949.

14 vols. (1.5 l.f.).   BV 624-637.

The Indianapolis real estate firm of Spann and Rassman was formed in 1960 from the merger of the John S. Spann Company and the Emil C. Rassman Company, both founded in 1860.

The collection consists of the John S. Spann Company's account books listing all property sold, buyers and sellers, and prices.

A-344. SPARKS, JEREMIAH BURRIS (1808-1886). PAPERS, 1839-1878.

1 ms. box.   Inventory.   M 260.

Sparks was a licensed exhorter for the Methodist Episcopal Church in Indiana (ca.1832-1848); licensed preacher, Indiana Conference, Methodist Episcopal Church (1850-1852); and itinerant preacher, Southeast Indiana Conference (1852-1880).

The collection includes Sparks's notebooks containing his diary entries, sermon texts, records of contributions, and other information regarding his work as an itinerant preacher in southeastern Indiana (1843-1878); notes for 210 sermons; 4 letters from 1854 regarding the condition of churches in Indiana; and receipts and other personal financial papers.

A-345. SPEED, EDWARD B. (1825-1864). PAPERS, 1863-1883.

29 items.   SC 1383.

Speed was a LaGrange County physician (1856-1864); and assistant surgeon, 44th Indiana Regiment (1864).

The collection includes correspondence between Speed and his wife while he served in the Union Army in Kentucky and Tennessee during the Civil War (1864); military documents relating to Speed's service; and legal papers of Speed's wife's family.

A-346. SQUIER, EPHRAIM GEORGE (1821-1888). PAPERS, 1842-1900.

2 ms. boxes.   Calendar.   M 262.
Microfilm.

Journalist and ethnologist. Squier was a newspaper editor in Albany, N.Y. (1842), Hartford, Conn. (1844-1845), and Chillicothe, Ohio (1845); U.S. charge d'affaires to Central America (1849); chief editor, Frank Leslie Publishing House, and director of the project "Frank Leslie's Pictorial History of the American Civil War" (1861-1862); U.S. commissioner to Peru (1863-1865); consul general of Honduras to New York City (1868); archaeologist and ethnologist, author of *Ancient Monuments of the Mississippi Valley* (1847) and *Aboriginal Monuments of the State of New York* (1851); and author of numerous works on the history and ethnology of Central America.

The collection consists of Squier's correspondence regarding his research and writings on American Indians and Central America; correspondence regarding his political and business interests in Central America, including papers regarding the general operations of the American embassy; his newspaper publishing career; and personal letters regarding his family's health.

Correspondents include Nathaniel P. Banks, James Gordon Bennett, Lewis Cass, Samuel S. Cox, William Parker Cutler, Henry Winter Davis, James Dixon, Edward Everett, Hamilton Fish, Benson J. Lossing, Joel Munsell, George F. Peabody, George P. Putnam, Whitelaw Reid, Alexander Hamilton Rice, William H. Seward, Pierre Soule, Philip Henry Stanhope, Charles Sumner, George Ticknor, Nicholas Trubner, and Gideon Welles.

A-347. STANFIELD, EDWARD P. (b.1843). LETTERS, 1861-1865.

73 items. Calendar. SC 1395.

Stanfield was a resident of South Bend, St. Joseph Co.; and 1st lieutenant and adjutant, 48th Indiana Regiment (1861-1865).

The collection consists of letters Stanfield wrote to his family in South Bend while he was serving with the Union Army in Tennessee, at Vicksburg, and in Georgia.

A-348. STAR MILL COMPANY. RECORDS, 1889-1919.

15 vols. (1.5 l.f.). BV 371-385.

The Star Mill Company operated a gristmill in Huntingburg, Dubois Co.

The records consist of the company's account books (1889-1919) and order books (1903-1911).

A-349. STARR, WILLIAM C. (1822-1897). PAPERS, 1861-1878.

86 items. Partial Calendar. SC 1400.

Starr was a Richmond, Wayne Co., Quaker; manager of saltworks at Pomeroy, Ohio (1855), and Mason City, Va. (1861); colonel, 9th West Virginia Regiment (1861-1865); and manufacturer of saddlery hardware, Richmond, Ind. (1865-1897).

The collection consists primarily of letters written during the Civil War, including correspondence between Starr and his wife in Richmond, and correspondence between Starr's wife and friends and relatives in Ohio and West Virginia. Also included are family and business letters from Ohio and Pennsylvania written after the war. Approximately half of the items are photostatic copies.

A-350. STATE FLORISTS ASSOCIATION OF INDIANA. RECORDS, 1887-1965.

1 ms. box, 8 vols. (1 l.f.). M 322, BV 1790-1797.

The State Florists Association of Indiana was founded in 1904 as the principal professional organization for the state's florists.

The collection consists of the minutes, membership lists, and financial records of the State Florists Association and its two predecessors, the Society of Indiana Florists and the Indianapolis Florists Club.

A-351. STEELE, THEODORE L. (1905-). COLLECTION, 1875-1946.

2 ms. boxes, 10 vols. (1 l.f.). Inventory. M 263, BV 1726-1735.

Steele, an Indianapolis architect and grandson of artist T. C. Steele, donated this collection to the Historical Society in 1974.

The collection includes minutes of the College Corner Literary Club, Indianapolis (1875-1897), and the Browning Society, Indianapolis (1895-1913); notebook and reminiscences of Selma N. Steele, wife of Indiana painter

T. C. Steele (1912-1934); notebook of reminiscences of Helen McKay Steele, Indianapolis (1946); post-Civil War reminiscences of antislavery work in Jennings and Jefferson counties, and work with ex-slaves in Cairo, Ill., during the Civil War; papers of Horace McKay relating to Woodruff Place and the Consumers Gas Trust Company, Indianapolis (1903-1915); and Record of the County and Township Committee, Indiana Republican State Central Committee (1878).

A-352. STEPHENSON, DAVID CURTIS (1891-1966). PAPERS, 1922-1928.

7 ms. boxes.   Calendar.   M 264.

Ku Klux Klan leader. Stephenson was leader of the Indiana Ku Klux Klan (1922-1925); King Kleagle for most of the midwestern states and Grand Dragon of the Realm of Indiana (1923-1925); broke away from the national Ku Klux Klan (1924); political ally of Indiana Republican governor Edward L. Jackson during 1924 election; and served prison term for murder of Madge Oberholtzer (1925-1956).

The bulk of the collection consists of depositions, hearing transcripts, and other official documents relating to Stephenson's 1925 murder trial. Also included are a number of Stephenson's letters and documents relating to his work with the Klan and the Republican Party (1923-1925); notes on Stephenson's murder trial made by Marion County prosecutor William H. Remy; and Marion County Grand Jury reports on the investigation into corruption charges against Gov. Edward L. Jackson (1927).

Correspondents include Hiram Wesley Evans, Simeon D. Fess, Edward L. Jackson, James E. Watson, and Roy West.

A-353. STOCKDALE, WILLIAM (fl.1845-1910). PAPERS, 1865-1910.

33 items.   SC 1412:

Stockdale was an English immigrant to America in the early 1860s; soldier in the Union Army during the Civil War; farmer near Ogden, Henry Co. (1870s-1880s); and resident of Greenfield, Hancock Co. (1890s-1910).

The collection consists of personal letters to Stockdale written by his family in Manchester, England.

A-354. STOCKWELL, ROBERT (fl.1815-1860). ACCOUNT BOOKS, 1819-1842.

4 vols. (.75 l.f.). BV 363-366.

Stockwell was a Princeton, Gibson Co., store owner (1815-ca.1850) and founder of the Stockwell Collegiate Institute, Tippecanoe Co. (1859).

The collection consists of Stockwell's account books for his Princeton store.

A-355. STOREY, THOMAS J. (1796-1878). PAPERS, 1823-1880.

186 items. Calendar. SC 1419.

Storey was a farmer and merchant in Jennings County.

The collection consists of receipts, land deeds, and other financial documents relating to Storey's business activities in Jennings County and southeast Indiana. Also included is an 1857 notebook containing records of Storey's horse breeding business.

A-356. STOUT, MARTHA (d.1913). PAPERS, 1834-1936.

120 items. Partial Calendar. M 265.

Stout was a schoolteacher in Greenwood, Johnson Co. (1857); and wife of Harvey S. Jaques (d.1912), a schoolteacher and store owner in Whitcomb, Franklin Co.

The collection consists of Stout's correspondence with family, friends, and Harvey Jaques during the time she was teaching school; letters from Franklin County soldiers serving in the Civil War; her correspondence with her children and other family members from the 1890s to the 1910s; and receipts, bills, and other financial and legal documents from the late nineteenth century. Also included is an essay on farming techniques and the care of fruit trees (ca.1860).

A-357. STREIGHTOFF, FRANK HATCH (1886-1935). PAPERS, 1894-1948.

8 ms. boxes.   Inventory.   M 267.

Educator. Streightoff was a professor of economics and business administration at DePauw University, Greencastle, Putnam Co. (1912-1918), the College of Emporia, Kans. (1919-1920), and Indiana University Extension, Indianapolis (1920-1935); secretary, Literature and Peace Committee, Western Yearly Meeting of Friends; and author, *Distribution of Incomes in the United States* (1912), and coauthor, with Frances Doan Streightoff, of *Indiana: A Social and Economic Survey* (1916). The collection also includes the papers of his wife, Frances Doan Streightoff (1885-1969), an Indianapolis civic leader and president, Marion County League of Women Voters.

The papers include correspondence between Streightoff and his wife (1915-1919); Streightoff's correspondence regarding the Literature and Peace Committee, including the Committee's disarmament petition (1924-1931); papers relating to his work with the Society of Friends Church in Indianapolis and Plainfield, Hendricks Co.; papers relating to the teaching and book publishing professions, including correspondence with various teacher placement agencies and universities; and papers relating to Earlham College, Richmond, Wayne Co. (1919-1927). Also included are Frances Doan Streightoff's papers relating to the League of Women Voters in the 1920s; and her graduate school thesis from the University of Illinois (1911).

A-358. STUART, JAMES ARTHUR (1880-1975). PAPERS, 1907-1965.

2 ms. boxes.   Inventory.   M 268.

Stuart was a reporter (1905-1921), managing editor (1923-1946), and editor (1946-1960) of the *Indianapolis Star*; and editorial director, *Rocky Mountain News* and the *Denver Times* (1921-1923).

The collection consists primarily of Stuart's correspondence regarding his newspaper work in Indianapolis and Denver, including letters from writers regarding proposed articles and letters of appreciation for stories.

Correspondents include George Ade, Albert J. Beveridge, Claude Bowers, William Lowe Bryan, Irwin S. Cobb, Charles W. Fairbanks, John Watson Foster, Harold W. Handley, J. Frank Hanly, Will H. Hays, Herbert Hoover, Kin Hubbard, Edward L. Jackson, Robert Underwood Johnson, John W. Kern, Thomas R. Marshall, Meredith Nicholson, Samuel M. Ralston, Arthur R. Robinson, Booth Tarkington, Henry Watterson, Matthew Welsh, and William Allen White.

A-359. STUCKEY, WILLIAM ROBERTS (1838-1864). LETTERS, 1861-1864.

1 ms. box. Inventory. M 269.

Stuckey was a farmer near Lynnville, Warrick Co., and a soldier in the 42nd Indiana Regiment serving in Kentucky, Tennessee, and Georgia.

The collection consists of letters Stuckey wrote to his wife in Lynnville while he was serving in the Union Army.

A-360. STYER, WILLIAM (1832-1890). PAPERS, 1862-1863, 1881.

1 ms. box. Inventory. M 400.

Styer was a Kokomo, Howard Co., businessman and mill owner; 2nd lieutenant in the 89th Indiana Regiment (1862-1863); commander of military prison at Fort Pickering, near Memphis, Tenn. (1863); and discharged from the army for medical reasons (1863).

The collection consists primarily of Styer's Civil War letters to his wife in Kokomo, discussing army life, his responsibilities as commander of the military prison at Fort Pickering, and family financial matters. Also included are papers relating to an attempted robbery of Styer's mill in Kokomo in 1881.

A-361. SULLIVAN, JEREMIAH (1794-1870). LETTERS, 1843-1870.

1 ms. box, 4 vols. (5 l.f.).   M 270, BV 367-370.
Microfilm.

Sullivan was a Madison, Jefferson Co., attorney (1816-1870); member, Indiana House of Representatives (1819-1820); Indiana Supreme Court Justice (1837-1846); and active member of the Indiana Whig and Republican parties.

The collection consists of Sullivan's letters to his son, Algernon Sydney Sullivan, a student at Hanover College, Jefferson Co. (1843-1844), and Miami College, Ohio (1845); and an attorney at Cincinnati, Ohio (1849-1857), and New York City (1857-). The letters relate to Sullivan's Indiana Supreme Court work, the legal profession, affairs at Madison and Hanover College, the Mexican War, Indiana and national politics, and family business. Also included are letters relating to Algernon S. Sullivan's arrest for treason for attempting to defend a captured Confederate pirate (1861); and A. S. Sullivan's ledgers for his law practice in Cincinnati, Ohio (1849-1851, 1856) and for his personal finances in Cincinnati (1853-1854) and New York City (1857).

A-362. SUMMERS, FRANK WALLACE (ca.1925-). PAPERS, 1940-1946.

3 ms. boxes.   M 272.

Summers served with the 4th Troop Carrier Squadron, 62nd Troop Carrier Group, Army Air Force, during World War II.

The collection includes correspondence between Summers and his sister and friends in Indianapolis while he was serving in the Air Force at McClellan Field, Calif. (1941-1942); and in North Africa, Sicily, and Italy (1942-1945). Also included are newsletters, pamphlets, and other printed materials prepared for servicemen and a notebook of news releases and other papers regarding Summers's squadron.

A-363. TALBERT, MARTHA WHITE (1826-1890). DIARIES, 1845-1879.

1 ms. box.   M 275.

Talbert was a member of the Society of Friends in Westfield, Hamilton Co. (1826-1864), and Minneapolis, Minn. (1864-1890); and wife of physician Aaron B. Talbert.

The collection consists of Talbert's diaries recording her life in Westfield and Minnesota, including accounts of Quaker meetings and antislavery activities.

A-364. TARKINGTON, BOOTH (1869-1946). COLLECTION, 1927-1946.

1 ms. box.   M 274.

Tarkington was an Indianapolis writer, author of *Penrod* (1914), *The Magnificent Ambersons* (1918), *Alice Adams* (1921), and numerous other novels, short stories, and plays.

The collection consists of miscellaneous Tarkington letters and manuscripts, including a radio script, "Let's Look Before We Leap," on continuing the draft after World War II (1945); a manuscript of the article, "Christmas This Year" (1945); and transcripts of the correspondence between Tarkington and Indianapolis politician Carleton B. McCulloch.

The collection includes Tarkington's letters to Edward Bok, Fabien Sevitzky, Abris Silberman, and Samuel J. Woolf.

A-365. TARKINGTON, BOOTH (1869-1946). PAPERS, 1894-1962.

1 oversize box.   Calendar.   OM 100.

Tarkington was an Indianapolis writer, author of *Penrod* (1914), *The Magnificent Ambersons* (1918), *Alice Adams* (1921), and numerous other novels, short stories, and plays.

The collection consists primarily of letters Tarkington wrote from his summer home in Kennebunkport, Maine, to his niece, Margaret Booth Jameson, her husband, Donald Jameson, and their daughters in Indianapolis (1938-1945). In his letters Tarkington wrote of family and local matters, dispensed advice, and gave his political views on Fascism, Communism, the New Deal, and World War II. The collection also includes his "Notes for Nieces," pieces of advice on growing up; letters to the Jamesons from his wife and secretary; and correspondence between Susanah Tarkington and Albert D. Van Nostrand regarding a proposed biography of Tarkington (1949-1952).

A-366. TARKINGTON, SUSANAH (1870-1966). DIARIES, 1898-1932.

1 ms. box (6 vols.).   M 411.

Tarkington, born Susanah Kiefer in Dayton, Ohio, married writer Booth Tarkington in 1912.

The collection consists of her diaries for the years 1898, when she was a young woman in Dayton; 1913, shortly after she married Tarkington; 1925, when the Tarkingtons toured Europe and North Africa (1925); and 1929-1932.

A-367. THOMAS, ANNE BUTLER (fl.1880-1931). PAPERS, 1880-1925.

1 ms. box.   Inventory.   M 378.

Thomas was the daughter of educator Ovid Butler of Indianapolis and wife of David Owen Thomas of Minneapolis, Minn.

The collection includes Thomas's diaries (1880-1884) and letter books (1881-1885) regarding her social life, education, and experiences with suitors at Vassar College, N.Y. (1880), and Indianapolis. There is also a diary of her trip to Japan, India, and Ceylon (1924-1925).

A-368. THOMAS, JAMES S. (b.1834). LETTERS, 1861-1864.

54 items.   Calendar.   SC 1448.

Thomas was from Zionsville, Boone Co., and served as a sergeant in the 10th Indiana Regiment during the Civil War.

The collection consists of letters Thomas wrote to his sister in Zionsville while he served with the Union Army in Tennessee, Mississippi, and Georgia.

A-369. THOMPSON, RICHARD WIGGINTON (1809-1899). PAPERS, 1838-1899.

46 items.   Inventory.   SC 1914.

Thompson was an attorney in Bedford, Lawrence Co. (1834-1843), and Terre Haute, Vigo Co. (1843-1899); Whig member, U.S. House of Representatives (1841-1843, 1847-1849); secretary of the navy under Rutherford B. Hayes (1877-1880); and lobbyist and attorney for a number of railroad companies.

The collection includes letters to Thompson from G. B. Roberts of the Pennsylvania Railroad Company regarding Thompson's work on the company's behalf (1871-1882); miscellaneous letters to Thompson regarding Indiana politics (1838-1849), business interests of Thompson's clients in Illinois and Iowa (1846-1847), and Thompson's work representing the claims of the Wisconsin Menominee Indians (1851-1855); and Thompson's legal briefs (ca.1842, ca.1870) regarding Francis Vigo's claims against the U.S. government for his support of George Rogers Clark's expedition during the American Revolution.

Correspondents include Josephus Collett, Charles Dewey, Noah Noble, J. N. Phipps, and G. B. Roberts.

A-370. THORNTON, HENRY P. (1783-1865). PAPERS, 1816-1864.

1 ms. box.   Inventory.   M 277.

Attorney and politician. Thornton was an attorney in Kentucky and Madison, Jefferson Co. (1817-1820), Lexington, Scott Co. (1820-1825), Salem, Washington Co. (1825-1835), New Albany, Floyd Co. (1835-1855), and Bedford, Lawrence Co. (1855-1865); Whig member, Indiana House of Representatives (1831-1832, 1836-1837); and delegate, Indiana Constitutional Convention (1850-1851).

The collection includes court docket books for Thornton's cases in the Indiana Supreme Court (1848-1854) and in circuit courts in Floyd, Clark, Lawrence, and other southern Indiana counties (1852-1856); correspondence and documents regarding his legal business, including his work on behalf of War of 1812 veterans; papers relating to the 1850 Indiana Constitutional Convention; and personal financial records.

Correspondents include William H. English and James F. D. Lanier.

A-371. TRASK, GEORGE KELLOGG (d.1911). PAPERS, 1855-1901.

41 items.   Calendar.   SC 1468.

Trask was editor of the railroad column for the *Indianapolis Journal* (1871-1911).

The collection consists of letters to Trask regarding railroad business and his newspaper column, primarily from the period 1886-1893.

Correspondents include Elijah Walker Halford, George C. Hitt, and Harry S. New.

A-372. TUCKER, ROBINA SHARPE (1848-1930). AUTOBIOGRAPHY.

1 ms. box.   M 278.

Tucker was prominent in Indianapolis society; wife of Hannibal Smith Tucker (1844-1904), founder of the Tucker Glove Company in Indianapolis.

Tucker's autobiography concentrates on her early years growing up and attending school in Indianapolis during the 1850s and 1860s; visiting Missouri in the mid-1850s; and participating in Indianapolis social life in the 1860s and 1870s.

A-373. TUTEWILER, HENRY W. (1842-ca.1920). PAPERS, 1864-1920.

1 ms. box, 1 folder.   Inventory.   M 279, SC 1475.

Tutewiler was a lieutenant in the 17th Indiana Regiment (1862-1865), Indianapolis city treasurer (1872-1876), shoe salesman (1876-1885), and undertaker (1885-1920).

The papers include letters to Tutewiler from his fiancee and his father in Indianapolis during the last year of the Civil War and from army friends immediately after the war (1865-1866); patriotic songs, some written by Tutewiler and his son (1860s-ca.1900); and family business papers. Also included are photostatic copies of Tutewiler's diaries from Indianapolis (1859-1860) and while serving in the Union Army in Tennessee and Georgia (1863-1865).

Correspondents include John T. Wilder.

A-374. ULRICH, DANIEL (1794-1885?). PAPERS, 1796-1904.

49 items.   Calendar.   SC 1481.
Microfilm.

Ulrich was a farmer in Bedford County, Pa., and Hagerstown, Wayne Co., Ind. (1822-1885); and a member of the Church of the Brethren.

The collection consists of Ulrich family business papers from Pennsylvania (1796-1829); Ulrich's business papers and family correspondence while he lived in Wayne County (1830-1874); and correspondence (1877-1904) of Ulrich's son, Daniel D. Ulrich (1834-1912), a Wayne County farmer.

A-375. UNION REGULAR BAPTIST CHURCH. RECORDS, 1827-1962.

9 vols. (.75 l.f.).   SC 1807, BV 1980-1988.

The Union Regular Baptist Church was active in North Salem, Hendricks Co., from 1827 to 1952.

The collection consists of minutes and other church records (1827-1952), including records of the church's Sunday schools (1914-1935). Also included are articles of incorporation for the North Salem Baptist Church (1962).

A-376. URBANA (OHIO) BANKING COMPANY. PAPERS, 1815-1860.

133 items. SC 55.

The bulk of the papers are from the period 1835-1844 and consist of letters to the Urbana Banking Company in Urbana, Ohio, from Indiana businessmen and bankers. The letters describe economic conditions in Indiana and Ohio and discuss business and banking matters.

Correspondents include Noah Noble.

A-377. U.S. INFANTRY. FIRST INFANTRY COMPANY, SECOND OFFICERS TRAINING CAMP. RECORDS, 1919-1963.

1 ms. box. M 281.

The First Infantry Company, Second Officers Training Camp, was an organization of World War I veterans who had been trained together at Fort Benjamin Harrison, Indianapolis, in 1917, and served during the war in the First Infantry Company of the U.S. Infantry.

The collection includes the organization's correspondence, minutes, and meeting attendance lists.

A-378. USHER, NATHANIEL R. (1855-1931). PAPERS, 1871-1884.

1 ms. box. M 282.

Usher was a native of Vincennes, Knox Co.; a graduate of the U.S. Naval Academy, Annapolis, Md. (1875); and an officer in the U.S. Navy, reaching the rank of rear admiral (1911).

The collection consists primarily of letters Usher wrote to his family in Vincennes while he was attending the Naval Academy (1871-1875) and while serving as a midshipman on a naval cruise to Japan and China (1876-1877).

A-379. VAN DYKE, AUGUSTUS M. (1838-1918). PAPERS, 1860-1920.

1 ms. box.   Calendar.   M 284.

Van Dyke was a Vincennes, Knox Co., attorney (1860-1861); sergeant (1861) and lieutenant (1862-1863), 14th Indiana Regiment, Army of the Potomac; and assistant adjutant general, 4th Division, 15th Corps, Army of the Tennessee (1864-1865).

The collection consists of Van Dyke's Civil War letters to his family in Ripley County and to his fiancee, Alice Kent, in Jefferson County, while he served in Virginia and Georgia. The collection also includes Van Dyke's letters from Vincennes (1860-1861); and his letters to his fiancee from Nashville, Tenn., where he attempted to start a business (1866).

A-380. VAN PELT, MATHIAS C. (d.1878). PAPERS, 1825-1888.

2 ms. boxes.   Calendar.   M 286.

Van Pelt was a merchant in Shelbyville, Shelby Co. (1833-1836), and in Cincinnati, Ohio (1839-1878).

The bulk of the collection consists of Van Pelt's family correspondence from the period 1850-1878, including letters from relatives in St. Paul, Decatur Co., and New Albany, Floyd Co.; and correspondence between Van Pelt's daughter Edna and her fiance, Alfred Buckingham, while he was serving in the Civil War as a surgeon in the 77th Pennsylvania Regiment (1862) and at the post hospitals at Camps Butler and Douglas, Ill. (1864-1865). Also included is a small amount of Van Pelt's business correspondence, primarily from the period 1833-1850.

Correspondents include Edward A. Hannegan and James F. D. Lanier.

A-381. Vance, Samuel C. (d.1830). Papers, 1788-1902.

6 ms. boxes.   Calendar.   M 283.
Microfilm.

Soldier, merchant, and land speculator. Vance was an officer in the U.S. Army serving in the Northwest Territory (1791-1802); deputy paymaster of the U.S. Army stationed at Fort Washington, near Cincinnati (1799-1802); established town of Lawrenceburg, Ind. (1802); merchant and land speculator at Lawrenceburg, Dearborn Co. (1803-1830); Dearborn County clerk (1803-1813); and register, U.S. Land Office at Fort Wayne, Allen Co. (1823-1829). The collection also includes papers of his son, Lawrence M. Vance (1816-1863), partner of Hervey Bates in a general merchandise store in Indianapolis (1838); and a contractor for the construction of the Lawrenceburg and Upper Mississippi Railroad (1852-1853) and other railroad lines.

The bulk of the papers are from the period 1799-1893. Included are Samuel Vance's papers relating to the U.S. Army in the West and his administration of the Paymaster's Office; the establishment and functioning of his Lawrenceburg mercantile business, in partnership with former U.S. Army officer James Dill (1772-1838); his land interests; the Fort Wayne Land Office; and early Indiana and Ohio politics. Also included are papers of Lawrence Vance and his family, including papers relating to Vance's Indianapolis business and real estate dealings in the 1840s and 1850s and the construction of the Lawrenceburg and Upper Mississippi Railroad; accounts for home furnishings; and letters from his sons: Samuel, a student at Wabash College, Crawfordsville, Montgomery Co. (1855-1857), and major, 70th Indiana Regiment serving in Kentucky and Tennessee (1861-1863); Harvey, an officer at the headquarters of the 3rd Division, Army of the Tennessee (1862-1864); George, a sailor on the U.S.S. *Peosta*, stationed on the Ohio and Mississippi rivers (1863); and Laddie, a student at Wabash College (1870-1873). Postwar papers include family correspondence and financial papers, including letters from friends in northwest Florida (1876-1883).

Correspondents include Conrad Baker, Henry Ward Beecher, Jacob Burnet, Francis Costigan, Isaac Craig, Henry Dearborn, James Dill, Thomas Ewing, Calvin Fletcher, Albert Gallatin, Alexander Hamilton, Allen Hamilton, John Francis Hamtramck, William Hendricks, Gen. Washington Johnston, Nicholas Longworth, James McHenry, Nathaniel Massie, Return Jonathan Meigs, Samuel Merrill, James Noble, Noah Noble, Robert Dale Owen, Benjamin Parke, Zebulon Pike, Arthur St. Clair, Jr., John Cleves Short, Solomon

Sibley, Caleb Swan, William Wells, James Wilkinson, Thomas Hill Williams, and Andrew Wylie.

A-382. VANDERBURGH COUNTY MISCELLANEOUS PAPERS, 1815-1910.

1 ms. box.   M 335.

The collection consists of papers from several families and businesses in Evansville and Vanderburgh County. Included are personal and business letters (1863-1875) to Evansville lawyer and railroad developer John Ingle, Jr. (1812-1875); letters to the Vickery Brothers, Evansville grocers, from affiliated stores in Vincennes, Knox Co. (May 1867), and Rockport, Spencer Co. (1873-1876), regarding business conditions and product orders; personal letters to the Keen family from Petersburg, Pike Co. (1851-1897); and receipts and land documents, most from the 1860s.

A-383. VEATCH, JAMES C. (1819-1895). PAPERS, 1843-1895.

7 ms. boxes.   Inventory.   M 287.

Attorney, soldier, and public official. Veatch was a Rockport, Spencer Co., attorney (1840-1895); Spencer County school examiner (1838-1848, 1854-1859) and auditor (1841-1855); manager, *Rockport Herald* (1843); president, Rockport and Gentryville Plank Road Company (1843); Republican candidate for Congress (1856, 1868); member, Indiana House of Representatives (1860); delegate, Republican National Convention (1860, 1884); colonel, 25th Indiana Regiment (1861-1862); promoted to brigadier general, U.S. Volunteers (1862); commanding officer, District of Memphis, Tenn. (1863-1864); adjutant general of Indiana (1869-1870); and collector of Internal Revenue, First District of Indiana (1870-ca.1884).

The collection includes Veatch's correspondence regarding his pre-Civil War political and business interests in Spencer County; Veatch's Civil War correspondence, consisting of official military correspondence, letters regarding his administration of Memphis, and letters from Indiana regarding the political and military situation in the state; and postwar correspondence regarding Republican Party politics on the local and national level (1866-1884), his position as collector of Internal Revenue, and Civil War veterans affairs. Also included are Veatch's Civil War diary (January-July 1864); four letter books containing copies of his letters regarding political matters and his duties as collector (1870-1890); and his histories of the 25th Indiana Regiment and the Battle of Shiloh.

Correspondents include Conrad Baker, John Watson Foster, James A. Garfield, Walter Q. Gresham, Elijah M. Halford, Benjamin Harrison, Alvin P. Hovey, Oliver P. Morton, John C. New, Albert G. Porter, Daniel D. Pratt, William Tecumseh Sherman, and Lew Wallace.

A-384. VIGO, JOSEPH MARIA FRANCESCO (1747-1836). PAPERS, 1751-1841.

4 ms. boxes.　　　　　　　　Calendar.　　　　　　　　M 289.
Microfilm.

Merchant. Vigo was born in Mondovi, Italy; served in the Spanish army at New Orleans; established as a fur trader at St. Louis (1772); entered into secret business partnership with Spanish lieutenant governor Fernando de Leyba (1778); provided financial and intelligence assistance to George Rogers Clark during and after the American expedition against the British posts at Kaskaskia and Vincennes (1778-1779); moved to Vincennes, Knox Co. (1783); associated with the Miami Company and Todd, McGill & Company in the fur trade during the 1780s; traded with American merchants on the East Coast (1790s); served as colonel, Knox County Militia (1790-1810); assisted Anthony Wayne and William Henry Harrison in negotiations with Indians; and elected trustee, Vincennes University (1806).

The collection consists of Vigo's business and personal papers, primarily from the period 1783-1820. Included are papers relating to the fur trade at Vincennes, Fort Wayne, Detroit, and Montreal; Vigo's relations with John Askin and the Miami Company; his business dealings with the Piankashaw and other midwestern Indians; his land transactions at Vincennes, particularly regarding the donation lands granted by Congress in 1789 to the old French inhabitants of Vincennes; financial affairs of the French inhabitants of the Illinois Country and the American settlers around Vincennes; his work on behalf of Gens. Anthony Wayne and William Henry Harrison; and his efforts to collect repayment from Congress for his loans to George Rogers Clark during the American Revolution. Also included is the inventory of the estate of Fernando de Leyba (1780).

The collection includes papers of John Askin, John Badollet, Bishop Simon Brute de Remur, Lewis Cass, August Chouteau, John Ewing, John Hay Farnham, Pierre Gibault, John Francis Hamtramck, William Henry Harrison, Andrew Holmes, General Washington Johnston, John Law, Manuel Lisa, Pierre Menard, Benjamin Parke, Bartholomei Tardiveau, and William Wells.

A-385. VINCENNES MISCELLANEOUS PAPERS, 1769-1908.

1 ms. box.   M 290.

The collection consists of land documents, stock certificates, and family papers relating to people in Vincennes, Knox Co. Included are papers of the Foulks family (1852-1899), including letters of Samuel MeKee from Hanover College (1853-1855); constitution, bylaws, and minutes of the Vincennes Baseball Association (1882-1883); deeds and property transactions for land in the Vincennes area, principally from the period 1788-1858; and photocopies of the proceedings of the trustees of the Borough of Vincennes (1815-1816). In addition, there are papers relating to John Gibson, William Henry Harrison, Gen. Washington Johnston, and Francis Vigo.

A-386. VONNEGUT, CLEMENS (1824-1906). ACCOUNT BOOKS, 1859-1864.

2 vols. (.25 l.f.).   BV 387-388.

Vonnegut was a German immigrant and an Indianapolis hardware dealer.

The collection consists of Vonnegut's hardware store account books (1859-1864).

A-387. WABASH AND ERIE CANAL. RECORDS, 1839-1852.

11 items, 2 vols. (.25 l.f.).   SC 1515, BV 340a&b.

The states of Ohio and Indiana began construction of the Wabash and Erie Canal in the 1830s in order to provide a navigable waterway between Lake

Erie and the Ohio River, following the Maumee and Wabash rivers. The canal was completed in 1856 and was abandoned by 1875.

The collection includes minutes and reports of the Appraisers of Damages (1851-1852) responsible for determining the amount due to owners of lands damaged in the construction of the canal; lists of lands selected for the canal (1839); and letters declining invitations to the opening of the stretch of the canal between Toledo, Ohio, and Lafayette, Tippecanoe Co., Ind., held at Fort Wayne, Allen Co., July 4, 1843, including letters from William C. Bouck, Henry Clay, Richard M. Johnson, Samuel B. Ruggles, Winfield Scott, Martin Van Buren, Daniel Webster, and Levi Woodbury.

A-388. WADE FAMILY. PAPERS, 1831-1918.

2 ms. boxes. Inventory. M 328.

The Wade family included Isaac Ferris Wade (1811-1898), publisher and editor of the *Crawfordsville Record*, Montgomery County; his son, Harrison Heaton Wade (183?-1918), a soldier in the 11th Indiana Regiment, and a Lafayette, Tippecanoe Co., businessman after the Civil War; and H. H. Wade's daughters, Margaret Alethia Wade (1866-1939) and Lucy Wallace Wade (186?-1924).

The papers include the diaries of Lucy Wade (1890), Margaret Wade (1890-1897), and Harrison Wade (1918) describing everyday life in Lafayette; a listing of plays presented at the Lafayette Grand Opera House (1889-1892); scrapbooks of theater programs and playbills, most from Lafayette and Richmond, Wayne Co.; Civil War letters from Harrison H. Wade to his family (1861); family business papers (1831-1871); and a Wade family history.

A-389. WAINWRIGHT, WILLIAM A. (b.1832). PAPERS, 1862-1864.

1 ms. box. M 291.

Wainwright was a Noblesville, Hamilton Co., businessman; and quartermaster of the 75th Indiana Regiment (1862) and assistant quartermaster, Nashville, Tenn. (1864).

The collection consists of vouchers, lists, and other documents relating to supplies for the 75th Indiana Regiment (October-December 1862) and a small number of documents relating to army supplies at Nashville, Tenn.

A-390. WALKER, MADAM C. J. (1867-1919). COLLECTION, 1911-1979.

80 ms. boxes, 48 vols. (42 l.f.). Inventory. M 399.
Restricted.

Businesswoman. Madam C. J. (Sarah Breedlove) Walker was a laundress in St. Louis (1880s-1890s); manufacturer and seller of hair products for black women in St. Louis, Denver (1905-1906), Pittsburgh (1908-1910), and Indianapolis (1910); business incorporated as Madam C. J. Walker Manufacturing Company in Indianapolis (1911); owner of factory in Indianapolis and director of nationwide network of agents and beauty schools; prominent black philanthropist; resident of New York City from 1916, but company remained headquartered in Indianapolis. Also prominent in the company were her daughter A'Lelia Walker Robinson (1885-1931), president of the company (1919-1931) and a prominent social figure in Harlem during the 1920s; Freeman B. Ransom (1882-1947), company attorney (1911-1947) and general manager (1918-1947), and prominent black leader in Indianapolis; and Robert Brokenburr (1886-1974), company general manager (1947-1955) and chairman of the board (1945-1974), Indianapolis attorney, and Republican member, Indiana State Senate (1940-1948, 1952-1956).

The collection consists of records and correspondence of the Madam C. J. Walker Manufacturing Company and its principal officers. The company's correspondence includes Freeman B. Ransom's correspondence on the operations of the company with Madam Walker and A'Lelia Walker Robinson (1912-1931); his correspondence with other members of the Walker family, Walker Company employees and agents, and business associates regarding the company, real estate, and other business interests; correspondence and business papers of Madam Walker (1911-1919) and A'Lelia Walker Robinson (1911-1931); and correspondence of other Walker Company officers (1918-1977). The company's business records include financial records (1916-1968), orders and inquiries (1918-1977), delinquent accounts (1956-1958), payrolls (1913-1917), advertising (1912-1970), company yearbooks and almanacs (1924-1949), newsletters (1927-1932, 1948-1968), convention materials for Walker agents (1917-1953), and press releases and clippings (1917-1970). Also included are records of businesses associated with the Walker Company, including records of the Walker Beauty Schools (1923-1973), consisting of student records, financial records, and yearbooks for schools in Indianapolis (1945-1965), Chicago, Kansas City, Washington, D.C., and Tulsa, Okla.; records of the Walker Company Benevolent Association, an organization for Walker agents, including records of its unions in Newark and Atlantic City, N.J., Baltimore, Md., Cincinnati, Ohio, Knoxville, Tenn., and New York and White Plains, N.Y. (1927-1970); and records of businesses housed in the Walker Building in Indianapolis, including the Walker Theater (1927-1946), the Walker Realty Company (1927-1965), the Walker Casino (1929-1931), the Walker Drug Company (1929-1953), and the Coffee Pot (1951-1955).

A-391. WALLACE, LEW (1827-1905). PAPERS, 1799-1923.

36 ms. boxes, 2 vols. (9.5 l.f.).   Calendar.   M 292, BV 1751-1752.
Microfilm.

Author, soldier, and politician. Wallace was a lieutenant, 1st Indiana infantry during the Mexican War (1846-1847); a lawyer in Covington, Fountain Co. (1850-1853), and Crawfordsville, Montgomery Co. (1853-1905); Democratic member, Indiana State Senate (1857-1859); Indiana adjutant general (1861); colonel, 11th Indiana Regiment (1861); general and division commander in the Union Army (1862-1865); fought at Fort Donelson and Shiloh (1862); organized defenses of Cincinnati (1862-1863); commander, Middle Division, Baltimore, Md. (1864); led Union Army at Battle of Monocacy (July 1864); member of the court-martial which tried the conspirators in the Lincoln assassination (1865); president of commission which tried Henry Wirz, commander of the Andersonville Prison, Ga. (1865); involved in acquiring arms and men for Mexican rebels fighting the French (1865-1867); Republican candidate for Congress (1870); member of committee to oversee counting of disputed ballots in Florida, Louisiana, and South Carolina after 1876 presidential election; governor of New Mexico Territory (1878-1881); U.S. minister to Turkey (1881-1885); author, *The Fair God* (1873), *Ben Hur* (1880), *The Prince of India* (1893), and *Lew Wallace, an Autobiography* (1906); and lecturer.

The bulk of the collection is from the period 1846-1906 and consists of Wallace's correspondence with his wife and son, retained copies of Wallace's business and professional letters, and letters to Wallace and his family. Included are Wallace's letters from Mexico (1846-1847); letters to his wife describing his work during the Civil War, in Mexico (1865-1867), New Mexico (1878-1881), Turkey (1885), and on his tours throughout the United States (1886-1887, 1894); Wallace's official correspondence relating to the Civil War, New Mexico and the Lincoln County Wars, and Turkey; his business correspondence relating to Mexico (1865-1867), his publishing and lecture work, and his business interests in Crawfordsville, Indianapolis, and New Mexico; his notebooks relating to the 1876 elections, New Mexico, Turkey, and his lecture tours; a manuscript of his autobiography; his drawings of Wirz and the Lincoln conspirators; inventory of books in his library (1899); and clippings and scrapbooks relating to his career.

Also included are papers of Wallace's wife, Susan Elston Wallace (1830-1907), consisting of family correspondence, her letters to her son from Europe, Turkey, and Egypt (1881-1882), and correspondence with publishers regarding her own writings; letter books of Wallace's son and business agent, Henry Lane Wallace (1853-1926), relating to the family's business interests, and a lawsuit involving Wallace and his publisher, Harper & Brothers, against producers Klaw and Erlanger regarding the theatrical production of *Ben Hur*; papers of Wallace's father-in-law, Isaac C. Elston (1794-1867) of Crawfordsville, primarily relating to Elston's interests in developing Michigan City, LaPorte Co. (1830-1849); and Elston family correspondence, primarily from the period 1864-1866 from Crawfordsville, Cincinnati, and Washington, D.C.

Correspondents include Stephen Vincent Benet, James G. Blaine, William H. Bonney (Billy the Kid), Don Carlos Buell, Edward Canby, William Cannon, Jose M. J. Carvajal, William E. Chandler, Schuyler Colfax, Francis Marion Crawford, George W. Curtis, Caleb Cushing, Henry Winter Davis, Porfirio Diaz, William M. Evarts, Charles W. Fairbanks, Calvin Fletcher, Frederick T. Frelinghuysen, John C. Fremont, James A. Garfield, Lucretia Garfield, Richard J. Gatling, Ulysses S. Grant, Henry W. Halleck, Murat Halstead, Marcus A. Hanna, Benjamin Harrison, Edward Hatch, Rutherford B. Hayes, William Randolph Hearst, William Hendricks, William R. Holloway, Alvin P. Hovey, Jose Maria Iglesias, Frederick Knefler, Mary Hannah Krout, Henry S. Lane, Abraham Lincoln, Robert T. Lincoln, Benson J. Lossing, George W. McCrary, John A. Mclernand, Robert H. Milroy, George W. Morgan, Oliver P. Morton, Reuben D. Mussey, Edward F. Noyes, Robert Dale Owen, James B. Pond, Albert G. Porter, John Baptist Purcell, Whitelaw Reid, William S. Rosecrans, Carl Schurz, Winfield Scott, William H. Seward, William F. Shanks, John Sherman, William Tecumseh Sherman, Edmund Kirby Smith, John J. Speed, Edwin M. Stanton, Herman Sturm, John M. Thayer, Maurice Thompson, Will Henry Thompson, Benjamin H. Ticknor, John Tipton, John George Walker, David Wallace, Albert S. White, and Henry Lane Wilson.

A-392. WEAVER, JACOB (fl. 1814-1824). LETTERS, 1814-1824.

22 items.   Calendar.   SC 1548.

Weaver was a farmer and winemaker near Vevay, Switzerland Co.

The collection consists of letters from Weaver in Switzerland County, to his brothers and father in Ulster Co., N.Y. The letters describe farming and vine-growing techniques, prices, and the problems of starting a new settlement.

A-393. WEER, PAUL (1886-1956). PAPERS, 1940s-1956.

3 ms. boxes.   Inventory.   M 293.

Weer was curator of the Eli Lilly Archaeological Collection (1932-1956); writer on midwestern Indians; and contributor to *Walam Olum* (1954), the study of the tribal chronicle of the Delaware Indians.

The collection consists primarily of Weer's research notes and writings on midwestern Indians, including his manuscript biography of Stockbridge Indian leader Capt. Hendrick Aupaumut (1757-1830); manuscript "Brief History of New France"; research notes, letters, and papers on the Walam Olum and Constantine Rafinesque; notes and writings on the Moravian mission to the Delaware Indians; and miscellaneous notes on midwestern Indians.

Correspondents include Glenn Black and Eli Lilly.

A-394. WHITEWATER CANAL ASSOCIATION. RECORDS, 1941-1964.

4 folders.   SC 1567.

The Whitewater Canal Association was organized in 1941 by Brookville, Franklin Co., banker John P. Goodwin to preserve and restore the Whitewater Canal.

The records include the association's minutes (1941-1946); correspondence relating to meetings and work on the canal (1941-1946); financial information

(1942-1945); a report on activities (1964); and clippings and promotional material about the canal.

A-395. WILDMAN, JAMES A. (1834-1900). PAPERS, 1860-1898.

47 items. Inventory. SC 1575, OM 63.

Wildman was a merchant and farmer in Kokomo, Howard Co., and Indianapolis; Howard County auditor (1859-1865); Republican member, Indiana House of Representatives (1869); Indiana state auditor (1873-1875); part owner, Central Bank, Indianapolis (1874-1882); and Indianapolis postmaster (1881-1885).

The collection consists primarily of documents relating to Wildman's government positions, receipts for his contributions to the Indianapolis Board of Trade's mortuary benefit fund (1884-1895), and letters regarding Republican Party politics on the state and national levels (1883-1898).

Correspondents include Charles W. Fairbanks, Marcus A. Hanna, Benjamin Harrison, and Richard W. Thompson.

A-396. WILEY, JAMES JEROME (1822-1894). PAPERS, 1833-1925.

12 ms. boxes. Calendar. M 294.

Wiley was a farmer and sawmill operator at Metamora, Franklin Co.

The collection consists of family correspondence and business documents of Wiley and his father James Wiley (1795-1874), a Metamora farmer. Included are letters from family members in Wapello County, Iowa (1850-1884), Neosho and Smith counties, Kans. (1873-1893), and Switzerland County, Ind. (1867-1886); correspondence between Wiley and his business partners in a sawmill operation in Scott County, Miss. (1873-1875); letters of Wiley's daughter and son-in-law, Caroline and Edgar O'Hair, of Brookville, Franklin Co., and Indianapolis (1881-1925); family letters to Wiley's sister-in-law, Caroline Hawkins, of Laurel, Franklin Co., primarily from Indianapolis and Richmond, Wayne Co. (1891-1925); a large quantity of receipts for household goods purchased from Franklin County merchants; legal and business documents relating to the Wileys' farming and mill interests; business documents relating to Franklin County schools (1806-1843); and correspondence, business documents, and advertising from manufacturers of farm and mill equipment.

A-397. WILKINSON, ASBURY (1818-1909). PAPERS, 1837-1892.

1 ms. box., 7 vols. (.66 l.f.). Inventory. M 295, BV 1753-1757.

Wilkinson was a student at Indiana Asbury University, Greencastle, Putnam Co. (1838-1840); minister, Indiana Conference, Methodist Episcopal Church (1840-1878); and circuit rider through southern and eastern Indiana.

The bulk of the papers are from the period 1837-1866 and include letters to Wilkinson from relatives, friends, and fellow ministers writing from Indiana Asbury University, Whitewater Female College in Centerville, Wayne Co., Indianapolis, and Franklin, Dearborn, Harrison, Pike, and Shelby counties. Also included are Wilkinson's journals which describe his work as a circuit rider in Dearborn, Fayette, Jefferson, Perry, Pike, Posey, Rush, Scott, Shelby, Switzerland, Warrick, Washington, and Wayne counties (1840-1853).

A-398. WILLIAMS, HERBERT (1795-1867). COLLECTION, 1826-1893.

1 folder, 3 vols. (.25 l.f.). SC 1581, BV 87.

Williams was a farmer in Brooklyn, Conn., and Michigan City, LaPorte Co. (1836-1867).

The collection consists of Williams's account books for his farms in Connecticut and LaPorte County (1826-1852); and "Glimpses of My Mother's Life" (1893) by Williams's daughter, Ellen Williams, giving an account of her mother's life in Massachusetts and Connecticut prior to coming to Indiana in 1836.

A-399. WILLIAMS, PETER W. (1816-1902). PAPERS, 1849-1891.

2 ms. boxes.   Calendar.   M 298.

Williams was engaged in the shipment of hay and grain by flatboat from Aurora, Dearborn Co., to New Orleans, La.

The bulk of the papers are from the period 1849-1861 when Williams was spending much of his time as New Orleans agent for his shipping companies. The papers consist of correspondence, primarily business letters from his partners in Indiana, and receipts, accounts, bills of lading, and other business papers.

A-400. WILLIAMS, SAMUEL (1786-1859). PAPERS, 1817-1897.

2 ms. boxes.   Inventory.   M 301.

Public official. Williams was deputy marshal of Ohio during the War of 1812; clerk, General Land Office, Washington, D.C. (1814-1815); chief clerk for the Surveyor General of the Lands North-West of the Ohio River (1815-1845), located in Chillicothe, Ohio (1815-ca.1828), and Cincinnati (ca.1828-1845); and active in the Methodist Church.

The collection consists principally of Williams's personal and business correspondence from the period 1826-1859, including correspondence regarding the operations of the Surveyor General's office and the mapping and surveying of land in the Old Northwest, particularly Indiana; correspondence with Austin W. Morris of Indianapolis regarding the mapping of Indiana in the 1830s; letters from Samuel Widney, a DeKalb County farmer, regarding business and religion (1837-1842); and letters of his son, E. T. Williams, an architect and temperance advocate living in Chillicothe (1836-1840), Dover, Tenn. (1840-1851), and Greensburg, Decatur Co. (1851-1859). Also included are letters from authors concerning manuscripts submitted to the Western Methodist Book Concern, Cincinnati, Ohio (1860-1897).

A-401. WILLIAMS, SAMUEL PORTER (1814-1897). PAPERS, 1846-1892.

1 ms. box.   Inventory.   M 300.

Williams was a Lima, LaGrange Co., merchant (1836-1897); owned branch store in Blandinsville, Ill. (1848-1855); established LaGrange Bank of Lima (1853); president, Lima branch of the State Bank of Indiana (1856); and trustee, Wabash College, Crawfordsville, Montgomery Co.

The collection includes Williams's diaries recording bank business in Lima (1863-1864); letters from the Indiana state auditor's office regarding LaGrange bank notes (1854-1863); letters of Caleb Mills regarding Wabash College affairs (1860-1862); expense books for Williams's store in Blandinsville (1849-1852); additional notebooks recording accounts (1846-1857); and certificates of deposit for the LaGrange Bank (1854-1856).

A-402. WILLIAMS, WORTHINGTON B. (1815-1891). FAMILY PAPERS, 1812-1926.

5 ms. boxes.   Calendar.   M 302.

Williams was raised in Poughkeepsie, N.Y., and was a farmer near Putnamville, Putnam Co. (1836-1891). Other family members whose papers figure prominently in the collection are Williams's father-in-law, Isaac Reed (1788-1858), a theology student in New York and Connecticut (1814-1817), itinerant Presbyterian minister in Kentucky, Indiana, Illinois, and Ohio (1817-1858), and author of *The Christian Traveller* (1828); and Williams's son, Josiah C. Williams (d.1900), lieutenant and captain in the 27th Indiana Regiment serving in Maryland and Virginia (1861-1863) and Tennessee and Georgia (1863-1864), and army provost marshal at Tullahoma, Tenn. (1864).

The largest section of the collection contains the papers of Josiah Williams, consisting of his letters to his father while attending school in Poughkeepsie (1851-1858) and while serving in the Union Army (1861-1865), his army diaries (1861-1864), official military correspondence and papers, and a copy of a report by Brig. Gen. Thomas H. Ruger on the Atlanta Campaign (April-September 1864). The collection also includes Civil War letters of Josiah's brother, Edwin Williams, 115th Indiana Regiment serving in Kentucky and Tennessee (1863-1864), and uncle, George W. Reed, 27th Indiana serving in Virginia and Maryland (1861-1862); papers of Isaac Reed, including his diaries from New York, Kentucky, and Indiana (1814-1818, 1850), family and business letters (principally 1845-1854), a prospectus for a girls school in Terre Haute run by the Reeds (1845), and manuscripts of thirty-nine sermons; and other personal letters of the Williams family (1839-1926), including letters from Putnamville, from Williams's father in Poughkeepsie (1839-1864), and from his daughter and son-in-law, Gertrude and Edwin Williamson, during their trip to Europe and Palestine (1886-1887).

Correspondents include Baynard R. Hall, Caleb Mills, and Albert S. White.

A-403. WOMAN'S FRANCHISE LEAGUE OF INDIANA. RECORDS, 1917-1919.

32 items. SC 1761.

The Woman's Franchise League, predecessor of the League of Women Voters, was a leader in the women's suffrage movement in Indiana.

The collection consists of league records from the period 1917-1919, including printed suffrage campaign leaflets and training material for campaign workers; correspondence from the league's state headquarters in Peru, Miami Co.; financial reports; and clippings on the suffrage movement.

A-404. WOMAN'S IMPROVEMENT CLUB. RECORDS, 1903-1981.

1 ms. box. M 432.

The club, organized in 1903, promotes civic activities and sponsors self-improvement programs for black women in Indianapolis. Among the club's activities was the sponsorship of an open-air camp near Indianapolis for black tuberculosis patients (1905).

The records include minutes (1909-1918); account books (1924-1931, 1959-1965); letters regarding club activities (1911-1926, 1976-1981); membership lists; and club constitutions.

A-405. WOMAN'S PRESS CLUB OF INDIANA. RECORDS, 1913-1978.

10 ms. boxes, 2 vols. (2.75 l.f.).   Inventory.   M 373, BV 1991-1993.

The Woman's Press Club of Indiana started in 1913 as a social and professional organization for women reporters and writers and is a charter member of the National Federation of Press Women (1937).

The records consist of the club's minutes and correspondence (1913-1976); financial reports and papers (1913-1976); membership and attendance lists (1942-1974); publications such as the *Mid Day Moon* (1915-1916) and the *Monthly Bulletin* (1935-1976); scrapbooks (1913-1947); and clippings on the activities of the club and its members (1971-1976).

A-406. WOMEN IN COMMUNICATIONS, INC., INDIANAPOLIS CHAPTER. RECORDS, 1915-1981.

6 archival boxes, 2 ms. boxes (6.5 l.f.).   Inventory.   M 375.

Women in Communications, Inc., was founded in 1909 as Theta Sigma Phi, a national college honorary society for women in journalism. It has been active in providing training in communications work, in promoting professional recognition for women in the communications field, and lobbying for legislation relating to communications and equal rights for women. The name Women in Communications, Inc., was adopted in 1972. The Indianapolis Chapter was started in 1928 by students at Butler, Indiana, and DePauw universities.

The records include bylaws and constitutions (1918-1977); minutes (1941-1977); financial statements and reports, including account and receipt books (1934-1970s); correspondence; clippings and scrapbooks; membership lists and initiation materials (1939-1980); papers relating to the WIC's scholarship, membership, and awards programs for young people (1923-1978); meeting materials and reports, including WIC regional conferences (1976-1979); WIC-sponsored contests and awards (1950s-1970s); publicity guides and public relations materials; and local and national publications such as the national *Matrix* magazine (1915-1918), the national *Newsletter* (1941-1980), and the Indianapolis chapter's newsletter, *File* (1950-1981).

A-407. WORDEN, CHARLES J. (1892-1948). COLLECTION, 1836-1940.

1 ms. box.   M 306.

Worden was the nephew of Marshall W. Wines and grand-nephew of Marshall S. Wines, the two principal figures in the collection. Marshall S. Wines (d.1842) was a Fort Wayne, Allen Co., miller; contractor on the Wabash and Erie Canal in Indiana and Ohio (1836-1842); Allen County associate judge (1837-1841); and Democratic member, Indiana House of Representatives (1841-1842). His son, Marshall W. Wines (fl.1841-1928) was a clerk in a Fort Wayne dry goods store (1856-1861); clerk in the Pension Office, Washington, D.C. (1862-1863); and captain, 152nd Indiana Regiment (1865).

The collection consists primarily of the papers of Marshall S. Wines, his wife Elizabeth, and his son Marshall W. (1836-1866). Included is the elder Wines's correspondence from Indianapolis and Fort Wayne regarding his work on the canal and family matters (1836-1842); family letters to Elizabeth Wines from Fountain and Lawrence counties, Ind., and Washington, D.C. (1842-1851); family letters (1857-1859) of Attica, Fountain Co., merchant Jacob F. Hoffman, including letters from his trip to New Orleans; letters (1861-1866) to Marshall W. Wines from Indiana politicians regarding Fort Wayne politics, Wines's career, and personal matters; documents relating to Wines's work with the 152nd Indiana Regiment (1865); and a letter from Franklin D. Roosevelt to Wines regarding the 1928 presidential election.

Correspondents include Charles Case, James A. Cravens, Andrew J. Hamilton, Thomas A. Hendricks, William S. Holman, James Whitcomb Riley, and Franklin Delano Roosevelt.

A-408. WRIGHT, WILLIAMSON (1814-1896). PAPERS, 1833-1890.

1 ms. box.   Calendar.   M 307.

Wright was an attorney in Lancaster, Ohio (1835), and Logansport, Cass Co. (1835-1891); Whig member, Indiana State Senate (1840-1843); candidate for U.S. Congress (1849); and president, Cincinnati, Logansport, and Chicago Railroad (1853).

The collection consists primarily of deeds, receipts, and legal papers of Wright and his clients in Cass County and northern Indiana (1835-1850). Also included is a small amount of political correspondence (1840-1849).

Correspondents include Daniel R. Bearss, William H. English, Joseph G. Marshall, Samuel C. Sample, and John Tipton.

A-409. YOUNG, W. L. (fl.1900s-1910s). ACCOUNT BOOKS, 1909, 1916.

3 vols. (.25 l.f.).   BV 391-393.

Young managed a general store in Shannondale, Montgomery Co.

The collection consists of Young's daybooks for 1909 and 1916 and a ledger for 1916.

A-410. ZULAUF, JOHN (1818-1873). PAPERS, 1835-1873.

1 ms. box, 4 vols. (.75 l.f.).   Partial Calendar.   M 308, BV 1769-1772.

Businessman. Zulauf was born in Thurgan, Switzerland; clerked for banks and manufacturing firms in England, France, and other European countries; employed to represent from 1846-1873 the Swiss heirs of John Fischli (d.1838), a Clark County, Ind., landowner; opened a lace and silk importing store in Louisville, Ky. (1848); and appointed Swiss consul to the western states (1848).

The bulk of the papers are German language letters to Zulauf from his family and employers in Switzerland from the period 1835-1866. Also included are correspondence, depositions, and other legal and financial papers relating to Zulauf's work in Clark County and the Indiana state legislature on behalf of the Fischli heirs (1846-1856); letters from the Rothschild brothers in Paris regarding Zulauf's financial transactions (1856-1858); ledgers recording his work on the Fischli estate (1850-1870); and business papers and ledgers for his personal business and real estate interests in Louisville and Clark County (1848-1873).

COLLECTIONS
OF THE
INDIANA DIVISION,
INDIANA STATE LIBRARY

B-1. ABORN, MARY J. (fl.1852-1927). COLLECTION, 1815-1908.

1 ms. box.   L 1.

Aborn was a Marshfield, Warren Co., historian and wife of physician Dr. Orin Aborn (1826-1885).

The largest part of the collection consists of papers of Ebenezer F. Lucas (1807-1871), a businessman in Williamsport and State Line City, Warren Co.; clerk, Warren County Circuit Court (1838); Warren County treasurer (1842); engineer and superintendent, Wabash and Erie Canal (1842-1846); and assistant marshal to aid in taking the 8th U.S. Census (1860). Lucas's papers include his correspondence regarding the operation of the Wabash and Erie Canal; correspondence, surveys, and legal documents relating to his business and land interests in Warren County; and papers relating to the 1860 census. The collection also includes Aborn's correspondence and writings relating to early Warren County history and the removal of Indians from Indiana; two scrapbooks of clippings on Warren County history from the 1880s, pasted in on Dr. Aborn's account books from the 1850s and 1870s; and record of the treasurer for [Warren County?] school district #1 (1834).

Correspondents include Henry W. Ellsworth, Elisha Gale English, Allen Hamilton, Edward A. Hannegan, Joseph E. McDonald, Daniel Mace, David Turpie, James Whitcomb, and William Wesley Woollen.

B-2. ADAIR, E. ROSS (1907-). PAPERS, 1950-1970.

169 archival boxes, 12 ms. boxes (173 l.f.).   Inventory.

Politician. Adair was an attorney in Fort Wayne, Allen Co. (1933-1950); 2nd lieutenant in Army Quartermaster Corps in Europe (1941-1945); Republican member, U.S. House of Representatives (1951-1971); member of the House Foreign Relations Committee and the House Veterans Affairs Committee; U.S. Ambassador to Ethiopia (1971-1974); member of the board, Hillsdale College, Mich.; and member of the board, Delta Sigma Phi fraternity.

The collection consists primarily of Adair's congressional papers (1950-1970). Included are Adair's Foreign Affairs Committee papers (1958-1970), including papers relating to Vietnam, Cuba, NATO, U.S. policy toward Africa, and other foreign policy issues; Veterans Affairs Committee papers (1960-1970), including papers and legislation on pensions, health programs, and other veterans benefits; papers regarding federal programs in Adair's district, including defense contracts to local firms, air service to Fort Wayne and other cities, highway construction, flood control on the Maumee River, and the economic development of Fort Wayne; correspondence, reports, and legislation on other domestic and foreign issues before Congress; papers relating to Adair's congressional trips to Inter-Parliamentary Union meetings in Europe (1959-1967), and trips to the Far East (1953-1955), the Mideast (1966), Africa (1968), and Vietnam (1970); constituent requests for assistance and information; papers relating to Adair's election campaigns (1950-1970); newsletters, press releases, broadcasts, speeches, and other publicity items; and papers relating to Hillsdale College and the Delta Sigma Phi fraternity.

B-3. ALLIANCE AMUSEMENT COMPANY. RECORDS, 1931-1968.

21 l.f.

The Alliance Amusement Company was a Chicago-based corporation which operated theaters and fast-food restaurants in the Midwest.

The collection consists of records of the company's Indiana operations, including theaters in a number of Indiana towns and McDonald's restaurants in Fort Wayne, Allen Co., and other places. Included is correspondence and business records regarding the management, supplies, expenses, and accounting for the subsidiary businesses (1949-1968); papers regarding theater openings, promotions, and bookings for films and live shows (1942-1959); and minutes and financial records of affiliated theaters in Marion, Grant Co., Kokomo, Howard Co., Frankfort, Clinton Co., Anderson, Madison Co., Terre Haute, Vigo Co., Delphi, Carroll Co., Fowler, Benton Co., Connersville, Fayette Co., and Fort Wayne.

B-4. ALTROCCHI, JULIA COOLEY (1893-1972). PAPERS, 1933-1958.

4 ms. boxes. L 245.

Altrocchi was a Berkeley, Calif., poet, novelist, and lecturer; and author of *Wolves against the Moon*, a novel based upon the life of Joseph Bailly (1774-1835), a northwestern Indiana Indian trader.

The collection is made up of papers relating to *Wolves against the Moon*, including research correspondence and notes, a manuscript of the book, reviews, and correspondence with Harold S. Latham and others at The MacMillan Company, the book's publisher. Also contained are notes and a manuscript on the Fort Dearborn, Ill., massacre.

B-5. AMERICAN LUNG ASSOCIATION OF CENTRAL INDIANA. RECORDS, 1913-1976.

74 l.f.

The association was organized in 1913 as the Marion County Tuberculosis Association to combat tuberculosis and promote public health legislation. The association sponsored research into tuberculosis and lung diseases; sponsored checkups and tests; and operated the Sunnyside Sanatarium at Oaklandon (1917-1967). In 1971 the association was restructured as the Central Indiana Tuberculosis and Respiratory Disease Association and became the American Lung Association of Central Indiana in 1973.

Association records include reports, studies, statistics, financial records, correspondence, and printed materials relating to the organization's programs for combating tuberculosis and lung diseases, including Christmas Seal campaigns; health programs; education programs for professionals and lay persons; nutrition camps (1930s); X-ray and other testing programs; relationships with hospitals and other health and charitable organizations in Marion County, especially the Marion County Division of Public Health; and rehabilitation and assistance for TB patients. In addition there are association annual reports, board meeting minutes, and financial records; correspondence and reports of Sunnyside Sanatarium (1917-1967) and the Indianapolis Flower Mission (1949-1952); X-ray results and analyses of individual cases of TB, including reports on potential draftees who claimed TB disabilities during World Wars I and II, and treatments and testings of TB at the Marion County Jail (1956); legislation; committee papers; materials from the state and national tuberculosis associations; papers regarding the restructuring of the association in the late 1960s; scrapbooks (1916-1975); and films, film strips, posters, and other educational materials.

B-6. AMERICAN NEGRO EMANCIPATION CENTENNIAL AUTHORITY, INDIANA DIVISION. RECORDS, 1962-1963.

2 folders. S 1506.

The American Negro Emancipation Centennial Authority was organized to commemorate the one hundredth anniversary of the Emancipation Proclamation.

The records include newsletters, flyers, programs, press releases, church bulletins, and clippings relating to the Authority's work and the Emancipation Proclamation Luncheon in Indianapolis (December 1962) and the Century of Negro Progress Exposition in Indianapolis (October 1963). Also contained are speeches by Indiana University President Elvis Stahr, Jr., and U.S. State Department official Samuel Z. Westerfield, Jr., and a scrapbook on the Authority's activities kept by state chairman Willard B. Ransom.

B-7. ANDERSON, CALEB (b.1814). PAPERS, 1856-1889.

32 items. S 22.

Anderson operated a flour mill in Ladoga, Montgomery Co.

The collection is made up of Anderson's diaries (1875, 1881, 1884-1885) recording the weather, prices, and his accounts; other family letters and business papers; correspondence of John T. Anderson regarding his work as agent of the Louisville, New Albany & Chicago Railroad in Ladoga (1864-1865); and John T. Anderson's record book of goods woven at the Ladoga mills (1882-1887).

B-8. ANDREW & COOKE. ACCOUNT BOOKS, 1839-1852.

6 vols. (.75 l.f.). V 193.

The firm of Andrew & Cooke owned a general store in Darlington, Montgomery Co.

The collection includes account books and daybooks for the Andrew & Cooke store (1839-1841); an account book for the Jenners & Sergeant general store in Darlington (1843-1847); and an account book for an unidentified general store in Darlington (1851-1852).

B-9. ARTHUR, CHRISTOPHER (1833-1898). ACCOUNT BOOKS, 1882-1899.

2 vols.   V 1.

Arthur was a physician in Portland, Jay Co.

The collection consists of his medical account books (1882-1899); and articles of association, bylaws, and minutes of the board of the Equitable Accident and Mutual Aid Life Association, Portland.

B-10. BAILEY, LOUIS J. (1881-1962). PAPERS, 1916-1934.

2 folders.   Inventory.   S 50.
Microfilm.

Bailey was librarian of the Gary (Lake Co.) Public Library (1908-1922); director of the Indiana State Library, Indianapolis (1922-1936); and chief librarian, Queensborough Public Library, New York (1936-1953).

The collection consists primarily of papers relating to books, Indiana history, and American and Indiana libraries, collected during Bailey's time as Indiana State Library Director. Included are brochures, pamphlets, articles, clippings, correspondence, speeches, and memoranda.

B-11. BAILLY DE MESSEIN, JOSEPH (1774-1835). PAPERS, 1794-1940.

5 ms. boxes.   Inventory.   L 5.

Merchant. Bailly was a fur trader at Michilimackinac (1793-1812) and southwest Michigan and northwest Indiana (1812-1835); established trading post and missionary center near Chesterton, Porter Co. (1822); and maintained trading centers at Baton Rouge, La., and Montreal, Canada.

The collection consists primarily of Bailly's accounts, financial journals, and inventory books relating to his fur trade business (1794-1835). Also included are retained copies of a small number of his letters relating to business (1800-1801); letters and other papers relating to the settlement of his estate (1836); account book for the Chicago and Lake Superior Mining Company (1846-1847); and letters and notes of Julia Cooley Altrocchi relating to her research on Bailly.

B-12. BAINBRIDGE, EUGENE (1911-1972). PAPERS, 1953-1972.

13 archival boxes, 1 ms. box (13.4 l.f.).

Politician. Bainbridge was involved in the oil business in East Chicago and Munster, Lake Co. (1933-1971); secretary-treasurer, Oil Dealers, Inc. (1953-1971); president, E. H. Bainbridge Supply Company (1965-1971); Democratic member, Indiana State Senate (1953-1961, 1965-1972); and director, Indiana Department of Public Works and Supplies (1961-1965).

The collection consists principally of papers relating to Bainbridge's career in the Indiana State Senate. Included are correspondence, legislation, reports, and other papers relating to issues before the Indiana Senate, such as public employees' and teachers' retirement funds, the highway department, reapportionment, development of port facilities (1969), abortion, and education reform and school financing (1965-1971); papers relating to Lake County issues before the Senate, including airport construction in the county; and election campaign material (1956-1972), including papers relating to his 1970 primary campaign for the U.S. Congress. In addition there are business papers relating to the Bainbridge Supply Company and Oil Dealers, Inc. (1960s); newspapers and scrapbooks relating to Indiana politics and Lake County; and constituent correspondence of Bainbridge's son, Phillip Bainbridge, while serving in the Indiana House of Representatives (1969).

B-13. BAKER, CHARLES T. (b.1871). LETTERS, 1936-1941.

70 items. S 53.

Baker was owner and publisher of the newspaper *Grandview Monitor*, Grandview, Spencer Co. (1905-1942); and a historian of southern Indiana and Abraham Lincoln.

The collection consists of Baker's letters to Thelma Murphy of Indianapolis on Spencer County history and Abraham Lincoln's Indiana years.

B-14. BAKER, IDA STRAWN (b.1876). PAPERS, 1912-1940.

1 ms. box. L 6.

Artist. Baker was an Indianapolis artist; president, Waldcraft Laboratories, Inc. (1930-ca.1942), an Indianapolis art and craft supply business; and active in the Waldcraft Center, a nonprofit group offering assistance to artists and professional help in crafts and frescoes.

The collection consists of Baker's diaries and sketchbooks, including a diary of a 1925 trip to Europe, and diaries (1938-1940) recording her daily life and business affairs; and sketchbooks showing scenes in California (1912) and of World War I army camps in Kentucky, Michigan, and Ohio (1917-1918).

B-15. BALLARD, MRS. CHARLES W. COLLECTION, 1827-1930.

1 ms. box. L 7.

Ballard, the wife of Roachdale, Montgomery Co., collector Charles W. Ballard, donated the collection to the Indiana State Library in 1965.

The collection consists of letters, documents, and other papers relating to a number of Montgomery County families. Included are letters to Caleb H. R. Anderson, Ladoga, from relatives in Indianapolis and Minnesota (1852-1856); letters to Ellen Dinneen[?], Crawfordsville, from her son in the 158th Indiana Regiment during the Spanish-American War (1898), and from other family members in Cincinnati, Ohio (1898), and Gas City, Grant Co. (1901-1902); and letters of other families from Waveland, Montgomery Co. (1885), Bogota, Ill. (1883), Louisville, Ky. (1890-1894), San Jose, Calif. (1884-1890), Baltimore, Md. (1886), and other places.

B-16. BALTZELL, ROBERT C. (1879-1950). PAPERS, 1904-1936.

2 ms. boxes.   L 8, L 248.

Baltzell was a Princeton, Gibson Co., attorney (1904-1925); judge, Gibson County Circuit Court (1920-1925); U.S. District judge, Indianapolis (1925-1950); and active in Republican Party affairs.

The collection includes four scrapbooks documenting Baltzell's career, particularly as a federal judge trying murder, bootlegging, and other cases, including the murder trial of George W. Barrett for killing an F.B.I. agent (1935-1936). Also included is a notebook listing his cases, the names of jurors, and the trial results (1932-1935).

B-17. BALZ, ARCADA (1880?-1973). PAPERS, 1928-1968.

2 ms. boxes.   L 9.

Politician and civic leader. Balz was active in the Indiana Federation of Women's Clubs, serving as president (1935-1937); president, New Harmony Memorial Commission (1939-1950s); Republican member, Indiana State Senate (1943-1950); and wife of Frederick C. Balz (d.1954), owner of Star Millinery Company, Indianapolis.

The papers are made up of Balz's correspondence, notes, articles, and other materials relating to the Indiana Federation of Women's Clubs, the New Harmony Memorial Commission and the preservation of the Fauntleroy House there (1934-1964), her work in the Indiana State Senate, and her family history research. Also included are her notebooks of meeting notes, speech outlines, and personal notes (1940-1959); a paper on the Edgeworthalean Society, a woman's club in Bloomington, Monroe Co. (1841-1844); and family correspondence (1964-1968).

B-18. BARNETT FAMILY. PAPERS, 1850-1955.

1 ms. box.   L 11.

The collection includes papers of George Barnett (1827-1892), a Winamac, Pulaski Co., merchant; and Henry J. Barnett (fl.1904-1939), a Winamac farmer and poultry dealer.

The collection consists of Barnett family correspondence, including letters to George Barnett and his family from Winamac (1851-1866), Belleville, Ill. (1859-1903), and Logansport, Cass Co. (1861-1870); George Barnett's letters to his wife while on business in St. Louis and New Orleans (1859-1868); letters to Henry J. Barnett from his brother, Ambrose Barnett, a hotelkeeper in Grand Rapids and Muskegon, Mich. (1904-1928); letters of J. P. Barnett while serving in the Indiana State Legislature in Indianapolis (1869); and other family papers.

B-19. BARNHART, HENRY A. (1858-1934). PAPERS, 1880-1940.

13 ms. boxes.   Partial Inventory.

Publisher, politician, and businessman. Barnhart was Fulton County Auditor (1885-1887); owner of the *Rochester Sentinel* (1886-1924); president and manager, Rochester Telephone Company (1895-1934); Democratic member, U.S. House of Representatives (1908-1919); president, Indiana Telephone Association (ca.1924-1934) and the National Telephone Association (1901-1903); president, Northern Indiana Editorial Association (ca.1905); director, Indiana State Prison, Michigan City (1893-1896); and appointed trustee of State Hospital for the Insane (1903).

The collection consists primarily of Barnhart's business and political correspondence, including his correspondence as owner of the *Rochester Sentinel* regarding operational costs, advertising, the paper's editorials and news stories, and the Northern Indiana Editorial Association (1890s-ca.1906); his correspondence as president of the Rochester Telephone Company regarding operational costs, rates, and regulations of the telephone industry, employee relations, and the work of the Indiana Telephone Association and the National Telephone Association (1906-1934); and his political correspondence, principally his congressional constituent letters dealing with local politics, political appointments, and national issues such as the war in Europe, the National Security League, and women's suffrage. Additional material includes correspondence and family documents; his scrapbooks and mementos; and two manuscript humor newspapers (1881).

Correspondents include John A. M. Adair, W. A. Banta, Winfield T. Durbin, Benjamin F. Shively, John B. Stoll, and J. M. Studebaker.

B-20. BARNHART, HUGH A. (1892-). PAPERS, 1898-1964.

26 ms. boxes.   Inventory.

Businessman and public servant. Barnhart was the son of Henry A. Barnhart of Rochester, Fulton Co.; served in the U.S. Army during World War I; publisher, *Rochester Sentinel* (1919-1961); president, Rochester Telephone Company (1934-1976); member and director, Indiana State Highway Commission (1932-1933); Democratic nominee for U.S. Congress (1936); Excise Administrator of Indiana, part of the Alcoholic Beverage Commission (1937-1941); director, Indiana State Department of Conservation (1941-1945); director, Public Service Company of Indiana, an electric utility company (1950s); board of directors, U.S. Independent Telephone Association (1950s-1960s), president (1958-1959); committee member, "Little Hoover" Committee, which reorganized state government agencies in Indiana (1952-1953); and director, Communications Division, Business and Defense Administration, U.S. Department of Commerce (1955).

The collection consists principally of Barnhart's business and political papers from the period 1932-1964. Included is his correspondence as a member of the State Highway Commission (1932-1933); correspondence, speeches, campaign literature, and other materials relating to political campaigns in 1934 and 1936; financial papers of the Indiana Telephone Association (1933-1935); correspondence with the Cole Brothers/Clyde Beatty Circus, in which Barnhart had a financial interest (1930s-1950s); correspondence, reports, and complaints filed in his office as Excise Administrator of Indiana; correspondence, financial records, and minutes of meetings of the Governors Advisory Committee of the Commission on Interstate Cooperation, which dealt with liquor control and other issues; field examiner reports, minutes of meetings, annual reports, and other records of the Indiana Department of Conservation (1941-1948); correspondence and business reports of the *Rochester Sentinel* (1930s-1940s); correspondence and reports of the "Little Hoover" Committee, particularly papers relating to the determination of which state agencies would regulate flood control and water resources (1952-1953); reports and correspondence of the Rochester Telephone Company (1937-1963); reports, minutes, and papers of the U.S. Independent Telephone Association and the Bell Acquisition Committee, primarily regarding the sale or acquisition of local telephone companies (1943-1964); annual reports of the Public Service Company of Indiana (1951-1955); and papers relating to Barnhart's work in the U.S. Department of Commerce (1955). Also included are Barnhart's personal and family correspondence; correspondence, scrapbooks, and financial records from his service in the U.S. Army (1917-1918); papers relating to the settlement and operation of the Henry Barnhart estate (1933-1940); and personal expense records (1937-1952).

Correspondents include Alben W. Barkley, Glenn Griswold, Charles A. Halleck, Louis Ludlow, Ken Maynard, Sherman Minton, Eugene Pulliam, Henry F. Schricker, M. Clifford Townsend, and Herman B Wells.

B-21. BARTHOLOMEW, ORION (b.1838?). PAPERS, 1854-1894.

82 items. S 72.

Attorney and soldier. Bartholomew was the son of a Danville, Hendricks Co., physician; a student at Indiana Asbury University, Greencastle, Putnam Co. (1856-1861); soldier and officer in the 7th Indiana (3 month) Regiment (1861), and 70th Indiana Regiment serving in Kentucky and Tennessee (1862-1864); lieutenant colonel, 15th United States Colored Infantry, serving in Tennessee, Virginia, and Texas (1864-1865); and attorney in Charion, Iowa.

The bulk of the collection consists of Bartholomew's letters to his family in Danville, written while he was attending Indiana Asbury University and serving in the Civil War (1856-1862). Also included are letters from his brother, Levi Bartholomew, from Indiana Asbury (1862) and the 7th and 117th Indiana regiments (1862-1863); letters from his brother, Frank Bartholomew, from Indiana Asbury (1866-1867); and an 1894 letter from DePauw University (formerly Indiana Asbury).

B-22. BARTON, JOSEPH T. (1813-1889). PAPERS, 1809-1927.

1 ms. box. L 12.

Barton was a farmer in western Virginia and near Mier, Grant Co. (1848-1889).

The papers include family letters from Harveysburg, Ohio (1849-1888), Shenandoah County, Va. (1854-1887), Parkersburg, (West) Va. (1853-1875), and Warren County (1885) and Mier, Ind. (1885). The collection also includes family business papers, including receipts and estate administration papers of Barton's son, John T. Barton (b.1851); and a farm account book (1900-1927).

B-23. BATES, HELEN S. COLLECTION, 1841-1932.

5 folders.   S 77.

Bates, from Ashley in Dekalb and Steuben counties, donated this collection of family papers in 1967.

The collection primarily contains the letters of the Hammond family of Fort Wayne, Allen Co., and Swan, Noble Co. (1841-1867). Included are letters from Daniel Hammond (d.1849), a barrel maker in Americus, Tippecanoe Co. (1847-1849); from Charles and Sarah (Hammond) Bruce, laborers in Fort Wayne and Swan (1841-1867); and from family members in Mishawaka, St. Joseph Co. (1845-1850). The collection also includes teachers' licenses and other family and school documents relating to the Orr family in Dekalb and Steuben counties (1869-1904); a history of the Orr family; a notebook listing engineers and firemen hired on the Wabash railroad (1857-1898); and two issues of Ashley newspapers (1916, 1932).

B-24. BEAMER, JOHN V. (1896-1964). PAPERS, 1918-1964.

15 ms. boxes.   Inventory.

Politician. Beamer served in the U.S. Army during World War I; representative for the Century Company, school textbook publishers (1921-1928); vice-president and general manager of Wabash Baking Powder and Chemical Company (1928-1941); vice-president and sales manager of Union Rock Wool Corporation, Wabash (1935-1942); owner of farm in Wabash County; Republican member, Indiana House of Representatives (1949-1950); member, U.S. House of Representatives (1951-1959), serving on House Interstate and Foreign Commerce Committee; and member, National Selective Service Appeal Board (1960-1961).

The collection consists principally of papers relating to Beamer's career in Congress (1951-1959), including correspondence with constituents on political issues and bills before Congress; correspondence, reports, memoranda, and clippings regarding legislation on flood control in the Upper Wabash Valley, interstate traffic safety, the construction of a Wabash airport (1957), the construction of a natural gas pipeline, and other legislation sponsored by Beamer; his newsletters and press releases; campaign records, including publicity, financial records, election statistics, and clippings (1952-1958); photos and clippings regarding Beamer's trip to South America with the House Interstate and Foreign Commerce Committee (1951); and correspondence regarding speaking engagements. Also included is correspondence regarding legislation considered by the Indiana General Assembly (1949); correspondence regarding Republican Party politics (1959-1962) and Beamer's support for legislation prohibiting false advertising of decorative and simulated wood products (1961-1963); and personal correspondence, including Beamer's letters to his sons (1948-1950).

Correspondents include E. Ross Adair, Frank W. Boykin, Charles A. Buckley, Homer Capehart, George Craig, Clifford Davis, Brady Gentry, Harold W. Handley, Oren Harris, Vance Hartke, J. Harry McGregor, Edmund S. Muskie, Richard O. Ristine, Kenneth A. Roberts, John Taber, Robert A. Taft, Earl Wilson, Robert E. Wilson, and Charles A. Wolverton.

B-25. BEARD, JOHN (1842?-1888). ACCOUNT BOOKS, 1876-1885.

5 vols. (.5 l.f.). V 4.

Beard owned a grocery and general store in Franklin, Johnson Co.

The collection consists of Beard's store account books.

B-26. BEARSS, DANIEL R. (1809-1884). PAPERS, 1830-1942.

1 ms. box, 10 vols. (1.33 l.f.). L 13, V 5.

Politician and businessman. Bearss was a storekeeper, farmer, and businessman in Peru, Miami Co. (1834-1884); Whig and Republican member, Indiana House of Representatives (1841-1844) and Indiana Senate (1855-1857, 1861-1863, 1875-1877); owner of extensive real estate in the Peru area; and director, Indianapolis, Peru and Chicago Railroad.

The collection mostly contains Bearss' receipts, invoices, land documents, and account books relating to his business and land interests in Peru. Among the items are account books for his transactions with the Miami Indians (1838-1842), his Peru general store (1835-1845), and a Peru sawmill (1851-1853); a letter book containing copies of his letters relating to his claims against the Indians and other business matters, including letters to David Wallace and Albert S. White (1839-1845); receipts, invoices, and accounts for Bearss' general store, including his accounts with New York suppliers in the 1830s; a small number of letters on family matters and Miami County politics; and an account book for farm labor (1875-1942).

B-27. BEELER, JOSEPH (1797-1851). PAPERS, 1821-1918.

1 ms. box. L 14

Beeler was a farmer and stockbreeder in Decatur Township, Marion Co. (1822-1851). He was the father of Fielding Beeler (1823-1895), a Marion County farmer and businessman; officer, Marion County Agricultural Society (1850s); and Republican member, Indiana House of Representatives (1868).

The collection contains family letters to the Beelers, including letters to Joseph Beeler from Truro, Ohio (1837-1842,) and Holt County, Mo. (1846-1850); letters from his brother, George Beeler, describing the Illinois legislature (1833) and Burlington, Iowa (1836-1838); letters to George Beeler in Indianapolis from Mineral Point, Wis. (1859-1860); letters to the John Marvis family, Decatur County, Ind., from relatives in Shelby County, Ky. (1823-1830); and two letters from a World War I soldier. Also included are diaries of George M. Beeler, Joseph Beeler's son, written while he was a student in Lancaster, Mass. (1855-1856); Joseph Beeler's account book (1836-1849); Fielding Beeler's account books (1847-1879); records of the Northport and Mars Hill Gravel Road Company (1863-1890) and the Spring Valley Road Company (1863-1890); copies of Fielding Beeler's diaries (1845-1847, 1864); constitution for the Newton and Spring Valley Horse Thief Detecting Company (ca.1855); farm leases and indentures for Joseph Beeler (1834-1851); and school copybooks (1860-1869).

B-28. BEESON, ISAAC W. (1789-1871). PAPERS, 1816-1942.

11 ms. boxes. Inventory. L 354.

Farmer and merchant. Beeson was a Quaker farmer, merchant, and wheelwright in Guilford County, N.C.; and lived intermittently in Dalton, Wayne

Co., Ind. (1822-1833), before settling permanently there in 1833. He was the father of Benjamin Branson Beeson (1843-1902), a Dalton farmer and stock raiser; general store owner (ca.1880-1886); officer of the Dalton Turnpike Company and the Hagerstown and Blountsville Turnpike Company (1876-1880s); president of the Wayne, Henry, and Randolph County Agricultural Association (1880s); charter member of the Nettle Creek Grange (1870); and publisher of the Prohibitionist newspaper, the *Richmond* (Wayne Co.) *Enterprise* (1891-1897).

The collection consists primarily of correspondence and financial and legal papers of Isaac and Benjamin Beeson. Included are Isaac Beeson's correspondence with family and friends in North Carolina (1829-1866), including correspondence between Beeson and his fiancee (1836-1837); his correspondence regarding Quakerism and the antislavery Friends, road building and other internal improvements, and farming and other business interests; drafts of his letters on religion, ethics, and slavery, including his letters to Gerrit Smith and Abraham Lincoln; his essays on religion, slavery, agriculture, and education; and business receipts and documents relating to landholdings. The Benjamin Beeson papers include correspondence and other items relating to his farms and agricultural associations, including a large amount of material relating to the Grange (1870-1897); and correspondence and business papers involving his dry goods store in the 1880s and the *Richmond Enterprise* in the 1890s.

B-29. BELL, ADDISON W. (1831-1900). PAPERS, 1807-1965.

1 archival box, 1 ms. box (1.33 l.f.).   Inventory.   L 15.

Bell was a farmer and store owner in Rosedale, Parke Co., and owner of a grocery and farm implement business in Terre Haute, Vigo Co. (1889-1900).

The bulk of the collection is from the period 1889-1900 and consists of account books, receipts, invoices, and other business papers relating to Bell's Terre Haute store. In addition there is an account book (1868-1894) of Bell's Parke County store; an account book (1884-1890) of his son-in-law, Albert McMullin (d.1897), a Vigo County farmer; family financial papers and a small number of letters of Bell's daughter, Lona McMullin, and her children in Terre Haute (1900-1965); and a McMullin family diary and stockbreeding record (1906-1907).

B-30. BELL, JOHN (1816-1880). ACCOUNT BOOKS, 1839-1870.

11 vols. (1 l.f.). V 6.

Bell was a farmer and merchant in Mount Pleasant, Jay Co. (1837-1880); and operated a general store from 1839 to 1855, when he sold the store to his brother, Lewis Bell.

The collection consists of Bell's general store account books, principally from the period 1839-1855.

B-31. BELLAMY, FLAVIUS J. (1838-1874). PAPERS, 1861-1864.

196 items. S 100.

Bellamy was a Craig, Switzerland Co., attorney; sergeant in the 45th Indiana Regiment (3rd Indiana Cavalry) (1861-1864); and Republican member, Indiana Senate (1867-1869).

The collection consists primarily of Bellamy's letters to his family in Switzerland County, written while he was serving with the Army of the Potomac in Maryland, Virginia, and Pennsylvania. Also included is Bellamy's diary (1863).

B-32. BENCE FAMILY. PAPERS, 1790-1885.

2 folders. S 1841.

The Bence family members were farmers in Jefferson County, Ky. In 1853 Philip Bence (1801-1882) moved to a farm in Washington Township, Putnam Co.

The collection is made up of the Bence family's land documents and other business papers for Jefferson County, Ky. (1790-1852), and Putnam County, Ind. (1853-1885). Also included is an appraisal of Philip Bence's estate (1882).

B-33. BEVERIDGE, ALBERT J. (1862-1927). PAPERS, 1893-1926.

1 ms. box. L 16.

Beveridge was an Indianapolis attorney (1887-1899); Republican member, U.S. Senate (1899-1911); chairman, Progressive National Convention (1912); and author, *Life of John Marshall* (1916-1919) and other political and historical works.

The collection consists principally of Beveridge's letters (1893-1914) to John C. Shaffer (1853-1943), publisher of the *Chicago Evening Post* (1901-1931) and the *Indianapolis Star*, and president of a syndicate owning the Indianapolis street railways (1888-1893). Included are letters from Beveridge as Shaffer's lawyer handling the dissolution of the Indianapolis street railways syndicate (1893) and letters on personal and political matters (1897-1914). Also included are Beveridge's manuscript for his speech on the Philippines (June 8, 1900); copies of additional speeches; and letters from Beveridge to a number of other people regarding political affairs and his research on the life of Abraham Lincoln.

B-34. BEVINGTON, ELIZABETH. COLLECTION, 1861-ca.1940.

2 folders.   Partial Inventory.   S 113.

Bevington, of Terre Haute, Vigo Co., sold this collection to the Indiana State Library in 1974.

The collection includes fifteen letters to Hannah Johnson, Centerburg, Ohio, from George Johnson, 65th Ohio Regiment, and Amos Johnson, 4th Ohio Regiment (1861-1865); other Civil War-era letters from Hamilton County, Ind., and the 46th Indiana Regiment; certificates of the Indiana Statehouse Building Association (1896-1899); certificates of the Mapel Oil Company, Terre Haute (1914); teachers' licenses and other school papers (1872-1914); and advertisements for lectures and theatrical performances in Terre Haute.

B-35. BIGLER, NICODEMUS (1829-1900). PAPERS, 1874-1899.

1 ms. box.   Calendar.   L 346.

Bigler was a cobbler and general laborer in Goshen, Elkhart Co. (1874-1877, 1883-1900), and near Bremen, Marshall Co. (1877-1883).

The collection consists of Bigler's letters to his children in Darke County, Ohio. The letters include discussions of the Elkhart and Marshall counties area; Bigler's shoe repair, farm labor, and other work; religious groups in the area, including Dunkards and Mennonites; and family problems.

B-36. BLAKE, JAMES S. (1791-1870). PAPERS, 1826-1847.

31 items.   S 130.

Blake was an Indianapolis businessman (1821-1870); operated ginseng company (1826-1828); officer, Steam Mill Company (1828); member, board of directors, Madison and Indianapolis Railroad; and president, State Board of Agriculture (1835).

The collection is mostly made up of correspondence and receipts relating to Blake's ginseng business, including his correspondence with Isaac Elston of Crawfordsville, Montgomery Co., and Isaac Higham [?] of Philadelphia, Pa. Also included is an 1833 letter from Michael Bright relating to the Jeffersonville (Clark Co.) Railroad Company.

B-37. BORDEN, WILLIAM WESLEY (1823-1906). PAPERS, 1715-1902.

1 ms. box.   L 17.

Geologist and educator. Borden was a farmer, geologist, and educator in New Providence (Borden), Clark Co.; assistant to the Indiana State Geologist (1873-1876); organized Colorado mining firm of Borden, Tabor & Company (1878); and established and directed the Borden Institute, a college at New Providence (1880-1906).

The bulk of the collection consists of business papers of Borden's father, John Borden (d.1824) and other ancestors. Included are land and business documents from Massachusetts (1715-1815), New London and Windham counties, Conn. (1766-1809), Newport County, R.I. (1798-1813), and Clark County, Ind. (1809-1906); accounts of the Troy, Mass., Cotton and Woolen Mill Company (1813-1815); W. W. Borden's letters and a scrapbook of notes and clippings on his geological work in the 1870s; speech of James Beggs, candidate for the Indiana Territorial Legislature (1816); and an account of a duel in Alabama (1837). The collection also contains the papers of John M. Johnston (b.1805), a Brookville, Franklin Co., judge including letters to Johnston from Thomas A. Hendricks, Oliver P. Morton, Noah Noble, and James Whitcomb.

B-38. BRADLEY & FLETCHER. ACCOUNT BOOKS, 1832-1837.

3 vols. (.25 l.f.). V 147.

The firm of Bradley and Fletcher owned a general store in Indianapolis from 1832 to 1837. The firm included Wilford Ungles, Henry Bradley, and Stoughton A. Fletcher.

The collection consists of the store's account books.

B-39. BRADSHAW, WILLIAM (fl.1816-1855). PAPERS, 1816-1867.

145 items. S 157.

Bradshaw was a farmer in Augusta County, Va. (1816-1838), and a farmer and miller in Indianapolis (1839-1855).

The collection consists of Bradshaw's receipts, land papers, and other documents dealing with his Virginia and Indiana business interests; and correspondence relating to family matters and his land and business interests in Indiana.

B-40. BRANHAM, DAVID C. (1812-1877). PAPERS, 1812-1905.

1 ms. box. L 18.

Railroadman and politician. Branham was a farmer, contractor, and railroadman in North Madison, Jefferson Co.; superintendent of the Jeffersonville, Madison and Indianapolis Railroad for twelve years; contractor for building the Shelbyville and Rushville Railroad, the Cincinnati and Martinsville Railroad, and other lines; and Whig and Republican member of the Indiana House of Representatives (1855-1867, 1873) and the Indiana Senate (1877).

The collection includes Branham's letters to his wife written while he was supervising railroad construction in the Martinsville, Morgan Co., area (1867-1868); his diaries discussing politics, railroad work, and personal business (1861, 1866-1867, 1869, 1873); family letters written during the Civil War; legal and business papers of Branham's mother, Mary Branham, Madison (1838-1847); minutes of the Soldiers Aid Society, North Madison (1862-1864); diary of S. H. Cobb, Branham's assistant while building a railroad line from Martinsville to Gosport, Owen Co. (1868); diary of Branham's son, William Branham (1904-1905); and reminiscences of life in early Indiana by Col. John Vawter.

B-41. BRANHAM, DAVID MCCLURE (fl.1883-1929). ACCOUNT BOOKS, 1893-1929.

20 vols. (3 l.f.). V 11.

Branham operated a general store in Elizabethtown, Bartholomew Co. (1893-1929).

The collection consists of Branham's store account books (1893-1929).

B-42. BRATTON BROTHERS FUNERAL HOME. RECORD BOOKS, 1901-1947.

14 vols. (2.5 l.f.). V 58.

The Bratton Brothers Funeral Home was located in Lebanon, Boone Co.; it was the successor to the firm of Cory and Bratton.

The collection consists of the firm's record books, containing accounts for each funeral and vital information and causes of death for the deceased.

B-43. BRAYTON, JOHN. COLLECTION, 1861-1907.

46 items. S 160.

Dr. John Brayton of Indianapolis donated this collection to the Indiana State Library in 1943.

The collection consists primarily of papers of Oliver P. Morton (1823-1877), governor of Indiana (1861-1867) and U.S. Senator (1867-1877). Included are letters to and from Morton relating to the Civil War, his U.S. Senate term, and personal matters, including his letters to his wife and children (1870-1874). Also included are personal letters to Mrs. Morton (1897-1903); and a letter from Albert J. Beveridge to A. W. Brayton (1907).

Correspondents include Schuyler Colfax, Henry W. Halleck, Andrew Johnson, George B. McClellan, Joaquin Miller, William H. Seward, Caleb Smith, Edwin M. Stanton, Lew Wallace, and Richard Yates.

B-44. BRICK, ABRAHAM LINCOLN (1860-1908). PAPERS, 1853-1950.

6 ms. boxes.

Politician and attorney. Brick was the son of St. Joseph County farmer William W. Brick; attended Cornell University in Ithaca, N.Y. (1880-1881), and Yale University in New Haven, Conn. (1881-1882); attorney in South Bend, St. Joseph Co. (1883-1908); prosecuting attorney for St. Joseph and LaPorte counties (1866-1868); delegate, Republican National Convention (1896); and member, U.S. House of Representatives (1899-1908), serving on the committees for appropriations, territories, military affairs, and naval affairs.

The papers include Brick's personal correspondence, including his letters to his daughter, Estelle, from Washington, D.C. (1901-1908), and his letters to his father from Cornell and Yale universities (1880-1882); correspondence regarding the merchant marine, the Panama Canal, and other issues with which he dealt in Congress (1899-1908); his political and patriotic speeches (1890-1908); clippings, brochures, and reports on the construction of the Panama Canal (1907); invitations to social events in Washington, D.C.; and bills and receipts for personal expenses in South Bend and Washington. Also included are love letters and poems written by William W. Brick to his fiancee, Elizabeth Calvert of South Bend (1854-1857); correspondence of A. L. Brick's widow, Anna, including letters of condolence written at her husband's death (1908), correspondence and other papers relating to the settlement of his estate (1908-1912), and personal correspondence (1912-1926); and letters of Brick's daughter, Estelle Brick, including personal and family correspondence (1930-1950), and correspondence regarding her publication of *Addresses and Speeches of Abraham Brick* (1938) and *The Letters of a Father to His Daughter* (1940).

Correspondents include Albert J. Beveridge, Edgar D. Crumpaker, Charles W. Fairbanks, Cornelia Fairbanks, Victor H. Metcalf, James Overstreet, and Peter Studebaker.

B-45. BRIGHAM, HAROLD FREDERICK (1897-1971). PAPERS, 1936-1955.

1 ms. box, 4 folders. (.8 l.f.). S 164, L 282.

Brigham was librarian, Free Public Library, Louisville, Ky. (1931-1942); and director, Indiana State Library, Indianapolis (1942-1962).

The collection contains Brigham's correspondence as director of the Indiana State Library (1942-1955), including correspondence relating to the library's activities during World War II; outlines and copies of his speeches; notes, correspondence, and papers relating to his research on Lewis and Clark; copies of three papers Brigham presented to the Indianapolis Literary Club; Indiana Library Association papers (1936-1939); and State Library bibliographies.

B-46. BROTHERHOOD OF LOCOMOTIVE ENGINEERS, AUXILIARY #552. RECORD BOOKS, 1915-1969.

6 vols. (.33 l.f.). V 125, V 174.

The auxiliary's membership consisted of the wives of the members of the Brotherhood of Locomotive Engineers union in Indianapolis.

The collection includes minutes of the auxiliary's meetings (1936-1956); and membership and dues records (1915, 1947-1969).

B-47. BROWN, AUSTIN H. (1828-1903). PAPERS, 1830-1901.

2 ms. boxes.   L 19.

Politician and businessman. Brown was the son of William J. Brown (1805-1857), Democratic member of U.S. Congress (1843-1845, 1849-1851); student, Indiana Asbury University, Greencastle, Putnam Co. (1844-1845); clerk, U.S. Auditor's Office, Washington, D.C. (1845-1850); publisher, *Indiana State Sentinel*, Indianapolis (1850-1855); Marion County Auditor (1855-1859); acting manager, Metropolitan Theater, Indianapolis (1858-1861); assistant to Indiana Adjutant General (1861-1866); Collector of Internal Revenue, Indianapolis (1866-1869); Marion County Clerk (1875-1879); chief of Horse Claims Division, U.S. Treasury Department (1887-1889); member, Indianapolis City Council (1861-1875); and Indiana representative, Democratic National Committee (1876-1889).

The collection consists primarily of Brown's personal and business correspondence, including letters from his father, William J. Brown (1844-1851); from his brother, naval officer George Brown (1835-1913), including letters from the U.S. Naval School (1849) and while on duty (1849-1879); from his sisters in Indianapolis and Amity, Johnson Co. (1844-1852), and attending school at St. Mary-of-the-Woods, Vigo Co. (1844-1845); from his cousin, John Ferguson, in Cincinnati, Ohio (1848-1850); from relatives in Martinsville, Morgan Co., and Milroy, Rush Co. (1845-1848); and from his son, Austin Brown, Jr., working with the Hecla Mining Company and Blue Bird Mining Company in Montana (1881-1892). Also included is correspondence regarding Brown's work with the federal government (1848-1850); letters to President Grover Cleveland recommending Brown for a federal appointment (1885); Brown's report on his discovery of fraudulent claims in the Horse Claims Division (1887); Brown's paper on the history of the Indianapolis Masonic lodge (1883); a biographical sketch of George Brown; financial papers (1830-1844) of Brown's father-in-law, Alexander W. Russell, including his book of accounts with the Indianapolis Branch Bank (1833-1844); a scrapbook of theatrical programs and announcements for the Metropolitan Theater (1870s) pasted into a letter book of personal and business letters of William Watson, an official of the Lafayette and Indianapolis Railroad in Indianapolis (1861); and Masonic and Democratic Party programs, cards, and other printed materials.

Correspondents include Jesse Bright, George Brown, William J. Brown, Edward T. Cox, John Wesley Davis, John D. Defrees, Byron K. Elliott, Arthur

P. Gorman, Isaac P. Gray, Thomas A. Hendricks, Joseph E. McDonald, George F. Parker, William F. Vilas, Robert J. Walker, and James Whitcomb.

B-48. BROWN, LYNDSAY (d.1954). PAPERS, 1818-1937.

1 ms. box. L 20.

Brown, a graduate of Indianapolis High School (1876), an Indianapolis attorney, and operator of an abstract of title business (1876-1926), donated this collection to the Indiana State Library.

The collection includes an Indiana High School Alumni Association record book (1875-1883); programs for meetings of the Indianapolis High School Alumni Association and for high school commencements (1875-1891); and Brown's account of the Ohio River flood at Jeffersonville, Clark Co. (1937). Also included are papers of Brown's father, Ignatius Brown (1831-1903), and grandfather, Hiram Brown (1792-1853), including papers on waterwheels and mills in Indianapolis (1818-1869); the Marion County Commissioners' report on the Mauks Ferry Road (1823-1824); letters to Ignatius Brown regarding road construction in the Pleasant Run area of Indianapolis (1898); and programs, badges, and invitations to reunions of "The Old Seminary Boys" (1878-1886).

B-49. BROWN, O. V. (d.1966). COLLECTION, 1806-1966.

7 ms. boxes, 11 vols. (4.75 l.f.).   Inventory.   L 21, V 12.

Brown owned a lumber company in Dale, Spencer Co.; and was a collector of historical documents and artifacts on Abraham Lincoln and southern Indiana.

The collection contains Brown's correspondence and other papers pertaining to his research on Lincoln, southern Indiana, and Indiana Indians; and documents which he collected relating to these topics. Included in the material collected are Civil War letters to Marion Thurman, Spencer County, from family members serving in the 25th and 48th Indiana regiments (1861-1865); statements concerning Lincoln's family in Indiana, collected by Brown from southern Indiana residents (1933-1960); photostats of letters from David

Turnham, Dale, to William Herndon regarding Lincoln's Indiana years (1865-1866); and numerous clippings, brochures, programs, pamphlets, speeches, poems, and other materials relating to Lincoln and Lincoln memorials in southern Indiana. The collection also includes account books for the *Rockport Democrat* (1869-1883); the William C. Jackson G.A.R. post in Spencer County (1884-1926); Spencer County school register (1844-1850); register of the Occidental Hotel, Rockport (1906); account book of freight received by the Bergenroth Brothers, Troy, Perry Co. (1908-1915); and accounts of several Ohio River steamboats (1900-1918).

B-50. BRUCE, DONALD C. (1921-1969). PAPERS, 1960-1964.

25 l.f.

Bruce was an Indianapolis radio executive; Republican member, U.S. House of Representatives (1961-1965); candidate for Republican nomination for U.S. Senate (1964); and one of the founders of the American Conservative Union.

The collection consists of Bruce's congressional papers (1960-1964), including correspondence, reports, and legislation regarding Vietnam, United Nations involvement in the Congo and Angola, Cuba and Communist activity in Latin America, foreign aid, un-American activities, military preparedness, the 1961 Education Bill, and Bruce's bill to limit U.S. Supreme Court rulings. Also included are printed and audio tape copies of Bruce's speeches; films of his speeches and other appearances; his newsletters; analysis of the 1964 election; and scrapbooks on foreign affairs.

B-51. BRUNER, MARGARET E. (1886-1971). PAPERS, 1865-1971.

4 archival boxes. Inventory.

Bruner was a poet and columnist in New Castle, Henry Co.; published poems in the *Indiana Poetry Magazine, Ave Maria, Magnificat, Howe's Christmas Album*, and *The Circle;* had separate volumes of her poetry published by the Christopher Publishing House, Boston; member, editorial committee, *American Poetry Magazine;* and author of weekly column "In Thoughtful Mood" for the *New Castle News Republican* (1946-1971).

The collection includes Bruner's correspondence with her publishers (1930s-1971); her diaries (1941, 1946, 1948, 1950-1952); personal correspondence and correspondence regarding her work (1919-1971); copies of her poetry, essays, short stories, and her newspaper articles and columns (ca.1916-1971); and family documents and genealogy.

B-52. BRUTUS FAMILY. PAPERS, 1839-1951.

59 items. S 185.

The collection includes family letters to Dora Conrad Brutus of Milroy, Rush Co., and Kokomo, Howard Co. (1881-1896), including letters from Homer, Rush Co., Hobbs, Tipton Co., and Downeyville and St. Paul, Decatur Co.; letters to Frank Pfaffenberger, Seymour, Jackson Co. (1904-1907); letters to Carter Cox, Jamestown, Boone Co., from North Carolina and Springfield, Mo. (1839-1844); and Christmas cards to the Brutus family (1925-1951).

B-53. BUCK, ELLA E. (fl.1874-1889). PAPERS, 1874-1889.

64 items. S 188.

Buck lived in Schuylkill County, Pa.

The collection consists of family letters to Buck from her cousins, principally Sadie and Mary Dawalt, in Denver, Miami Co., and North Manchester, Wabash Co. (1874-1889).

B-54. BURGESS, JOHN KLINE (1874-1929). PAPERS, 1920-1924.

1 ms. box. L 22.

Burgess was a banker and real estate dealer in New Castle, Henry Co. (1910-1919), and Indianapolis (1919-1929); and shareholder trustee for the Knox County Oil Company (1920-1924).

The collection consists of Burgess' papers relating to the Knox County Oil Company, an unsuccessful oil drilling operation near Wheatland and Bruceville, Knox Co. Included is correspondence, financial papers, and minutes of the shareholders meetings.

B-55. BURNETT, JEROME C. (1833-1891). TRAVEL ACCOUNT, 1870.

1 ms. box. L 24.

Burnett was an Indianapolis newspaperman and lecturer.

The collection consists of Burnett's account of a trip to Denver, Colo., and the Rocky Mountains, entitled "Six months in saddle and camp, or roughing it in the Rockies in 1870; an account of a six month sojourn in the Rocky Mountains of Colorado in 1870." The account was written in 1872.

B-56. BUTLER, AMOS W. (1860-1937). PAPERS, 1818-1931.

3 ms. boxes. L 25.

Businessman, ornithologist, and civic leader. Butler was a Brookville, Franklin Co., businessman (1880s-1896); ornithologist, Indiana Department of Geology and Natural Resources (1896-1897); secretary, Indiana Board of State Charities (1897-1923); president, National Conference of Charities and Corrections (1906-1907); president, American Prison Association (1909-1910); and founding member, Indiana Academy of Science (1885) and president (1895).

The collection consists primarily of business papers of Butler, his father, William W. Butler (1810-1903), and other Brookville businessmen. Included are correspondence and financial papers relating to the Brookville and Metamora Hydraulic Company (1866-1896), of which Butler and his father were principal officers; letter book of Butler, his father, and other businessmen regarding Brookville real estate dealings and Republican Party politics (1876-1890); papers relating to the estate of Henry C. Gallion of Brookville (1858-1869); and account books for Brookville dry goods stores owned by Theodore Reifel (1866-1868) and William Reynolds (1866-1869). Also included are Butler's papers relating to the Indiana Centennial, for which he served as chairman of the Charities and Correction Committee (1915-1916); other papers relating to the National Conference of Charities and Corrections (1915), the Indiana Academy of Science, and charities in Indianapolis; notes and papers on Indians in Indiana; notes on students at Brookville College in the mid-nineteenth century; and a bibliography of Butler's writings on ornithology and charity and corrections.

B-57. BUTLER, JOHN H. (1812-1900). PAPERS, 1847-1906.

1 folder. S 200.

Butler was an attorney in Salem, Washington Co. (1839-1866), and New Albany, Floyd Co. (1866-1868); appointed judge of the 27th Judicial District of Indiana (1868); and father of Noble C. Butler.

The collection contains indentures, receipts, and other business documents pertaining to Butler's land and business interests in Jefferson and Floyd counties. Included are letters of Arthur Hawhe, a Chicago real estate dealer, regarding his business dealings with Butler (1869-1872).

B-58. BUTLER, NOBLE CHASE (1844-1933). PAPERS, 1820-1937.

2 ms. boxes. L 26.

Attorney. Butler was the son of John H. Butler; New Albany, Floyd Co., attorney with the firm of Butler, Gresham and Butler; register of bankruptcy in New Albany (1867-1879); clerk of the U.S. District and Circuit Courts in Indianapolis (1879-1922); and lecturer at the Indiana Law School (1902-1928).

The collection consists primarily of letters to Butler from the period 1870-1933. Included are letters on politics and legal affairs from Walter Q. Gresham (1832-1895), federal judge and secretary of state under Grover Cleveland (1893-1895); a large number of family letters, including letters from his son Noble Butler, Jr., written while he was a student at Rose Polytechnic Institute, Terre Haute (1898); letters from his daughters in Oberlin, Ohio, Ithaca, N.Y., and Summit, N.J.; and letters regarding the mental illness of his son (1907). Also included are a small number of Butler family legal documents and letters

(1820-1869); and receipts for numerous Butler family purchases, principally in Indianapolis (1880-1900).

B-59. BUTLER, THADDEUS (1846-1915). PAPERS, 1848-1906.

1 ms. box. L 27.

Newspaperman. Butler was editor and publisher of newspapers in Wabash, Wabash Co. (1872-1884), and Andrews and Huntington, Huntington Co. (1884-1914); and special agent, Office of Indian Affairs, U.S. Department of the Interior, to make payment of annuities and take a census of the Miami Indians (1880-1882).

The collection principally consists of Butler's papers dealing with his work among the Miami Indians (1880-1882). Included is his correspondence and instructions from the Office of Indian Affairs, and copies of his census and payment records for the Miami Indians in Indiana, Kansas, the Indian Territory (Oklahoma), and other areas.

B-60. CAMPBELL, C. ALFRED (1895-1973). PAPERS, 1875-1972.

1 ms. box.   Inventory.   L 28.

Campbell was an Indianapolis automobile executive and member, Indianapolis Literary Club.

The collection consists of Campbell's correspondence, writings, and material collected for his 1952 paper for the Indianapolis Literary Club on Hoosier humorist Kin Hubbard (d.1930). Included is Campbell's correspondence with people who knew Hubbard; copies of articles and clippings on Hubbard; and a copy of Campbell's paper on Hubbard, "Give Us Back Our Hillbillies." There is also a small amount of later correspondence on Hubbard.

B-61. CAPEHART, HOMER E. (1897-1979). PAPERS, 1944-1963.

168 archival boxes.   Inventory.

Politician. Capehart was president, the Capehart Corporation, Fort Wayne, Allen Co. (1927-1932); vice-president, the Wurlitzer Company, Cincinnati,

Ohio (1933-1940); chairman of the board, Packard Manufacturing Company, Indianapolis (1930s); owner of Capehart Farms, Washington, Daviess Co.; and Republican member, U.S. Senate (1944-1963), serving on the Foreign Relations Committee, Committee on Aeronautics and Space Sciences, Joint Committee on Defense Production, and the Banking and Currency Committee.

The collection consists of Capehart's senatorial papers (1944-1963), particularly papers relating to national defense, the Banking and Currency Committee, the Interstate and Foreign Commerce Committee, and the Foreign Affairs Committee. Military and Defense Department papers include papers relating to Indiana soldiers serving in World War II and Korea, and living conditions in camps and bases during the Korean War (1951); legislation, reports, and correspondence on defense spending, the Defense Production Acts (1950s), the establishment of the Air Force Academy (1948-1957), the U.S. Guided Missile program (1958), the Mutual Security Program (1955), Universal Military Training Bill (1948), civil defense, military surpluses, and other defense matters; and papers relating to military installations in Indiana, including the Jefferson Proving Grounds, Crane Naval Ammunition Depot, and Bunker Hill Naval Air Station.

Also included are Banking and Currency Committee papers relating to the Securities and Exchange Commission, the FDIC, the Federal Reserve System, the Office of Price Administration (1945-1947), the Reconstruction Finance Corporation (1946-1953), the federal budget (1947-1962), and general committee information; Interstate and Foreign Commerce Committee papers relating to aviation and aeronautics, radio and television licenses, the 1948 bill limiting the power of radio stations, the Atomic Energy Commission, the Federal Power Commission, foreign oil and oil shortages (1947-1950), railroads, the Federal Trade Commission, fair trade legislation, and interstate highways; Foreign Affairs Committee papers relating to NATO, the Korean War, the St. Lawrence Seaway, Capehart's proposed European Recovery Program (1948-1949), foreign aid bills, his Latin American trip (1953), and Israel and the Middle East; papers on labor legislation, including the Fair Employment Act (1948), minimum wage legislation (1961), disability payments, and the Department of Labor; papers relating to federal housing programs, including the 1954 Housing Act, FHA and VA loans, and Capehart's Depreciation and Amortization bill (1957-1958); papers relating to federal agricultural programs, including the Rural Electrification Administration, the creation of an International Food Community to send surplus food to the needy, the Farmer's Home Administration, and Capehart's 1959 farm bill; and papers relating to flood control in Indiana. Other topics covered include

Alaskan statehood, anti-communism, federal aid to education, the Food and Drug Administration, immigration and naturalization, the Niagara Falls development (1951-1954), the U.S. Post Office, the Public Welfare Act (1953), the Small Business Committee, and taxes.

The collection also includes constituent correspondence on current issues before Congress; requests for information and assistance; press releases, radio broadcast scripts, speeches, voter surveys, clippings, scrapbooks, and other publicity items; Republican Party contributors lists; and his voting records.

Correspondents include Hubert H. Humphrey and R. Sargent Shriver.

B-62. CARLETON, EMMA (1850-1924). PAPERS, 1889-1935.

39 items. S 218.

Carleton was a poet and writer of humorous essays in Indianapolis (1875-1888) and New Albany, Floyd Co. (1888-1924).

The collection includes letters to Carleton from Indianapolis poet and newspaperman Daniel L. Paine (1830-1895), regarding Indianapolis life, the works of other Indiana writers, including James Whitcomb Riley, and advice on Carleton's writing (1889-1895). In addition, there are a small number of Carleton's poems, both manuscript and printed; and excerpts from Carleton's writings published in the newspaper column "Hoosier Listening Post" by Kate Milner Rabb (1935).

B-63. CARR, MICHAEL W. (1851-1922). PAPERS, 1882-1970.

3 ms. boxes. L 351.

Carr was a writer and newspaperman; editor of the *Toledo* (Ohio) *Review* (1873-1879); correspondent and editor, *Indiana Sentinel* (1880s); author, *History of Catholicity in Indiana* (1898), *History of Catholicity in Northern Ohio and in the Diocese of Cleveland* (1903); and histories of Catholic churches in a number of smaller Indiana towns (1887-1898).

The largest part of the collection contains Carr's letters to his wife and son in Indianapolis, written while he was working in Cleveland and northern Ohio on his history of the Catholic church in that area (1899-1904). The collection also includes school papers and family letters of his wife, Carrie Sargent Carr of Chicago, including letters from family and friends in the Chicago area and Waukesha, Wis. (1883-1910), and letters regarding her marriage to a Catholic (1887-1889); and letters of Carr's son, Cyril Carr, written to his parents while he was attending St. Joseph's College in Rensselaer, Jasper Co. (1908-1910), and serving as a dentist with the American Army in France (1918-1919). Also included are letters to Cyril Carr from a French woman in Paris (1919-1924), and papers regarding an army correspondence course (1927-1928).

B-64. CARSON FAMILY. PAPERS, 1825-1915.

144 items.   S 230.

The Carson family included Jacob Carson (d.1856?), a Quaker farmer in Highland County, Ohio, and Decatur Township, Marion Co., Ind. (1844-1856); and his son, Uriah Carson (fl.1801-1865), a farmer in Marion County (1829-ca.1865).

The collection consists primarily of correspondence among the Carson family, particularly letters to Uriah Carson from the period 1829-1865. Included are letters from Highland and Wyandotte counties, Ohio (1829-1858), Winneshiek, Adair, and Keokuk counties, Iowa (1855-1865), and Clinton, Howard, and other Indiana counties (1852-1855), and an 1825 letter from New Garden, Wayne Co., Ind. Also included are epistles from meetings of women Friends in Virginia and Ohio addressed to the Yearly Meeting of Women Friends in Indiana, and extracts from the minutes of the meetings of the Indiana Yearly Meeting of Women Friends (1840-1852).

B-65. CEJNAR, JOHN A. (1895?-1975). PAPERS, 1917-1947.

1 ms. box.   L 29.

Cejnar was Indianapolis bureau chief of the International News Service (1926-1934); and public relation officer with the American Legion and editor, *Indiana Legionnaire* (1934-1964).

The collection consists primarily of Cejnar's correspondence, notes, and news stories for the International News Service, including his stories and interview notes pertaining to gangster John Dillinger and Dillinger's father (1934), and his stories on inventions by Indiana people. Also included are papers of Cejnar's wife relating to her work with the American Association of University Women (1934-1938), the Indianapolis Council of Social Agencies, the League of Women Voters, and other clubs and social service agencies in Indianapolis (1931-1947).

B-66. CENTURY CLUB OF INDIANAPOLIS. RECORDS, 1889-1935.

2 ms. boxes, 2 folders (1 l.f.). L 200, S 2209.

The Century Club of Indianapolis was founded in 1888 as a social and literary club for men.

The records include minutes of meetings (1889-1910); roll book of members (1897-1899); yearbooks (1890-1927); programs (1899-1933); correspondence regarding membership (1903-1912, 1924-1927); correspondence of Louis J. Bailey, director of the Indiana State Library, dealing with the planning of club programs for the following year (1929-1930); and other membership, financial, and program information.

B-67. CHAMBERLIN & CHASE. ACCOUNT BOOKS, 1811-1853.

9 vols. (.75 l.f.). V 32.

The firm of Chamberlin and Chase operated a sawmill in Terre Haute, Vigo Co. (1820s-1840s).

The collection consists principally of account books and order books for the sawmill in the 1830s and 1840s, including an order book describing the projects for which the lumber was purchased. In addition there are accounts for labor performed (1811-1820s).

B-68. CHENOWETH, JOHN T. (1833-1903). ACCOUNT BOOKS, 1860-1910.

2 ms. boxes (43 vols.). L 30.

Chenoweth was a physician in Cincinnati, Ohio (1860), Huntsville, Randolph Co., Ind. (1861-1863), Williamsburg, Wayne Co. (1863-1875), and Winchester, Randolph Co. (1875-1903).

The collection consists of account books for Chenoweth's medical practice (1860-1903), including his joint practice with his son, Forrest A. Chenoweth (1858-1926) during the years 1886-1903; and Forrest A. Chenoweth's account books (1903-1910). The accounts list daily patient visits, charge per visit, and occasional brief notations on the reason for the visit.

B-69. CHITTENDEN, GEORGE F. (1830-1915). PAPERS, 1831-1913.

2 ms. boxes. L 31.

Politician, physician. Chittenden was a physician in Hartsville, Bartholomew Co. (1853-1855), Milford, Decatur Co. (1855-1858), and Anderson, Madison Co. (1858-1915); assistant surgeon and surgeon, 16th Indiana Regiment serving in Maryland, Kentucky, Tennessee, and Louisiana (1861-1864); examining surgeon, Indiana State Enrollment Board (1864); Republican member, Indiana House of Representatives (1869); commissioner, Indiana State Hospital for the Insane (1873); and delegate, Republican National Convention (1880).

The collection is composed primarily of Chittenden's correspondence, including letters between Chittenden and his fiancee and wife, Amanda Branham of Vernon, Jennings Co. (1853-1858); correspondence between Chittenden and his wife, their parents, and other family members during the Civil War (1861-1865); letters to Chittenden regarding Republican Party affairs and the 1880 Republican National Convention; correspondence regarding his work with the Indiana Hospital for the Insane; letters of Chittenden, his wife, and other family members to his son Edgar, a student at DePauw University, Greencastle, Putnam Co. (1883-1884); Chittenden's correspondence regarding military pensions (1897-1908); and letters from family and friends in Ravenna, Ohio (1873-1888), Clarinda, Iowa (1858-1861), and other towns in the

Midwest. Also contained are the Civil War letters of Preston Branham, 16th Indiana Regiment.

B-70. CHRIST CHURCH CATHEDRAL. RECORDS, 1840-1977.

18 l.f.   Restricted.

Christ Church was the first Episcopalian Church in Indianapolis. The first church building was constructed on the Indianapolis Circle in 1838, and it was replaced by the current church building in 1858. In 1954 it became the cathedral for the Episcopal Diocese of Indianapolis.

Records include church bulletins amd special service programs (1888-1977); Christ Church *Chimes* (1931-1945), Christ Church *Bulletin* (1924-1930), and other publications of the church; financial records (1855-1867, 1920-1972); indentures, mortgages, blueprints, and other records relating to church property (1840-1950s); correspondence (1930s-1960s), including correspondence pertaining to Josiah K. and Eli Lilly's involvement with the church; attendance records (1941-1950); confirmation class records (1932-1947); parish reports (1950s); and scrapbooks and histories of the church (1857-1972). In addition, there are records of the Sewing Guild (1842-1947); minutes of the Women's Auxiliary meetings (1907-1954); and minutes of the League of Service meetings (1921-1924).

B-71. CHURCH HISTORY—BAPTIST. RECORDS, 1798-1912.

1 archival box.   L 189.

The collection consists of records, both originals and copies, of a number of Indiana Baptist churches. Among the records are those for Baptist churches at Attica, Fountain Co. (1870-1899); Aurora, Dearborn Co. (1871-1883); Bloomington, Monroe Co. (1825-1890); Brown's Wonder Church, Boone Co. (1840-1873); Ebenezer and Clear Creek, Morgan Co. (1830-1891); Eel River District Association, Putnam Co. (1825-1851); Lick Creek, Fayette Co. (1814-1912); Little Mt. Zion Church, Warrick Co. (1869-1882); Little Pigeon Creek, Warren Co. (1816-1840); Mt. Zion Church, Floyd Co. (1831-1833); Poison Creek, Perry Co. (1888-1909); Silver Creek, Clark Co. (1798-1837); and Wolcottville, Noble Co. (1837-1868).

B-72. CITIZENS HISTORICAL ASSOCIATION. RECORDS, 1933-1952.

1 ms. box.   L 321.

The Citizens Historical Association was organized in Indianapolis in 1934 to establish a national library of historical and biographical information. The executive director of the organization was Lyman Davidson (1879-1952), and board members included Indianapolis banker Felix McWhirter (1886-1983) and *Indianapolis News* correspondent and editor Stephen Noland (1887-1962). The association disbanded in 1952.

The records include the minutes of board of directors meetings, financial reports, and correspondence of Davidson, Noland, and others regarding the work of the association.

B-73. CIVIL WAR. CLAIMS FOR VETERANS, 1864-1866.

1 folder.   S 2614.

The collection is made up of correspondence, forms, depositions, and other legal papers of a number of Indiana Civil War veterans filing claims with the U.S. Treasury for back pay. The collection includes papers for Arthur Bonwell, 85th Indiana Regiment; Joseph C. Freeman, 97th Indiana Regiment; Christian Keck, 21st Indiana Regiment; Charles Lockman, 126th Indiana Regiment; William Miller, 17th Indiana Regiment; William Perryman, 9th Indiana Regiment; and Nicholas Smith, 17th Indiana Regiment.

B-74. CLARK & CLARK. ACCOUNT BOOKS, 1895-1924.

3 vols. (.25 l.f.).   V 240.

J. W. Clark and his son were veterinary surgeons in Columbia City, Whitley Co.

The collection consists of the firm's account books (1895-1912, 1923-1924).

B-75. CLARK, JOHN G. (1836-1910). PAPERS, 1856-1878.

5 folders. S 1839.

Clark was a Frankfort, Clinton Co., businessman; major and colonel, 26th Indiana Regiment (1861-1865); regiment commander (1862-1865); and Clinton County treasurer (1866-1870).

The collection is largely composed of correspondence, invoices, and other business papers relating to Clark's real estate interests in Humboldt, Eureka, and Wyandotte, Kans., Beatrice, Nebr., and Magnolia, Iowa (1866-1878). The collection also includes correspondence and financial papers relating to Clark's business affairs in Toledo, Ohio (1860); correspondence regarding the 26th Indiana Regiment (1865); and family letters (1856).

B-76. CLARKE, GRACE JULIAN (1865-1938). PAPERS, 1857-1938.

3 ms. boxes. L 33.

Clarke was the daughter of Congressman George W. Julian (1817-1899); resident of Irvington, Marion Co. (1873-1938); graduate of Butler University, Indianapolis (1884, 1885); active in women's suffrage movement and women's clubs; founded Irvington Woman's Club (1892); chairman, general committee, National American Woman Suffrage Association meeting in Indianapolis (1899); president, Indiana Federation of Clubs (1909-1911); board member and national press chairman, General Federation of Women's Clubs (1912-1916); organized Woman's Franchise League of Indiana (1912); wrote column on women's clubs for *Indianapolis Star* (1911-1929); head, women's division, Federal Employment Bureau of Indianapolis (1916); active worker on behalf of the League of Nations and disarmament groups (1919-1925); member, Indianapolis City Plan Commission (1931-1933); and author, *George W. Julian* (1923) and other books and articles on her father.

The bulk of the collection consists of Clarke's correspondence for the period 1891-1934, including papers relating to the women's suffrage movement in Indiana and nationally, the National American Woman Suffrage Association, and the Woman's Franchise League (1891-1917); her correspondence relating to her work with the General Federation of Women's Clubs (1912-1916) and Indiana women's clubs; correspondence and speech notes relating to the League of Nations and organizations working on behalf of the League, such as the Pro-League Independents and the League to Enforce Peace (1919-1922); papers regarding the Indiana Democratic Party's 1920 campaign; correspondence with historians in Indiana, Ohio, and at the Library of Congress regarding her historical research and the papers of George W. Julian and her grandfather, Congressman Joshua R. Giddings (1795-1864); and correspondence and meeting minutes relating to the Indianapolis City Plan Commission (1931-1933). Also included are letters addressed to May Wright Sewall regarding woman's suffrage (1880-1899); minutes of the meetings of the Equal Suffrage Society of Indianapolis (1878-1880); Clarke's scrapbooks of newspaper clippings, programs, and leaflets relating to woman's suffrage (1878-1884, 1915); programs and leaflets of the National American Woman Suffrage Association (1884-1900); Clarke's eulogy of May Wright Sewall (1920); her memorandum book of notes and clippings on the League of Nations; her class notes as a Butler University freshman (1880); and a memorial to Grace Julian Clarke by May Louise Shipp (1938).

Correspondents include Susan B. Anthony, Albion Fellows Bacon, Claude Bowers, Hilton U. Brown, Francis F. Browne, Carrie Chapman Catt, Charles E. Coffin, Jacob Piatt Dunn, Worthington C. Ford, William Dudley Foulke, Francis J. Garrison, Ida Husted Harper, Caroline Scott Harrison, Mary G. Hay, Herbert Houston, Daniel Wait Howe, J. Franklin Jameson, Ester Everett Lafe, Harlow Lindley, William O. Lynch, Carleton McCulloch, Paul V. McNutt, Harry S. New, Meredith Nicholson, Benjamin Strattan Parker, Anna (Mrs. P. V.) Pennybacker, Samuel Ralston, James Ford Rhodes, James Whitcomb Riley, May Wright Sewall, May Louise Shipp, J. H. Short, Lucius B. Swift, William Howard Taft, Thomas Taggart, Booth Tarkington, Harriet Taylor Upton, Zerelda Wallace, James E. Watson, Woodrow Wilson, and James A. Woodburn.

B-77. CLAYPOOL HOTEL. RECORDS, 1947-1967.

6 ms. boxes. L 325.

The Claypool Hotel was one of the leading hotels in downtown Indianapolis from its opening in 1903 until its closing in 1967. The hotel building was razed in 1969.

The papers date principally from the years 1947-1960 when the hotel was managed by W. Bryan Karr, and the hotel was affiliated with the National Hotel Company of Galveston, Tex. Included is Karr's correspondence with the National Hotel Company staff regarding hotel finances, auditing procedures, supplies, and construction work; his correspondence with hotel patrons, suppliers, advertisers, and other hotel owners regarding hotel business; and his memos to the hotel staff (1959). In addition there are reports, blueprints, memos, and correspondence regarding hotel renovations and the installation of new furnishings in the 1950s; papers relating to the rental of office and display space in the hotel by airlines and other businesses; applications and references for employees (1960); papers regarding the Indianapolis "500" Festival and the "500" Festival Association (1957); bulletins and papers of the Indiana Hotel Association and the American Hotel Association (1959-1960); menus, directories, signs, and other printed materials used in the Claypool Hotel and its restaurants; and a 1948 survey of hotel wages in Indianapolis.

B-78. CLIO CLUB. RECORDS, 1878-1937.

2 ms. boxes.

The Clio Club is an Indianapolis women's literary and social club. It was organized by Quaker women as Indianapolis Conversation Club No. 3 in 1878; it became the Friends History Club in 1888, and the Clio Club in 1889.

The records consist of the organization's minute books (1878-1937) and yearly program calendars (1888-1935).

B-79. COATS, NELLIE M. (1888-1977). PAPERS, 1859-1973.

4 folders.   S 269.

Coats was a librarian with the Indiana State Library, Indianapolis (1923-1959); librarian, Indiana Academy of Science (1934-1977); and producer of weekly radio program in Indianapolis (1960s).

The collection includes letters to Coats from a number of World War II soldiers, including Grant Robbins of the 14th Air Force and 21st Photo Squadron, serving in China and India (1942-1946); letters from an American soldier in West Germany (1969-1970); her correspondence regarding the preservation of the Pine Hills nature preserve, Montgomery County (1961); letters from the Tippecanoe County Democratic Central Committee regarding the duties of state employees in the 1936 and 1940 elections; Coats's notes and writings on Woodruff Place in Indianapolis; and a small number of nineteenth-century family papers.

B-80. COBURN, JOHN (1825-1908). PAPERS, 1850-1904.

1 ms. box, 11 vols. (1.5 l.f.). L 34, V 59.

Politician and attorney. Coburn was an Indianapolis attorney; colonel, 33rd Indiana Regiment (1861-1864), general (1865); Whig member, Indiana House of Representatives (1850-1851); Republican member, U.S. House of Representatives (1867-1875), serving as chairman of the Committee on Military Affairs and on the Committee on Banking and Currency; and justice, Montana Territory Supreme Court (1884-1885).

The collection contains nine of Coburn's letter books (1879-1903), chiefly relating to his Indianapolis law practice, but also including letters on Republican Party politics, local civic activities, and Indiana history; correspondence regarding Coburn's work as a congressman, including letters regarding political appointments and his work on banking and military affairs; other correspondence regarding politics; correspondence and financial papers relating to the settlement of the estate of Augustus Coburn, including papers relating to land in Ontonagon County, Mich., and mining claims in the West (1850-1865); Coburn's memorandum books containing addresses, legal case notes, receipts, and cures for diseases (1904-1905); a scrapbook of the 1867 political campaign; Coburn's account book (1865); an article by Coburn on riots in Indianapolis and other Indiana towns during the Civil War; and notes and drafts of speeches.

B-81. COCKEFAIR, ELISHA (fl.1812-1860). PAPERS, 1851-1959.

1 ms. box. L 35.

Cockefair owned farms near Everton, Fayette Co., and in Harmony Township, Union Co.

The collection includes letters of the Cockefair family in Everton, principally to Alice Keltner in Anderson, Madison Co. (1895-1911); papers of Charles

Masters of Connersville, Fayette Co., including his canceled checks (1917-1939) and his papers relating to his work raising money in Fayette County for the Indiana University Memorial Fund (1922); and letters of Mary Alice Masters from Connersville (1922) and Washington, D.C. (1938), and from California while she was serving in the military (1942). Also included are school notes and exercises of Elisha and Laf Cockefair (1860, 1889), history class notes of Charles Masters at Indiana University (1906-1907), and school notes and papers of Mary Alice Masters; and receipts of Elisha Cockefair (1851-1859).

B-82. COFFIN & CAINS. ACCOUNT BOOKS, 1848-1859.

7 vols.   V 13.

Coffin & Cains was a general store in Economy, Wayne Co.

The collection consists of the store's account books (1848-1859).

B-83. COGSWELL, STACY H. (d.1906). PAPERS, 1864-1909.

2 folders.   S 279.

Cogswell was an Indianapolis carpenter and served in the 13th Indiana Regiment during the Civil War.

The collection consists primarily of papers regarding Cogswell's efforts to obtain a Civil War pension (1888-1901). Also included are programs, reunion announcements, and rosters of Grand Army of the Republic posts and meetings in Indianapolis (1885-1899).

B-84. COLFAX, SCHUYLER (1823-1885). PAPERS, 1757-1926.

1 ms. box.   L 36.

Colfax was deputy auditor, South Bend, St. Joseph Co. (1841-1849); publisher and part owner, *St. Joseph Valley Register* (1845-1863); one of the organizers of the Republican Party in Indiana; member, U.S. House of Representatives (1855-1869); Speaker of the House (1863-1869); Vice-President under U. S. Grant (1869-1873); implicated in the Credit Mobilier scandal; and popular lecturer.

The collection consists primarily of Colfax's correspondence from the period 1841-1884, including letters to Colfax regarding Whig and Republican Party politics in Indiana and nationally; letters from Indiana officers in the Civil War regarding promotions and assignments; Colfax's letters on routine business as Speaker of the House and Vice-President; his letters pertaining to speaking engagements; letters to his wife regarding his role in the Credit Mobilier affair (1875); and letters regarding his inheritance from his grandfather, William Colfax (1841). Also included are a memorandum of a meeting with Stephen A. Douglas on the Kansas issue (1857); notes and drafts of speeches and articles, including an 1871 article on his opposition to a bill in 1857 increasing Congress' power to subpoena witnesses; invitations to dinners and parties in Washington; and the manuscript of a speech on Colfax written by Lew Wallace (1898). The collection also contains papers of William Colfax (d.1838), including papers regarding his Revolutionary War Service and militia posts in Bergen County, N.J., his letter regarding New Jersey troops in the War of 1812, and letters to his son, Schuyler Colfax (1814-1822); letter of Colfax's father, Schuyler Colfax, to his wife from St. Croix, V.I. (1822); letters to Colfax's son, Schuyler Colfax, Jr. (d.1925), principally letters of introduction for a trip to Europe (1907); and genealogical information on the Colfax family.

Correspondents include Albert J. Beveridge, Abraham L. Brick, Anson Burlingame, Robert Carter, John C. Clark, Roscoe Conkling, Charles A. Dana, John D. Defrees, Charles Dick, Stephen A. Douglas, John C. Fremont, Horace Greeley, Horatio King, Benson J. Lossing, Alexander K. McClure, Robert H. Milroy, Daniel D. Pratt, Whitelaw Reid, Elihu Root, Winfield Scott, William H. Seward, John Sherman, H. S. Spaulding, Charles Sumner, and R. W. Woodbury.

B-85. COTTMAN, GEORGE STREIBE (1857-1941). PAPERS, 1857-1937.

1 ms. box. L 39.

Cottman was a printer in Irvington, Marion Co.; founder and publisher, *Indiana Quarterly Magazine of History* (1905); author of numerous articles and pamphlets on Indiana history and nature study; and author, *A Centennial History and Handbook of Indiana* (1915).

The collection consists primarily of Cottman's correspondence from the period 1891-1937, including correspondence with other Indiana and midwestern writers regarding his work; correspondence regarding the *Indiana Quarterly Magazine of History* and research in Indiana history; and letters dealing with the Western Association of Writers. Also included are drafts of a number of Cottman's speeches and articles, among them his work on the history of newspapers in Indiana; papers of Cottman's father, John Cottman, regarding his role with the 19th Indiana Regiment during the Civil War, and regarding his farm near Beech Grove, Marion Co.

Correspondents include Albert J. Beveridge, Isaac Blackford, Emma Carleton, Hamlin Garland, Clara E. Laughlin, John Uri Lloyd, Solomon Meredith, Merrill Moores, Harry S. New, Meredith Nicholson, Benjamin Strattan Parker, Bruce Rogers, Caroline Dale Snedeker, T. C. Steele, Booth Tarkington, W. H. H. Terrell, Maurice Thompson, and James A. Woodburn.

B-86. Cox, Elisha (d. 1847?). Papers, 1812-1860.

3 folders. S 2052.

Cox was a farmer near Lawrenceburg, Dearborn Co.

The collection consists principally of Cox's receipts from the period 1820-1843. Also included is an account book for T. S. Miller's general store (1839-1848); and copies of War of 1812 militia rolls for Indiana companies under Capt. Frederick Sholts and Capt. James McGuire.

B-87. Crosier, Adam (1805-1887). Papers, 1840-1902.

257 items. S 2059.

Crosier was a farmer and surveyor in Laconia, Harrison Co.

The collection consists primarily of letters to Crosier from his son, Edward S. Crosier (d.1891), a student in Louisville, Ky. (1853), and Ann Arbor, Mich.

(1856); a doctor with the U.S. Army Hospital at New Albany, Floyd Co. (1864-1865); a New Albany physician (1865-1869); employee in the Surveyor's Office of the U.S. Custom House at Louisville (1870-1885); and owner of a druggist and chemist shop in New Albany (1887-1891). Also included are other family letters from Battle Creek, Mich. (1856-1862), Knoxville, Iowa (1858-1861), Seneca (1860-1863) and Geneva, N.Y. (1882-1888), Ford County, Ill. (1870-1871), Jacksonville, Oreg. (1882-1884), and a number of Harrison County towns; letters of several Indiana soldiers serving in the Civil War; letters to Adam Crosier pertaining to his surveying work (1856); letters to Lafe Crosier in Laconia regarding family affairs and agricultural implements (1888-1889); and an 1866 campaign circular of Walter Q. Gresham.

B-88. CROSS, GEORGE WASHINGTON (b.1816). PAPERS, 1821-1868.

183 items. S 324.

Cross was a clerk and businessman in Montezuma, Parke Co.

The collection consists primarily of Cross' receipts and other financial papers from the period 1831-1852. In addition, there are two account books of a Montezuma laundress (1851-1862); a patent deed for an improved clothes dryer (1868); and a survey of land belonging to Addison Cross in Ross County, Ohio (1821).

B-89. CRUMPACKER, SHEPARD J. (1917-). PAPERS, 1940-1956.

7 ms. boxes. Inventory.

Crumpacker is a South Bend, St. Joseph Co., attorney (1941-); Republican member, U.S. House of Representatives (1951-1957), serving on the Judiciary Committee; and U.S. delegate to the NATO Conference in Paris, France (1955).

The collection consists primarily of Crumpacker's congressional papers (1951-1956), including correspondence, reports, legislation, and other papers pertaining to the automobile industry and a federal investigation of monopolistic practices in the industry, Electoral College reform, patent law reform, defense procurement practices, international copyright laws, UNESCO, air defense policy, trade restrictions to protect the American tuna industry, and matters before the Judiciary Committee. Also included are papers relating to local issues, including the Calumet River bridge (1952), and Lake Central Airlines in South Bend (1955); papers concerning his 1954 election campaign; Republican National Committee correspondence (1953-1954); and his newsletters, speeches, and appointments.

B-90. CUNNINGHAM, JOSEPH (1853-1906). PAPERS, 1893-1941.

5 ms. boxes. L 364.

Cunningham was a Loree, Miami Co., farmer; breeder of Poland China swine and Barred Plymouth Rock poultry; Democratic member, Indiana House of Representatives (1899); and member, State Board of Agriculture (1902-1905).

The collection includes Cunningham's correspondence with breeders regarding pedigrees, markets, and livestock sales (1897-1905); correspondence regarding the Indiana State Fair (1901-1905); and bills, receipts, and other business papers relating to farm and stock breeding operations (1897-1905). In addition there are papers of his daughter, Ora Cunningham Turner, including her school notebooks; letters to her from parents and friends while she was a student at Marion College, Marion, Grant Co. (1893-1895); letters from her fiance, Eli Barton Turner (1893-1895); and account book listing livestock sales (1905-1909) and farm accounts (1930s-1941).

B-91. CURTIS, DANIEL (1853-1902). ACCOUNT BOOKS, 1879-1914.

3 vols. (.5 l.f.). V 14.

Curtis was a farmer and tile manufacturer in Wingate, Montgomery Co.

The collection consists of account books for his farm and tile businesses, principally from the period 1879-1887.

B-92. DALRYMPLE, JOSEPH W. (fl. 1870-1912). PAPERS, 1858-1891.

100 items.   S 2603.

Dalrymple was a Rising Sun, Ohio Co., dealer in hay, grain, and produce; associated with firm of Bush and Dalrymple (1875-1881); and worked as firm's agent in New Orleans, Memphis, and other Mississippi River towns.

The collection includes Dalrymple's letters to his wife written while he was on business in Mississippi River towns in Louisiana, Mississippi, Tennessee, Arkansas, and Illinois (1870-1881); letters from his partner, J. W. Bush, from Rising Sun (1875-1881); letters and invoices from merchants in Cincinnati, New Orleans, Louisville, Natchez, Miss., and Cairo, Ill. (1871-1880); and letters to Dalrymple regarding a mill property in Sistersville, W.Va. (1890). In addition there are Civil War letters of G. W. Lamb, 45th Indiana Regiment (1863); letters to Dalrymple's wife, Jennie Seward, from a school friend in Lawrenceburg, Dearborn Co. (1865-1867); and letters from Mrs. R. H. Bowen of Calvert County, Md., to her son (1864-1865).

B-93. DANNER, MRS. A. V. COLLECTION, 1847-1927.

37 items.   S 2602.

Danner was the wife of a Vevay, Switzerland Co., hardware store owner; and was active in the Switzerland County Historical Society.

The collection primarily contains shipping bills for the steamboat "Wisconsin" and a number of other steamboats operating from Cincinnati, New Orleans, Louisville, and Madison, Lawrenceburg, and Vevay, Ind. (1847-1857). Also included are Mrs. Danner's letters and a newspaper clipping regarding the steamboat "Jacob Strader" (1927); and two Indiana railroad tickets (1852).

B-94. DAVIS, JEFFERSON COLUMBUS (1828-1879). PAPERS, 1826-1873.

4 ms. boxes, 1 vol. (1.75 l.f.).   Inventory.   L 41, V 9.

Soldier. Davis was born in Clark County, Ind.; served with the 3rd Indiana Regiment during the Mexican War; appointed 2nd lieutenant, 1st Artillery,

U.S. Army (1848); stationed at Fort Sumter during the siege (1861); served in quartermaster's department, Indianapolis (May-August 1861); appointed colonel, 22nd Indiana Regiment (August 1861); promoted to brigadier general (November 1861); commanded troops in Missouri (1861-1862), Tennessee (1862-1863), Georgia (1864), and the Carolinas (1865); commanding officer, District of Kentucky (1865-1866); colonel, 23rd U.S. Infantry (1866); and fought in Modoc War, Oregon (1873).

The collection consists principally of Davis's official Civil War papers, particularly receipts, bills, requisitions, and other documents relating to his work in the quartermaster's department in Indianapolis (May-August 1861). Also contained is official correspondence regarding his duties in Missouri and Tennessee, including a letter book containing retained copies of his telegrams to Gen. John C. Fremont and others (1861); letters and military inspection reports sent to him while he was with the 14th Army Corps in South Carolina (February-March 1865); ration and provision reports on Kentucky state troops (October-November 1865); his correspondence as commander of the District of Kentucky, including correspondence regarding claims of Kentucky residents against the army (1866); his account books for personal items (1868-1870); a translation of a German article on the Modoc War (ca.1875); and eighteen maps (1826-1872), most from the Civil War.

Correspondents include William P. Benton, Will Cumback, Samuel R. Curtis, John C. Fremont, Ulysses S. Grant, Alvin P. Hovey, George B. McClellan, Oliver P. Morton, Lazarus Noble, John Pope, William S. Rosecrans, Winfield Scott, Franz Sigel, James C. Veatch, Lew Wallace, Thomas Wood, and Richard Yates.

B-95. DEAM, CHARLES C. (1865-1953). PAPERS, 1896-1952.

24 ms. boxes.   Partial Calendar.

Botanist. Deam was a Bluffton, Wells Co., botanist, specializing in the collection and identification of plant species; Indiana State Forester (1909-1913, 1917-1928); and author of numerous articles and books on plants, including *Trees of Indiana* (1918), *Indiana Woodlands and Their Management* (1922), *Grasses of Indiana* (1929), and *Flora of Indiana* (1940).

The bulk of the collection consists of Deam's correspondence with botanists regarding the collection, identification, and reproduction of plants. Also included is Deam's correspondence with publishers, research assistants, and reviewers regarding his research and publications; correspondence and papers relating to his trips to Florida, Mexico, and Central and South America to collect plant specimens; correspondence and papers relating to the Indiana Academy of Science, of which Deam was one of the founding members; correspondence with county agents, businesses, and schoolteachers regarding speaking engagements and consulting work; papers relating to his position as State Forester; papers relating to Deam's involvement with the Democratic Party, and his involvements in the fights against pollution and in favor of the state's acquisition and preservation of wilderness land; and personal correspondence with family members.

Correspondents include H. H. Bartlett, N. L. Britton, Homer Capehart, Stanley Coulter, W. W. Eggleston, George W. Gillie, J. M. Greenman, G. Grossman, A. S. Hitchcock, Richard Lieber, Warren T. McCray, Kenneth K. Mackenzie, Thomas Riley Marshall, Francis W. Pennell, Gene Stratton Porter, Robert Ridgeway, L. S. Sargent, and Paul Weatherwax.

B-96. DEBS, EUGENE V. (1855-1926). PAPERS, 1895-1935.

1 ms. box.   Inventory.   L 230.

Labor and Socialist Party leader. Debs was a Terre Haute, Vigo Co., railroad man and labor leader; officer, Brotherhood of Locomotive Firemen (1880-1893); president, American Railway Union (1893-1897); leader of national strike against the Great Northern Railway (1894), and a leader in the Pullman Strike and boycott (1894); presidential candidate, Social Democratic Party (1900), and the Socialist Party (1904, 1908, 1912, 1920); convicted of violating the Espionage Act for his opposition to American involvement in World War I (1918), and served time in federal prison (1919-1921).

The collection consists primarily of correspondence of Socialist Party Executive Secretary Otto Branstetter with and regarding Debs during the period 1920-1923, including letters regarding amnesty for Debs and other people imprisoned for their opposition to the war; and letters regarding Socialist Party politics and Debs's role in the party following his release from prison. Also included are Debs's writings on the labor movement; his essay on Elizabeth Cady Stanton (1922); statements of Debs and others on their opposition to the war (1918); a scrapbook of newspaper articles regarding Debs's 1923 speaking tour; copies of Debs's letters to Cleveland, Ohio, socialist leader

Peter Witt (1895-1924) and Terre Haute socialist Shubert Sebree (1914-1920); clippings, printed articles, and other published material on Debs; and booklets "Ballad of Gene Debs" by Sarah Cleghorn (1928) and "At Death of Debs" by J. Howard Flowers (1926).

Correspondents include Roger Baldwin, Theodore Debs, Albert DeSilver, Irwin St. John Tucker, George S. Viereck, and Bertha Hale White.

B-97. DELAWARE COUNTY. JAIL MATRON'S DIARY, 1935-1938.

1 ms. box (4 vols.). L 210.
Restricted.

The collection is made up of the work diaries of an unidentified jail matron in Muncie, Delaware Co., during the years 1935-1938. The matron's responsibilities primarily involved relief assistance to the poor in Muncie, rather than work with jail inmates.

B-98. DENNIS, DAVID W. (1912-). PAPERS, 1969-1974.

121 l.f. Partial Inventory.

Dennis is a Richmond, Wayne Co., attorney (1935-); Republican member, Indiana House of Representatives (1947-1949, 1953-1957); and member, U.S. House of Representatives (1969-1975), serving on the House Judiciary Committee.

The collection consists of Dennis's congressional papers (1969-1974), including constituent correspondence, legislation, reports and publications, his newsletters and press releases, and Judiciary Committee papers. Included are papers relating to the Nixon impeachment proceedings (1974), immigration and illegal aliens, Electoral College reform, reorganization of the federal judiciary, crime, and other matters before the House Judiciary Committee; Dennis's testimony before the Government Operations Committee regarding Executive Privilege and the War Powers Bill (1973); and papers relating to state and district concerns, including the Delaware County Airport, flood control, aid and grants for local projects, and support for state colleges and universities. Also included are papers concerning the Republican Congressional Committee Task Force, the Republican Congressional Committee Conference, and Republican Party campaign materials.

B-99. DENTON, WINFIELD K. (1896-1971). PAPERS, 1913-1971.

16 archival boxes, 2 ms. boxes, 15 vols. (23 l.f.).   Inventory.

Politician. Denton was a soldier in the U.S. Army Air Corps during World War I; attorney in Evansville, Vanderburgh Co. (1922-1971); Democratic Party chairman in Evansville (1925); prosecuting attorney, Vanderburgh Co. (1932-1936); member, Indiana House of Representatives (1937-1942), House minority leader (1941); officer in the Judge Advocate General's Department, Wright Field, Ohio (1942-1945); and member, U.S. House of Representatives (1949-1953, 1955-1967). He was the son of George K. Denton (1864-1926), Evansville lawyer and Democratic congressman (1917-1918).

The largest part of the collection consists of Denton's congressional papers (1949-1966), including correspondence, advertising, and other papers from his election campaigns (1946-1967); reports, correspondence, and other papers relating to legislation which he introduced (1949-1966), such as bills on veterans benefits, aid to farmers, and flood control and other projects in southern Indiana; papers regarding his trips to Europe for the NATO Parliamentary Conferences (1962-1966) and to the South Pacific on congressional business (1964-1966); political speeches and statements; newsletters, radio broadcasts, reports, and statements issued for constituents; and his pocket diaries (1957-1966). Also included are papers relating to legal cases handled by Denton and his father in Evansville (1913-1969), particularly suits against insurance companies for failure to pay benefits, and a suit brought against the state of Kentucky for failure to pay agreed amount for construction work on the Kentucky Turnpike (1960-1962); his military papers from World War I and World War II, including his letters to his parents (1918), a pilot's logbook (1918), and orders, vouchers, transfers, and other official papers (1918-1926, 1942-1946); personal financial records (1952-1961); and scrapbooks (1927-1971).

Correspondents include Birch Bayh, Roger D. Branigin, Dennis Chavez, James M. Hanley, Wayne L. Hayes, Estes Kefauver, John W. McCormack, George Mahan, Edmund Muskie, J. Edward Roush, and Stewart L. Udall.

B-100. DICKERSON, JOHN WILLIAM (1948-). LETTERS, 1966-1969.

1 ms. box.   L 264.

Dickerson, from Knightstown, Henry Co., served in the United States Army during the period 1966-1969. His assignments included training at Fort Leonard Wood, Mo., and Fort Sill, Okla. (June 1966-February 1967); active duty in Vietnam with C Battery, 3rd Battalion, 18th Artillery (May 1967-April 1968), Company A, 5th Battalion, 46th Infantry (August-November 1968), and with a Mobile Advisory Team working with Republic of Vietnam troops (November 1968- April 1969). In April 1969 he was wounded in action and returned to the United States.

The collection consists primarily of Dickerson's letters from the army to his parents in Knightstown. The letters describe his training, army life, Vietnam, his travels in Australia, and family matters. Also included are issues of the *Hook and Star*, newsletter of the 3rd Battalion, 18th Artillery (1967-1968).

B-101. DICKINSON, JESSE L. (1906-1982). PAPERS, 1942-1965.

19 ms. boxes.

Politician. Dickinson was a South Bend, St. Joseph Co., social worker (1928-1935); employee of the federal Works Progress Administration (1935-1941); employee of Bendix Corporation (1941-1945); owner-operator of shoe repair service (1950-1957); director, South Bend Housing Authority (1958-1972); Democratic member, Indiana House of Representatives (1943-1959) and Indiana State Senate (1959-1961); member, Negro Defense Workers Council (1942); member, U.S. Fair Employment Practices Commission (1945-1946, 1953-1954); member, Indiana Commission on Aging and Aged (1955-1969); and member, Indiana Civil Rights Commission (1963-1970).

The largest part of the collection consists of Dickinson's constituent correspondence while he was serving in the state legislature (1943-1961), particularly constituents' views on pending legislation. Also included are papers pertaining to prison conditions, the state penal system, and Dickinson's work as chairman of the Senate Committee on Benevolent and Penal Institutions (1961); and papers relating to his work with the South Bend Housing Authority, the Indiana Commission on Aging and Aged, and the Indiana Association for Mental Health.

B-102. DILLARD, FRED ELWOOD (1894-). PAPERS, 1868-1971.

1 ms. box, 1 vol. (.5 l.f.).   Inventory.   L 44.

Dillard was a schoolteacher at French Lick, Orange Co. (1914-1950s); owned property in Patoka Township, Crawford Co., and lived near Birdseye, Dubois Co.; and served in the U.S. Army in Europe during World War I.

Included are World War II letters of Dillard's sons Max (1920-1943), a pilot with the U.S. Navy in the Pacific, and Charles with the Air Transport Command; letters to Max and Charles Dillard from their parents and family (1943-1945); Max Dillard's Indiana University grade reports (1938), and papers relating to his military enlistment, training, and death, including his 1942 flight instruction record book; Fred Dillard's reminiscences; a Dillard family history; Patoka Township, Crawford Co., tax receipts of Dillard (1929-1967), Benjamin and Sarah Carroll (1868-1881), and Jacob Painter (1892-1918); Fred Dillard's postcards acquired in Europe, including some written to his family in Indiana (1918-1919); and a family scrapbook of school and service records, and newspaper clippings on the family.

B-103. DILLON, JOHN BROWN (1807?-1879). PAPERS, 1861-1886.

1 ms. box.   L 45.

Historian and civil servant. Dillon was editor, *Logansport* (Cass Co.) *Canal-Telegraph* (1834-1842); Indiana State Librarian (1845-1851); secretary, State Board of Agriculture (1850s); clerk, U.S. Department of the Interior (1863-1871) and the House Military Affairs Committee (1871-1875); secretary, Indiana Historical Society (1859-1879); author, *History of Indiana* (1843) and other works on the history of Indiana, Indians, and the Old Northwest.

The collection consists principally of Dillon's historical notes on people and events relating to the early exploration and settlement of Indiana and the Old Northwest. Also included is a scrapbook of Dillon's letters published in newspapers on the Civil War, the Republican Party, and Indiana history (1861-1876); letters to Dillon regarding the Indiana Historical Society, the Indiana Sanitary Fair (1864), and Dillon's historical work; and a memorial of John Coburn on the life of Dillon (1886).

Correspondents include Horace P. Biddle, John Coburn, and Calvin Fletcher.

B-104. DOWLING, THOMAS (1806-1876). PAPERS, 1850-1874.

50 items. S 372.

Politician, newspaperman, and businessman. Dowling was a Terre Haute, Vigo Co., newspaper publisher (1832-1845); Whig member, Indiana House of Representatives, serving six terms between 1836 and 1849; trustee, Wabash and Erie Canal (1850s); member, Terre Haute City Council (1867-1871); officer, Terre Haute Savings Bank (1869-1876); and Vigo County Commissioner (1873).

The collection includes letters regarding the operation and finances of the Wabash and Erie Canal (1850-1854); correspondence with Daniel W. Voorhees regarding a disagreement over a railroad lawsuit (1873); reports on expenditures of New Albany and Terre Haute schools (1868); bids and bills for construction of a building in Terre Haute (1864); and other business papers (1864-1869).

Correspondents include Charles Butler, John Dowling, and Daniel W. Voorhees.

B-105. DUBOIS, JESSE KILGOUR (1811-1876). PAPERS, 1833-1920.

130 items. S 384.

Politician and businessman. Dubois was a farmer, merchant, and land dealer in Lawrenceville and Springfield, Ill.; Lawrence County, Ill., justice of the peace (1833); Whig member, Illinois State Legislature (1834-1844); Receiver of Public Moneys, U.S. General Land Office, Palestine, Ill. (1849-1853); Lawrence County judge (1853-1856); and Illinois State Auditor (1856-1864?).

The collection contains Dubois's correspondence and business papers pertaining to his work as Receiver of Public Moneys (1849-1853); papers relating to his land investments and interests in land drainage (1840s-1850s); correspondence and other papers relating to the Illinois State Auditor's office and the presidential campaigns of 1860 and 1864; copies of his letters and petitions to Abraham Lincoln (1856-1861); correspondence regarding Lincoln's life; notes on the Dubois family, including Dubois's father, Toussaint Dubois (d.1816) of Vincennes, Knox Co.; and correspondence of the Huntington family of Springfield, Ill. (1880-1920).

Correspondents include J. Butterfield, O. M. Hatch, John Hay, James Shields, Lyman Trumbull, Daniel W. Voorhees, Jesse Weik, and Elisha Whittlesey.

B-106. DUFOUR FAMILY. PAPERS, 1762-1917.

1 ms. box.   Inventory.   L 46.

The Dufour Family, from Canton de Vaud, Switzerland, settled in Kentucky and Switzerland County, Ind. The principal members of the family were John James Dufour (1763-1827), who established a colony and vineyard near Lexington, Ky. (1798), sponsored a second colony and vineyard in Switzerland County (1802), and wrote *The American Vine Dresser's Guide* (1826); and his brother, John Francis Dufour (1783-1850), who settled in Kentucky (1801) and Vevay, Switzerland Co. (1809), and served as Vevay postmaster (1810-1835), Switzerland County clerk and recorder (1814), probate judge (1839), and member of the Indiana House of Representatives (1828-1829).

The collection includes John James Dufour's daybook of expenses and travel notes (1796-1826), and his instructions and reports for his work in America (1796-1804); maps of the Swiss colony and Vevay (1802-1836); an 1810 description of New Switzerland; John Francis Dufour's correspondence and appointments to public office; a 1917 transcript of David Dufour's account of his 1801 voyage from Switzerland to America; and articles by Perret Dufour (1807-1884) on the early history of Switzerland County and the Dufour family (1869, 1876). A number of the documents were published in Perret Dufour's *The Swiss Settlement of Switzerland County* (Indiana Historical Commission, 1925).

B-107. DUNN, JACOB PIATT (1855-1926). PAPERS, 1888-1920.

2.5 l.f.   Inventory.   L 47.

Historian. Dunn was an Indianapolis attorney (1876-1879, 1884-1888); prospector and journalist in Colorado (1879-1884); secretary, Indiana Historical Society (1886-1924); writer for the *Indianapolis Sentinel* (1893-1904) and other Indianapolis newspapers; Indiana State Librarian (1889-1893); and historian, author of *Massacre of the Mountains* (1886), *Indiana, a Redemption from Slavery* (1888), *True Indian Stories* (1908), and *Indiana and Indianans* (1919).

The collection consists of Dunn's papers relating to his research on Indiana Indians, including his English-Miami Indian dictionary on index cards; stories and texts in Miami, collected from Miami Indians by Dunn and others, primarily in the period 1906-1916; Dunn's notes and essays on Miami language, religion, and customs; a copy of the Peoria-French dictionary in the John Carter Brown Library, Providence, R.I., with Dunn's notes and writings comparing Peoria and Miami languages; Dunn's reading notes on Indiana Indians, in preparation for his book *True Indian Stories;* his study of the Lenox Library Peoria manuscript; letters from Chippewa Indian ministers in northern Minnesota to Rev. J. A. Gilfillan, in Chippewa with Gilfillan's translations (1880s-1890); and a small amount of Dunn's correspondence relating to his work on Miami Indians. The collection inventory was published as *Jacob Piatt Dunn: His Indian Language Studies and Indian Manuscript Collection* by Caroline Dunn (Indiana Historical Society *Prehistory Research* Series, v.1, no.2, Dec. 1937).

B-108. DUNN, TEMPLE H. (1846-1920). PAPERS, 1855-1950.

1 ms. box.   L 262.

Educator. Dunn was a student at Hartsville Commercial School, Hartsville, Bartholomew Co. (1866-1867); a schoolteacher at Hartsville and Columbus, Bartholomew Co. (1867-1873), Brownsburg, Hendricks Co. (1874), Fort Wayne, Allen Co. (1876-1880), and Crawfordsville, Montgomery Co. (1880s); school principal, Quincy, Ill. (1895-1903); principal, Marengo, Crawford Co. (ca.1910-1913, 1917-1920); superintendent, Indiana Soldiers' and Sailors' Orphans' Home, Knightstown, Henry Co. (1913-1917); associated with the Alton Furniture Company, Alton, Crawford Co. (1890); and resident of Soldiers' Home, Dayton, Ohio (1904-ca.1909).

The collection consists primarily of Dunn's correspondence from the period 1866-1919. Included are Dunn's letters to his brother, William R. Dunn, an Alton furniture maker (1866-1880); letters to his daughter, written while he was living at the Soldiers' Home (1904-1909); letters to Dunn from W. R. Dunn, principally when working with Peckinpaugh, Harrison & Company, an Alton wagon company (1892-1897); and other family letters from Jamestown, Boone Co. (1878), and from Wells College, N.Y. (1919). Additional materials include Dunn's correspondence with other educators regarding his efforts to find a position (1891-1893); business receipts (1880-1890); and his notes on Roman history (1880).

B-109. DuShane, James (fl.1870-1915). Papers, 1828-1949.

4 ms. boxes, 24 vols. (4 l.f.). L 48, V 47.

Educator and attorney. DuShane was a teacher, high school principal (1875-1878), and school superintendent (1878-1891) in South Bend, St. Joseph Co.; South Bend lawyer specializing in patent law, in partnership with father-in-law Andrew Anderson in firms of Anderson and DuShane (1890s) and Anderson, DuShane and Crabill (1897-1906), and in his own firm (1906-1915); secretary for the South Bend Power Company (1900), the St. Joseph and Elkhart Power Company (1902-1903), and the Berrien Springs (Mich.) Water Power Company (1903); invested in oil leases in Kansas and Indiana, in partnership with J. P. Heasley (1902-1908); and owned summer home in Macatawa, Mich. (1910-1915).

The papers contain DuShane's correspondence, principally from the period 1890-1914, including correspondence regarding DuShane's interests in the South Bend area power companies (1895-1903); letters from J. P. Heasley and others dealing with his oil investments in Kansas and in Jay, Adams, and Delaware counties, Ind. (1902-1904); correspondence and patent specifications relating to his work as a patent attorney (1888-1914); letters from his son, Donald DuShane, school superintendent at Madison, Jefferson Co. (1910-1914); and correspondence regarding family matters and his personal business affairs. Also included are DuShane's business letter books (1899-1907); his teacher's and superintendent's record books (1870-1891); personal account books (1874-1875, 1900-1915); record book of Heasley and DuShane (1904-1908); guardianship record book (1890-1907); minutes of the Liberty Township Teachers' Institute, St. Joseph Co. (1885-1895); letter book and account book of the South Bend Pad and Comb Company (1895-1897); letters of William H. Hobbs, a Spanish-American War soldier serving at Tampa, Fla., and Havana, Cuba (1898-1899); a 1949 scrapbook on Chapin family history, including letters and documents of Horatio Chapin, South Bend, from the 1820s and 1830s; and legal papers of Ellen Colfax, widow of Schuyler Colfax (1885-1887).

Correspondents include Abraham Lincoln Brick, Frederick P. Delefield, Charles W. Fairbanks, Charles W. Miller, and Charles H. Tennery.

B-110. DYNES, HARRY B. (1884-1968). PAPERS, 1873-1945.

1 ms. box, 1 folder.   L 256, S 397.

Dynes was an executive with the Equitable Life Assurance Society of America, Indianapolis; Republican member, Indiana House of Representatives (1917); secretary, Indiana Selective Service Association (1921); and conciliator for the U.S. Labor Department in the 1920s and 1930s. Also included are papers of K. C. Adams (d.1956), who served as an official with the United Mine Workers of America until 1948, including service as publicity director for the UMW, based in Indianapolis (1913-1918), and editor of the *United Mine Workers Journal* until 1948.

The bulk of the collection consists of Adams's correspondence during the period 1916-1917 when he was working as publicity director of the United Mine Workers in Indianapolis. The correspondence includes both letters to Adams and retained copies of Adams's letters, and regards organizing activities of the UMW; strikes and other labor conflicts in coalfields in Colorado, Utah, Oklahoma, Pennsylvania, West Virginia, and other places; the role of the UMW in the 1916 presidential election; the involvement of the UMW with the American Committee on War Finance and other groups concerned with labor's role in World War I; and correspondence with the Committee on Industrial Relations, the National Labor Defense Council, and other pro-labor groups. The collection also contains a Dynes family scrapbook, primarily of Indianapolis Republican Party programs, election tickets, ribbons, broadsides, and other campaign material (1873-1923); papers relating to the Indiana Selective Service Association (1918-1921); correspondence regarding the visit of David Lloyd-George to Indianapolis (1923); letters to Dynes from World War II soldiers (1942); and a collection of Indianapolis clippings and cards, including newspaper stories regarding a 1927 Indianapolis trolley-truck accident (1924-1945).

Correspondents include Dante Barton, Samuel W. Gompers, William P. Harvey, Edward Keating, John L. Lewis, Frank Morrison, Phillip Murray, Scott Nearing, Paul Paulsen, Amos Pinchot, George P. West, John P. White, and Thomas J. White.

B-111. EGGLESTON, EDWARD (1837-1902). PAPERS, 1868-1920.

79 items. S 410.

Author. Eggleston was a resident of Vevay, Switzerland Co., and other southeast Indiana towns; pastor in a series of small churches in Minnesota (1857-1866); journalist; editor and corresponding editor, *Sunday School Teacher* (1867-1873); pastor, Church of Christian Endeavor, Brooklyn, N.Y. (1874-1879); novelist and historian; and author of *The Hoosier Schoolmaster* (1871) and other novels, and *A History of the United States and Its People* (1888) and other historical works.

The bulk of the collection consists of letters to Eggleston from the period 1892-1902 regarding his writing and lecturing, illustrations for his works, and social engagements. Also included are family letters from Eggleston and his brothers to his cousin, Evelyn Craig of Vevay (1901-1920); a lengthy letter about Eggleston's family and his boyhood by his brother, George Craig Eggleston (1886); and scattered letters written by Eggleston.

Correspondents include Leonard W. Bacon, Henry Ward Beecher, James Bryce, Rebecca Harding Davis, Harry Fenn, Richard W. Gilder, Washington Gladden, Edward Everett Hale, William Dean Howells, Samuel Pennybacker, Frederic Remington, James Whitcomb Riley, Charles Dudley Warner, and Frances E. Willard.

B-112. ELDER, ROMENA O. (fl.1912-1966). COLLECTION, 1857-1942.

1 ms. box, 26 vols. (2.5 l.f.). L 50, V 60.

Elder, born Romena Oehler, lived in Indianapolis and Greenwood, Johnson Co., and was married to Marion G. Elder (d.1958), an Indianapolis florist. She donated this collection to the Indiana State Library in 1966.

The collection consists principally of account books and other financial records of Roman Oehler (1841-1920), a German immigrant who owned an Indianapolis jewelry store (ca.1865-1900) and managed property in Indianapolis and Greenwood. Oehler's records include account books for his jewelry store (1875-1900); accounts for the Senate Hotel, Indianapolis, and other rental property which he and his family managed (1895-1929); personal and family accounts (1879-1925); and papers relating to purchases of property (1872-1879). Additional materials include the papers and accounts of Marion County farmer Alexander M. Hannah (1821-1895), including his farm account books (1857-1888), other accounts and receipts (1860-1895), and letters of Ingram Fletcher regarding land speculation in the Orlando, Florida, area (1884-1888); account books of the Virginia Avenue Building and Loan Association, Indianapolis (1873-1927); and account book of the Southport and Indianapolis Gravel Road Company (1860-1888).

B-113. ELLIS, FRANK (b.1842). PAPERS, 1906-1910.

2 folders. S 420.

Politician and attorney. Ellis was an officer in the 84th Indiana Regiment during the Civil War (1862-1865); attorney in Muncie, Delaware Co.; Republican; mayor of Muncie (1883-1891); U.S. Commissioner (1898-1910); and judge, 46th Judicial Circuit.

The papers include Ellis's correspondence regarding state and local Republican Party politics; papers regarding the Society of the Army of the Cumberland, a Civil War veterans organization to which he belonged; letters from his daughter, a student at the University of Chicago (1909); a small amount of correspondence regarding his legal business; and personal and business bills and receipts.

Correspondents include John A. M. Adair, James P. Goodrich, Isaac H. Gray, Nathan P. Hawkins, James A. Hemenway, and Gen. William Harrison Kemper.

B-114. EMBREE, LUCIUS C. (1853-1932). PAPERS, 1786-1933.

13 ms. boxes. L 52.

Attorney. Embree was an attorney in Princeton, Gibson Co. (1877-1932); active in state and local Republican Party politics; unsuccessful candidate for

Indiana Supreme Court (1914); served on Pueblo Lands Board, Santa Fe, N.Mex., working on Indian land claims (1926-1928); and vice-president, Southwest Indiana Historical Society (1920s). Embree was the grandson of Elisha Embree (1801-1863), Gibson County lawyer and farmer, Whig member of the Indiana State Senate (1833-1835), judge of the 4th Judicial Circuit Court of Indiana (1835-1845), and member of the U.S. House of Representatives (1847-1849); and son of James T. Embree (1826-1867), Princeton lawyer and officer in the 58th Indiana Regiment during the Civil War.

The collection contains business, political, and personal papers of Elisha, James T., and Lucius Embree. Elisha Embree papers include receipts, accounts, land indentures, and other financial papers relating to his land and business interests; correspondence pertaining to his legal business in Princeton, Evansville, and other southwestern Indiana towns, including retained copies of Embree's letters and correspondence of his partners Samuel Hall and Charles Phillips; correspondence regarding Whig and Republican politics in Indiana (1833-1863); his correspondence regarding politics and constituent problems during his term in Congress (1847-1849); personal correspondence, including letters from family in Tompkinsville, Ky. (1820s), and from father-in-law David Robb in LaPorte County, Ind. (1833-1834); account books for his legal and personal business (1836-1859); notebooks recording letters sent and other business done while serving in Congress; his speeches on the state legislature (1835), on temperance (1842), and on various issues before Congress; papers regarding the Gibson County Seminary (1826-1830); and his estate inventory (1863).

James T. Embree papers include his letters to his father, written while he was a student at Indiana Asbury University, Greencastle, Putnam Co. (1847-1850); his graduation address from Indiana Asbury (1850); correspondence and financial papers relating to his business interests in southwestern Indiana, including an account book for the Evansville Steam Flour Mill Company (1852-1857); a letter book containing copies of his legal correspondence (1857-1861); his Civil War letters to his wife, written from Kentucky, Tennessee, and Mississippi (1862-1863); reports on the 58th Indiana Regiment's casualties at Murfreesboro (1862), and on the 58th's actions at Chickamauga (1863); military papers and letters of his brother, David Embree, an officer in the 42nd Indiana Regiment; and letters of his sister in Topeka, Kans. (1862).

Lucius C. Embree papers include correspondence regarding his legal practice in Princeton and southwestern Indiana, including numerous cases involving railroad property in Gibson County (1877-1926); correspondence regarding state and local Republican Party politics, including letters regarding Embree's attempts to secure a federal appointment (1881-1926); correspondence regarding Gibson County history and the Southwestern Indiana Historical Society (1920-1928); reports and papers regarding the work of the Pueblo Lands Board (1926-1928); letters to Embree from William H. Trippett, an attorney in Deer Lodge and Anaconda, Mont. (1887-1924); Embree's commonplace books containing notes on legal cases (1878, 1883); Master Commissioner's Docket, Gibson Circuit Court, for when Embree was master commissioner (1881-1905); and genealogical material on the Embree and Robb families.

Correspondents include Thomas H. Adams, Conrad Baker, Charles I. Battell, Albert J. Beveridge, Isaac Blackford, William C. Bobbs, Emmett F. Branch, Joseph R. Burton, Calvin Coolidge, George W. Crawford, Edgar D. Crumpacker, W. H. Cullop, Harry M. Daugherty, John D. Defrees, Charles Denby, George K. Denton, Henry S. Dodge, Thomas Dowling, Charles T. Doxey, Winfield T. Durbin, Byron K. Elliott, William H. English, Charles W. Fairbanks, George W. Faris, Simeon D. Fess, John H. Foster, John Watson Foster, Newton W. Gilbert, James P. Goodrich, Horace Greeley, Walter Q. Gresham, A. J. Halford, J. Frank Hanley, Benjamin Harrison, Will H. Hays, William Heilman, Guy T. Helvering, James A. Hemenway, Alvin P. Hovey, Henry Hurst, John E. Iglehart, James H. Jordan, Samuel Judah, John Worth Kern, Henry S. Lane, John Law, Abraham Lincoln, James Lockhart, Oscar R. Luhring, Claude Matthews, Charles W. Miller, Leander Monks, Merrill Moores, Austin W. Morris, Harry S. New, Noah Noble, Robert Owen, Robert Dale Owen, William Owen, William Prince, Samuel Ralston, Woodfin D. Robinson, Benjamin F. Shively, Caleb B. Smith, Truman Smith, Lyman Stickney, Elihu Stout, Richard W. Thompson, William A. Twigg, James E. Watson, John Sharp Williams, Albert W. Wishard, Joseph A. Wright, and Bennett H. Young.

B-115. ENGLISH, HENRY K. (1853-1939). COLLECTION, 1854-1931.

1 ms. box.   L 53.

English was an Indianapolis painter and interior decorator. He was the son of Joseph K. English (b.1824), an Indianapolis painter (1850-ca.1900); member, Indianapolis City Council (1857-1859); and Indianapolis City Treasurer (1861-1865).

The collection consists primarily of accounts and organizational records belonging to Joseph K. English, including an account book for his painting business (1854-1862); other receipts, checks, and bills; broadsides and letters of the U.C., an anti-Copperhead organization in Indianapolis (1862); record book of the Indianapolis City Treasurer (1861-1865); minutes of the Fall Creek and Warren Township Gravel Road Company (1864-1878); accounts of the Marion County Association for the Detection of Horse Thiefs (1865-1867); and record book of the Center Township Citizens Draft Fund, which raised money for volunteer bonuses so that the military draft would not be needed in Indianapolis (1864). Also included is a typescript, "Recollections of the Past," a paper based on an interview with Henry K. English in 1931; and a 1910 labor contract between the Master Painters' Association of Indianapolis and the Brotherhood of Painters, Decorators, and Paperhangers of America.

B-116. EPISCOPAL DIOCESE OF INDIANAPOLIS. RECORDS, 1834-1978.

81 l.f. Inventory.
Restricted

The diocese was organized in 1838 as the Diocese of Indiana, representing Episcopalian parishes from throughout the state. In 1898 the northern third of the state was split off to form a separate diocese, and in 1903 the diocese for the central and southern parts of the state became the Diocese of Indianapolis. The diocese's cathedral was the All Saints Church in Indianapolis from 1912 to 1947, and the Christ Church in Indianapolis since 1954.

The bulk of the collection consists of diocesan records from the 1950s to the 1970s, particularly during the tenure of Bishop Joseph P. Craine (1959-1977). Included is correspondence with clergy and postulants concerning status, positions, and general church business; bishop's office records, including correspondence, speeches, and addresses; diocesan committee records, including the budget, executive, and personnel committees; financial and operational reports of parishes and missions within the diocese; correspondence, financial records, meeting minutes, reports, and other records of diocesan and Episcopalian agencies and departments, such as Waycross Retreat Center, University Canterbury Association and Canterbury College in Danville, United Episcopal Charities, Home for the Aging, Urban Center, Episcopalian Young Churchmen, Episcopalian Churchwomen, Diocesan General Convention, Standing Commission on Structure of the National Church, Diocesan Council, Cathedral Arts, and Forward, Inc., an inner city project; papers relating to city and state interdenominational agencies, including the Church Federation of Greater Indianapolis, Indiana Council of Churches, and the Christian Theological Seminary; correspondence and other papers regarding its companion diocese, the Diocese of Haiti; and marriage judgement records (1959-1973). In addition there are parish histories and newspaper clippings (1834-1891); Bishop George Upfold's ordinations, baptisms, and marriages (1850-1862); diocesan publications (1884-1908); documents pertaining to church property in the late nineteenth century; and scrapbooks (1931-1939).

B-117. EVANS, GEORGE (1802-1863). LETTERS, 1839-1840.

2 folders. S 437.

Evans was a Spiceland, Henry Co., farmer; member, Society of Friends; and Democrat member, Indiana State Senate (1848-1851).

The collection consists of Evans's letters to his family and friends in Spiceland, written during his trip visiting Quaker meetings in northern Indiana, Michigan, Canada, New York, Connecticut, Rhode Island, Massachusetts, and New Jersey (1839-1840). Evans was accompanied by Quaker minister and abolitionist Charles Osborn (1775-1850). The collection includes original letters and transcripts.

B-118. EVERMANN, BARTON W. (1853-1932). LETTERS, 1906-1932.

40 items. S 442.

Educator. Evermann was a teacher and school superintendent at Burlington, Carroll Co. (1880s); professor of biology, Indiana State Normal School, Terre Haute (1886-1891); ichthyologist with U.S. Bureau of Fisheries (1891-1914); museum director, California Academy of Sciences, San Francisco (1914-1932); director, Steinhart Aquarium, San Francisco (1922-1932); and author, with David Starr Jordan, of *The Fishes of North and Middle America* (1896, 1900), and numerous other works on ichthyology.

The collection consists of letters from Evermann to his niece, Ava Evermann (fl.1906-1961), a resident of Burlington, Carroll Co. (1906-1911), and Kokomo, Howard Co. (1911-1932). The letters, written from Washington, D.C. (1906-1908), and San Francisco (1914-1932), discuss bird watching, Evermann's activities, and family matters.

B-119. EWING, WILLIAM GRIFFITH (1801-1854) AND EWING, GEORGE WASHINGTON (1804-1866). PAPERS, 1818-1889.

56 ms. boxes, 32 vols. (29.5 l.f.).　　　Calendar.　　　L 323, L 316, V 48.

Merchants. The Ewing brothers were partners in the firm of W. G. and G. W. Ewing Company, a trading house based in Fort Wayne, Allen Co. (1827-1854). The company's activities included fur trading in Indiana, Michigan, and the West, in association with the firm of Suydam, Sage & Company of New York (1820s-ca.1850); trading with Indians in northern Indiana, Iowa, Wisconsin, Minnesota, Missouri, and Kansas (1820s-1860s); real estate investments in Fort Wayne, Chicago, Minnesota, St. Louis, and elsewhere in the Midwest; and general merchandise business in Fort Wayne and other northern Indiana towns. William Griffith Ewing was based in Fort Wayne (1822-1854); director, Fort Wayne Branch, Indiana State Bank; Whig member, Indiana State Senate (1838-1841); and unsuccessful candidate for the U.S. House of Representatives (1847). George Washington Ewing was located at Fort Wayne (1822-1830, 1854-1866), Logansport, Cass Co. (1830-1839), Peru, Miami Co. (1839-1846), and Westport and St. Louis, Mo. (1846-1854); and Democratic member, Indiana State Senate (1836-1840).

The collection is made up largely of the Ewings' correspondence, accounts, receipts, legal documents, and other papers relating to their business interests (1825-1866), particularly the Indian trade, the fur trade, and real estate. Indian trade papers include correspondence, letter books, and accounts pertaining to their trade with the Potawatomi and Miami Indians in northern Indiana and Kansas (1820s-1850s), the Sac and Fox Indians in Wisconsin and Iowa (1840s-1850s), the Menominee Indians in Wisconsin (1850s), the Winnebago, Chippewa, and Sioux Indians in Minnesota (1850s-1860s), and the Osage and Shawnee Indians in Missouri and Kansas (1840s-1850s); papers dealing with the Ewings' involvement in the removal of Indians from Indiana, Michigan, Wisconsin, and Minnesota (1820s-1850s); their correspondence with the U.S. Commissioners for Indian Affairs and other federal officials regarding federal Indian policy, the actions of federal Indian agents, and the Ewings' claims against the Indians (1820s-1850s); W. G. Ewing's letters from Washington,

D.C., regarding his lobbying on behalf of Indian traders (1840s-1850s); and their account books, including ledgers for their posts at St. Peter's, Minn. (1845-1847), and Westport, Mo. (1852-1865).

Fur trade papers include correspondence, letter books, and accounts relating to their fur trading operations in Indiana, Michigan, and the West (1820s-1850s); correspondence and accounts with their agent, Suydam, Sage & Company of New York (1825-ca.1850); papers relating to their competition and agreements with the American Fur Company and Pierre Chouteau & Company (1820s-1850s); and correspondence regarding the fur markets in England and Germany. Real estate papers include correspondence, deeds, receipts, and other papers regarding the Ewings' property in Fort Wayne, northern Indiana, Chicago, Missouri, and Minnesota (1820s-1860s); papers relating to the Wabash and Erie Canal, and canal lands purchased by the Ewings (1830s); book of plat maps and lists of sales for the Ewing Addition in Fort Wayne (1823-1859); and real estate books for Winona and St. Paul, Minnesota (1856-1857).

Additional items include correspondence, accounts, and letter books relating to the administration of the Ewings' estates (1854-1889), including the settlement of accounts and the management of the family's property in the Middle West; correspondence and accounts for their general merchandise business in northern Indiana, including a daybook for their store in Peru, Indiana (1836-1840); correspondence pertaining to state and national politics (1820s-1850s); family correspondence, particularly regarding family finances (1820s-1880s); receipts and other personal expense documents; and business papers of their father, Alexander Ewing, a Fort Wayne trader (1818-1827).

Correspondents include James Abbott, William Barton, Edward Bates, Daniel R. Bearss, Samuel Brenton, Jesse D. Bright, Michael G. Bright, Alexander W. Buel, William Allen Butler, Lewis Cass, Charles W. Cathcart, Pierre Chouteau, Jr., Charles Conrad, Alexis Coquillard, T. Hartley Crawford, Thomas Dowling, Ebenezer Dumont, John Dumont, John W. Edmunds, Richard Smith Elliott, Graham N. Fitch, Gabriel Franchere, Alexander Fraser, William Godfroy, Allen Hamilton, Samuel Hanna, Edward A. Hannegan, Hyacinth Lasselle, John Law, Luke Lea, Jonathan McCarty, Hugh McCulloch, George W. Manypenny, William Medill, David Olmsted, Abel C. Pepper, John Pettit, John U. Pettit, John S. Phelps, Trusten Polk, Daniel D. Pratt, James Rariden, James M. Ray, Solon Robinson, Henry Sibley, Oliver H. Smith, Madison Sweetser, Cyrus Taber, John Test, Richard W. Thompson,

John Tipton, David Turpie, John P. Usher, Hugh S. Walsh, James Whitcomb, Albert S. White, Isaac White, and William Windom.

B-120. FEIGHTNER, HAROLD C. (1892-1969). PAPERS, 1920-1968.

4 ms. boxes.   Partial Inventory.   L 55.

Journalist. Feightner was a reporter and editor for the *Huntington Press*, Huntington County (1911-1917); political reporter for the *Indianapolis Star* and the *Indianapolis Times* (1919-1922); legislative and political reporter for the *Indianapolis News*, and writer of a syndicated column on Indiana politics (1922-1934); executive director, Indiana Brewers Association (1934-1966); and consultant for the United States Brewers Association and the Beer Distributors of Indiana, Inc. (1966-1968).

The collection consists of Feightner's papers on the Indiana Brewers Association and papers relating to the Ku Klux Klan in Indiana. The Indiana Brewers Association papers include Feightner's correspondence relating to the regulation of the brewing industry (1945-1966); drafts and revisions of the Codified Alcoholic Beverage Statute, prepared for the Indiana General Assembly (1966); Feightner's newsletters and reports on alcoholic beverage bills in the Indiana legislature (1965); his speeches, writings, and notes on the history of alcoholic beverages and the regulation of alcohol; minutes and financial statements of Regional Board #9 (Indiana), of the Brewing Industry of the United States (1933-1935); financial records of the Indiana Brewers Association (1963-1965); and his correspondence with publishers regarding his work "Politics, Prohibition, and Repeal," on the history of alcohol regulation in Indiana.

Also included are papers Feightner collected on the Ku Klux Klan in Indiana during the 1920s, including pamphlets and circulars written by Indiana Klan leader D. C. Stephenson; constitution, bylaws, and pamphlets issued by the Indiana and the national Klan; newspaper articles about Stephenson, the Klan, and corruption charges against Indiana politicians at the time; and a folder of newspaper clippings, notes, and letters regarding corruption charges against Indiana governor Warren T. McCray.

B-121. FISHER, RUSSELL V. (fl.1926-1948). PAPERS, 1926-1940.

1 folder. S 467.

Fisher was a resident of Culver, Marshall Co.

The collection consists primarily of letters, notes, and writings of Howard Walton Clark (1870-1941), ichthyologist with the U.S. Bureau of Fisheries (1904-1923) and with the California Academy of Sciences (1923-1941), and author, with Barton W. Evermann, of *Lake Maxinkuckee, a Physical and Biological Survey* (1920). Included are Clark's letters to Fisher and his family regarding his scientific work and personal matters; Clark's letters and reports regarding his participation in the California Academy of Sciences' expedition to the Galapagos Islands in 1932; and an essay on a Brown County, Ind., trip in the 1930s.

B-122. FOGLEMAN, IDA (fl.1874-1950). PAPERS, 1859-1950.

4 folders. S 474.

Fogleman was the daughter of David Fogleman (1828-1906), a Mooresville, Morgan Co., farmer and businessman; student in Terre Haute, Vigo Co., Greencastle, Putnam Co., and Indiana University, Bloomington, Monroe Co. (1892-1898); and schoolteacher in Mooresville.

The collection includes David Fogleman's letters to his fiancee and wife, Maggie Moore Fogleman (1869-1880); letters to Maggie Fogleman from relatives in Champaign, Ill. (1870s), and Kansas City, Mo. (1880s); letters to Ida Fogleman from her parents while she was in school in Terre Haute, Greencastle, and Bloomington (1892-1898); her letters to her parents from a summer camp at Vawter Park, Kosciusko Co., near Lake Wawasee (1897), and from school in Bloomington (1897-1898); letters from family and friends in California and Indiana (1900-1920); a personal expense book (1875-1886); Ida Fogleman's school memory book (1882-1886); a memory book from a birthday party for her (1934); and her instructions to her estate executor (1939-1950).

B-123. FOSTER, MRS. OREN. COLLECTION, 1827-1939.

8 folders.   S 485.

Mrs. Oren Foster, of Tipton Co., Ind., donated this collection to the State Library in 1955.

The collection consists principally of the papers of the Henry Harper family of Adams County, Ohio (1835-1842), and Versailles, Ripley Co., Ind. Among the items are letters to Harper from his family in Carmichaels, Pa. (1836-1850s); letters to the Harpers from the Swearingen family in Winchester, Ill. (1849-1868); letters from the Charles H. Nettleton family in Winona County, Minn. (1857-1882); Civil War letters of James Harper, a soldier in the 37th Indiana Regiment serving in Tennessee (1863-1864); James Harper's letters to his family from his farm in Sharpsville, Tipton Co. (1865-1870); family letters and letters on family history to Mrs. Howard Harper, Sedalia, Mo., from her cousin, Nellie Harper of Gary, Lake Co. (1913-1916); and Harper family receipts and land documents (1827-1868).

B-124. FOULKE, WILLIAM DUDLEY (1848-1935). PAPERS, 1849-1931.

2 ms. boxes.   L 56.

Reformer and author. Foulke was an attorney in New York (1870-1876) and Richmond, Wayne Co. (1876-1935); Republican member, Indiana State Senate (1883-1885); president, American Woman's Suffrage Association (1885-1890); officer, Indiana Civil Service Reform Association (1885-1890); member, U.S. Civil Service Commission (1901-1903); editor, *Evening Item*, Richmond (1909-1912); president, National Municipal League (1910-1915); member, platform committee, Progressive Party (1912); president, National Civil Service Reform League (1923-1924); and author, *Life of Oliver P. Morton* (1899), *A Hoosier Autobiography* (1922), and *Lucius B. Swift, American Citizen* (1930).

The collection includes Foulke's correspondence relating to civil service reform, the women's rights movement, Indiana and national Republican Party politics, the Progressive Party in 1912 and 1916, American involvement in the Philippine Islands, and his work on behalf of American preparedness in World War I, and on behalf of the World Court, the League to Enforce Peace, and the League of Nations; copies of his extensive correspondence with

Theodore Roosevelt regarding civil service reform and Republican and Progressive Party politics (1890-1917); correspondence and papers relating to Foulke's research on Oliver P. Morton; his articles and speeches on civil service and electoral reform, women's rights, World War I, prohibition, toleration, and other subjects; and minutes of the Indiana Civil Service Reform Association (1885-1890). Also included are papers (1849-1863) of Indiana Civil War governor Oliver P. Morton (1823-1877), including letters from members of the Indiana congressional delegation regarding a proposed peace conference with the South in the spring of 1861.

Correspondents include George Ade, William O. Barnard, Thomas Francis Bayard, Albert J. Beveridge, Alice Stone Blackwell, Henry B. Carrington, Grace Julian Clarke, John Coburn, Joseph M. Dixon, G. Cary Eggleston, Charles W. Fairbanks, William P. Fishback, John Watson Foster, Emma Goldman, James P. Goodrich, Horace Greeley, Pleasant Hackleman, Murat Halstead, J. Frank Hanly, Benjamin Harrison, Mary Lord Harrison, Albert Bushnell Hart, Robert R. Hitt, William R. Holloway, Julia Ward Howe, Harold L. Ickes, Hiram W. Johnson, Robert Underwood Johnson, George W. Julian, George Kennan, John Worth Kern, David Kilgore, Count Carl Mannerhein, John Mitchell, Oliver P. Morton, Meredith Nicholson, Godlove Orth, Gifford Pinchot, Samuel Ralston, James Whitcomb Riley, Theodore Roosevelt, May Wright Sewall, Thomas C. Slaughter, Caleb B. Smith, Theodore C. Steele, Lucius B. Swift, William Howard Taft, David Turpie, James E. Watson, and Henry Lane Wilson.

B-125. FRANKLIN COUNTY GENERAL STORE. ACCOUNT BOOKS, 1839-1843.

2 vols. (.25 l.f.). V 153.

The collection consists of account books for a general store in Metamora, Franklin Co.

B-126. FREEZ, F. (fl.1841-1860). ACCOUNT BOOKS, 1841-1853.

3 vols. (.25 l.f.). V 50.

Freez was a blacksmith in Preble County, Ohio.

The collection consists of Freez's account books (1841-1853).

B-127. GARDEN CLUB OF INDIANA. RECORDS, 1931-1983.

9 l.f.

The Garden Club was founded in 1930 as part of the Indiana Federation of Art Clubs. It became an independent organization in 1932 as the Indiana Federation of Garden Clubs and became the Garden Club of Indiana in 1935. The club is for people interested in horticulture, flower arranging, conservation, and landscaping, and it has been involved in the beautification of highway roadsides, the improvement of the environment, and the sponsorship of Junior Garden Clubs.

The records include minutes of board and committee meetings, chairmen's and district directors' reports, and convention programs and reports (1932-1983); financial statements (1946-1964); scrapbooks of newspaper clippings, programs, and other items about the club (1931-1983); papers relating to the Blue Star Memorial Highway Award (1979) and the club's environmental improvement program (1971); video and audio tapes; and awards.

B-128. GARVER, JOHN JAMES (1845-1900). ACCOUNT BOOKS, 1880-1900.

3 vols. (.25 l.f.).   V 15.

Garver was an Indianapolis physician.

The collection consists of Garver's account books listing patients, reasons for visits, charges, and some prescriptions.

B-129. GASKINS, BERNICE. COLLECTION, 1864-1924.

2 folders.   S 505.

Gaskins, of Bloomington, Monroe Co., donated this collection to the State Library in 1972.

The collection consists of the papers of the Gaskins family of Ellettsville, Monroe Co. Included are letters from Anna Sage, Gosport, Owen Co., to her fiance, Tobe A. Gaskins, in Weldon, Ill., Indianapolis, and Ellettsville (1909-1911); Gaskins family letters (1911-1920), including letters from Dupont, Jefferson Co., and letters from soldiers serving in the U.S. Army in World War I; documents relating to Gaskins family landholdings in Monroe County (1879-1892); and a ledger book containing the constitution, minutes, and accounts of the Valley Exchange Telephone Company (1918-1924), organized by the farmers of Washington, Bloomington, and Beanblossom townships, Monroe Co.

B-130. GATES, RALPH F. (1893-1978). PAPERS, 1941-1975.

27 l.f.   Partial Inventory.

Gates was an attorney in Columbia City, Whitley Co. (1917-1978); naval officer in World War I; Indiana commander, American Legion (1931); Republican State Chairman (1941-1944); governor of Indiana (1945-1949); and Republican National Committeeman (1947-1961).

The collection consists of correspondence, speeches, reports, and legislation from Gates's term as governor, including papers relating to the Alcoholic Beverage Commission, the Indiana State Highway Commission, the Tax Study Commission, flood control, veterans' affairs, and labor and the Standard Oil strike in Whiting (1945). Also included are papers relating to the Republican National Committee and the Republican Party in Indiana (1940s-1960s); papers pertaining to Gates's campaign for governor (1944); scrapbooks (1944-1950); and personal correspondence.

Correspondents include E. Ross Adair, Homer Capehart, George N. Craig, Dwight D. Eisenhower, and William E. Jenner.

B-131. GIDDINGS, LURA MARIA (1825-1871). PAPERS, 1840-1870.

1 ms. box.   L 332.

Giddings was the daughter of Joshua R. Giddings (1795-1864), antislavery leader, Whig and Republican congressman from Ohio (1839-1859), and U.S. consul general to Canada in Montreal (1861-1864).

The collection includes Joshua Giddings's letters to his daughter, wife, and other members of his family, written from Washington, D.C. (1840-1858), and Montreal, Canada (1862-1864); journals of Joshua Giddings (1852-1860); journals of Lura Maria Giddings (ca.1860-1870), including journals of a trip from Cleveland to Lake Superior (1867-1868) and journals written at Philadelphia and London (1869-1870); and her biography of her father, along with several of his brief memoirs.

B-132. GLOVER, JOSEPH (1782-1844). PAPERS, 1805-1881.

1 folder.   S 518.

Glover was clerk and bookkeeper of the Kentucky State Prison; farmer in Lawrence County, Indiana (ca.1816-1844); Lawrence County sheriff (1818-1822, 1826-1828, 1831-1835); and member, Indiana House of Representatives (1822-1823).

The collection consists primarily of business papers from the period 1805-1842, including personal and prison receipts from Kentucky (1805-1810); Lawrence County court and sheriff's papers (1820s-1830s); land and business papers from Lawrence County; rules and membership list of a Lawrence County association for suppressing counterfeiting and horse stealing (ca.1819); and a petition on behalf of Indiana judge John H. Thompson (ca.1839).

B-133. GRAND ARMY OF THE REPUBLIC. GEORGE H. THOMAS POST #17. RECORDS, 1880-1934.

1 ms. box, 10 vols., 1 folder (2 l.f.).   L 201, V 127, V 175, S 1941.

The George H. Thomas Post was the Indianapolis chapter of the Grand Army of the Republic, an organization of Union Army veterans.

The collection is made up of minutes of meetings (1890-1908, 1927-1933); dues and membership records (1880-1933); ledgers and other financial records (1893-1933); memorials written on members' deaths (1882-1905); meeting attendance records (1926-1933); books of GAR rituals and services; and correspondence and other papers regarding membership (1932-1934). Also included are photocopies of minutes of Johnson Post #368 in Montpelier, Blackford Co. (1884-1894).

B-134. GRANT COUNTY WAR HISTORY COMMITTEE. RECORDS, 1919-1921.

1 folder.   S 1667.

The Grant County War History Committee worked with the Indiana Historical Commission to collect service records of Grant County's soldiers and sailors who died in World War I. The records were published in the Grant County section of the Historical Commission's *Gold Star Honor Roll. A Record of Indiana Men and Women Who Died in the Service of the United States and the Allied Nations in the World War* (1921).

The collection consists primarily of the correspondence of Mrs. George A. Southall (1866-1969), chairman of the Grant County War History Committee, regarding service records of Grant County soldiers and sailors. In addition there are Indiana Historical Commission War History Records forms, filled out for a number of Grant County servicemen.

B-135. GRAY, WILLIAM H. (fl.1845-1866). PAPERS, 1836-1881.

31 items.   S 534.

Gray was a farmer in Cumberland, Marion Co.

The papers include letters to Gray from relatives in Amelia, Ohio (1848-1851), Jacksonville, Oregon Territory (1854), and from a soldier serving with the 45th Indiana Regiment (3rd Cavalry) in Virginia (1863); also Gray's tax receipts (1845-1866).

B-136. GRIFFIN, DANIEL F. (1833-1865). PAPERS, 1861-1883.

1 ms. box.   L 60.

Griffin, from New Albany, Floyd Co., was a major and colonel in the 38th Indiana Regiment, serving in Kentucky, Tennessee, and Georgia (1861-1864).

The collection is composed of forty-four original Civil War letters from Griffin to his wife in New Albany; typed transcripts of 277 of his Civil War letters to his wife; and a notebook containing notes on regimental accounts and several hand drawn maps.

B-137. HAMILTON, ALLEN (1798-1864). PAPERS, 1817-1932.

12 archival boxes, 21 ms. boxes (20.4 l.f.). L 62.

Merchant and Indian trader. Hamilton was an emigrant from Ireland to Canada and Pennsylvania (1817); resident of Lawrenceburg, Dearborn Co. (1820-1823), and Fort Wayne, Allen Co. (1823-1864); deputy clerk, U.S. Land Office at Fort Wayne (1823); Allen County sheriff (1824-1826); Fort Wayne postmaster (1825-1831); county auditor, clerk, and recorder (1831-1838); merchant, partner in firm of Hamilton and Taber (1820s-1830s) and Hamilton and Williams (1840s-1850s), involved in trade with Indians in northern Indiana; member, U.S. commission to negotiate treaties with Miami Indians (1834, 1838); member, commission to extinguish Indian titles in Indiana (1840); U.S. Indian Agent to Miami Indians (1841-1845); Whig delegate, Indiana Constitutional Convention (1850-1851); Democratic member, Indiana State Senate (1859-1861); and president of Fort Wayne branch, State Bank of Indiana, and of the Allen Hamilton National Bank in Fort Wayne.

The collection consists principally of Hamilton's business papers and correspondence from the period 1825-1860. Included are receipts, legal papers, accounts, and business correspondence of the firm of Hamilton and Taber, including Cyrus Taber's letters to Hamilton from Logansport, Cass Co. (1830s), receipts and accounts for trade with the Miami Indians (1820s-1830s), and accounts and business correspondence with merchants in Indiana, Cincinnati, Louisville, and New York, including the New York firm of Suydam, Jackson & Company; his correspondence regarding Miami Indian treaties and trade in the 1830s, and papers regarding the settlement of the estate of Miami Chief Francis Godfroy (1840s); his correspondence as U.S. Indian Agent to the Miamis (1841-1845), including retained copies of his letters to the U.S. Commissioner of Indian Affairs and other federal officials; receipts, accounts, and business correspondence of the firm of Hamilton and Williams (1840s-1850s); correspondence and business papers regarding Hamilton's other business interests, including railroads, canals, banking, and land acquisitions in Allen, Cass, Blackford, Huntington, and Marshall counties; and correspondence regarding state and national politics (1820s-1860s), including correspondence pertaining to internal improvements in Indiana (1830s) and Whig Party politics (1848), and letters from his brother-in-law, William S. Holman, regarding Democratic Party politics and the U.S. Congress in the 1850s and 1860s. Also included is correspondence and business papers relating to the settlement and administration of Hamilton's estate; correspondence and personal business papers of his son, Andrew H. Hamilton (1834-1895), including papers relating to his time as a student at Wabash College and in Goettingen, Germany (1850s), and correspondence from constituents while he was a Democratic member of the U.S. House of Representatives (1875-1879); papers pertaining to Andrew Hamilton's estate, particularly papers of his wife, Phoebe, who served as executrix; Hamilton family correspondence (1820s-1920s); and papers regarding the Olds Wagon Works in Fort Wayne (1881-1910).

Correspondents include Thomas H. Blake, Jesse D. Bright, Michael G. Bright, T. Hartley Crawford, John D. Defrees, John Dowling, Thomas Dowling, John B. Duret, Henry C. Ellsworth, George W. Ewing, William G. Ewing, Francis Godfroy, Samuel Hanna, Andrew J. Harlan, Thomas A. Hendricks, William Hendricks, Jesse L. Holman, William S. Holman, Edmond O. Hovey, Henry S. Lane, James F. D. Lanier, Ebenezer F. Lucas, Jonathan McCarty, Hugh McCulloch, Samuel Merrill, Samuel Milroy, Elias Murray, Abel C. Pepper, Daniel D. Pratt, George H. Proffit, James Rariden, Joseph Richardville, William Rockhill, Samuel C. Sample, Caleb B. Smith, Oliver H. Smith, John Test, Richard W. Thompson, John Tipton, David Wallace, Nathaniel West, Albert S. White, Charles White, Jesse L. Williams, Daniel Worth, and Joseph A. Wright.

B-138. HARRISON, BENJAMIN (1833-1901). PAPERS, 1841-1900.

4 ms. boxes.   L 63.

Politician and attorney. Harrison was an Indianapolis attorney (1854-1901); Indianapolis city attorney (1857); reporter, Indiana Supreme Court (1860-1862, 1864-1868); officer in the 70th Indiana Regiment (1862-1865), reaching the rank of brigadier general; Republican candidate for governor of Indiana (1876); member, Mississippi River Commission (1879-1881); U.S. Senator and Chairman, Senate Committee on Territories (1881-1887); President of the United States (1889-1893); Republican nominee for President (1892); served as senior counsel for Venezuela before arbitration tribunal in Paris during boundary dispute with England (1899); and writer and speaker on public affairs.

The bulk of the collection consists of invoices and receipts for Harrison's personal and household expenses in Indianapolis (1893-1897), and for expenses incurred in the construction of his Indianapolis home (1874-1875). In addition, there are Harrison's letters (1896-1900) to his Indianapolis friend and law partner, W. H. H. Miller, regarding Republican Party politics, Harrison's legal work in the Venezuelan boundary dispute, investments, and family and personal matters; correspondence regarding a federal appointment for his son, Russell B. Harrison (1875-1881); correspondence and invitations relating to the Harrisons' social life in Washington, D.C. (1889-1893); scattered correspondence regarding politics and Harrison's writings; an 1864 letter of Harrison's wife, Caroline Scott Harrison, to her brother; 1888 campaign badges, broadsides, and other material; political notebooks containing names and notes on political supporters (1881); duplicates of Harrison papers in the Library of Congress; and "Catalogue of Library and Index to Vocal and Instrumental Music," by Lizzie Lord, Caroline Scott Harrison's niece (1866).

Correspondents include Edward Bok, Horatio C. Burchard, John S. Clarkson, Roscoe Conkling, Will Cumback, Winfield T. Durbin, Melville W. Fuller, E. M. Halford, Joseph B. Hawley, Alexander Heron, Robert Underwood Johnson, Nathan Kimball, Louis T. Michener, John F. Miller, William H. H. Miller, Col. K. G. Shryock, George Alfred Thompson, Albion Tourgee, and William Windom.

B-139. HARRISON, I. MERRITT (1886-1973). COLLECTION, 1856-1900.

5 vols. (.5 l.f.).   V 82.

Harrison, an Indianapolis architect, donated this collection to the State Library in 1935.

The collection includes letter books of Richmond, Wayne Co., businessman Timothy Harrison, containing copies of his correspondence as secretary of the Missionary Board and secretary of the Executive Committee on Education, Indiana Yearly Meeting of Friends (1871-1876); minute book of the Union of Christian Endeavors, New Castle, Henry Co. (1891-1900); minute book of the White Water Auxiliary of the Indiana Bible Association of Friends, Wayne County (1857-1870); and account book for William G. Johnson's general store in Raysville, Henry Co. (1856-1858).

B-140. HARRISON, MARY LORD (1858-1948). PAPERS, 1901-1947.

40 items.   S 599.

Harrison was the second wife of President Benjamin Harrison (1833-1901); and resident of New York City after 1901.

The collection consists principally of Harrison's letters (1936-1947) to Cyril Clemens, president of the International Mark Twain Society, Webster Groves, Mo., regarding her life, the life of Benjamin Harrison, and their literary acquaintances. In addition, there is a letter from Harrison to Charles W. Fairbanks thanking him for his kindness during President Harrison's illness (1901), and several of her autographs on envelopes.

B-141. HARRYMAN, SAMUEL K. (1826-1877). LETTERS, 1862-1865.

48 items.   S 603.

Soldier. Harryman, of Mooresville, Morgan Co., was a lieutenant in the 70th Indiana Regiment, serving in Kentucky, Tennessee, Georgia, and the Carolinas (1862-1865); and aide-de-camp to General William T. Ward, commander of the 1st Division, 11th Army Corps (1864), and the 1st Brigade, 3rd Division, 20th Army Corps (1864-1865).

The collection consists of Harryman's Civil War letters to Margaret Moore, Mooresville, Ind. (1862-1865).

B-142. HARTLEY, HARRY D. (ca.1882-1959). PAPERS, 1925-1951.

2 ms. boxes.   L 273.

Hartley was the president of Pioneer Coal and Shaft Company, Piqua, Ohio, and president of the Piqua Savings Bank (to 1925); president, Turner Glass Company, Indianapolis (ca.1926-1930); handled family's investments and worked as a business consultant, Indianapolis (1930s); and served on War Rationing Board, Indianapolis, during World War II.

The collection consists of Hartley's correspondence and papers regarding his family's property (1925-1940), particularly property in Kokomo, Howard Co., which was leased for an A & P grocery store in 1930; correspondence regarding his proposed book on the contributions of Indiana people to the development of the United States and western civilization (1939-1951); letters relating to an Indianapolis talk given by Arthur E. Morgan on his investigations into the Tennessee Valley Authority (1939); transcripts of the meetings of the Forward Club, organized by Hartley (1928, 1938); a scrapbook of clippings, pictures, and letters on the Reeves Pulley Company of Columbus, Bartholomew Co., which manufactured automobiles in the early twentieth century; a scrapbook of clippings and brochures relating to television and other inventions (1928-1944); and brochures on New Harmony, the J. F. D. Lanier Home in Madison, Jefferson Co., and Boulder Dam.

Correspondents include Carl Fisher and Frederick Van Nuys.

B-143. HARVEY, RALPH (1901-). PAPERS, ca.1920-1984.

23 archival boxes, 36 vols. (31 l.f.).　　　　　　　　Inventory.

Politician. Harvey was a farmer in Henry County; Henry County Councilman (1932-1942); Republican member, Indiana House of Representatives (1942-1947); elected to U.S. Congress to fill vacancy caused by death of Raymond S. Springer (1947); member, U.S. House of Representatives (1947-1959, 1961-1967), serving on the House Committee on Expenditures; member, U.S. Board of Forest Appeals (1970-1974); and author, *Autobiography of a Hoosier Congressman* (1975).

The collection consists primarily of Harvey's congressional papers (1947-1967), including correspondence with constituents on legislative and political issues, such as agriculture, care for the aged, foreign aid, and taxes; reports, publications, surveys, and other materials on small business, foreign and domestic agriculture and the work of the Food and Agricultural Organization of the United Nations, and other issues before Congress; reports, publications, and other materials regarding Harvey's congressional trips to South and Central America (1955) and Asia and West Africa (1964); his speeches, press releases, interviews, and newsletters; information on his voting record and on legislation which he introduced in Congress; and constituent requests for information and assistance. Also included are Harvey's diaries (1944-1984); his scrapbooks (1920-1966); copies of his articles for the *Eastern Indiana Farmer* (1950s-1960s); and constituent correspondence of Congressman Raymond S. Springer (1940-1947).

B-144. HASELTINE, ROSS J. (1833-1892). PAPERS, 1863-1866.

47 items. S 621.

Haseltine was a merchant in New Paris, Ohio, and Kokomo, Howard Co. (1864-1892); and lieutenant and captain in the 69th Ohio Regiment, serving in Tennessee (1863-1865).

The collection includes Haseltine's reports on equipment and supplies for his company during the Civil War, principally from 1863; and his correspondence with the U.S. Treasury Department regarding information in his equipment reports (1866).

B-145. HAWK, ALETHA GRACE (b.1882). PAPERS, 1918-1941.

74 items. S 612.

Businesswoman and humanitarian. Hawk worked for the American Red Cross, serving as secretary to Frederic M. Ayres (1872-1940), director of supplies and surplus, in Washington, D.C. (1918-1919), and Paris, France (1919); held a variety of positions with L. S. Ayres & Company, an Indianapolis department store, including secretary to the president and executive secretary (1919-1953); and active in the Women's Overseas Service League (1920s-1940s), serving as president, editor of the national magazine *Carry On*, and Indianapolis service chairman (1941).

The collection consists principally of Hawk's letters to her family in Indianapolis from Washington, D.C., and Europe, describing her work with the Red Cross and as a volunteer working with wounded servicemen at Walter Reed Hospital, and describing her travels through France, Switzerland, Belgium, and Germany (1918-1919). Also included is her 1921 letter describing the visit of Marshall Ferdinand Foch to Indianapolis; two letters to Hawk from a

French refugee describing conditions in occupied France (1940-1941); and Hawk's poetry.

B-146. HAWLEY, RANSOM (1802-1889). PAPERS, 1824-1899.

8 ms. boxes.　　　　　　　　　　　　　　　　　　　　　　　　L 64.

Minister. Hawley was a graduate of Auburn Theological Seminary, Auburn, N.Y. (1828); Presbyterian missionary and minister in Indiana, serving at Washington, Daviess Co. (1828-1834), Bloomington, Monroe Co. (1834-1841), and Putnamville, Putnam Co. (1841-1879); and resident of Terre Haute, Vigo Co. (1879-1889). Hawley's family included his son, Henry M. Hawley (1834-1914), an employee of the Evansville and Crawfordsville Railroad Company in Terre Haute; his son, Ransom E. Hawley (b.1844), a student at Wabash College, Crawfordsville, Montgomery Co. (1862-1865), and Lane Seminary, Cincinnati, Ohio (1867-1868), soldier in the 133rd Indiana Regiment (1863), and a Presbyterian minister in Cincinnati (1868-1873), Kentland, Newton Co. (1873-1874), Cleves, Ohio (1874-1880), Washington, Daviess Co. (1880-1888), Hastings and St. Paul, Minn. (1888-ca.1898), and Edinburg, Johnson Co. (1898); and his daughter, Lucy Ing (1837-1881), a teacher in Evansville, Vanderburgh Co. (1860s), married missionary John Ing (1870), missionary and teacher in China (1870-1874) and Hirosaki, Japan (1874-1878).

The collection consists primarily of Hawley's family and professional correspondence, including correspondence with his family in Bridgeport, Conn., while he was a student at Auburn Seminary (1825-1828); correspondence of Hawley and his wife in Indiana with their families in Bridgeport (1828-ca.1880); letters to Hawley from Presbyterian ministers and other church people in southern and central Indiana (1828-ca.1880); letters and appointments from the Board of Missions of the General Assembly of the Presbyterian Church, from the American Home Missionary Society, and the American Sunday School Union (1825-ca.1860); Hawley's correspondence with his children, including his letters to Ransom E. Hawley (1860-1889), and letters to Hawley from Henry Hawley in Terre Haute, from Lucy Ing in Bridgeport, Conn. (1853), Evansville (1860s), China and Japan (1873-1878), and Salt Springs, Mo. (1880-1881), and from Ransom E. Hawley at Wabash College (1862-1864), in the 133rd Regiment in Alabama (1863), at Lane Seminary (1867-1868), and at his churches in Ohio, Indiana, and Minnesota (1868-1898); and letters from other members of the Hawley family in Asheville,

N.C. (1870s), Seymour, Jackson Co., and North Vernon, Jennings Co. (1870s-1880s), and other places in the Midwest. Additional items include Ransom Hawley's journals of his ministerial work (1832-1836); list of his sermons (1837-1883); his travel journal for a trip from Bloomington to Bridgeport, Conn. (1835); his memorandum book (1851); Ransom E. Hawley's diaries (1867-1889); and a Hawley family scrapbook (1824-ca.1885) containing articles on the American Home Missionary Society, John and Lucy Ing's articles on missionary work in China and Japan, and documents and articles relating to Hawley's church work.

Correspondents include Henry Ward Beecher, Benjamin Harrison, Edmund O. Hovey, Caleb Mills, Isaac Reed, and Andrew Wylie.

B-147. HAYS, WILL H. (1879-1954). PAPERS, 1857-1954.

130 l.f. Inventory and partial calendar.

Attorney, politician, and motion picture executive. Hays was a native of Sullivan, Sullivan Co.; graduate of Wabash College, Crawfordsville (1900); lawyer in Sullivan firm of Hays and Hays (1900-1954); Sullivan city attorney (1910-1913); chairman, Republican State Committee (1914-1918); chairman, Indiana State Council of Defense (1917-1918); chairman, Republican National Committee (1918-1921); campaign manager for Warren G. Harding (1920); U.S. Postmaster General (1921-1922); president (1922-1945) and advisor (1945-1950), Motion Picture Producers and Distributors of America; member, board of directors, Chicago & Eastern Illinois Railroad, Bedford Stone and Construction Company, and other companies; member, board of trustees, Wabash College (1919-1954); national president, Phi Delta Theta fraternity (1920-1922); chairman, Near East Relief Commission (appointed 1922); and chairman, Layman's Committee, Presbyterian Board for Ministerial Relief.

The collection includes Hays's correspondence, speeches, scrapbooks, and notebooks, principally from the period 1914-1954. His political papers include correspondence and other papers regarding his work as Indiana and national Republican Party chairman; his work with the State Council of Defense during World War I; his efforts to unite the liberal and conservative wings of the Republican Party for the 1920 election, including his correspondence with Theodore Roosevelt on the party's future (1918-1919); his efforts to attract women voters to the party by working with woman suffrage organizations and the Anti-Saloon League; his work on behalf of Warren G. Harding's presidential campaign, including papers regarding campaign finances, the support of interest groups, and the operations of state campaign committees; his work as U.S. Postmaster General, including papers regarding postal appointments, post office policies, and air mail, rural mail service, and other post office operations; and his involvement in Republican Party affairs from the 1920s to the 1950s, particularly the 1940 national convention and his support of Wendell Willkie.

His papers as president of the Motion Picture Producers and Distributors of America (MPPDA) include minutes of meetings; policy statements, such as censorship policies; MPPDA financial statements and reports; Hays's annual reports as president (1926, 1932-1945); his speeches regarding the motion picture industry; and papers regarding issues before the MPPDA, including conduct of movie personnel, distribution monopolies and unfair competition, taxes on the film industry, the distribution of American films abroad, copyright protection, the motion picture industry during World War II, and the use of motion pictures for educational purposes. Also included is correspondence, transcripts of hearings, and photostats of exhibits relating to a 1947 case involving American film companies' claims against French distributors for royalties owed from the period 1939-1945, in which Hays served as arbitrator.

Also contained are Hays's papers regarding his business interests in the Chicago and Eastern Illinois Railroad (1920s-1950s), the Bedford Stone Company, various coal companies in southwestern Indiana, the U.S. Potash Company, and banks in Sullivan, Indianapolis, California, and New York; personal correspondence, including letters from his father, John T. Hays, while Hays was attending Wabash College (1896-1900), and correspondence with friends and relatives in Sullivan, Indianapolis, and other Indiana cities; and papers regarding Hays's work with cultural and charitable institutions, including Wabash College, Phi Delta Theta fraternity, the Near East Relief Commission (1920s-1930s), the Theodore Roosevelt Memorial Association, the Red Cross, and the Presbyterian Board for Ministerial Relief, which worked to rebuild Presbyterian churches and missions in Asia and the Pacific after World War II. The collection also includes scrapbooks of clippings, press releases, speeches, and other items dealing with Hays's career, and with Republican Party affairs, the U.S. Post Office, and the motion picture industry; and outlines, notes, and drafts of his autobiography, published as *Memoirs* (1955).

Correspondents include George Ade, Ingrid Bergman, Albert J. Beveridge, Oscar E. Bland, Styles Bridges, Richard E. Byrd, Eddie Cantor, Homer

Capehart, John C. Chaney, Calvin Coolidge, Cecil B. DeMille, Stoughton A. Fletcher, Ralph F. Gates, James P. Goodrich, Charles Halleck, Warren G. Harding, James A. Hemenway, Ted Herron, Herbert Hoover, Charles Evans Hughes, Joseph P. Kennedy, Henry Cabot Lodge, Medill McCormick, Warren T. McCray, Harry S. New, Meredith Nicholson, Mary Pickford, Will Rogers, Theodore Roosevelt, Alfred E. Smith, Delavan Smith, Harlan F. Stone, William Howard Taft, Thomas Taggart, Booth Tarkington, Arthur H. Vandenberg, Albert H. Vestal, Booker T. Washington, James E. Watson, Thomas Watson, Raymond E. Willis, and Henry Lane Wilson.

B-148. HAZELWOOD LUMBER COMPANY. ACCOUNT BOOKS, 1890-1914.

2 vols. (.5 l.f.). V 232.

The Hazelwood Lumber Company was located in Anderson, Madison Co.

The collection consists of the company's account books.

B-149. HECKER, EDWARD J. (1868-1945). PAPERS, 1892-1945.

2 ms. boxes. L 65.

Educator, printer, and politician. Hecker was a teacher at the Indiana School for the Deaf, Indianapolis (ca.1888-ca.1905); printer, with Hecker Brothers, Irvington, Marion Co. (1899-1930s); active in Marion County Republican Party politics; founding member and officer of the Irvington Republican Club; appointed to advisory board to the mayor of Indianapolis (1911); unsuccessful candidate for the Indiana General Assembly (1912, 1916); Warren Township Trustee, Marion Co. (1918-1926); Indiana deputy secretary of state (1925, 1927, 1929); unsuccessful candidate for U.S. Congress (1934); and wrote column of wit and verses for the *Indianapolis News*.

The collection consists of Hecker's correspondence (1892-1945), including his correspondence regarding education for the deaf; his election campaigns in 1912, 1916, and 1934; his work as Warren Township Trustee; local Republican Party politics (1910s-1930s); and family matters. In addition there are account books from Hecker Brothers printing company (1899-1923); his writings, including fictional, inspirational, humorous, and political pieces; newspaper clippings regarding Hecker's career and political campaigns; papers relating to the Irvington Republican Club; and papers pertaining to the reorganization of the Indianapolis Street Railways Company (1932).

Correspondents include Richard Lieber, Louis Ludlow, Frederick Polley, Stephen Marion Reynolds, and Arthur R. Robinson.

B-150. HEDRICK, MRS. WEST. COLLECTION, 1855-1868.

26 items. S 625.

Mrs. West Hedrick, of Salem, Washington Co., donated this collection to the Indiana State Library in 1930.

The collection consists of family letters to Elizabeth J. Roby (ca.1828-1905), a resident of Salem, Washington Co. Included are letters from cousins William and Agnes Scott of Smyrna, Iowa, and from other family in Xenia, Ill., principally from the period 1861-1866, regarding farm life and family matters.

B-151. HELM, THOMAS B. (1822-1889). DIARIES, 1862-1888.

1 ms. box (26 vols.). L 66.

Helm was a teacher in Logansport, Cass Co. (1844-1873); Cass County civil engineer (1856-ca.1870); Cass County probate commissioner (1856-1868); and author, *History of Cass County, Indiana* (1886), and histories of other Indiana counties.

The collection contains Helm's diaries (1862-1888), primarily consisting of his detailed daily descriptions of weather conditions in Logansport. The diaries also include scattered references to Cass County events and Helm's family affairs.

B-152. HELMS, HAMET N. (1814-1892). PAPERS, 1823-1890.

1 ms. box, 2 vols. (.67 l.f.). L 132, V 84.

Helms was a physician (1839-1874) and a farmer (1874-1892) in Carlisle, Sullivan Co.; medical partner of Dr. John W. Davis (1839-1841); and married Mary A. Davis (1939).

The collection is made up of Helms's family correspondence (1840-1881), including correspondence with the Davis family in Carlisle, Pa., and Baltimore, Md. (1840-1851); correspondence between Helms and his wife (1847-1848); letter of John Lee Davis, officer in the U.S. Navy, from Macao, China (1849); and letters of Dr. J. W. Davis, Lansing, Iowa (1881). Also included are Helms's account books, containing accounts for his medical practice (1856-1865, 1870-1874) and his farm (1874-1878); Helms's 1879 reminiscence about his early years as a physician in Sullivan County; miscellaneous accounts for his medical practice (1864-1865); and a Methodist testimonial and letter regarding Methodist practices, Chambersburg, Pa. (1823, 1827).

B-153. HENDRICKS, ALLAN (1864-1949). COLLECTION, 1816-1939.

2 folders. S 634.

Hendricks, an Indianapolis attorney, donated this collection to the Indiana State Library in 1937 and 1939. He was the son of Abram W. Hendricks (1822-1887), an attorney in Madison, Jefferson Co. (1847-1866), and Indianapolis (1866-1887); law partner of Thomas A. Hendricks in Indianapolis firm of Hendricks, Hord and Hendricks; member, Indiana House of Representatives (1852-1853); Republican candidate for Indiana Supreme Court (1858); and secretary, Committee of Safety during 1877 Indianapolis railroad strike.

The collection consists primarily of Abram Hendricks's papers, including his correspondence on Indiana politics (1859-1870); minutes of the Indianapolis Committee of Safety during the 1877 railroad strike; letters of Heinrich Schliemann to Hendricks, Hord and Hendricks regarding his property in Indianapolis (1870-1871); Hendricks's receipts and invoices for personal expenses, particularly clothing, in Madison (1851-1866); a chart of the organization of the Union Army at Vicksburg (1863); and papers of the Indianapolis Insurance Company (1868). Also included is Allan Hendricks's recollections of the Indianapolis Portfolio Club (1939).

Correspondents include Conrad Baker, William M. Dunn, Walter Q. Gresham, Winslow S. Pierce, Albert Gallatin Porter, and Heinrich Schliemann.

B-154. HERON, ALEXANDER (1827-1900). PAPERS, 1870-1900.

40 items.   S 641.

Heron was a farmer in Brookville, Franklin Co.; and served as secretary of the Indiana State Board of Agriculture (1872-1891).

The collection consists primarily of family letters from the period 1873-1878 and includes letters from Heron at the Indiana State Board of Agriculture, Indianapolis, to his family in Brookville (1873-1878); other family letters written from Brookville in the 1870s; and business letters to Heron regarding agriculture and agricultural fairs (1870-1890).

B-155. HERRON, GEORGE. COLLECTION, 1868-1936.

3 folders.   S 645.

Herron, of Noblesville, Hamilton Co., donated this collection to the Indiana State Library in 1967.

The collection includes political papers of Albert W. Trittipo (fl.1877-1936), a farmer at Fishers, Hamilton Co. Among the items are Democratic Party pollbooks kept by Trittipo for Fishers precinct, Hamilton Co. (1918-1930); election tickets for the Democratic, Republican, Prohibition, Union Labor, and National parties (1868-1888); newspaper clippings on Indiana and national politics (1880s-1930s); a small amount of correspondence regarding agricultural business (1877-1880s) and Democratic Party politics (ca.1900-1936); and Trittipo's notes on election returns.

B-156. HERSHEY, JEREMIAH (1839-ca.1922). DIARIES, 1873-1922.

2 ms. boxes (47 vols.).   L 68.

Hershey was a surveyor in Vincennes, Knox Co. (1868-1871); Vincennes city civil engineer (1871-ca.1903); and surveyor and contractor in Knox County (1900s-1910s).

The collection consists of Hershey's diaries (1873-1922) in which he wrote of his professional work, family matters, local politics and events, economic conditions, weather reports, and medicine.

B-157. HIBBEN FAMILY. PAPERS, 1850-1926.

1 ms. box.   L 69.

The Hibben family included James S. Hibben (1822-ca.1879), a dry goods retail and wholesale merchant in Rushville, Rush Co. (ca.1850-1865), and Indianapolis (1865-ca.1879), and founder of the Indianapolis wholesale dry goods firm of Hibben, Hollweg and Company; and Thomas E. Hibben (1893-1952), an architect in Indianapolis in the 1920s and a soldier in World War I.

The collection includes letters from James Hibben, Rushville, to his wife (1853-1856); invitations and social announcements, Rush County (1850s); other scattered family letters (1853-1912), including a letter from Sun Valley, Calif. (1853), and a letter on Indianapolis real estate (1912); Thomas E. Hibben's geographical description of the European front during World War I; letters to Hibben from the Indiana National Guard regarding meetings (1923); and personal accounts of the West family (1881-1885).

B-158. HINES, CYRUS C. (1830-1901). PAPERS, 1855-1873.

1 ms. box.   L 70.

Hines was an Indianapolis attorney (1854-1885), associated with Benjamin Harrison and Albert Gallatin Porter in the 1870s and 1880s; officer in the 24th Indiana Regiment and the 57th Indiana Regiment (1861-1863); Marion County farmer (1863-1866); and Indianapolis circuit court judge (1866-1872).

The collection is largely made up of the records of the Mars Hill and Indianapolis Gravel Road Company and the Bluff Creek Gravel Road Company, for both of which Hines served as an officer. Included are the companies' articles of association, minutes of meetings, correspondence, receipts, accounts, contracts, and officer election results (1861-1871). Also included are receipts and accounts for Hines's personal expenses and family expenses.

B-159. HISS, WILLIAM H. (1868-1907). PAPERS, 1858-1904.

1 ms. box, 27 vols. (2.75 l.f.).   L 71, V 51.

Businessman. Hiss was a graduate of DePauw University, Greencastle, Putnam Co. (1894); teacher at Central Academy, Plainfield, Hendricks Co. (1891-1892); Plainfield funeral director and dealer in furniture and agricultural implements (1894-1904), in company started by his father, Sebastian Hiss (ca.1858); and secretary and president, Indiana Funeral Directors' Association (1903-1904).

The collection includes account books for the Hiss funeral, furniture, and agricultural implement businesses (1858-1904); letter books of Sebastian and William Hiss containing business correspondence (1883-1899); register of funerals (1892-1902); register of invoices (1897-1899); and loose bills, receipts, and school report cards.

B-160. HOLLIDAY, JOHN H. (1846-1921). COLLECTION, 1850-1880.

35 items.   S 670.

Holliday, an Indianapolis newspaper editor and businessman, donated this collection to the Indiana State Library in 1922.

The collection includes papers relating to Indianapolis's quotas for volunteers during the Civil War (1864-1865); Indianapolis mayor John Caven's correspondence with the U.S. War Department regarding the number of Civil War soldiers provided by Indiana (1880); a speech on the payment of a bounty to the troops of the 17th Indiana Regiment (ca.1865); and scattered business papers of Caven (1850-1877).

Correspondents include John Caven, John Coburn, Ebenezer Dumont, Oliver P. Morton, Alexander Ramsey, W. H. H. Terrell, and Richard W. Thompson.

B-161. HOLMAN, WILLIAM STEELE (1822-1897). PAPERS, 1838-1894.

1 ms. box.   L 73.

Politician and attorney. Holman was an attorney in Aurora and Lawrenceburg, Dearborn Co.; Dearborn County probate judge (1843-1847); Democratic member, Indiana House of Representatives (1851-1852); member, U.S. House of Representatives for sixteen terms from 1859 to 1897; and chaired, at various times, House committees on Appropriations, Public Buildings and Grounds, and Inquiry into Indian Affairs.

The collection contains correspondence and petitions from constituents addressed to Holman in Congress (1865-1890); other scattered congressional papers of Holman, including papers relating to the U.S. Mint (1876), floods at Aurora (ca.1885), and government appointments; Holman's letters to his son, William Steele Holman, Jr., regarding Dearborn County politics (1894); Holman family letters, including letters to Holman's wife from her cousin in San Jose, Calif. (1886), and a letter from W. S. Holman, Jr., to his wife from the Chicago Columbian Exposition (1893); notes on Holman's speech on the policies of the Democratic Party (ca.1865); Holman's mailing lists of constituents receiving congressional and government publications; notes and clippings relating to southeastern Indiana election returns (1878-1890); and account book and diary of Richard Holman, a beginning attorney at Aurora (1837-1839).

B-162. HORAN, MICHAEL E. (1806-1844). PAPERS, 1825-1888.

60 items. S 682.

Horan was a businessman in Dublin, Ireland (1820s-1836), and Leesburg, Kosciusko Co. (1837-1844).

The collection is made up of family letters from Ireland (1825-1840); letters of introduction for Horan written by Irish businessmen to acquaintances in the United States (1836); tax receipts, merchant licenses, a will, and other business papers of Horan in Kosciusko County (1837-1844); Civil War veterans papers and pension papers of Horan's son-in-law, Hiram F. Berst, of Warsaw, Kosciusko Co. (1863-1888); and a brief Potawatomi Indian vocabulary list (ca.1840).

B-163. HORSE THIEF DETECTIVE ASSOCIATION. WARREN TOWNSHIP, MARION COUNTY. RECORDS, 1858-1933.

1 ms. box. L 202.

The Horse Thief Detective Association was a vigilante group active in many Indiana towns and counties from the early 1850s through the 1920s. During the 1920s it became associated with the Ku Klux Klan in Indiana.

The collection consists of records of the Horse Thief Detective Association in Warren Township, Marion Co. Included are minutes of meetings (1858-1933); receipt books for expenditures (1892-1933); roll book of members (1914-1932); a certificate of appointment as constable (1920); petition for constable powers (ca.1920); and badges.

B-164. HOUSTON, GUS (b.1850). DIARIES, 1876-1892.

1 ms. box (9 vols.). L 74.

Houston was a schoolteacher and surveyor at Bedford, Lawrence Co. (1876-ca.1880); surveyor in Pueblo, Colo., area (ca.1880-1890); and surveyor in Bedford (1890-1892).

Houston's diaries consist of brief entries describing his daily activities, his surveying work in Bedford and in Colorado, and religious and political meetings he attended (1876-1892).

B-165. HOVEY, EDMUND OTIS (1801-1877). PAPERS, 1826-1877.

1 ms. box.   Inventory.   L 75.

Minister and educator. Hovey was a graduate of Dartmouth College (1828) and Andover Seminary (1831); ordained Presbyterian missionary (1831); with wife, Mary Carter Hovey, moved from Vermont to Coal Creek, Fountain Co. (1831-1832); Presbyterian minister in Fountain County and western Indiana (1832-1834); one of the founders of Wabash College, Crawfordsville, Montgomery Co. (1832); Wabash College trustee (1832-1877); worked as agent for the college, raising money in the East (1834-1835); professor of rhetoric, geology, and other subjects at Wabash College (1834-1877); and college financial officer and agent (1830s-1850s).

The collection consists principally of Hovey family letters, including correspondence between Hovey and his fiancee (1831); letters of Hovey and his wife to their families in the East describing their trip from Vermont to Indiana, and their living conditions in Fountain County (1831-1834); correspondence between Hovey and his wife while he was traveling through the East raising money for Wabash College, and she was staying with family in Owego, N.Y. (1834-1835); and correspondence between Hovey and his wife while she was in Crawfordsville, and he was traveling on behalf of the college to Madison and New Albany, Ind. (1839), and New York, Philadelphia, Boston, Washington, D.C., and Vermont (1841-1869). Also included are transcripts of letters written by Hovey to his family while he was a student at Dartmouth College (1826-1827) and Andover Seminary (1828-1831); by Hovey and his wife in Indiana to their families in the East (1831-1858); and by Hovey to Charles White, regarding White's appointment as Wabash College president (1841-1842), and other college matters (1846-1859).

B-166. HOWARD, DONALD D. PAPERS, 1944-1946.

1 ms. box.   L 76.

Howard, of Evansville, Vanderburgh Co., served in the U.S. Navy (1944-1946), including service in the 4th Joint Assault Signal Company in the South Pacific and on Okinawa (1944-1945), and on the U.S.S. *Bergen* near Okinawa, Korea, China, and the Philippines (fall 1945).

The collection is composed of World War II letters from Howard to his parents, Louise and George Howard in Evansville, written from the South Pacific, Okinawa, China, Korea, the Philippines, California, and Fort Benjamin Harrison, Indianapolis (1944-1946); and correspondence of his parents with their daughter, Marilyn, a student at Indiana University, Bloomington (1945), and their daughter, Mrs. R. C. Datzman, a medical technician and wife of a physician in Detroit, Mich., and Carlisle, Pa. (1945-1946).

B-167. HOWE, FRANCIS (1811-1850). FAMILY PAPERS, 1817-1919.

1 ms. box.   L 77.

Howe was a Chicago businessman; husband of Rose Bailly (1813-1891), daughter of French fur trader Joseph Bailly de Messein of Porter County.

The collection also includes papers of Rose Bailly Howe, a resident of Baillytown, Porter Co., after her husband's death, and property owner in Porter County and Chicago, including downtown Chicago; and her daughters, Rose Howe (1842-1879), a student at St. Mary-of-the-Woods Academy, Vigo Co., a girls school run by the Sisters of Providence (1855-1860), and Frances R. Howe (1851-1917), a student at St. Mary-of-the-Woods Academy (1860-1869), a resident of Baillytown, Porter Co., and author of *Story of a French Homestead in the Old Northwest* (1907), and other works on the Bailly family and the history of northwestern Indiana.

The collection consists principally of Howe family correspondence and business papers, including Francis Howe's letters to his fiancee Rose Bailly (1841); Rose Bailly Howe's correspondence with her daughters at St. Mary-of-the-Woods Academy (1855-1869); correspondence with her daughter Rose living in Chicago (1861-1868); letters of her cousin Caroline A. Chase in Detroit, Mich., and Windsor, Ontario (1851-1868), and of her sister, Mother Mary Cecilia of the Sisters of Providence, St. Mary-of-the-Woods (1859-1890); letters of members of the Howe family to relatives during their tour of Catholic shrines in Europe and Palestine (1869-1874); correspondence and business papers relating to the Howes' investments in Chicago (1847-1890s), particularly correspondence with Chicago banker and attorney J. Young Scammon in the 1880s; correspondence of Francis R. Howe regarding Bailly family history, the upkeep of the Bailly home, and the Catholic church in northern Indiana, including correspondence with Rev. H. F. Joseph Kroll of Fort Wayne (1904-1916); correspondence of Frances R. Howe with her adopted daughter in Los Angeles, Calif. (1908-1917); and correspondence, receipts, and business papers relating to the Howes' property in Porter County. The collection also contains estate and other business papers of Joseph Bailly de Messein (1817-1838), including an inventory of his estate; and letters regarding the Bailly family's business affairs from John Whistler and Joel H. Wicker in Chicago (1838-1869).

B-168. HUDNUT, WILLIAM H. (1932-). PAPERS, 1972-1974.

51.4 l.f.   Inventory.

Politician. Hudnut was a Presbyterian minister in Buffalo, N.Y. (1957-1960), and Annapolis, Md. (1960-1963); senior minister, Second Presbyterian

Church, Indianapolis (1963-1972); Republican member, U.S. House of Representatives (1973-1975), serving on the Appropriations Committee and the Public Health and Environment Subcommittee; and mayor of Indianapolis (1975-).

The collection consists of Hudnut's congressional papers (1972-1974), including correspondence, reports, and other papers relating to his committee work on appropriations for government operations, and on public health and environmental issues; papers regarding Indianapolis interests, including the Weir Cook Airport, Ft. Benjamin Harrison, the Naval Avionics Facility, Lockefield Gardens, Environmental Protection Agency regulations, Amtrak service, and revenue sharing; correspondence pertaining to constituent problems and concerns; correspondence and papers regarding other matters before Congress, including the War in Vietnam, busing, Watergate, abortion, the energy crisis, foreign trade, and the health professions; papers relating to his 1972 election campaign; constituent correspondence of his administrative assistant; constituent requests for information and publications; patronage position recommendations; and invitations and appointments.

B-169. HUDSON, HUBERT (b.1921). PAPERS, 1893-1969.

8 ms. boxes.

Hudson owned Hudson Sales Company, an Attica, Fountain Co., department store (1950s-1960s). The collection also includes papers of David Park Drummond (b.1922), a resident of Janesville, Wis. (1930s), and Indianapolis (1939-1940s); a student at Butler University, Indianapolis (1940); serviceman in the U.S. Navy Air Corps during World War II (1942-1945), stationed at Bunker Hill Naval Air Station in Miami County, Ind., and in Rhode Island, Florida, and California.

The collection includes David Drummond's personal correspondence (1934-1945), including letters from family and friends while he was attending school in Janesville and Indianapolis (1934-1940); and letters to him while he was in the service, including letters from his family in Janesville, Indianapolis, and Crawfordsville, Montgomery Co., and from friends in the service in California, Indiana, and Rhode Island. Hubert Hudson papers include his personal and financial papers (1947-1969); sales materials relating to the Hudson Sales

Company of Attica (1954-1969); and family and business papers of Hudson's in-laws, the Compton family, of Newport, Ky. (1920s-1930s).

B-170. HUTCHINSON, DAVID (1812-1891). PAPERS, 1836-1896.

26 items.   S 707.

Physician. Hutchinson received medical training at Edinburg University, Scotland, and at Indiana University, Bloomington (1854); practiced medicine in Mooresville, Morgan Co. (1854-1865), and Winterset and Council Bluffs, Iowa (1865-1891); appointed Indiana Military Agent at Nashville, Tenn., responsible for the care of Indiana's sick and wounded soldiers (1862-1863); and served as surgeon, 30th Indiana Regiment (1863).

The collection contains documents attesting to Hutchinson's medical training in Scotland, Indiana, and Iowa (1836-1885); correspondence and documents relating to his military service in the Civil War, including his letter of instructions from Indiana governor Oliver P. Morton regarding his duties as Indiana Military Agent at Nashville (1862); and letters to his son from Winterset, Iowa (1884-1887).

B-171. HYNES, WILLIAM DUNN (1840-ca.1912). LETTERS, 1826, 1862-1865.

25 items.   S 709.

Hynes was the son of Thomas W. Hynes, a Presbyterian minister in Greenville, Ill.; soldier in the 22nd Illinois Regiment in Tennessee, Kentucky, and Georgia during the Civil War; and Indianapolis businessman.

The collection consists principally of Hynes's letters to his father, written while he served in the 22nd Illinois (1862-1865), and including letters written after his capture by Confederate troops (December 1864-May 1865). In addition, there is a hand-drawn map of the battlefield at Peach Tree Creek, Ga. (July 1864); and a letter to Hynes's grandfather, William R. Hynes of Bardstown, Ky., from Florida territorial governor William P. Duval regarding Florida politics (1826).

B-172. INDIANA ACADEMY OF SCIENCE. RECORDS, 1885-1912.

1 ms. box.   L 203.

The Indiana Academy of Science was organized in 1885 by citizens in Indiana interested in science. Its purpose has been to encourage scientific research and to promote interaction among people engaged in scientific work.

The records include minutes of the academy's meetings from its founding in 1885 through 1912; a 1909 membership list; and a small amount of correspondence and notes regarding the academy's activities.

B-173. INDIANA DEPARTMENT OF PUBLIC WELFARE. COLLECTION, 1847-1961.

1 ms. box.   L 196.

The Indiana Department of Public Welfare transferred this collection to the Indiana State Library.

The collection contains correspondence, minutes, reports, and a history of the Indiana Association of County Welfare Directors (1942-1961); a history of the Indiana State Board of Charities (ca.1901); a history of the Indiana Department of Public Welfare (ca.1938); correspondence and reports of the State Board of Charities and its secretary, Amos W. Butler (1890-1916), including correspondence and reports on reformatories, juvenile courts, child care, and a number of Indianapolis charities, among them the Charity Organization Society, the Mothers Aid Society, the Summer Mission for Sick Children, and the Citizens Humane Society; transcripts of Dorothea Dix's memorial to Congress requesting a grant of land for the relief and support of the indigent insane (1848), and a transcript of her report on Indiana jails and poor asylums (1847); and correspondence, reports, and papers regarding child health care, insane asylums, and homes for the feeble-minded (1898-1940).

B-174. INDIANA DUNES STATE PARK. COLLECTION, 1917-1929.

2 folders.   S 2112.

The Indiana Dunes State Park, Porter Co., was started in the mid-1920s with purchases of land authorized by the Indiana General Assembly in 1923, and by a number of private gifts of land.

The collection consists primarily of papers of the National Dunes Park Association, based in Gary, Lake Co., concerning its efforts to make the dunes land into a state park. Among the items are correspondence, bylaws, and articles of association of the National Dunes Park Association; minutes of the Chicago committee of the association; and bylaws of the Gary chapter of the association.

B-175. INDIANA FEDERATION OF ART CLUBS. RECORDS, 1928-1983.

1 ms. box, 2 vols. (.5 l.f.).

The federation was founded in 1926 as a statewide organization to foster appreciation of art. It coordinates and assists in sponsoring art organizations and shows in the state.

The records include the federation's bulletins (1933-1983); annual convention programs and tour information (1928-1978); yearbooks (1969-1971, 1974); and scrapbooks of clippings relating to federation activities (1937-1939, 1966-1970).

B-176. INDIANA FEDERATION OF CLUBS. RECORDS, 1890-1982.

18 l.f.   Inventory.
Restricted.

The federation was formed in 1906 from a merger of the Indiana Union of Literary Clubs and the Indiana State Federation of Women's Clubs. The federation has concentrated on civic programs which are beyond the capability of individual clubs. It has worked for the separation of the girls' industrial school from the men's prison, the introduction of domestic science and manual training into the schools, the creation of public playgrounds, the preservation of Turkey Run State Park, the acquisition of the Fauntleroy home in New Harmony, the licensing of nursing homes, and housing legislation. The federation currently includes over 300 member clubs and nearly 9,000 members, and it is a member of the General Federation of Women's Clubs.

The federation records are composed of trustee and executive committee minutes (1912-1966); convention programs (1907-1982); yearbooks (1906-

1982); financial records (1936-1971); correspondence and reports (1910s-1970s); programs of the study and work of the IFC (1910s-1977); issues of the IFC magazine *Indiana Club Woman* (1921-1978); and programs, newspaper clippings, and material on the history of the club (1920s-1970s). Also included are correspondence, speeches, and other papers of federation leaders Arcada Balz (1930s-1940s) and Virginia Claypool Meredith (1890s-1936); yearbooks, minutes, and other records of the Indiana Union of Literary Clubs and the Indiana State Federation of Women's Clubs (1890-1906); histories and reports of district clubs (1950s-1960s); minutes, membership records, and scrapbooks of the 7th District Club, Indianapolis (1918-1936); records of the IFC Junior Conference (1946-1961); papers relating to the General Federation of Women's Clubs (1913-1980); and records of INFO (Indiana Forum), an organization to inform citizens on current issues and to solicit opinions (1970-1977).

B-177. INDIANA FEDERATION OF SOCIAL WORK CLUBS. RECORDS, 1941-ca.1951.

3 archival boxes.

The federation was organized in 1941 as a professional and social organization for social workers. It was affiliated with the National Social Work Club Committee, and it was active into the 1950s.

The records include the federation's newsletters, minutes of meetings, committee papers, membership listings, and correspondence regarding club operations, manuals, and legislation affecting social workers. Additional items are minutes of meetings of the Budget Committee and the National Board of the YMCA (1943-1948); and papers of the U.S.O. and other organizations associated with the YMCA in the 1940s.

B-178. INDIANA LIBRARY ASSOCIATION. RECORDS, 1893-1984.

38 l.f.
Restricted.

The ILA was organized in 1891 to promote library interests in Indiana. The ILA supports legislation to benefit libraries and the welfare of librarians in the state, sponsors state and district conferences for librarians, and awards scholarships and loans to students working to pursue careers as librarians. The ILA is affiliated with the American Library Association.

The records include reports, minutes, correspondence, and publicity for ILA state conferences (1893-1977) and district meetings (1944-1978); secretary's record books containing minutes, programs, and reports (1925-1943, 1970-1974); executive board minutes (1940s-1970s); Legislative Committee records, including Indiana House and Senate bills, correspondence, and reports (1920s-1980s); Scholarship and Loan Committee records, including applications and loan records (1950s-1970s); records of the Publicity, Budget, Conference, Auditing, and other committees (1930s-1970s); records of the College and University Section and the Small Library Group (1950s-1970s); financial records (1932-1975); correspondence regarding the American Library Association and National Library Week; issues of the ILA magazine, *Focus on Indiana Libraries* (1967-1973), and *Focus* advertising correspondence (1963-1976); and scrapbooks of programs and publicity (1928-1930, 1950s-1960s).

B-179. INDIANA LIBRARY TRUSTEES ASSOCIATION. RECORDS, 1909-1978.

8 l.f.
Restricted.

The association was founded in 1909 by library trustees in the state to promote the welfare of Indiana libraries, and library work in general. The ILTA has worked with the Indiana Library Association on library issues, including librarian training and certification, benefits and pensions for librarians, and codification of Indiana library laws.

The records include the secretary's books, containing meeting minutes, correspondence, programs, and printed materials (1909-1968); treasurer's books (1928-1978); reports, minutes, and correspondence regarding committees and conferences (1947-1977); ILTA newsletters (1957-1975); and presidents and vice-presidents files (1971-1973).

B-180. INDIANA REPUBLICAN EDITORIAL ASSOCIATION. RECORDS, 1895-1953.

6 l.f.

The association was founded in 1878 by newspaper editors in the state affiliated with the Republican Party. The purpose of the association has been to serve as a professional organization for newspaper editors and to promote the interests and principles of the Republican Party.

The records include minutes of meetings (1895-1948); correspondence regarding meetings and speakers; correspondence with Republican Editorial Associations in other states, with the Indiana Republican State Central Committee, and with association members; committee reports and resolutions; papers delivered at the meetings; financial records; membership lists; and 75th anniversary materials, including press releases, clippings, and scrapbooks.

B-181. INDIANA SOCIETY FOR MENTAL HYGIENE. RECORDS, 1915-1959.

1 ms. box. L 205.

The Indiana Society for Mental Hygiene was founded in 1916 to promote education on mental disease and mental deficiency and to improve the care and treatment of the mentally ill and the mentally handicapped. In 1952 the society became the Indiana Association for Mental Health.

The records contain correspondence of the society's secretaries regarding annual meetings and the reorganization of the society in 1940 (1915-1941); correspondence with the Indiana Federation of Clubs and the Indiana State Library regarding the preparation of a package library of books on mental health (1935-1936); copies of papers on mental illness presented at the annual meetings in 1920, 1932, and 1940-1941; shorthand notes on the 1920 annual meeting sessions; clippings, programs, and press releases, mostly relating to annual meetings (1932-1941); news bulletins (1949-1950); and a legislative bulletin of the Indiana Association for Mental Health (1959).

Correspondents include Amos W. Butler.

B-182. INDIANA STATE ASSOCIATION OF PARLIAMENTARIANS. RECORDS, 1943-1971.

2 ms. boxes, 8 vols. (3 l.f.). Inventory.

The association is the Indiana chapter of the National Association of Parliamentarians. It was chartered in Indianapolis in 1943 as an organization for people interested in parliamentary law, and it has been active in teaching parliamentary procedures to clubs and businesses.

The records consist of the minutes of the association's regular and board meetings (1943-1969); yearbooks (1961-1969); annual meeting programs (1944-1971); and issues of the *Indiana Parliamentarian* (1962-1971). Also included are records of the Rose Marie Cruzan Parliamentary Club (1946-1971), Indianapolis, including scrapbooks, minutes of meetings, bylaws, and directories.

B-183. INDIANA STATE COMMISSION FOR THE REORGANIZATION OF SCHOOL CORPORATIONS. RECORDS, 1958-1969.

11 archival boxes. Inventory.

The Indiana General Assembly authorized the formation of the School Reorganization Commission in 1959 to oversee the consolidation of the state's school corporations in order to produce a more efficient, less expensive school system. The commission operated from 1959 to 1969, and during that time the number of school systems in the state was reduced from 966 to 321.

The largest part of the collection consists of reorganization papers from individual counties, including plans, reports, local committee meeting minutes, financial papers, surveys, and correspondence with the commission. Additional materials concern the records of the commission office, including minutes of meetings (1959-1965), correspondence regarding meetings, studies, and court cases (1959-1965); programs and reports (1960-1967); and studies and reports from other states.

B-184. INDIANA STATE CONFERENCE ON SOCIAL WORK. RECORDS, 1936-1968.

2 ms. boxes. L 207.

The Indiana State Conference on Social Work was founded in 1890 as a professional organization for people engaged in social work and related fields.

The records contain minutes of board and committee meetings (1938-1957); correspondence of the conference's secretaries regarding annual meetings of the conference, state and national meetings of the Child Welfare League, state and national legislation relating to social work, the work of regional social work groups and associated professional groups in Indiana, and issues of interest to the social work profession (1937-1959); annual meeting programs (1936-1956); copies of papers delivered at annual meetings, including papers on relief work, health care, child care, and the history and programs of social work organizations and agencies in Indiana (1937-1943); and newsletters and reports (1937-1968). In addition, there are transcripts of annual reports and correspondence of White's Manual Labor Institute, Wabash County (1863-1952), and a history of the Indiana State Board of Charities.

B-185. INDIANA STATE GRANGE. COLLECTION, 1869-1952.

1 archival box, 13 vols. (3 l.f.). L 290, V 186, V 260.

The Indiana State Grange of the Order of Patrons of Husbandry was organized in the early 1870s as part of the national Grange movement for cooperation among farmers and the regulation of railroads. Since the 1870s the Grange has functioned as a social and educational society for farmers.

The collection is made up of records of the state grange and its subordinate granges. State grange records include applications from local granges for permission to organize (1869-1904); information sheets on subordinate granges in the state (1873-1895); records of dues and other receipts collected from subordinate granges (1911-1939, 1951-1952); printed constitutions and official rosters (1891-1952); reorganization forms and membership applications (ca.1910-ca.1940); records of 6th degrees conferred by the state grange (1888-1898); ledger listing accounts for county granges (1877-1889); and an error book listing corrections in state grange accounts (1876-1893). Subordinate grange records include minutes and financial records for granges in Adamsboro, Cass Co., Cleveland Twp., Elkhart Co., and Old Oak and Washington, Daviess Co. (1873-1949).

B-186. INDIANA TAXPAYERS ASSOCIATION. RECORDS, 1918-1974.

153 l.f.

The association was founded in 1923 to work for the reduction of public expenses and taxes of state and local governments in Indiana. The association compiles statistics on budgets and taxes for schools, public utilities, and governments; issues publications and press releases; and lobbies for the reduction of spending and taxes.

The collection consists primarily of financial statistics regarding taxes and government expenditures from the 1930s to 1974, including statistics on school spending in the state (1950s-1970s); on county tax rates and valuations, county budgets, and city and county expenditure reports (1918-1972); on valuation and tax rates on pipeline, oil, and gas companies (1960s), and public utility and railroad assessments (1920s-1970s); on alcohol, motor vehicle, cigarette, and other taxes; and on bond issues (1930s-1960s). Additional material includes association business records, including annual reports (1923-1971); board of directors minutes (1930s-1970s); press releases (1960-1967); financial records (1940s-1970s); correspondence with members and with taxpayer organizations in other states (1930s-1970s); and printed materials issued by the association (1940s-1970s).

B-187. INDIANA WEAVERS' GUILD. RECORDS, 1943-1983.

2 ms. boxes, 2 vols. (1 l.f.).

The Indiana Weavers' Guild was organized in 1943 for people interested in weaving. The guild offers demonstrations, exhibits, and publications on weaving.

The records include the secretary's books and minutes of board meetings (1943-1981); membership applications, directories, and attendance records (1945-1980); newspaper clippings (1950s-1970s); correspondence and committee reports (1945-1957, 1973-1979); and a history of the guild (1983).

B-188. INDIANAPOLIS BUSINESS AND PROFESSIONAL WOMEN'S CLUB. RECORDS, 1912-1979.

15.5 l.f.   Inventory.

The club started in 1914 as the Business Women's Section of the Woman's Department Club. In 1927 the section merged with the Women's City Club to form the IBPWC. The club serves as a meeting place for business and professional women; is active in civic affairs, particularly the Anti-Crime Crusade and the School Drop-out Program; and offers scholarships to young women.

The records are made up of the club's meeting minutes (1927-1978); membership applications and lists (1946-1977); correspondence, reports, and other papers of the presidents, other officers, and committees (1943-1979); financial records (1927-1979); scrapbooks (1928-1959); issues of the club magazine and other publications (1950-1969); and publications of state and national businesswomen's organizations. Also included are minutes, scrapbooks, and yearbooks of the Woman's Department Club and the Indianapolis Women's City Club (1912-1927).

B-189. INDIANAPOLIS CHAIN AND STAMPING COMPANY. INVOICES, 1899-1905.

3 vols.   V 191.

The company manufactured bicycle chains in Indianapolis. In 1900 it became the American Bicycle Company, and by 1903 it was the Diamond Chain Factory of the Federal Manufacturing Company.

The collection consists of scrapbooks of invoices sent to the company by its suppliers.

B-190. INDIANAPOLIS COUNCIL OF WOMEN. RECORDS, 1886-1984.

6 l.f.

The council was organized in 1892 under the leadership of May Wright Sewall as the Local Council of Women of Indianapolis. The ICW aims to establish better communications among women's clubs in Indianapolis, and it has worked for women's suffrage, temperance, consumer interests, women's retirement and old age security programs, performing and fine arts programs, the abolition of child labor, the establishment of juvenile courts and vocational schools, and for educational and legal rights for women.

The records include minutes of board and assembly meetings (1892-1981); treasurers' records (1941-1968); yearbooks (1929-1984); annual reports and organization histories (1924-1976); presidents' books (1966-1976); programs and newspaper clippings (1928-1976); records of related organizations, such as the National Council of Women, the International Council of Women, and the Indiana State Council of Women (1929-1976); and papers relating to May Wright Sewall.

B-191. INDIANAPOLIS GERMAN LITERARY CLUB. RECORDS, 1893-1918.

2 vols. (.5 l.f.) V 188.

The club was founded in 1889 as an Indianapolis woman's club for the study of German literature. In 1894 it became the Indianapolis Deutsch-Literarischer Klub.

The records consist of the club's programs, constitutions, and minutes of meetings. The records from 1893-1894 are in English; the rest are in German.

B-192. INDIANAPOLIS MATINEE MUSICALE. RECORDS, 1877-1982.

4 archival boxes, 11 ms. boxes, 2 vols. (8.5 l.f.). Inventory.

The Indianapolis Matinee Musicale, organized in 1877, is the second oldest women's music club in the United States. The organization has promoted American music and the work of American composers, sponsored recitals, and granted scholarships to music students. It was involved in the founding of the Indianapolis Symphony Orchestra (1930), and it is affiliated with the National Federation of Music Clubs.

The records contain the organization's yearbooks (1877-1978); officers' reports and records (1881-1970); scrapbooks (1929-1969); programs and publications (1895-1980); records of the IMM Choral Ensemble (1929-1959); records of the Student Junior Programs and Awards (1946-1980); and records of the Alumnae Section (1955-1976).

B-193. INDIANAPOLIS TYPOGRAPHICAL UNION NO. 1. RECORDS, 1883-1981.

9 l.f.   Inventory.

The Indianapolis Typographical Union was incorporated in 1840 as an association of Indianapolis area printers; it joined with other typographical unions to form the National Typographical Union (1852). The union is the local affiliate of the National (later International) Typographical Union (1852-) and has worked for the improvement of wages and working conditions for printers, trained apprentice printers, provided burial, pension, and other benefits to its members, and worked with other unions on issues of common interest to labor.

The records contain minutes of union meetings (1883-1971), including reports of officers and committees, resolutions, papers relating to grievances and contracts, and correspondence with newspaper publishers and other unions; membership applications (1946-1967); dues payment books (1969-1978); record of traveling cards issued and accepted (1956-1973); correspondence and papers relating to contract negotiations with the *Indianapolis Star* and the *Indianapolis News* (1925-1971); publications of the International Typographical Union, including the ITU *Bulletin* (1921-1939, 1963-1967, 1971-1973), contract agreements (1951-1959), minimum wages and hours data (1971-1980), official directories (1973-1981), and index to the executive council decisions and appeals (1949-1978); and other publications on union rules, contracts, and the printing craft.

Correspondents include Hilton U. Brown, James M. Lynch, and Eugene Pulliam.

B-194. INDIANAPOLIS U.S.O. COUNCIL. RECORDS, 1941-1947.

1 archival box.

The Indianapolis U.S.O. Council was organized in May, 1941, to provide recreational activities for military personnel stationed in Indianapolis. The council received funds from the National War Board and provided funds and coordination for the local constituent agencies which provided the actual facilities and activities. The principal local agencies were the YMCA, the YWCA, National Catholic Community Service, the Jewish Welfare Federation, the Salvation Army, and the National Travelers Aid Association. The council was dissolved in 1946.

The records include minutes of board of directors meetings; committee reports, including reports of the postwar planning committee; financial records, including records of the U.S.O. canteen at Union Station; papers relating to the relations between the council and the local constituent agencies; correspondence of council chairman J. J. Kiser; correspondence with U.S.O. national and regional headquarters in New York and Chicago; and papers relating to recreational facilities for black soldiers.

B-195. INGALLS STONE COMPANY. RECORDS, 1887-1981.

15 l.f.

The company was founded in Oneonta, N.Y., in 1887 by Charles Cleveland Ingalls. It was moved to Binghamton, N.Y., in 1899, and to Bedford, Lawrence Co., in 1910. The company operated stone quarries and mills in Lawrence, Owen, and Monroe counties, supplying stone for many well known buildings, including the Lincoln Memorial. During World War II, the company manufactured armaments through the Ingalls Steel Division. The company was liquidated in 1976.

The records include minutes of board of directors meetings (1920-1966); scrapbooks containing advertising materials and newspaper clippings about the company and the Ingalls family; cash books (1902-1937); letter book of Charles Ingalls (1898-1899); stock certificate book (ca.1918-ca.1938); and property documents, business correspondence, and employee records, principally from the period 1940-1975.

B-196. JACKSON, AMOS WADE (1904-1972). PAPERS, 1847-1972.

23 l.f.

Jackson was a Versailles, Ripley Co., attorney (1925-1972); Ripley County prosecutor (1937-1940); associate justice, and justice, Indiana Supreme Court (1959-1971); president, Bank of Versailles; and president, Jackson Abstracts, Inc. Jackson was the son of Rowland H. Jackson (1872-1957), a Versailles attorney (1901-1957) and Democratic member, Indiana State Senate (1911-1917).

The collection contains papers relating to Jackson's legal cases in Ripley County (1931-1964); Ripley County land title abstracts from Jackson Abstracts, Inc. (1945-1949, 1951-1953); his casebook as Ripley County prosecutor (1937-1940); political correspondence regarding gun control (1967-1972), fluoridation of water (1956-1963), and nonpartisan election of U.S. Supreme Court justices (1963); papers regarding the sale of land in Cape Canaveral, Fla. (1962-1963); television editorial scripts (1965-1972); and Ripley County Bar Association papers (1930s-1970s). Also included are papers of his father, Rowland H. Jackson, including constituent correspondence, petitions, and legislation relating to his work in the 1917 State Senate session; newspaper clippings relating to Senate business (1911-1915); title abstracts, receipts, and other business papers (1911-1916); personal correspondence, scrapbooks, recipes, and other materials relating to Mrs. R. H. Jackson's hobby of chrysanthemum growing (1950s-1960s); and Jackson family legal papers (1847-1891).

B-197. JACKSON, THOMAS (ca.1838-ca.1908). PAPERS, 1855-1908.

2 folders. S 716.

Jackson was a farmer near Nora, Marion Co., and private and sergeant in the 8th Indiana Cavalry (39th Indiana Regiment) (1861-1865).

The collection includes Jackson's Civil War diary of a march from Nashville, Tenn., to Atlanta, Ga. (July-August 1864); papers regarding Civil War pensions for Jackson and other men who served in his regiment (1891-1908); diary and memo books (1866-1876, 1884); receipts and business papers; and a small amount of family correspondence.

B-198. JACOBS, ANDREW, JR. (1932-). PAPERS, 1969-1970.

1 ms. box. Inventory.

Jacobs is an Indianapolis attorney (1958-); and Democratic member, U.S. House of Representatives (1965-1973, 1975-).

The collection includes invitations to conferences, banquets, and speaking engagements; mailings to constituents; speeches; and news releases.

B-199. JAYNE, SEELY (d.1862). CIVIL WAR LETTERS, 1861-1862, 1889.

26 items. S 716.

Jayne was a farmer near North Vernon, Jennings Co.; served in the 6th Indiana Regiment in Kentucky and Tennessee (1861-1862); and killed at Stone River, Tenn. (December 31, 1862).

The collection consists of Jayne's Civil War letters to his wife in North Vernon and an 1889 letter from the U.S. War Department regarding Jayne's death.

B-200. JENCKES, VIRGINIA ELLIS (1877-1975). PAPERS, 1918-1951.

4 ms. boxes.

Politician. Jenckes was engaged in farming in the Terre Haute, Vigo Co., area (1912-1940s); secretary, Wabash Valley Improvement Association (1926-1932); Democratic member, U.S. House of Representatives (1933-1939), serving on the Civil Service, District of Columbia, and Mines & Mining committees; delegate to the Interparliamentary Union, Paris, France (1937); and lobbyist for Catholic organizations.

The collection consists principally of Jenckes's congressional papers (1933-1938), including correspondence, reports, and other papers relating to the Agriculture Waste Recovery Project (1933-1934) and other efforts to help farmers during the Depression; flood control on the Wabash and White rivers; railroads; women's rights; education; and communists in America, including Jenckes's opposition to communist radio broadcasts. Also included are papers relating to her political campaigns (1934-1938), the meeting of the 1937 Interparliamentary Union, including a transcript of Jenckes's speech to the

Union; political correspondence (1938-1940); and newspaper clippings, principally relating to politics (1932-1949).

Correspondents include J. Edgar Hoover, Louis M. Howe, Eleanor Roosevelt, and Franklin D. Roosevelt.

B-201. JOHNSON, JEREMIAH (1792-1876). PAPERS, 1815-1851.

2 folders. S 723.

Johnson was a storekeeper, farmer, and tavern keeper in Indianapolis and Bridgeport, Marion Co. (1820-ca.1855), and Hendricks County (ca.1855-1876); and member, Indiana House of Representatives (1834-1835).

The collection consists primarily of Johnson's receipts, promissory notes, contracts, and land documents relating to his business affairs in Marion County (1820-1851). The collection also includes a small amount of business and family correspondence, and an 1824 petition by the citizens of Indianapolis to have Johnson made their agent to oversee the planning of a town cemetery.

B-202. JOHNSON, JOHN (d.1905). PAPERS, 1853-1933.

1 ms. box. L 283.

Johnson owned a brickmaking company in Castleton, Marion Co.; and served as secretary of the Keystone Lodge of the Free and Accepted Order of Masons (1870s-1890s).

The collection contains minutes, reports, and financial documents of the Keystone Masonic Lodge (1863-ca.1900); receipts, estate papers, and other financial papers of Johnson and his family (1853-1933), including personal financial papers of his son, Albert Johnson of Indianapolis; and family correspondence.

B-203. JOHNSTON, MARGARET AFFLIS (1907-1967). PAPERS, 1933-1967.

4 archival boxes. Inventory.

Politician. Johnston was Deer Creek Township trustee, Delphi, Carroll Co. (1930-1934); Carroll County Democratic Party vice-chairman (1930-1938); Second Congressional District vice-chairman (1932-1941); Democratic candidate for Congress, opposing Rep. Charles Halleck (1946); state probation director (1941-1945, 1949-1953); member, Indiana Women's Prison Parole Board (1954-1967); Indiana Democratic National Committeewoman (1960-1964); president, Indiana Women's Democratic Club (1965-1967); married to Delphi druggist William A. Afflis (d.1945); moved to Indianapolis (1949); and married Leroy O. Johnston (1951).

The collection consists principally of Johnston's political and business correspondence and papers, including papers as Deer Creek Township trustee (1933); Democratic Party campaign materials (1936-1940s); correspondence and papers as state probation director, including probation division reports, legislation, papers on national and local conferences, and parole requests (1943, 1948-1953); papers relating to her 1946 congressional campaign; papers regarding her work on the Board of Parole of the Indiana Women's Prison, including minutes of meetings and reports (1953-1960s); Indiana and national Democratic Party press releases, reports, and correspondence (1960-1967), including papers pertaining to her work as Indiana Democratic National Committeewoman, and with the Women's National Committee; and her political speeches (1930s-1960s). Also included is her personal correspondence, including correspondence and mementos of her son, professional wrestler William F. Afflis ("Dick the Bruiser") (1940s-1960s); personal financial papers (1940s-1950s); and appointment books and notebooks (1938, 1942, 1960).

Correspondents include Andrew Jacobs, John F. Kennedy, and Matthew E. Welsh.

B-204. JONES, WILLIAM F. (1813-1890). PAPERS, 1827-1890.

1 ms. box. L 86.

Businessman and politician. Jones was a farmer, merchant, and contractor in Hartford City, Blackford Co. (1842-1852), and Muncie, Delaware Co. (1852-1890); Democratic member, Indiana House of Representatives (1846-1847);

officer, Fort Wayne and Southern Railroad Company (1848); Muncie school trustee (1854-1864); and Republican mayor of Muncie (1877-1879).

The collection includes letters to Jones from family members in Warren and Clinton counties, Ohio (1848-1850s), and from his daughter and son-in-law in Greenfield, Mo. (1870-1879); correspondence regarding his land and business interests in Blackford and Delaware counties; correspondence regarding the Fort Wayne and Southern Railroad Company and other railroad companies in Ohio and Indiana (1848-1860s); correspondence regarding state and national politics (1840s-1870s); receipts and other business papers; and a girl's diary (1888-1889).

Correspondents include Thomas Dowling, William H. English, Andrew J. Harlan, Austin W. Morris, William Rockhill, Oliver H. Smith, and Samuel Taggart.

B-205. JULIAN, GEORGE WASHINGTON (1817-1899). PAPERS, 1789-1902.

4 ms. boxes, 4 vols. (2.25 l.f.). L 81, V 53.

Politician. Julian was a native of the Centerville, Wayne Co., area; teacher in Mercer County, Ill. (1839); attorney in Centerville (1843); Whig member, Indiana House of Representatives (1845-1846); Free Soil (1849-1851) and Republican (1861-1871) member, U.S. House of Representatives; Free Soil Party nominee for Vice-President of the United States (1852); antislavery writer and speaker; associated with Radical Republicans in U.S. Congress in 1860s; married Laura Giddings, daughter of antislavery leader Joshua Giddings (1863); joined the Liberal Republican movement and supported Horace Greeley for president (1872); later joined the Democratic Party; moved to Irvington, Marion Co., and established law practice (1873); writer and speaker on politics, reform, and women's suffrage; law partner of William A. Meloy in Washington, D.C. (1879-1884); surveyor general of New Mexico Territory (1885-1889); and author of *Political Recollections* (1884) and *The Life of Joshua R. Giddings* (1892).

The collection includes Julian's correspondence with his wife, Laura Giddings Julian (1864-1884), written while he was serving in Congress, working as an attorney in Washington, D.C., and while on speaking tours; family correspondence of Laura Giddings Julian (1857-1884), including letters to her from her father, Joshua R. Giddings, written while he was serving in Congress and as U.S. consul general to Canada in Montreal (1861-1864), and correspondence between her and her sister in Washington, D.C., Montreal, and Ohio; other Julian family correspondence, including his correspondence with his brothers in Centerville (1838-1839) and Iowa (1840s), and with his daughter, Grace Julian Clarke (1870s-1890s); correspondence regarding Indiana and national politics, women's rights, Julian's legal work, and his speeches and writings, including retained copies of his letters; and copies of his correspondence with Edward L. Pierce pertaining to their biographies of Joshua Giddings and Charles Sumner (1885-1898). Also included are Julian's journals (1869-1899); his memoranda books containing notes on expenses, notes for speeches and campaigns, and newspaper clippings (1850-1858, 1868); his scrapbook of clippings on Zachary Taylor for the 1848 election; his school notes on law and history (1839); his manuscript of his book *Political Recollections*; journal of the family's trip to New Mexico, written by his daughter, Grace Julian Clarke (1885); Julian's speeches and speech notes; and an account book from an Irvington grocery store and meat market (1877-1878).

Correspondents include W. H. Barnum, Benjamin Butler, Salmon P. Chase, Charles F. Coffin, Schuyler Colfax, Francis J. Garrison, Joshua R. Giddings, Stephen S. Harding, Abram S. Hewitt, Robert G. Ingersoll, Oliver P. Morton, Samuel W. Parker, Andrew L. Robinson, Samuel J. Tilden, William W. Wick, and William W. Woollen.

B-206. KETCHAM, JACOB (fl.1840-1873). PAPERS, 1818-1896.

1 ms. box.   L 82.

Ketcham was a farmer in Daviess County.

The collection includes letters to Ketcham and his wife from family members, particularly family in Salem, Ohio (1866-1881); receipts, real estate appraisals, and promissory notes (1840-1880s); and an account book of Richard Heacock, Salem, Ohio (1818-1836), which includes newspaper clippings from the 1880s.

B-207. KING, ELIJAH (d.1879?). ACCOUNT BOOKS, 1847-1863.

8 vols. (1 l.f.).   V 280.

King owned a general store in Bethlehem (later Carmel), Hamilton Co. (1846-1879).

The collection consists of King's store account books.

B-208. KLING, FLORA GARDINER (b.1858). COLLECTION, 1888-1938.

4 ms. boxes, 1 vol. (2 l.f.).   Index.   L 344.

Kling was a collector of autographs and bookplates in Mt. Vernon, Posey Co.

The collection includes letters to Kling, principally from the period 1900-1915, from writers, poets, illustrators, and musicians responding to her letters about their work, and to her requests for examples of their bookplates; correspondence regarding her collection of bookplates, particularly with other bookplate collectors; and her bookplate collection.

Correspondents include Louis Adamic, George Ade, Ambrose Bierce, Samuel Langhorne Clemens, Richard Harding Davis, Theodore Dreiser, Thomas A. Edison, Max Ehrmann, Charles W. Fairbanks, Hamlin Garland, Rube Goldberg, Clara E. Laughlin, George Barr McCutcheon, John T. McCutcheon, and Meredith Nicholson.

B-209. KRESGE, FLOYD LESLIE (1885-1957). PAPERS, 1901-1957.

3 ms. boxes.   Inventory.   L 85.

Kresge worked in Scranton, Pa. (1901-1904); manager of S. S. Kresge store in Indianapolis (1904-1916, 1924-ca.1957) and Fond du Lac, Wis. (ca.1920-1924); treasurer, J. D. Williams Company, jobbers for confectioners and stationers, Scranton, Pa. (1916-ca.1920); and cousin of Sebastian S. Kresge, president of the S. S. Kresge Company.

The collection consists principally of Kresge's business and personal correspondence from the period 1903-1924, and includes his correspondence with S. S. Kresge Company officials in Detroit, Mich., regarding the operation of his stores in Indianapolis and Fond du Lac, and correspondence with Kresge store managers in other cities (1904-1924); financial reports and other business papers of the S. S. Kresge Company and its Indianapolis store (1904-1924); family correspondence, particularly from Kresge's brother who operated a dairy farm near Ransom, Pa., and from other family members in Scranton; his papers relating to real estate and other business interests in Scranton,

Indianapolis, and Fond du Lac; and Christmas cards and letters to Kresge and his family (1912-1957).

Correspondents include Sebastian S. Kresge.

B-210. LACROIX, MARCELLE D. (fl. 1847-1879). PAPERS, 1847-1886.

1 ms. box, 11 vols. (1.5 l.f.).   L 87, V 74.

Lacroix was a dealer in dry goods and wheat at Vincennes, Knox Co.

The collection consists of Lacroix's business papers, including his correspondence regarding wheat shipments from Vincennes with merchants in New Orleans, Cincinnati, and Evansville (1850s), and New York, Baltimore, St. Louis, Cincinnati, and Chicago (1860s-1870s); bills of lading and other documents relating to his dealings with steamboat companies and railroads; and his company letter books (1862-1876), account books (1849-1872), and records of wheat purchases and sales (1862-1874). Also included is a record of a lottery held during the Vincennes orphans festival (1866).

B-211. LANDGREBE, EARL F. (1916-). PAPERS, 1969-1974.

71 archival boxes.

Politician. Landgrebe was president of trucking firms in Valparaiso, Porter Co. (1943-); director, First Federal Savings and Loan Association, Valparaiso (1952-1970); Republican member, Indiana State Senate (1959-1968); and member, U.S. House of Representatives (1969-1975).

The collection consists of Landgrebe's congressional papers (1969-1974), including correspondence, reports, and legislation regarding the Consumer Protection Act (1974), the Elementary and Secondary Education Act (1973), the Food and Drug Administration, the Tax Reform Act (1969), the Pollution Control Act (1971), farm bills (1969-1974), Watergate, the War in Vietnam, defense spending, abortion, the draft, foreign aid, railroads, public land use, poverty programs, the Pueblo Incident, and other issues before Congress; papers relating to his district, including the construction of the Bailly Nuclear

Reactor, pollution of Lake Michigan, the Indiana Dunes National Lakeshore Park, the development of the lakeshore, the Chicago, South Shore and South Bend Railroad, and grants for local programs and studies; papers relating to Landgrebe's attempts to distribute Bibles in the Soviet Union (1972); correspondence regarding constituent problems; newsletters, press releases, and information released by his office; papers relating to his election campaigns, his voting record, and the Republican Party; and requests for publications, invitations, and papers relating to his office operations.

B-212. LASSELLE FAMILY. PAPERS, 1713-1904.

18 ms. boxes, 97 vols. (13 l.f.).   Partial Calendar.   L 127, V 91.

The Lasselle family included Hyacinth Lasselle (1777-1843), a French trader at Fort Wayne, Allen Co. (1794-1796), at various points along the Wabash River (1797-1805), at Vincennes, Knox Co. (1805-1833), and at Logansport, Cass Co. (1833-1840); lieutenant in the Indiana militia (1812) and the U.S. Rangers (1813-1815); temporary commander of Fort Harrison, near present-day Terre Haute, Vigo Co. (1814-1815); appointed major general in Indiana Militia (1825); married Julia Bosseron, daughter of Vincennes trader Francis Bosseron (d.1791). Lasselle's children included Charles B. Lasselle (1819-1908), a student at Indiana University, Bloomington (1836-1839), law student under Daniel D. Pratt (1839-1842), Logansport lawyer (1842-1908), prosecuting attorney in Cass County (1847-1850), Democratic member of the Indiana House of Representatives (1863-1865) and the Indiana State Senate (1869-1871), mayor of Logansport (1880s), Cass County probate commissioner (1890s); Stanislaus Lasselle (1811-1853), publisher of the *Logansport Canal Telegraph* (1834-1836), partner of Benjamin Polke in dry goods firm of Lasselle & Polke in Delphi, Carroll Co. (1837-ca.1842), lieutenant and captain in the 1st Regiment, Indiana Volunteers in the Mexican War (1846-1848), participated in the California Gold Rush, and operated dry goods business near San Francisco (1849-1853); Hyacinth Lasselle, Jr. (1806-1876), a lawyer and merchant in Vincennes and Logansport, and publisher, with historian John B. Dillon, of the *Logansport Telegraph* (1836-1849); and Jacques Magloire Lasselle (1817-1851), a student at Indiana University, Bloomington (1834-1836), lawyer in Logansport (1841-1851), a sergeant in the 1st Regiment of Indiana Volunteers during the Mexican War (1846-1848), and judge of the Cass County Probate Court (1851).

The collection consists of personal and business papers of the Hyacinth Lasselle family, and papers of a number of Vincennes families connected with the

Lasselles through family or business relations, including the French merchants Francis Bosseron and Antoine Marchal. The Hyacinth Lasselle papers include his account books (1798-1843); receipts, contracts, land documents, and other legal and business documents from Vincennes and Logansport (1796-1843); business correspondence, primarily regarding the Indian trade and Lasselle's land interests; papers relating to his service in the War of 1812 (1812-1815), including correspondence and orders from Col. William Russell, papers pertaining to Fort Harrison, and muster rolls, equipment returns, and other official military papers relating to Lasselle's company; Indiana militia papers from Knox and Cass counties (1820s-1830s); papers relating to St. Francis Xavier Catholic Church in Vincennes (1817-1825); papers relating to the case of *Lasselle* v. *Polly*, a woman of color, concerning the right to own slaves in Indiana (1820); business papers of the Terre Haute Company, regarding land sales and development of the site of Terre Haute (1820-1824); and plat maps of land in Cass County and neighboring counties (1830s-1850s).

Charles B. Lasselle papers include his correspondence with his family while he was a student at Indiana University (1836-1839); his business letters, contracts, and other documents relating to his legal business in Cass County and northern Indiana (1846-1880s); his account books (1847-1895); letters from family members in Fort Wayne, Logansport, and Peru, Miami Co., Monroe, Mich., and Louisiana (1840s-1870s); papers relating to the family's land claims based upon an 1826 treaty with the Potawatomi Indians (1840s-1860s); correspondence regarding Democratic Party politics and the work of the Indiana legislature (1860s-1870s), including correspondence regarding treason charges against Lambdin P. Milligan; letters to Lasselle from William P. Lasselle, an officer in the 9th Indiana Regiment, and other Civil War soldiers; his letters to his fiancee (1870); his letter book for his law business (1870-1877); correspondence of Lasselle and T. C. Buntin of Terre Haute regarding family claims based upon Francis Bosseron's Revolutionary War service (1878-1880s); Lasselle's papers as Cass County probate commissioner (1888-1904); correspondence regarding his interests in early Indiana history; his historical writings, including essays on the life of John Tipton (1851), and the history of Fort Wayne (1850), Cass County (1859), and the early French in Indiana; and his meteorological records made at Logansport (1836-1883).

Stanislaus Lasselle papers include account books, bills, statements of account, receipts, and business correspondence of the Lasselle & Polke dry goods company (1836-ca.1842); his journal of a boat trip from Logansport to Vicksburg, Miss. (1840); his correspondence with his sister in Logansport while he was serving in the Mexican War (1846-1848), including his letters from camp in New Albany, Floyd Co., and from Texas and Mexico; certificates of disability, muster rolls, and other military papers for his company; his drawings of camps and battlefields in Mexico; summary of remarks made by Henry S. Lane at a dinner given by Lasselle in Matamoros, Mexico (1847); a diary of his trip to California (1849); his letters to his family from the San Francisco, Calif., area (1852); and account books for his California store (1851-1857).

Hyacinth Lasselle, Jr., papers include his business accounts in Logansport (1830s-1840s); his letters regarding family business written from New Orleans (1840-1841); and letters to his wife, written primarily from Washington, D.C., while he was seeking federal appointments and pursuing Indian claims (1848-1854). Jacques M. Lasselle papers include his correspondence with his family while he was a student at Indiana University (1834-1836); and his correspondence with his sister while he served in the Mexican War.

The collection also contains papers relating to the early history of Vincennes, principally from the period 1760-1815. Included are papers of Hyacinth Lasselle's father, Jacques, and brothers Jacques, Francois, and Antoine (1790-1830), including their correspondence regarding the fur trade at Detroit and Vincennes (1803-1810), and their business accounts, including their accounts with Hyacinth Lasselle; papers of Francis Bosseron, including his account books (1777-1791), his correspondence regarding the fur trade (1778-1791), receipts, accounts, and other business documents (1763-1791), his accounts with Leonard Helm and other members of George Rogers Clark's army at Vincennes (1778-1780), and transcripts of documents relating to Bosseron's involvement with Clark's campaign; papers of French immigrant and Vincennes merchant Antoine Marchal (d.1816), including his correspondence with his partner, Louis Nicolas Fortin of New Orleans and Baton Rouge, La. (1801-1816), his business correspondence with merchants in St. Louis, Kaskaskia, Fort Wayne, and Kentucky, including Pierre Menard and Manuel Lisa (1798-1816), his accounts and other business papers (1795-1816), his account book (1798-1800), his accounts with the Compagnie du Scioto (1790), and his estate papers (1816-1819).

Also included are papers of Vincennes merchant Francois Bizayon (d.1810), including his account book (1807-1810), receipts and other business papers (1801-1810), and his estate papers (1810-1812); papers of Cape Girardeau trader Louis Lorimier, including business letters, receipts, and accounts (1781-1805); military and business papers of Capt. Robert Buntin (1793-1812), including military letters and orders to Buntin at Fort Knox from officers at Fort Washington (1795-1797), and receipts, contracts, and other Vincennes business papers (1797-1812); letters to merchant David Gray at Vincennes, from his associates George Sharp and George Ironside at Miamis

(1786-1787); military papers of Pierre Andre, captain in the 1st Indiana Militia Regiment (1811-1813) and the U.S. Rangers (1813-1815), including his correspondence on military matters with Col. William Russell, Lasselle, Ensign David Gregg, and others at Vincennes and Fort Harrison (1813-1815), and provision returns and other business documents for his company (1811-1815); papers of Ensign David Gregg of the U.S. Rangers, stationed at Vincennes and Fort Harrison, including letters from his family in Kentucky, military letters from Col. William Russell, and papers relating to Fort Harrison (1813-1819); plat maps for the town of Vincennes, drawn by U.S. surveyor Samuel Baird (1792); and marriage contracts, land contracts, receipts, and other legal and financial documents for people in Vincennes.

The collection includes documents and letters of Samuel Baird, Horace P. Biddle, James Bigger, J. J. Bingham, Bishop Simon Brute de Remur, John C. Calhoun, Lewis Cass, John T. Chunn, Schuyler Colfax, Alexis Coquillard, John D. Defrees, John Brown Dillon, Thomas Dowling, Lyman C. Draper, Toussaint Dubois, George G. Dunn, Jacob P. Dunn, William H. English, George W. Ewing, John Ewing, Graham N. Fitch, Bishop Benedict Joseph Flaget, Alexander Fraser, Pierre Gibault, John Gibson, Gabriel Godfroy, Isaac P. Gray, John Francis Hamtramck, John Cleves Symmes Harrison, William Henry Harrison, Thomas A. Hendricks, Joseph Henry, Daniel Wait Howe, Henry Hurst, Jonathan Jennings, General Washington Johnston, John Rice Jones, Joseph H. Lane, John Law, Manuel Lisa, Louis Lorimier, William McIntosh, Mahlon D. Manson, Pierre Menard, William H. H. Miller, Lambdin P. Milligan, Benjamin Parke, Samuel Parry, John U. Pettit, Thomas Posey, Daniel D. Pratt, William Prince, Frederick Rapp, James Brown Ray, John Francis Rivet, William Russell, Louis St. Ange, Adhemar St. Martin, Samuel C. Sample, Benjamin Sebastian, Solomon Sibley, Thomas Smith, Elihu Stout, W. H. H. Terrell, John Tipton, John Todd, David Turpie, Henry Vanderburgh, Francis Vigo, James Whitcomb, Albert S. White, William W. Wick, James D. Williams, George Winter, and Simon Yandes.

B-213. LAUCK, ANTHONY J. (1908-). PAPERS, 1908-1973.

2 ms. boxes. L 88.

Priest and artist. Lauck is the son of Anthony P. Lauck, an Indianapolis funeral director; graduate of the John Herron School of Art, Indianapolis (1936); entered the Congregation of the Holy Cross (1937), and ordained a Catholic priest (1946); graduate of University of Notre Dame, Notre Dame, St. Joseph

Co. (1942); member of the art department, University of Notre Dame (1950-); department chairman (1960-1967); appointed director of Notre Dame Art Gallery (1962); and sculptor.

The papers include family correspondence, primarily from the period 1937-1950, including letters to Lauck from his family in Indianapolis; from his sister Marie Lauck, an Indianapolis probation officer (1935-1948), lawyer (1955-), and Indiana State Senator (1964-1968); and from John Lauck, an officer in the 5th Marine Division, serving at Camp LeJeune, N.C., the South Pacific, and Japan (1944-1946). Also included is Lauck's correspondence regarding his sculpture and sculpting commissions, art exhibitions at which his work was on exhibit, art magazines, and his work with the Notre Dame Art Department and the Notre Dame Art Gallery (1950-1968); catalogs for exhibitions at which his work was displayed (1953-1968); sketches for his sculptures; and correspondence with other priests and church officials, primarily from the period 1937-1950.

Correspondents include Ralph Fabri and Theodore Hesburgh.

B-214. LAYMAN, DANIEL W. (1808-1887). ACCOUNT BOOKS, 1835-1872.

4 vols., 11 items (.5 l.f.). V 275.

Layman was a physician in Putnamville, Putnam Co.

The collection includes account books for his medical practice (1835-1836, 1850-1872); and personal receipts and accounts (ca.1850-ca.1870).

B-215. LEACH, JOSHUA (fl.1849-1885). PAPERS, 1831-1883.

1 ms. box. L 242.

Leach was secretary and financial agent for the Cincinnati and Indianapolis Junction Railroad Company, based in Connersville, Fayette Co. (1850s-1860s).

The collection contains letters to Leach from his brother, James Leach, a lawyer in Stamping Ground and New Castle, Ky., regarding politics, railroad and land business, and family matters (1853-1860); letters from relatives in Weatherford, Tex. (1860-1861, 1883), and Natchez, Miss. (1867-1868); Cincinnati and Indianapolis Junction Railroad Company papers regarding the purchase and appraisal of land, company finances, lawsuits, and other legal and financial matters (1853-1867); and papers regarding land in Union County (1831-1838).

B-216. LEAGUE OF WOMEN VOTERS OF INDIANA. RECORDS, 1910-1978.

60 l.f.

The League of Women Voters was formed from the National American Woman Suffrage Association in 1920 after women won the right to vote. The league has worked to protect voting rights and has provided information on government operations, public issues, and election procedures and candidates. The League of Women Voters of Indiana is affiliated with the national League of Women Voters.

The largest part of the collection consists of reports, press releases, and correspondence regarding issues studied by the Indiana League (1920s-1960s), including child welfare and child labor; conservation; Indiana constitutional reform; crime, penal reform, and juvenile delinquency; inflation, unemployment, and other economic issues; the United Nations, the Marshall Plan and other foreign policy issues; social services and public welfare; education; status of women in society; labor laws affecting women; public and mental health; and taxes. In addition, there are administrative records of the state league and local chapters, particularly the Indianapolis chapter, including records of state conferences and other state meetings (1929-1960); minutes of state board meetings (1950-1959); financial records (1926-1961); information kits distributed by the league (1940s-1960s); local league organization reports (1929-1942); bylaws, handbooks, annual reports, press releases, and other organizational materials (1920s-1970s); scrapbooks (1920s-1940s); newsletters (1921-1970s); and papers relating to the national league and its annual conventions (1921-1971). The collection also includes correspondence, legislation, legal briefs, and reports of the Woman's Franchise League of Indiana, relating to the campaign for woman's suffrage (1910-1919).

Correspondents include Albert J. Beveridge, Claude Bowers, Carrie Chapman Catt, Grace Julian Clarke, Charles W. Fairbanks, James P. Goodrich, Will Hays, John Worth Kern, Harry S. New, and Samuel Ralston.

B-217. LIEBER, CARL H. (1866-1929). PAPERS, 1910-1925.

32 items. S 2826.

Lieber was treasurer of the H. Lieber Company, an art supply store in Indianapolis; involved in organizing the John Herron Art Institute and other art activities in Indianapolis; and chairman, art committee, Paul Dresser Memorial Association (1924-1925).

The collection includes Lieber's correspondence regarding the Civic Improvement Committee of the Indianapolis Commercial Club (1910); the founding of the Indiana Little Theater Society, associated with the John Herron Art Institute (1915-1916); and the planning of a memorial to composer Paul Dresser in Terre Haute, Vigo Co. Among the items is an article on Dresser by Max Ehrmann and drawings of proposed memorials to Dresser.

Correspondents include William Fortune and Lorado Taft.

B-218. LIEBER, RICHARD (1869-1944). PAPERS, 1920-1924.

1 ms. box (665 items). Index. L 90.

Lieber was a German immigrant to the United States (1891); Indianapolis newspaperman and businessman; president, Merchants and Manufacturers Insurance Bureau, Indianapolis (1912-1939); Director, Indiana Department of Conservation (1919-1933); and active in the Indiana Republican Party.

The papers consist of Lieber's personal and political correspondence, including retained copies of his own letters, primarily from the period 1921-1923. Included is correspondence regarding the German-American community, including correspondence with politicians and editors of German-language newspapers regarding the community's political interests, its involvement with German relief efforts, and its opposition to the French occupation of Germany; correspondence regarding Republican Party politics, particularly with Harry S. New and Medill McCormick; family correspondence, including letters from his relatives in Dusseldorf, Germany; correspondence and business papers relating to his personal expenses and investments; papers pertaining to the Merchants and Manufacturers Insurance Bureau; and correspondence regarding his work as director of the Indiana Department of Conservation.

Correspondents include John T. Adams, Oscar E. Bland, Theodore Brentano, Harry M. Daugherty, Frederick W. Elven, Otto N. Frenzel, James P. Goodrich, Hans Hackel, Will H. Hays, Bernard G. Heyn, William G. Irwin, Medill McCormick, Paul Mueller, Harry S. New, Meredith Nicholson, Kate Milner Rabb, and James E. Watson.

B-219. LIEBER, RICHARD (1869-1944). PAPERS, 1892-1958.

16 ms. boxes. Inventory. L 91.

Conservationist, businessman, and newspaperman. Lieber was a German immigrant to the United States (1891); writer for the *Indianapolis Journal* and the *Tribune* (1892-1900); associated with James R. Ross & Company, importers and jobbers (1905-1918); president, Merchants and Manufacturers Insurance Bureau, Indianapolis (1912-1939); chairman, Indiana State Parks Commission (1915-1939); military secretary to Indiana governor James P. Goodrich, with rank of colonel (1917-1921); director, Indiana Department of Conservation (1919-1933); chairman, Indiana Lincoln Union (1927-1944); director, Indiana World's Fair Commission (1932-1933); consultant for the National Parks Service (1930s-1944); member, National Park Service Advisory Board on National Parks, Historic Sites, Buildings and Monuments (1930s-1944); member, National Conference of State Parks; and author, *America's Natural Wealth: A Study of the Use and Abuse of Our Resources* (1942).

The collection is made up principally of Lieber's correspondence and papers from the period 1933-1944. Included are his papers relating to the Indiana Lincoln Union (1897-1943), consisting of papers pertaining to the location of Nancy Hanks Lincoln's grave (1897-1925), minutes of Union meetings (1928-1943), and Lieber's correspondence with committee members, architects, and sculptors regarding the construction of a Lincoln memorial in Spencer County; his papers as a consultant to the National Park Service (1933-1944), including correspondence with Park Service officials, reports and itineraries of Lieber's inspection tours of state and national parks, correspondence regarding Park Service plans for restoring New Harmony, and his travel vouchers; his papers as a member of the National Park Service Advisory Board (1936-1944), consisting of minutes of meetings, reports on Park Service activities, and correspondence; papers relating to other organizations with which Lieber was involved, such as the Indiana World's Fair Commission (1932-1933), the American Planning and Civic Association (1939-1943), and the National Conference on State Parks (1932-1944); papers pertaining to his book *America's Natural Wealth* (1938-1942), including the manuscript of the book, correspondence relating to its research and publication, and reviews; his correspondence regarding state and national Republican Party politics, conservation, state parks, flood control in the Ohio Valley (1937), the reorganization plan for the U.S. Interior Department (1937-1938), and the Civilian Conservation Corps (1941-1943); his family correspondence (1896-1945), including correspondence with his family in Germany (1896-1941); his speeches on conservation, state parks, politics, Germans, and patriotism (1918-1944); scrapbooks on German social activities in Indianapolis (1892-1900); and brochures and pamphlets on Indiana and state parks.

Correspondents include Louis Adamic, Charles A. Beard, Thomas Hart Benton, Herbert E. Bolton, Claude Bowers, Paul V. Brown, William Lowe Bryan, Stanley Coulter, Charles C. Deam, James P. Goodrich, Warren G. Harding, Will H. Hays, J. I. Holcomb, Cordell Hull, Harold L. Ickes, Waldo G. Leland, Harry G. Leslie, Josiah K. Lilly, Medill McCormick, Harry S. New, Meredith Nicholson, Gifford Pinchot, Henry F. Schricker, Thomas Taggart, M. Clifford Townsend, Tom Wallace, and Evans Woollen.

B-220. LLOYD, PEARL (b.1885). PAPERS, 1869-1956.

1 ms. box.   Inventory.   L 92.

Lloyd was a grade school teacher in Indianapolis.

The papers contain letters to Lloyd from family and fellow schoolteachers (1923-1956); her receipts, bills, and other personal financial documents (1921-1956); school compositions of Lloyd and others (1869-1920); and documents and clippings relating to Lloyd's family and Indianapolis schoolteachers.

B-221. LOWES, WILLIAM R. (fl.1861-1884). PAPERS, 1862-1864.

26 items.   S 856.

Lowes was a resident of Acton, Marion Co.; and private in the 70th Indiana Regiment in Tennessee and Georgia (1862-1865).

The papers include Lowes's Civil War letters to his wife in Acton; and letters of other soldiers to Lowes and his family (1862-1864).

B-222. LUTEN, DANIEL B. (1869-1946). PAPERS, 1908-1934.

1 ms. box.   L 93.

Engineer. Luten was president of Luten Engineering Company in Indianapolis, consulting on the construction of concrete bridges (1900-1932); president of Daniel B. Luten Manufacturing Company, Indianapolis (1932-1946); and member of the board of directors of the Emergency Work Committee, Inc., a private organization of Indianapolis businessmen which attempted to provide work for the city's unemployed during the Depression.

The papers consist primarily of reports and minutes of meetings of the Emergency Work Committee, Inc. (1930-1934). Also included is a partial register of persons who visited the Charles W. Fairbanks headquarters during the 1908 Republican National Convention; and Luten's notes for the American Plan-Open Shop-Conference in Fort Wayne, Ind. (1928).

B-223. LUTHER, JAMES H. (1814-1893). PAPERS, 1861-1889.

1 ms. box.   L 94.

Luther was a farmer and businessman in Crown Point, Lake Co. (1849-1893); Lake County Auditor (1860-1868); and active in the Spiritualist movement. Luther's sons included John E. Luther, a private and lieutenant in the 20th Indiana Regiment, serving in Virginia (1861-1864), regimental adjutant (1863-1864), employee of McCormick Reaper Company in Galesburg, Ill., and Indianapolis (1868-1879), businessman in Troy, Ohio (1879-1882), and Crown Point (1880s); Amos Origen Luther, a corporal in the 20th Indiana Regiment (1861-1864), agent and engineer for railroad companies in Kokomo, Howard Co. (1866), St. Louis, Mo. (1869-1871), Cedar Rapids, Iowa (1872), and in Colorado (1872-1880s); and Albert W. Luther (d.1875), a musician in the 20th Indiana Regiment, serving in Virginia (1861-1864) and Washington, D.C. (1863-1864), soldier in the 151st Indiana Regiment, serving in Tennessee (1865), laborer in Chicago, Ill. (1867-1868), and printer in Lincoln, Winchester, and Springfield, Ill. (1869-1871), in St. Louis (1872-1874), and Modesto, Calif. (1874-1875).

The papers consist primarily of Luther's family correspondence, including Civil War letters from his sons serving in Virginia (1861-1864), Washington, D.C. (1863-1864), and Tennessee (1865); letters from his sons working in

Indiana, Illinois, Ohio, Iowa, Minnesota, Colorado, and California (1866-1886); Luther's letters to his wife, written while he was attempting to establish a business in the San Francisco, Calif., area (1869-1870); letters from John E. Luther in Crown Point to his father visiting family in Colorado and California (1884-1886); letters of other family members, including Abraham Smith, a spiritualist teacher in Sturgis, Mich. (1861-1881); and letters from grandchildren in California and Colorado (1888-1889).

B-224. MCBRIDE, CHARLES S. (1855?-1929). ACCOUNT BOOKS, 1918-1925.

6 vols. (.25 l.f.). V 99.

McBride was an officer in the Union Trust Company, Indianapolis, and retired to live in Irvington, Marion Co. (1910s).

The collection consists of account books recording the family's daily expenses (1918-1925).

B-225. MCCLURE, WILLIAM S. (b. 1822/23). PAPERS, 1861-1900.

179 items. S 881.

McClure, of Madison, Jefferson Co., was an officer in the 3rd Indiana Cavalry (45th Indiana Regiment), serving in the Army of the Potomac (1861-1864); appointed colonel, 9th Indiana Cavalry (121st Indiana Regiment), but declined appointment and resigned from army (February 1864).

The collection contains military orders, including orders issued from the offices of generals George Meade, Henry W. Halleck, and Alfred Pleasonton; military communications, muster rolls, commissions, and other official military papers; McClure's pension papers (1884-1900); papers pertaining to the military service of Dr. William J. McClure of Madison (b.1807?), who served as Commissary of Subsistence in Washington, D.C. (1862); and personal correspondence and correspondence relating to the McClures' appointments during the Civil War.

Correspondents include William M. Dunn, Lazarus Noble, and W. H. H. Terrell.

B-226. McCray, Warren T. (1865-1938). Memoirs, 1865-1926[1927].

2 ms. boxes. L 96.
Microfilm.

Businessman, farmer, and politician. McCray was connected with the Discount and Deposit Bank in Kentland, Newton Co. (1880-ca.1920), president (1913-ca.1920); operated chain of grain elevators in northern Indiana; farmer near Kentland; nationally-known breeder of Hereford cattle; Republican governor of Indiana (1921-1924); resigned as governor following conviction for mail fraud (1924); and served three years in federal prison in Atlanta, Ga. (1924-1927).

The collection consists of McCray's memoirs, written shortly after his release from prison, describing his boyhood and family, his agricultural and business interests, his political campaigns and governorship, his trial on mail fraud charges, and his term in federal prison.

B-227. McCrea, Henry (ca.1851-1908). Logbooks, 1872-1873.

5 vols. (.25 l.f.). V 273.

McCrea was an officer in the U.S. Navy (1866-1908); and midshipman on the U.S.S. *Pensacola* (1872-1873).

The collection includes logbooks for the U.S.S. *Pensacola*, kept by McCrea, on the ship's voyage from San Francisco, Calif., to Panama, Peru, and Chile (January 1872-April 1873); and a volume of calculations and nautical reckonings written by McCrea (1872).

B-228. McCullough, Jacob S. (ca.1836-1897). Papers, 1861-1864.

6 vols. (.25 l.f.). S 876.

McCullough was a teacher in Rush County (1850s); private in the 37th Indiana Regiment, serving in Kentucky, Tennessee, and Georgia (1861-1864); and a bookkeeper in Indianapolis after the war.

The collection contains McCullough's Civil War diaries (1861-1864); and an order book for the 37th Regiment (1861-1862).

B-229. McGan, Thomas J. (1844-1911). Record Books, 1844-1911.

8 vols. (1 l.f.). V 94.

McGan was a farmer and jewelry store owner in Russellville, Putnam Co.

The collection includes account books and an inventory of goods for McGan's jewelry store (1904-1911); accounts of the guardianship of his nephew, William T. Sennett (1894-1900); account books for the Putnam County stock raising and farming operations of his father, James McGan (1844-1870); diaries of his brother, Benjamin F. McGan, a Putnam County farmer (1864-1866, 1874); and diary of William T. Sennett regarding farm life and his work selling telephones (1902-1905).

B-230. McGraw, John S. (fl.1857-1905). Letters, 1863.

61 items. S 887.

McGraw was a blacksmith in Richmond, Wayne Co.; and lieutenant, captain, and colonel in the 57th Indiana Regiment, serving in Kentucky, Tennessee, Georgia, and Texas (1861-1866).

The collection consists of McGraw's Civil War letters to his wife and children in Richmond, Ind., written from Murfreesboro, Pelham, and Chattanooga, Tenn., in 1863.

B-231. MCLAUGHLIN, MARY GODOWN (MRS. H. C.) (b.1868?). PAPERS, 1861-1951.

3 ms. boxes.   L 98.

McLaughlin was the daughter of John M. Godown (1833-1911), an engineer in Fort Wayne, Allen Co., for the Pittsburgh, Fort Wayne, and Chicago Railroad (1850s-1860s), a lieutenant in the 12th Indiana Regiment (1861-1865), and secretary and treasurer of the Statehouse Board, responsible for planning and constructing a new state capitol building (1880s).

The collection includes Godown's Civil War letters to his fiancee, Francis Fairbank of Lowell, Mass., written from Maryland and Virginia (1861-1862), from Kentucky, Tennessee, Mississippi, and Georgia (1862-1864), and from a Confederate prison camp in South Carolina (1864-1865); letters to her from Fort Wayne (1865-1866); Godown's reminiscences of his early life and his Civil War years; and reminiscences of Mary Godown McLaughlin, principally of growing up in Indianapolis.

B-232. MCNEELY, JAMES H. (1828-1902). PAPERS, 1847-1863.

144 items.   S 901.

Newspaperman. McNeely was a printer and newspaper publisher in Lawrenceburg, Dearborn Co. (1846, 1849), Cincinnati, Ohio (1847-1849), and Indianapolis (1850-1859); part owner and editor, *Evansville* (Vanderburgh Co.) *Journal* (1859-1866); Evansville postmaster (1861-1867); and owner and editor of *Evansville Journal* (1883-1902).

The papers consist of letters to McNeely from friends, principally newspapermen, in Lawrenceburg, Indianapolis, and Terre Haute, Vigo Co., and Dayton and Cincinnati, Ohio (1847-1854); and a large number of personal and business receipts and bills, principally from businesses in Indianapolis (1850-1860) and Evansville (1860-1863).

B-233. MARION COUNTY BIBLE SOCIETY. RECORDS, 1824-1844.

26 items. S 2200.

The Marion County Bible Society, associated with the American Bible Society, sold inexpensive bibles in the Indianapolis area. It worked with the Indianapolis Sabbath School Union which taught reading and religion.

The papers contain accounts of the Bible Society (1827-1834), including accounts of customers who purchased bibles, and accounts kept by Samuel Merrill when he worked as the society's agent; and records of the Indianapolis Sabbath School Union (1824-1844), including reports of the superintendent and the board of directors, lists of students, and drafts of a history of the Union (1844).

B-234. MARKLE, AUGUSTUS R. (b.1869). COLLECTION, 1774-1867.

1 ms. box. L 99.

Markle was an electrical engineer in Terre Haute, Vigo Co.; author of a series of articles on Terre Haute history, "When Terre Haute was Young," in the *Terre Haute Star* (1931-1954). He was the descendant of Abraham Markle (1770-1826), a miller in New York and Canada; officer in the U.S. Army during the War of 1812; recipient of federal land grant in Vigo County, Ind., in payment for military service; and Vigo County settler (1816) and participant in founding of Terre Haute.

The collection consists primarily of Abraham Markle's contracts, receipts, land documents, court papers, and other legal and financial documents relating to his business affairs in New York, Canada, and Vigo County (1811-1826). Also included are photostats of original documents, mostly from the National Archives, relating to the land grants given to Canadians who served in the U.S. Army during the War of 1812, and particularly to Markle's claims in Vigo County; and Vigo County commissioners records, justice of the peace records, court records, licenses to do business, and other official county records relating to taxes, roads and canals, and land ownership.

B-235. MARSH, HENRY C. (b.1838). PAPERS, 1861-1915.

90 items. S 905.

Marsh was a farmer near Muncie, Delaware Co.; private and hospital steward, 19th Indiana Regiment, serving in Virginia and Maryland (1861-1865); Muncie postmaster (1866-1875); and active in the Grand Army of the Republic and other veterans organizations.

The collection includes Marsh's Civil War letters to his father, John Marsh, a Muncie banker (1862); Marsh's war diaries (1862-1863); letters to Marsh from his father in Muncie (1861); letters to John Marsh from Lt. W. H. McDonald, 29th Indiana Regiment, serving in Tennessee (1862); correspondence and other papers relating to pension claims of Marsh and other veterans of the 19th Regiment (1886-1888); and papers relating to reunions of the 19th Regiment (1911-1915).

B-236. MARSHALL, THOMAS RILEY (1854-1925). PAPERS, 1860-1932.

4 ms. boxes, 6 vols. (2.25 l.f.). L 100, V 95.

Politician. Marshall was a graduate of Wabash College, Crawfordsville, Montgomery Co. (1873); lawyer, Columbia City, Whitley Co. (1876-1909); active in the Indiana Democratic Party; governor of Indiana (1909-1913); Vice-President of the United States under Woodrow Wilson (1913-1921); member, U.S. Coal Commission (1922); and author, *Recollection of Thomas R. Marshall* (1925).

The collection contains Marshall's speeches on Democratic Party politics and state and national affairs (1880s-1925), his speeches to Masons and other fraternal organizations, and speeches on law, schools, and history; manuscript draft of his *Recollections*; scrapbooks containing clippings of his newspaper columns on foreign affairs and current events (1921-1922, 1925), his obituaries (1925), newspaper stories on his gubernatorial campaign (1908), and family news (1890s); political correspondence (1908-1925), and letters of condolence written at his death; addresses and messages as governor to the state legislature (1909-1913); invitations, programs, menus, inauguration materials, and other memorabilia as vice-president (1913-1921); his school compositions and notebook from Wabash College (1868-1872); and family correspondence from Lewis County, Mo. (1860s).

Correspondents include Evangeline Booth, William E. Borah, William Jennings Bryan, Baron de Cartier, Calvin Coolidge, Stephen A. Douglas, Solomon B. Griffin, Warren G. Harding, Thomas A. Hendricks, Jules Jusserand, Helen Keller, Robert Lansing, Meredith Nicholson, John J. Pershing, Albert C. Ritchie, Elihu Root, William Howard Taft, Henry Van Dyke, Edith Bolling Wilson, and Woodrow Wilson.

B-237. MARY RIGG CENTER. RECORDS, 1911-1964.

1 archival box, 1 vol. (1.25 l.f.).   L 310, V 242.

The Mary Rigg Center, a neighborhood center in Indianapolis, was the successor to the Immigrant's Aid Association (1911-1923), the American Settlement (1923-1939), and the Southwest Social Center (1939-1961). In its early years the center worked with immigrants on the Indianapolis west side (1911-1939). In 1961 it was named for Mary Rigg (ca.1888-1971), director of the American Settlement and the Southside Social Center (1924-1961).

The records contain reports on group activities (1937-1942); annual reports (1929-1947); bills and financial records (1942-1965); account book (1949-1955); American Settlement Day Nursery applications (1934); newsletters of the American Settlement (1936-1938) and the Southwest Social Club's Women's Auxiliary (1940-1952); membership lists and accounts of the Immigrant's Aid Association (1911-1918); and newspaper clippings about a 1957 highway fraud case in Indiana.

B-238. MASTELLER, MRS. PAUL (CLARA) (fl.1909-1956). PAPERS, 1903-1956.

1 ms. box.   L 103.

Clara Schroeder Masteller grew up in Freelandville, Knox Co., and married Paul Masteller, an Indianapolis printer.

The collection consists primarily of Masteller's correspondence regarding the history of the Schroeder and Sanders families, principally 1930s-1956, and including retained copies of her own letters, and letters from family members in Freelandville, other cities in the United States, and Germany. In addition there are notes on family history and Masteller's personal and family correspondence.

B-239. MASTERS, FRANK S. (b.1872). PAPERS, 1915-1952.

1 ms. box.　　　　　　　　　　　　　　　　　　　　　　　　　L 102.

Masters was a farm implement and supply dealer in Brookville, Franklin Co. (1895-1922); secretary-treasurer and general manager, White Water Valley National Farm Loan Association (1923-1940s); and owner of farms in Franklin and Wayne counties.

The papers include Masters's correspondence and contracts with manufacturers of farm machinery, fertilizers, and other farm equipment and supplies (1915-1918); account books for Masters's farm tenants; and his reports of examination of the White Water Valley National Farm Loan Association, prepared for the U.S. Farm Credit Administration (1937-1939).

B-240. MATTHEWS, CLAUDE (1845-1898). PAPERS, 1836-1907.

ca.115 items.　　　　　　　　　　　　　　　　　　　　　　　　S 931.

Politician. Matthews was a graduate of Centre College, Danville, Ky. (1867); married Martha Whitcomb (1868), daughter of former Indiana governor James Whitcomb (1795-1852); farmer and livestock breeder near Clinton, Vermillion Co.; Democratic member, Indiana House of Representatives (1877); Indiana secretary of state (1891-1893); and governor of Indiana (1893-1897).

The papers include letters and a petition addressed to Governor Matthews regarding the coal miners' strike in southern Indiana, including communications from county sheriffs, Grand Army of the Republic posts, and miners' organizations (1894); correspondence dealing with the Pullman Strike and rioting in Lake County (1894); and correspondence as governor regarding the determination of the Indiana-Kentucky border, the Indiana State Fair, the extradition of criminals, and other official matters. Also included is personal correspondence of Matthews and his wife (1882-1907); correspondence regarding a portrait of Gov. James Whitcomb (1895); financial papers of Whitcomb (1836-1850); Matthews's political and patriotic speeches; his oration

"Obligation of the World to Literature," from Centre College (1867); and a fragment of a journal for sightseeing in southern California (ca.1900).

Correspondents include John P. Altgeld, George W. Ferris, William M. Fishback, Isaac P. Gray, Mary Hannah Krout, Albert Gallatin Porter, John G. Rich, and Adlai E. Stevenson.

B-241. MEDICAL AND DENTAL SERVICES, INC., FORT WAYNE. RECORDS, 1903-1973.

5 archival boxes, 4 vols. (5.5 l.f.).   Inventory.

Medical and Dental Services, Inc., was organized in Fort Wayne, Allen Co., as the Hope Hospital Free Bed Fund in 1903 to provide medical care for the indigent. It was renamed the Hospital and Home Service Association (1918); became the medical agency of the Fort Wayne Community Chest (1926); consolidated with the Sick Children's Aid Society (1928); reorganized as the Medical and Dental Service, Inc. (1952); and closed (1973).

The records include minutes of committee, board, and annual meetings (1930-1959); financial records, including account books (1928-1960), audit reports (1926-1959), budgets (1929-1960), monthly financial statements (1928-1959), tax materials (1934-1960), and insurance and retirement papers for employees (1934-1961); monthly and annual statistical reports (1926-1959); papers regarding casework and the Case Committee (1943-1959); general correspondence (1946-1960); publicity materials and newspaper clippings (1931-1959); and papers relating to the work of the Social Planning Council in Fort Wayne (1933-1958). Also included are minutes of the Children's Ward Association, later known as the Sick Children's Aid Society (1907-1926); and minutes of the Women's Hope Hospital Association (1915-1929).

B-242. MENDON SABBATH SCHOOL. RECORDS, 1888-1921.

1 ms. box (7 vols.).   L 191.

The Mendon Sabbath School was a Methodist school in Fall Creek Township, Hancock Co.

The collection consists of the school's minute books (1888-1921).

B-243. MENGER, CORNELIUS H. (fl.1917-1939). PAPERS, 1899-1957.

4 ms. boxes.　　　　　　　Inventory.　　　　　　　L 105.

Soldier. Menger was a cadet in the U.S. Coast Guard Academy (1917); resident of New York City (1917); served as an officer in the U.S. Army, stationed in France (1917-1919); officer in the ordnance department, U.S. Army, stationed at Jackson, La. (1919), Watertown, Mass. (1920-1922), and Birmingham, Ala. (1922-1928); employee of the Alabama Power Company (1929-1932?); officer in the Army Reserve, at Fort Sheridan, Ill. (1935), and Fort Knox, Ky. (1938); camp inspector with the National Park Service (1936-1937); employee of International Harvester in Indianapolis (1938-1939); and married Jean Hornstein of New York City (1920).

The collection consists primarily of Menger's letters to his fiancee and wife, Jean Hornstein Menger (fl.1914-1969). Included are letters written while Menger was in the service and she was living with her family in New York (1917-1920); his letters while he was traveling on behalf of the War Department and the Alabama Power Company, written from Birmingham, New York City, Boston, Washington, D.C., Cleveland, and Columbus, Ohio, and Pensacola, Fla. (1922-1932); his letters while he was with the Army Reserve (1935, 1938); and his letters to her in Bridgeport, Marion Co., and Indianapolis, while he was with the National Park Service in Omaha, Nebr., and during his camp inspection tours in the West (1936-1937). In addition there are letters to Jean Hornstein from other soldiers serving in World War I.

B-244. MERRILL, SAMUEL (1831-1924). PAPERS, 1850-1924.

1 ms. box.　　　　　　　　　　　　　　　　　　　L 106.

Publisher and diplomat. Merrill was the son of Indianapolis banker and bookseller Samuel Merrill (1792-1855); Indianapolis publisher and bookseller, with firm of Bowen-Merrill (1852-ca.1890); captain and lt. colonel, 70th Indiana Regiment, serving under Benjamin Harrison (1862-1865); and consul general at Calcutta, India (1889-1893).

The collection consists principally of Merrill's Civil War papers, including his letters to his wife and sister in Indianapolis from Kentucky, Tennessee, Georgia, and South Carolina (1862-1865); his war diary (1863); and orders, clothing, equipment records, and other official military papers (1862-1865). Also included are business papers of Merrill and his family (1850-ca.1900), including papers of his father; essays on Indiana's state capitals and on the early schools of Indianapolis, probably written by Merrill's sister, Catherine Merrill; and an 1898 oration by James Cooley Fletcher.

B-245. MESSLER, JAMES W. (1830-1894). PAPERS, 1858-1896.

35 items.   S 946.

Messler grew up on farms in Ohio and Indiana; was a miner and merchant in Australia (1853-1858); farmer near Frankfort, Clinton Co. (1858-1894); and a private in the 100th Indiana Regiment during the Civil War (1862-1865).

The papers include Messler's letters from Frankfort to his brother, Henry P. Messler, in Oxford, Ohio (1858-1860); family letters to Henry Messler from College Corner, Ohio (1859-1860); and letters to Charles L. Harper, Frankfort, from family and friends in Indiana, Missouri, and Dallasburg, Ky. (1881-1883).

B-246. MEYER, JAMES H. (1895-1967). PAPERS, 1922-1959.

22 ms. boxes.   Inventory.

Meyer was an attorney in Evansville, Vanderburgh Co. (1923-1967); Vanderburgh County deputy prosecuting attorney (1932-1935); prosecuting attorney (1936-1943); attorney for the Evansville Housing Authority (1951-1953, 1958); and Democratic candidate for judge of the Superior Court (1946).

The collection is made up primarily of depositions, summonses, transcripts of testimony, court decisions, correspondence, notes, and other papers pertaining to Meyer's legal cases, including criminal cases which he handled as a prosecutor; civil and criminal cases in which he was involved as a private attorney; and cases on behalf of the Evansville Housing Authority, particularly regarding the collection of delinquent rents. Also included are grand jury depositions regarding the closing of the Lincoln Bank in Evansville (1931); political brochures, clippings, and correspondence; legal publications, reports, and clippings; correspondence regarding possible changes in the jury system (1955); an article by Meyer on capital punishment (1938); and personal financial papers.

Correspondents include Winfield K. Denton and Paul V. McNutt.

B-247. MILLER, ISAAC (1807-1881?). PAPERS, 1806-1904.

80 items.   S 962.

Miller was a farmer in Lebanon County, Pa. (1830-1854), and Fayette County (1850s), Rush County (1860-1869), and Hamilton County (1870-1881), Ind.

The collection consists of Miller's business receipts, tax receipts, land records, and other financial documents from Pennsylvania and Indiana (1830-1881); and receipts for the estate of Henry Miller, Lebanon County, Pa. (1829-1837).

B-248. MILLER, OSCAR G. (1866-1957). PAPERS, 1824-1968.

8 ms. boxes, 1 vol. (4 l.f.).   Inventory.

Miller was a teacher in Greensburg, Decatur Co. (1880s); graduate of DePauw University, Greencastle, Putnam Co. (1891); Greensburg attorney (1891-1957); mayor of Greensburg (1902); and husband of Clara Lambert (1866-1957). His family included his father-in-law, Paschal T. Lambert (1831-1916), a clerk in Greensburg (1853), resident of Albia and other towns in Iowa (1853-1875), abstractor of real estate titles in Greensburg (1875-1916), and director of a Greensburg building and loan association; and Miller's brother-in-law, Edward M. White, an attorney in Muncie and Indianapolis, and assistant state attorney general (1910s-1920s).

The papers consist of correspondence, diaries, and business papers of Miller and his family. Included are letters to Clara Lambert Miller (1885-1950), among them letters from Albia, Iowa (1885-1886), from the Saunders family in Shepardsville, Ky. (1895-1950), and from friends in America while the Millers were traveling in Europe (1913, 1927); family correspondence of the

Miller, Lambert, and White families (1888-1932); diaries of Clara Miller (1897-1943), including diaries of her trips to California (1908), Europe (1913), Pittsburgh (1927), and West Virginia (1930), and diaries of her daily life in Greensburg (1897-1899, 1930-1932, 1936, 1943); Oscar Miller's accounts of his trips to California (1909) and Iowa (1947); real estate business papers of Paschal T. Lambert for property in Decatur County (1834-1921); other family real estate papers for land in Decatur, Rush, and Marion counties (1824-1946); P. T. Lambert's reminiscences of childhood in Indiana and account of his trip to California (1903); diaries of other Lambert family members (1927-1928, 1935); poems and writings by Clara Miller; and autograph album for Oscar Miller's friends (1882-1896).

B-249. MILLER, VALETTE (1870?-1958). COLLECTION, 1784-1885.

1 ms. box. L 107.

Miller was the wife of Dr. T. R. White, pastor of the Meridian Heights Presbyterian Church, Indianapolis (1920s-1934), and chaplain of the Indiana Reformatory at Pendleton (1934-1950s). She was the great granddaughter of Indiana governor Noah Noble (1794-1844), and granddaughter of Alexander H. Davidson (d.1863?), an Indianapolis schoolteacher and businessman, and member of the executive committee of the Indiana Constitutional Union Party (1860).

The collection includes receipts and financial papers of Noah Noble (1820-1844); Noble's will and estate inventory (1844); personal correspondence of Noble's daughter, Catherine Noble Davidson (1839-1851); correspondence of Alexander H. Davidson regarding the Constitutional Union Party in the election of 1860; letters to Davidson from his son and brother in Lexington, Va. (1861); autograph album of Catherine Noble Davidson (1836-1851); autograph books signed by members of the U.S. House of Representatives (1857-1858); Noble family land and legal documents from Virginia and Kentucky (1784-1815); and newspaper clippings on politics and the Civil War (1841-1868).

Correspondents include John J. Crittenden, William Henry Harrison, John James Hayden, Michael C. Kerr, Robert Dale Owen, Caleb B. Smith, Oliver H. Smith, and Richard W. Thompson.

B-250. MILLER, WILLIAM HENRY HARRISON (1840-1917). PAPERS, 1874-1919.

1 ms. box, 14 vols. (2 l.f.).   L 108, V 101.

Miller was an attorney in Fort Wayne, Allen Co. (1866-1874), and Indianapolis (1874-1889, 1893-1917); law partner of Benjamin Harrison (1874-1889); and Attorney General of the United States in Harrison administration (1889-1893).

The papers include Miller's letter books (1875-1909), containing his correspondence regarding his legal work, his work as Attorney General of the United States, and personal and financial matters; indentures, mortgages, abstracts of title, and other legal documents regarding his property ownership in Indianapolis (1874-1906); correspondence, reports, and financial papers regarding the construction and maintenance of buildings in Indianapolis owned by Miller (1895-1906); letters of condolence to his wife and children at his death (1917); an engagement book for Miller and his wife in Washington, D.C. (1890-1891); Miller's speeches on politics, morality, and the law; his ledger book recording his trustee accounts (1901-1911); and a report to the U.S. Circuit Court on the case of *James R. Jessup* v. *Wabash, St. Louis and Pacific Railway Company* (1907?).

Correspondents include Albert J. Beveridge, Oscar Bohlen, Mary Lord Harrison, and James E. Watson.

B-251. MITCHELL, EDWARD A. (1910-1979). PAPERS, 1946-1949.

27 ms. boxes.   Inventory.

Politician and businessman. Mitchell was vice-president and general manager of Hesmer Foods, Inc., Evansville, Vanderburgh Co. (1937-1946), president (1946-1979); lt. commander, U.S. Navy, in command of underwater demolition team during World War II; Republican member, U.S. House of Representatives (1947-1949); and Vanderburgh County councilman (1949-1951).

The collection consists of Mitchell's congressional papers (1946-1949), including correspondence regarding veterans claims and benefits and papers relating to Mitchell's service on the House Veterans Committee; correspondence and legislative papers regarding bills introduced or supported by Mitchell, including the Taft-Hartley Act, the elimination of the tax on oleomargarine, the abolition of the War Assets Administration, and changes in the Chinese Immigration Law; his correspondence with constituents concerning the work of federal agencies, including complaints and requests for information and assistance; constituent correspondence regarding current events and legislation before Congress; his speeches in Congress and before civic and political groups; press releases and other publicity issued by his office; papers relating to his 1946 and 1948 congressional campaigns; papers pertaining to his work as an anti-Communist; and correspondence regarding his resignation from the Jewish Congressional Advisory Board (1947). Also included are papers relating to the 1947 Evansville mayoral election.

Correspondents include Omar N. Bradley, Homer Capehart, Charles A. Halleck, and Joseph McCarthy.

B-252. MOORE, SAMUEL (1799-1889). PAPERS, 1823-1953.

3 ms. boxes, 13 vols. (3.25 l.f.).   L 110, V 73, V 76, V 96.

Merchant. Moore was a merchant in Washington County (1818-1823); founder of Mooresville, Morgan Co. (1824); owner of dry goods stores in Mooresville (1824-ca.1868); involved in pork packing and shipping of agricultural products to Cincinnati and New Orleans; and operator of gristmill near Mooresville (1830s-1840s).

The collection consists principally of Moore's business papers from the period 1823-1860, including his correspondence, invoices, receipts, shipping lists, and inventories of goods documenting his dealings with merchants in Madison, Jefferson Co. (1830-1850s), New Orleans (1833-1855), Cincinnati (1829-1850s), Louisville (1824-1830s), and Philadelphia and Pittsburgh (1842-1850s); store account books for the firms of Moore and Worthington (1834, 1837), Samuel Moore & Company (1840-1860), and Moore, Griggs & Cook (1853-1864); Moore's indentures, deeds, and other land documents, including plats and other documents dealing with the development of Mooresville (1823-1880s); Moore's notebook listing expenses of transporting a herd of horses to market in Virginia (1833); his journal and account book from his trip to New Orleans (1837-1838); memorandum book of pork and lard shipped to merchants in Pittsburgh (1847-1849); stock certificates and other papers relating to his investments in the Madison and Indianapolis Railroad, and the Indianapolis and Bellefontaine Railroad (1840s-1850s); and other receipts, invoices, and business papers. Additional items include family correspondence from Muhlenberg and Worthington, Ky. (1829-1834), Mooresville (1829-1880s), Newport, Vermillion Co. (1829-1838), Washington County (1830s-1840s), and from Moore's daughters attending school in Madison (1846-1848); personal letters to his daughter, Margaret Moore (1860s-1870s); memory book and school essays of his daughter, Martha Jane Moore (1845-1848); correspondence regarding state and national politics, the Whig Party in Indiana, and the work of the Indiana state legislature (1830s-1850s); Moore's family correspondence and personal financial documents (1860s-1880s); and correspondence and notes of Thomas S. Moore of Robinson, Ill., and Mrs. Charles W. Hollandsworth of Canton, Ill., regarding family history (1914-1953).

Correspondents include Hervey Bates, Thomas H. Blake, Jesse D. Bright, James F. D. Lanier, Nicholas McCarty, Joseph Moore, and David Wallace.

B-253. MOORES, CHARLES W. (1862-1923). SPEECHES, 1901-1908.

26 items.   S 982.

Moores was an Indianapolis attorney; member, Indiana Board of School Commissioners (1901-1909), vice-president (1903-1908) and president (1908-1909); author of books for schoolchildren on Abraham Lincoln, Christopher Columbus, and Indiana history.

The collection consists of Moores's speeches (1901-1908), including his speeches at Indianapolis school openings and graduations; speeches on Abraham Lincoln, Benjamin Harrison, and teachers and education; and a speech to the German American Teachers Association.

B-254. MORTON, OLIVER PERRY (1823-1877). PAPERS, 1855-1909.

6 ms. boxes.   L 113.

Politician. Morton was a Centerville, Wayne Co., attorney (1847-1860); one of the founders of the Republican Party in Indiana; candidate for governor of the People's (Republican) Party (1856); elected lieutenant governor of Indiana (1860); became governor upon resignation of Henry S. Lane (January 1861); governor of Indiana (1861-1867); U.S. Senator (1867-1877); associated with the Radical Republicans in Congress; chairman of the Senate Committee on Elections and Privileges (1873-1874); and member of the electoral commission to determine the outcome of the presidential voting in several southern states (1876-1877).

The collection consists principally of Morton's speeches and notes for speeches on Republican politics, the Civil War, secession, Reconstruction, and other state and national political issues. Also included is Morton's correspondence (1859-1877), including his questions to Indiana's delegates to the Peace Convention, and the delegates' responses (1861); political correspondence as governor and U.S. Senator; correspondence regarding Louisiana politics and the disputed U.S. Senate election (1873-1876), including letters and newspaper clippings sent by Louisiana governor William P. Kellogg; and letters from Indiana and the rest of the nation regarding Morton's position on the 1876 presidential election and the work of the electoral commission (January-February 1877). The collection also contains Morton's personal finance books (1863-1875); letters to his son, Oliver T. Morton, describing Morton's career for a proposed biography (1884-1886); papers relating to the Morton monument in Indianapolis, including letters of Morton's widow (1900-1909); and contemporary copies of Lew Wallace's correspondence with Jose M. J. Caravajal regarding an American military expedition to Mexico (1865).

Correspondents include James G. Blaine, John Brough, Salmon P. Chase, Schuyler Colfax, William P. Fishback, John Watson Foster, George F. Hoar, Alvin P. Hovey, John J. Ingalls, William P. Kellogg, Nathan Kimball, Henry S. Lane, William L. McMillan, Jeptha D. New, Godlove Orth, Robert Dale Owen, William S. Rosecrans, Lionel A. Sheldon, Caleb B. Smith, James C. Veatch, and Joseph A. Wright.

B-255. MOWREY, WALTER LEVI (ca.1897-1953). PAPERS, 1917-1947.

ca.90 items. S 997.

Mowrey was a graduate of Purdue University (1920); farmer in Hancock County (1920-ca.1943) and Lawrence Township, Marion Co. (ca.1943-1953);

and teacher of vocational agriculture and athletic director, Warren Central High School, Marion Co. (1923-1953).

The papers are made up of Mowrey's grade and class reports from Purdue University (1917-1920), and from schools where he did additional course work (1923-1947); his teaching certificates and teaching contracts (1920-1947); and diplomas and other educational certificates (1911-1943).

B-256. MYERS, WALTER D. (1882-1973). PAPERS, 1908-1969.

1 ms. box. Inventory. L 115.

Myers was an Indianapolis attorney (1907-1963); Indianapolis city attorney (1913-1925); Democratic candidate, U.S. Senate (1928); speaker, Indiana House of Representatives (1931-1933); and assistant postmaster general of the United States (1940-1953).

The collection contains Myers's political speeches (1928-1931), including speeches for his 1928 Senate race; correspondence and other papers relating to Democratic Party politics and Myers's career in Indianapolis and with the U.S. Post Office (1908-1969); and newspaper and magazine clippings relating to Myers's career and the Democratic Party.

Correspondents include Charles W. Fairbanks, Frederick Landis, H. L. Mencken, Franklin D. Roosevelt, Matthew E. Welsh, and Claude R. Wickard.

B-257. NATURE STUDY CLUB OF INDIANA. RECORDS, 1903-1970.

3 ms. boxes, 2 archival boxes, 2 vols. (3.5 l.f.). L 227, V 190.

The Nature Study Club of Indiana was organized in Indianapolis in 1908 to promote the love and study of nature, and to conserve Indiana's scenery, flora, and fauna; incorporated in 1913 with the additional responsibility of administering Woollen's Garden of Birds and Botany in Indianapolis after the death of William Wesley Woollen; and sponsored nature tours and supported the establishment of state parks and nature preserves.

The collection consists principally of Nature Club records from the period 1908-1940 and includes meeting minutes (1908-1938); correspondence, announcements, and reports on outings (1908-1940); publications of the club, including the monthly *From the Buzzers Roost* (1914-1915), the monthly *Nature Study Club of Indiana* (1926-1930), the quarterly *The Hoosier Outdoors* (1919-1970), and the club's yearbooks (1908-1931); papers relating to Woollen's Garden of Birds and Botany; papers relating to the Guthrie Memorial Forest in Jennings County, administered by the club (1927-1937); registration books for visitors to Woollen's Gardens (1906-1939); club financial records (1937-1941); and halftone cuts used in club publications.

Correspondents include Charles C. Deam, Kate Milner Rabb, and William Wesley Woollen.

B-258. NAYLOR, ISAAC (1790-1873). PAPERS, 1818-1888.

3 folders (28 items). S 1009.

Attorney. Naylor was a resident of Charlestown, Clark Co. (1805-1833); soldier in Battle of Tippecanoe (1811); lawyer at Charlestown (1817-1833) and Crawfordsville, Montgomery Co. (1833-1873); judge, 1st Judicial Circuit (1837-1852?); and active in Whig Party politics and in the Independent Order of Freemasons.

The collection includes Naylor's reminiscences of pioneer life in Clark County, the Battle of Tippecanoe, and the Pigeon Roost Massacre; an autobiographical sketch (1852); his Masonic speeches at Madison, Jefferson Co. (1823), and Charlestown (1826); his political speeches (1840s); his judicial opinions (1848, 1851); manuscript of resolutions passed at the Tippecanoe Battlefield reunion (1840); political letters; and Mary Naylor's reminiscence of moving the state capital from Corydon to Indianapolis.

Correspondents include Walter Q. Gresham, Benjamin Harrison, Jonathan Jennings, and Zachary Taylor.

B-259. NEW, HARRY S. (1858-1937). PAPERS, 1869-1938.

1 ms. box. L 299.

Politician and newspaperman. New was the son of Indianapolis newspaperman and Republican politician John C. New; reporter, editor, and publisher, *In-*

dianapolis Journal (1878-1903); Republican member, Indiana State Senate (1896-1900); captain, U.S. Army during the Spanish American War (1898); member, Republican National Committee (1900-1912), chairman (1907-1908); member, U.S. Senate (1917-1923); and Postmaster General of the United States under Presidents Harding and Coolidge (1923-1929).

The papers contain New's correspondence regarding state and national politics, including correspondence regarding the 1912, 1920, and 1924 presidential elections, his appointment and work as U.S. Postmaster General (1923-1929), and Indiana politics, especially in the late 1920s and 1930s; New's notes on the significance and background of many of the letters in the collection, written in the early 1930s; his reminiscences on the 1896, 1908, and 1912 presidential elections, on the 1898 election of Albert J. Beveridge to the U.S. Senate, on the 1924 Republican National Convention, on the development of the airmail system during his term as Postmaster General, and on William Howard Taft, Warren G. Harding, Calvin Coolidge, James Whitcomb Riley, and Lew Wallace; and his essays on Caleb Smith and Civil War general John L. Clem. The collection also contains historical documents collected by New, including letters of Schuyler Colfax and Oliver P. Morton; and letters of John K. Gowdey to Marcus A. Hanna regarding the 1896 presidential election.

Correspondents include George Ade, Bernard M. Baruch, Nicholas Murray Butler, Arthur Capper, Schuyler Colfax, Charles Curtis, Harry M. Daugherty, Charles G. Dawes, Edwin Denby, John K. Gowdy, Marcus A. Hanna, Warren G. Harding, Will H. Hays, Charles D. Hilles, George C. Hitt, Herbert Hoover, James M. Huff, Henry O. Johnson, Frank B. Kellogg, Robert Lansing, Henry Cabot Lodge, Andrew W. Mellon, Oliver P. Morton, John C. New, Meredith Nicholson, Bill Nye, Henry C. Payne, Elihu Root, Frederick E. Schortemeier, Leslie W. Shaw, Henry L. Stimson, William Howard Taft, Booth Tarkington, James E. Watson, John W. Weeks, and Frank B. Willis.

B-260. NEW CASTLE CEMETERY ASSOCIATION. RECORDS, 1859-1895.

2 folders (172 items). S 2638.

The New Castle Cemetery Association was incorporated in 1858 for the purpose of providing burial ground for people in the New Castle vicinity; and owned and operated the South Mound Cemetery in New Castle.

The records consist of treasurers' and secretaries' reports, bills, receipts, documents relating to the sale of burial plots, and other business documents of the association (1859-1895), particularly from the period 1888-1893 when New Castle attorney Thomas B. Redding (1831-1895) was serving as secretary and superintendent.

B-261. NICHOLSON, ROBERTA WEST (1903-). PAPERS, 1861-1957.

2 archival boxes.   Inventory.   L 320.

Social worker and politician. Nicholson was an Indianapolis social worker; served as director, Marion County Works Progress Administration, Women's and Professional Division (1930s), and in administrative posts in other social work agencies; Democratic member, Indiana House of Representatives (1935-1936); member of Parole Board, Indiana Girls School (1956-1961); wife of Indianapolis insurance executive Meredith Nicholson, Jr. (1902-1968); and daughter-in-law of writer Meredith Nicholson (1866-1947).

The papers contain Nicholson's family correspondence, including correspondence between Nicholson and her husband (1947-1952), letters of her daughter Eugenie Nicholson Fox from the University of Iowa (1951-1952) and Chicago (1954), letters of her son Meredith Nicholson, III, while he was serving in the U.S. Army at the Army Finance Center in St. Louis, and in the officers' school at Fort Riley, Kans. (1951-1954), letters from her mother in North Carolina and Battle Creek, Mich. (1949-1951), and letters to Meredith Nicholson, Jr., from his children in Indianapolis (1942-1944); political letters to Roberta Nicholson while she was serving in the Indiana legislature, including letters regarding her bill prohibiting suits for alienation of affections (1935); her political speeches, advertisements, and other materials (1934-1957); correspondence of Meredith Nicholson, Jr., with attorney Kurt Pantzer regarding investments (1941-1948); family photographs and newspaper clippings; and genealogical materials regarding the Nicholson and other families. Also contained are letters and poems of Meredith Nicholson (1890-1940), including letters to Indianapolis writer May Louise Shipp, and letters written while he was serving as an American diplomat in South America (1930s); clippings on writers Booth Tarkington and James Whitcomb Riley; and an 1861 handwritten newspaper.

B-262. NOBLE, LAZARUS (ca.1826-1879). PAPERS, 1860-1869.

1 ms. box.   L 117.

Noble was a Vincennes, Knox Co., businessman; adjutant general of Indiana during the Civil War (1861-1865); and clerk of the Indiana Supreme Court (1864-1868).

The collection consists primarily of Noble's business correspondence and papers from the period 1864-1868 while he was living in Indianapolis. Included are correspondence and papers relating to the Indianapolis Copper Mining Company in which he was an investor, including letters from the company agent in the Sault Ste. Marie area (1865-1867); letters regarding his Vincennes business interests, particularly from his in-laws John and Samuel Judah; requests for assistance in obtaining state and federal appointments, including letters from former Union soldiers living in Louisiana; and letters regarding bounties for soldiers in the 21st Indiana Regiment (1865-1866). Also included is family correspondence from Vincennes; and correspondence regarding his family's trip to Montreal, Canada, in 1865.

B-263. NOBLE, NOAH (1794-1844). PAPERS, 1816-1844.

6 ms. boxes.   Calendar.   L 118.

Businessman, attorney, and politician. Noble was a lawyer, farmer, and businessman in Brookville, Franklin Co. (ca.1811-1825); member, Indiana House of Representatives (1825); receiver of public monies, Indianapolis Land Office (1825-1829); involved in steam mill company and tannery in Indianapolis (ca.1828); Michigan Road commissioner (1830); governor of Indiana (1831-1837), elected as a Henry Clay supporter (1831) and as a Whig (1834); as governor, promoted extensive program of canal, road, and railroad building; member, Indiana Internal Improvements Board, overseeing construction of the Whitewater Canal, the Wabash and Erie Canal, the Madison and Indianapolis Railroad, and other road and railroad construction projects (1839-1841); Indiana Fund Commissioner (1841-1842); and owner of farm near Indianapolis.

The collection is composed of Noble's political correspondence (1828-1844), including correspondence regarding state and national Whig politics, his campaigns for governor, and letters from Indiana's congressmen regarding national politics; his papers as member of the Internal Improvements Board, including receipts and bills for work performed and supplies provided to the projects, and correspondence regarding claims against the state, possibilities of employment on projects, and the operations of the board and its major projects, including the Madison and Indianapolis Railroad, the Whitewater Canal, and the Wabash and Erie Canal; his papers as Indiana Fund Commissioner, principally his correspondence regarding the state's debts arising from the Internal Improvements projects, and including his correspondence with eastern and British investors, correspondence pertaining to his meetings with investors in New York (1841), and his answers to the Indiana Senate Investigating Committee's questions relating to the actions of the state's agents (1841-1842); his correspondence and receipts as Receiver of Public Monies in the Indianapolis Land Office (1826-1829); and personal business papers (1821-1844), including correspondence regarding his trip to Texas and his Texas investments (1843-1844). Also included are Noble's papers as governor, including correspondence regarding Indiana Indians, including the purchase of Indian land and the removal of Indians from the state, and fears of an Indian uprising in northern Indiana during the Black Hawk War (1832); papers relating to internal improvements, including project survey reports and receipts for work performed (1835-1837); correspondence regarding appointments to state positions; petitions and correspondence dealing with criminals and requests for clemency; and petitions to the governor regarding local issues.

Correspondents include John Badollet, Samuel Bigger, Michael G. Bright, David Burr, Henry Clay, John Wesley Davis, John Dowling, George H. Dunn, Paris C. Dunning, Elisha Embree, John Ewing, John Hay Farnham, Graham N. Fitch, George Graham, William Graham, William Hendricks, Samuel Judah, James F. D. Lanier, Robert Lucas, Jonathan McCarty, Joseph G. Marshall, Samuel Merrill, James Noble, David Dale Owen, Robert Dale Owen, Samuel W. Parker, Daniel D. Pratt, Daniel G. Read, Caleb B. Smith, Oliver H. Smith, Milton Stapp, Jeremiah Sullivan, John Test, John Tipton, and Omer Tousey.

B-264. NOLAND, STEPHEN C. (1887-1962). PAPERS, 1938-1950.

ca.86 items. S 2313.

Noland was a writer (1914-1917, 1919-1933) and editor (1934-1949) for the *Indianapolis News*; publisher, Marion County *Mail* (1950-ca.1960); and editor in chief and officer, Citizens Historical Association (1934-1952).

The papers consist entirely of Noland's correspondence and papers for the Citizens Historical Association (1938-1950), including his correspondence with executive director Lyman Davidson regarding the work of the organization and its field agents, and financial reports, circulars, and other papers of the association.

B-265. OGG, ADAMS LEE (1827-1904). PAPERS, 1836-1936.

ca.132 items.   S 1028.

Ogg was an attorney and businessman in Greenfield, Hancock Co., and Indianola, Iowa (1850s); captain, 3rd Iowa Regiment, serving in Missouri, Tennessee, and at Vicksburg, Miss. (1861-1863); lawyer in Greenfield (ca.1865-1904); and married Mary E. Longnaker of Greenfield (1861).

The collection contains primarily Ogg and Longnaker family correspondence, including correspondence between Ogg and his wife while he was serving in the Civil War and she was at Greenfield or in Iowa (1862-1863); correspondence with her family in Greenfield (1861-1863); other Longnaker and Ogg family correspondence, principally from the period 1854-1871, including letters from Iowa and Greenfield; diaries and memoranda of expenditures of Mary E. Ogg (1859-1878); and clippings of Kate Milner Rabb's "A Hoosier Listening Post" columns from the *Indianapolis Star*, containing excerpts from the Ogg Civil War-era letters (1936).

B-266. OLDS, WILLIAM C. (1845-1893). PAPERS, 1862-1865.

ca.55 items.   S 1029.

Olds was from Covington, Fountain Co., and served as a corporal and sergeant in the 63rd Indiana Regiment (1862-1865).

The papers consist of Olds's Civil War letters to his father, Frank A. Olds of Covington, written from Kentucky, Tennessee, Georgia, and North Carolina (1862-1865).

B-267. OLIN, FRANK W. (1853-1941). PAPERS, 1832-1940.

4 ms. boxes. L 301.

Businessman. Olin attended City Academy in Indianapolis (1860s); worked for the Howe Sewing Machine Company in Peru, Miami Co. (1872-1875), and Indianapolis (1875-1882, 1884-1885); engaged in the typewriter business in Indianapolis (1886-1897); engaged in the life insurance business (1897-1917); involved in establishing the State Automobile Insurance Association (1917), and worked for the association (1917-1941); and active in Indianapolis civic organizations.

The collection includes Olin's diaries (1877, 1897-1898, 1922-1939); correspondence, circulars, and reports from organizations with which Olin was associated, including the Indianapolis Commercial Club and the Indianapolis Chamber of Commerce (1902-1920s), the Indianapolis Civic League (1908), the YMCA (1909-1913), the Layman's Missionary Movement and its Indianapolis convention in 1916, the American Rights Committee (1916), and the Indianapolis Home for Aged Women (1921-1935); political papers, containing papers relating to the Republican Party in Indianapolis (1900s-1910s), and the Citizens' Non-Partisan Movement (1913); insurance and other business papers, including papers relating to the Indiana Association of Life Underwriters (1908); Olin's business letter book (late 1880s); and an unpublished literary magazine of the City Academy, edited by Olin (1869). Also included are miscellaneous legal and financial documents from LaPorte County (1832-1870s).

B-268. OLIVER, REECE A. (1891-1966). PAPERS, 1914-1950.

ca.70 items. S 1032, S 2318.

Oliver was from Akron, Fulton Co.; taught school in the Philippine Islands (1914-1930s); field manager for the American Red Cross' China Famine Relief operation; worked for the Philippine Board of Education (1930s); officer in the U.S. Army during World War II, and fought with the Philippine guerrillas; and U.S. official in the Philippines (1946-1950).

The collection consists primarily of Oliver's letters from the Philippines and China (1914-1950) to his brother, Kenneth A. Oliver, an Akron farmer, and other family members. Included are his letters regarding the Philippine schools, the effect of World War I on the Philippines, his work in China with the Red Cross, and conditions in the Philippines before and after World War II. Also contained are Kenneth Oliver's expense and account books (1915-1925); brochures, clippings, and other printed items relating to the Philippines; and a pamphlet, *Drill Manual for Philippine Cadets*, by Reece Oliver (1924).

B-269. ORTH, GODLOVE S. (1817-1882). LETTERS, 1845-1881.

59 items. S 1033.

Politician and attorney. Orth was an attorney in Lafayette, Tippecanoe Co. (1839-1882); Whig member, Indiana State Senate (1843-1849), president pro tem of the Senate (1845-1846); delegate, Know Nothing National Convention (1856); Commissioner, Washington Peace Conference (1861); Republican member, U.S. House of Representatives (1863-1873, 1879-1882); and U.S. Minister to Austria-Hungary (1875-1876).

The collection is made up principally of Orth's letters to Schuyler Colfax (1845-1878), particularly from the period 1845-1854, and discussing Whig, Know Nothing, and Republican Party politics, the work of the Indiana General Assembly, and other state and national issues. The collection also contains photostats of Orth's letters to James A. Garfield (1880-1881) and others. The letters to Colfax were published in the *Indiana Magazine of History* (1943-1944).

B-270. OSGATHARP, HARLAND L. (b.1887). DIARIES, 1942-1945.

1 ms. box. Inventory. L 120.

Soldier and government worker. Osgatharp was from Otwell, Pike Co.; served in the medical corps of the U.S. Army during World War I; worked in Civilian Conservation Corps camps in Oregon (1941-1942); and private, U.S. Army during World War II (1942-1945), serving in the 50th Station Hospital and the 99th Field Hospital at Camp Lee, Va. (1942-1943), North Africa (1943), and Italy (1944-1945).

The collection consists of Osgatharp's diaries from the period January 1942-December 1945, describing his work in the Civilian Conservation Corps camps in Oregon; his enlistment and training in the U.S. Army in Texas, Michigan, and Virginia (1942-1943); his service in military hospitals in Virginia, North Africa, and Italy (1942-1945); his return to Otwell, Ind. (December 1945); and his reminiscences of service in World War I. Also included is an undated address book.

B-271. OSGOOD, HOWARD G. (d. 1913). PAPERS, 1858-1912.

1 ms. box, 4 vols. (1 l.f.).   L 121, V 92.

Osgood was a physician in Gosport, Owen Co. (1858-1913).

The papers include Osgood's account books for his medical practice in Gosport (1858-1866); his correspondence, receipts, and other documents regarding his business affairs (1858-1912); and mortgages, deeds, and tax receipts for farmland which he owned in Owen, Monroe, and Floyd counties (1869-1911).

B-272. OTT, JOHN (b.1823?). PAPERS, 1858-1905.

3 vols., 18 items (.5 l.f.).   V 105, S 1034.

Ott, a German immigrant, manufactured furniture in Indianapolis.

The collection includes account books for Ott's furniture business (1858-1878); price lists and inventories of furniture for the L. W. Ott Company of Indianapolis (1900-1905); and personal business papers of the Ott family (1864-1880s).

B-273. OWEN, ROBERT DALE (1801-1877). PAPERS, 1826-1904.

3 ms. boxes.   Partial Calendar.   L 122.

Author and politician. Owen was the son of reformer Robert Owen (1777-1858); accompanied his father to establish experimental community at New Harmony, Posey Co. (1825); editor of social reform journals, including the *New Harmony Gazette,* the *New York Free Enquirer,* and *The Crisis* (1820s-1830s); Democratic member, Indiana House of Representatives, from Posey

County (1836-1839, 1851-1852); member, U.S. House of Representatives (1843-1847); U.S. charge d'affaires and minister to Naples, Italy (1853-1858); writer and speaker on social, political, and philosophical issues, including emancipation, women's rights, and spiritualism; and married Lottie Walton Kellogg of New York (1876).

The collection contains Owen's correspondence and writings (1826-1877), and correspondence of Lottie Kellogg Owen and the Kellogg family of New York and Philadelphia (1827-1904). The Owen papers include his family correspondence, including his correspondence with Robert Owen (1852-1854), his daughter Rosamond (1872-1877), and Lottie Kellogg (1872-1877), and a letter regarding New Harmony from his brother, William Owen (1827); his correspondence pertaining to spiritualism and his spiritualist writings (1859-1877); letters of condolence and other papers regarding the death of Robert Owen (1858); his correspondence with publishers, particularly from the 1870s, dealing with his autobiography and his play about Pocahontas "Sixteen Hundred and Seven"; his writings regarding Texas annexation, slavery, reconstruction, women's rights, the Indiana school law of 1852, and other issues; the manuscript of his play "Sixteen Hundred and Seven"; and his Chickasaw Indian dictionary and phrase book (1828). The Kellogg family papers include Lottie Kellogg Owen's correspondence and papers regarding the settlement of Robert Dale Owen's estate (1877-1880s); correspondence of Lottie Kellogg and her sisters with friends, suitors, and family members (1839-1900); and correspondence of Alexander Osbourn of Philadelphia (1835-1853), including letters from his wife in New York (1835-1837), and letters to his wife, Jennie Kellogg Osbourn, written from Ohio, Kentucky, and New Orleans (1853). Also contained is a letter from Mary Wollstonecraft Shelley to Frances Wright (1830).

Correspondents include Henry Ward Beecher, Augustus C. Dodge, William Dean Howells, Anne Henrietta Leonowens, Robert Owen, William Owen, Harriet Beecher Stowe, and Nicholas P. Trist.

B-274. PALMER HOUSE. RECORD BOOKS, 1845-1853.

2 vols. (.25 l.f.).　　　　　　　　　　　　　　　　　　　　　　　　V 140.

The Palmer House was an Indianapolis hotel.

The collection includes the hotel's guest register (1845-1848) and its account book listing daily expenses and receipts (1851-1853).

B-275. PANTZER, KURT F. (1892-1979). PAPERS, 1878-1979.

50 l.f.   Partial Inventory.

Attorney and civic leader. Pantzer was a student at Wabash College, Crawfordsville, Montgomery Co., and Harvard University, Mass. (1909-1920); captain, U.S. Infantry (1917-1919); lawyer in New York (1920-1922) and Indianapolis (1922-1979); member of Indianapolis law firm of Barnes, Hickam, Pantzer and Boyd (1940-1979); lecturer, Indiana University School of Law (1955-1966); member, Republican National Finance Committee (1956-1966); finance chairman for Richard Nixon's 1968 Indiana primary campaign; chairman, Indiana Republican Finance Committee, and co-founder of the Indianapolis Republican Finance Committee; member of board of directors of numerous companies, including the American States Life Insurance Company, the Morgan Packing Company, and Inland Container Company; trustee of Tudor Hall School and Butler University, Indianapolis; and active in civic and arts organizations.

The collection consists primarily of Pantzer's papers relating to his political, legal, and civic work. Materials on politics include papers relating to state and national Republican Party politics, and the state and national Republican Finance Committees (1940s-1970s); Richard Nixon's presidential campaigns (1968, 1972); presidential campaigns of Robert Taft (1947-1952) and Barry Goldwater (1964); his support for Sherman Minton's appointment to the U.S. Supreme Court (1949); his involvement with foreign affairs organizations, including the American Committee on United Europe (1947-1951) and the Council on Foreign Relations (1940s-1950s); and his work against the Communist Party in the United States and Indiana (1942-1950s). Materials on Pantzer's legal work include papers regarding his role as a special master in the dispute between New York and New Jersey over use of the Delaware River water (1940s-1960s); his involvement with the writing of the Uniform Commercial Code, and his work with the National Conference of Commissions on Uniform State Laws (1940s-1970s); his work with the American, Indiana, and Indianapolis Bar Associations, and the Bar Association of the 7th District U.S. Court of Appeals (1940s-1970s); his work with the estate of Meredith Nicholson, Jr. (1936-1948); and his law classes and seminars (1940s-1960s). Materials on his civic activities include papers pertaining to the Harrison Community Project, involving the conversion of Fort Benjamin Harrison, Indianapolis, into a peacetime military base (1946-1950s); and papers relating to Indiana and Indianapolis civic and educational organizations, including Butler University and the construction of Clowes Hall (1947-1979), Wabash College (1920s-1970s), Tudor Hall School (1942-1950s), the Associated Colleges of Indiana (1940s-1970s), the Indianapolis Museum of Art (1960s), the Art Association of Indianapolis (1940s-1970s), the John Herron Art Institute (1960s), the Indianapolis Theatre Association and Starlight Musicals (1948-1959), the Indianapolis Symphony Orchestra (1940s-1960s), the Indiana Lincoln Foundation (1957-1977), the Meridian Street Foundation (1960s-1970s), Delta Tau Delta Fraternity (1930s-1960s), and the Sagamore of the Wabash Award (1946-1977). The collection also includes family papers, including Pantzer's correspondence while a student at Wabash College and Harvard University (1909-1920), and as an officer in the U.S. Army at Louisville, Ky. (1917-1919); and letters from his mother's family in Germany (1878-1930s).

Correspondents include George N. Craig, William E. Jenner, Sherman Minton, Richard M. Nixon, and Robert A. Taft.

B-276. PARKER, BENJAMIN STRATTAN (1833-1911). PAPERS, 1844-1923.

4 ms. boxes. L 123.

Writer and politician. Parker was a farmer and teacher in Henry County (1850s-1860s); Lewisville, Henry Co., grocer and grain dealer (1863-1874); editor and publisher, *New Castle Mercury* (1875-1882) and the *Knightstown Banner* (1885-1888); Republican presidential elector (1880); U.S. Consul to Sherbrooke, Canada (1882-1885); Henry County Clerk (1888-1892); Republican member, Indiana House of Representatives (1901); poet and short story writer; coeditor, with E. B. Heiney, of *Poets and Poetry of Indiana* (1900); and president, Western Association of Writers.

The collection consists of Parker's correspondence and writings, including his correspondence with E. B. Heiney and publishers regarding *Poets and Poetry of Indiana* (1897-1900); correspondence pertaining to the Western Association of Writers, Parker's poetry and prose writing, his newspaper work, and requests for advice on writing (1870s-1890s); correspondence regarding Republican Party politics (1870s-1880s); correspondence relating to James Whitcomb Riley (1890s-1910s); and family correspondence (1844-1870s), including letters regarding Whig Party politics from Samuel W. Parker to Isaac Parker (1844-1852). The collection also contains Parker's historical writings on the National Road, the early history of Indiana and the Midwest, Quakers, education in Indiana, western social customs, and the natural and political history of Henry County; his short stories, primarily stories published in boys' magazines; biographical sketches of Indiana writers and residents of Henry County; and poetry by Parker and other Indiana poets.

Correspondents include J. G. Bourinot, Thomas M. Browne, George S. Cottman, John M. Dickey, Edmund Eitel, Hewitt H. Howland, Daniel L. Paine, Samuel W. Parker, W. W. Pfrimmer, John J. Piatt, and Maurice Thompson.

B-277. PAUL V. MCNUTT FOR PRESIDENT IN 1940 CLUB, INC. RECORDS, 1936-1937.

1 ms. box. L 293.

The club was organized in Indianapolis in 1936 to promote the candidacy of Indiana governor Paul V. McNutt for the Democratic nomination for President in 1940.

The records include minutes of meetings, officers' correspondence, financial records, legal papers, and membership information (1936-1937).

B-278. PECK, SARAH CAROLINE (fl.1893-1914). PAPERS, 1859-1913.

3 vols., 33 items (.25 l.f.). V 107, S 1047.

Peck was the wife of William J. Peck, a Brookville, Franklin Co., general store owner; and resident of Indianapolis (1895-1914).

The collection includes her business correspondence regarding the management of her property in Muncie, Delaware Co., Connersville, Fayette Co., and Tipton, Tipton Co. (1893-1896); her diaries (1907-1911, 1913); and account books for her husband's general store in Brookville (1859-1873).

B-279. PENDLETON UNIVERSALIST CHURCH. RECORDS, 1859-1929.

4 vols. (.25 l.f.). V 112.

The church was organized as the Union Universalist Church of Pendleton and Huntsville, Madison Co., in 1859; it closed in 1929.

The records consist of the minutes of the church meetings (1859-1929); baptism and death records (1859-1927); and the treasurer's book (1912-1928).

B-280. PERING FAMILY. PAPERS, 1821-1920.

96 items. S 1052.

The Pering family lived in Bloomington, Monroe Co. The family included Alfred H. Pering, a teacher at Salem, Washington Co. (1852-1853), and a resident of Bloomington.

The collection includes Alfred Pering's correspondence with his fiancee, Eda Carter, while he was in Salem and she was in Bloomington (1852-1853); his letters to her while he was traveling to Louisville, Philadephia, and Atlantic City (1869); land documents of the Pering and Carter families in Monroe and Washington counties (1821-ca.1900); newspaper clippings (1829-1920); other family and business letters; and transcripts of letters written by Pering's father, Cornelius Pering, from Bloomington to his family in England (1833).

B-281. PIERCE-KRULL FAMILY. PAPERS, 1834-1963.

8 archival boxes. Inventory. L 353.

The Pierce-Krull family included Theresa Vinton Pierce Krull (1877-1963), a graduate of Vassar College (1900), an Indianapolis clubwoman, a feature writer for the *Indianapolis Star*, and a lecturer and writer on educational, historical, and political topics; her husband, Frederic Krull (1876-1961), an Indianapolis singer, voice instructor, and composer, whose works included music for James Whitcomb Riley's poems; her father, Henry Douglas Pierce (1848-1929), an Indianapolis lawyer and businessman who was a director of railroad companies in Indiana and New York, a director of the Nicaragua Maritime Canal Company, and a journalist writing on European and South American affairs; and her grandfather, Winslow S. Pierce (1819-1888), a physician in Illinois, California, and Indianapolis (1840s-1888), comptroller of the State of California (1851), and businessman involved in real estate, railroad development, and Democratic Party politics in Indiana (1854-1888).

The collection includes family correspondence (1834-1963), writings, financial records, journals, and scrapbooks. Family correspondence includes correspondence of the John Moore family of Ellisville, Geneseo, and Rock Island, Ill. (1834-1870), including letters from family members in St. Louis, Mo., California, Madison, Jefferson Co., and Shelbyville, Shelby Co.; letters, and transcripts of letters, of W. S. Pierce in Yuba City, Calif., to his wife and son in Indiana and Illinois (1850-1854); correspondence between W. S. Pierce in Indianapolis and his son, Henry D. Pierce, at Princeton University (1865-1866); W. S. Pierce's business correspondence regarding his real estate and railroad interests in Indiana, and state and national Democratic Party politics, particularly in regard to his brother-in-law, Thomas A. Hendricks (1860s-1870s); correspondence of H. D. Pierce with his fiancee and wife, Elizabeth Vinton (1874-1880s), including letters written during his trips to Europe and California in the 1880s; correspondence of Elizabeth Vinton while she was a student at Vassar College (1871-1874); family correspondence of Theresa Pierce (1890s), including her letters from Vassar College (1899-1900); her correspondence with her fiance, Frederic Krull, while he was in Columbia, Mo. (1904-1906); letters of Douglas Pierce while a student at Harvard Law School (1906-1908); Theresa Krull's correspondence regarding the Vassar College Alumnae Association, and the association's work for women's suffrage and the training of nurses for service during World War I; her correspondence relating to her involvement with Indianapolis organizations, such as the Indianapolis Propylaeum, the Indiana Federation of Clubs, and the Indianapolis Woman's Club; her correspondence pertaining to her historical, genealogical, and patriotic interests; and correspondence regarding Frederic Krull's work.

The family's writings include Frederic Krull's musical compositions; Theresa Krull's articles and lectures on women's clubs and midwestern history; Henry D. Pierce's articles and speeches (1895-1926), principally on Europe, South America, and Nicaragua; typed manuscript of Booth Tarkington's story "The Last Sunday"; Charles Holman-Black's memoirs of growing up in Indianapolis in the late nineteenth century; and an unpublished novel by Frederic Krull.

The collection also contains Theresa Krull's journals (1892-1947); account books of the Vinton family of Indianapolis (1852-1875); receipts, land documents, and other family business documents of the Moore, Pierce, Vinton, and Krull families (1840-1949); family school essays and report cards (1840-1899); scrapbooks of Theresa and Frederic Krull (1922-1947); newspaper clippings relating to family members and their interests (1867-1963); programs, pamphlets, and other materials relating to Indianapolis organizations (1888-1956); pamphlets and other printed materials regarding the proposed canal across Nicaragua (1893-1928); and genealogical materials.

Correspondents include George S. Boutwell, Thomas A. Hendricks, Eli Lilly, Horatio Seymour, and Elihu B. Washburne.

B-282. POLK SANITARY MILK COMPANY. RECORDS, 1904-1961.

1 ms. box, 4 vols. (1 l.f.). L 212, V 98.

The Polk Sanitary Milk Company was an Indianapolis dairy from 1893 to 1962.

The records contain the company's account books (1904-1938) and microfilm of its drivers' route sheets. Also included are records of the Mecca Realty Company of Indianapolis (1916-1933), owned by the Polk family, including the company's articles of association, minutes of stockholders' meetings, and papers relating to the Citizens Brewery Company property.

B-283. POPLAR RIDGE HORSE THIEF AND DETECTIVE COMPANY. RECORDS, 1875-1925.

1 ms. box. L 213.

The Poplar Ridge Horse Thief and Detective Company operated in the Carmel, Hamilton Co., area; it was associated with other horse thief detective associations in Indiana which were active from the early 1850s through the 1920s as officially recognized vigilante groups.

The records include minutes of the company's meetings (1875-1925) and membership records (1900-1910).

B-284. PORTER, ALBERT GALLATIN (1824-1897). PAPERS, 1874-1896.

11 ms. boxes, 6 vols. (5 l.f.). L 125.

Porter was an Indianapolis attorney (1845-1897); Republican member, U.S. House of Representatives (1859-1863); governor of Indiana (1881-1885); minister to Italy (1889-1891); and spent last part of his life working on a history of Indiana.

The collection consists primarily of Porter's historical papers, including unfinished drafts of his history of Indiana; his notes and sketches on various topics in Indiana history, such as the Civil War, internal improvements, education, churches, the state constitutions, Indians, the Battle of Tippecanoe, and Indiana governors and other prominent people in the state; Porter's notes and contemporary letters and affidavits relating to the treason trials in Indiana during the Civil War; and his correspondence regarding his requests for information about the early history of the state. The collection also includes Porter's political speeches (1870s-1890s); his journal as minister to Italy; correspondence of W. H. H. Terrell regarding Republican Party politics and Indiana history (1870s-1880s); Terrell's notebooks for the 1880 Indiana election; Richard Owen's "Brief History of the Social Experiment at New Harmony" (1887); and documents relating to a Vincennes slave case (1817).

Correspondents include Schuyler Colfax, Eli Lilly, Samuel Merrill, Godlove S. Orth, Joseph F. Tuttle, and Simon Yandes.

B-285. PORTER-GRIFFIN FAMILY PAPERS, 1823-1975.

13 archival boxes, 111 vols. (33 l.f.).   Partial Inventory.

The Porter-Griffin family included William A. Porter (1800-1884), a graduate of Miami University, Ohio (1827), superintendent of the Harrison County Seminary in Corydon, Ind. (1827-1829), Corydon lawyer (1829-1884), Harrison County probate judge (1829-1833), Whig member, Indiana House of Representatives (1836-1837, 1845-1848), Speaker of the House (1847-1848), and member, Indiana State Senate (1848-1851); Patrick Griffin (1831-1917), a worker in McGrain & Meadows iron foundry in Louisville, Ky. (1846-1852), dry goods store operator in California (1852-1865), owner of dry goods store in Corydon, with brother-in-law Thomas McGrain, Jr. (ca.1866-ca.1887), Harrison County treasurer (1889-1893), owner of M. Griffin & Company dry goods store, Corydon (1897-1917), and husband of William Porter's daughter, Helen; and Daniel Patrick Griffin (1885-1975), son of Patrick Griffin, graduate of Purdue University Pharmacy School (1905), pharmacist in Indianapolis, Cincinnati, and Norfolk, Va. (1905-1912), worked in family dry goods business in Corydon (1912-1966), and president of company (1951-1966).

The William Porter material includes papers relating to his legal cases, especially estate settlements and civil suits (1829-1883); personal correspondence when he was a student at Miami University (1826); papers relating to the Harrison County Seminary (1827-1829); his correspondence while serving in the state legislature, including letters from Samuel Hall of Princeton, Gibson Co., regarding legislation for the Alton, Mt. Carmel & New Albany Railroad (1849-1850); Civil War letters from Porter's nephew, Ethan Andrews, serving in Tennessee, Arkansas, and Virginia (1862-1865); and correspondence of his daughters Helen and Aurelia in the 1860s, including their correspondence with family members, and correspondence while students at the Oxford (Ohio) Female College and the Glendale (Ohio) Female College. The Griffin family papers include bills, receipts, and ledgers from the firm of Griffin and McGrain (1865-1887); Patrick Griffin's personal and family correspondence (1860s-1917); ledger from his business in California (ca.1864); papers of the Corydon Artesian Well Company (1870s); Patrick Griffin's insurance policies, checks, and other personal financial documents (1880-1889); and expense book of Helen Porter Griffin (1884-1889).

Daniel P. Griffin papers consist of correspondence with his parents and family (1900-1950s), including his letters from Purdue University (1903-1905); letters to Griffin from servicemen in World War I and II; papers relating to his World War I service, including his involvement with the Chemical Warfare Service; and correspondence regarding his activities with the Corydon Presbyterian Church (1910s-1975) and with the Indiana Republican State Committee (1910s). The collection also contains papers of Griffin's brother Maurice, including his papers as treasurer of the Harrison County Cyclone Relief Committee (1917), and papers on the Chautaqua in Corydon (1914-1917); papers of the Rupp family in Corydon (1840s-1890s); personal correspondence and financial papers (1910s-1950s) of Griffin's sister, Helen O'Leary, and her husband, including political items from Chicago, Ill. (1910s-1920s); correspondence of the Bickel family, German immigrants living in Lanesville, Harrison Co. (1860s); Civil War papers of Daniel Griffin of the 38th Indiana Regiment, including a history of the 38th Regiment; ledgers of Corydon businesses, including R. W. Heth & Bros., Thomas J. Ryan, and Paul Sieg; papers relating to the Corydon Masonic Lodge (1850s-1975); and local history papers and memorabilia on Corydon and the Porter-Griffin home.

B-286. PRATT, DANIEL D. (1813-1877). PAPERS, 1816-1901.

50 ms. boxes. L 128.

Attorney and politician. Pratt was a teacher in Rising Sun, Ohio Co. (1832); law clerk in office of Calvin Fletcher in Indianapolis (1833-1836); lawyer in

Logansport, Cass Co. (1836-1877); Whig member, Indiana House of Representatives (1850-1853); member, Republican State Executive Committee (1860); secretary, Republican National Committee (1860); elected to U.S. House of Representatives (1868); U.S. Senator (1869-1875), member of Senate committees on Pensions, Claims, and the District of Columbia; and U.S. Commissioner of Internal Revenue (1875-1876).

The collection consists primarily of Pratt's legal and political papers from the period 1831-1877. His legal papers include correspondence, briefs, legal and financial documents, and notes regarding his cases in Logansport and northern Indiana, and pertaining to the collection of debts for eastern law firms; papers relating to the settlement of the estate of Sen. John Tipton of Logansport (1830s-1840s); correspondence and legal papers relating to the affairs of Indian traders in northern Indiana, including the W. G. and G. W. Ewing Company of Fort Wayne with which Pratt was associated in the 1830s and 1840s; and correspondence and papers regarding other legal interests of Pratt, including railroads, the Wabash and Erie Canal, land development in Iowa and other western states, and criminal cases. Political papers include letters to Pratt from federal office-seekers, particularly from Indiana (1869-1875); correspondence regarding the work of the state legislature (1851-1853); correspondence regarding state and national elections, particularly the 1860, 1868, 1872, and 1876 elections; letters to Pratt regarding his work on the Pensions and Claims Committees, and issues before the U.S. Senate (1869-1876); and correspondence regarding the state and national Republican Party.

In addition, there are literary and temperance addresses delivered by Pratt in Rising Sun, Indianapolis, and Logansport (1832-1840s); papers relating to the Logansport school system (1860s), including classroom record books (1865-1867); family correspondence, including letters from his son, Charles D. Pratt, regarding the family's legal business while Pratt was in the U.S. Senate; Pratt's diary and expense records from a trip to New York (1854) and while traveling with the circuit court (1844-1854, 1861); journal of his son, James P. Pratt, while a student at Wabash College, Crawfordsville, Montgomery Co. (1857-1858); and legal correspondence and papers of Logansport attorney William T. Wilson (1877-1901).

Correspondents include Oakes Ames, Conrad Baker, William W. Belknap, Horace P. Biddle, James T. Bryer, Charles Butler, Ovid Butler, John C. Calhoun, Henry P. Coburn, John Coburn, Schuyler Colfax, Roscoe Conkling, Will Cumback, John D. Defrees, Thomas Dowling, George H. Dunn, John B. Duret, George W. Ewing, William G. Ewing, Hamilton Fish, Graham N. Fitch, Calvin Fletcher, John Watson Foster, James S. Frazier, James A. Garfield, Isaac P. Gray, Walter Q. Gresham, Benjamin Harrison, John James Hayden, Thomas A. Hendricks, Barnabas C. Hobbs, George Washington Julian, Henry S. Lane, Hyacinth Lasselle, John H. Lathrop, Robert Milroy, Oliver P. Morton, Thomas A. Nelson, John B. Niles, Noah Noble, Cyrus Nutt, Godlove S. Orth, John U. Pettit, Gilbert A. Pierce, Albert Gallatin Porter, William Tecumseh Sherman, Thomas C. Slaughter, Caleb B. Smith, Benjamin Spooner, Robert S. Taylor, Richard W. Thompson, Henry C. Thornton, John Tipton, Spear S. Tipton, David Turpie, Joseph F. Tuttle, John P. Usher, Cyrus Vigus, Daniel W. Voorhees, Albert S. White, and Simon Yandes.

B-287. PRESTON, NATHANIEL (1809-1871). PAPERS, 1821-1918.

2 ms. boxes, 7 vols. (1.5 l.f.). L 129, V 144.

Preston was a teacher in Licking County, Ohio (1831-1834), Vincennes, Knox Co. (1835-1836), and Terre Haute, Vigo Co. (1836-1837); clerk (1837-1842) and cashier (1842-1849), Terre Haute Branch of the State Bank of Indiana; and farmer near Terre Haute (1850-1871).

The collection consists of Preston's family correspondence, including letters from his brother in Marshall, Mich. (1832-1847), and his sister in Brandon, Vt. (1837-1851); correspondence regarding the Terre Haute Branch of the State Bank of Indiana (1840s); Preston's personal account books (1835-1871); his roll books of students (1836-1837); his diary (1842-1862); and record of protested bills of exchange at the Terre Haute Branch of the State Bank (1838-1840). In addition, there are family letters to his daughter, Margaret Preston of Terre Haute, including letters from her brother, William Preston, an assistant paymaster in the U.S. Navy, from Washington, D.C., and from South America (1870-1875), and letters from a World War I soldier in Camp Shelby, Miss., and France (1917-1918); and William Preston's Civil War discharge and pension papers (1863-1869), papers regarding his appointment to the Navy (1869-1875), his diary (1874), and a record book of equipment and stores issued to sailors (1874-1875).

B-288. PRICHETT, JOHN (1803-1884). JOURNALS, 1849-1851.

1 ms. box. L 130.

Prichett was a physician in Centerville, Wayne Co.; and participant in the California Gold Rush (1849-1851).

Prichett's journals cover his trip from Centerville to California by steamboat on the Ohio and Missouri rivers, and overland from Independence, Mo.; his life in the mining camps near Yuba City and Sacramento, Calif.; and his return trip by ship from San Francisco, through Panama, to New Orleans.

B-289. PROHIBITION PARTY OF INDIANA. RECORDS, 1943-1972.

5.3 l.f.

The Prohibition Party of Indiana is the state branch of the national Prohibition Party. The national party was organized in 1869 for the purpose of working for the prohibition of the manufacture, importation, and sale of intoxicating liquors. The Indiana party has run candidates for state office since 1884 and has been involved in education on the dangers of alcohol abuse.

The collection consists principally of party records from the period 1952-1972, and contains state and national party newsletters (1962-1972); campaign and convention materials, press releases, and campaign financial records (1952-1968); literature regarding alcohol abuse and the rehabilitation of alcoholics; correspondence with party candidates and religious and temperance groups (1960s); and Prohibition Party financial support cards (1966-1968). Also included are records of the Goshen, Elkhart Co., Anti-Liquor Association (1943-1944).

B-290. REAGAN, CHARLES M. (b.1864). PAPERS, 1851-1927.

ca.53 items.   S 1099.

Reagan was an Indianapolis attorney.

The collection includes correspondence regarding Reagan's efforts to secure a federal appointment (1918); correspondence regarding the War of 1812 military career of Thomas Askern of Pennsylvania (1927); histories of Quaker meetings in the Indianapolis area, and obituaries of their members; and Reagan family legal documents.

Correspondents include David Starr Jordan, Merrill Moores, and Harry S. New.

B-291. RECORDS, WILLIAM H. (b. 1837). DIARIES, 1862-1865, 1904.

1 ms. box.   L 131.

Records was a farmer from Montmorency, Tippecanoe Co., and Rising Sun, Ohio Co.; and private and corporal in the 72nd Indiana Regiment (1862-1865), serving in the mounted infantry in Kentucky, Tennessee, Mississippi, Alabama, and Georgia.

The collection contains Records's Civil War diaries (1862-1865); letters and other papers relating to his service; a transcript of his diary for the period 1862-1863; and his diary from Rising Sun (1904).

B-292. REDDING, THOMAS B. (1831-1895). PAPERS, 1844-1918.

2 ms. boxes.   L 336.

Redding was an attorney in New Castle, Henry Co. (1855-1895), and Chicago, Ill. (1858-1860); sold county maps in Henry County and Racine, Wis. (1857-1859); and scientist, member of American Society of Microscopy and other scientific organizations.

The papers consist primarily of correspondence, receipts, indentures, contracts, and other papers relating to Redding's legal business in Henry County and central Indiana, including papers regarding land transfers, debt collections, and Civil War pensions. Also contained are his correspondence and papers regarding the sale of county maps in Henry County and Wisconsin (1857-1860); papers relating to his personal business interests in Henry County; papers pertaining to his scientific work and patent inquiries; and family correspondence.

B-293. RICE, MARY. COLLECTION, 1864-1918.

ca.140 items.   S 2607.

Rice donated this collection to the Indiana State Library in 1935. The principal figure in the collection is Hiram Maine (fl.1864-1918), a soldier in the

3rd Illinois Cavalry during the Civil War; a printer and journalist in Council Bluffs, Iowa, and Harlan, Allen Co. (1880s-1890s); and author of articles on social and political reform for the *Chicago Express* (1880s).

The collection consists principally of Hiram Maine's family correspondence, including his Civil War letters from Louisiana, Tennessee, Mississippi, and Fort Snelling, Minn., to his parents in Galva, Ill. (1864-1865); letters to Maine and his parents from his brothers in Leavenworth, Kans., Page County, Iowa, and Goshen, Elkhart Co., and letters to Maine from his family in Galva (1864-1873); correspondence regarding his newspaper work, including letters from the *Chicago Express* and from labor unions; and letters to stockholders in the La Cobriza Mining Company in Sonora, Mexico (1907-1913).

Correspondents include Simon Pokagon and C. C. Post.

B-294. RICHARDSON, LEWIS BRADFORD (fl.1910-1951). PAPERS, 1874-1947.

3 folders. S 1112.

Richardson was a poet and engineer in Trafalgar, Johnson Co.

The collection is made up of Richardson's poetry; his personal legal and financial documents (1918-1947); and papers regarding the history of his family.

B-295. RICHARDSON, MILDRED KNIGHT. COLLECTION, 1827-1899.

1 ms. box. L 133.

Richardson, of Indianapolis, deposited this collection with the Indiana State Library in 1929. The principal figure in the collection is Elias W. H. Beck (1822-1888), a physician in Delphi, Carroll Co. (1845-1888); assistant surgeon, 1st Indiana Regiment in the Mexican War, and assistant surgeon at the general hospital at Matamoros, Mexico (1846-1847); physician in California (1850); surgeon, 45th Indiana Regiment (3rd Cavalry), and surgeon in chief, 1st Division, Cavalry Corps, Army of the Potomac (1861-1864); married Francis Milroy (1848), daughter of Delphi founder Samuel Milroy (1780-1845), and brother of Civil War general Robert Milroy (1816-1890).

The collection contains Beck's letters to Francis Milroy Beck from Texas and Matamoros, Mexico (1846-1847), from California (1850), and from Virginia and Maryland during the Civil War (1861-1864); family letters to Samuel Milroy and his wife (1827-1842); and letters from Beck's son, Walter M. Beck, written while serving as a physician with the 13th Minnesota Regiment in the Philippines during the insurrection (1898-1899).

Correspondents include Richard M. Johnson and Robert H. Milroy.

B-296. RIGG, MARY (ca.1888-1971). PAPERS, 1924-1964.

2 ms. boxes.   Inventory.   L 134.

Rigg was an Indianapolis social worker; director of the American Settlement, a settlement house for immigrants on the Indianapolis west side (1924-1939), and its successor, the Southwest Social Center, a neighborhood center on the southwest side (1939-1961).

The papers include letters to Rigg from World War II servicemen who had been active in the American Settlement (1942-1945); reports on Indianapolis social work activities (1924-1939); attendance and financial records for American Settlement activities (1936-1940); financial records for the Southwest Social Center (1940-1964); and cards, clippings, and other personal material of Rigg.

B-297. RILEY, JAMES WHITCOMB (1853-1916). COLLECTION, 1876-1940.

1 ms. box.   L 135.

Riley was a poet, best known as a writer of Hoosier dialect verse; resident of Indianapolis; author of *Raggedy Man* (1907), *The Little Orphant Annie Book* (1908), *The Old Swimmin Hole and Other Poems* (1912), and numerous other books of poetry.

The collection includes Riley's letters to Kentucky author Madison Cawein (1891-1906); other letters and manuscript poems written by Riley; printed copies of Riley's poems and letters; and essays and newspaper stories about Riley.

B-298. ROBINSON, WILLIAM H. (1845-1868). PAPERS, 1862-1897.

28 items. S 1133.

Robinson was from North Madison, Jefferson Co.; private in the 54th Indiana Regiment during the Civil War (1862-1865); and worked in the Provost Marshal's office in Pulaski, Tenn. (1864).

The collection includes Robinson's Civil War letters to his family, written from Camp Morton, Ind. (1862), and from Tennessee and Alabama (1864-1865); Civil War-era letters from other family members, including letters to Robinson from home; and family letters from the 1890s.

B-299. ROCKWOOD, WILLIAM (1874-1945). COLLECTION, 1808-1884.

ca.90 items. S 1807.

Rockwood was an Indianapolis businessman; he donated this collection to the Indiana State Library in 1937.

The collection contains papers of the Heaton and Wade families of Middletown, Ohio, and Crawfordsville, Montgomery Co. (1808-1884), and papers relating to the Indiana State Bank and other Indiana banks (1835-1856). The Heaton and Wade family papers include letters from Alethea Wade, wife of Crawfordsville newspaper publisher Isaac F. Wade, to her mother, Mary Heaton, in Middletown, Ohio (1832-1841); other family letters to Mary Heaton, including letters from St. Anthony, Minn. (1858-1861); and family and business correspondence of Isaac Wade. The banking papers contain reports, financial statements, and correspondence regarding the operations of the Indiana State Bank and other banks in Indiana and Ohio.

Correspondents include Hervey Bates, James F. D. Lanier, Samuel Merrill, Bethuel F. Morris, and James M. Ray.

B-300. ROSS MEAT MARKET. ACCOUNT BOOKS, 1916-1917.

2 vols. (.25 l.f.). V 146.

The Ross Meat Market was located in Ambia, Benton Co.

The collection consists of the market's account books (1916-1917).

B-301. ROUDEBUSH, RICHARD (1918-). PAPERS, 1965-1976.

25 archival boxes. Inventory.

Politician. Roudebush was a demolition specialist in the U.S. Army during World War II (1941-1944); farmer near Noblesville, Hamilton Co.; partner in a livestock commission business; chairman, Indiana Veterans Commission (1954-1960); national commander, Veterans of Foreign Wars (1957-1958); Republican member, U.S. House of Representatives (1961-1971); Republican candidate for the U.S. Senate (1970); and assistant deputy administrator, U.S. Veterans Administration (1971-1976).

The collection consists primarily of Roudebush's congressional papers from the 90th Congress (1967-1969), including correspondence, reports, and other papers relating to legislation on agriculture, air traffic safety, the Indiana Dunes National Lakeshore, housing programs and other civil rights measures, defense spending, crime, flood control in the Colorado River Basin and the Wabash River Valley, air pollution control, the Job Corps, and veterans benefits; correspondence and papers regarding other issues before Congress, such as the seating of Rep. Adam Clayton Powell, the nomination of Abe Fortas as Chief Justice of the Supreme Court, the War in Vietnam, the National Aeronautics and Space Administration, lowering the voting age to eighteen, and the House Un-American Activities Committee; correspondence with the Ball Brothers Company of Muncie, Delaware Co., pertaining to food production and food preservation legislation; papers regarding the Republican National Committee and the 1968 Republican National Convention; constituents' correspondence on current events and requests for information and assistance;

campaign papers from his 1968 congressional campaign, and records of contributions to his 1966 and 1968 campaigns; financial and administrative records from his congressional office; retained copies of his letters of condolence to the families of soldiers who died in Vietnam; and papers relating to his efforts to obtain a pardon for a court-martialed soldier in Vietnam. Also included are retained copies of his letters to constituents during the 91st Congress (1969-1970); and his speeches as an official of the Veterans Administration.

Correspondents include Roger D. Branigin, Earl Butz, John Ehrlichman, Vance Hartke, Melvin Laird, Richard Lugar, John McCormick, Armin H. Meyer, Wilbur D. Mills, Edmund S. Muskie, Richard M. Nixon, R. Sargent Shriver, and Roscoe Turner.

B-302. RULE, LUCIEN V. (1871-1948). PAPERS, 1922-1941.

3 folders.　　　　　　　　　　　　　　　　　　　　　　S 1815, S 2141.

Minister and author. Rule was a Presbyterian minister in Kentucky and southern Indiana (1908-1948); chaplain, Indiana State Reformatory, Jeffersonville, Clark Co. (ca.1914-1923); home mission pastor, New Albany Presbyterian Church (1923-1940s); historian of the Synod of Indiana (1930s); poet, and author of works on Presbyterian history and on prisons and prison reform.

The collection includes Rule's correspondence (1922-1923) regarding the Presbyterian Church in southern Indiana and Kentucky, his historical and prison writings, and family and personal matters; and his essays on early Presbyterian missionaries in Kentucky and Indiana, written in the 1930s.

B-303. SABBATH SCHOOL UNION SOCIETY. RECORDS, 1806-1873.

87 items.　　　　　　　　　　　　　　　　　　　　　　　　　　S 2708.

The Indianapolis Sabbath School Union was started by Isaac Coe in 1823 to provide religious instruction for the town's children.

The union's records contain annual reports (1824-1831), attendance lists, constitution, and correspondence of Coe and other officers with affiliated organizations in other towns. Also included is a history of the union (1873); papers of the First Presbyterian Church of Indianapolis (1841-1853); and an annual report of the Marion County Temperance Society (ca.1835).

B-304. SCHLICHTE, EDWARD J. (fl.1909-1925). ACCOUNT BOOKS, 1909-1925.

8 vols. (.25 l.f.). V 272.

Schlichte owned a dry goods and grocery store in Connersville, Fayette Co.

The collection consists of the store's account books.

B-305. SCHNEIDER, WILLIAM (fl.1850-1894). PAPERS, 1850-1902.

1 ms. box, 8 vols. (1.25 l.f.). L 341, V 128.

Schneider owned general stores in the German community of St. Wendel, Posey Co. (1850-ca.1890); and operated a store in partnership with George Naas (1862-1872).

The collection includes Schneider's general store account books (1850-ca.1890); account books for the Schneider and Nass store (1862-1872); and Schneider's miscellaneous business and personal papers (1850-1902).

B-306. SCHRADER, CHRISTIAN (ca.1841-1920). PAPERS, 1900-1931.

4 folders. S 815.

Schrader was an Indianapolis china merchant (ca.1860-ca.1910); resident of Madison, Jefferson Co. (ca.1911-1920); and artist, noted for his pictures of Indianapolis in the mid-nineteenth century.

The collection includes Schrader's correspondence with Demarchus Brown of the Indiana State Library regarding his drawings and their sale to that institution (1916-1917); his reminiscences and notes accompanying the drawings; his reminiscences of life in Indianapolis in the mid-nineteenth century (1913); clippings of newspaper stories on Indianapolis history, illustrated with Schrader's drawings (1900-1912); and letters of Schrader's daughters about him and his drawings (1930-1931).

B-307. SCOTT, MARGARET M. (ca.1873-1964). PAPERS, 1873-1950.

2 ms. boxes.   L 139.

Scott was a journalist for the *Indianapolis News* (1892-1910s); free lance writer in Indianapolis; started literary studio, In-Var, for teaching young writers (1920s); and awarded gold medallion for achievement from national Theta Sigma Phi sorority (1960).

The papers consist primarily of Scott's essays, short stories, unpublished novels, and her correspondence regarding her writing (1920s-1930s). Also included are papers regarding the work of the Indiana Lincoln Memorial Association (1920s); a scrapbook of newspaper stories by and about her (1910s-1920s); and poetry of her father, John Scott.

B-308. SCOTUS GAUL PICTI. RECORDS, 1892-1899.

1 ms. box.   L 214.

Scotus Gaul Picti was a Brookville, Franklin Co., fraternal organization founded in 1892 to provide entertainment and to promote Brookville. It disbanded in 1899.

The records include the minutes of meetings (1892-1899), constitution and bylaws, rituals, membership lists, and financial documents.

B-309. SEEHAUSEN, PAUL (ca.1896-1965). PAPERS, 1935-1965.

4 ms. boxes.   Inventory.   L 140.

Educator. Seehausen was an Indianapolis social studies teacher (1930s); consultant for social studies, Indiana Department of Education (ca.1944-1950);

coordinator of adult education for Indiana University (ca.1944-1950); director of adult education and the summer school, Valparaiso University, Valparaiso, Porter Co. (1950-1961); resident of Nashville, Brown Co. (1961-1965); and author, *Land of the Great Lakes* (1958) and other articles and textbooks.

The collection includes Seehausen's correspondence regarding his work on *Land of the Great Lakes* and other textbook projects (1950-1964); correspondence, newsletters, programs, and other papers relating to adult education programs (1947-1964); his annual reports on adult education programs submitted to Indiana University (1945-1949); notes, reports, speeches, and other papers on education, civics, state and national history, the teaching of social studies, and Valparaiso University; and personal correspondence.

B-310. SHACKELFORD, RALPH (1909-1983). PAPERS, 1843-1977.

8 l.f.

Shackelford was a resident of the Broad Ripple section of Indianapolis; employee of Naval Avionics; active member of the Masonic Lodge; and son of Mary Bessie Van Scyoc Shackelford (1882-1966), and grandson of John W. Van Scyoc (1836-1919), a Marion County justice of the peace, owner of a threshing business, and a business management advisor.

The collection consists of Shackelford and Van Scyoc family personal and legal papers. Included are papers of John W. Van Scyoc, including records of his threshing business, his business management firm, and his justice of the peace office; papers of Bessie Van Scyoc Shackelford, including her personal correspondence (1890s-1966), her diary (1895-1897), and school records (1890s); and papers of Ralph Shackelford, including school records (1920s-1930s), and his personal correspondence (1930s). In addition there are papers relating to the history of Broad Ripple and the Masonic Lodge in Indianapolis; and business correspondence of the Indianapolis collection agency of White, Wright and Boleman (1931-1932).

B-311. SHADES INN. GUEST REGISTERS, 1898-1921.

2 vols. (.25 l.f.). V 119.

The inn was built in 1887 by the Garland Dells Mineral Springs Association as part of a health spa and resort at the current site of Shades State Park,

Montgomery Co. It was purchased by Joseph W. Frisz in 1916 and became a state park in 1947.

The collection is made up of the inn's guest registers (1898-1921).

B-312. SHAW, WILLIAM (d. ca.1873). PAPERS, 1827-1874.

49 items. S 1172.

Shaw emigrated with his family from Scotland to Vevay, Switzerland Co. (1817); worked as a farmer and merchant in Vevay; and married Linda Rous, whose family emigrated from Yorkshire, England, to Switzerland County in 1814.

The collection consists of family letters to Shaw and his wife from their families in Scotland and England (1827, 1856-1874).

B-313. SHEPARDSON FAMILY. PAPERS, 1819-1897.

ca.105 items.   Calendar.   S 2696.

The Shepardson family included Otis Shepardson (1791-1843), a farmer in Windham County, Vt., and Mongo, LaGrange Co., Ind. (1835-1843); his sons, Elijah Shepardson (1820-1897), a soldier in the Confederate Army during the Civil War, and a steamboat pilot and laborer in St. Louis, Mo. (1867-1893), Lorenzo Dow Shepardson (1829-1906) and Pliny Shepardson (b.1824), farmers and miners in Oregon and Washington (1850s-1900s), and Samuel Shepardson (b.1839), a Mongo businessman, and a sergeant in the 30th Indiana Regiment (1861-1864); and his daughter, Susan Shepardson Freligh (1832-1900), a resident of Mongo.

The collection includes Otis Shepardson's land and business documents from Vermont and LaGrange County (1819-1843); letters of Pliny and Lorenzo Dow Shepardson from Washington and Oregon (1855-1872); Samuel Shepardson's Civil War letters from Kentucky and Tennessee (1861-1864); Elijah Shepardson's letters from St. Louis (1867-1893); letters to Susan Freligh from her children in Oregon (1877-1883); and Susan Freligh's letters home while visiting Washington and Oregon (1896-1897).

B-314. SHEPHERD, JAMES NELSON (1838-1895). PAPERS, 1860-1866.

1 ms. box.   L 311.

Shepherd was a Vigo County farmer and stockbreeder (1860-1895); sergeant, 31st Indiana Regiment, serving in Kentucky and Tennessee (1861-1862); and Vigo County treasurer (1865-1869).

The papers include Shepherd's Civil War diary (1861-1862); his letters to his fiancee, Arminda Rhyan of New Goshen, Vigo Co. (1860-1862); Civil War letters to Shepherd from his brother, Thomas E. Shepherd of the 31st Indiana (1862); and Shepherd's farm ledgers (1864-1866), including his record of shipments made on the steamboat "Sultana" (1864).

B-315. SHORT, LUTHER (1845-1925). PAPERS, 1833-1914.

49 items.   S 1181.

Soldier, attorney, and editor. Short was a resident of Springville, Lawrence Co. (1845-1860); corporal, 43rd Indiana Regiment, serving in Missouri and Arkansas (1861-1864); attorney in Arkansas (1871-1874) and in Franklin, Johnson Co. (1874); editor, *Franklin Democrat* (1879-1892); Democratic member, Indiana House of Representatives (1891); and trustee, Indiana Soldiers' and Sailors' Orphan's Home (1911).

The collection consists primarily of Short's Civil War correspondence, including letters to Short from his father and friends in Springville (1862-1864), and his letters home from Arkansas (1863-1864). In addition, there are papers relating to the Indiana Soldiers' and Sailors' Orphan's Home (1911); papers relating to a Masonic Home in Franklin (1914); other personal correspondence and papers (1867-1914); and a farm account book (1833-1836).

B-316. SHORTRIDGE, NORMAN H. (1898-1978). PAPERS, 1933-1942.

1 ms. box.   L 142.

Shortridge was an officer in the U.S. Army (1917-1919, 1933-1954); and officer in the Civilian Conservation Corps at Fort Benjamin Harrison, Indianapolis, and at Nashville, Brown Co. (1933-1942).

The papers consist of orders, rosters, accounts, and requisitions relating to Shortridge's work in the Civilian Conservation Corps in Indiana (1933-1942).

B-317. SHRYER, JOHN D. (d.1872?). ACCOUNT BOOKS, 1830-1871.

4 vols. (.33 l.f.).   V 131.

Shryer owned a general store in Jeffersonville, Clark Co.

The collection consists of Shryer's store account books.

B-318. SILVER, THOMAS (fl.1828-1856). PAPERS, 1828-1866.

1 ms. box.   L 143.

Silver owned a general merchandise store and mill in Pendleton, Madison Co. (1828-ca.1856).

The collection consists primarily of Silver's receipts, accounts, deeds, and other business papers for his Pendleton store and his personal affairs (1828-1852), including his accounts with wholesale merchants in Cincinnati and Philadelphia, and a daybook for his store (1838-1842). Also included are receipts, accounts, and other business papers (1830s-1852) for Pendleton merchant William Silver (ca.1803-1888).

B-319. SIMPSON, JOHN R. (1834-1906). PAPERS, 1822-1875.

1 ms. box.   L 144.

Attorney. Simpson was the son of attorney A. J. Simpson of Paoli, Orange Co.; student at Westfield Academy, Mass. (1852-1855); attorney and businessman in Paoli (1850s-1865, 1870-1906), Davenport, Iowa (1865-1868), and New York State (1868-1870); and Orange County clerk (1875-1883).

The collection consists primarily of letters to Simpson from family and friends in Paoli while he was a student in Massachusetts (1852-1855). Also included are other family letters to Simpson (1851-1875); and business papers of the Campbell family of Paoli (1822-1850s).

B-320. SINKER-DAVIS COMPANY. RECORD BOOKS, 1882-1922.

7 vols. (1.75 l.f.).   V 217, V 241.

The Sinker-Davis Company of Indianapolis manufactured boilers, engines, saws, and other machine equipment. It was founded in the early 1850s by Edward T. Sinker (1820-1871), and it continued in business into the late 1950s.

The collection consists of the company's books showing orders received (1891-1922); and a book of orders from Texas (1882-1888).

B-321. SINKS, DANIEL (fl.1829-1868). PAPERS, 1825-1879.

70 items.   S 1194.

Sinks was a grocer and businessman in Indianapolis.

The papers include Sinks's business and tax receipts, land indentures, and contracts (1829-1868); papers relating to his business connections with James Sulgrove of Indianapolis (1825-1840s); and daybooks of three Indianapolis teachers, listing their students (1845-1849).

B-322. SLACK, JAMES R. (1818-1881). PAPERS, 1837-1882.

1 ms. box.   Calendar.   L 145.

Attorney, soldier, and politician. Slack was an attorney in Huntington, Huntington Co. (1840-1881); Democratic member, Indiana State Senate (1851-1852, 1859-1861); colonel, 47th Indiana Regiment (1861-1864); general (1864-1865); Union commander at Memphis, Tenn. (June-July 1862), and Helena, Ark. (July-December 1862); brigade commander during Vicksburg campaign (1863), and in Louisiana, Mississippi, and Alabama (1864-1865);

commander of troops patrolling the Mexican border (summer 1865); and Huntington County Circuit Court judge (1872-1881).

The collection consists primarily of Slack's Civil War letters to his wife in Huntington, written from Kentucky, Missouri, Tennessee, Arkansas, Louisiana, Mississippi, Alabama, and Texas (1861-1865). Also included is his diary written during the siege of Mobile, Ala. (March-May 1865); and other family correspondence and business papers.

B-323. SMITH, BENJAMIN WILSON (1830-1921). PAPERS, 1856-1949.

1 ms. box.   L 146.

Smith was an educator in Dearborn, Porter, White, Tippecanoe, and Marion counties (1840s-1910s); Republican candidate for Indiana Superintendent of Public Instruction (1872); member, Indiana House of Representatives (1883-1887); and postmaster, Lafayette, Tippecanoe Co. (1889-1893).

The collection includes Smith's writings on the history of Warrick, Spencer, and White counties, Ind., and Harrison County, W.Va.; his history of the postal system; his accounts of his 1846 trip from Virginia to White County, Ind.; his history of Manchester Academy in Dearborn County; and his autobiography. Also included is his scrapbook of clippings and notes on politics (1856-1860); his advice to students in Dearborn County (1859); DAR applications from his family (1894, 1940s); correspondence of his daughter regarding family history (1900s); and papers regarding the Civil War service of his brother-in-law Oliver Smith Rankin, who served as a spy for the Union Army.

B-324. SMITH, RUTH BURGESS LEBO (1884-1954). PAPERS, 1854-1958.

2 ms. boxes.   Inventory.   L 147.

Smith was the wife of Charles Smith (1878-1963), who was a graduate of DePauw University, Greencastle, Putnam Co. (1902), and a Methodist minister in Fort Wayne, Allen Co. (1929-1944), Tipton, Tipton Co., and other northern Indiana towns.

The collection includes letters from Charles Smith to Ruth Lebo written from DePauw University and other places (1902-1905); Smith family correspondence (1905-1958); Ruth Lebo Smith's diary and letters to her family from her trip to Palestine and Europe (1933); her papers and diplomas from Tipton, Ind. (1890s); newspaper and magazine articles regarding Charles Smith's work with the Methodist church; and letters of the Burgess family (1854-1880), particularly letters from Alexander Burgess in Arcadia, Hamilton Co., to his family in Centerville, Wayne Co.

B-325. SMITH, SAMUEL A. (b. ca.1821). PAPERS, 1835-1902.

ca.45 items. S 1211.

Smith was a farmer and businessman near Bloomington, Monroe Co.

The collection consists primarily of Smith's business papers from the period 1847-1869, including indentures and other land documents from property in Monroe and Orange counties; and correspondence with business associates in Louisiana (1848-1851).

B-326. SMITH, WILLIAM HENRY (1830-1911). ACCOUNT BOOKS, 1881-1910.

3 vols. (.25 l.f.). V 133.

Smith was a physician in Leesville and Bedford, Lawrence Co.

The collection includes his account books for his medical practice (1883-1910), and for his real estate and other business interests (1881-1900).

B-327. SMITH & COMPANY. ACCOUNT BOOKS, 1862-1865.

2 vols. (.25 l.f.). V 132.

Smith & Company was a dry goods store in Mooresville, Morgan Co.

The collection includes a scrapbook of bills from the store's wholesale suppliers, principally from Indianapolis and Madison, Jefferson Co. (1862-1864); and a daybook (1863-1865).

B-328. SOULE, JOSHUA (d.1853). PAPERS, 1837-1853.

ca.40 items. S 1222.

Soule was an Indianapolis dentist (1830s-1853); and town board president (1837-1838).

The papers consist primarily of Soule's correspondence with his fiancee, Eliza Lawson of Lebanon, Ohio (1838). Also included are letters to Soule regarding Democratic Party politics (1843-1844); and other family papers.

Correspondents include William Brown, Andrew Kennedy, and James Whitcomb.

B-329. SPRING MILL STATE PARK. COLLECTION, 1835-1918.

2 ms. boxes. Inventory. L 225.

Spring Mill State Park is located in Lawrence County. The collection was formerly at the park and was transferred to the State Library by the Indiana State Museum.

The collection contains business papers and correspondence (1859-1896) of Jonathan Turley (b.1827), a farmer and miller who owned the Spring Mill property in the 1870s and 1880s. In addition there is a copybook of Benjamin Standish of Livonia, Washington Co. (1857-1871); a Civil War diary of Thomas Armes, 24th Indiana Regiment (1862); and an account book for a general store in Woodland (now Mitchell), Lawrence Co. (1853-1854).

B-330. SPRINGER-BRAYTON FAMILY. PAPERS, 1820-1969.

7 ms. boxes.

The Springer-Brayton family included William H. Springer (1829-1915), a tinner and farmer in Oakland City, Gibson Co. (1850s-1887), and Washington, Daviess Co. (1887-1915), and an officer in the 38th Indiana Regiment (1861-1864); his daughter, Ella Springer Sears (1850-1876), wife of Jesse M. Sears (1847-1873), a music teacher in southern Indiana and Kentucky; his daughter, Carrie Springer Brayton (1860-1934), wife of Chicago bookkeeper John Brayton (d.1941); and Carrie Brayton's daughter, Margaret Brayton

(1895-), a graduate of National Kindergarten College, Chicago (1916), a kindergarten instructor in Chicago (1920s), and kindergarten education instructor at Ball State Teachers College, Muncie, Delaware Co. (1932-1960s).

The collection principally consists of the personal correspondence of the Springer and Brayton families from the period 1842-1940. Included are William Springer's letters to his wife while serving in the Union Army in Kentucky, Tennessee, and Georgia (1861-1864); letters from Jesse Sears to Ella Springer (1869), and letters of Ella Sears to her parents (1870-1871); correspondence between John Brayton in Chicago and Valparaiso, Porter Co., and his fiancee, Carrie Springer, in Washington, Evansville, Vanderburgh Co., New Albany, Floyd Co., and Paducah, Ky. (1884-1891); correspondence between the Springers in Washington and the Braytons in Chicago (1892-1910); letters to Margaret Brayton and her sister, Ruth, from World War I soldiers (1917-1919); letters from Ruth Brayton to her parents while she was working for the Salvation Army at Camp Grant, Ill. (1919); and letters to Margaret Brayton in Chicago and Muncie from family and friends (1920s-1930s). Also included are letters from N. M. Springer in California (1852-1853); correspondence and legal documents of the Brayton family in Warren County, N.Y. (1820-1850s), and Chicago (1850s-1880s); business documents of the Springer family in Paoli, Orange Co. (1834-1850s); business papers and correspondence of W. H. Springer, including papers relating to his Civil War service (1860s-1915); Margaret Brayton's journals (1915-1917, 1924); Margaret Brayton's correspondence and papers regarding her education and teaching positions (1910s-1960s); and poems and short stories written by John Brayton.

B-331. STAR GROCERY. ACCOUNT BOOKS, 1888-1909.

4 vols. (.5 l.f.). V 218.

The Star Grocery was located in Broad Ripple, Marion Co.

The collection consists of the store's account books.

B-332. STAUDT, CARL (d. ca.1939). PAPERS, 1881-1919.

3 folders. S 1242.

Staudt and his brother, John M. Staudt, were from Indianapolis and served as privates in the U.S. Army in Europe during World War I.

The papers consist primarily of Carl and John Staudt's World War I letters to their family from Camp Sherman, Ohio, Camp Merritt, N.J., and from France (1918-1919). Also included are letters from their family in Indianapolis during the war; and clippings regarding the family (1881-1918).

B-333. STEELE, SELMA NEUBACHER (1870-1945). PAPERS, 1906-1940.

14 ms. boxes.   Inventory.   L 148.

Steele was an art teacher in Indianapolis; in 1907, married painter Theodore Clement (T. C.) Steele (1847-1926); established home and studio, called "House of the Singing Winds" in Brown County; and active in the Indiana Federation of Art Clubs and other arts organizations.

The collection consists principally of her correspondence from the period 1926-1940, including correspondence regarding T.C. Steele's paintings and exhibitions of his work; her shawl collection; her maintenance of the Brown County property; her activities in the Indiana Federation of Art Clubs and other organizations; and family, personal, and social affairs.

Correspondents include Alfred M. Brooks, William Lowe Bryan, Mary Q. Burnet, Frank Hohenberger, Josiah K. Lilly, and Herman B Wells.

B-334. STEPHENSON, DAVID CURTIS (1891-1966). PAPERS, 1925-1933.

1 archival box.   Inventory.   L 246.

Stephenson was the leader of the Indiana Ku Klux Klan (1922-1925); King Kleagle for most of the midwestern states and Grand Dragon of the Realm of Indiana (1923-1925); broke away from the national Ku Klux Klan (1924); political ally of Indiana Republican governor Edward L. Jackson during 1924 election; and served prison term for murder (1925-1956).

The papers principally consist of contemporary copies of Stephenson's prison correspondence, made for Indiana State Prison warden Walter Daly (1925-1933). Included is Stephenson's correspondence with his attorneys, supporters, and family regarding his attempts to gain release, prison conditions, the Ku Klux Klan, Indiana politics, and personal business. Also contained are letters to Daly regarding Stephenson; letters to and from Stephenson which were retained by prison officials; depositions and other court documents relating to Stephenson's case; and newspaper clippings regarding Stephenson and corruption in Indiana during the late 1920s.

Correspondents include Court Asher, Gutzen Borglum, Clarence Darrow, and Edward A. Rumely.

B-335. STOLL, JOHN B. (1843-1926). PAPERS, 1854-1926.

1 ms. box. L 149.

Newspaper editor and political writer. Stoll emigrated with his family from Germany to Pennsylvania (1853); owner and publisher, *Ligonier* (Noble Co.) *Banner* (1866-1913); owner and editor of the *South Bend* (St. Joseph Co.) *Times* (1883-1912); also associated with Democratic newspapers in LaPorte and Elkhart; organized Democratic State Editorial Association (1881); writer and speaker on behalf of the Indiana and national Democratic parties; and author, *History of the Indiana Democracy, 1816-1916* (1917).

The collection contains letters to Stoll regarding state and national Democratic Party politics (1866-1920), including correspondence relating to the 1870 and 1872 campaigns, and letters from German Democrats in the state; correspondence regarding newspapers in northern Indiana and the work of the Democratic State Editorial Association; correspondence pertaining to Stoll's work on the history of the Democratic Party in Indiana (1910s); and his political speeches and writings.

Correspondents include Henry A. Barnhart, Albert J. Beveridge, Schuyler Colfax, John D. Defrees, Thomas Dowling, William H. English, Charles W. Fairbanks, William P. Fishback, Isaac P. Gray, Thomas A. Hendricks, David B. Hill, William S. Holman, John Worth Kern, Michael C. Kerr, Frederick Landers, Thomas R. Marshall, Claude Matthews, James A. Mount, William H. O'Brien, Henry B. Payne, Samuel M. Ralston, Horatio W. Seymour, Benjamin F. Shively, James R. Slack, Thomas Taggart, David Turpie, Daniel W. Voorhees, and Woodrow Wilson.

B-336. STOOPS, HARRY M. (1866-1936). PAPERS, 1817-1958.

4 ms. boxes.   Inventory.   L 150.

Stoops was a teacher and businessman in Brookville, Franklin Co., and officer in the Franklin County Historical Society, and researcher in family and Franklin County history.

The papers include Stoops's correspondence regarding his research on the history of the Stoops and related families (1919-1932); letters from Amos W. Butler, principally regarding Franklin County history (1923-1935); his essays on Indian mounds and Franklin County history (1889-1929); land documents, receipts, and other business documents of Stoops's family in Franklin County (1820-1937); copies of documents which he collected on the Vincent, Wilson, Martin, Williams, and Trotter families of Franklin County; programs for Brookville and Brookville College activities (1856-1928); and letters to Lizzie Johnston of Portland, Maine, from relatives in Brookville and Hagerstown, Wayne Co. (1868).

B-337. STOVER, URBAN C. (b.1867). PAPERS, 1918-ca.1943.

1 ms. box.   L 151.

Stover was an attorney in Ladoga, Montgomery Co., and Indianapolis (1893-1940s); and deputy attorney general of Indiana (1934-1945).

The papers consist principally of family letters written during World War I, including letters to Stover from his son, Harney W. Stover, from the Great Lakes Naval Training Station (July-October 1918), and from France and New York (November 1918-January 1919); and letters from Daniel Stover, a lawyer with the Judge Advocate's Office in France (1918), and Harney B. Stover, an officer in the Field Artillery in France (1918). Also included is Stover's "History of the Office of Attorney General in Indiana" (ca.1943).

B-338. STOWMAN, CHARLES W. (d.1873). ACCOUNT BOOKS, 1851-1907.

5 vols. (.33 l.f.).   V 137.

Stowman owned a mill and a farm in Jefferson Twp., Miami Co., and was a dealer in agricultural products.

The collection includes account books for his mill and agricultural businesses (1851-1873); an account book for a shoemaker and repairer in Jefferson Twp. (1861-1870); and brief farm accounts for C. B. Stowman (1903-1907).

B-339. STUTESMAN, JAMES FLYNN (1860-1917). PAPERS, 1868-1916.

1 ms. box.   L 152.

Diplomat, attorney, and politician. Stutesman was a lawyer in Peru, Miami Co. (1884-1885, 1893-1906), Indianapolis (1906-1910), and Washington, D.C. (1910-1917); examiner, U.S. Department of Justice (1891-1893); Republican member, Indiana House of Representatives (1895, 1901-1903); U.S. Minister to Bolivia (1908-1910); U.S. commissioner general to Central America and the West Indies for the Panama-Pacific Expedition (1913); and worked for the Republican National Headquarters in Chicago during the 1916 presidential election.

The papers consist principally of Stutesman's correspondence regarding Republican Party politics, his work in Central and South America, and his attempts to secure federal appointments. Among the material is his correspondence regarding the 1916 Republican presidential campaign, particularly in California and the West; his papers regarding his work for the Panama-Pacific Exposition, including his reports, and copies of his communications with the heads of state in Central America and the West Indies (1913-1914); correspondence regarding Bolivian affairs (1908-1912); his correspondence regarding federal appointments (1884-1916); and report of Lafayette attorney Will R. Wood on his trip to Cuba with Stutesman (1901).

Correspondents include Walter R. Bacon, Albert J. Beveridge, Willis H. Booth, William M. Bowen, Nicholas Murray Butler, John Watson Foster, Newton W. Gilbert, James P. Goodrich, Walter Q. Gresham, Will H. Hays, John J. Ingalls, Charles B. Landis, Louis T. Michener, Charles C. Moore, Harry S. New, George W. Prince, Fred E. Sims, and James N. Tyner.

B-340. SULGROVE, LESLIE (d.1939). PAPERS, 1816, 1870-1894.

1 ms. box.   L 153.

Sulgrove was an Indianapolis newspaperman (1870s-1880s); and resident of Helena, Mont. (1887-1939).

The papers principally contain correspondence, receipts, and treasurer's book for the Crescent Society and the Alumni Society of Indianapolis High School (1871-ca.1885), in which Sulgrove served as an officer. Also included are receipts and correspondence regarding his personal business; school essays; programs for Indianapolis social events; and a ciphering book of John D. Brackenridge, Bath County, Ky. (1816).

B-341. SULLIVAN, WILLIAM G. (1884-1959). PAPERS, 1930s-1957.

2 ms. boxes. Inventory. L 154.

Sullivan was an Indianapolis businessman; board member, Art Association of Indianapolis; and author, *English's Opera House* (1960).

The papers consist mostly of Sullivan's research notes and writings, including notes and a manuscript biography of nineteenth-century Indiana playwright Joseph Arthur; notes and manuscript history of the English Opera House in Indianapolis; notes on theatrical performances by John Wilkes Booth; biographical sketches of English artist John Flaxman, writer Prosper Merimee, sculptor John Rogers, and composer Georges Bizet; and drafts of his letters on literary topics.

B-342. SWIFT, LUCIUS BURRIE (1844-1929). PAPERS, 1851-1931.

4 ms. boxes. L 155.

Reformer. Swift was a soldier in a New York regiment during the Civil War; graduate of the University of Michigan (1870); principal and superintendent of schools, LaPorte, LaPorte Co. (1872-1879); Indianapolis lawyer (1879-1929); leader in civil service reform movement; editor and publisher, *Civil Service Chronicle* (1889-1896); member of board and officer, National Civil Service Reform League (1880s-1929); trustee, Citizens Gas Company, Indianapolis (1905-1929); member, 1st Sanitary Commission, Indianapolis (1917-1923); and author, *Germans in America* (1915) and *How We Got Our Liberties* (1928).

The collection consists primarily of Swift's correspondence from the period 1885-1908 relating to his work with federal civil service reform, including correspondence relating to the work of the National Civil Service Reform League; Swift's publication of the *Civil Service Chronicle;* federal appointments in Indiana and elsewhere; the work of the U.S. Civil Service Commission; and the role of reformers in state and national elections. Also contained is correspondence regarding Swift's involvement with progressive Republicans, particularly Theodore Roosevelt and Albert J. Beveridge; correspondence pertaining to his work in the campaign to prepare the United States for war with Germany (1914-1918), and reactions to his pamphlets *Germans in America* (1915) and *America's Debt to England* (1917); correspondence regarding tariff reform (1908-1912); papers relating to the Citizens Gas Company and the Indianapolis Sanitary Commission (1920s); papers regarding his lecturing and writing on historical and reform topics (1910s-1920s); his letters to his wife (1885-1916), primarily written from the East while he was attending reform and political meetings, including meetings with Theodore Roosevelt; his diaries written during a meeting of the National Civil Service Reform League (1889), during a meeting to discuss the creation of a reform political party (1892), and on a trip to Massachusetts (1897); his journal (1875-1888) containing notes on LaPorte, starting a law practice in Indianapolis, politics, and reminiscences of his Civil War experiences; and drafts of his letters and essays on reform and politics.

Correspondents include Albert J. Beveridge, Eliza A. Blaker, Charles J. Bonaparte, James H. Breasted, William Lowe Bryan, Edward Cary, French Ensor Chadwick, Edward P. Clark, George William Curtis, Richard Henry Dana, Dorman B. Eaton, Charles W. Fairbanks, William Farnam, William Fortune, John Watson Foster, William Dudley Foulke, James P. Goodrich, John K. Gowdy, Albert Bushnell Hart, William Dean Howells, Louis G. Howland, Charles Evans Hughes, Jules Jusserand, George Kennan, Henry S. Lea, Francis E. Leupp, Henry Cabot Lodge, Arthur O. Lovejoy, George W. McAneny, Franklin MacVeagh, William Henry Harrison Miller, Oliver T. Morton, Henry Raymond Mussey, Meredith Nicholson, Walter H. Page, William Potts, Edith Kermit Roosevelt, Theodore Roosevelt, John C. Rose, Carl Schurz, Francis Lynde Stetson, Moorfield Storey, Mark Sullivan, Charles P. Taft, William Howard Taft, Frank William Taussig, Oswald Garrison Villard, James W. Wadsworth, William English Walling, Everett Wheeler, Horace White, Charles R. Williams, Wong Kai Kah, and James A. Woodburn.

B-343. TAGGART, THOMAS T. (1856-1929). PAPERS, 1858-1950.

2 archival boxes, 3 ms. boxes, 30 vols. (15 l.f.).

Politician. Taggart was Marion County auditor (1886-1894); chairman, Democratic State Committee (1892-1894); mayor of Indianapolis (1895-1901); member, Democratic National Committee (1900-1912), chairman (1900-1908); appointed U.S. Senator from Indiana to fill unexpired term (1916); purchased Grand Hotel, Indianapolis (1893); head of syndicate which purchased the French Lick Springs Hotel, a resort and health spa in Orange County (1901); and member of the board of directors, French Lick Springs Hotel (1901-1929), chairman (1924-1929).

The collection includes Taggart's scrapbooks (1895-1920) containing newspaper clippings regarding his political career, the French Lick Springs Hotel, and the 1915 trial of Taggart and others for election fraud; political correspondence, including correspondence from his term in the U.S. Senate (1916), and correspondence with Samuel Ralston regarding Ralston's campaign for the Democratic presidential nomination (1924); records of the French Lick Springs Hotel (1887-1928), including correspondence, contracts, financial documents, minutes of board meetings of the French Lick Springs Company (1887-1901), and hotel register (1908-1909); papers relating to Taggart's threatened libel actions against the *Indianapolis News* and others (1914), and Edna Ferber (1926); correspondence with A. C. Sallee regarding Sallee's proposed biography of Taggart (1920s); and personal correspondence and correspondence of Taggart's children (1874-1950), particularly correspondence of his son, Thomas D. Taggart (1886-1949). In addition, there is a register for the Grand Hotel, Indianapolis (1898); and a scrapbook on Taggart's wife's family (1859-1905).

Correspondents include Claude Bowers, Warren G. Harding, Will H. Hays, Kin Hubbard, Cordell Hull, William G. Irwin, Carleton B. McCulloch, Meredith Nicholson, Samuel Ralston, Franklin D. Roosevelt, Alfred E. Smith, Edith Bolling Wilson, and Evans Woollen.

B-344. TARKINGTON, BOOTH (1869-1946). PAPERS, 1892-1951.

37 items. Calendar. S 1282.

Tarkington was an Indianapolis writer and author of *Penrod* (1914), *The Magnificent Ambersons* (1918), *Alice Adams* (1921), and numerous other novels, short stories, and plays.

The papers consist of miscellaneous letters and manuscripts of Tarkington, including letters of Tarkington and his wife to Indianapolis journalist Mary Dyer Lemon (1931-1936); his letters to the Silberman brothers, art dealers in New York (1934-1944); his answers to questions about American art and literature; and typescripts of essays and poems.

B-345. TAYLOR, ROBERT S. (1838-1918). PAPERS, 1860-1918.

14 archival boxes, 27 vols. (18 l.f.).

Attorney. Taylor was an attorney in Fort Wayne, Allen Co. (1860-1918); judge of the court of common pleas, Allen County (1869-1870); Republican member, Indiana House of Representatives (1871-1872); Republican candidate for U.S. House of Representatives (1874, 1880) and for the Indiana State Senate (1897, 1899); member, U.S. Mississippi River Commission (1881-1914); specialist in patent law, particularly with regard to utilities; chairman, American Bar Association Committee on Patents, Trade-Mark, and Copyright Law (1909); and trustee, Wabash College, Crawfordsville, Montgomery Co.

The papers consist principally of Taylor's legal correspondence, particularly regarding his work on patent cases. Among the material is correspondence regarding patent cases involving the Fort Wayne Electric Company, Westinghouse, General Electric, American Bell Telephone Company, and other utilities and companies (ca.1878-1914); correspondence regarding his cases in the Fort Wayne area involving property, contracts, and civil suits (1860-ca.1880); and correspondence regarding the work of the ABA Committee on Patent, Trade-Mark, and Copyright Law, particularly its effort to create a Court of Patent Appeals (1906-1911). Also included is Taylor's correspondence regarding Republican Party politics, the Mississippi River Commission (1881-1914), his work as trustee of Wabash College, his membership in the Indiana Club of Chicago, and his songwriting (1914-1918); and his letter books, including twenty-five volumes containing copies of his legal correspondence (1868-1915), one volume of political correspondence (1871-1888), and one volume of correspondence and reports for the Mississippi River Commission (1881-1914).

Correspondents include Jane Addams, George Ade, Conrad Baker, Albert J. Beveridge, Charles J. Bonaparte, J. C. Burrows, Schuyler Colfax, Shelby M. Cullom, Edward Denby, Henry W. Diederich, Charles W. Fairbanks, Frederick P. Fish, William Dudley Foulke, Lindley M. Garrison, Newton W. Gilbert, James P. Goodrich, Walter Q. Gresham, J. Frank Hanly, Judson Harmon, Benjamin Harrison, Elwood Haynes, James A. Hemenway, Merica Hoagland, Samuel Insull, William G. Irwin, John Worth Kern, Frederick Landis, Harry G. Leslie, Henry Cabot Lodge, Frank Lowden, Louis Ludlow, Thomas R. Marshall, William H. H. Miller, W. H. Moody, Edward Moseley, Harry S. New, John C. New, Richard Olney, Benjamin Strattan Parker, George F. Peabody, Daniel D. Pratt, Redfield Proctor, John Sherman, Clement Studebaker, John Studebaker, William Sulzer, William Howard Taft, Frank L. O. Wadsworth, Lew Wallace, Booker T. Washington, James E. Watson, and William Wesley Woollen.

B-346. TAYLOR, TUCKER W. (1854-1901). PAPERS, 1870-1904.

2 ms. boxes. L 235.

Taylor was a resident of Greencastle, Putnam Co.; graduate of DePauw University, Greencastle (1878); private secretary to W. C. DePauw (1880-1884) and Dr. John Clark Ridpath (1888-1897); and poet, author of *Songs of Old Sileural; a Potpourri of Poetical Putnam* (1897).

The collection includes Taylor's poems; correspondence regarding his poetry (1880s-1890s); and papers of his brother, Dr. James H. Taylor (1852-1944), including his essays on diphtheria, dysentery, and other medical topics, and his address to the graduating class of the Medical College of Indiana (1900).

B-347. TERRE HAUTE SCHOOL SOCIETY. RECORDS, 1829-1834.

53 items. S 2778.

The Terre Haute School Society sponsored the construction and operation of a school in Terre Haute, Vigo Co.

The records include lists of subscribers to the society, receipts for construction of the schoolhouse (1829-1831), and minutes of meetings.

B-348. THOMPSON, RICHARD WIGGINTON (1809-1900). PAPERS, 1818-1900.

2 ms. boxes.   Partial Calendar.   L 158.

Politician. Thompson was a lawyer in Bedford, Lawrence Co. (1834-1843), and Terre Haute, Vigo Co. (1843-1900); Whig and Republican; member, Indiana House of Representatives (1834-1836) and Indiana Senate (1836-1838); member, U.S. House of Representatives (1841-1843, 1847-1849); commandant at Camp Thompson, Terre Haute, and provost marshal of Terre Haute district during the Civil War; Collector of Internal Revenue, 7th Indiana District (1864-1865); Secretary of the Navy under Rutherford B. Hayes (1877-1880); chairman, American Committee of the Panama Canal Company (1880); director, Panama Railroad Company (1881-1889); and author, *The Papacy and the Civil Power* (1876) and other anti-Catholic works.

The collection is made up of Thompson's political correspondence, including correspondence regarding state and national Whig and Republican Party politics, and Thompson's role in political campaigns (1840s-1880s); letters from constituents during his terms in Congress regarding political appointments and local politics (1841-1849); Civil War correspondence, including correspondence pertaining to state and national politics, and Thompson's duties in Terre Haute (1861-1865); his correspondence as Secretary of the Navy, including letters from congressmen and others making recommendations for appointments, and correspondence regarding naval contracts and policies (1877-1880); and his correspondence regarding a canal across Panama (1880-1881). In addition, there is correspondence regarding his legal work, including the settlement of Shawnee, Menominee, and other Indian claims (1850s), railroads and the Wabash and Erie Canal (1850s-1880s), and Vigo County land; his correspondence with his wife and parents (1830-1853); correspondence with Harper & Brothers regarding *The Papacy and the Civil Power* (1876-1880); political speeches (1840s-1880s); his essay on Henry A. Wise; his notebook of expenses, and notes for speeches (1865); his wife's diary (1838); and correspondence between relatives in Adair County Ky., and Culpepper County, Va. (1818-1830).

Correspondents include Conrad Baker, John J. Barbour, Henry W. Blair, Newton Booth, Henry V. Boynton, Jesse D. Bright, Thomas M. Browne, Joseph G. Cannon, Henry B. Carrington, John M. Clayton, Thomas R. Cobb, Francis M. Cockrell, Thomas Corwin, James H. Cravens, Charles A. Dana, Henry Winter Davis, John G. Davis, John W. Davis, John D. Defrees, Charles Devens, Charles Dewey, John B. Dillon, John Dowling, Thomas Dowling, George G. Dunn, William M. Dunn, William M. Evarts, Charles W. Fairbanks, Graham N. Fitch, John Watson Foster, Henry A. Glidden, Walter Q. Gresham, E. M. Halford, Wade Hampton, John J. Hayden, Thomas A. Hendricks, Barnabas C. Hobbs, William R. Holloway, Elisha M. Huntington, Robert G. Ingersoll, Nathan Kimball, Henry S. Lane, John Law, William G. Le Duc, John A. Logan, George W. McCrary, David McDonald, Joseph E. McDonald, Edward W. McGaughey, Wayne MacVeagh, Willie P. Mangum, George W. Manypenny, William L. Marcy, Joseph G. Marshall, Elijah B. Martindale, Stanley Matthews, William H. H. Miller, Austin W. Morris, Oliver P. Morton, Lazarus Noble, Noah Noble, Godlove Orth, Daniel D. Pratt, Alexander Ramsey, John Clark Ridpath, James M. Robinson, William K. Rogers, Harvey D. Scott, Jesse Seligman, Joseph Seligman, Frederick W. Seward, John Sherman, Jeremiah Sullivan, W. H. H. Terrell, John P. Usher, John Vawter, Daniel W. Voorhees, James Whitcomb, Albert S. White, Washington C. Whitthorne, William W. Wick, and Joseph A. Wright.

B-349. THORNTON, WILLIAM WHEELER (1851-1932). PAPERS, 1871-1931.

4.5 ms. boxes. L 159, L 309, S 1312.

Thornton was an attorney in Logansport, Cass Co. (1876-1880), Crawfordsville, Montgomery Co. (1883-1889), and Indianapolis (1889-1932); deputy attorney general of Indiana (1880-1882); judge, Superior Court of Marion County (1914-1922); and author of numerous books and articles on law.

The papers include his manuscript for a book of political documents, principally from nineteenth-century America; manuscript of his biography of early Indiana jurist Isaac Blackford; articles on the judicial system of Indiana and the Northwest Territory; an essay on French general Michel Ney in America; and correspondence regarding politics and his legal and historical writings (1871-1903).

B-350. 325th FIELD ARTILLERY ASSOCIATION. RECORDS, 1918, 1940-1942.

3 folders.   S 1620.

The association held reunions for veterans who served with the 325th Field Artillery in World War I.

The records include correspondence, minutes, reply cards, and publicity for the 1940 and 1941 association meetings in Indiana, held in honor of Wendell Willkie who had served in the regiment.

B-351. TIPTON, JOHN (1786-1839). PAPERS, 1806-1858.

18 ms. boxes.   Calendar.   L 160.

Militia officer, politician, Indian agent, and land speculator. Tipton was a farmer and merchant in Harrison County (1807-1823); Harrison County justice of the peace (1811); officer in the Indiana militia (1811-1820s), serving at the Battle of Tippecanoe and in engagements against the Indians during the War of 1812; Harrison County sheriff (1816-1819); member, Indiana House of Representatives (1820-1822); member, commission to select site for state capital (1820); member, commission to mark the Indiana-Illinois boundary (1821); director, Corydon branch of the Indiana State Bank (1821); federal agent to the Indians of the Upper Wabash, based at Fort Wayne, Allen Co. (1823-1828), and Logansport, Cass Co. (1828-1831); member, U.S. Senate (1831-1839), associated with pro-Jackson Party; directed removal of Potawatomi Indians from Indiana (1838); and elected grand master of the Grand Lodge of Masons in Indiana (1820, 1828).

The collection consists principally of Tipton's papers from the period 1810-1839, including letters to Tipton, his retained copies of outgoing letters, and his business papers. Included is correspondence pertaining to the operations of the Indiana militia in the 1810s; political correspondence regarding the work of the state legislature (1820s-1830s), his senatorial elections (1831, 1832), appointments to federal office (1831-1839), and local, state, and national issues, particularly internal improvements, Indian policy, and banking; correspondence regarding his work as Indian agent (1823-1831), including treaty negotiations, trading practices with the Miami and Potawatomi Indians, and federal Indian policy; correspondence regarding the removal of the Potawatomi Indians from Indiana (1838); correspondence relating to his personal business interests, particularly land development in Logansport and along the Wabash River; correspondence regarding the Masonic Lodge in Indiana; and family correspondence, including letters of his daughter, Matilda Tipton, written from school in Cincinnati (1826-1827), and correspondence with his son, Spear S. Tipton, a student and lawyer in Madison, Jefferson Co. (1828-1839). Also included are Tipton's journals of the Tippecanoe Expedition (1811), the Driftwood Expedition against the Indians along the White River (1812), his trip to locate the Owen County seat (1820), his trip to locate a site for the Indiana state capital (1820), his trip to mark the Indiana-Illinois boundary (1821), and his trip to Washington, D.C., with Miami and Potawatomi Indian chiefs (1826); accounts of annuities and treaty provisions paid to the Indians; and receipts, contracts, accounts, and other papers pertaining to his personal business interests. The collection also contains business papers and correspondence of his son, Spear S. Tipton (1814-1847), including papers relating to the settlement of John Tipton's estate; correspondence regarding his personal business interests and Cass County politics; and letters from his half-brother, George T. Tipton, written while a student at Wabash College, Crawfordsville (1844-1846). Many of Tipton's papers were published in *The John Tipton Papers* (Indianapolis: Indiana Historical Bureau, 1942. 3v.).

Correspondents include William B. Astor, James Barbour, Joseph Bartholomew, Hervey Bates, Daniel R. Bearss, James S. Blake, Thomas H. Blake, Ratliff Boon, Jesse D. Bright, Bishop Simon Brute de Remur, John C. Calhoun, Israel T. Canby, Lewis Cass, Marston G. Clark, William Conner, John Wesley Davis, John D. Defrees, Charles Dewey, John B. Dillon, John Dowling, Thomas Dowling, Lyman C. Draper, George H. Dunn, John B. Duret, Isaac C. Elston, George W. Ewing, John Ewing, Thomas Ewing, William G. Ewing, Graham N. Fitch, Calvin Fletcher, Davis Floyd, Allen Hamilton, Hugh Hanna, Samuel Hanna, Edward A. Hannegan, William Henry Harrison, John Hays, William Hendricks, Edmond O. Hovey, Tilghman A. Howard, Elisha M. Huntington, Jonathan Jennings, Richard M. Johnson, General Washington Johnston, James F. D. Lanier, Jonathan McCarty, Nicholas McCarty, Isaac McCoy, Thomas L. McKenney, Pierre Menard, Samuel Merrill, Samuel Milroy, Austin W. Morris, Elias Murray, James Noble, Noah Noble, Benjamin Parke, Abel C. Pepper, John U. Pettit, William Polke, Thomas Posey, Daniel D. Pratt, James Rariden, James Brown Ray, James M. Ray, John B. Richardville, Joseph Richardville, Solon Robinson, William Rockhill, Samuel Sample, Oliver H. Smith, Jeremiah Sullivan, Cyrus Taber, Waller Taylor, John Test, Henry P. Thornton, Edward Tiffin, David Wallace, James Whitcomb, Albert S. White, William W. Wick, and William Woodbridge.

B-352. TUCKER, JAMES M. (1908-). PAPERS, 1938-1940.

1 ms. box.   Inventory.   L 233.

Tucker is a Paoli, Orange Co., attorney (1932-); Republican; and Indiana Secretary of State (1938-1942).

The papers include his correspondence regarding speaking engagements (July-October 1940) and personal expenses (1938-1940).

B-353. TURLEY, JONATHAN (b.1827). PAPERS, 1851-1934.

3 ms. boxes, 13 vols. (2.25 l.f.).   Partial Inventory.   L 161, V 184.

Turley was a farmer in Mitchell, Lawrence Co.; and owned and operated Daisy Spring Mill (now in Spring Mill State Park), where he distilled brandy and whiskey and operated a lime kiln.

The collection consists principally of Turley's business papers relating to Lawrence County land and his mill, distillery, and lime kiln operations (1866-1896), including correspondence regarding the remodeling and sale of his mill; correspondence with business associates in Louisville, Ky.; account books for his mill and distillery operations (1859-1919); his diaries and expense books (1851-1883); and receipts, contracts, and accounts. Also contained is family correspondence (1864-1934), including Civil War letters from his brother, Benjamin Turley, serving in the Veteran Reserve Corps in Evansville, Vanderburgh Co. (1864-1865), and from other soldiers serving in Texas, Alabama, and Louisiana; letters from relatives in Illinois and Kansas (1870s-1890s); and letters to his daughters, Lida and Jennie Turley (1890s-1934), including letters from San Diego, Calif., East St. Louis, Ill., Fort Andrews, Mass., and Terre Haute, Vigo Co., and Indianapolis, Ind.; minute book, treasurer's book, and roll book for the Big Springs Grange, Lawrence Co. (1874-1876); and farm record books (1895-1922).

B-354. TURNBULL, DAVID C. COLLECTION, 1836-1966.

1 ms. box.   L 163.

The Indiana State Library acquired this collection from Turnbull of Mishawaka, St. Joseph Co. (1966-1969).

The collection includes letters of Indiana Civil War soldiers (1861-1865); business and legal documents relating to Kosciusko County (1836-1849), St. Joseph County (1847-1916), and other counties; correspondence of Alexander Grant of Cass County, Mich. (1871-1875), the Bidwell family of Niles, Mich., and Brownsville, Tex. (1937-1940), and the Ackerman family of Niles (1940-1947); and documents relating to the Studebaker Company of South Bend, St. Joseph Co. (1856-1886).

B-355. TURPIE, DAVID (1829-1907). PAPERS, 1875-1903.

1 ms. box. L 164.

Turpie was a lawyer in Carroll, White, and Cass counties (1849-1872), and in Indianapolis (1872-1907); Democratic member, U.S. Senate (1863, 1887-1899); and author, *Sketches of My Own Time* (1903).

The papers include a manuscript copy of *Sketches of My Own Time*; minutes of Fiat Lux, an Indianapolis literary society to which Turpie belonged (1875-1876); and Turpie's speeches on literary and political matters, including lectures given to Fiat Lux in the 1870s.

B-356. UNTHANK, SUSAN B. (fl. 1855-1924). PAPERS, 1837-1924.

3 folders. S 1332.

Unthank, born Susan B. Hunt, was a resident of Spiceland, Henry Co.; and in 1861 married Josiah T. Unthank (1837-1919), a Quaker carpenter in Spiceland, and part-time instructor at White's Indiana Manual Labor Institute, a Quaker training school for Indians, blacks, and indigent whites in Wabash County.

The papers include letters to the Unthanks from Indian students at White's Institute, and from former students living in Wyoming, Missouri, Oklahoma, Kansas, and the Dakotas (1879-1905); family letters to Susan Hunt Unthank from relatives in Richmond, Wayne Co., Lebanon, Boone Co., and other places (1855-1866); an 1859 diary; letters to the Unthanks from Civil War soldiers; Unthank family accounts (1837-1851); and family business papers (1840s-1850s).

B-357. UPFOLD, GEORGE (1796-1872). PAPERS, 1796-1926.

1 ms. box.   Inventory.   L 165.

Upfold was an Episcopalian priest in New York City (1820-1831), Pittsburgh, Pa. (1831-1850), and Lafayette, Tippecanoe Co. (1850-1854); bishop of the Episcopal church in Indiana (1849-1865); and resident of Indianapolis (1857-1872).

The papers include Upfold's diaries describing his church duties and the parishes he visited in Indiana (1854-1870); his letters to his wife and daughter written during his tours of Indiana parishes (1850-1864); and papers relating to his service in parishes in New York and Pittsburgh. Also included are personal letters of the Bingham family, written from New York City (1822-1846), Lafayette (1851-1860s), and Germany (1900). Bishop Upfold's daughter married Joseph Bingham.

B-358. VANDERBILT, JAMES CORNELIUS (ca.1840-1880). LETTERS, 1861-1864.

1 ms. box.   L 166.

Vanderbilt was a plasterer in New Albany, Floyd Co., and Harrison County; and private in the 23rd Indiana Regiment (1861-1864).

The collection consists of Vanderbilt's Civil War letters to his mother and aunt in New Albany, written while serving in Missouri, Kentucky, Tennessee, Louisiana, Mississippi, Alabama, and Georgia.

B-359. VAN HOOK, JAMES M. (1844-1927). PAPERS, 1801-1907.

2 ms boxes.   Inventory.   L 308.

Van Hook was a private in the 77th Indiana Regiment during the Civil War; resident of Charlestown, Clark Co. (1860s-1870s, 1890s); and orange grower in Florida (1880s, ca.1900-1927).

The collection includes Van Hook's papers, including correspondence regarding his activities with the Freemasons, the Grand Army of the Republic, and the Clark County Historical Society (1870s-1907); papers regarding his business interests near Gainesville and Ft. Meade, Fla. (1883-1899); and his notes and writings on the early history of Clark County. Also contained are miscellaneous Clark County papers, including indentures and other land documents (1801-1900); papers of the John Denny family of Charlestown, particularly Denny's accounts and business papers (1818-1840s), and letters of Margaret Denny to her brother serving in the Union Army (1864-1865); and reminiscences and letters on life in early Indiana written for the Clark County Historical Society (1873-1874). The collection also includes diaries of Joshua Leach, financial agent and secretary for the Cincinnati and Indianapolis Junction Railroad Company, based in Connersville, Fayette Co. (1854-1866).

B-360. VAN PELT, FRANCIS MARION (1838-1929). PAPERS, 1860-1929.

5 ms. boxes. Inventory. L 168.

Soldier and businessman. Van Pelt was an officer in the 17th Indiana Regiment (1861-1865), serving in Wilder's Brigade in Tennessee; employee of the Chicago, Burlington, and Quincy Railroad in Galesburg, Ill. (1865-1870); married Amanda Slater, Galesburg (1868); worked in the post office, internal revenue service, and private business in Atlanta, Ga. (1870-1893); resident of Anderson, Madison Co. (1895-1929); Anderson justice of the peace (1902-1908?, 1919-1929); active in Civil War veterans organizations; and state commander, Grand Army of the Republic (1925).

The collection includes Van Pelt's family correspondence (1863-1929), particularly letters from Van Pelt and his wife in Atlanta, Ga. (1870-1892), and letters from relatives in Galesburg and Wataga, Ill. (1878-1907), Creston, Iowa (1878-1909), Lincoln, Nebr. (1894), Taiban, N.Mex. (1908-1909), and Pittsburg and Yeoman, Carroll Co. (1863-1865, 1883-1896), Anderson, Madison Co. (1873-1909), and Monticello, White Co. (1879-1890); orders, quartermasters reports, and other official military papers of Van Pelt and the 17th Indiana (1862-1865); papers regarding veterans activities, including letters to Van Pelt from John T. Wilder (1903-1917), reunion record books and scrapbooks for the 17th Indiana and Wilder's Brigade (1880-1925), and Van Pelt's speech as GAR commander (1925); family scrapbooks (1910s); and record book of the Anderson Township Progressive Club, for which Van Pelt was secretary. In addition there are papers of Van Pelt's son-in-law, Henry M. Phipps, and his family, containing Phipps's letters to his wife in Indianapolis from New York, England, and France while he was working with the YMCA during World War I (1918-1919); and diaries (1890-1921) of George A. Phipps, a farmer near Pendleton, Madison Co.

B-361. VESTAL, ALBERT H. (1875-1932). PAPERS, 1899-1940.

5 ms. boxes. L 352.

Vestal was an attorney in Anderson, Madison Co. (1896-1932); Republican member, U.S. House of Representatives (1917-1932); and served as Republican whip in Congress (1923-1931).

The collection contains invitations, programs, and announcements for social events in Washington, D.C. (1927-1932); newspaper and magazine clippings regarding Vestal's work in Congress; diary of his trip to California and Alaska (1927); speeches; record of assistance given to World War I soldiers and their families from his district; and a journal and copies of newspaper headlines made by Vestal (1917). Also included are papers of his wife, consisting of her diaries (1920, 1925-1932); correspondence and other papers regarding her work with the Wendell Willkie Notification Committee, principally regarding the planning for the official notification ceremony in Elwood, Indiana, August 17, 1940; her family and personal business correspondence (1932-1938); and reports on clothing production by Red Cross volunteers in Anderson (1932-1933).

B-362. WADE, WILLIAM H. (1906-1971). PAPERS, 1949-1971.

3 archival boxes. Inventory.

Wade was a newspaper reporter for several papers in Indiana, Ohio, and Michigan in the 1930s and 1940s; writer for the *Anderson* (Madison Co.) *Herald* (1948-1971); wrote column "Folklore" for the *Herald* (1949-1971); contributor of articles to boys' magazines; and author, *Ghost Ship* (1950s).

The collection includes Wade's correspondence regarding folklore and his newspaper columns (1949-1971); copies of his articles for the *Anderson Herald*; his speeches on folklore and other topics (1940s-1960s); notes, newsletters, magazine and newspaper articles, and other published items collected by

Wade for his articles and for his work on folklore; correspondence with his son; and notes on Anderson and Anderson High School for his newspaper articles.

B-363. WAGGAMAN, JOHN STANLEY. COLLECTION, 1963-1969.

7 ms. boxes.   Inventory.   L 171.

Waggaman was associated with the Bureau of Institute Research, Indiana University, Bloomington.

The collection consists of articles, pamphlets, newsletters, reports, questionnaires, clippings, and correspondence relating to the functioning of the Indiana General Assembly, collected or prepared by Waggaman for Bureau studies. Included is material on legislative and congressional district reapportionment in Indiana and other states (1963-1968); compensation for legislators; the organization and functioning of the General Assembly; and recommendations for improving the legislature.

B-364. WAHL, HENRY E. (1914-). PAPERS, 1865-1945.

1 ms. box.   L 172.

Wahl was the son of H. E. Wahl, a Bloomington, Monroe Co., baker; graduate of Indiana University, Bloomington (1936); businessman in Indianapolis (1936) and Lansing, Mich. (1937); officer in the U.S. Navy during World War II, serving in the Pacific; and member of staff of the Indiana University Halls of Residence (1955-).

The papers include letters to Wahl from his parents in Bloomington (1936-1945); letters to his parents during World War II (1943-1945), including letters from Wahl and his wife in California, Hawaii, and the Pacific, and letters from Donald Wahl, a naval officer serving in the Pacific. In addition there is a notebook containing a diary of a trip from Evansville, Vanderburgh Co., to Nashville, Tenn. (1865), and accounts for a schoolteacher in Gibson County (1866); and family business papers and correspondence of the Wampler family in Bloomington (1910-1927).

B-365. WALKER, JOHN MANN (1874-1960). PAPERS, 1848-1960.

8 ms. boxes.   L 369.

Methodist minister. Walker was a student at DePauw University, Greencastle, Putnam Co. (ca.1893-1896), and Maryville Seminary, Maryville, Mo. (1897); instructor at DePauw (1899-1901); student at Boston (Mass.) University School of Theology (ca.1902-1903); Methodist Episcopal minister in Massachusetts (1903-1905), French Lick, Orange Co. (1905), Greencastle (1908-1910), Indianapolis (1910-1912), and New Albany, Floyd Co. (1910s); superintendent of the Methodist Episcopal Church districts in Connersville, Fayette Co. (ca.1919-1926), Evansville, Vanderburgh Co. (1926-1930), and Bloomington, Monroe Co. (1930-1938); and part-time Methodist minister in Massachusetts (1950s). He was the son of Francis Walker (1831-1914), a Methodist minister in southern Indiana (1857-1874), and owner of a nursery in New Albany (1874-1914).

The collection consists principally of Walker's family correspondence from the period 1893-1941, including correspondence between Walker and his parents in New Albany (1895-1911); correspondence between Walker and his fiancee and wife, Nora Severinghaus Walker (1894-1919), including her letters from New Albany and Louisville, Ky. (1902-1919), and from her trip to Europe (1903); Walker's letters to his daughters (1919-1941); letters to Walker from family and friends in New Albany, Greencastle, and other places (1896-1938); and letters to Nora Walker from family and friends (1893-1927), particularly from Evansville and Seymour, Jackson Co., Ind., and Denver, Colo. (1893-1912). Also included is Walker's autobiography, written in the late 1940s; his sermons and addresses; his journal (1915); a book of testimonials written by Bloomington district churches upon his retirement as superintendent in 1938; and reminiscences of growing up in New Albany, written by his brothers and sisters (1950s-1960).

The collection also contains papers of his father, Francis Walker, including his letters to his family while attending Ohio Wesleyan University in Delaware, Ohio (1851), and while serving as a Methodist minister in southern Indiana (1860s); letters to him from other Methodist ministers and DePauw University officials (1860s-1910s); his school essays from the Clermont (Ohio) Academy (1840s); his sermons; autobiographical notes (1899); and letters of his wife, Mary Graham Walker, written to her family in New Albany from Leesville, Lawrence Co. (1861), Brownstown, Jackson Co. (1863-1864), Newburgh, Warrick Co. (1865), Gentryville, Spencer Co. (1866), Cannelton, Perry Co. (1868-1871), and Mt. Vernon, Posey Co. (1872-1873).

B-366. WALLACE, LEW (1827-1905). PAPERS, 1848-ca.1905.

1 ms. box. L 173.

Wallace was an attorney in Crawfordsville, Montgomery Co.; major general in the Union Army; organized defense of Cincinnati (1862); and author, *Ben Hur* (1880), *Lew Wallace, an Autobiography* (1906), and other works.

The papers consist principally of Wallace's military papers from September, 1862, pertaining to the defense of Cincinnati and northern Kentucky. Included is correspondence of Wallace and his staff regarding the defense and administration of the area, a report on the defense of the Ohio River, and other reports and official papers. Also included are a small number of miscellaneous letters written by Wallace.

B-367. WATERS, JOHN T. (1867-ca.1943). PAPERS, 1815-1917.

1 ms. box. L 175.

Waters, son of Isaac Waters, was a furniture maker and undertaker in Pittsboro, Hendricks Co. (1880s-1913); and carpenter in Indianapolis (ca.1914-ca.1943).

The collection contains account books for the Waters furniture store (1885-1891, 1904-1908) and funeral business (1875-1891); Isaac Waters's account of fines collected as justice of the peace (1881-1883); John T. Waters's business papers and correspondence (1882-1917), including receipts and correspondence regarding his bicycling interests (1880s-1890s), and family letters from Brownsburg, Hendricks Co., and Lebanon, Boone Co. (1888-1889); and copies of Waters family papers and letters (1815-1874).

B-368. WAYNE COUNTY MEDICAL SOCIETY. RECORDS, 1864-1930.

1 ms. box, 1 vol. (.5 l.f.). L 350, V 298.

The Medical Society was a professional organization for physicians in Wayne County. In 1923 it merged with the Union County Medical Society to form the Wayne-Union County Medical Society.

The records include minutes of meetings (1864-1930), containing summaries of papers and discussions, and reports on society business; secretary's account book (1888-1900); papers delivered at meetings; lists of members; and the constitution for the Social Service Bureau of Richmond, Wayne Co. (1917).

B-369. WELSH, MATTHEW E. (1912-). PAPERS, 1941-1978.

79 l.f. Inventory.
Restricted.

Politician and attorney. Welsh was an attorney in Vincennes, Knox Co. (1937-1960); Democratic member, Indiana House of Representatives (1941-1943); officer, U.S. Navy (1943-1946); U.S. attorney, Southern District of Indiana (1950-1952); member, Indiana State Senate (1955-1960); governor of Indiana (1961-1965); member, National Governors Conference Executive Committee (1963); chairman, U.S. Interstate Oil Compact Commission (1963); Democratic National Committeeman from Indiana (1964-1965); candidate in the 1964 Indiana presidential primary, running against George Wallace of Alabama; chairman, U.S.-Canadian International Joint Commission, dealing with common waterway problems (1966-1970); member, Indianapolis law firm (1965-); co-chairman, State Constitutional Revision Commission (1967-1972); Democratic candidate for governor (1972); and author, *View from the State House: Recollections and Reflections* (1981).

The collection contains Welsh's papers as governor, including his correspondence on local and national issues, his correspondence with Indiana's congressional delegation on state needs, reports and budgets of state agencies and commissions, legislation, speeches, schedules, press releases, newspaper clippings, recommendations, appointments, and awards; correspondence, surveys, financial records, and other papers relating to the Indiana Democratic Party (1961-1965), particularly papers relating to Roger Branigin's 1964 campaign for governor, and Welsh's campaign against George Wallace in the 1964 presidential primary; correspondence, reports, meeting minutes, publications, clippings, and other papers relating to the Interstate Oil Compact Commission (1961-1964), particularly regarding cooperation between businesses and state regulatory agencies on the conservation of oil and natural gas; papers of the U.S.-Canadian International Joint Commission, particularly relating to the pollution of the Great Lakes (1966-1970); correspondence, speeches, press releases, and other papers relating to his 1972 campaign for governor against Otis Bowen; papers relating to his 1960 campaign for governor, and to the

1960 Democratic presidential primary and general election campaigns; his speeches, press releases, and other papers as U.S. attorney for the Southern District of Indiana, as Indiana State Senator, and as unsuccessful candidate for the 1956 Democratic nomination for governor; vouchers, orders, and other papers relating to his service in the U.S. Navy and Naval Reserve (1943-1950s); and materials collected for Welsh's book *View from the State House*. Also included are photographs, videotapes, films, and audiotapes (1956-1972); and papers relating to Birch Bayh's 1976 presidential campaign.

Correspondents include E. Ross Adair, Birch Bayh, John Brademas, William G. Bray, Edmund G. Brown, Donald C. Bruce, Earl Butz, Winfield K. Denton, Vance Hartke, Ralph Harvey, Lyndon B. Johnson, Robert F. Kennedy, Ray J. Madden, Nelson A. Rockefeller, George Romney, Richard Roudebush, J. Edward Roush, and Earl Wilson.

B-370. WESLER, CHARLES H. (b.1866). COLLECTION, 1830-1846, 1937-1949.

29 items. S 2328.

Wesler was a resident of Batesville, Ripley Co., and involved in the campaign to restore the Whitewater Canal.

The collection contains receipts and business correspondence of George Tousey, a Lawrenceburg, Dearborn Co., merchant (1830-1846); and Wesler's writings, including his reminiscences of the Whitewater Canal as a young man in Lawrenceburg, and his history of the canal and canal floods (1937-1949).

B-371. WESTERN ASSOCIATION OF WRITERS. PAPERS, 1891-1907.

1 ms. box. L 217.

The Western Association of Writers was founded in Indiana in 1886 in order to promote the work of writers in the Midwest and West, and to encourage and assist in the development of young writers. Members included James Whitcomb Riley, Maurice Thompson, and Lew Wallace.

The collection consists principally of the correspondence of members George S. Cottman and Amos W. Butler regarding meetings and programs of the association. Also included are programs, constitution and bylaws, and newspaper clippings about the association.

Correspondents include Ida Mae Davis, William P. Fishback, Eli Lilly, Benjamin S. Parker, John Clark Ridpath, and William H. Venable.

B-372. WETHERILL, CHARLES MAYER (1825-1871). PAPERS, 1817-1863.

66 items.   S 1387.

Wetherill was a chemist in Philadelphia (1840s-1850s); resident of Lafayette, Tippecanoe Co. (1857-1862); chemist, U.S. Department of Agriculture (1862) and the Smithsonian Institute, Washington, D.C. (1863-1866); and professor of chemistry, Lehigh University, Pa. (1866-1871).

The papers include letters to Wetherill in Washington from residents of Lafayette regarding the work of the Lafayette Union Club in combating disloyalty during the Civil War (1862-1863); Wetherill's journal and receipts from his trip from New York City to Niagara Falls, Montreal, and New England (1844-1845); letters of advice from Charles Wetherill, Philadelphia, to his brother William, a student at Mount Airy, Pa. (1817-1818); and broadsides and other printed documents of the Union Club (1862-1863).

B-373. WHARTON, WILLIAM L. (b.1851). PAPERS, 1855-1886.

49 items.   S 1388.

Wharton was a student at Indiana Asbury University (DePauw University), Greencastle, Putnam Co. (1871-1877); student at Indiana University Medical School, Bloomington (1880-1882); and physician in Matthews (New Cumberland), Grant Co. (1880s).

The papers include letters to Wharton from his family in Marion, Grant Co., and other places while he was a student at Indiana Asbury; letters from Indiana Asbury students to his father, William Wharton, a retired farmer in Marion (1870s); and an 1855 letter from Clark County.

B-374. WHITE, THOMAS R. (1869-1973). PAPERS, 1938-1940.

27 items.   S 1394.

White was a Presbyterian minister in Indianapolis (1920-1934); and chaplain, Indiana Reformatory, Pendleton, Madison Co. (1934-1946).

The collection includes letters to White from inmates and former inmates of the Indiana Reformatory (1938-1939); and an annual report of his activities as chaplain (1940).

B-375. WHITMER, JACOB (d.1927). PAPERS, 1927-1930.

2 folders.   S 1398.

Whitmer was a farmer near Shelbyville, Shelby Co.

The collection contains correspondence, inventories, expense sheets, and other papers relating to the administration of Whitmer's estate (1927-1930); and papers on Indiana plants, churches, and other local topics (1920s).

B-376. WILDER, JOHN THOMAS (1830-1917). PAPERS, 1858-1884.

3 folders.   S 2600.

Soldier and businessman. Wilder was a mill operator in Greensburg, Decatur Co. (1852-1860); lieutenant colonel, colonel, and brigadier general during the Civil War; commander of the 17th Indiana Regiment (1862-1865) and Wilder's Brigade in Tennessee (1862-1865); and built and operated Roane Iron Works at Rockwood, Tenn. (1867-1917).

The collection consists principally of Wilder's Civil War correspondence, including letters from his wife in Greensburg (1861-1864) and relatives at Lawrenceburg, Dearborn Co. (1858-1862); correspondence regarding the operations of his regiment and brigade; correspondence pertaining to the political situation in Indiana and Washington, D.C., during the war; orders and other official military documents; and topographical maps. Also included is correspondence regarding his ironworks in Tennessee and his involvement with veterans organizations.

Correspondents include Schuyler Colfax, William S. Holman, Henry S. Lane, Robert H. Milroy, Oliver P. Morton, and W. H. H. Terrell.

B-377. WILEY FAMILY. PAPERS, 1845-1912.

3 folders.   Inventory.   S 1410.

The Wiley family included James Jerome Wiley (1822-1894), a farmer and sawmill operator at Metamora, Franklin Co.; and his father, James Wiley (1795-1874), a Metamora farmer.

The papers include indentures, tax receipts, and other business papers of the Wiley family (1845-1890), and newspapers and publications (1845-1912).

B-378. WILLIAMS, CHARLES T. (d.1930?). PAPERS, 1897-1931.

1 ms. box, 7 vols. (1.25 l.f.).   L 177, V 204.

Williams was an Indianapolis attorney.

The collection consists principally of records of Williams's law practice from the period 1922-1930, including letter books, receipt books, account books, and copies of papers filed in the Marion County Probate Court. Also included are estate papers for the Hightshoe family of Marion County (1900-1917).

B-379. WILLIAMS CREEK BAPTIST CHURCH. RECORDS, 1832-1940.

1 ms. box.   L 342.

The Williams Creek Regular Baptist Church was located in Harrison Twp., Fayette Co.; the church property was sold in 1940.

The records consist of minutes of the church meetings, 1832-1940, containing reports on church activities and church members.

B-380. WILLIAMSPORT DEBATING SOCIETY. RECORDS, 1840-1861.

35 items. S 2845.

The society was active in Williamsport, Warren Co., from 1840 to 1843; its members debated current issues and held mock legislatures.

The records include constitution and minutes of the society (1840-1843); constitution, articles of agreement, and minutes of the Williamsport McClure Workingmen's Institute (1857-1861); constitution of the Williamsport Young Men's Literary Association (1858); and court documents for a Warren County case (1858).

B-381. WILLIS, RAYMOND E. (1875-1956). PAPERS, 1936-1950.

3 ms. boxes. Calendar. L 179.

Politician and newspaperman. Willis was editor and publisher of the *Angola* (Steuben Co.) *Magnet* (1898-1907) and the *Angola Steuben Republican* (1907-1938); president, Steuben Printing Company (1925-1941, 1947-ca.1956); Republican member, Indiana House of Representatives (1919-1921); Republican candidate for U.S. Senate (1938, 1940); and U.S. Senator from Indiana (1941-1947).

The collection consists principally of Willis's political correspondence from the period 1938-1947, particularly correspondence regarding his campaigns for nomination and election as U.S. Senator (1938, 1940, 1946). Also contained are papers as U.S. Senator, including correspondence regarding the Cannelton Flood Control Project, U.S. relations with Yugoslavia, and other issues; his voting records (1941-1944); papers regarding his appointments to the service academies; and a scrapbook of newspaper stories about Sen. Sherman Minton, Willis's Democratic opponent in the 1940 election (1938-1940).

Correspondents include Dean Acheson, Bert Andrews, Court Asher, William G. Bray, Hugh Butler, Ralph F. Gates, James P. Goodrich, Charles A. Halleck,

Warren T. McCray, Felix M. McWhirter, Arthur R. Robinson, Arthur Vandenberg, and James E. Watson.

B-382. WILLOUGHBY, AURELIUS (1843?-1922). PAPERS, 1861-1917.

1 ms. box.   L 303.

Willoughby was regimental quartermaster for the 39th Indiana Regiment (8th Indiana Cavalry), serving in Tennessee, Kentucky, Alabama, Georgia, and North Carolina (1861-1865); U.S. Internal Revenue agent in northeastern Georgia (1866-1868); and merchant in Vincennes, Knox Co. (1868-1922).

The collection consists principally of Willoughby's Civil War diaries (1861-1865). Also included are discharge papers, memorabilia, and personal business papers (1864-1917); and a manuscript history of Company H, 39th Indiana (ca.1910).

B-383. WILSON, WILLIAM (d.1920). DIARIES, 1881-1920.

16 vols. (.75 l.f.).   V 156.

Wilson was a farmer in Frankfort, Clinton Co.

Wilson's diaries include descriptions of farm life, social activities, and economic conditions; and his personal financial accounts.

B-384. WILSON, WILLIAM T. (1854-1943). PAPERS, 1817-1942.

3 ms. boxes, 10 vols. (2 l.f.).   L 315, V 222.

Wilson was a Logansport, Cass Co., attorney (1875-1930s); assistant in law office of Daniel D. Pratt (1875-1876); and member, board of directors, First National Bank of Logansport (1877-1930s). Wilson was the son of Logansport merchant Thomas H. Wilson (1818-1877), founder with Phillip Pollard of the mercantile firm of Pollard & Wilson in Logansport (1840); and president of the Logansport National Bank (1865-1877).

The collection consists of papers of William T. Wilson, Thomas H. Wilson, and Daniel D. Pratt. William T. Wilson papers include an account book for his law firm (1877-1898); and his correspondence, writings, and collected papers (1817-1942) regarding the history of the Presbyterian church in Logansport and Cass County, and Presbyterian minister Martin M. Post (d.1876). Thomas H. Wilson papers contain an account book, business correspondence, and financial papers of the firm of Pollard and Wilson (1840s-1850s), including business letters from Samuel Rees in Connersville, Fayette Co., and Des Moines, Iowa (1853-1855); and papers relating to the Logansport National Bank (1865-1870s). Daniel D. Pratt papers include account books for his legal practice in Logansport (1843-1874); correspondence between Pratt in Washington, D.C., and W. T. Wilson in Logansport regarding Pratt's legal and personal business (1875-1876); papers pertaining to Pratt's legal and personal business (1840-1870s); and papers relating to the administration of Pratt's estate (1881-1902). Also included are papers relating to land and business dealings in Connersville, Fayette Co. (1817-1830s); and legal depositions relating to the property of the Barron family in Logansport (1926-1927).

Correspondents include George W. Ewing and Allen Hamilton.

B-385. WINCHESTER, JOHN S. (1819-1898). PAPERS, 1863-1895.

2 folders.   S 1442.

Winchester was a Methodist Episcopal preacher in southeastern Indiana, particularly in the Greensburg, Decatur Co., area (1842-1898).

The collection includes letters to Winchester from family members in Franklin, Johnson Co., Carthage, Rush Co., and Pope County, Ill., regarding family business and religion (1863-1873); and invitations, announcements, and other social materials (1871-1895).

B-386. WINTIN, GENDRON M. (1894-1962). NOTEBOOKS, 1932-ca.1962.

1 ms. box.   L 274.

Wintin was president and curator of the Shelby County Historical Museum.

The collection consists of her notebooks on Shelby County history and family history, including copies of newspaper stories and reminiscences on Shelby County in the nineteenth century.

B-387. WOLCOTT, ANSON (1819-1907). PAPERS, 1870-1876.

30 items. S 1447.

Wolcott was a lawyer, businessman, and land speculator from New York; founder of Wolcott, White Co. (1858); Republican member, Indiana State Senate (1867-1869); and active in Greenback Party (1876).

The collection consists principally of correspondence, depositions, and other papers relating to Wolcott's claims against the U.S. government for the loss of his steamship "Fawn" during the Civil War (1870-1873). Also included is a printed circular explaining his reasons for refusing the Greenback nomination for governor (1876).

B-388. WOLFF, HERMAN CLARK (1890-1955). PAPERS, 1898-1910.

3 folders. S 2692.

Wolff was a graduate of Wabash College, Crawfordsville, Montgomery Co. (1910); a student at Harvard University, Mass. (1910); and insurance executive in Indianapolis.

The papers contain letters to Wolff in Indianapolis from his grandfather, Julius T. Clark, in Topeka, Kans. (1898-1907); letters from his fiancee, Florence Flickinger, in Indianapolis (1909-1910); papers relating to his time at Wabash College; and dance programs, theater tickets, and other social materials (1906-1910).

B-389. WOMAN'S RELIEF CORPS. INDIANA DEPARTMENT. GEORGE H. THOMAS POST #20. RECORDS, 1885-1943.

2 archival boxes. L 216.

The Woman's Relief Corps was the women's auxiliary to the Civil War veterans' organization, the Grand Army of the Republic. The corps provided relief for Union veterans and their families, contributed to programs for Spanish-American War and World War I soldiers, sponsored scholarships, and promoted patriotism. The George H. Thomas Post #20, based in Indianapolis, disbanded in 1942.

The records include the post's minute books (1891-1935), cashbooks (1886-1942), ledgers (1885-1932), letter books (1885-1889, 1900), membership rolls (1885-1939), and general orders issued from the state headquarters (1885-1909, 1922-1923).

B-390. WOODFILL, JAMES M. (b.1854). ACCOUNT BOOKS, 1889-1914.

9 vols. (1.75 l.f.). V 231.

Woodfill owned a men's clothing store in Greensburg, Decatur Co. (1889-1897). After his retirement in 1897, his sons operated the store under the name J. M. Woodfill's Sons.

The collection consists of the store's account books (1889-1914).

B-391. WOODWARD, WILLIAM (fl.1847-1848). LETTERS, 1847-1848.

24 items. Calendar. S 1453.

Woodward was a store clerk in Michigan City, LaPorte Co. (1847-1848), and South Bend, St. Joseph Co. (1848).

The collection consists of Woodward's letters to his family in Middleton, Conn., describing his trip from Connecticut to Indiana by way of Buffalo, N.Y., and Cleveland, Ohio, and describing conditions in Indiana.

B-392. WORKMAN, HAZEL (fl.1936-1965). COLLECTION, 1846-1936.

65 items. S 1457.

Workman, a resident of Indianapolis, donated this collection to the Indiana State Library in 1965.

The collection consists principally of receipts, land documents, and personal documents (1854-1895) of James L. Kyte (b.1831) of Hendricks County and Indianapolis.

B-393. WRIGHT, ANNA W. (d.1931). COLLECTION, 1855-1911.

4 vols., 3 folders, (.75 l.f.).   S 2444, V 212.

Wright was the daughter of Jacob T. Wright (1816-1891), an Indianapolis businessman and chairman of the Republican State Central Committee (1864-1868).

The collection includes letters to Gov. Oliver P. Morton pertaining to the recruitment of black troops for Indiana regiments during the Civil War (1861-1864); papers of the Union State Central Committee, an Indianapolis Republican organization (1864-1866); letters from Oliver P. Morton to Jacob Wright regarding the 1868 Republican National Convention (1866-1868); family letters of Jacob Wright (1855-1860s); letters from national politicians to Louis T. Michener responding to his requests for them to speak in Indiana during the 1890 election campaign; account books for the George Tomlinson general merchandise store in Southport, Marion Co. (1855-1858); a scrapbook of programs, clippings, correspondence, and photographs of the Girls' Classical School of Indianapolis, particularly materials relating to its principal, May Wright Sewall (1891-1906); and scrapbooks of late nineteenth-century newspaper clippings.

Correspondents include William B. Allison, Albert J. Beveridge, Charles A. Boutelle, John Coburn, Shelby M. Cullom, Will Cumback, William P. Fishback, Robert M. LaFollette, William H. H. Miller, Oliver P. Morton, L. E. Payson, Gilbert A. Pierce, Preston B. Plumb, Thomas B. Reed, John C. Spooner, W. H. H. Terrell, Richard W. Thompson, and Daniel W. Voorhees.

B-394. WRIGHT, JOSEPH ALBERT (1810-1867). PAPERS, 1843-1931.

2 ms. boxes.   L 183.

Politician and diplomat. Wright was an attorney in Rockville, Parke Co.; Democratic member, Indiana House of Representatives (1833-1834, 1836-

1837) and the Indiana State Senate (1839-1840); member, U.S. House of Representatives (1843-1845); governor of Indiana (1849-1857); U.S. Minister to Prussia (1857-1861, 1865-1867); Republican after 1861; and member, U.S. Senate (1862-1863).

The collection includes letters to Wright in Washington from his family in Rockville (1843-1844); letters from his district regarding local and national politics (1844); letters to Wright as Indiana governor regarding appointments, railroad development, the Indiana State Bank, criminal cases, agricultural societies, and politics (1849-1857); letters to him as minister to Prussia (1857-1861), including letters from Americans traveling in Europe, and letters from American diplomats; letters to him as U.S. Senator (1862-1863) regarding appointments and local politics; and programs, invitations, and other social and diplomatic materials from his time in Prussia. The collection also contains family correspondence of Wright's son, Albert J. Wright, a general merchandise dealer in Sparta, Oreg. (1891-1931), particularly letters from his brother, John C. Wright, an Indianapolis businessman (1916-1925); and a partial biography of Joseph A. Wright (ca.1906).

Correspondents include Conrad Baker, George Bancroft, John C. Breckenridge, James Buchanan, Nahum Capen, Lewis Cass, Salmon P. Chase, Schuyler Colfax, Francis Costigan, George M. Dallas, William H. English, Edward Everett, Allen Hamilton, Thomas A. Hendricks, William S. Holman, Erastus Hopkins, Alvin P. Hovey, Andrew Johnson, Henry S. Lane, Joseph Lane, John Law, James R. McDonald, John Y. Mason, Catherine Merrill, Oliver P. Morton, Charles Nordhoff, David Dale Owen, Daniel G. Read, Addison Roache, Richard Rush, William H. Seward, and Alexander W. Thayer.

B-395. WRIGHT, WILLIAMSON (1814-1896). PAPERS, 1837-1865.

23 items.   S 1465.

Wright was a lawyer in Logansport, Cass Co. (1835-1896); Whig member, Indiana State Senate (1840-1843); and director, Lake Michigan, Logansport, and Ohio River Railroad Company.

The papers include correspondence regarding Wright's legal business, particularly correspondence regarding his cases involving Indian claims, roads, railroads, and canals and canal lands; political correspondence regarding issues before the Indiana General Assembly and Whig and Republican Party politics; and correspondence relating to his involvement with railroad companies.

Correspondents include Schuyler Colfax, Graham N. Fitch, Daniel D. Pratt, John Sherman, and Cyrus Vigus.

B-396. WYATT, ROBERT H. (1903-1975). PAPERS, 1921-1970.

7 l.f.
Restricted.

Educator. Wyatt was a teacher in the Noble County and Fort Wayne, Allen Co., schools (1920-1938); president, Fort Wayne Teachers Association (1931-1935); president, Indiana State Federation of Public School Teachers (1935-1938); executive secretary, Indiana State Teachers Assocation (1938-1971); and president, National Education Association (1964).

The collection consists principally of papers relating to the Indiana State Teachers Association. Included are transcripts of the ISTA annual general and business sessions (1921-1929); and papers regarding the work of ISTA from the period 1948-1970, including papers dealing with the construction of the ISTA building in Indianapolis (1956), school financing and government aid, teachers' benefits, integration of the Indianapolis schools, and ISTA positions on state and federal legislation concerning education. The collection also contains Wyatt's speeches; clippings and press releases; materials relating to educational conferences and Wyatt's 1962 campaign for NEA president; and his personal correspondence (1968-1970).

B-397. YANDES, DANIEL (d.1877). PAPERS, 1833-1891.

ca.70 items.   Inventory.   S 1479.

Yandes was associated with his uncle, Daniel Yandes (1793-1878) in Yandes & Company, a wholesale dealer in hides and leathers in Indianapolis.

The collection consists primarily of Yandes family correspondence from the period 1833-1869, including letters from Yandes and his brother, Lafayette Yandes, in Indianapolis, to his sister, Anne Hampson, in Fairfield County,

Ohio (1836-1861); letters from Lafayette Yandes's wife and widow from Havana, Cuba, and Indianapolis (1850); and correspondence of the Hampson family in Birmingham and Centerville, Iowa (1855-1869).

B-398. ZIG ZAG CYCLE CLUB. RECORDS, 1895-1897.

1 ms. box. L 218.

The club started as the Indianapolis Cycle Club in 1895 and became the Zig Zag Cycle Club in 1896. The club promoted bicycle outings and races; provided social activities for cyclists; and lobbied on behalf of better roads.

The records include club minutes (1895-1897); register of members; a copy of the club's proposed legislation on improving state roads; and clippings and pictures on bicycle events.

B-399. ZION, ROGER H. (1921-). PAPERS, 1966-1974.

76 archival boxes. Inventory.

Politician. Zion was an employee of Mead Johnson & Company (1945-1966), director of sales training and professional relations (1965-1966); international marketing consultant for the city of Evansville (1966); Republican member, U.S. House of Representatives (1967-1975), member of House committees on Public Works, Internal Security, International Trade Task Force, and chairman of the Energy and Resources Task Force; and author, *Keys to Human Relations in Selling* (1963).

The collection consists of Zion's congressional papers (1967-1974), particularly constituent correspondence regarding abortion, civil rights, busing, environmental protection, inflation, firearms control, crime, the impeachment of Richard Nixon, the seating of Rep. Adam Clayton Powell, and other political and social issues; correspondence and papers relating to the War in Vietnam, including anti-war protests, the My Lai massacre, American prisoners of war, and Zion's trip to Paris with other congressmen to discuss the release of American prisoners with the North Vietnamese (1970-1971); correspondence and papers relating to other federal legislation, programs, and agencies, including programs relating to railroads, mining, trucking, agriculture, flood control, improvements in the Wabash Valley watershed, revenue sharing, Medicare, the Alaska Pipeline, national defense, the work of the Department of Health, Education and Welfare (HEW) and the Department of Housing and Urban Development (HUD), and work programs such as Manpower Administration, Job Corps, and the Office of Economic Opportunity; correspondence regarding constituent problems and requests; campaign papers, including information on contributions; newsletters; and recommendations on positions.

NOTES ON INDEX USAGE

The alpha-numerical entries in this index refer to the collection designations used in this guide rather than page numbers. "A" before a number indicates it is an Indiana Historical Society collection, while "B" means it is found in the Indiana State Library. Included are listings for collections, individuals and corporations, places, and major subject headings.

Collection names are indicated by all caps, and the specific location is listed first and italicized. Specific businesses, law firms, etc., are listed individually with the location (when known) in parenthesis. Names of books are italicized while printed articles and essays are in quotations.

Indiana cities and towns are listed both individually and by county; for example, Lafayette is listed as Lafayette, Tippecanoe County, and Tippecanoe County-Lafayette. Because of the large number of references under Indianapolis, it is located only under the city and not under Marion County. Non-Indiana cities are listed only under their state or foreign countries. States and foreign countries are organized by general references, subjects, or events, followed by cities or counties.

In order to accommodate a broad range of subject search strategies, subject indexing was done hierarchically, with broad terms subdivided by narrow terms. To locate material on a topic, identify the likely broad term from the list below, and then check the subdivisions for related headings. For example, materials on blacksmiths may be found under "Business—blacksmiths," and the references for canals may be found by searching under "Transportation—canals." It may be of additional help for the user to know that Indiana and United States governments are grouped by executive, judicial, and legislative branches, while Civil War references are listed by individual regiments and subjects, as well as a separate entry under the individual states from where the letters were written or the events occurred. Some of the larger subject references, such as family life and politics, are divided chronologically by the following dates: -1815; 1816-1849; 1850-1879; 1880-1909; 1910-1945; 1946- . Business is organized by both type (hotels, general stores, etc.) and dates.

Listed below are the major subject headings.

Abolition	Labor and Trades
Agriculture	Land
American Revolution	Law
Archaeology and Anthropology	Libraries
	Literature and Drama
Architecture	Maps
Art	Medicine
Autographs	Mexican War
Banking, Finance, & Economics	Music
Blacks	Newspapers
Business	Northwest Territory
Civil War	Organizations
Communalism	Politics
Communications	Publishing
Conservation	Religion
Crime	Science
Diaries	Slavery
Education	Spanish-American War
Engineering	Temperance and Prohibition
Entertainment	
Family Life	Transportation
Genealogy	Travel Accounts
Historic Preservation	United States Government
History and Biography	Vietnam War
Humor	War of 1812
Immigrants	Welfare and Correction
Indiana	Women
Indiana State Government	World War I
Indianapolis	World War II
Indians	

INDEX

A.D. COOK COMPANY (Lawrenceburg): *A-1*
A & P Grocery Store (Kokomo): B-142
Abbott, James: B-119
ABERNATHY, JOHN: *A-2*
Abolition: A-53, A-83, A-101, A-111, A-342, A-363, B-28, B-117
ABORN, MARY J.: *B-1*
Acheson, Dean: B-381
Ackerman family: B-354
Acton, Marion Co.: B-221
ADAIR, E. ROSS: *B-2*, B-24, B-130, B-369
Adair, John A. M.: B-19, B-113
Adamic, Louis: B-208, B-219
Adams, Herbert Baxter: A-341
Adams, John: A-250, A-272
Adams, John Quincy: A-272
Adams, John T.: B-218
Adams, K. C.: B-110
ADAMS, MARCELLUS M.: *A-3*
Adams, Thomas H.: B-114
Adams County: A-143, B-109
Adamsboro, Cass Co.: B-185
Addams, Jane: A-172, B-345
Addresses and Speeches of Abraham Brick: B-44
Ade, George: A-272, A-315, A-322, A-358, B-124, B-147, B-208, B-259, B-345
Adkins, Alphonso: A-9
Afflis, Margaret — see JOHNSTON, MARGARET AFFLIS
Afflis, William F. ("Dick the Bruiser"): B-203
Africa: B-143
Agriculture:
   -1815: A-237, A-261, A-374, A-392, B-32
   1816-1849: A-4, A-37, A-51, A-111, A-131, A-171, A-207, A-237, A-261, A-264, A-265, A-270, A-321, A-328, A-355, A-374, A-392, A-398, B-22, B-26, B-27, B-28, B-32, B-39, B-86, B-112, B-135, B-229, B-247, B-315, B-325, B-394

   1815-1879: A-4, A-10, A-17, A-19, A-28, A-48, A-51, A-63, A-90, A-104, A-111, A-131, A-135, A-138, A-157, A-171, A-207, A-227, A-238, A-247, A-259, A-264, A-265, A-270, A-295, A-321, A-328, A-355, A-356, A-374, A-396, B-22, B-26, B-27, B-28, B-32, B-35, B-39, B-81, B-91, B-112, B-135, B-150, B-154, B-155, B-185, B-197, B-226, B-229, B-247, B-314, B-325, B-329, B-338, B-353, B-394
   1880-1909: A-4, A-17, A-28, A-48, A-49, A-104, A-157, A-217, A-247, A-259, A-265, A-292, A-295, A-296, A-313, A-321, A-355, A-374, A-396, B-22, B-26, B-28, B-29, B-32, B-35, B-85, B-87, B-90, B-91, B-112, B-154, B-155, B-185, B-197, B-226, B-247, B-329, B-338, B-353, B-360, B-383
   1910-1945: A-17, A-49, A-74, A-231, A-247, A-295, A-296, B-22, B-26, B-28, B-61, B-85, B-90, B-185, B-200, B-209, B-226, B-239, B-353, B-360, B-375, B-383
   1946-: A-231, B-61, B-185
Aid to Soldiers' Families: A-156
AIKEN, OLIVER PERRY: *A-4*
Akron, Fulton Co.: B-268
Alabama: B-37
   Civil War: A-21, A-213, B-146, B-298, B-322, B-353, B-358, B-382
   Birmingham: B-243
   Mobile (Civil War): A-88, A-106, B-322
Alabama Power Commission: B-243
Alaska: A-102, A-336, B-361
Albion, Noble Co.: A-26
Aldrich, William: A-341
Alice Home Hospital (Lake Forest, Ill.): A-337

425

Allan, Chilton: A-91
ALLEN, EDWARD B.: *A-5*
Allen County: A-181, B-137
   Fort Wayne: A-40, A-132, A-141, A-163, A-187, A-237, A-286, A-384, A-387, A-407, B-2, B-3, B-23, B-108, B-119, B-137, B-167, B-212, B-222, B-231, B-241, B-286, B-324, B-345, B-351
   Harlan: A-39, B-293
ALLIANCE AMUSEMENT COMPANY (Chicago): *B-3*
Allison, William B.: A-302, B-393
Allison, Young: A-112
Altgeld, John P.: B-240
Alton, Mt. Carmel & New Albany Railroad: B-285
ALTROCCHI, JULIA COOLEY: *B-4*, B-11
Ambia, Benton Co.: B-300
Amboy, Miami Co.: A-49
American Association of University Women: B-65
American Bar Association: B-275, B-345
American Bell Telephone Company: B-345
American Bicycle Company (Indianapolis): B-189
American Committee on United Europe: B-275
American Corporation for Investors: A-337
American Friends Service Committee: A-49
American Fur Company: B-119
American Home Missionary Society: B-146
American Hotel Association: B-77
American Jewish Relief Committee: A-309
American Lung Association: A-6
AMERICAN LUNG ASSOCIATION OF CENTRAL INDIANA: *B-5*
AMERICAN LUNG ASSOCIATION OF INDIANA: *A-6*
AMERICAN NEGRO EMANCIPATION CENTENNIAL AUTHORITY, INDIANA DIVISION: *B-6*

American Nurses Association: A-186
American Peace Society: A-112
American Planing and Civic Association: B-219
American Poetry Magazine: B-51
American Red Cross: A-7, A-12, A-84, A-112, B-145, B-147, B-268, B-361
AMERICAN RED CROSS, INDIANAPOLIS AREA CHAPTER: *A-7*, A-112
American Revolution: A-8, A-16, A-101, A-286, A-287, B-84, B-212
   Illinois Campaign: A-101, A-286
   quartermaster corps: A-287
   veterans claims: A-8, A-303, A-369, A-384
   7th Virginia Regiment: A-303
   8th Virginia Regiment: A-101
American Rights Committee: B-267
American Settlement (Indianapolis): B-296
American Settlement Day Nursery (Indianapolis): B-237
American Society of Civil Engineers: A-108
American Sunday School Union: B-146
America's Debt to England: B-342
America's Natural Wealth: B-219
Americus, Tippecanoe Co.: B-23
Ames, Oakes: B-286
Amity, Johnson Co.: B-47
ANDERSON, CALEB H.R.: *B-7*, B-15
Anderson, John T.: B-7
Anderson, Madison Co.: A-268, A-302, A-324, A-340, B-3, B-69, B-81, B-148, B-360, B-361, B-362
Anderson *Herald:* B-362
Anderson High School: B-362
Anderson Township Progressive Club (Madison Co.): B-360
Andover Seminary (Vt.): B-165
ANDREW & COOKE, (Darlington): *B-8*
Andrews, Bert: B-381
Andrews, Ethan: B-285
Angola, Stuben Co.: B-381
Anthony, Susan B.: B-76
Anti-Saloon League: B-147
Appeal to Reason: A-312

INDEX

Arcadia, Hamilton Co.: B-324
Archaeology and Anthropology: A-346, A-393
Architecture: A-98, A-319, A-320, A-400
Arizona: A-59
Arkansas: A-288, B-92
　Civil War: A-85, A-143, A-234, A-259, B-285, B-314, B-322
　White County: A-318
Armes, Thomas: B-329
ARMSTRONG, JOHN: *A-8*, A-147, A-272, A-286
ARMSTRONG, JOHN H.: *A-9*
Armstrong, Tabitha — see Lockhart, Tabitha Armstrong
Armstrong, William G.: A-8
Armstrong, William G., Jr.: A-8
Art: A-128, A-157, A-178, A-237, B-14, B-208, B-213, B-217, B-275, B-306, B-333, B-341, B-344
Arthur, Chester: A-272
ARTHUR, CHRISTOPHER: *B-9*
Arthur, Joseph: B-341
Asher, Court: B-334, B-381
Ashley, Dekalb Co.: B-23
Ashton, Samuel A.: A-10
ASHTON, WILLIAM A.: *A-10*
Asia: B-143, B-147
Askern, Thomas: B-290
Askin, John: A-384
Associated Press: A-341
Astor, William B.: A-351
"At Death of Debs": B-96
ATALANTIAN JOURNAL, 1845-1848: *A-11*
Atlantic Ocean: A-54
Attica, Fountain Co.: A-23, A-140, A-251, A-407, B-71, B-169
Auburn Theological Seminary (New York): B-146
Audubon Society: A-336
Aupaument, Hendrick: A-83, A-393
Aurora, Dearborn Co.: A-67, A-334, A-399, B-71, B-161
Austin and Northwestern Railroad: A-146
Australia: A-317, B-100
Austria: A-216
Autographs: A-232, A-272, B-249

Ave Maria: B-51
Ayres, Elias: A-152
AYRES, FREDERIC MURRAY: *A-12*, B-145

Bacon, Albion Fellows: B-76
Bacon, Leonard W.: B-111
Bacon, Walter R.: B-339
Badollet, John: A-282, A-384, B-263
Badollet, Margaret — see Caldwell, Margaret Badollet
BAILEY, ELISHA T.: *A-13*
BAILEY, LOUIS J.: *B-10*, B-66
BAILEY, SARAH: *A-14*
BAILLY DE MESSIN, JOSEPH: *B-11*, B-4, B-167
Bailly, Mother Mary Cecilia: B-167
Bailly, Rose — see Howe, Rose Bailly
Bailly Nuclear Reactor: B-211
BAINBRIDGE, EUGENE: *B-12*
Bainbridge, Phillip: B-12
Bainbridge, Putnam Co.: A-72, A-231
Bainbridge Gravel Road Company: A-231
Bainbridge Supply Company (Lake Co.): B-12
Baird, Samuel: A-302, B-212
BAKER, CHARLES T.: *B-13*
BAKER, CONRAD: *A-15*, A-57, A-237, A-266, A-272, A-381, A-383, B-114, B-153, B-286, B-345, B-348, B-394
BAKER, EVAN: *A-16*
BAKER, HENRY: *A-17*
BAKER, IDA STRAWN: *B-14*
Baker, John H.: A-52
Baker, Ray Stannard: A-176
Baker, William: A-15
Baker, Hord & Hendricks (Indianapolis): A-15
Baldwin, Roger: B-96
BALL, TIMOTHY HORTON: *A-18*
Ball Brothers Company (Muncie): B-301
"Ballad of Gene Debs": B-96
Ballard, Bertha — see BERTHA BALLARD HOME ASSOCIATION
BALLARD, MRS. CHARLES W.: *B-15*
Ballard, William H.: A-31
Baltimore and Ohio Southwestern (Railway) Company: A-276

BALTZELL, ROBERT C.: *B-16*
BALZ, ARCADA (Mrs. Frederick): *B-17*, B-176
Bancroft, George: A-272, B-394
Bank of Vincennes: A-302
Banking, Finance, & Economics: A-8, A-42, A-101, A-103, A-111, A-123, A-165, A-171, A-229, A-258, A-266, A-267, A-302, A-337, A-376, A-381, A-401, A-410, B-112, B-137, B-147, B-167, B-246, B-287, B-299, B-310, B-321 B-351, B-384
Banks, Charles E.: A-312
Banks, Nathaniel P.: A-346
BANTA, ROBERT M.: *A-19*
Banta, W. A.: B-19
BAPTIST CHURCH. LAUGHERY ASSOCIATION: *A-20*
Baptist Church-History — see CHURCH HISTORY-BAPTIST
Baptist Church, Williams Creek — see WILLIAMS CREEK BAPTIST CHURCH
Barbour, James: A-147, B-351
Barbour, John J.: B-348
Barkely, Alben W.: B-20
BARKER, ISAAC: *A-21*
BARNARD, HARRY EVERETT: *A-22*
Barnard, Marion Harvie: A-22
Barnard, William O.: B-124
BARNES COLLECTION, 1833-1925: *A-23*
Barnett, Ambrose: B-18
Barnett, George: B-18
Barnett, Henry J.: B-18
Barnett, J. P.: B-18
BARNETT FAMILY: *B-18*
BARNHART, HENRY A.: *B-19*, B-20, B-335
BARNHART, HUGH A.: *B-20*
Barnum, W. H.: B-205
Barrett, George W.: B-16
Barrett, Joseph H.: A-341
Barron family: B-384
Barrymore, Lionel: A-327
Bartholomew, Frank: B-21
Bartholomew, Joseph: A-101, B-351
Bartholomew, Levi: B-21

BARTHOLOMEW, ORION: *B-21*
Bartholomew County: A-37, A-181, A-261, A-293
  Columbus: A-73, B-108, B-142
  Elizabethtown: A-77, B-41
  Hartsville: B-69, B-108
Bartlett, H. H.: B-95
BARTMESS, JACOB W.: *A-24*
Barton, Clara: A-237
Barton, Dante: B-110
Barton, John T.: B-22
BARTON, JOSEPH T.: *B-22*
Barton, William: B-119
Barton, William E.: A-176
Baruch, Bernard M.: B-259
Bates, Edward: B-119
BATES, HELEN S.: *B-23*
Bates, Hervey: A-111, A-267, A-307, B-252, B-299, B-351
Batesville, Ripley Co.: B-370
Battell, Charles I.: B-114
Bayard, John Francis: A-57
Bayard, Samuel: A-57
Bayard, Thomas Francis: B-124
Bayh, Birch: A-288, B-99, B-369
Bays, Lee: A-60
BEAMER, JOHN V.: *B-24*
Beard, Charles A.: B-219
BEARD, JOHN: *B-25*
BEARSS, DANIEL R.: *A-25, B-26*, A-408, B-119, B-351
Beck, Elias W. H.: B-295
Beck, Francis Milroy: B-295
Beck, Walter M.: B-295
Bedford, Lawrence Co.: A-76, A-94, A-117, A-369, B-164, B-195, B-326, B-348
Bedford Stone and Construction Company: A-309
Beech Grove, Marion Co.: A-63, A-342, B-85
Beecher, Catherine E.: A-111
Beecher, Henry Ward: A-272, A-275, A-381, B-111, B-146, B-273
BEECHER, JOHN SLOANE: *A-26*
Beecher, Truman: A-26
Beeler, Fielding: B-27
Beeler, George M.: B-27
BEELER, JOSEPH: *B-27*
BEEM, DAVID ENOCH: *A-27*

INDEX 429

Beeson, Benjamin: B-28
BEESON, ISAAC W.: *B-28*
BEESON, THOMAS: *A-28*
Beeson family: A-109
Beggs, James: B-37
Belgium: B-145
Belknap, William W.: B-286
BELL, ADDISON: *B-29*
Bell, John (1797-1869): A-272
BELL, JOHN (1816-1880): *B-30*
Bell, Lona — see McMullin, Lona Bell
BELLAMY, FLAVIUS: *B-31*
Belleville, Hendricks Co.: A-55
Ben Hur: A-391
Bence, Philip: B-32
BENCE, ROBERT: *A-29*
BENCE FAMILY PAPERS, 1790-1885: *B-32*
Benet, Stephen Vincent: A-391
Bennett, James Gordon: A-346
Benton, Thomas Hart: A-272, B-219
Benton, William P.: B-94
Benton County: A-295
  Ambia: B-300
  Fowler: A-295, B-3
Bergenroth Brothers (Troy): B-49
Bergman, Ingrid: B-147
Berrien, John M.: A-272
BERRYMAN, NELSON: *A-30*
Berryman, Thomas: A-30
Berst, Hiram F.: B-162
BERTHA BALLARD HOME ASSOCIATION (Indianapolis): *A-31*
BERTHIER, ALEXANDRE: *A-32*
Bethany, Parke Co.: A-88
Bethell, Eliza — see Warren, Eliza Bethell
Bethell, Thomas F.: A-33
Bethell, Union: A-33
BETHELL-WARREN FAMILY: *A-33*
Bethlehem, Clark Co.: A-8
Bethlehem (Carmel), Hamilton Co.: B-207
BEVAN, PHILIP: *A-34*
BEVERIDGE, ALBERT J.: *B-33*, A-52, A-68, A-102, A-148, A-176, A-272, A-322, A-336, A-358, B-43, B-44, B-84, B-85, B-114, B-124, B-147, B-216, B-250, B-259, B-335, B-339, B-342, B-345, B-393
BEVINGTON, ELIZABETH: *B-34*
Bickel family: B-285
Bicknell, George A.: A-52
Biddle, Horace P.: A-15, B-103, B-212, B-286
Biddle, Nicholas: A-272
Bidwell family: B-354
Bierce, Ambrose: B-208
Big Creek Ditching Company, White Co.: A-334
Big Springs Grange, Lawrence Co.: B-353
Bigger, James: B-212
Bigger, Samuel: A-272, B-263
BIGLER, NICODEMUS: *B-35*
Billings, Thomas M.: A-304
"Billy the Kid" — see Bonney, William H.
Bingham, Joseph: B-357
Bingham family: B-357
Birdseye, Dubios Co.: B-102
Birkbeck, Morris: A-198, A-302
Bizayon, Francois: B-212
Bizet, Georges: B-341
Black, Glenn: A-393
Black, Jeremiah: A-283
Blackford, Isaac: A-136, B-85, B-114, B-349
Blackford County: A-200, B-137
  Hartford City: B-204
  Montpelier: B-133
Blacks: A-64, A-105, A-153, A-177, A-188, A-268, A-271, A-316, A-390, A-404, B-6, B-101, B-194, B-356, B-393 — See also Slavery
Blackwell, Alice Stone: B-124
Blaine, James G.: A-52, A-164, A-302, A-341, A-391, B-254
Blair, Henry W.: B-348
Blair, Montgomery: A-272
BLAIR, WILLIAM WYLIE: *A-35*
BLAKE, JAMES S.: *B-36*, B-351
Blake, Thomas H.: A-91, B-137, B-252, B-351
Blaker, Eliza A.: B-342
Blanchard, John: A-266
Blanchard, Jonathan: A-286

Bland, Oscar E.: B-147, B-218
Bledsoe, Jesse: A-147
BLEDSOE FAMILY: *A-36*
Blennerhassett, Harman: A-272
Blethen, Alden J.: A-341
Bloomfield, Greene Co.: A-58
Bloomingsport, Randolph Co.: A-296
Bloomington, Monroe Co.: A-111,
    A-216, A-275, A-338, B-17,
    B-71, B-146, B-280, B-325,
    B-364, B-365 — See also Indiana
    University
Blount, Willie: A-272
Blue Bird Mining Company (Mont.):
    B-47
Blue Star Memorial Highway Award:
    B-127
Bluff Creek Gravel Road Company
    (Marion Co.): B-158
Bluffton, Wells Co.: B-95
Board of Women Managers (Indianapolis): A-188
BOAZ, MIGNON: *A-37*
Boaz, Simeon: A-37
Bobbs, William C.: B-114
Bohlen, Oscar: B-250
Bok, Edward: A-145, A-272, A-364,
    B-138
Boleman, White, and Wright Collection
    Agency — see White, Wright
    and Boleman Collection Agency
Bolivia: B-339
Bolling, Edith — see Wilson, Edith
    Bolling
Bolton, Herbert E.: B-219
Bolton, Sarah T.: A-150, A-334
Bonaparte, Charles J.: B-342, B-345
Bonaparte, Napoleon: A-32
Bond, Joshua: A-237
Bonney, William H. ("Billy the Kid"):
    A-391
Bonwell, Arthur: B-73
Bookplates: B-208
Boon, Ratliff: A-101, A-272, B-351
Boone, Victoria — see Douglass, Victoria Boone
Boone County
    Brown's Wonder Church: B-71
    Dover: A-88
    Eagle Village: A-245

Jamestown: B-52, B-108
    Lebanon: B-42, B-356, B-367
    Zionsville: A-368
Boone family: A-89
Booth, Evangeline: B-236
Booth, John Wilkes: B-341
Booth, Margaret — see Jameson, Margaret Booth
Booth, Newton: A-11, A-311, B-348
Booth, Willis H.: B-339
Borah, William E.: B-236
Borden, John: B-37
Borden, Lydia: A-38
BORDEN, WILLIAM WESLEY:
    A-38, B-37
Borglum, Gutzen: B-334
Borinstein Home (Indianapolis): A-204
Bosseron, Francis: B-212
BOSTON, DELBERT D.: *A-39*
Boston, Ella Furney: A-39
Boston Society of Civil Engineers:
    A-108
Bouck, William C.: A-387
Boulder Dam: B-142
Bouquet, Henry: A-341
Bourinot, J. G.: B-276
Boutelle, Charles A.: B-393
Boutwell, George S.: B-281
BOWEN, GEORGE WASHINGTON: *A-40*
Bowen, Otis R.: A-288, B-369
Bowen, Mrs. R. H.: B-92
Bowen, William M.: B-339
Bowers, Claude: A-358, B-76, B-216,
    B-219, B-343
BOWLUS, EZRA: *A-41*
Bowman, Abraham: A-101
Bowman, Isaac: A-101
Bowman, John: A-101
Bowman, Joseph: A-101
Boyd, John P.: A-272
BOYD, LINNAES C.: *A-42*
Boykin, Frank W.: B-24
Boyle, James: A-164
Boynton, Charles A.: A-337, A-341
Boynton, Henry V.: A-164, A-341,
    B-348
Brackenridge, John D.: B-340
Brademas, John: B-369
Bradley, Omar N.: B-251

INDEX

BRADLEY & FLETCHER (Indianapolis): *B-38*
BRADSHAW, WILLIAM: *B-39*
Branch, Emmett F.: B-114
Brandon, Henry Judah: A-210
Brandon-Judah family — see JUDAH-BRANDON FAMILY
BRANDT, MARIE ESTER: *A-43*
Branham, Amanda — see Chittenden, Amanda Branham
BRANHAM, DAVID C.: *B-40*
BRANHAM, DAVID MCCLURE: *B-41*
Branham, Mary: B-40
Branham, Preston: B-69
Branham, William: B-40
Branigin, Roger D.: A-288, B-99, B-301, B-369
Branstetter, Otto: B-96
BRATTON BROTHERS FUNERAL HOME (Lebanon): *B-42*
Bray, William G.: B-369, B-381
Brayton, A. W.: B-43
Brayton, Carrie Springer: B-330
Brayton, John (d.1941): B-330
BRAYTON, DR. JOHN (fl.1943): *B-43*
Brayton, Margaret: B-330
Brayton, Ruth: B-330
Brayton-Springer family — see SPRINGER-BRAYTON FAMILY
Brazelton, Beulah — see GRAY, BEULAH BRAZELTON
Brazelton family: A-127
Brazil: A-29, A-111
Brazil, Clay Co.: A-248
Breasted, James H.: B-342
Breckenridge, S. M.: A-302
Breckinridge, John C.: B-394
Brenton, Samuel: B-119
Bretano, Theodore: B-218
Brewing Industry of the United States: B-120
Brewster, Benjamin H.: A-145
BRICK, ABRAHAM LINCOLN: *B-44*, B-84, B-109
Brick, Anna: B-44
Brick, Estelle: B-44
Brick, William W.: B-44
Bridgeport, Marion Co.: B-201, B-243
Bridges, Styles: B-147

"Brief History of New France": A-393
"Brief History of the Social Experiment at New Harmony": B-284
Briggs, Benjamin: A-72
Briggs, John: A-302
BRIGHAM, HAROLD FREDERICK: *B-45*
Bright, Jesse D.: A-91, A-101, A-215, A-232, A-237, A-272, B-47, B-119, B-137, B-252, B-348, B-351
Bright, Michael G.: A-81, A-215, B-36, B-119, B-137, B-263
BRITTON, ALEXANDER THOMPSON: *A-44*
Britton, N. L.: B-95
Broad Ripple, Marion Co.: B-310, B-331
Brooks, Alfred M.: B-333
Brooks, Erastus: A-341
Brookston, White Co.: A-215
Brookville, Franklin Co.: A-8, A-123, A-135, A-157, A-265, A-394, A-396, B-37, B-56, B-154, B-239, B-278, B-308, B-336
Brookville and Metamora Hydraulic Company: B-56
Brookville College: A-123, B-56, B-336
Brookville National Bank: A-123
BROTHERHOOD OF LOCOMOTIVE ENGINEERS AUXILIARY: *B-46*
Brotherhood of Painters, Decorators, and Paperhangers of America: B-115
Brough, John: A-266, A-341, B-254
Brouillet, Michael: A-237
Brown, Austin, Jr.: B-47
BROWN, AUSTIN H.: *B-47*, A-81
Brown, Clay: A-302
Brown, Demarchus: B-306
Brown, Edmund G.: B-369
BROWN, EUNICE A.: *A-45*
Brown, George: B-47
BROWN, HILTON ULTIMUS: *A-46*, A-337, B-76, B-193
Brown, Hiram: A-302, B-48
Brown, Ignatius: B-48
Brown, James: A-302, A-326
Brown, John: A-8

INDEX

Brown, John Carter: A-108 — See also John Carter Brown Library
BROWN, LYNDSAY: *B-48*
BROWN, O. V.: *B-49*
Brown, Paul V.: B-219
Brown, William: B-328
Brown, William J.: A-81, B-47
Brown and McCrea Company — see MCCREA AND BROWN COMPANY
Brown County: A-58, B-121, B-333
 Nashville: B-309, B-316
Brown University (R.I.): A-22, A-111, A-210
Browne, Francis F.: A-341, B-76
Browne, Thomas M.: A-52, B-276, B-348
Browne and Cheney (Winchester): A-62
Browning Society (Indianapolis): A-351
Brown's Wonder Church, Boone Co.: B-71
Brownsburg, Hendricks Co.: B-108, B-367
Brownstown, Jackson Co.: A-201, B-365
Bruce, Charles: B-23
BRUCE, DONALD C.: *B-50*, B-369
Bruce, Sarah Hammond: B-23
Bruceville, Knox Co.: B-54
BRUCKER, MAGNUS: *A-47*
BRUNER, ALFRED WILSON: *A-48*
BRUNER, MARGARET E.: *B-51*
Bruté de Remur, Bishop Simon: A-57, A-384, B-212, B-351
Brutus, Dora Conrad: B-52
BRUTUS FAMILY PAPERS, 1839-1951: *B-52*
Bryan, William Jennings: B-236
Bryan, William Lowe: A-102, A-358, B-219, B-333, B-342
Bryce, James: B-111
Bryer, James T.: B-286
Buchanan, James: A-272, B-394
BUCK, ELLA E.: *B-53*
Buck, Solon J.: A-176
Buckingham, Alfred: A-380
Buckley, Charles A.: B-24
Buel, Alexander W.: B-119
Buell, Don Carlos: A-391
BUNDY, CHESTER E.: *A-49*
Buntin, Robert: A-237, B-212

Buntin, T. C.: B-212
Burbank, Lucinda — see Morton, Lucinda Burbank
Burbank, Luther: A-134
Burchard, Horatio C.: B-138
Burgess, Alexander: B-324
BURGESS, JOHN KLINE: *B-54*
Burgess family: B-324
Burlingame, Anson: B-84
Burlington, Carroll Co.: B-118
Burnet, Jacob: A-8, A-147, A-272, A-286, A-381
Burnet, Mary Q.: B-333
BURNETT, JEROME C.: *B-55*
Burnside, Ambrose E.: A-108
Burpee-Johnson Company: A-309
Burr, Aaron: A-272
Burr, David: B-263
Burrows, J. C.: B-345
Burton, Joseph R.: B-114
Bush, J. W.: B-92
Business: A-8, A-25, A-57, A-75, A-79, A-111, A-229, A-230, A-334, A-336, A-346, A-354, A-382, B-88, B-162, B-167, B-169, B-201, B-226, B-267, B-285, B-325, B-326, B-370, B-394
 alcoholic beverage: B-120
 automobile: B-142
 beauty products: A-390
 blacksmiths: A-301, B-126
 booksellers: B-233
 cabinetmakers: A-122
 carpenters: A-132, A-207
 casket manufacturing: A-191
 cigar company: A-337
 clothing stores: B-390
 construction: A-98, B-34, B-112
 coopers: A-122
 dairies: B-282
 department stores: B-209
 distillers: B-353
 drug company: A-390
 drugstores: B-87
 dry goods: A-79, A-159, A-331, A-410, B-28, B-56, B-210, B-212, B-252, B-304, B-327
 farm equipment: B-29, B-159, B-239, B-338
 farm seed: A-74

INDEX 433

Business—*Continued*
  film industry: B-147
  florists: A-350
  funeral homes & cemeteries: A-191,
    A-373, B-42, B-159, B-260,
    B-367
  fur trade: A-286, A-384, B-11,
    B-119, B-212
  furniture: B-159, B-272, B-367
  general merchants: A-26, A-33,
    A-70, A-78, A-89, A-90, A-125,
    A-158, A-169, A-245, A-306,
    A-384, A-401, B-137
  general stores: A-2, A-8, A-13, A-54,
    A-61, A-70, A-94, A-115, A-118,
    A-152, A-202, A-245, A-251,
    A-262, A-328, A-330, A-381,
    A-409, B-8, B-25, B-26, B-28,
    B-30, B-38, B-41, B-82, B-86,
    B-119, B-125, B-139, B-207,
    B-278, B-305, B-317, B-318,
    B-329, B-393, B-394
  ginseng: B-36
  grain: B-92
  groceries: A-122, A-124, A-306,
    A-382, B-142, B-205, B-304,
    B-321, B-331
  hardware stores: A-248, A-273, A-386
  horse breeding: A-355
  hotels: A-66, A-98, A-101, A-258,
    B-18, B-49, B-77, B-112, B-274,
    B-311, B-343
  insurance: A-87, A-116, A-260, B-9,
    B-218, B-267
  ironworks: B-376
  jewelers: B-112, B-229
  lime kiln: B-353
  lumber: B-148
  manufacturing: A-1, A-23, A-65,
    A-67, B-56, B-91, B-109,
    B-189, B-320
  meat markets: B-300
  medicine: A-82
  mills: A-73, B-7, B-48, B-338
    cotton: A-180
    flour: A-212, A-257, A-360, B-7,
      B-48, B-114, B-234, B-318,
      B-329, B-338, B-353
    grist: A-348, B-252
    hosiery: A-152

    saw: A-149, A-396, B-26, B-67,
      B-377
    textile: B-7, B-37
    woolen: A-132, A-212, B-37
  mining: A-95, A-98, A-222, B-47,
    B-80, B-110, B-147, B-240,
    B-262, B-288, B-293
  monument company: A-281
  oil: B-12, B-34, B-54, B-109
  orange growers: B-359
  packing: B-252
  painting: B-115
  pork slaughterhouse: A-251
  printers: B-149, B-223
  real estate: A-62, A-63, A-101, A-171,
    A-309, A-381, A-390, B-56,
    B-75, B-112, B-119, B-248,
    B-252, B-278, B-282, B-326
  restaurants: A-390, B-3, B-77
  road building: A-72, A-92, A-171,
    A-231, A-313, B-27, B-115,
    B-158
  saddlery hardware: A-349
  salesmen: B-229
  shipping: A-4, A-33, A-72, A-214,
    A-399, B-252
  shoe makers: B-338
  shoe sales: A-95, A-169
  shoe stores: A-258, A-373
  silversmiths: A-70
  steamboat: B-49
  stockyards: A-189, A-309
  stone quarries: A-309, B-195
  tailors: A-309
  tanners: A-243, A-309
  taverns: A-124, A-301
  theaters: A-390, B-3
  threshing: B-310
  toy stores: A-262
  traders: B-212, B-286, B-351
  typewriter company: A-337, B-267
  utilities: A-52, A-258, A-309, A-351,
    B-19, B-20, B-109, B-129, B-342,
    B-345
  wagonmakers: B-108, B-137, B-354
  wine production: A-392
  -1815: A-8, A-54, A-70, A-124,
    A-125, A-159, A-214, A-286,
    A-336, A-376, A-381, A-384,

434 INDEX

Business—*Continued*
  -1815—*cont.*
    A-392, B-11, B-37, B-67,
    B-212, B-234, B-351
  1816-1849: A-25, A-26, A-54, A-57,
    A-61, A-73, A-75, A-78, A-94,
    A-98, A-111, A-115, A-118,
    A-122, A-124, A-125, A-132,
    A-149, A-152, A-158, A-159,
    A-169, A-171, A-180, A-207,
    A-222, A-229, A-230, A-243,
    A-245, A-251, A-257, A-262,
    A-266, A-267, A-301, A-306,
    A-328, A-331, A-336, A-346,
    A-354, A-376, A-381, A-384,
    A-392, A-399, A-410, B-8,
    B-11, B-23, B-26, B-30, B-36,
    B-38, B-40, B-56, B-67, B-82,
    B-86, B-87, B-119, B-125,
    B-126, B-137, B-162, B-201,
    B-207, B-212, B-233, B-248,
    B-252, B-286, B-287, B-288,
    B-299, B-317, B-318, B-321,
    B-325, B-351, B-353, B-370,
    B-384
  1850-1879: A-2, A-4, A-13, A-23,
    A-25, A-62, A-65, A-72, A-75,
    A-78, A-79, A-89, A-90, A-92,
    A-95, A-98, A-101, A-111,
    A-115, A-132, A-149, A-152,
    A-158, A-165, A-169, A-171,
    A-180, A-189, A-202, A-212,
    A-229, A-230, A-231, A-243,
    A-245, A-251, A-257, A-262,
    A-266, A-267, A-270, A-273,
    A-280, A-302, A-306, A-313,
    A-328, A-331, A-334, A-337,
    A-346, A-349, A-355, A-373,
    A-381, A-382, A-386, A-399,
    A-401, A-410, B-7, B-8, B-18,
    B-25, B-26, B-27, B-28, B-30,
    B-56, B-57, B-67, B-75, B-82,
    B-87, B-92, B-112, B-114,
    B-115, B-119, B-126, B-137,
    B-139, B-158, B-159, B-162,
    B-205, B-207, B-210, B-212,
    B-223, B-248, B-252, B-262,
    B-272, B-274, B-278, B-285,
    B-286, B-299, B-305, B-317,
    B-318, B-321, B-325, B-327,
    B-329, B-338, B-353, B-354,
    B-367, B-376, B-377, B-384,
    B-393
  1880-1909: A-1, A-4, A-23, A-52,
    A-62, A-65, A-66, A-67, A-79,
    A-82, A-89, A-90, A-95, A-101,
    A-149, A-152, A-165, A-169,
    A-180, A-189, A-191, A-202,
    A-231, A-243, A-248, A-257,
    A-258, A-260, A-273, A-280,
    A-281, A-309, A-330, A-337,
    A-346, A-348, A-350, A-351,
    A-360, A-373, A-399, A-409,
    B-7, B-9, B-18, B-25, B-28,
    B-29, B-33, B-34, B-41, B-42,
    B-49, B-56, B-57, B-87, B-91,
    B-92, B-108, B-109, B-112,
    B-119, B-137, B-142, B-148,
    B-149, B-159, B-162, B-189,
    B-195, B-209, B-226, B-229,
    B-248, B-267, B-272, B-278,
    B-282, B-293, B-305, B-310,
    B-311, B-320, B-326, B-329,
    B-331, B-338, B-343, B-345,
    B-353, B-354, B-359, B-367,
    B-376, B-377, B-390, B-394
  1910-1945: A-1, A-42, A-66, A-74,
    A-82, A-87, A-103, A-116,
    A-149, A-180, A-189, A-191,
    A-248, A-258, A-273, A-281,
    A-309, A-337, A-348, A-350,
    A-351, A-373, A-390, A-409,
    B-3, B-14, B-18, B-41, B-42,
    B-49, B-54, B-129, B-142,
    B-147, B-148, B-149, B-195,
    B-209, B-218, B-226, B-239,
    B-243, B-246, B-248, B-278,
    B-282, B-293, B-300, B-304,
    B-310, B-320, B-342, B-343,
    B-345, B-376, B-390, B-394
  -1946: A-1, A-87, A-116, A-180,
    A-189, A-191, A-197, A-309,
    A-350, A-390, B-3, B-12, B-20,
    B-77, B-147, B-169, B-195,
    B-209, B-239, B-260
BUTLER, AMOS W.: *A-50, B-56,*
  B-173, B-181, B-336, B-371
Butler, Anne (fl. 1856): A-52
Butler, Anne (fl. 1880-1931) — see
  THOMAS, ANNE BUTLER

Butler, Benjamin: A-272, B-205
Butler, Charles: A-91, B-104, B-286
BUTLER, FRANK: *A-51*
Butler, Hugh: B-381
Butler, Jesse: A-51
BUTLER, JOHN H.: *B-57*, A-52
Butler, Mann: A-286
Butler, Nicholas Murray: A-172, B-259, B-339
Butler, Noble, Jr.: B-58
BUTLER, NOBLE CHASE: *A-52, B-58*, A-15, A-145
BUTLER, OVID: *A-53*, A-111, A-210, A-229, B-286
Butler, Robert: A-51
BUTLER, THADDEUS: *B-59*
Butler, William Allen: B-119
Butler, William W.: B-56
Butler University (Indianapolis) (formerly Northwestern Christian University): A-46, A-53, A-322, B-76, B-275
Butterfield, C. W.: A-341
Butterfield J.: B-105
Butz, Earl: B-301, B-369
Bynum, William D.: A-52
Byrd, Richard E.: B-147
Byrneville, Harrison Co.: A-34

Cable, Joseph: A-91
Cady, Elizabeth — see Stanton, Elizabeth Cady
Cains & Coffin — see COFFIN & CAINS
Caldwell, Albert G.: A-54
CALDWELL, JOHN: *A-54*
Caldwell, John, Jr.: A-54
Caldwell, Margaret Badollet: A-54
Calhoun, John C.: A-147, A-187, A-272, B-212, B-286, B-351
California: A-59, A-72, A-95, A-110, A-128, A-209, A-222, A-302, B-14, B-81, B-122, B-147, B-166, B-167, B-169, B-212, B-223, B-240, B-248, B-281, B-295, B-330, B-361, B-364
   gold rush: A-98, A-135, A-263, B-288
   World War II: B-166, B-169, B-364
   Altedena: A-110

Hollywood: B-147
Long Beach: A-240
Los Angeles: A-216, B-147, B-167
McClellan Field (World War II): A-362
Modesto: B-223
Sacramento: B-288
San Diego: B-353
San Francisco: A-263, B-118, B-212, B-223, B-227, B-288
San Jose: A-221, B-15, B-161
Santa Barbara: A-172
Sun Valley: B-157
University of California-Berkley: A-110
Yuba City: B-281, B-288
California Academy of Sciences: B-121
Calkins, William H.: A-164
Calumet River: B-89
Calumet and War Club: A-71
Calvert, Elizabeth: B-44
Cambridge City, Wayne Co.: A-264
Cameron, Simon: A-272
CAMPBELL, C. ALFRED: *B-60*
CAMPBELL, LEANDER M.: *A-55*
Campbell family: B-319
Canaan, Jefferson Co.: A-235
Canada: B-117
   War of 1812: B-234
   British Columbia: A-174
   Lake Nipigon: A-219
   Manitoba
      Stuartburn: A-318
      Winnipeg: A-219
   Ontario
      Windsor: B-167
   Quebec: A-102
      Montreal: A-384, B-131, B-205, B-262, B-372
Canby, Edward: A-391
Canby, Israel T.: A-229, B-351
Canfield, Cass: A-172
Cannelton, Perry Co.: A-180, B-365
Cannelton Cotton Mills: A-180
Cannelton Flood Control Project: B-381
Canning, George: A-272
Cannon, Joseph G.: B-348
Cannon, William: A-391
Canterbury College (Danville): B-116

436 INDEX

Cantor, Eddie: B-147
CAPEHART, HOMER E.: *B-61*, A-127, B-24, B-95, B-130, B-147, B-251
Capen, Nahum: A-101, A-154, B-394
Capper, Arthur: B-259
Caravajal, Jose M. J.: A-391, B-254
Caribbean: A-317
CARLETON, EMMA: *B-62*, B-85
Carleton, Guy: A-286
Carmel, Hamilton Co.: B-283
CARNAHAN, JAMES R.: *A-56*
Carnegie, Andrew: A-237
Carondolet, Francisco Luis Hector de: A-326
Carr, Carrie Sargeant: B-63
Carr, Cyril: B-63
CARR, MICHAEL W.: *B-63*
Carrington, Henry B.: A-15, B-124, B-348
Carroll, Benjamin: B-102
Carroll, John: A-286
Carroll, Sarah: B-102
Carroll, William: A-272
Carroll County
   Burlington: B-118
   Deer Creek Township: B-203
   Delphi: A-245, B-3, B-203, B-212, B-295
   Pittsburg: B-360
   Yeoman: B-360
Carson, Uriah: B-64
CARSON FAMILY PAPERS, 1825-1915: *B-64*
Carter, Eda: B-280
Carter, Mary — see Hovey, Mary Carter
Carter, Robert: B-84
Carthage, Rush Co.: B-385
Cartier, Baron de: B-236
Cary, Edward: B-342
Case, Charles: A-407
Cass, Jonathan: A-286
Cass, Lewis: A-83, A-101, A-147, A-272, A-346, A-384, B-119, B-212, B-351, B-394
Cass Cigar Manufacturing Company: A-337
Cass County: A-23, B-137, B-351
   Adamsboro: B-185

Logansport: A-23, A-91, A-408, B-18, B-119, B-137, B-151, B-212, B-286, B-349, B-351, B-384, B-395
Castleman, J. B.: A-302
Castleton, Marion Co.: B-202
"Catalogue of Library and Index to Vocal and Instrumental Music": B-138
Cathcart, Alice Morrison: A-277
Cathcart, Charles W.: A-237, B-119
Cathedral Arts (Indianapolis): B-116
Catlin, George: A-272
Catt, Carrie Chapman: B-76, B-216
Cauthorn, Henry S.: A-57, A-173
Caven, John: A-111, B-160
CAVINS, ELIJAH C.: *A-58*
Cavins, Samuel: A-58
Cawein, Madison: B-297
Cecilia, Mother Mary — see Bailly, Mother Mary Cecilia
Cedar Lake, Lake Co.: A-18
Cedar Lake Lyceum, Lake Co.: A-18
CEJNAR, JOHN A.: *B-65*
Center Township Citizens Draft Fund (Indianapolis): B-115
Centerville, Wayne Co.: A-9, A-220, A-263, B-205, B-288, B-324
Central America: A-346, B-95, B-143, B-339
Centre College (Danville, Ky.): B-240
CENTURY CLUB OF INDIANAPOLIS: *B-66*
Century of Negro Progress Exposition: B-6
Ceramics: A-157
Ceylon: A-367
Chadwick, French Ensor: B-342
CHAMBERLAIN, JOSEPH WRIGHT: *A-59*
Chamberlain, Orville Tryon: A-59
Chamberlain, Tully: A-59
CHAMBERLAIN & CHASE (Terre Haute): *B-67*
Chandler, William E.: A-391
Chandler, Zachariah: A-341
CHANEY, JOHN CRAWFORD: *A-60*, A-102, B-147
Chapin, Horatio: B-109
Chapin family: B-109

INDEX

Chapman, Carrie — see Catt, Carrie Chapman
Charity Organization Society (Indianapolis): A-103, B-173
Charlestown, Clark Co.: A-8, A-34, A-78, B-258, B-359
Chase, Caroline A.: B-167
Chase, Ira C.: A-272
Chase, Salmon P.: A-272, B-205, B-254, B-394
Chase & Chamberlain — see CHAMBERLAIN & CHASE
Chautauqua: B-285
Chavez, Dennis: B-99
CHEEK, WILLIAM V.: *A-61*
Chemical Warfare Service: B-285
CHENEY, JOHN J.: *A-62*
Cheney, Person Colby: A-145
Cheney, Mrs. P. C. (Person Colby): A-145
Cheney and Watson (Winchester): A-62
Chenoweth, Forest A.: B-68
CHENOWETH, JOHN T.: *B-68*
Chicago and Atlantic Railroad: A-164
Chicago and Eastern Illinois Railroad: B-147
Chicago and Lake Superior Mining Company: B-11
Chicago Evening Post: B-33
Chicago Express: B-293
Chicago, South Shore and South Bend Railroad: B-211
Child Welfare League: B-184
Children's Aid Association (Indianapolis): A-103
Children's Ward Association (Ft. Wayne): B-241
Chile: B-227
China: A-378, B-79, B-146, B-166, B-268
  Macao: B-152
Chittenden, Amanda Branham: B-69
Chittenden, Edgar: B-69
CHITTENDEN, GEORGE F.: *B-69*
Chouteau, August: A-237, A-272, A-384
Chouteau, Pierre, Jr.: B-119 — See also Pierre Chouteau & Company
Christ Church *Bulletin:* B-70
CHRIST CHURCH CATHEDRAL (Indianapolis): *B-70*

Christ Church Chimes: B-70
Christ Church League of Service: B-70
Christ Church Sewing Guild: B-70
Christ Church Women's Auxiliary: B-70
Christian Endeavor Convention (Ft. Wayne): A-132
Christian Theological Seminary (Indianapolis): B-116
"Christmas This Year": A-364
Christopher Publishing House (Boston): B-51
Chunn, John T.: B-212
Church Federation of Greater Indianapolis: B-116
CHURCH HISTORY-BAPTIST: *B-71*
Churchman, Mrs. F. M.: A-63
CHURCHMAN, FRANCIS MCCLINTOCK: *A-63*
Churchman, Frank F.: A-63
Churchman, William H.: A-63
Cincinnati and Indianapolis Junction Railroad Company: B-215, B-359
Cincinnati Commercial: A-341
Cincinnati Gazette: A-341
Cincinnati, Hamilton and Dayton Railway Company: A-276
Cincinnati Type of the Times: A-341
The Circle: B-51
Cist, Charles: A-8
Citizens Brewery Company: B-282
CITIZENS FORUM (Indianapolis): *A-64*
Citizens Gas Company (Indianapolis): A-258, B-342
CITIZENS HISTORICAL ASSOCIATION: *B-72*, B-264
Citizen's Humane Society (Indianapolis): B-173
Citizen's Non-Partisan Movement: B-267
Citizens' Street Railway Company (Muncie): A-200
Civil Service: B-342
Civil Service Chronicle: B-342
Civil War: A-14, A-138, A-156, A-201, A-295, A-356, A-391, B-80, B-87, B-153, B-160, B-170, B-285, B-342, B-354, B-356, B-359, B-366, B-387, B-393

Civil War—*Continued*
  Army of the Tennessee
    3rd Division: A-381
    4th Division: A-379
  U.S. Volunteers: A-264, A-383
  14th Army Corps: B-94
  14th U.S. Colored Infantry: A-271
  49th U.S. Colored Infantry: A-271
  109th U.S. Colored Infantry: A-335
  1st U.S. Veterans Volunteer Engineers: A-21
  3rd Illinois Cavalry: B-293
  22nd Illinois Regiment: B-171
  17th Indiana Battery: A-329
  6th Indiana Regiment: B-199
  7th Indiana Regiment: A-170, B-21
  8th Indiana Regiment: A-259
  9th Indiana Regiment: A-305, B-73, B-212
  10th Indiana Regiment: A-368
  11th Indiana Regiment: A-289, A-388, A-391
  12th Indiana Regiment: B-231
  13th Indiana Regiment: A-216, B-83
  14th Indiana Regiment: A-27, A-58, A-168, A-228, A-379
  16th Indiana Regiment: B-69
  17th Indiana Regiment: A-278, A-373, B-73, B-160, B-360, B-376
  18th Indiana Regiment: A-85, A-168
  19th Indiana Regiment: A-264, A-274, B-85, B-235
  20th Indiana Regiment: B-223
  21st Indiana Regiment: A-88, A-106, A-133, B-73, B-262
  22nd Indiana Regiment: A-80, B-94
  23rd Indiana Regiment: A-47, B-358
  24th Indiana Regiment: A-33, A-213, B-329
  25th Indiana Regiment: A-383, B-49
  26th Indiana Regiment: A-142, B-75
  27th Indiana Regiment: A-97, A-402
  29th Indiana Regiment: B-235
  30th Indiana Regiment: B-313
  31st Indiana Regiment: A-88, B-314
  33rd Indiana Regiment: A-29, A-88, A-111, A-247
  37th Indiana Regiment: A-294, B-123, B-228
  38th Indiana Regiment: A-325, B-136, B-285, B-330
  39th Indiana Regiment: A-24, B-197, B-382
  41st Indiana Regiment: A-129
  42nd Indiana Regiment: A-359, B-114
  43rd Indiana Regiment: B-315
  44th Indiana Regiment: A-345
  45th Indiana Regiment: A-3, B-31, B-92, B-135, B-225, B-295
  46th Indiana Regiment: B-34
  47th Indiana Regiment: A-143, B-322
  48th Indiana Regiment: A-347, B-49
  50th Indiana Regiment: A-234
  54th Indiana Regiment: B-298
  57th Indiana Regiment: A-206, A-208, A-269, A-291, B-230
  58th Indiana Regiment: A-35, B-114
  60th Indiana Regiment: A-41
  63rd Indiana Regiment: A-252, B-266
  67th Indiana Regiment: A-213
  69th Indiana Regiment: A-259, A-329
  70th Indiana Regiment: A-145, A-205, A-271, A-381, B-21, B-141, B-221, B-244
  71st Indiana Regiment: A-5
  72nd Indiana Regiment: A-88, A-140, B-291
  74th Indiana Regiment: A-59
  75th Indiana Regiment: A-241, A-340, A-389
  77th Indiana Regiment: A-96
  79th Indiana Regiment: A-170, A-209
  82nd Indiana Regiment: A-244
  83rd Indiana Regiment: A-206
  85th Indiana Regiment: A-160, B-73
  86th Indiana Regiment: A-56
  89th Indiana Regiment: A-360
  97th Indiana Regiment: B-73
  115th Indiana Regiment: A-111, A-402
  117th Indiana Regiment: B-21
  119th Indiana Regiment: A-143
  121st Indiana Regiment: B-225
  124th Indiana Regiment: A-220
  126th Indiana Regiment: B-73
  128th Indiana Regiment: A-113
  133rd Indiana Regiment: B-146
  137th Indiana Regiment: A-168
  147th Indiana Regiment: A-21, A-220

INDEX

Civil War—*Continued*
  151st Indiana Regiment: B-223
  152nd Indiana Regiment: A-407
  3rd Iowa Regiment: B-265
  13th Iowa Regiment: A-19
  8th Michigan Regiment: A-242
  4th Ohio Regiment: B-34
  65th Ohio Regiment: B-34
  69th Ohio Regiment: B-144
  113th Ohio Regiment: A-109
  77th Pennsylvania Regiment: A-380
  9th West Virginia Regiment: A-349
  Andersonville (Ga.) Prison: A-291, A-391
  Atlanta Campaign: A-402
  Camp Butler (Ill.): A-380
  Camp Carrington (Indianapolis): A-21
  Camp Douglas (Ill.): A-380
  Camp Morton (Indianapolis): A-41, A-302, A-339, B-298
  Camp Thompson (Terre Haute): B-348
  Camp Vigo (Vigo Co.): A-168
  Chancellorsville, Battle of: A-58
  Confederate soldiers: A-229, A-302
  Copperheads: B-115
  draft: B-115
  Fort Pickering Prison (Tenn.): A-360
  Fredericksburg, Battle of: A-58
  medical corps: A-29, A-35, A-47, A-160, A-207, A-220, A-278, A-345, B-69, B-170, B-225, B-235, B-295
  Morgan's Raid: A-15, A-101, A-229
  navy: A-381
  newspapers: B-103
  nurses: A-216
  politics: A-5, A-229, B-43, B-84, B-254, B-262, B-348, B-376, B-393
  prisoners: A-111, A-229, A-291, A-302, A-360, A-361, B-171, B-231
  provost marshals: A-221
  Quaker response to: A-129
  quartermaster department: A-389, B-94, B-360
  Shiloh, Battle of: A-383
  spies: B-323
  treason: A-15, A-361, B-212, B-284, B-372
  Veteran Reserve Corps: B-353
  veterans: A-3, A-58, A-80, A-94, A-112, A-126, A-133, A-216, A-254, A-373, A-383, B-49, B-69, B-73, B-83, B-113, B-133, B-162, B-225, B-235, B-240, B-262, B-287, B-292, B-330, B-359, B-360, B-376, B-389
  Wilder's Brigade: B-360, B-376
  — See also individual states
CIVIL WAR. CLAIMS FOR VETERANS: *B-73*
Civilian Conservation Corps (CCC): B-219, B-270, B-316
Clark, Edward P.: B-342
Clark, George Rogers: A-8, A-286, B-212
Clark, Howard Walton: B-121
Clark, J. W.: B-74
Clark, John C.: B-84
CLARK, JOHN G.: *B-75*
Clark, Jonathan: A-8, A-101
Clark, Julius T.: B-388
Clark, Marston G.: A-101, A-125, B-351
Clark, William: A-8, A-125, A-237, A-272, A-286
CLARK & CLARK (Columbia City): *B-74*
Clark County: A-78, A-80, A-101, A-370, A-410, B-37, B-258, B-359, B-373
  Bethlehem: A-8
  Charlestown: A-8, A-34, A-78, B-258, B-359
  Clark's Grant: A-121
  Jeffersonville: A-8, A-9, A-101, A-121, A-125, A-308, A-331, B-36, B-48, B-302, B-317
  New Providence/Borden: A-38, A-330, B-37
  Silver Creek: B-71
Clark County Historical Society: B-359
CLARKE, GRACE JULIAN: *B-76*, B-124, B-205, B-216
Clarke, William: A-302
CLARKE, WILLIAM HORATIO: *A-65*
Clark's Grant, Clark Co.: A-121

INDEX

Clarkson, John S.: B-138
Clay, Green: A-147, A-272
Clay, Henry: A-147, A-264, A-272, A-326, A-341, A-387, B-263
Clay County
  Brazil: A-248
Claypool, Virginia — see Meredith, Virginia Claypool
CLAYPOOL HOTEL (Indianapolis): *A-66, B-77*
Claysville, Washington Co.: A-213
Clayton, John M.: B-348
Clear Creek, Morgan Co.: B-71
Cleghorn, Sarah: B-96
Clem, John L.: B-259
Clemens, Cyril: B-140
Clemens, Samuel Langhorne: B-208
Clendenin, David: A-272
Clermont (Ohio) Academy: B-365
Cleveland, Grover: A-101, A-272, B-47
Cleveland (Ohio) Female Seminary: A-266
Cleveland Township, Elkhart Co.: B-185
Clinton, Vermillion Co.: A-228
Clinton County: A-131, B-64
  Frankfort: B-3, B-75, B-245, B-383
  Middlefork: A-265
CLIO CLUB: *B-78*
Clowry, Robert C.: A-341
Clyde Beatty Circus — see Cole Brothers/Clyde Beatty Circus
Coal Creek, Fountain Co.: B-165
COATS, NELLIE M.: *B-79*
COBB, DYAR: *A-67*
Cobb, Howell: A-272
Cobb, Irwin S.: A-358
Cobb, John: A-67
Cobb, S. H.: B-40
Cobb, Thomas R.: B-348
Cobb's Iron and Nail Company (Aurora): A-67
Coburn, Augustus: B-80
Coburn, Henry: A-29
Coburn, Henry P.: B-286
COBURN, JOHN: *B-80*, A-15, B-103, B-124, B-160, B-286, B-393
Cochran, Charles F.: A-8
COCKEFAIR, ELISHA: *B-81*
Cockefair, Laf: B-81

Cockrell, Francis M.: B-348
Cockwell, Sidney: A-172
Coe, Isaac: B-303
Coffeen, E. W.: A-230
COFFIN, CHARLES EMMET: *A-68*, A-101, B-76
Coffin, Charles F.: A-15, A-111, B-205
Coffin, Elijah: A-111, A-266
Coffin, William G.: A-229
COFFIN & CAINS (Economy): *B-82*
COGSWELL, STACY H.: *B-83*
Cole, Cornelia — see Fairbanks, Cornelia Cole
Cole Brothers/Clyde Beatty Circus: B-20
Coleman, Christopher B.: A-176, A-336
Colescott, J. A.: A-225
Colfax, Ellen: B-109
COLFAX, SCHUYLER: *A-69, B-84*, A-15, A-25, A-52, A-59, A-111, A-136, A-145, A-164, A-229, A-232, A-264, A-272, A-302, A-391, B-43, B-205, B-212, B-254, B-259, B-269, B-284, B-286, B-335, B-345, B-376, B-394, B-395
Colfax, Schuyler, Jr.: B-84
Colfax, William: B-84
College Corner Literary Club (Indianapolis): A-351
Collett, Josephus: A-369
Collot, Victor: A-286
Colorado: A-142, B-110, B-223
  Colorado Springs: A-174
  Denver: B-55, B-365
  Fort Sedgewick: A-137
  Pueblo: B-164
Colorado River: B-301
Columbia City, Whitley Co.: B-74, B-130, B-236
Columbus, Bartholomew Co.: A-73, B-108, B-142
Columbus, Piqua, and Indiana Railroad: A-307
Columbus and Indianapolis Railroad: A-307
Combs, Leslie: A-272
Commission on Indian Affairs: A-229
Commission on Uniform State Laws: B-275

INDEX 441

Committee on Industrial Relations: B-110
Communalism: A-237, A-250, A-282, B-17, B-142, B-273, B-284
Communications
  telephone: B-19, B-20, B-129, B-229, B-345
Communism: A-365, B-200, B-251, B-275
Community Nutrition Report: A-183
Compagnie du Scioto: A-70, B-212
Compton family: B-169
Congressional Medal of Honor: A-59
Conkling, Roscoe: A-272, B-84, B-138, B-286
Connecticut: A-236, B-117
  Bridgeport: B-146
  Brooklyn: A-398
  Hartford: A-346
  Middleton: B-391
  New London County: B-37
  Windham County: B-37
  Yale University: A-107, A-210, B-44
Conner, William: B-351
Connersville, Fayette Co.: A-45, A-115, A-118, A-157, A-158, B-3, B-81, B-215, B-278, B-304, B-359, B-365, B-384
Conservation: B-20, B-95, B-168, B-218, B-219, B-257
Constitutional Union Party: B-249
Consumers Gas Trust Company (Indianapolis): A-351
Contemporary Literary Club: A-315
Continental Congress: A-272
Converse, Miami Co.: A-49
Cook, A.D. Company – see A. D. COOK COMPANY
Cook, Jacob: A-209
Cooke & Andrew – see ANDREW & COOKE
Cooley, Julia – see ALTROCCHI, JULIA COOLEY
Coolidge, Calvin: A-272, B-114, B-147, B-236, B-259
Cooper, James Fenimore: A-272
Coquillard, Alexis: B-119, B-212
Corcoran, William W.: A-81
Cornell University (N.Y.): B-44
Corwin, Thomas: B-348

Corydon, Harrison Co.: A-89, A-90, A-303, B-285
Corydon Artesian Well Company: B-285
Corydon Masonic Lodge: B-285
Corydon Presbyterian Church: B-285
Costigan, Francis: A-381, B-394
COTTMAN, GEORGE STREIBE: *B-85*, B-276, B-371
Cottman, John: B-85
Coulter, Stanley: A-102, B-95, B-219
Council on Foreign Relations: B-275
COUPIN, CLAUDE ANTOINE GABRIEL: *A-70*
Covington, Samuel: A-237
Covington, Fountain Co.: A-140, A-245, B-266
Cox, Carter: B-52
Cox, Edward T.: A-15
COX, ELISHA: *B-86*
Cox, Jacob D.: A-229
Cox, Samuel S.: A-346
Cox Multi-Mailer Company: A-337
Craig, Evelyn: B-111
Craig, George N.: B-24, B-130, B-275
Craig, Isaac: A-8, A-286, A-287, A-381
CRAIN, JACOB R.: *A-71*
Craine, Joseph P.: B-116
Crandell, Agnes: A-138
CRANE, ABIATHAR: *A-72*
Crapo, Henry H.: A-15
Cravens, J. J.: A-111
Cravens, James A.: A-101, A-407
Cravens, James H.: B-348
Cravens, John R.: A-229
Crawford, Francis Marion: A-391
Crawford, George W.: B-114
Crawford, T. Hartley: B-119, B-137
Crawford, W. S.: A-111
Crawford, William H.: A-147, A-187, A-272
Crawford County
  Leavenworth: A-34, A-77
  Patoka Township: B-102
Crawfordsville, Montgomery Co.: A-23, A-74, A-79, A-130, A-131, A-229, A-230, A-275, A-295, A-332, A-388, A-391, B-15, B-36, B-108, B-165, B-169,

INDEX

Crawfordsville — *Continued*
   B-258, B-299, B-366 — See also Wabash College
Crawfordsville and Wabash Railroad: A-229
Crawfordsville Land Office: A-229
CRAWFORDSVILLE SEED COMPANY: *A-74*
Credit Mobilier: B-84
Crescent Society (Indianapolis): B-340
Crevecoeur, Michel Guillaume St. Jean de: A-286
Crime: A-161, A-290, A-352, A-360, B-16, B-65, B-96, B-97, B-101, B-132, B-163, B-173, B-203, B-216, B-226, B-240, B-246, B-263, B-301, B-334, B-374
Crittenden, John J.: A-272, B-249
Croghan, George: A-286
Croghan, William: A-125, A-286
Crosby, John Schuyler: A-146
CROSIER, ADAM: *B-87*
Crosier, Lafe: B-87
Cross, Addison: B-88
CROSS, GEORGE WASHINGTON: *A-75, B-88*
Cross, Sharon: A-75
CROWE, EUGENE BURGESS: *A-76*, A-258
Crown Point, Lake Co.: A-225, B-223
Crumpacker, Edgar D.: B-44, B-114
CRUMPACKER, SHEPARD J.: *B-89*
Cruzan, Rose Marie — see Rose Marie Cruzan Parliamentary Club
Cuba: A-260, B-339
  Havana: A-250, B-109, B-397
Cullom, Shelby M.: A-341, B-345, B-393
Cullop, W. H.: B-114
Culver, Marshall Co.: B-121
Cumback, Will: A-5, A-15, A-52, A-229, A-232, A-272, B-94, B-138, B-286, B-393
Cumberland, Marion Co.: A-301, B-135
CUNNINGHAM, JOSEPH: *B-90*
Cunningham, Ora — see Turner, Ora Cunningham
CURRAN, CHARLES W.: *A-77*
Curti, Merle: A-176
Curtis, Charles: B-259

CURTIS, DANIEL: *B-91*
Curtis, George William: A-391, B-342
Curtis, Samuel R.: B-94
Curts, Susan Shockley: A-329
Curts family: A-329
Cushing, Caleb: A-272, A-391
Cutler, Manasseh: A-272, A-286
Cutler, William Parker: A-346

DAILY, DAVID W.: *A-78*
Daily, Philip: A-78
Daisy Spring Mill, Lawrence Co.: B-353
Dakotas: B-356
Dale, Spencer Co.: B-49
Dallas, Alexander J.: A-147, A-272
Dallas, George M.: B-394
Dalrymple, Jennie — see Seward, Jennie Dalrymple
DALRYMPLE, JOSEPH W.: *B-92*
Dalton, Wayne Co.: B-28
Daly, Walter: B-334
Dana, Charles A.: A-341, B-84, B-348
Dana, Richard Henry: B-342
DANNER, MRS. A. V.: *B-93*
Danville, Hendricks Co.: A-55, A-155, B-21, B-116
DARBY, ORANGE V.: *A-79*
Darlington, Montgomery Co.: B-8
Darrow, Clarence: B-334
Dartmouth College (N.H.): A-216, A-266, B-165
Datzman, Mrs. R. C.: B-166
Daugherty, Harry M.: B-114, B-218, B-259
Daughters of Temperance: A-259
Daughters of the American Revolution (D.A.R.): A-102, A-235, A-336, B-323
Davidson, Alexander H.: B-249
Davidson, Catherine Noble: B-249
Davidson, Lyman: B-72, B-264
Daviess County: B-206
  Washington: B-146, B-185, B-330
Davis, Clifford: B-24
Davis, David: A-302
Davis, Henry Winter: A-302, A-346, A-391, B-348
Davis, Ida Mae: B-371
Davis, Jefferson: A-272

INDEX

DAVIS, JEFFERSON COLUMBUS: *A-80, B-94*, A-15
DAVIS, JOHN GIVAN: *A-81*, A-72, B-348
Davis, John Lee: B-152
Davis, John W. (fl.1830s-1840s): B-152
Davis, John Wesley (1799-1859): A-101, A-232, B-47, B-263, B-351
Davis, Mary A. — see Helms, Mary A. Davis
Davis, Rebecca Harding: B-111
Davis, Richard Harding: B-208
Davis family: B-152
Davis-Sinker Company — see SINKER-DAVIS COMPANY
Dawalt, Mary: B-53
Dawalt, Sadie: B-53
Dawes, Charles G.: B-259
DAWSON, GOVERNOR GREENUP ("Harry"): *A-82*
Dawson Concert Company: A-82
Dayton, Jonathan: A-147
Dayton and Muncie Traction Company: A-200
DEAM, CHARLES C.: *B-95*, B-219, B-257
Dean, Edward: A-83
Dean, John (1736-1824): A-83
Dean, John (1813-1863): A-83
Dean, Mary: A-83
Dean, Thomas: A-83
DEAN FAMILY: *A-83*
Dearborn, Henry: A-147, A-272, A-286, A-381
Dearborn County: A-206, A-397
 Aurora: A-67, A-334, A-399, B-71, B-161
 Lawrenceburg: A-1, A-4, A-61, A-95, A-159, A-165, A-173, A-302, A-308, A-381, B-86, B-92, B-93, B-161, B-232, B-370, B-376
 Logan: A-207
 Manchester Academy: B-323
DEBS, EUGENE V.: *B-96*, A-302, A-312 — See also "At Death of Debs" and "Ballad of Gene Debs"
Debs, Theodore: A-312, B-96
Decatur County: B-27, B-248
 Downeyville: B-52

Greensburg: A-67, A-119, A-294, A-333, A-400, B-248, B-376, B-385, B-390
 Milford: B-69
 St. Paul: A-380, B-52
Decatur Township, Marion Co.: B-27, B-64
Declaration of Independence: A-272
Deer Creek Township, Carroll Co.: B-203
Defrees, John D.: A-15, A-25, A-57, A-81, A-229, A-302, B-47, B-84, B-114, B-137, B-212, B-286, B-335, B-348, B-351
Dekalb County: A-400, B-23
 Ashley: B-23
 Orangeville: A-149
DELAPLANE, MARGARET LANDON: *A-84*
Delassus, Charles: A-147
Delaware, Wilmington: A-91
Delaware County: A-181, A-200, A-329, B-109
 Muncie: A-23, A-122, A-146, A-200, A-214, A-291, B-97, B-113, B-204, B-235, B-278, B-301, B-330
 New Cincinnati: A-122
 Selma: A-274
DELAWARE COUNTY. JAIL MATRON'S DIARY: *B-97*
Delaware River: B-275
Delefield, Frederick P.: B-109
Delphi, Carroll Co.: A-245, B-3, B-203, B-212, B-295
Delta Sigma Phi: B-2
Delta Tau Delta: B-275
DeMille, Cecil B.: A-147
Democratic National Committee: B-203
Democratic Party:
 1816-1849: A-78, A-165, A-237, A-283, B-47, B-328, B-351, B-394
 1850-1879: A-57, A-81, A-91, A-95, A-101, A-119, A-154, A-165, A-215, A-237, A-254, A-283, A-407, B-47, B-137, B-161, B-212, B-240, B-281, B-335, B-394

Democratic Party—*Continued*
  1880-1909: A-57, A-95, A-101,
    A-154, A-165, A-173, A-254,
    A-283, B-95, B-155, B-236,
    B-240, B-335, B-343
  1910-1945: A-51, A-76, A-95, A-249,
    A-285, A-407, B-76, B-79, B-95,
    B-155, B-196, B-200, B-236,
    B-256, B-261, B-277, B-343
  1946-: B-12, B-95, B-99, B-198,
    B-203, B-256, B-269
Democratic State Central Committee:
  A-101
Democratic State Editorial Association:
  B-335
Democratic Woman's National Committee: B-203
Denby, Charles: B-114
Denby, Edward: B-345
Denby, Edwin: B-259
DENNIS, DAVID W.: *B-98*
Dennison, William: A-272
Denny, Ebenezer: A-8
DENNY, GILBERT H.: *A-85*
Denny, John: B-359
Denny, Margaret: B-359
Denton, George K.: B-114
DENTON, WINFIELD K.: *B-99*,
  B-246, B-369
Denver, Miami Co.: B-53
Denver Times: A-358
DePauw, W. C.: A-101
DePauw University (formerly Indiana
  Asbury): A-52, A-57, A-111,
  A-123, A-144, A-151, A-288,
  A-310, A-311, A-334, A-357,
  A-397, B-21, B-69, B-114,
  B-324, B-365, B-373 — See also
  Greencastle, Putnam County
DeSilver, Albert: B-96
Deutschen Allgemeinen Protestantischen Waisenvereins: A-300
Devens, Charles: B-348
Devine, Edward T.: A-172
Dewey, Charles: A-8, A-302, A-369,
  B-348, B-351
Dewey, George: A-283
Diamond Chain Factory (Indianapolis):
  B-189

Diaries
  -1815: A-8, A-402
  1816-1849: A-18, A-34, A-77, A-111,
    A-123, A-125, A-219, A-222,
    A-250, A-344, A-363, A-402,
    B-161, B-212, B-287, B-348
  1850-1879: A-10, A-17, A-28, A-29,
    A-33, A-34, A-43, A-52, A-55,
    A-57, A-77, A-104, A-111,
    A-123, A-128, A-148, A-156,
    A-157, A-207, A-219, A-227,
    A-228, A-238, A-264, A-295,
    A-313, A-321, A-344, A-363,
    A-402, B-7, B-27, B-40, B-146,
    B-151, B-156, B-197, B-229,
    B-270, B-287, B-342, B-353,
    B-356, B-357, B-359, B-364
  1880-1909: A-17, A-34, A-104,
    A-132, A-134, A-148, A-157,
    A-264, A-265, A-285, A-295,
    A-313, A-321, A-366, A-367,
    A-388, B-7, B-29, B-40, B-146,
    B-151, B-156, B-197, B-204,
    B-229, B-248, B-278, B-291,
    B-342, B-353, B-360, B-383
  1910-1945: A-17, A-22, A-102,
    A-116, A-132, A-157, A-285,
    A-313, A-366, A-367, A-388,
    B-14, B-51, B-97, B-143, B-156,
    B-248, B-270, B-278, B-360,
    B-361, B-383
  1946- : A-132, A-295, B-51, B-143
  Civil War: A-58, A-59, A-168, A-170,
    A-205, A-228, A-271, A-278,
    A-294, A-383, A-402, B-31,
    B-228, B-244, B-291, B-314,
    B-322, B-329, B-382
The Diaries of Donald Macdonald: A-250
The Diary of Calvin Fletcher: A-111
Diaz, Porfirio: A-391
Dick, Charles: B-84
"Dick the Bruiser" — see Afflis, William F.
DICKERSON, JOHN WILLIAM:
  B-100
DICKES, JOHN THOMAS: *A-86*
Dickey, John M.: B-276
Dickey, Marcus: A-315
DICKINSON, JESSE L.: *B-101*
Dickinson College (Pa.): A-98

Dictionary of the United States Congress: A-232
Diederich, Henry W.: B-345
Dies, Martin: A-172
Dill, Elizabeth: A-308
Dill, James: A-308, A-381
Dillard, Charles: B-102
DILLARD, FRED ELWOOD: *B-102*
Dillard, Max: B-102
Dillinger, John: B-65
DILLON, JOHN BROWN: *B-103*, A-8, A-229, A-302, B-212, B-348, B-351
Dime Savings and Loan (Indianapolis): A-103
Dinneen, Ellen: B-15
Diocesan Council (Episcopal): B-116
Diocesan General Convention (Episcopal): B-116
DISABILITY INCOME INSURANCE COMPANY (Indianapolis): *A-87*
Dix, Dorothea: B-173
Dixon, James: A-346
Dixon, Joseph M.: B-124
Doan, Frances — see Streightoff, Frances Doan
Dodd, William E.: A-176
Dodge, Augustus C.: B-273
Dodge, Henry S.: B-114
Donahue, Patrick: A-91
Donaldson, Thomas: A-341
DOOLEY, RUFUS: *A-88*
Dorsey, James: A-282
Douglas, Stephen A.: A-272, B-84, B-236
DOUGLASS, BENJAMIN PENNEBAKER: *A-89*, A-90
Douglass, Ephraim: A-286
DOUGLASS, SAMUEL WALTER: *A-90*
Douglass, Victoria Boone: A-89
Dover, Boone Co.: A-88
Dover, Wayne Co.: A-342
DOWLING, JOHN: *A-91*, A-81, A-232, B-104, B-137, B-263, B-348, B-351
DOWLING, THOMAS: *B-104*, A-91, B-114, B-119, B-137, B-204, B-212, B-286, B-335, B-348, B-351

Down Our Way: A-210
Downeyville, Decatur Co.: B-52
Doxey, Charles T.: B-114
Drake, Daniel: A-8, A-272
Draper, Lyman C.: A-57, A-272, A-341, B-212, B-351
Dreer, Ferdinand J.: A-282
Dreiser, Theodore: B-208
Dresser, Paul: B-217 — See also Paul Dresser Memorial Association
Driftwood Expedition: B-351
Drill Manual For Philippine Cadets: B-268
Driscoll, Frederick: A-341
Drummond, David Park: B-169
Drummond, Thomas: A-52
Dublin, Wayne Co.: A-92
DUBLIN AND NEW CASTLE TURNPIKE COMPANY: *A-92*
DUBOIS, JESSE KILGOUR: *B-105*
Dubois, Toussaint: A-223, B-105, B-212
Dubois County: A-93
  Birdseye: B-102
  Huntingburg: A-348
DUBOIS COUNTY MISCELLANEOUS RECORDS, 1853-1908: *A-93*
Duden, Alice Harvie: A-22
Duden, Hans: A-22
Dudley, William Wade: A-164
Dufour, David: B-106
Dufour, Francis: A-272
Dufour, John James: A-120, B-106
Dufour, Perret: B-106
DUFOUR FAMILY PAPERS: *B-106*
Dumont, Ebenezer: A-15, A-229, A-267, B-119, B-160
Dumont, John: A-15, A-237, A-302, B-119
Dumont, Julia: A-267
Dunbar, John: A-303
Duncan, John M.: A-253
Dunn, Caroline: B-107
Dunn, George: A-95
DUNN, GEORGE GRUNDY, SR.: *A-94*, B-212, B-348
Dunn, George Grundy, Jr.: A-94
Dunn, George H.: B-263, B-286, B-351
Dunn, Isaac: A-95
Dunn, Jacob, Sr. (1811-1890): A-95

DUNN, JACOB PIATT (1855-1924):
    A-95, B-107, A-229,
    A-237, A-337, B-76, B-212
Dunn, Moses F.: A-94
DUNN, TEMPLE H.: *B-108*
DUNN, WILLIAM H.: *A-96*
Dunn, William M.: A-8, A-150,
    A-229, B-108, B-153, B-225,
    B-348
Dunn, William R.: B-108
Dunn, Williamson: A-8
Dunn & Dunn (Bedford): A-94
Dunning, Paris C.: A-15, A-272,
    B-263
Dupont, Jefferson Co.: B-129
Durbin, Winfield T.: A-52, A-102,
    A-272, B-19, B-114, B-138
Duret, John B.: B-137, B-286, B-351
DuShane, Donald: B-109
DUSHANE, JAMES: *B-109*
Duval, William P.: B-171
Dyer, Charles E.: A-52
Dykeman, D. D.: A-23
DYNES, HARRY B.: *B-110*

Eagle Village, Boone Co.: A-245
Earlham College (Richmond): A-357 —
    See also Richmond, Wayne
    County
Early Engagements: A-150
Eastern Indiana Farmer: B-143
Eaton, Dorman B.: B-342
Eaton, John H.: A-272
Ebenezer, Morgan Co.: B-71
Eckert, Thomas T.: A-341
Economy, Wayne Co.: A-259, B-82
Eddy, Norman: A-81
Edgeworthalean Society (Bloomington):
    B-17
Edinburgh, Johnson Co.: A-30, B-146
Edison, Thomas A.: B-208
Edmunds, John W.: B-119
Education
    administration and faculty: A-23,
        A-26, A-36, A-46, A-48, A-55,
        A-63, A-72, A-100, A-111,
        A-129, A-144, A-153, A-174,
        A-175, A-177, A-182, A-185,
        A-195, A-203, A-221, A-228,
        A-231, A-237, A-253, A-271,
        A-275, A-284, A-334, A-356,
        A-357, A-401, B-109, B-149,
        B-213, B-220, B-253, B-255,
        B-275, B-285, B-287, B-309,
        B-321, B-330, B-345, B-347,
        B-356, B-364, B-396
    adult: B-309
    colleges:
      -1815: A-302
      1816-1849: A-18, A-36, A-43, A-57,
        A-91, A-98, A-107, A-111,
        A-144, A-203, A-236, A-302,
        A-310, A-311, A-361, A-397,
        B-47, B-114, B-146, B-165,
        B-212, B-285, B-351, B-372
      1850-1879: A-18, A-27, A-30, A-36,
        A-43, A-52, A-53, A-54, A-56,
        A-57, A-108, A-111, A-123,
        A-140, A-151, A-203, A-210,
        A-216, A-265, A-266, A-271,
        A-284, A-310, A-312, A-334,
        A-337, A-361, A-381, A-385,
        A-397, B-21, B-56, B-137,
        B-146, B-165, B-236, B-240,
        B-281, B-285, B-286, B-319,
        B-336, B-365, B-373
      1880-1909: A-18, A-22, A-39, A-46,
        A-52, A-91, A-123, A-210,
        A-231, A-246, A-288, A-310,
        A-337, B-21, B-44, B-58, B-63,
        B-69, B-76, B-81, B-90, B-113,
        B-122, B-147, B-281, B-285,
        B-324, B-336, B-365
      1910-1945: A-46, A-52, A-100,
        A-110, A-231, A-246, A-337,
        A-357, B-81, B-102, B-108,
        B-166, B-255, B-275, B-281,
        B-336, B-345, B-365, B-388
      1946-: A-46, A-153, A-255, A-322,
        B-261, B-275
    law school: A-297, B-281
    medical school: A-111, A-174, A-243,
        A-246, A-268, A-293, A-302,
        B-170, B-346
    school records: A-100, A-156, A-253,
        A-314, A-332, A-396, B-1, B-23,
        B-27, B-34, B-49, B-81, B-104,
        B-114, B-159, B-244, B-281,
        B-286, B-287, B-321, B-380
    school reorganization: B-183

INDEX 447

Education—*Continued*
  schools: A-36, A-67, A-78, A-132, A-148, A-153, A-156, A-175, A-182, A-253, A-259, A-277, A-314, A-402, B-169, B-252, B-253, B-267, B-268, B-275, B-323, B-340, B-351, B-356, B-365
  summer camps: A-304, A-327
EDWARDS, GEORGE: *A-97*
Edwards, Ninian: A-101, A-272
Eel River District Association (Putnam Co.): B-71
EGGLESTON, EDWARD: *B-111*, A-272, A-322
Eggleston, G. Cary: B-124
Eggleston, George Craig: B-111
Eggleston, J. C.: A-302
Eggleston, W. W.: B-95
Egypt: A-162, A-317, A-391
Ehrlichman, John: B-301
Ehrmann, Bess: A-176
Ehrmann, Max: B-208, B-217
Eisenhower, Dwight D.: B-130
Eisenhower, Julia Nixon: A-288
Eitel, Edmund: A-112, B-276
Elder, Alex: A-98
Elder, Amelia Line: A-98
Elder, Clifford: A-67
ELDER, JOHN: *A-98*
Elder, John R.: A-98
Elder, Oliver C.: A-67
ELDER, ROMENA O.: *B-112*
Elder, Samuel: A-98
Elizabethtown, Bartholomew Co.: A-77, B-41
Elkhart County: A-305, B-35
  Cleveland Township: B-185
  Goshen: B-35, B-289, B-293
Elkhart County Anti-Liquor Association: B-289
Ellettsville, Monroe Co.: B-129
Ellicott, Andrew: A-272
Elliott, Byron K.: B-47, B-114
ELLIS, FRANK: *B-113*
Ellis, Martha — HOPKINS, MARTHA ELLIS
Ellis, Virginia — see JENCKES, VIRGINIA ELLIS
Ellsworth, Henry C.: B-137

Ellsworth, Henry W.: B-1
Elston, Isaac C.: A-81, A-229, A-230, A-391, B-36, B-351
Elston, Susan — see Wallace, Susan Elston
Elven, Frederick W.: B-218
ELY, JAMES M.: *A-99*
Embree, David: B-114
Embree, Elisha: A-136, A-232, A-264, B-114, B-263
Embree, James T.: B-114
EMBREE, LUCIUS C.: *B-114*, A-176
Emergency Work Committee, Inc.: B-222
Engineering: A-108, A-174
England: A-10, A-22, A-198, A-250, B-119, B-263, B-280, B-312
  control of Old Northwest: A-286
  World War I: B-360
  World War II: A-127
  Cheshire
    Norwich: A-127
  London: A-116, B-131
  Manchester: A-353
Engleman, Anna Ulen: A-100
ENGLEMAN, JAMES OZRO: *A-100*
English, Charles: A-318
English, Elisha Gale: A-101, B-1
English, Helen Orr: A-101
ENGLISH, HENRY K.: *B-115*
English, Joseph K.: B-115
English, William E.: A-101
ENGLISH, WILLIAM HAYDEN: *A-101*, A-15, A-173, A-232, A-264, A-272, A-370, A-408, B-114, B-204, B-212, B-335, B-394
English Hotel and Opera House (Indianapolis): A-101, B-341
English's Opera House: B-341
Entertainment
  casinos: A-390
  circuses: B-20
  medicine shows: A-82
  motion pictures: A-327, B-147
  sewing: A-332
  sports: A-219, A-385, B-203, B-367, B-398
  theaters: A-390, A-391, B-3, B-34, B-47

Environmental protection: B-127
EPISCOPAL DIOCESE OF INDIANAPOLIS: *B-116*, B-70
Episcopalian Churchwomen: B-116
Episcopalian Young Churchmen: B-116
Equal Rights Ammendment: A-288
Equal Suffrage Society of Indianapolis: B-76
Equitable Accident and Mutual Aid Life Association (Portland, Ind.): B-9
Equitable Life Assurance Society: A-116
Esarey, Logan: A-176
Eugene, Vermillion Co.: A-332
Europe: A-108, A-391, B-145, B-248
  tours:
    1850-1879: B-167
    1880-1909: A-83, A-162, A-174, A-317, A-402, B-84, B-281, B-365
    1910-1945: A-123, A-366, B-14, B-248, B-324
Eustis, William: A-147, A-272
EVANS, GEORGE: *B-117*
Evans, Hiram Wesley: A-352
Evans, M. Stanton: A-288
Evansville, Vanderburgh Co.: A-4, A-15, A-33, A-57, A-176, A-382, B-99, B-114, B-146, B-166, B-210, B-232, B-246, B-251, B-330, B-353, B-364, B-365, B-399
Evansville and Crawfordsville Railroad: A-136, B-146
Evansville and Illinois Railroad: A-136
Evansville Housing Authority: B-246
Evansville Steam Flour Mill Company: B-114
Evarts, William M.: A-391, B-348
Everett, Edward: A-346, B-394
Everett, Ester — see Lafe, Ester Everett
Evermann, Ava: B-118
EVERMANN, BARTON W.: *B-118*
Everton, Fayette Co.: B-81
Ewing, Alexander: B-119
Ewing, George W.: A-25, B-119, B-137, B-212, B-286, B-351, B-384
Ewing, John: A-57, A-91, A-237, A-266, A-272, A-384, B-263, B-351
Ewing, Thomas: A-147, A-237, A-272, A-381, B-351

Ewing, William G.: A-8, B-137, B-286, B-351
EWING, WILLIAM GRIFFITH, AND EWING, GEORGE WASHINGTON: *B-119* — See also W. G. and G. W. Ewing Company

Fabri, Ralph: B-213
Facism: A-365
Fairbank, Francis: B-231
Fairbanks, Adelaide: A-102
FAIRBANKS, CHARLES WARREN: *A-102*, A-46, A-52, A-60, A-134, A-164, A-237, A-260, A-302, A-322, A-337, A-341, A-358, A-391, A-395, B-44, B-109, B-114, B-124, B-140, B-208, B-216, B-222, B-256, B-335, B-342, B-345, B-348
Fairbanks, Cornelia Cole: A-102, B-44
Fall Creek and Warren Township Gravel Road Company (Marion Co.): B-115
Fall Creek Township, Hancock Co.: B-242
Fallen Timbers, Battle of: A-286
Family Life
  -1815: A-29, A-72, A-198, A-266, A-302, A-308
  1816-1849: A-8, A-14, A-18, A-26, A-27, A-29, A-38, A-57, A-59, A-72, A-91, A-98, A-107, A-111, A-114, A-117, A-123, A-130, A-142, A-144, A-152, A-175, A-198, A-201, A-203, A-216, A-222, A-236, A-243, A-265, A-266, A-267, A-270, A-275, A-288, A-301, A-302, A-323, A-332, A-333, A-335, A-374, A-391, A-402, A-407, B-22, B-27, B-28, B-47, B-52, B-64, B-114, B-131, B-135, B-146, B-152, B-165, B-204, B-249, B-273, B-276, B-280, B-287, B-295, B-299, B-312, B-313, B-330, B-348, B-354, B-356, B-394, B-397
  1850-1879: A-8, A-9, A-14, A-19, A-27, A-29, A-30, A-33, A-38,

INDEX

Family Life—*Continued*
  1850–1879—*cont.*
    A-45, A-57, A-59, A-72, A-75,
    A-81, A-83, A-88, A-89, A-91,
    A-98, A-111, A-114, A-117,
    A-129, A-130, A-137, A-138,
    A-142, A-143, A-145, A-150,
    A-152, A-171, A-174, A-175,
    A-198, A-201, A-203, A-210,
    A-216, A-218, A-222, A-227,
    A-228, A-242, A-243, A-253,
    A-259, A-265, A-266, A-267,
    A-275, A-288, A-302, A-321,
    A-323, A-333, A-335, A-349,
    A-353, A-356, A-374, A-380,
    A-385, A-391, A-396, A-402,
    A-407, B-7, B-15, B-18, B-21,
    B-22, B-23, B-26, B-28, B-35,
    B-40, B-43, B-52, B-64, B-69,
    B-86, B-92, B-108, B-122,
    B-123, B-131, B-135, B-146,
    B-150, B-151, B-152, B-154,
    B-156, B-157, B-165, B-167,
    B-204, B-205, B-206, B-215,
    B-223, B-226, B-245, B-252,
    B-262, B-265, B-273, B-275,
    B-276, B-280, B-281, B-285,
    B-287, B-293, B-299, B-312,
    B-313, B-330, B-348, B-353,
    B-354, B-356, B-360, B-365,
    B-373, B-385, B-393, B-397
  1880–1909: A-9, A-14, A-22, A-23,
    A-27, A-30, A-39, A-63, A-83,
    A-89, A-98, A-111, A-114,
    A-129, A-130, A-137, A-138,
    A-142, A-143, A-145, A-150,
    A-174, A-175, A-201, A-210,
    A-217, A-228, A-243, A-247,
    A-253, A-259, A-275, A-288,
    A-295, A-296, A-299, A-318,
    A-321, A-323, A-324, A-333,
    A-335, A-353, A-356, A-374,
    A-385, A-391, A-396, A-402,
    B-7, B-15, B-18, B-22, B-29,
    B-35, B-52, B-58, B-63, B-81,
    B-86, B-105, B-108, B-111,
    B-118, B-122, B-123, B-151,
    B-156, B-157, B-161, B-167,
    B-205, B-206, B-215, B-219,
    B-223, B-226, B-245, B-265,
    B-273, B-275, B-280, B-281,
    B-285, B-298, B-313, B-323,
    B-324, B-330, B-342, B-353,
    B-354, B-360, B-365, B-367,
    B-388
  1910–1945: A-22, A-27, A-39, A-83,
    A-110, A-114, A-142, A-174,
    A-210, A-211, A-228, A-285,
    A-295, A-296, A-315, A-335,
    A-353, A-356, A-357, A-365,
    A-396, A-402, B-18, B-29,
    B-52, B-63, B-81, B-105, B-108,
    B-111, B-118, B-122, B-123,
    B-156, B-157, B-167, B-169,
    B-209, B-218, B-219, B-226,
    B-261, B-275, B-280, B-281,
    B-285, B-324, B-330, B-342,
    B-353, B-354, B-360, B-365
  1946– : A-110, A-114, A-315, B-17,
    B-29, B-52, B-169, B-209, B-261,
    B-281, B-285, B-324, B-330,
    B-354
FAMILY SERVICE ASSOCIATION
  OF INDIANAPOLIS: *A-103*
Family Welfare Society (Indianapolis):
  A-103
Faris, George W.: B-114
Farmers and Merchants Bank (Madison,
  Ind.): A-302
Farnham, John Hay: A-125, A-302,
  A-384, B-263
Farnham, William: B-342
Farquhar, John: A-15
Farrand, Max: A-176
Farwell, Charles B.: A-237, A-341
Farwell, John V.: A-341
FAUCETT, THOMAS: *A-104*
Fauntleroy House (New Harmony):
  B-17
"Fawn" (steamship): B-387
Fayette County: A-157, A-397, B-247
  Connersville: A-45, A-115, A-118,
    A-157, A-158, B-3, B-81, B-215,
    B-278, B-304, B-359, B-365,
    B-384
  Everton: B-81
  Harrison Township: B-379
  Lick Creek: B-71
  Waterloo: A-118
Fayette County Fair: A-158

Fearing, Paul: A-8
Feasel, Calvin: A-329
FEDERATION OF ASSOCIATED CLUBS, INC.: *A-105*
FEIGHTNER, HAROLD C.: *B-120*
Female Moral Society (Brothertown, N.Y.): A-83
Fenn, Harry: B-111
Ferber, Edna: B-343
Ferguson, John: B-47
Ferris, George W.: B-240
Ferry Hall, (Lake Forest (Ill.) University): A-337
Fess, Simeon D.: A-352, B-114
Fiat Lux: B-355
Filene, Edward A.: A-285
Fillmore, Millard: A-272
Finney, Charles J.: A-23
First Congregational Church Sewing Circle (Terre Haute): A-128
FIRST INDIANA HEAVY ARTILLERY REGIMENT: *A-106*
First National Bank (Indianapolis): A-101
Fischli, John: A-410
Fish, Frederick P.: B-345
Fish, Hamilton: A-346, B-286
Fishback, William M.: B-240
Fishback, William P.: B-124, B-254, B-335, B-371, B-393
Fisher, Carl: B-142
FISHER, RUSSELL V.: *B-121*
Fishers, Hamilton Co.: B-155
Fitch, Graham N.: A-81, A-101, A-232, A-272, B-119, B-212, B-263, B-286, B-348, B-351, B-395
Fitch, Marshall Montgomery: A-107
FITCH, MAY LOUISE: *A-107*
FITZGERALD, DESMOND: *A-108*
Flaget, Bishop Benedict Joseph: B-212
FLANNER, HENRY BEESON: *A-109*
FLANNER, HILDEGARDE: *A-110*
Flanner, Janet: A-110
Flanner, Orpha Tyler: A-109
Flanner family: A-109
Flanner House (Indianapolis): A-268
Flat Rock, Shelby Co.: A-211
Flaxman, John: B-341
Fletcher, Allen M.: A-29

FLETCHER, CALVIN: *A-111*, A-229, A-302, A-381, A-391, B-103, B-286, B-351
Fletcher, Ingram: B-112
Fletcher, James Cooley: A-29, A-111, B-244
Fletcher, Lydia Bates: A-29
Fletcher, Miles: A-111
Fletcher, Sarah Hill: A-111
Fletcher, Stephen Keyes: A-111
Fletcher, Stoughton A.: B-147
Fletcher, William B.: A-111, A-293
Fletcher & Bradley — see Bradley & Fletcher
Flickinger, Florence: B-388
Flint, Steuben Co.: A-242
Florida: A-174, A-381, B-95
  Cape Canaveral: B-196
  Ft. Meade: B-359
  Gainesville: B-359
  Orlando: B-112
  Pensacola: B-243
  Tampa: B-109
Florida territory: B-171
Flowers, J. Howard: B-96
Floyd, Davis: A-272, B-351
Floyd County: A-370, B-57, B-271
  Mt. Zion Church: B-71
  New Albany: A-38, A-52, A-107, A-117, A-125, A-152, A-215, A-280, A-325, A-380, B-58, B-87, B-104, B-136, B-165, B-212, B-302, B-330, B-358, B-365
Foch, Ferdinand: B-145
Focus on Indiana Libraries: B-178
Fogelman, David: B-122
FOGELMAN, IDA: *B-122*
Fogelman, Maggie Moore: B-122
Folklore: B-362
Foraker, Joseph B.: A-164
Ford, Betty: A-288
Ford, Henry: A-172
Ford, Worthington C.: A-176, B-76
Fort Adams (Miss.): A-286
Fort Benjamin Harrison (Indianapolis): B-166, B-168, B-275, B-316
Fort Dearborn (Ill.): B-4
Fort Finney (Ohio): A-8, A-286
Fort Hamilton (Ohio): A-8

Fort Harrison (Terre Haute): B-212
Fort Jefferson (Ohio): A-101, A-286
Fort Knox (Vincennes): A-286
Fort Pitt (Pa.): A-8
Fort St. Clair (Ohio): A-286
Fort Washington (Ohio): A-8, A-147
Fort Wayne, Allen Co.: A-40, A-132, A-141, A-163, A-187, A-237, A-286, A-384, A-387, A-407, B-2, B-3, B-23, B-108, B-119, B-137, B-167, B-212, B-222, B-231, B-241, B-286, B-324, B-345, B-351
Fort Wayne and Southern Railroad Company: A-101, B-204
Fort Wayne Electric Company: B-345
Fort Wayne Land Office: A-381
Fortas, Abe: B-301
Fortin, Louis Nicolas: B-212
Fortnightly Literary Club: A-315
FORTUNE, WILLIAM: *A-112*, A-176, B-342
Forward Club: B-142
Forward, Inc. (Indianapolis): B-116
Foster, Abiel: A-286
Foster, John H.: B-114
Foster, John Watson: A-15, A-52, A-102, A-164, A-176, A-302, A-358, A-383, B-114, B-124, B-254, B-286, B-339, B-342, B-348
FOSTER, MRS. OREN: *B-123*
FOULKE, WILLIAM DUDLEY: *B-124*, A-52, A-164, A-210, B-76, B-342, B-345
Foulks family: A-385
Fountain City, Wayne Co.: A-226
Fountain County: A-131, A-261, A-407
 Attica: A-23, A-140, A-251, A-407, B-71, B-169
 Coal Creek: B-165
 Covington: A-140, A-245, B-266
Fowler, Benton Co.: A-295, B-3
Fox, Eugenie Nicholson: B-261
France: A-70, B-63, B-145, B-218, B-349
 colonization in North America: A-70
 influence in Old Northwest: A-286
 Napoleonic era: A-32, B-349
 World War I: A-12, A-49, A-114,
  B-63, B-145, B-218, B-287, B-332, B-337, B-360
 Grenoble: A-57
 Paris: A-70, A-410
Franchere, Gabriel: B-119
Frankfort, Clinton Co.: B-3, B-75, B-245, B-383
Franklin, Johnson Co.: A-18, A-19, A-20, A-36, A-205, B-25, B-315, B-385
Franklin College (formerly Indiana Baptist Manual Labor Institute): A-18, A-20, A-36
Franklin County: A-10, A-157, A-356, A-397
 Brookville: A-8, A-123, A-135, A-157, A-265, A-394, A-396, B-37, B-56, B-154, B-239, B-278, B-308, B-336
 Laurel: A-396
 Metamora: A-202, A-396, B-125, B-377
 Springfield: A-328
 Union: A-328
 Whitcomb: A-356
FRANKLIN COUNTY GENERAL STORE: *B-125*
Franklin Turnpike Company: A-123
Fraser, Alexander: B-119, B-212
FRASER, DWIGHT: *A-113*
Fraser, Joshua: A-113
Frazier, James S.: B-286
Freelandville, Knox Co.: B-238
Freeman, Joseph C.: B-73
FREEZ, F.: *B-126*
Freligh, Susan Shepardson: B-313
Frelinghuysen, Frederick T.: A-391
Fremont, Jesse Benton: A-272
Fremont, John C.: A-80, A-391, B-84, B-94
French Lick, Orange Co.: B-102, B-343, B-365
French Lick Springs Hotel: B-343
Frenzel, Otto N.: B-218
Friends Boarding House for Girls (Indianapolis): A-31
Friends History Club: B-78
Friendsville Academy (Tenn.): A-129
From the Buzzers Roost: B-257
Fry, John: A-114

FRY-RHUE FAMILY: *A-114*
FRYBARGER, GEORGE: *A-115*
Frybarger, W. W. — see W. W. Frybarger & Company
Fullen, Samuel: A-301
Fuller, Hector: A-116, A-312
FULLER, JOHN LOUIS HILTON: *A-116*
Fuller, Melville W.: A-52, B-138
Fulton County
  Akron: B-268
  Rochester: B-19, B-20
Funeral Supply Credit Association: A-191

Gage, Thomas: A-286
Galapagos Islands: B-121
Gale, Joseph: A-117
Gale, Joseph W.: A-117
GALE, WAKEFIELD: *A-117*
Gallatin, Albert: A-147, A-272, A-381
Gallion, Henry C.: B-56
GALLION, NATHAN D.: *A-118*
Gallipolis: A-70
Gano, John S.: A-8, A-147, A-272
GARDEN CLUB OF INDIANA: *B-127*
Gardiner, Flora — see KLING, FLORA GARDINER
Garfield, James A.: A-69, A-145, A-164, A-272, A-341, A-383, A-391, B-269, B-286
Garfield, Lucretia: A-391
Garland, Hamlin: A-272, B-85, B-208
Garner, John Nance: A-172
Garrison, Francis J.: B-76
Garrison, Lindley M.: B-345
Garrison, William Lloyd: A-272
GARVER, JOHN JAMES: *B-128*
Gary, Lake Co.: B-123, B-174
Gas City, Grant Co.: B-15
GASKINS, BERNICE: *B-129*
Gaskins, Tobe A.: B-129
Gaskins family: B-129
GATES, RALPH F.: *B-130*, A-231, B-147, B-381
Gatling, Richard J.: A-391
Gause, Eli: A-237
GAVIN, JAMES: *A-119*
Gavin and Miller (Greensburg): A-119

Gayoso, Manuel de Lemos: A-286
Genealogy: A-3, A-9, A-51, A-79, A-125, A-127, A-150, A-169, A-216, A-229, A-288, A-336, B-17, B-51, B-84, B-102, B-105, B-106, B-114, B-123, B-167, B-238, B-252, B-261, B-281, B-294, B-336
General Electric Corporation: B-345
General Federation of Women's Clubs: B-76, B-176
Gentry, Brady: B-24
Gentryville, Spencer Co.: B-365
Geology: B-37
Georgetown (Ky.) Female Collegiate Institute: A-107
Georgia
  Civil War: A-21, A-24, A-29, A-47, A-59, A-80, A-113, A-145, A-160, A-205, A-206, A-208, A-220, A-244, A-252, A-259, A-269, A-291, A-294, A-340, A-347, A-359, A-368, A-373, A-379, A-402, B-136, B-141, B-197, B-221, B-228, B-231, B-244, B-266, B-330, B-358, B-382
  Andersonville (Civil War): A-291, A-391
  Atlanta: B-360
  Atlanta (Civil War): B-197
  Chickamauga (Civil War): A-56, B-114
  Peach Tree Creek (Civil War): B-171
German American Teachers Association: B-253
Germans in America: B-342
German Protestant Orphan Association: A-300
Germany and Germans: A-47, A-175, A-216, A-262, A-300, A-321, B-79, B-112, B-119, B-145, B-191, B-218, B-219, B-238, B-275, B-285, B-335, B-357
  World War I: A-114, B-145
  Dusseldorf: B-218
  Goettingen: B-137
  Kleingartach: A-175
  Prussia: B-394
Gerry, Elbridge: A-272

GEX OBUSSIER, LOUIS: *A-120*
Gibault, Pierre: A-384, B-212
Gibson, John: A-101, A-147, A-272, A-286, A-302, A-385, B-212
GIBSON, THOMAS WARE: *A-121*
Gibson Circuit Court: B-114
Gibson County: A-252, B-114, B-364
  Oakland City: B-330
  Princeton: A-35, A-136, A-137, A-278, A-354, B-16, B-114, B-285
Gibson County Seminary: B-114
Giddings, Joshua R.: B-76, B-131, B-205
Giddings, Laura — see Julian, Laura Giddings
GIDDINGS, LURA MARIA: *B-131*
GILBERT, JOHN ALSOP: *A-122*
Gilbert, Newton W.: B-114, B-339, B-345
Gilder, Richard W.: B-111
Gilfillan, Rev. J. A.: B-107
Gill, Caleb: A-206
Gillie, George W.: B-95
Gilpin, Henry D.: A-147, A-272
Girl's Classical School (Indianapolis): B-393
"Give Us Back Our Hillbillies": B-60
Gladden, Washington: B-111
Gladstone, William: A-272
Glendale (Ohio) Female College: B-285
Glidden, Henry A.: B-348
"Glimpses of My Mother's Life": A-398
GLOVER, JOSEPH: *B-132*
Godfroy, Chief Francis: B-137
Godfroy, Gabriel: B-212
Godfroy, William: B-119
Godown, John M.: B-231
Godown, Mary — see MCLAUGHLIN, MARY GODOWN
Goforth, William: A-8
Goldberg, Rube: B-208
Goldman, Emma: B-124
Goldwater, Barry: A-288
Gompers, Samuel W.: B-110
Goodrich, James P.: A-272, B-113, B-114, B-124, B-147, B-216, B-218, B-219, B-339, B-342, B-345, B-381

Goodrich, Watson, and Macy — see Watson, Macy, and Goodrich
GOODWIN, JOHN PEMBERTON: *A-123*
Goodwin, John R.: A-123
Goodwin, Mattie Shirk: A-123
Goodwin, Samuel: A-123
Goossens, Eugene: A-327
Gorman, Arthur P.: B-47
Goshen, Elkhart Co.: B-35, B-289, B-293
Gosport, Owen Co.: A-133, B-129, B-271
Gowdy, John K.: A-102, B-259, B-342
GRAETER, CHRISTIAN: *A-124*
Graeter, Frederick: A-124
Graham, George: B-263
GRAHAM, JOHN KENNEDY: *A-125*
Graham, Mary — see Walker, Mary Graham
Graham, William: B-263
Grand Army of the Republic (G.A.R.): A-58, A-112, A-126, A-133, A-216, A-254, B-49, B-83, B-133, B-240, B-359, B-360, B-389
GRAND ARMY OF THE REPUBLIC. GEORGE H. THOMAS POST: *B-133*
GRAND ARMY OF THE REPUBLIC. NELSON TRUSLER POST NO. 60: *A-126*
Grand Hotel (Indianapolis): B-343
Grand Rapids and Indiana Railroad Company: A-240
Grandview, Spencer Co.: B-13
Grange (Patrons of Husbandry): A-292, B-28, B-185, B-353
Granger, Francis: A-272
Grant, Alexander: B-354
Grant, Ulysses S.: A-164, A-272, A-391, B-94
Grant County: A-6, A-181, A-342, B-134
  Gas City: B-15
  Marion: B-3, B-90, B-373
  Mier: B-22
  Sims: A-23
GRANT COUNTY WAR HISTORY COMMITTEE: *B-134*

GRAY, BEULAH BRAZELTON: *A-127*
Gray, David: B-212
Gray, Horace: A-52
Gray, Isaac H.: B-113
Gray, Isaac P.: A-272, B-47, B-212, B-240, B-286, B-335
Gray, James: A-253
GRAY, MARION H.: *A-128*
GRAY, WILLIAM H.: *B-135*
Gray family: A-127
Graydon, James Weir: A-302
Greeley, Horace: A-229, A-272, B-84, B-114, B-124
Green, Cyrus: A-129
Green, Duff: A-91
GREEN, MIRIAM WILSON: *A-129*
GREEN, REUBEN: *A-130*
Green, Robert: A-130
Greenback Party: B-387
Greencastle, Putnam Co.: A-144, B-122, B-346, B-365 — See also DePauw University
Greene, Nathaniel: A-287, A-303
Greene County: A-97
  Bloomfield: A-58
  Worthington: A-17
Greenfield, Hancock Co.: A-3, A-114, A-245, A-353, B-265
Greenman, J. M.: B-95
Greensburg, Decatur Co.: A-67, A-119, A-294, A-333, A-400, B-248, B-376, B-385, B-390
Greenwood, Johnson Co.: A-356, B-112
Gregg, David: B-212
Gregg, Harvey: A-111
Gresham, Walter Q.: A-15, A-52, A-101, A-164, A-229, A-302, A-383, B-58, B-87, B-114, B-153, B-258, B-286, B-339, B-345, B-348
GRIFFIN, DANIEL F.: *B-136*
Griffin, Daniel P.: B-285
Griffin, Helen — see O'Leary, Helen Griffin
Griffin, Helen Porter: B-285
Griffin, Maurice: B-285
Griffin, Patrick: B-285
Griffin, Solomon B.: B-236
Griffin and McGrain (Corydon): B-285

GRIFFITH, THORNTON: *A-131*
Grills, Henry S.: A-132
GRILLS, MERTON W.: *A-132*
Grimmessy family: A-291
GRIMSLEY, JAMES: *A-133*
Griswald, Glenn: B-20
Griswold, George: A-302
Grossman, G.: B-95
Grosvenor, Charles Henry: A-164
Guthrie, Wayne: A-288
Guthrie Memorial Forest, Jennings Co.: B-257
Gwathmey, John: A-101

HACK, ELIZABETH JANE MILLER: *A-134*
Hackel, Hans: B-218
Hackelman, Pleasant: B-124
Hackleman, William R.: A-135
HACKLEMAN-TOWNER FAMILY: *A-135*
Hagerstown, Wayne Co.: A-28, A-132, A-222, A-374, B-336
Hagerstown and West River Turnpike Association: A-132
Hagerstown Canal Office: A-132
Hagerstown Mining Company: A-222
Haiti: A-95, A-210
  Episcopal Diocese: B-116
Haldeman, Walter N.: A-341
Hale, Bertha — see White, Bertha Hale
Hale, Edward Everett: A-282, B-111
Halford, E. M.: A-383, B-138, B-348
Halford, Elijah Walker: A-52, A-312, A-371
Hall, Baynard R.: A-402
Hall, Rev. J. Wesley: A-102
Hall, James: A-303
Hall, John A.: A-131
HALL, SAMUEL (1797-1862): *A-136*, B-114, B-285
HALL, SAMUEL (1848-1869): *A-137*
Halleck, Charles A.: B-20, B-147, B-251, B-381
Halleck, Henry W.: A-80, A-391, B-43, B-225
Halstead, Murat: A-164, A-341, A-391, B-124
Hambrecht, George P.: A-176

INDEX 455

Hamilton, Alexander: A-272, A-286, A-287, A-381
HAMILTON, ALLEN: *B-137*, A-229, A-264, A-381, B-1, B-119, B-351, B-384, B-394
Hamilton, Andrew H.: B-137
Hamilton, Andrew J.: A-407
Hamilton, Henry: A-272
HAMILTON, JOHN WATTS: *A-138*
Hamilton, Phoebe: B-137
Hamilton, Steuben Co.: A-26
Hamilton and Taber (Fort Wayne): B-137
Hamilton and Williams (Fort Wayne): B-137
Hamilton County: A-342, B-34, B-247
  Arcadia: B-324
  Bethlehem (Carmel): B-207
  Carmel: B-283
  Fishers: B-155
  Noblesville: A-389, B-301
  Roberts Settlement: A-316
  Westfield: A-21, A-342, A-363
Hamlin, Hannibal: A-272
Hammond, Abram A.: A-81
Hammond, Charles: A-147
Hammond, Daniel: B-23
Hammond, Sarah — see Bruce, Sarah Hammond
Hampson, Anne Yandes: B-397
Hampson family: B-397
Hampton, Wade: B-348
Hamtramck, John Francis: A-8, A-237, A-272, A-286, A-302, A-381, A-384, B-212
Hancock, Winfield S.: A-101
Hancock County: A-114, A-139
  Fall Creek Township: B-242
  Greenfield: A-3, A-114, A-245, A-353, B-265
  New Palestine: A-99
  Sugar Creek Township: A-321
HANCOCK COUNTY MISCELLANEOUS PAPERS, 1828-1853: *A-139*
Handley, Harold W.: A-358, B-24
Hanley, James M.: B-99
Hanly, J. Frank: A-272, A-358, B-124, B-345
Hanna, Hugh: A-260, B-351

Hanna, Marcus A.: A-164, A-391, A-395, B-259
Hanna, Robert: A-140
HANNA, ROBERT BARLOW: *A-140*
HANNA, SAMUEL (1797-1866): *A-141*, B-119, B-137, B-351
Hanna, Samuel (fl.1880s): A-140
Hannaman, Rhode Ann Luse: A-243
Hannaman, William: A-243
Hannegan, Edward A.: A-59, A-81, A-91, A-229, A-267, A-272, A-380, B-351
Hanover, Jefferson Co.: A-43, A-125
Hanover College: A-43, A-52, A-107, A-361, A-385
Hansbrough, H. C.: A-102
Harding, Attila: A-142
Harding, Samuel S.: A-302
HARDING, STEPHEN SELWYN: *A-142*, B-205
Harding, Warren G.: A-272, B-147, B-219, B-236, B-259, B-343
Harlan, Allen Co.: A-39, B-293
Harlan, Andrew J.: A-91, B-137, B-204
Harlan, James: A-15
Harlan, John M.: A-46, A-52, A-164, A-337, A-341
Harmar, Josiah: A-8, A-272, A-286
Harmon, Judson: B-345
Harper, Charles L.: B-245
Harper, Henry: B-123
Harper, Mrs. Howard: B-123
Harper, Ida Husted: B-76
Harper, James: B-123
Harper, Nellie: B-123
HARPER, WILLIAM: *A-143*
Harper & Brothers Publishers: A-391, B-348
HARRAH, ALMIRA MARIA SCOTT: *A-144*
Harrah, Samuel B.: A-144
Harrah family: A-144
Harris, Oren: B-24
Harrison, Benjamin (1726-1791): A-272
HARRISON, BENJAMIN (1833-1901): *A-145*, *B-138*, A-44, A-52, A-102, A-136, A-164, A-260, A-272, A-302, A-311, A-312, A-383, A-391, A-395, B-114, B-124,

Harrison, Benjamin—*Continued*
    B-140, B-146, B-253, B-258,
    B-286, B-345
Harrison, Caroline Scott: A-145, A-272,
    B-76, B-138
HARRISON, I. MERRITT: *B-139*
Harrison, John Cleves Symmes: B-212
HARRISON, MARY LORD: *B-140*,
    A-145, B-124, B-250
HARRISON, RUSSELL B: *A-146*,
    A-145, B-138
Harrison, Timothy: B-139
HARRISON, WILLIAM HENRY:
    A-147, A-8, A-71, A-101, A-187,
    A-237, A-272, A-286, A-302,
    A-308, A-384, A-385, B-212,
    B-249, B-351
Harrison County: A-37, A-261, A-397,
    B-87, B-351
  Byrneville: A-34
  Corydon: A-89, A-90, A-303, B-285
  Laconia: B-87
  Lanesville: B-285
  Martinsburgh: A-34
Harrison County Cyclone Relief
    Committee: B-285
Harrison County Seminary: B-285
Harrison Township, Fayette Co.: B-379
Harrisville, Randolph Co.: A-292
HARRYMAN, SAMUEL K.: *B-141*
Hart, Albert Bushnell: B-124, B-342
Hartford City, Blackford Co.: B-204
Hartke, Vance: A-288, B-24, B-301,
    B-369
HARTLEY, HARRY D.: *B-142*
Hartsville, Bartholomew Co.: B-69,
    B-108
Harvard University: B-275, B-281
HARVEY, RALPH: *B-143*, B-369
Harvey, William P.: B-110
Harvie, Alice — see Duden, Alice
    Harvie
HASELTINE, ROSS J.: *B-144*
Hasselman, Lewis W.: A-148
Hasselman, Olive Eddy: A-148
HASSELMAN, OTTO H.: *A-148*
Hatch, Edward: A-391
Hatch, O. M.: B-105
Hawaii: A-317, B-364
Hawhe, Arthur: B-57

HAWK, ALETHA GRACE: *B-145*
HAWK, CHRISTOPHER L.: *A-149*
Hawkins, Caroline: A-396
Hawkins, John P.: A-271
Hawkins, Martha: A-110
Hawley, Henry: B-146
Hawley, Joseph B.: B-138
HAWLEY, RANSOM: *B-146*
Hawley, Ransom E.: B-146
Hay, John: A-102, B-105
Hay, Mary G.: B-76
Hayden, Henry J.: A-150
HAYDEN, JOHN JAMES: *A-150*,
    B-249, B-286, B-348
Hayden, Sarah Marshall: A-150
Hayes, Rutherford B.: A-15, A-164,
    A-272, A-302, A-341, A-391
Hayes, Wayne L.: B-99
Hayes, Webb: A-341
Haynes, Elwood: B-345
Hays, John: B-351
Hays, John T.: B-147
HAYS, WILL H.: *B-147*, A-176, A-358,
    B-114, B-216, B-218, B-219,
    B-259, B-339, B-343
HAZELWOOD LUMBER COM-
    PANY (Anderson): *B-148*
Hazlitt, Henry: A-176
Heacock, Richard: B-206
Hearst, William Randolph: A-391
Heasley, J. P.: B-109
Heasley and DuShane (South Bend):
    B-109
Heath, John W.: A-151
Heath, Robert: A-151
HEATH, WILLIAM P.: *A-151*
Heaton, Aletha — see Wade, Aletha
    Heaton
Heaton, Mary: B-299
Hebrew Ladies Benevolent Society:
    A-204
Heckenwelder, John: A-272
HECKER, EDWARD J.: *B-149*
Hecker Brothers Printing Company
    (Indianapolis): B-149
Hecla Mining Company (Mont.): B-47
HEDDEN, DAVID: *A-152*
Hedden, William H.: A-152
HEDRICK, MRS. WEST: *B-150*
Heilman, William: B-114

INDEX   457

Heiney, E. B.: B-276
Helena Daily Journal: A-146
HELLER, HERBERT LYNN: *A-153*, A-156
Helm, Leonard: B-212
HELM, THOMAS B.: *B-151*
HELMS, HAMET N.: *B-152*
Helms, Mary A. Davis: B-152
Helvering, Guy T.: B-114
Hemenway, James A.: A-52, A-102, A-176, A-337, B-113, B-114, B-147, B-345
Hemlock Lodge (Pine Hills): A-15
Hempstead, William S.: A-237
Hendricks, Abram: B-153
HENDRICKS, ALLAN: *B-153*
Hendricks, Hord and Hendricks (Indianapolis): B-153
HENDRICKS, THOMAS ANDREW: *A-154*, A-15, A-52, A-57, A-59, A-81, A-101, A-229, A-230, A-232, A-272, A-302, A-322, A-407, B-37, B-47, B-137, B-212, B-236, B-281, B-286, B-335, B-348, A-394
Hendricks, William: A-8, A-91, A-101, A-237, A-272, A-302, A-381, A-391, B-137, B-263, B-351
Hendricks County: A-155, A-335, A-342, B-392
  Belleville: A-55
  Brownsburg: B-108, B-367
  Danville: A-55, A-155, B-21, B-116
  Mill Creek: A-342
  North Salem: A-375
  Pittsboro: B-367
  Plainfield: A-299, A-342, A-357, B-159
  Sugar Grove: A-342
Hendricks County Fremont Club: A-55
HENDRICKS COUNTY MISCEL-
  LANEOUS PAPERS, 1830-
  1905: *A-155*
Henley, Miriam: A-129
Henley, Thomas J.: A-80
Hennegan, Edward A.: B-1, B-119
Henry, Charles L.: A-52
Henry, James: A-147
Henry, Joseph: A-101, B-212
Henry, Patrick: A-272, A-286

Henry County: A-132, A-153, A-156, A-221, A-342, B-143, B-276
  Knightstown: A-132, A-221, B-100, B-276
  New Castle: A-92, A-138, A-156, A-281, A-336, B-51, B-139, B-260, B-276, B-292
  Ogden: A-353
  Raysville: A-45, A-109, B-139
  Spiceland: A-259, B-117, B-356
Henry County Historical Society Museum: A-336
HENRY COUNTY MISCELLA-
  NEOUS PAPERS, 1812-1943: *A-156*
Henry County Nature Research Club: A-336
Henry County Seminary: A-156
HERON, ALEXANDER: *A-157*, *B-154*, B-138
HERON, JAMES: *A-158*
HERRON, GEORGE: *B-155*
Herron, George D.: A-312
Herron, Ted: B-147
Herron Art Institute (Indianapolis) — See John Herron Art Institute
HERSHEY, JEREMIAH: *B-156*
Hesburgh, Theodore: B-213
Heth, R. W. — see R. W. Heth & Brothers
Hewitt, Abram S.: B-205
Heyn, Bernard G.: B-218
Hibben, James S.: B-157
Hibben, Thomas E.: B-157
HIBBEN FAMILY: *B-157*
Higgenson, Thomas Wentworth: A-282
Higham, Isaac: B-36
Hightshoe family: B-378
Hill, David B: B-335
Hill, James J.: A-69
Hill, John Wesley: A-102
Hill, Sarah — see Fletcher, Sarah Hill
Hilles, Charles D.: B-259
Hillsdale College (Mich.): B-2
HINES, CYRUS C.: *B-158*, A-111
Hingston, Nicholas: A-70
Hispaniola Mining Company (Haiti): A-95
Hiss, Sebastian: B-159
HISS, WILLIAM H.: *B-159*

Historic Preservation: A-394, B-17, B-142
History and Biography: A-11, A-50, A-57, A-95, A-101, A-111, A-127, A-132, A-142, A-150, A-153, A-156, A-164, A-170, A-176, A-214, A-232, A-237, A-268, A-274, A-277, A-302, A-313, A-322, A-336, A-341, A-372, A-391, A-393, B-4, B-13, B-33, B-40, B-45, B-49, B-60, B-72, B-85, B-103, B-106, B-107, B-108, B-120, B-124, B-142, B-147, B-205, B-212, B-226, B-254, B-258, B-259, B-264, B-281, B-284, B-290, B-302, B-323, B-336, B-341, B-349, B-359, B-369, B-386, B-394
"A History of the Army of the Cumberland": A-170
"History of the Office of Attorney General in Indiana": B-337
Hitchcock, A. S.: B-95
HITCHCOCK, MOSES: *A-159*
Hite, Isaac: A-101
Hitt, George C.: A-371, B-259
Hitt, Robert R.: A-164, B-124
Hoagland, Merica: B-345
Hoar, George F.: B-254
Hobart, Garret A.: A-102
Hobbs, Barnabas C.: A-15, A-81, A-266, A-272, B-286, B-348
Hobbs, Tipton Co.: B-52
Hobbs, William H.: B-109
HOBBS, WILLIAM P.: *A-160*
Hodgdon, Samuel: A-8, A-147, A-272, A-286, A-287
HODGIN, EVERETT E.: *A-161*
Hoffman, Jacob F.: A-407
Hohenberger, Frank: B-333
Holcomb, J. I.: B-219
Hollandsworth, Mrs. Charles W.: B-252
HOLLIDAY, JOHN H.: *B-160*, A-52
HOLLIDAY, MARGARET YANDES: *A-162*
Holliday, William A.: A-111
HOLLOWAY, EMMA: *A-163*
HOLLOWAY, WILLIAM ROBESON: *A-164*, A-15, A-52, A-311, A-341, A-391, B-124, B-348

Holman, Jesse L.: B-137
Holman, Richard: B-161
HOLMAN, WILLIAM STEELE: *B-161*, A-91, A-101, A-165, A-173, A-232, A-272, A-302, A-407, B-137, B-335, B-376, B-394
Holman, William Steele, Jr.: B-161
Holman-Black, Charles: B-281
HOLMAN-O'BRIEN PAPERS: *A-165*
Holmes, Andrew: A-384
Home for the Aging (Episcopal): B-116
Homer, Rush Co.: B-52
Hook and Star: B-100
"Hoosier": A-95
"Hoosier Listening Post": B-62, B-265
The Hoosier Outdoors: B-257
Hoosier State Medical Association: A-268
HOOSIERS FOR PEACE: *A-166*
Hoover, Herbert: A-172, A-272, A-358, B-147, B-259
Hoover, J. Edgar: B-200
Hooverwood (Indianapolis): A-204
Hopkins, Erastus: B-394
Hopkins, Harry: A-172
HOPKINS, MARTHA ELLIS: *A-167*
HORAN, MICHAEL E.: *B-162*
Hord, Hendricks, and Hendricks — see Hendricks, Hord, and Hendricks
Hornstein, Jean — see Menger, Jean Hornstein
HORSE THIEF DETECTIVE ASSOCIATION: WARREN TOWNSHIP, MARION COUNTY: *B-163*
Houghton, Eugene: A-168
HOUGHTON, WILLIAM: *A-168*
Houston, George S.: A-81
HOUSTON, GUS: *B-164*
Houston, Herbert: B-76
Hovey, Alvin P.: A-15, A-272, A-383, A-391, B-94, B-114, B-254, B-394
HOVEY, EDMUND OTIS: *B-165*, A-271, B-137, B-146, B-351
Hovey, Mary Carter: B-165
HOWARD, DONALD D.: *B-166*
HOWARD, FREDERICK WILLIAM: *A-169*

INDEX

Howard, George: B-166
Howard, Louise: B-166
Howard, Marilyn: B-166
Howard, Tilghman A.: A-272, B-351
Howard County: A-6, A-342, B-64
   Kokomo: A-79, A-84, A-269, A-360, A-395, B-3, B-52, B-118, B-142, B-223
   Russiaville: A-49
   Tampico: A-269
   West Middleton: A-49
HOWE, DANIEL WAIT: *A-170*, B-76, B-212
Howe, Frances R.: B-167
HOWE, FRANCIS: *B-167*
Howe, Henry: A-341
Howe, Julia Ward: B-124
Howe, Louis M.: B-200
Howe, Rose: B-167
Howe, Rose Bailly: B-167
Howe's Christmas Album: B-51
Howells, William Dean: A-116, A-282, A-341, B-111, B-273, B-342
Howie, Hillis L.: A-304
Howland, Hewitt H.: B-276
Howland, Louis G.: A-52, B-342
HOWLAND, POWELL: *A-171*
Hubbard, Kin: A-68, A-358, B-60, B-343
HUDNUT, WILLIAM H.: *B-168*, A-288
HUDSON, HUBERT: *B-169*
Hudson Sales Company (Attica): B-169
Huff, James M.: B-259
Hughes, Charles Evans: A-68, B-147, B-342
Hull, Cordell: A-249, B-219
Hull, William: A-272
Humor: A-82, B-19, B-60, B-62
Humphrey, Hubert H.: B-61
Hunt, Susan B. — see UNTHANK, SUSAN B. (Hunt)
Hunter, Caroline Stokes: A-172
Hunter, Mae — see Weinstein, Mae Hunter
HUNTER, ROBERT: *A-172*, A-128
Hunter, Robert M. T.: A-272
HUNTER, WILLIAM D. II.: *A-173*, A-165
Huntingburg, Dubois Co.: A-348

Huntington, Elisha M.: B-348, B-351
Huntington, Huntington Co.: B-322
Huntington County: A-342, B-137
   Huntington: B-322
   Roanoke: A-241
Huntington family: B-105
Huntsville, Madison Co.: B-279
Huntsville, Randolph Co.: B-68
Huntzinger, William: A-170
Hurlbert, William Henry: A-341
Hurst, Henry: B-114, B-212
Husted, Ida — see Harper, Ida Husted
Hutchings, Agnes — see Zulauf, Agnes Hutchings
Hutchings, Frederick: A-174
Hutchings, Matilda Koehler: A-174, A-175
Hutchings, Robert: A-174, A-175
HUTCHINGS, WILLIAM DAVIES: *A-174*
HUTCHINGS-KOEHLER FAMILY: *A-175*
HUTCHINSON, DAVID: *B-170*
HYNES, WILLIAM DUNN: *B-171*
Hynes, William R.: B-171

Iceland Medicine Company (Indianapolis): A-82
Idaho: A-142
Ickes, Harold L.: B-124, B-219
IGLEHART, JOHN EUGENE: *A-176*, B-114
Iglesias, José Mariá: A-391
ILIFF, JAMES ARTHUR: *A-177*
Illinois: A-9, A-198, A-267, A-323, A-369, B-92, B-223, B-353
   Civil War: A-351, A-380, B-171, B-293
   government: B-27, B-105
   Alton: A-265, B-108
   Bellville: B-18
   Blandinsville: A-401
   Bloomington: A-140
   Bogota: B-15
   Cairo: A-108, A-264, A-351, B-92
   Camp Butler (Civil War): A-380
   Camp Douglas (Civil War): A-380
   Camp Grant: B-330
   Canton: B-252
   Champaign: B-122

Illinois—*Continued*
  Chicago: A-98, A-231, A-233, A-270,
    A-302, A-341, A-390, B-63,
    B-113, B-119, B-147, B-167,
    B-210, B-223, B-285, B-330
  Columbian Exposition: A-63,
    A-264, B-161
  Danville: A-138
  Decatur: A-100
  East St. Louis: B-353
  Effingham County: A-201
  Ellisville: B-281
  Ford County: B-87
  Fort Dearborn: B-4
  Fort Sheridan: B-243
  Galesburg: B-223, B-360
  Galva: B-293
  Geneseo: B-281
  Great Lakes Naval Training Station
    (World War I): B-337
  Kaskaskia: A-286, B-212
  Lake Forest: A-337
  Lawrence County: B-105
  Lincoln: B-223
  Pope County: B-385
  Robinson: B-252
  Rock Island: B-281
  Shawneetown: A-54, A-150
  Springfield: A-130, B-105, B-223
  Toledo: A-201
  Wataga: B-360
  Weldon: B-129
  Winchester: B-123, B-223
  Xenia: B-150
Illinois Country: A-384
Immigrants: A-47, A-57, A-120, A-198,
  A-204, A-239, A-321, A-353,
  B-112, B-162, B-191, B-218,
  B-237, B-272, B-285, B-312,
  B-335
Immigrant's Aid Association (Indianapolis): B-237
Independent Company of Rangers:
  A-230
Independent Order of Good Templars:
  A-228
India: A-271, A-367, B-79
Indiana (works on Indiana history):
  A-11, A-101, A-150, A-176,
  A-302, B-103, B-142, B-276,
  B-284
Indiana, a Redemption from Slavery: A-95
INDIANA ACADEMY OF SCIENCE:
  B-172, B-56, B-95
Indiana and Indianans: A-95
INDIANA ARTISTS' CLUB, INC.:
  A-178
Indiana Asbury University — see
  DePauw University
Indiana Association for Mental Health:
  B-101, B-181
Indiana Association of Life Underwriters: B-267
Indiana Baptist Manual Labor Institute
  (Franklin) — see Franklin
  College
Indiana Bar Association: B-275
Indiana Bible Association of Friends:
  B-139
Indiana Brewers Association: B-120
Indiana Centennial: B-56
INDIANA CENTRAL RAILWAY
  COMPANY: *A-179*
The Indiana Churchwoman: A-181
Indiana Civil Service Reform Association: B-124
Indiana Club of Chicago: B-345
Indiana Club Woman: B-176
Indiana Commission on Aging and
  Aged: A-199, B-101
Indiana Committee on Nursing: A-186
Indiana Conference of Tuberculosis
  Workers: A-6
Indiana Constitutional Convention
  (1850-51): A-101, A-277, A-370
INDIANA COTTON MILLS
  (Cannelton): *A-180*
Indiana Council of Christian Education:
  A-181
INDIANA COUNCIL OF
  CHURCHES: *A-181*, B-116
Indiana Council of Religious Education:
  A-181
INDIANA COUNTY SUPERINTENDENTS ASSOCIATION:
  A-182
Indiana Democratic Committee: B-203
Indiana Democratic Editorial Association: A-173

INDIANA DEPARTMENT OF PUB-
LIC WELFARE: *B-173*
INDIANA DIETETIC ASSOCIA-
TION: *A-183*
INDIANA DUNES STATE PARK:
B-174, B-211, B-301
INDIANA FEDERATION OF ART
CLUBS: *B-175*, B-333
Indiana Federation of Charity Organiza-
tions' Secretaries: A-103
INDIANA FEDERATION OF
CLUBS: *B-176*, A-288, B-181,
B-281
INDIANA FEDERATION OF
SOCIAL WORK CLUBS:
B-177
Indiana Federation of Women's Clubs:
B-17
Indiana Female Seminary (Indianapolis):
A-253
Indiana Forestry Association: A-102
Indiana Gazette (Vincennes): A-57
INDIANA GUARD RESERVE: *A-184*
Indiana High School Alumni Assoc.:
B-48
Indiana Historical Commission: A-176
Indiana Historical Society: A-95, A-111,
A-123, A-176, A-336, B-103
Indiana Hospital for the Insane: A-15,
B-69
Indiana Hotel Association: B-77
Indiana Hotel Keepers' Association:
A-66
Indiana Institute for the Education of
the Blind (Indianapolis): A-63
Indiana Internal Improvements Board:
B-263
Indiana Keramic Club: A-157
INDIANA LIBRARY ASSOCIATION:
B-178, B-45, B-179
INDIANA LIBRARY TRUSTEES
ASSOCIATION: *B-179*
Indiana Lincoln Foundation: B-275
Indiana Lincoln Memorial Association:
B-307
Indiana Lincoln Union: B-219
Indiana Little Theater Society: B-217
Indiana Magazine of History: B-85, B-269
Indiana National Guard: A-184, B-157

Indiana Normal School (Terre Haute):
A-39
Indiana Parliamentarian: B-182
Indiana Poetry Magazine: B-51
Indiana Reformatory (Pendleton): B-374
INDIANA REPUBLICAN EDITO-
RIAL ASSOCIATION: *B-180*
Indiana Republican State Central Com-
mittee: B-180, B-285
Indiana Sanitary Fair: B-103
Indiana School for Feeble-Minded
Youth (Fort Wayne): A-163
Indiana School for the Deaf (Indianapo-
lis): A-177
INDIANA SCHOOLMEN'S CLUB:
A-185
Indiana Selective Service Association:
B-110
INDIANA SOCIETY FOR MENTAL
HYGIENE: *B-181*
Indiana Soldiers' and Sailors' Orphan's
Home (Knightstown): B-108,
B-315
INDIANA STATE ASSOCIATION
OF PARLIAMENTARIANS:
B-182
Indiana State Bank: A-266, A-267,
A-302, B-299, B-394
  Terre Haute Branch: B-287
Indiana State Board of Agriculture:
A-157, B-154
Indiana State Board of Health: A-6
Indiana State Capitals: B-244, B-258,
B-351
Indiana State Capitol Building (Indian-
apolis): A-319
INDIANA STATE COMMISSION
FOR THE REORGANIZA-
TION OF SCHOOL CORPO-
RATIONS: *B-183*
INDIANA STATE CONFERENCE
ON SOCIAL WORK: *B-184*
Indiana State Council of Women: B-190
Indiana State Fair: A-157, B-90, B-240
Indiana State Federation of Women's
Clubs: B-176
Indiana State Government
Constitutional Convention (1850-
1851): A-101, A-277, A-370

Indiana State Gov. — *Continued*
  Executive: B-20, B-43
    Alcoholic Beverage Commission:
      B-20, B-120, B-130
    Conservation Dept.: B-20, B-95,
      B-218, B-219
    Department of Public Welfare:
      B-173
    Food and Drug Commission: A-22
    governor: A-15, A-164, A-272,
      B-43, B-130, B-226, B-240,
      B-254, B-263, B-284, B-369,
      B-394
    Highway Commission: B-20, B-130
    Internal Improvements Board:
      B-263
    Secretary of State: B-352
    state auditor: A-395, A-401
    State Board of Charities: A-188,
      B-173, B-184
    State Council on Defense (World
      War I): B-147
    State Treasurer: A-266, A-267
    Superintendent of Public Instruction: A-111, A-271
    Tax Study Commission: B-130
  Judicial
    Attorney General: B-337
    Probation Division: B-203
    Supreme Court: A-361, A-370
  Legislative (House): A-8, A-15, A-25,
    A-47, A-57, A-125, A-165,
    A-270, A-302, A-395, B-12,
    B-18, B-101, B-212, B-261,
    B-269, B-285, B-286, B-345,
    B-351, B-363, B-395
  Legislative (Senate): A-8, A-15, A-25,
    A-57, A-125, A-221, A-231,
    A-302, B-12, B-17, B-101,
    B-114, B-196, B-212, B-213,
    B-269, B-285, B-286, B-351,
    B-363, B-369, B-395
    Committee on Benevolent and
      Penal Institutions: B-101
    history: A-101
  School Reorganization Commission:
    B-183
INDIANA STATE GRANGE: *B-185*
Indiana State House Building Assoc.:
  B-34

Indiana State Library: A-123, B-10,
  B-45, B-181, B-306
INDIANA STATE NURSES ASSOCIATION: *A-186*
Indiana State Pension Association:
  A-133
Indiana State Prison: B-334
Indiana State Teachers Association:
  A-271, B-396
Indiana Sunday School Association: A-181
Indiana Sunday School Union: A-181
INDIANA TAXPAYERS ASSOCIATION: *B-186*
Indiana Telephone Assoc.: B-19, B-20
Indiana Territory: A-101, A-147, A-187,
  A-303, B-37
  militia: B-212, B-351
INDIANA TERRITORY COLLECTION, 1800-1818: *A-187*
Indiana Trudeau Society: A-6
Indiana Tuberculosis Council: A-6
Indiana Union of Literary Clubs: B-176
Indiana Union Traction Company:
  A-200
Indiana University: A-27, A-140, A-246,
  A-297, B-81, B-102, B-122,
  B-166, B-212, B-309 — See
  also Bloomington, Monroe
  County
Indiana University, Indianapolis Extension: A-357
Indiana University Memorial Fund:
  B-81
INDIANA WEAVERS' GUILD: *B-187*
Indiana Women's Prison: B-203
Indiana World's Fair Commission:
  B-219
Indiana Yearly Meeting of Anti-Slavery
  Friends: A-342
Indiana Yearly Meeting of Friends:
  B-139
Indiana Yearly Meeting of Women
  Friends: B-64
Indianapolis: A-29, A-42, A-63, A-68,
  A-110, A-111, A-119, A-148,
  A-157, A-170, A-211, A-218,
  A-233, A-240, A-249, A-253,
  A-263, A-269, A-275, A-288,
  A-301, A-302, A-315, A-317,

INDEX 463

Indianapolis—*Continued*
   A-335, A-365, A-367, A-372,
   A-373, A-396, A-397, A-400,
   B-27, B-38, B-48, B-58, B-62,
   B-65, B-66, B-110, B-112, B-145,
   B-231, B-232, B-243, B-244,
   B-256, B-278, B-281, B-316,
   B-321, B-360, B-388, B-392,
   B-397
  architecture: A-319, A-320
  art & artists: A-178, B-217, B-275,
   B-306, B-341, B-344
  attorneys: A-15, A-53, A-145, A-210,
   A-216, A-229, A-260, A-266,
   A-267, A-297, A-302, B-80,
   B-138, B-153, B-250, B-275,
   B-290, B-342, B-378
  Bertha Ballard Home: A-31
  Borinstein Home: A-204
  buses: A-197
  business: A-82, A-87, A-95, A-101,
   A-103, A-111, A-123, A-164,
   A-171, A-189, A-190, A-191,
   A-192, A-197, A-258, A-260,
   A-262, A-266, A-267, A-288,
   A-309, A-337, A-341, A-351,
   A-373, A-381, A-386, A-390,
   A-391, A-395, B-38, B-39, B-48,
   B-112, B-142, B-147, B-149,
   B-153, B-158, B-201, B-209,
   B-218, B-233, B-250, B-262,
   B-267, B-272, B-281, B-282,
   B-320, B-321, B-327, B-394
  Butler University: A-46, A-53, A-322,
   B-76, B-275
  Camp Carrington (Civil War): A-21
  Camp Morton (Civil War): A-41,
   A-302, A-339, B-298
  charities: A-31, A-64, A-84, A-103,
   A-105, A-112, A-188, A-195,
   A-196, A-204, A-268, A-279,
   B-173, B-222, B-237, B-267,
   B-295
  Christ Church Cathedral: B-70
  Citizens Gas Company: A-258, B-342
  City Academy: B-267
  Claypool Hotel: A-66, B-77
  Clowes Hall: B-275
  courts: B-16, B-378
  Dime Savings and Loan: A-103
  education: A-46, A-53, A-63, A-195,
   A-304, B-48, B-76, B-220,
   B-275, B-303, B-310, B-321,
   B-340, B-393
  English Hotel & Opera House:
   A-101, B-341
  factories: A-65, A-191, B-189
  First National Bank: A-101
  First Presbyterian Church: A-162,
   B-303
  Flanner House: A-268
  Fort Benjamin Harrison: B-166,
   B-168, B-275, B-316
  Friends Boarding House For Girls:
   A-31
  Girl's Classical School: B-393
  government and politics: A-112,
   A-161, A-193, A-288, A-395,
   B-48, B-76, B-115, B-153,
   B-201, B-256, B-267, B-310,
   B-342, B-343, B-393
  Grand Hotel: B-343
  history: A-95, B-306
  Hooverwood: A-204
  hospitals: A-268
  hotels: A-66, A-98, A-101, B-77,
   B-274, B-343
  Indiana Female Seminary: A-253
  Indiana Institute for the Education of
   the Blind: A-63
  Indiana School for the Deaf: A-177
  Indiana State Capitol Building: A-319
  Indiana University, Indianapolis Extension: A-357
  Institute for the Deaf and Dumb:
   A-177
  ISTA building: B-396
  Jewish community: A-204, A-309
  journalists, authors, and poets: A-95,
   A-134, A-148, A-170, A-285,
   A-288, A-313, A-320, A-322,
   A-364, A-365, B-307, B-340,
   B-341, B-344
  Kirschbaum Center: A-204
  land office: A-237
  letters from: A-83, A-107, A-109,
   A-114, A-130, A-150, A-157,
   A-210, A-231, A-233, A-243,
   A-262, A-263, A-266, A-275,
   A-288, A-333, A-400, A-407,

464 INDEX

Indianapolis—*Continued*
  letters from—*cont.*
    B-15, B-47, B-129, B-154,
    B-212, B-261, B-328, B-332,
    B-353, B-394, B-397
  Lockefield Gardens: B-168
  Marott Hotel: A-258
  Marott Shoe Store: A-258
  medicine and physicians: A-29, A-161,
    A-186, A-194, A-243, A-268,
    A-293, B-128, B-328
  Meridian Street Foundation: B-275
  musicians: A-327
  Naval Avionics Facility: B-168
  newspapers: A-46, A-116, A-164,
    A-237, A-320, A-337, A-341,
    A-358, A-371, B-33, B-72,
    B-193, B-265, B-343
  organizations: A-31, A-42, A-64,
    A-103, A-105, A-112, A-166,
    A-178, A-186, A-190, A-192,
    A-194, A-195, A-204, A-268,
    A-279, A-288, A-298, A-300,
    A-315, A-351, A-404, B-188,
    B-190, B-191, B-192, B-193,
    B-194, B-257, B-267, B-275,
    B-277, B-281, B-340, B-355,
    B-389, B-393, B-398
  orphanage: A-196, A-300
  police department: A-161
  post office: A-164, A-395
  railways: A-101, A-111, A-112, A-164,
    A-189, A-266, A-267, A-371,
    B-33, B-47, B-149, B-153
  Rainbow Divison Parade (1923): A-12
  real estate: A-63, A-309, A-343,
    A-390, B-153, B-157, B-282
  religion: A-95, A-162, A-204, A-253,
    A-310, A-357, B-70, B-116,
    B-290, B-303
  Soldier's and Sailor's Monument:
    A-319
  Starlight Musicals: B-275
  Supreme Court and State Office
    Building: A-15
  teachers: A-313
  theaters: A-101, B-275, B-341
  Union Inn Hotel: A-98
  Union Station: B-194
  Veterans Hospital: A-112

Walker Beauty School: A-390
Walker Building: A-390
Walker Manufacturing Company:
  A-390
Walker Theater: A-390
Weir Cook Airport: B-168
Woodruff Place: A-351, B-79
YMCA (Fall Creek Parkway Branch):
  A-268
YMCA (Senate Ave. Branch): A-268
Indianapolis "500" Festival: B-77
Indianapolis and Bellefontaine Railroad:
  A-111, B-252
Indianapolis and Fall Creek Gravel
  Road Company: A-171
Indianapolis and Springfield Plank
  Road: A-72
Indianapolis and Vincennes Railroad:
  A-108
INDIANAPOLIS ASYLUM FOR
  FRIENDLESS COLORED
  CHILDREN: *A-188*
Indianapolis Bar Association: B-275
Indianapolis Belt Railway: A-313
INDIANAPOLIS BELT RAILROAD
  AND STOCK YARDS COM-
  PANY: *A-189*, A-309
Indianapolis Benevolent Society: A-103
INDIANAPOLIS BOARD OF
  TRADE: *A-190*, A-309, A-395
Indianapolis Branch Bank: B-47
INDIANAPOLIS BUSINESS AND
  PROFESSIONAL WOMEN'S
  CLUB: *B-188*
Indianapolis Cable Street Railway Co.:
  A-164
INDIANAPOLIS CASKET COM-
  PANY: *A-191*
INDIANAPOLIS CHAIN AND
  STAMPING COMPANY:
  B-189
INDIANAPOLIS CHAMBER OF
  COMMERCE: *A-192*, A-112,
  B-267
Indianapolis, Cincinnati, and Lafayette
  Railroad: A-313
Indianapolis Citizens Street Railway
  Company: A-101
Indianapolis City Plan Commission:
  B-76

INDIANAPOLIS CITY RECORDS, 1943, 1946: *A-193*
Indianapolis Civic League: B-267
Indianapolis Commercial Club: A-112, A-192, B-217, B-267
Indianapolis Committee of Safety: B-153
Indianapolis Conversation Club #3: B-78
Indianapolis Copper Mining Company: B-262
Indianapolis Council of Social Agencies: B-65
INDIANAPOLIS COUNCIL OF WOMEN: *B-190*
Indianapolis Cycle Club: B-398
Indianapolis Deutsch-Literarischer Klub: B-191
Indianapolis Florists Club: A-350
INDIANAPOLIS FLOWER MISSION: *A-194*, B-5
INDIANAPOLIS FREE KINDERGARTEN AND CHILDREN'S AID SOCIETY: *A-195*
INDIANAPOLIS GERMAN LITERARY CLUB: *B-191*
Indianapolis Graduate Nurses Association: A-186
Indianapolis High School Alumni Society: B-340
Indianapolis Home for Aged Women: B-267
Indianapolis Insurance Company: B-153
Indianapolis Journal: A-371
Indianapolis Junior Chamber of Commerce: A-192
Indianapolis Land Office: B-263
Indianapolis Light Infantry: A-101
Indianapolis Literary Club: B-45, B-60
Indianapolis Masonic Lodge: B-47
INDIANAPOLIS MATINEE MUSICALE: *B-192*
Indianapolis Metropolitan YMCA: A-268
Indianapolis Monetary Committee: A-260
Indianapolis Museum of Art: B-275
Indianapolis News: A-46, A-116, A-237, A-337, A-341, B-72, B-193, B-343

INDIANAPOLIS ORPHANS ASYLUM: *A-196*
Indianapolis Portfolio Club: B-153
Indianapolis Propylaeum: B-281
Indianapolis Sabbath School Union: B-233, B-303
Indianapolis Sanitary Commission: B-342
Indianapolis Star: A-358, B-33, B-193, B-265
Indianapolis Street Railways Company: B-149
Indianapolis Symphony Orchestra: A-327, B-275
Indianapolis Theatre Association: B-275
Indianapolis Times: A-164, A-320
Indianapolis Trade Association: A-192
INDIANAPOLIS TRANSIT SYSTEM: *A-197*
INDIANAPOLIS TYPOGRAPHICAL UNION NO.1: *B-193*
INDIANAPOLIS U.S.O. COUNCIL: *B-194*
Indianapolis Union Railway Company: A-189
Indianapolis Woman's Club: B-281
Indianapolis Women's City Club: B-188
Indians: A-346 — See also *True Indian Stories*
  Brothertown tribe: A-83
  Chickasaw tribe: B-273
  Chippewa tribe: B-107, B-119
  Delaware tribe: A-187, A-393
  Fox tribe: B-119
  Menominee tribe: A-369, B-119, B-348
  Miami tribe: A-25, A-91, A-187, B-26, B-59, B-107, B-119, B-137, B-351
  Osage tribe: A-272, B-119
  Peoria tribe: B-107
  Piankashaw tribe: A-384
  Potawatomi tribe: A-25, B-119, B-162, B-212, B-351
  Sac tribe: B-119
  Shawnee tribe: B-119, B-348
  Sioux tribe: B-119
  Stockbridge tribe: A-393
  Winnebago tribe: B-119

Indians—*Continued*
    in Indiana: A-83, A-95, A-187, B-49, B-56, B-59, B-107, B-119, B-212, B-263, B-336
    in Iowa: B-119
    in Kansas: B-119
    in Midwest: A-393
    in Minnesota: B-119
    in Missouri: A-272, B-119
    in New York: A-83
    in South Dakota: A-175
    in Wisconsin: A-84, B-119
    agents: A-83, A-187, A-272, B-137
    claims: A-25, A-83, A-91, B-212, B-348, B-395
    education: A-175, A-393, B-356
    government control over: A-91, B-59, B-119, B-351
    languages: B-107
    removal: A-83, B-1, B-119, B-263, B-351
    trade: A-286, A-384, B-4, B-11, B-119, B-137, B-212, B-286, B-351
    treaties: A-147, A-187, A-286, A-302, B-137, B-351
    wars: A-8, A-95, A-101, A-147, A-272, A-286, B-4, B-263, B-351
        Battle of Fallen Timbers: A-286
        Battle of Tippecanoe: B-258, B-284, B-351
    Industrial Removal Office (Indianapolis): A-204
INFO: B-176
Ing, John: B-146
Ing, Lucy: B-146
Ingalls, Charles: B-195
Ingalls, John J.: B-254, B-339
Ingalls family: B-195
INGALLS STONE COMPANY (Bedford): *B-195*
Ingersoll, Charles J.: A-272
Ingersoll, Robert G.: A-52, B-205, B-348
INGLE, JOHN: *A-198*
Ingle, John, Jr.: A-176, A-198, A-382
Inglefield, Vanderburgh Co.: A-198
Ingram, Andrew: A-111

Institute for the Deaf and Dumb (Indianapolis): A-177
INSTITUTE ON RELIGION AND AGING: *A-199*
Insull, Samuel: B-345
International Council of Women: B-190
International Mark Twain Society: B-140
International News Service: B-65
International Typographical Union: B-193
Interparliamentary Union: B-200
INTERURBANS: *A-200*
Iowa: A-9, A-19, A-88, A-168, A-323, A-329, A-369, B-223, B-248, B-286
    Civil War: A-19, A-259, B-265
    Indians: B-119
    Adair County: B-64
    Afton: A-201
    Albia: B-248
    Birmingham: B-397
    Burlington: B-27
    Cedar Rapids: B-223
    Centerville: B-397
    Chariton: A-201
    Clarinda: B-69
    Council Bluffs: A-302, B-293
    Creston: B-360
    Dallas County: A-259
    Davenport: B-319
    Des Moines: B-384
    Indianola: B-265
    Keokuk County: B-64
    Knoxville: B-87
    Lansing: B-152
    Magnolia: B-75
    Page County: B-293
    Paton: A-296
    Silver Creek: A-242
    Smyrna: B-150
    University of Iowa: B-261
    Wapello County: A-396
    Winneshiek County: B-64
    Winterset: B-170
Iowa Conference Seminary (Mt. Vernon, Iowa): A-334
Iran — See Persia
Ireland: B-162
IRELAND, JAMES: *A-201*

Ironside, George: B-212
Irving, William: A-272, A-286
Irvington, Marion Co.: B-76, B-85,
 B-149, B-205, B-224
Irvington Republican Club: B-149
Irwin, William G.: B-218, B-343, B-345
Italy: A-229, A-239, A-302, B-284
 World War II: A-362, B-270

J.F.D. Lanier Home (Madison): B-142
JACKSON, AMOS WADE: *B-196*
Jackson, Andrew: A-147, A-272
Jackson, Edward L.: A-68, A-272,
 A-352, A-358
JACKSON, JOSEPH W.: *A-202*
Jackson, Rowland H.: B-196
Jackson, Mrs. Rowland H.: B-196
Jackson, Suydam, & Company — see
 Suydam, Jackson, & Company
JACKSON, THOMAS: *B-197*
Jackson Abstracts, Inc. (Versailles):
 B-196
Jackson County: A-342
 Brownstown: A-201, B-365
 Seymour: B-52, B-146, B-365
*Jacob Piatt Dunn: His Indian Language
 Studies and Indian Manuscript Collection:* B-107
"Jacob Strader" (steamboat): B-93
Jacobs, Andrew, Sr.: B-203
JACOBS, ANDREW, JR.: *B-198*,
 A-288
Jameson, Donald: A-365
Jameson, J. Franklin: B-76
Jameson, Margaret Booth: A-365
Jameson, Mary — see Judah, Mary
 Jameson
Jameson, Patrick Henry: A-210
Jamestown, Boone Co.: B-52, B-108
Japan: A-367, A-378, B-146, B-213
Jaques, Harvey: A-356
Jaques, Martha (Mrs. Harvey) — see
 STOUT, MARTHA
Jasper County: A-167
 Rensselaer: A-167, B-63
Jay County: A-24, A-143, A-237, A-342,
 B-109
 Mount Pleasant: B-30
 Portland: A-86, B-9
JAYNE, SEELY: *B-199*

Jean Sibelius Fund: A-327
Jefferson, Thomas: A-101, A-250,
 A-272, A-286
Jefferson County: A-23, A-96, A-351,
 A-379, A-397, B-57
 Canaan: A-235
 Dupont: B-129
 Hanover: A-43, A-125 — See also
  Hanover College
 Madison: A-43, A-174, A-175, A-219,
  A-235, A-237, A-266, A-361,
  B-40, B-93, B-109, B-142,
  B-153, B-165, B-225, B-252,
  B-258, B-281, B-327, B-351
 Manville: A-235
 North Madison: B-40, B-298
Jefferson Township, Miami Co.: B-338
Jeffersonville, Clark Co.: A-8, A-9,
 A-101, A-121, A-125, A-308,
 A-331, B-36, B-48, B-302,
 B-317
Jeffersonville Railroad Company: A-8,
 B-36
JENCKES, VIRGINIA ELLIS: *B-200*
JENKS, NATHAN: *A-230*
Jenner, William E.: A-231, B-130,
 B-275
Jenners & Sergeant (Darlington): B-8
Jennings, Jonathan: A-101, A-125,
 A-232, A-272, A-302, B-212,
 B-258, B-351
Jennings County: A-351, A-355
 Guthrie Memorial Forest: B-257
 North Vernon: A-212, B-146, B-199
 Vernon: B-69
Jerusalem: A-229
*Jessup v. Wabash, St. Louis and Pacific
 Railway Company:* B-250
Jewish Community Center Association
 (Indianapolis): A-204
Jewish Community Relations Council
 (Indianapolis): A-204
Jewish Congressional Advisory Board:
 B-251
Jewish Education Association (Indianapolis): A-204
Jewish Family and Children's Services
 (Indianapolis): A-204
Jewish Federation (Indianapolis): A-204

JEWISH WELFARE FEDERATION OF INDIANAPOLIS: *A-204*
  Women's/Young Matron's Divisions: A-204
John C. Spann Company (Indianapolis): A-343
John Carter Brown Library (Providence, R.I.): B-107
John Cleves Symmes Harrison v. *Frederick Rapp:* A-210
John Herron Art Institute (Indianapolis): B-217, B-275
The John Tipton Papers: B-351
Johnson, Albert: B-202
Johnson, Amos: B-34
Johnson, Andrew: A-272, B-43, B-394
JOHNSON, ANDREW JACKSON: *A-205*
Johnson, George: B-34
JOHNSON, GEORGE S.: *A-206*
Johnson, Hannah: B-34
Johnson, Harriet Eitel Wells: A-315
Johnson, Henry O.: B-259
Johnson, Henry V.: A-52
Johnson, Hiram W.: A-172, B-124
JOHNSON, JEREMIAH: *B-201*
JOHNSON, JOHN: *B-202*
Johnson, Lyndon B.: B-369
Johnson, Reverdy: A-272
Johnson, Richard M.: A-91, A-147, A-272, A-387, B-295, B-351
Johnson, Robert Underwood: A-285, A-341, A-358, B-124, B-138
Johnson, William G.: B-139
Johnson County
  Amity: B-47
  Edinburg: A-30, B-146
  Franklin: A-18, A-19, A-20, A-36, A-205, B-25, B-315, B-385
  Greenwood: A-356, B-112
  Trafalgar: B-294
Johnston, General Washington: A-223, A-381, A-384, A-385, B-212, B-351
Johnston, John M.: B-37
Johnston, Lizzie: B-336
JOHNSTON, MARGARET AFFLIS: *B-203*
Joint Defense Appeal: A-204
JOLLY, CHARLES: *A-207*

Jolly, William Henry: A-207
Jones, Aquilla: A-81, A-95
JONES, JAMES H.: *A-208*
Jones, John Rice: A-286, A-302, B-212
JONES, LUMAN: *A-209*
JONES, WILLIAM F.: *B-204*
Jordan, David Starr: B-290
Jordan, James H.: B-114
Judah, John: B-262
Judah, John Mantle: A-210
Judah, Mary Jameson: A-210
Judah, Samuel: A-210, B-114, B-262, B-263
JUDAH-BRANDON FAMILY: *A-210*
JULIAN, GEORGE WASHINGTON: *B-205*, A-15, A-229, A-232, A-272, A-302, B-76, B-124, B-286
Julian, Grace — see CLARKE, GRACE JULIAN
Julian, Laura Giddings: B-205
Jusserand, Jules: B-236, B-342

Kahn Tailoring Company (Indianapolis): A-309
Kaltenborn, H. V.: A-172
Kansas: A-9, A-28, A-72, A-125, A-130, A-201, A-259, A-329, B-109, B-353, B-356
  Indians: B-119
  politics: A-101, A-230, B-84
  Ft. Riley: B-261
  Ft. Scott: A-28
  Howard: A-140
  Humboldt: B-75
  Kickapoo: A-302
  Leavenworth: B-293
  Neosha County: A-396
  Smith County: A-396
  Topeka: B-114, B-388
  Wyandotte: B-75
Kansas-Nebraska Act: A-81
Karr, W. Bryan: B-77
KASER, MARY ETTA: *A-211*
Kealing, Joseph B.: A-102
Keating, Edward: B-110
Keck, Christian: B-73
Keeler, Hiram: A-91
Keen family: A-382
Kefauver, Estes: B-99

INDEX

Keithly, Earle J.: A-256
Kellar, Andrew J.: A-341
Kellar, John: A-212
KELLAR MILLS (North Vernon): *A-212*
Keller, Helen: B-236
KELLEY, DAVID: *A-213*
Kellogg, Frank B.: B-259
Kellogg, Jennie — see Osbourn, Jennie Kellogg
Kellogg, Lottie — see Owen, Lottie Kellogg
Kellogg, Miner K.: A-282
Kellogg, William P.: B-254
Keltner, Alice: B-81
Kemper, Dr. Arthur T.: A-214
KEMPER, GENERAL WILLIAM HARRISON: *A-214*, B-113
Kennan, George: B-124, B-342
Kennedy, Andrew: B-328
Kennedy, Edward M.: A-288
Kennedy, John F.: B-203
Kennedy, Joseph P.: B-147
Kennedy, Robert F.: B-369
Kent, Alice: A-379
KENT, PHINEAS MARTIN: *A-215*
Kent State University: A-100
Kentland, Newton Co.: B-146, B-226
Kentucky: A-55, A-89, A-101, A-125, A-326, A-402, B-212, B-240, B-249, B-273
  American Revolution: A-101
  authors: B-297
  Civil War: A-35, A-41, A-59, A-85, A-96, A-129, A-140, A-205, A-228, A-234, A-241, A-259, A-269, A-325, A-329, A-340, A-359, A-381, B-21, B-114, B-136, B-141, B-199, B-228, B-231, B-244, B-266, B-313, B-314, B-322, B-330, B-358, B-366, B-382
  legal cases: A-326, B-99
  religion: B-302
  World War I: A-114, B-14
  Adair County: B-348
  Bardstown: B-171
  Bath County: B-340
  Boone County: A-114, A-302
  Camp Taylor (World War I): A-114
  Covington: A-90, A-114
  Dallasburg: B-245
  Danville: B-240
  Fayette County: A-332
  Fort Knox: B-243
  Georgetown: A-8, A-107
  Jefferson County: A-29, B-32
  Livingston County: A-29
  Louisville: A-52, A-54, A-90, A-112, A-125, A-286, A-410, B-15, B-87, B-92, B-93, B-137, B-252, B-275, B-280, B-353, B-365
  Mayfield: A-82
  Maysville: A-229
  Muhlenberg: B-252
  New Castle: B-215
  Newport: B-169
  Paducah: B-330
  Pewee Valley: A-52
  Portland: A-280
  Shelby County: B-27
  Shepardsville: B-248
  Stamping Ground: B-215
  Tompkinsville: B-114
  Worthington: B-252
Kentucky State Prison: B-132
Kentucky Volunteers: A-101
Kepner, William: A-21
Kern, John Worth: A-52, A-358, B-114, B-124, B-216, B-335, B-345
Kerr, Michael C.: A-272, B-249, B-335
KETCHAM, JACOB: *B-206*
Ketcham, Jane Merrill: A-216, A-267
Ketcham, John (1782-1865): A-216
KETCHAM, JOHN LEWIS (1810-1869): *A-216*, A-266
Ketcham, William: A-216
Keystone Masonic Lodge (Marion Co.): B-202
Kickapoo Indian Medicine Company: A-82
Kiefer, Susanah — see TARKINGTON, SUSANAH (Kiefer)
Kilgore, Daniel: A-229
Kilgore, David: B-124
Kilgour, Jesse — see DUBOIS, JESSE KILGOUR
KILLIAN, JOHN M.: *A-217*
Kimball, Nathan: B-138, B-254, B-348
KINDER, TRUSTIN B.: *A-218*

Kinder family: A-218
KING, ELIJAH: *B-207*
King, Horatio: B-84
KING, JOHN LYLE: *A-219*, A-229
King, Rufus: A-272
KING, WILLIAM F.: *A-220*
King's Daughter Hospital (Madison, Ind.): A-174
Kingsbury, Jacob: A-187
KINLEY, ISAAC: *A-221*
Kipling, Rudyard: A-327
Kirschbaum Center (Indianapolis): A-204
Kiser, J. J.: B-194
Kittredge, Solomon: A-117
KLING, FLORA GARDINER: *B-208*
Knapp, Charles W.: A-341
Knefler, Frederick: A-15, A-391
Knerr, Valerie: A-57
Knight, Mildred — see RICHARDSON, MILDRED KNIGHT
Knightstown, Henry Co.: A-221, A-336, B-100, B-276
Knightstown Banner: B-276
KNODE, ARCHIBALD B.: *A-222*
Know Nothing Party: B-269
Knox, Henry: A-8, A-272, A-286, A-287, A-303
Knox County: A-223, A-261
 Bruceville: B-54
 Freelandville: B-238
 Vincennes: A-54, A-57, A-70, A-108, A-124, A-210, A-223, A-230, A-237, A-283, A-286, A-302, A-308, A-378, A-379, A-382, A-384, A-385, B-105, B-156, B-210, B-212, B-262, B-284, B-287, B-369, B-382
 Wheatland: B-54
Knox County Board of Commissioners: A-223
KNOX COUNTY MISCELLANEOUS PAPERS, 1764-1833: *A-223*
Knox County Oil Company: B-54
Koehler, Aurora: A-174, A-175
Koehler, Herman: A-174, A-175
Koehler, Herman C.: A-175
Koehler, Matilda — see Hutchings, Matilda Koehler

Koehler, Robert: A-175
Koehler, Septima: A-175
Koehler family: A-174, A-175
Koehler-Hutchings family — see HUTCHINGS-KOEHLER FAMILY
Kokomo, Howard Co.: A-79, A-84, A-269, A-360, A-395, B-3, B-52, B-118, B-142, B-223
Korea: A-152, B-166
Kosciusko County: B-354
 Leesburg: A-59, B-162
 Vawter Park: B-122
 Warsaw: B-162
Kossuth, Washington Co.: A-85
KRAMER, FRANK N.: *A-224*
KRESGE, FLOYD LESLIE: *B-209*
Kresge, S. S. Company — see S. S. Kresge Company
Kresge, Sebastian S.: B-209
Kroll, Rev. H. F. Joseph: B-167
Krout, Mary Hannah: A-391, B-240
Krull, Frederic: B-281
Krull, Theresa Pierce: B-281
Krull-Pierce family — see PIERCE-KRULL FAMILY
Ku Klux Klan: A-15, A-225, A-226, A-352, B-120, B-163, B-334
KU KLUX KLAN. CROWN POINT: *A-225*
KU KLUX KLAN. WAYNE COUNTY: *A-226*
Kyte, James L.: B-392

L. W. Ott Company (Indianapolis): B-272
Labor and Trades: A-189, B-23, B-26, B-35, B-38, B-46, B-47, B-67, B-77, B-96, B-110, B-130, B-147, B-153, B-187, B-193, B-240, B-293
La Cobriza Mining Company (Sonora, Mexico): B-293
Laconia, Harrison Co.: B-87
LACROIX, MARCELLE D.: *B-210*
Ladies Home Journal: A-145
Ladoga, Montgomery Co.: B-7, B-15, B-337
Lafayette, Tippecanoe Co.: A-73, A-75, A-79, A-151, A-169, A-209,

INDEX

Lafayette — *Continued*
    A-311, A-334, A-388, B-339, B-357, B-372 — see also Purdue University
  Grand Opera House: A-388
Lafayette and Indianapolis Railroad: B-47
Lafayette College (Easton, Pa.): A-312
Lafayette Union Club: B-372
Lafe, Ester Everett: B-76
LaFollette, Robert M.: B-393
LAFUSE, AGGIE: *A-227*
LaGrange, La Grange Co.: A-327
LaGrange Bank (Lima, Ind.): A-401
LaGrange Collegiate Institute (LaGrange Co.): A-203
LaGrange County: A-339, A-345
  LaGrange: A-327
  Lima: A-401
  Mongo: A-149, B-313
  Ontario: A-203
Laird, Melvin: B-301
Lake County: A-91, A-181, B-12
  Cedar Lake: A-18
  Crown Point: A-225, B-223
  Gary: B-123, B-174
  Pullman Strike: B-240
Lake Erie: A-339
Lake Erie, Evansville, and South Western Railway Co.: A-52
Lake Forest University (Ill.): A-337
Lake Michigan: B-211
Lamb, G. W.: B-92
Lambert, Clara — see Miller, Clara Lambert
LAMBERT, GEORGE WASHINGTON: *A-228*
Lambert, Paschal T.: B-248
Land
  documents: A-3, A-23, A-27, A-49, A-70, A-75, A-93, A-94, A-122, A-123, A-214, A-228, A-229, A-237, A-240, A-266, A-282, A-329, A-343, A-355, A-382, A-385, A-388, A-408, B-32, B-37, B-123, B-129, B-142, B-196, B-202, B-205, B-215, B-234, B-247, B-248, B-249, B-280, B-292, B-313, B-325, B-336, B-359, B-392
  speculation and development: A-8, A-70, A-83, A-101, A-111, A-146, A-174, A-229, A-230, A-237, A-266, A-267, A-272, A-286, A-302, A-307, A-318, A-342, A-381, B-1, B-26, B-28, B-39, B-57, B-75, B-105, B-112, B-114, B-137, B-167, B-212, B-215, B-252, B-263, B-281, B-286, B-351, B-395
  surveying: A-8, A-83, A-125, A-272, A-302, A-400, B-87, B-88, B-156, B-164, B-212, B-351
  title abstracts: A-121
Land of the Great Lakes: B-309
Landers, Frederick: B-335
LANDGREBE, EARL F.: *B-211*
Landis, Charles B.: A-102, B-339
Landis, Frederick: A-68, B-256, B-345
Landis, Kenesaw Mountain: A-52
Landon, Margaret — see DELAPLANE, MARGARET LANDON
LANE, HENRY SMITH: *A-229, A-230,* A-5, A-52, A-69, A-101, A-111, A-136, A-232, A-237, A-272, A-391, B-114, B-137, B-212, B-254, B-286, B-348, B-376, B-394
Lane, Joanna: A-229
Lane, Joseph H.: A-230, B-212
Lane, Nellie Ruth: A-231
LANE, OSCAR BRUCE: *A-231*
Lane Seminary (Cincinnati): B-146
Lanesville, Harrison Co.: B-285
Lanier, James F. D.: A-8, A-15, A-101, A-266, A-267, A-302, A-370, A-380, B-137, B-252, B-263, B-299, B-351 — See also J. F. D. Lanier Home
LANMAN, CHARLES: *A-232*
Lansing, Robert: B-236, B-259
LaPorte, LaPorte Co.: A-8, A-9, A-107, A-112, A-240, B-342
LaPorte County: B-114, B-267
  LaPorte: A-8, A-9, A-107, A-112, A-240, B-342
  Michigan City: A-59, A-107, A-229, A-237, A-391, A-398, B-391
  Noble Township: A-238

472 INDEX

LaPorte University (LaPorte Co.): A-18
Larrabee, William C.: A-101
Larrabee, William H.: A-250, A-258
Lasher, George W.: A-145
Lasselle, Antoine: B-212
Lasselle, Charles B.: A-237, B-212
Lasselle, Francois: B-212
Lasselle, Hyacinth: A-223, B-119, B-212, B-286
Lasselle, Hyacinth, Jr.: B-212
Lasselle, Jacques: B-212
Lasselle, Jacques, Jr.: B-212
Lasselle, Jacques M.: B-212
Lasselle, Stanislaus: B-212
Lasselle, William P.: B-212
Lasselle & Polk (Logansport): B-212
LASSELLE FAMILY PAPERS: *B-212*
Lasselle v. *Polly:* B-212
"The Last Sunday": B-281
Latham, Harold S.: B-4
Lathrop, John H.: B-286
LAUCK, ANTHONY J.: *B-213*
Lauck, John: B-213
Lauck, Marie: B-213
LAUGHLIN, CLARA E.: *A-233*, B-85, B-208
Laurel, Franklin Co.: A-396
Law
  attorneys: A-15, A-30, A-51, A-52, A-55, A-60, A-62, A-83, A-94, A-102, A-111, A-119, A-136, A-144, A-145, A-156, A-164, A-165, A-176, A-210, A-215, A-216, A-219, A-266, A-267, A-297, A-302, A-326, A-361, A-369, A-370, A-408, B-16, B-58, B-80, B-99, B-109, B-113, B-114, B-138, B-147, B-161, B-167, B-196, B-205, B-213, B-246, B-275, B-285, B-286, B-292, B-337, B-342, B-345, B-348, B-349, B-369, B-378, B-384, B-395
  cases: A-15, A-16, A-30, A-52, A-94, A-101, A-102, A-111, A-210, A-297, A-302, A-352, A-369, A-370, A-391, B-104, B-212, B-215, B-216, B-246, B-284, B-285, B-286, B-345, B-380
  courts: A-290, B-132
  judges: A-122, A-361, B-37, B-58, B-132
  legal documents: A-4, A-23, A-27, A-53, A-89, A-91, A-123, A-127, A-141, A-159, A-223, A-229, A-237, A-252, A-256, A-261, A-264, A-266, A-408, A-410, B-212, B-234, B-250, B-290
Law, John: A-8, A-57, A-81, A-136, A-267, A-302, A-384, B-114, B-119, B-212, B-348, B-394
Lawrence, Catherine — see RANDOLPH, CATHERINE LAWRENCE
Lawrence County: A-213, A-370, A-407, B-132, B-353
  Bedford: A-76, A-94, A-117, A-369, B-164, B-195, B-326, B-348
  Daisy Spring Mill: B-353
  Leesville: A-77, B-326, B-365
  Mitchell: B-353
  Spring Mill State Park: B-329
  Springville: B-315
  Woodland (Mitchell): B-329
Lawrenceburg, Dearborn Co.: A-1, A-4, A-61, A-95, A-159, A-165, A-173, A-302, A-308, A-381, B-86, B-92, B-93, B-161, B-232, B-370, B-376
Lawrenceburg and Upper Mississippi Railroad: A-381
Lawson, Eliza: B-328
Lawson, Victor F.: A-337, A-341
LAYMAN, DANIEL W.: *B-214*
Layman's Missionary Movement: B-267
Le Duc, William G.: B-348
Lea, Henry S.: B-342
Lea, Luke: B-119
Leach, James: B-215
LEACH, JOSHUA: *B-215*, B-359
League of Nations: B-76, B-124
League of Women Voters: A-357, B-65
LEAGUE OF WOMEN VOTERS OF INDIANA: *B-216*
League to Enforce Peace: B-76, B-124
Lear, Tobias: A-147, A-272
Leavenworth, Crawford Co.: A-34, A-77
Lebanon, Boone Co.: B-42, B-356, B-367

INDEX

Lebo, Ruth — see SMITH, RUTH BURGESS LEBO
Lee, Charles: A-237
Lee, Henry: A-303
Lee, Richard Henry: A-272
Leesburg, Kosciusko Co.: A-59, B-162
Leesville, Lawrence Co.: A-77, B-326, B-365
Legal Aid Society (Indianapolis): A-103
Legion of the United States: A-286
Leland, Waldo G.: B-219
Lemon, Mary Dyer: B-344
Lenox Library, Peoria manuscript: B-107
LEONARD, JOHN FINLEY THOMPSON: *A-234*
Leonowens, Anne Henrietta: B-273
Leslie, Harry G.: B-219, B-345
LeSueur, Charles-Alexandre: A-237, A-282
"Let's Look Before We Leap": A-364
The Letters of a Father to his Daughter: B-44
Leupp, Francis E.: B-342
Lewis, Chauncey B.: A-235
Lewis, John L.: B-110
Lewis, Mary: A-236
LEWIS, SAMUEL B.: *A-235*
LEWIS, WILLIAM: *A-236*
Lewis and Clark expedition: B-45
Lexington, Scott Co.: A-77, A-101, A-174
Leyba, Fernando de: A-384
Liberty, Union Co.: A-227
Liberty Township Teachers' Institute (St. Joseph Co.): B-109
Libraries: A-255, B-10, B-45, B-66, B-72, B-178, B-179, B-264
Lick Creek, Fayette Co.: B-71
Lick Creek, Orange Co.: A-342
LIEBER, CARL H.: *B-217*
LIEBER, RICHARD: *B-218, B-219,* B-95, B-149
Lightburn, Elsie Whitehurst: A-127
Ligonier, Noble Co.: B-335
Lilly, Eli: A-393, B-70, B-281, B-284, B-371
Lilly, Josiah K.: A-285, A-336, B-70, B-219, B-333
Lima, LaGrange Co.: A-401

Lincoln, Abraham: A-112, A-176, A-272, A-391, B-13, B-28, B-33, B-49, B-105, B-114, B-253
Lincoln, Nancy Hanks: A-112, B-219
Lincoln, Robert T.: A-391
Lincoln assassination trial: A-391
Lincoln Bank (Evansville): B-246
Lincoln County Wars (New Mexico): A-391
Lincoln Memorial (Spencer Co.): B-219
Lincoln Union: A-176
Linden, Montgomery Co.: A-284
LINDLEY, HARLOW: *A-237*, B-76
Lippmann, Walter: A-172
Lisa, Manuel: A-70, A-237, A-384, B-212
Literature and Drama: A-11, A-30, A-34, A-132, A-134, A-150, A-175, A-210, A-216, A-221, A-233, A-285, A-313, A-314, A-315, A-364, A-365, A-391, B-4, B-44, B-51, B-55, B-60, B-62, B-78, B-96, B-111, B-140, B-145, B-149, B-191, B-208, B-217, B-248, B-261, B-267, B-275, B-276, B-281, B-294, B-297, B-307, B-330, B-341, B-344, B-346, B-355, B-371
Literature and Peace Committee: A-357
Little Mt. Zion Church, Warrick Co.: B-71
Little Pigeon Creek, Warren Co.: B-71
Livingston, Edward: A-272
Livingston, John: A-136
Livonia, Washington Co.: B-329
LLOYD, JOHN A.: *A-238*
Lloyd, John Uri: B-85
LLOYD, PEARL: *B-220*
Lloyd-George, David: B-110
Lock Foundry and Machine Shop (Logansport): A-23
Lockhart, James: B-114
Lockhart, Tabitha Armstrong: A-8
Lockman, Charles: B-73
Lockridge, Ross: A-123
Lodge, Henry Cabot: B-147, B-259, B-342, B-345
Logan, Dearborn Co.: A-207
Logan, John A.: A-341, B-348

Logan, Nathaniel: A-16
Logansport, Cass Co.: A-23, A-91,
  A-408, B-18, B-119, B-137,
  B-151, B-212, B-286, B-349,
  B-351, B-384, B-395
Logansport National Bank: B-384
LOGGIA COLONIA ITALIANA,
  WAYNE COUNTY NO. 933:
  A-239
LOMAX, JOSEPH: *A-240*
Lomax, Joseph A.: A-240
Lomax, Mary: A-240
London, Joan: A-172
Long, John: A-283
Longnaker, Mary E. — see Ogg, Mary
  E. Longnaker
Longnaker family: B-265
Longworth, Nicholas: A-381
Loogootee, Martin Co.: A-168
LOOP, URIAH J.: *A-241*
Lord, Lizzie: B-138
Lord, Mary — see HARRISON, MARY
  LORD
Loree, Miami Co.: B-90
Lorimier, Louis: B-212
Losantville, Randolph Co.: A-28
Lossing, Benson J.: A-229, A-272,
  A-346, A-391, B-84
Louisiana: A-125, A-267, A-335, B-92,
  B-212, B-254, B-262, B-325
  Civil War: A-41, A-85, A-88, A-106,
    A-133, A-143, A-213, A-259,
    B-293, B-322, B-353, B-358
  Spanish retrocession to France: A-32
  World War I: A-114
  Baton Rouge: B-212
  Camp Beauregard (World War I):
    A-114
  Jackson: B-243
  New Orleans: A-4, A-78, A-250,
    A-257, A-302, A-333, A-399,
    A-407, B-18, B-92, B-93, B-210,
    B-252, B-273, B-288
  Shreveport: A-90
  Tullania: A-175
  Waterproof: A-266, A-275
Louisville, New Albany & Chicago Railroad: B-7
LOUNSBURY, GEORGE: *A-242*
Lovejoy, Arthur O.: B-342

Lovell, John: A-286
Lowden, Frank: B-345
LOWES, WILLIAM R.: *B-221*
Lucas, Ebenezer F.: B-1, B-137
Lucas, Robert: B-263
Ludlow, Louis: A-46, A-68, A-112,
  A-134, A-249, A-258, B-20,
  B-149
Lugar, Richard: A-288, B-301
Luhring, Oscar R.: B-114
LUSE, DOUGLASS: *A-243*
Luse, Douglass, Jr.: A-243
Luse, Elizabeth — see Paxton, Elizabeth
  Luse
Luse, Rhode Ann — see Hannaman,
  Rhode Ann Luse
Luse, Susan: A-243
LUTEN, DANIEL B.: *B-222*
LUTHER, JAMES H.: *B-223*
Luther, John E.: B-223
Lyall, Charles: A-272
Lynch, James M.: B-193
Lynch, William O.: B-76
Lynnville, Warrick Co.: A-359

MABREY, BENJAMIN BENN: *A-244*
McAneny, George W.: B-342
McArthur, Duncan: A-147
MCBRIDE, CHARLES S.: *B-224*
McCarty, Jonathan: A-91, B-119,
  B-137, B-351
McCarthy, Joseph: B-251
MCCARTY, NICHOLAS: *A-245*,
  A-111, B-252, B-351
McCarty, Richard: A-8
McClellan, George B.: B-43, B-94
McClure, Alexander K.: B-84
McClure, Dr. William J.: B-225
MCCLURE, WILLIAM S.: *B-225*
McClurg, Alexander C.: A-80
McCormack, John W.: B-99
MCCORMICK, CHARLES OWEN:
  A-246
McCormick, Cyrus: A-337
McCormick, Medill: A-337, B-147,
  B-218, B-219
McCormick Reaper Company: B-223
McCoy, Isaac: A-83, A-272, B-351
McCrary, George W.: A-391, B-348

INDEX

MCCRAY, WARREN T.: *B-226*,
  A-272, B-95, B-120, B-147,
  B-381
MCCREA, EDWARD T.: *A-247*
MCCREA, HENRY: *B-227*
MCCREA AND BROWN COMPANY
  (Brazil): *A-248*
MCCULLOCH, CARLETON BUEL:
  A-249, A-285, A-364, B-76,
  B-343
McCulloch, Hugh: A-272, B-119, B-137
McCulloch, Oscar C.: A-52, A-103
MCCULLOUGH, JACOB S.: *B-228*
McCutcheon, George Barr: B-208
McCutcheon, John T.: A-315, B-208
McDonald, David: B-348
MACDONALD, DONALD: *A-250*
MCDONALD, JAMES D.: *A-251*
McDonald, James R.: B-394
McDonald, Joseph E.: A-52, A-272, B-1,
  B-47, B-348
McDonald, W. H.: B-235
McDonald's Restaurants (Fort Wayne):
  B-3
Mace, Daniel: B-1
McGan, Benjamin F.: B-229
McGan, James: B-229
MCGAN, THOMAS J.: *B-229*
MCGARRAH, ANDREW J.: *A-252*
McGarrah family: A-252
McGaughey, Edward W.: B-348
MCGRAW, JOHN S.: *B-230*
McGrawsville, Miami Co.: A-23
McGregor, J. Harry: B-24
McGuire, James: B-86
McHenry, James: A-272, A-286, A-381
McIntosh, William: B-212
McKay, Helen — see Steele, Helen
  McKay
McKay, Horace: A-351
McKee, David R.: A-341
McKee, Samuel: A-385
McKenney, Thomas L.: A-272, B-351
Mackenzie, Kenneth K.: B-95
McKinley, William: A-102, A-164,
  A-272, A-341
McKinney, Thomas C.: A-83
MCLAUGHLIN, MARY GODOWN:
  B-231
MCLEAN, CHARLES G.: *A-253*

McLean, John: A-8
McLean, Margaret — see Todd, Margaret McLean
McLean, Mary Ann: A-253
MCLEAN, WILLIAM E.: *A-254*
Mclernand, John A.: A-391
Maclure, James: A-282
Maclure, William: A-237
MacMillan, Ernest: A-327
McMillan, William L.: B-254
MacMillan Publishing Company: B-4
McMillin, Albert: B-29
McMullin, Lona: B-29
MCNEELY, JAMES H.: *B-232*
McNutt, Paul V.: A-249, A-272, A-327,
  B-76, B-246, B-277 — See also
  PAUL V. MCNUTT FOR
  PRESIDENT IN 1940 CLUB,
  INC.
MacVeagh, Franklin: B-342
MacVeagh, Wayne: B-348
McWhirter, Felix M.: A-288, B-72,
  B-381
McWhirter, Felix T.: A-288
McWhirter, Susan — see OSTROM,
  SUSAN MCWHIRTER
McWhirter family: A-288
Macy, Watson, and Goodrich — see
  Watson, Macy, and Goodrich
Madam C. J. Walker Manufacturing
  Company (Indianapolis): A-390
Madden, Ray J.: B-369
Madison, James: A-101, A-147, A-272
Madison, Jefferson Co.: A-43, A-174,
  A-175, A-219, A-235, A-237,
  A-266, A-361, B-40, B-93,
  B-109, B-142, B-153, B-165,
  B-225, B-252, B-258, B-281,
  B-327, B-351
Madison and Indianapolis Railroad:
  A-266, A-267, A-302, B-252,
  B-263
Madison County: A-6, A-141, A-200,
  A-342
  Anderson: A-268, A-302, A-324,
    A-340, B-3, B-69, B-81, B-148,
    B-360, B-361, B-362
  Huntsville: B-279
  Pendleton: B-279, B-318, B-360
  Quincy (Elwood): A-340

INDEX

Maginness, E. A.: A-325
Magnificat: B-51
Mahaffy, Ellen: A-295
Mahan, George: B-99
Mailly, William: A-312
Maine
  Greenland: A-107
  Kennebunkport: A-365
  Portland: B-336
Maine, Hiram: B-293
Manchester Academy (Dearborn Co.): B-323
Mangum, Willie P.: B-348
Mannerhein, Count Carl: B-124
Manson, Mahlon D.: B-212
Manville, Jefferson Co.: A-235
Manypenny, George W.: B-119, B-348
Mapel Oil Company (Terre Haute): B-34
Maps: A-302, B-94, B-171, B-212, B-376
Marchal, Antoine: B-212
Marcy, William L.: A-81, A-147, A-272, B-348
Marietta, Shelby Co.: A-209
Marion, Grant Co.: B-3, B-90, B-373
Marion College (Marion, Ind.): B-90
Marion County: A-171, A-200, A-256, A-342, B-5, B-248, B-378
  Acton: B-221
  Beech Grove: A-63, A-342, B-85
  Bridgeport: B-201, B-243
  Broad Ripple: B-310, B-331
  Castleton: B-202
  Cumberland: A-301, B-135
  Decatur Township: B-27, B-64
  Indianapolis — see Indianapolis
  Irvington: B-76, B-85, B-149, B-205, B-224
  Nora: B-197
  Southport: B-393
  Warren Township: B-149, B-163
Marion County Agricultural and Horticultural Society: A-313
Marion County Association for the Detection of Horse Thiefs: B-115
MARION COUNTY BIBLE SOCIETY: B-233
Marion County Horse Company: A-171
MARION COUNTY LIBRARY: *A-255*

MARION COUNTY MISCELLANEOUS PAPERS, 1831-1917: *A-256*
Marion County Temperance Society: B-303
Marion County Tuberculosis Association: B-5
Markle, Abraham: B-234
MARKLE, AUGUSTUS R.: *B-234*
MARKLE, FREDERICK: *A-257*
MAROTT, GEORGE JOSEPH: *A-258*
Marott, Mrs. George: A-258
Marott Hotel (Indianapolis): A-258
Marott Shoe Store (Indianapolis): A-258
Mars Hill and Indianapolis Gravel Road Company: B-158
MARSH, HENRY C.: *B-235*
Marsh, John: B-235
Marshall, Alonso: A-259
Marshall, John: A-303
Marshall, Joseph G.: A-8, A-91, A-302, A-408, B-263, B-348
Marshall, Samuel S.: A-81
Marshall, Sarah — see Hayden, Sarah Marshall
Marshall, Swain: A-259
MARSHALL, THOMAS (1811-1901): *A-259*
MARSHALL, THOMAS RILEY (1854-1925): *B-236*, A-52, A-237, A-272, A-358, B-95, B-335, B-345 — See also *Recollections of Thomas R. Marshall*
Marshall County: B-35, B-137
  Culver: B-121
Marshall Plan: B-216
Martin, Joseph: A-172
Martin County
  Loogootee: A-168
Martin family: B-336
MARTINDALE, ELIJAH BISHOP: *A-260*, A-101, B-348
Martinsburg, Washington Co.: A-34
Martinsville, Morgan Co.: B-40, B-47
Marvis, John: B-27
MARY RIGG CENTER (Indianapolis): B-237 — See also, RIGG, MARY
Maryland: A-336
  Civil War: A-97, A-133, A-168,

INDEX 477

Maryland—*Continued*
  Civil War—*cont.*
    A-228, A-329, A-402, B-31,
      B-231, B-295
    Antietam battlefield memorial: A-58
    Baltimore: A-175, A-214, A-237,
      A-253, A-336, A-390, B-15,
      B-152, B-210
    Calvert County: B-92
    Frederick: A-174, A-175
    Frederick County: A-131
    Indian Head: A-22
    Sharpsburg: A-222
Mason, John Y.: B-394
Masonic Home (Franklin): B-315
Masonic Lodge: A-101, B-47, B-202,
  B-258, B-285, B-310, B-315,
  B-351, B-359
Massachusetts: A-72, A-111, A-174,
  A-267, A-398, B-37, B-117,
  B-319, B-342, B-365
  Adams: A-302
  Andover: A-108, A-210
  Berkley: A-72
  Boston: A-154, A-257, B-51, B-165,
    B-243, B-365
  Concord: A-29
  Dracut: A-29
  Fort Andrews: B-353
  Harvard University: B-275, B-281
  Lancaster: A-111, B-27
  Lowell: B-231
  Newton Theological Seminary: A-18
  North Wilbraham Academy: A-18
  Troy: B-37
  Watertown: B-243
  Wellesley: A-79
  West Springfield: A-18
  Westfield Academy: B-319
Massachusetts Indemnity Insurance
  Company: A-87
Massacres of the Mountains: A-95
Massie, Nathaniel: A-8, A-286, A-381
MASTELLER, MRS. PAUL (CLARA):
  B-238
Master Painters' Association of Indianapolis: B-115
Masters, Charles: B-81
MASTERS, FRANK S.: *B-239*
Masters, Mary Alice: B-81

MATTHEWS, CLAUDE: *B-240,*
  A-52, A-272, A-302, B-114,
  B-335
Matthews, Martha Whitcomb: B-240
Matthews, Stanley: B-348
Mauks Ferry Road: B-48
Maumee River: B-2
Maurice Thompson, Archer and Author:
  A-322 — See also Thompson,
  Maurice
MAY, GEORGE: *A-261*
MAYER, CHARLES: *A-262*
Maynard, Ken: B-20
Meade, George: B-225
Mecca Realty Company (Indianapolis):
  B-282
MEDICAL AND DENTAL SERVICES, INC. FORT WAYNE:
  B-241
Medical College of Indiana: B-346
Medical College of Ohio (Cincinnati):
  A-293
Medicine: A-230
  cardiology: A-268
  dentists: A-22, B-328
  dieticians and nutrition: A-183
  druggists and pharmaceuticals: A-82,
    A-230, A-325
  hospitals: A-337, B-145
  mental health: A-163, A-274, B-101,
    B-173, B-181
  nurses: A-186, A-216
  obstetrics: A-246
  organizations: A-6, A-7, A-172,
    A-183, A-194, B-5, B-101,
    B-145, B-147, B-173, B-181,
    B-241, B-368
  physicians: A-3, A-10, A-35, A-40,
    A-47, A-59, A-72, A-86, A-99,
    A-125, A-160, A-161, A-163,
    A-174, A-175, A-214, A-220,
    A-235, A-243, A-246, A-268,
    A-278, A-293, A-302, A-345,
    B-1, B-9, B-68, B-69, B-87,
    B-128, B-152, B-166, B-170,
    B-214, B-225, B-271, B-295,
    B-326, B-368
  technicians: B-166
  tuberculosis: A-6, A-172, A-175,
    A-194, B-5

Medicine — *Continued*
veterinarians: B-74
-1815: A-230
1816-1849: A-10, A-35, A-59, A-230,
A-302, B-170, B-173, B-214,
B-295, B-328
1850-1879: A-3, A-10, A-35, A-40,
A-47, A-59, A-72, A-99, A-125,
A-160, A-175, A-214, A-216,
A-220, A-230, A-235, A-243,
A-278, A-293, A-325, A-337,
A-345, B-1, B-68, B-69, B-87,
B-152, B-170, B-214, B-225,
B-271, B-295, B-368
1880-1909: A-3, A-6, A-22, A-35,
A-40, A-82, A-86, A-160, A-161,
A-174, A-186, A-194, A-214,
A-235, A-246, A-278, A-293,
A-325, A-337, A-345, B-9, B-68,
B-69, B-74, B-128, B-173,
B-241, B-271, B-295, B-326,
B-368
1910-1945: A-6, A-7, A-22, A-82,
A-86, A-161, A-163, A-172,
A-183, A-186, A-194, A-235,
A-246, A-268, A-274, A-293,
A-337, B-5, B-68, B-74, B-87,
B-145, B-147, B-173, B-181,
B-241, B-271, B-326, B-368
1946-: A-6, A-7, A-163, A-172,
A-183, A-186, A-194, A-246,
A-268, B-5, B-101, B-166,
B-181, B-241
Medill, Joseph: A-164, A-341
Medill, William: B-119
Mediterranean Sea: A-54
Meharry Medical College (Nashville, Tenn.): A-268
Meigs, Return Jonathan: A-147, A-272, A-286, A-381
Mellon, Andrew W.: B-259
Melrose, Rush Co.: A-2
Memoirs (Will H. Hays): B-147
Menard, Pierre: A-101, A-384, B-212, B-351
Mencken, H. L.: B-256
MENDON SABBATH SCHOOL (Hancock Co.): *B-242*
MENGER, CORNELIUS H.: *B-243*, A-315

Menger, Jean Hornstein: B-243
Menou, General: A-32
Merchants and Manufacturers Insurance Bureau (Indianapolis): B-218
Meredith, Henry: A-264
MEREDITH, SAMUEL CALDWELL: *A-263*
MEREDITH, SOLOMON: *A-264*, A-229, B-85
Meredith, Virginia Claypool: A-264, B-176
Mergenthaler Printing Company: A-341
Merimee, Prosper: B-341
Meriwether, David: A-81
MERRICK, JOHN: *A-265*
Merrick, John A.: A-265
Merrill, Catherine: A-210, A-216, A-266, B-244, B-394
Merrill, Jane — see Ketcham, Jane Merrill
Merrill, Julia — see MOORES, JULIA MERRILL
Merrill, Mina: A-266
MERRILL, SAMUEL (1792-1855): *A-266*, *A-267*, A-111, A-125, A-216, A-302, A-381, B-137, B-233, B-244, B-263, B-284, B-299, B-351
MERRILL, SAMUEL (1831-1924): *B-244*
Messler, Henry P.: B-245
MESSLER, JAMES W.: *B-245*
Metamora, Franklin Co.: A-202, A-396, B-125, B-377
Metcalf, Victor H.: B-44
Meteer, James: A-271
Metropolitan Theater (Indianapolis): B-47
Mexican Border Conflict: A-46
Mexican War: A-78, A-361, B-212
16th U.S. Regiment: A-33
1st Indiana Regiment: A-229, A-391, B-295
2nd Indiana Regiment: A-218, A-325
5th Indiana Regiment: A-135
medical corps: B-295
Mexico: A-391, B-95, B-254
Matamoros: B-212, B-295
Sonora: B-293
Meyer, Armin H: B-301

INDEX 479

MEYER, JAMES H.: *B-246*
Miami Company: A-384
Miami County: A-6, A-342
   Amboy: A-49
   Converse: A-49
   Denver: B-53
   Jefferson Township: B-338
   Loree: B-90
   McGrawsville: *A-23*
   Peru: A-25, A-51, A-403, B-26, B-119, B-212
Miami County Jefferson Club: A-51
Miami (Ohio) University: A-236, A-361, B-285
Miamis (fur trade): A-286
Michener, Louis T.: A-52, A-145, B-138, B-339, B-393
Michigan: A-73, A-174, B-14, B-117, B-119, B-270
   Civil War: A-242
   Ann Arbor: B-87
   Battle Creek: B-87, B-261
   Cass: A-342
   Cass County: B-354
   Detroit: A-187, A-384, B-166, B-167, B-209, B-212
   Grand Rapids: A-242, B-18
   Grand Traverse: A-342
   Hillsdale College: B-2
   Kalamazoo: A-240
   Marshall: B-287
   Michilimackinac: B-11
   Monroe: B-212
   Muskegon: B-18
   Niles: B-354
   Ontonagon County: B-80
   Sault Ste. Marie: B-262
   Sturgis: B-223
   University of Michigan: A-140
Michigan City, LaPorte Co.: A-59, A-107, A-229, A-237, A-391, A-398, B-391
Michigan Road: A-125
Middle East: A-162, B-147
Middlefork, Clinton Co.: A-265
MIDDLETON, HARVEY N.: *A-268*
Midland Transportation Corporation (Milwaukee): A-197
Mier, Grant Co.: B-22
Mifflin, Thomas: A-272, A-286

Milan, Ripley Co.: A-142
Milford, Decatur Co.: B-69
Mill Creek, Hendricks Co.: A-342
Miller, Charles W.: B-109, B-114
Miller, Clara Lambert: B-248
Miller, Elizabeth Jane — see HACK, ELIZABETH JANE MILLER
Miller, Henry: B-247
MILLER, ISAAC; *B-247*
Miller, Joaquin: B-43
Miller, John F.: B-138
MILLER, OSCAR G.: *B-248*
Miller, Ralph: A-134
MILLER, STEPHEN A.: *A-269*
Miller, T. S.: B-86
MILLER, VALETTE: *B-249*
MILLER, WILLIAM (ca. 1809-1879): *A-270*
Miller, William (fl. 1860s): B-73
MILLER, WILLIAM HENRY HARRISON: *B-250*, A-15, B-138, B-212, B-342, B-345, B-348, B-393
Millersville Gravel Road Company (Marion County): A-171
Milligan, Lambden P.: B-212
Milliken, James P.: A-302
Mills, Benjamin Marshall: A-271
MILLS, CALEB: *A-271*, A-266, A-267, A-302, A-401, A-402, B-146
Mills, John: A-286
Mills, Wilbur D.: B-301
Milner, Kate — see Rabb, Kate Milner
Milroy, Francis — see Beck, Francis Milroy
Milroy, Robert H.: A-15, A-229, A-391, B-84, B-286, B-295, B-376
Milroy, Rush Co.: B-47, B-52
Milroy, Samuel: B-137, B-295, B-351
Minnesota: A-9, A-264, B-15, B-107, B-119, B-223
   Indians: B-119
   religion: B-146
   Fort Snelling: B-293
   Hastings: B-146
   Minneapolis: A-363
   Red Wing: A-72
   St. Anthony: B-299
   St. Paul: B-119, B-146

INDEX

Minnesota — *Continued*
  St. Peters: B-119
  Winona: B-119, B-123
Minton, Sherman: A-249, A-285, B-20, B-275, B-381
Mishawaka, St. Joseph Co.: B-23
Mississippi: B-92
  Civil War: A-140, A-143, A-208, A-271, A-339, A-368, B-114, B-231, B-293, B-322, B-358
  World War I: B-287
  Camp Shelby (World War I): B-287
  Fort Adams: A-286
  Natchez: A-125, A-308, B-92, B-215
  Scott County: A-396
  Vicksburg: B-212
    Civil War: A-47, A-207, A-329, A-347, B-153, B-265
Mississippi River Commission: B-345
Mississippi Valley Conference on Tuberculosis: A-6
Missouri: A-28, A-45, A-272, A-329, A-372, B-119, B-245, B-356
  Civil War: A-85, A-143, A-259, B-94, B-265, B-322, B-358
  Indians: A-272, B-119
  Butler County: A-318
  Cape Girardeau: B-212
  Carroll County: A-28
  Columbia: B-281
  Greenfield: B-204
  Holt County: B-27
  Independence: B-288
  Kansas City: A-390, B-122
  Lewis County: B-236
  Maryville: B-365
  Miller County: A-318
  St. Charles: A-52
  St. Louis: A-30, A-145, A-150, A-286, A-384, B-18, B-119, B-210, B-212, B-223, B-261, B-281, B-313
    Civil War: A-259
  Salt Springs: B-146
  Sedalia: B-123
  Springfield: B-52
  Webster Groves: B-140
  Westport: B-119
MITCHELL, EDWARD A.: *B-251*
Mitchell, John: B-124

Mitchell, Lawrence Co.: B-353
MITTEN, ARTHUR G.: *A-272*
MOBLEY, CHARLES WILLIAM: *A-273*
Modoc War: B-94
Moley, Raymond: A-172
Mongo, LaGrange Co.: A-149, B-313
Monks, Leander: B-114
Monroe, James: A-147, A-272, A-286, A-303, A-341
Monroe County: A-234, B-271
  Bloomington: A-111, A-216, A-275, A-337, B-17, B-71, B-146, B-280, B-325, B-364, B-365 — see also Indiana University
  Ellettsville: B-129
Montana: A-146, B-47
  Anaconda: B-114
  Deer Lodge: B-114
  Helena: A-146
Montezuma, Parke Co.: A-75, B-88
Montgomery, William: A-81
Montgomery County: A-72, A-131, A-230, A-342
  Crawfordsville: A-23, A-74, A-79, A-130, A-131, A-229, A-230, A-275, A-295, A-332, A-388, A-391, B-15, B-36, B-108, B-165, B-169, B-258, B-299, B-366 — see also Wabash College
  Darlington: B-8
  Ladoga: B-7, B-15, B-337
  Linden: A-284
  New Richmond: A-247
  Pine Hills: A-15
  Pine Hills nature preserve: B-79
  Roachdale: B-15
  Shades Inn: B-311
  Shannondale: A-409
  Sugar River: A-342
  Waveland: A-88, B-15
  Wingate: B-91
Monticello, White Co.: B-360
Montpelier, Blackford Co.: B-133
Montmorency, Tippecanoe Co.: B-291
Moody, W. H.: B-345
Moore, Charles C.: B-339
Moore, Joseph: B-252

INDEX

Moore, Maggie — see Fogelman, Maggie Moore
Moore, Margaret: B-141, B-252
Moore, Martha Jane: B-252
Moore, Robert Walton: A-285
MOORE, SAMUEL: *B-252* — See also Samuel Moore and Company
Moore, Thomas S.: B-252
MOORE, WILLIAM ROBY: *A-274*
Moore and Worthington (Mooresville): B-252
Moore, Griggs & Cook (Mooresville): B-252
Moore family: B-281
MOORES, CHARLES W.: *B-253*, A-267
MOORES, JULIA MERRILL: *A-275*, A-266
Moores, Merrill: A-52, A-267, B-85, B-114, B-290
Mooresville, Morgan Co.: B-122, B-141, B-252, B-327
Moral Society (Brothertown, N.Y.): A-83
Morgan, Arthur E.: B-142
Morgan, George: A-8, A-286
Morgan, George W.: A-391
Morgan County: A-342
   Clear Creek: B-71
   Ebenezer: B-71
   Martinsville: B-40, B-47
   Mooresville: B-122, B-141, B-252, B-327
   West Union: A-342
Morrill, Justin: A-302
Morris, Austin W.: A-400, B-114, B-204, B-348, B-351
Morris, Bethuel F.: B-299
Morris, Catherine — see Morrison, Catherine Morris
Morris, Frank: A-23
MORRIS, HOWARD: *A-276*
Morrison, Alice — see Cathcart, Alice Morrison
Morrison, Catherine Morris: A-277
Morrison, Frank: B-110
MORRISON, JOHN IRWIN: *A-277*
Morton, Lucinda Burbank (Mrs. Oliver P.): B-43, B-254

MORTON, OLIVER PERRY: *B-254*, A-5, A-15, A-52, A-111, A-145, A-164, A-229, A-232, A-264, A-272, A-302, A-322, A-383, A-391, B-37, B-43, B-94, B-124, B-160, B-170, B-205, B-259, B-286, B-348, B-376, B-393, B-394 See also Oliver P. Morton Monument
Morton, Oliver T.: A-52, A-164, B-254, B-342
Moseley, Edward: B-345
Mothers Aid Society (Indianapolis): A-103, B-173
Motion Picture Exchange Operators: A-192
Motion Picture Producers and Distributors of America: B-147
Mount, James A.: A-52, A-102, A-272, B-335
Mount Pleasant, Jay Co.: B-30
Mount Vernon, Posey Co.: B-208, B-365
Mount Zion Church, Floyd Co.: B-71
Mowgli stories: A-327
MOWREY, WALTER LEVI: *B-255*
Mueller, Paul: B-218
Muhlenberg, John Peter: A-286
Muir, John: A-275
Muncie, Delaware Co.: A-23, A-122, A-146, A-200, A-214, A-291, B-97, B-113, B-204, B-235, B-278, B-301, B-330
Muncie, Anderson and Indianapolis Street Railroad Company: A-200
Muncie, Hartford and Fort Wayne Railway Company: A-200
MUNFORD, SAMUEL E.: *A-278*
Munsell, Joel: A-346
Murphy, Thelma: B-13
Murray, Elias: B-137, B-351
Murray, Phillip: B-110
Music: A-282, A-327, A-388, B-192, B-208, B-217, B-275, B-281, B-345
Muskie, Edmund S.: B-24, B-99, B-301
Mussey, Henry Raymond: B-342
Mussey, Reuben D.: A-391
Mutual Life Policyholders Association (Indianapolis): A-260

MUTUAL SERVICE ASSOCIATION
    INC. (Indianapolis): *A-279*
Mutual Service Journal: A-279
Myers, John D.: A-59
MYERS, WALTER D.: *B-256*

Naas, George: B-305
Nancy Hanks Lincoln Memorial: A-112
Nashville, Brown Co.: B-309, B-316
National American Woman Suffrage
    Association: B-76
National Brookville Bank: A-123
National Citizens' League for the Promotion of a Sound Banking System: A-42
National City Bank (New York): A-116
National Civil Service Reform League:
    B-342
National Conference of Charities and
    Corrections: A-103
National Conference on State Parks:
    B-219
National Council of Women: B-190
National Dunes Park Association: B-174
National Education Association: B-396
National Hotel Company: B-77
National Interfaith Coalition on Aging:
    A-199
National Labor Defense Council: B-110
National Party: B-155
National Road: B-276
National Security League: B-19
National Telephone Association: B-19
National Tuberculosis Association: A-6
Native Americans — see Indians
NATO: B-89, B-99
NATURE STUDY CLUB OF
    INDIANA: *B-257*
NAYLOR, ISAAC: *B-258*
Naylor, Mary: B-258
Near East Relief Commission: B-147
Nearing, Scott: B-110
Nebraska: A-9, A-329
    Beatrice: B-75
    Fort McPherson: A-137
    Greely County: A-318
    Lincoln: B-360
    Lincoln County: A-318
    Omaha: A-137, B-243

"Negro Education in Indiana from 1816
    to 1869": A-153
Nelson, Thomas A.: B-286
Nettleton, Charles H.: B-123
Neubacher, Selma — see STEELE,
    SELMA NEUBACHER
Nevada: A-59
NEW, HARRY S.: *B-259*, A-68, A-102,
    A-123, A-167, A-210, A-229,
    A-249, A-272, A-341, A-371,
    B-76, B-85, B-114, B-147, B-216,
    B-218, B-219, B-290, B-339,
    B-345
New, Jeptha D.: B-254
New, John C.: A-101, A-164, A-272,
    A-302, A-341, A-383, B-259,
    B-345
New Albany, Floyd Co.: A-38, A-52,
    A-107, A-117, A-125, A-152,
    A-215, A-280, A-325, A-380,
    B-58, B-86, B-104, B-136,
    B-165, B-212, B-302, B-330,
    B-358, B-365
NEW ALBANY AND PORTLAND
    FERRY COMPANY: *A-280*
New Albany Hosiery Mills: A-152
New Albany Water Works: A-52
New Bethel and Sugar Creek Gravel
    Road Company: A-313
New Castle, Henry Co.: A-92, A-138,
    A-156, A-281, A-336, B-51,
    B-139, B-260, B-276, B-292
New Castle and Dublin Turnpike Company — see DUBLIN AND
    NEW CASTLE TURNPIKE
    COMPANY
NEW CASTLE CEMETERY ASSOCIATION: *B-260*
NEW CASTLE MARBLE WORKS:
    A-281
New Castle Mercury: B-276
New Castle News Republican: B-51
New Cincinnati, Delaware Co.: A-122
New Deal: B-365
New England: A-22, B-372
New Garden, Wayne Co.: A-342, B-64
New Goshen, Vigo Co.: A-228, B-314
New Hampshire: A-145, A-267
    Alstead: A-72

INDEX 483

New Hampshire—*Continued*
  Dartmouth College: A-216, B-165
  Pembroke: A-117
New Harmony, Posey Co.: A-120,
    A-237, A-250, A-282, B-17,
    B-142, B-273, B-284
  Educational Society: A-282
  NEW HARMONY COLLECTION,
    1821-1880: *A-282*
New Harmony Memorial Commission:
  B-17
New Jersey: A-335, B-117, B-275
  American Revolution: B-84
  War of 1812: B-84
  World War I: B-337
  Atlantic City: A-390, B-280
  Bergen County: B-84
  Camp Merritt (World War I): B-332
  Newark: A-390
  Princeton University: A-111, B-281
  Summit: B-58
New Mexico: B-205
  Santa Fe: B-114
  Taiban: B-360
  Thoreau: A-304
New Mexico Territory: A-391
New Palestine, Hancock Co.: A-99
New Providence/Borden, Clark Co.:
  A-38, A-330, B-37
New Richmond, Montgomery Co.:
  A-247
New York: A-8, A-73, A-83, A-110,
    A-111, A-128, A-150, A-152,
    A-333, A-402, B-117, B-137,
    B-147, B-234, B-264, B-273,
    B-275, B-286, B-319, B-357
  Indians: A-83
  Albany: A-346
  Auburn: B-146
  Binghamton: B-195
  Bradford: A-144
  Brothertown: A-83
  Buffalo: B-391
  Cazenovia: A-91
  Cornell University: B-44
  Fort Plain: A-253
  Geneva: B-87
  Ithaca: B-58
  Lenox: A-159
  Marshall: A-83

New York City: A-8, A-54, A-98,
    A-164, A-361, A-390, B-147,
    B-165, B-210, B-243, B-337,
    B-357, B-372
  National City Bank: A-116
Niagara Falls: B-372
Oneonta: B-195
Onondaga County: A-59
Ontario County
  Victor: A-203
Owego: B-165
Poughkeepsie: A-402
Saratoga County: A-171
Seneca: B-87
Tuckahoe: A-307
Ulster County: A-392
Warren County: B-330
Wells College: B-108
White Plains: A-390
Newburgh, Warrick Co.: A-4, A-33,
  B-365
Newport, Vermillion Co.: B-252
Newport (Fountain City), Wayne Co.:
  A-130
Newspapers
 -1815: A-57
 1816-1849: A-57, A-71, A-91, A-98,
    B-232
 1850-1879: A-57, A-91, A-98, A-165,
    A-341, A-346, A-371, B-49,
    B-103, B-232, B-261, B-276,
    B-335
 1880-1909: A-46, A-116, A-146,
    A-164, A-165, A-173, A-237,
    A-337, A-341, A-358, A-371,
    B-19, B-28, B-33, B-49, B-180,
    B-193, B-276, B-293, B-335,
    B-340
 1910-1945: A-46, A-237, A-320,
    A-337, A-358, A-371, B-19,
    B-20, B-23, B-33, B-62, B-65,
    B-110, B-120, B-180, B-193,
    B-236, B-265, B-335, B-343
 1946- : B-51, B-100, B-143, B-180,
    B-193, B-358, B-362
 German-language: B-218
 history: B-85
 socialist: A-312

NEWTON AND SPRING VALLEY
    HORSE THIEF DETECTING
    COMPANY (Marion Co.): B-27
Newton County: A-23
  Kentland: B-146, B-226
Newton Theological Seminary (Mass.):
    A-18
Ney, Michel: B-349
NIBLACK, ALBERT P.: *A-283*
Niblack, William E.: A-283
Nicaragua: A-249, B-281
NICHOLS, WILLIAM MERRICK:
    A-284
Nicholson, Dorothy: A-285
Nicholson, Eugenie — see Fox, Eugenie
    Nicholson
NICHOLSON, MEREDITH: *A-285*,
    A-46, A-52, A-68, A-164, A-176,
    A-210, A-249, A-263, A-322,
    A-358, B-76, B-85, B-124,
    B-147, B-208, B-218, B-219,
    B-236, B-259, B-261, B-342,
    B-343
Nicholson, Meredith, Jr.: B-261
Nicholson, Meredith, III: B-261
NICHOLSON, ROBERTA WEST:
    B-261
Niles, John B.: B-286
Nixon, Julia — see Eisenhower, Julia
    Nixon
Nixon, Richard M.: B-98, B-275, B-301,
    B-399
Nixon, William Penn: A-341
Noble, Catherine — see Davidson,
    Catherine Noble
Noble, James: A-101, A-111, A-272,
    A-381, B-263, B-351
NOBLE, LAZARUS: *B-262*, A-5, A-15,
    A-145, A-210, B-94, B-225,
    B-348
NOBLE, NOAH: *B-263*, A-125, A-136,
    A-147, A-237, A-272, A-282,
    A-369, A-376, A-381, B-37,
    B-114, B-249, B-286, B-348,
    B-351
Noble County: A-339
  Albion: A-26
  Ligonier: B-335
  Swan: B-23
  Wolcottville: B-71

Noble Township, LaPorte Co.: A-238
Noblesville, Hamilton Co.: A-389,
    B-301
NOLAND, STEPHEN C.: *B-264*,
    B-72
Nora, Marion Co.: B-197
Nordhoff, Charles: B-394
North, William: A-286
North Africa: A-317, A-366
  World War II: A-362, B-270
North Carolina: A-130, A-301, B-28,
    B-52, B-261
  Civil War: A-24, A-206, A-216,
    A-220, B-141, B-266, B-382
  World War II: B-213
  Asheville: B-146
  Camp LeJeune (World War II):
    B-213
  Guilford County: A-130, B-28
North Dakota: B-356
North Madison, Jefferson Co.: B-40,
    B-298
North Manchester, Wabash Co.: A-163,
    B-53
North Salem, Hendricks Co.: A-375
North Salem Baptist Church (Hendricks
    Co.): A-375
North Vernon, Jennings Co.: A-212,
    B-146, B-199
North Wilbraham Academy (Mass.):
    A-18
Northern Indiana Editorial Association:
    B-19
Northport and Mars Hill Gravel Road
    Company (Marion Co.): B-27
Northwest Territory: A-8, A-101,
    A-147, A-237, A-272, A-286,
    A-381, A-400, B-103
  government and politics: A-286
NORTHWEST TERRITORY COL-
    LECTION, 1749-1838: *A-286*
Northwestern Christian University —
    see Butler University
"Notes for Nieces": A-365
Notre Dame, St. Joseph Co.: B-213
Notre Dame Art Gallery: B-213
Noyes, Edward F.: A-391
Nurses Associated Alumnae: A-186
Nutt, Cyrus: B-286
Nye, Bill: B-259

INDEX

Oakland City, Gibson Co.: B-330
O'Brien, Cornelius: A-1, A-123, A-165
O'Brien, William H.: A-165, B-335
O'Brien-Holman family — see HOLMAN-O'BRIEN PAPERS
Occidental Hotel (Rockport): B-49
Ochs, Adolph S.: A-341
Oehler, Roman: B-112
Oehler, Romena — see ELDER, ROMENA O.
Ogden, Henry Co.: A-353
OGG, ADAMS LEE: *B-265*
Ogg, Mary E. Longnaker: B-265
Ogle, William B.: A-128
Oglesby, Richard J.: A-15, A-272
O'Hair, Caroline Wiley: A-396
O'Hair, Edgar: A-396
O'HARA, JAMES: *A-287*, A-286
Ohio: A-8, A-237, A-267, A-336, A-349, B-205, B-223, B-273
  Civil War: A-109, B-34, B-144, B-366
  politics: A-341
  religion: B-64, B-146
  World War I: B-14
  Adams County: B-123
  Amelia: B-135
  Ashtabula County: A-339
  Camp Sherman (World War I): B-332
  Centerburg: B-34
  Chillicothe: A-346, A-400
  Cincinnati: A-8, A-10, A-54, A-90, A-111, A-119, A-125, A-164, A-174, A-175, A-189, A-257, A-293, A-308, A-341, A-361, A-380, A-390, A-391, A-400, B-15, B-47, B-68, B-93, B-137, B-146, B-210, B-232, B-252, B-351
    Civil War: B-366
  Clark County: A-342
  Cleveland: A-91, A-266, B-63, B-243, B-391
  Clermont: B-365
  Cleves: B-146
  Clinton County: A-342, B-204
  College Corner: A-270, B-245
  Columbiana County: A-109
  Columbus: B-243
  Darr Town: A-236
  Dayton: A-309, A-366, B-232
  Delaware: B-365
  Drake County: B-35
  Fairfield County: B-397
  Fallen Timbers, Battle of: A-286
  Findlay: A-39, A-149
  Fort Finney: A-8, A-286
  Fort Hamilton: A-8
  Fort Jefferson: A-101, A-286
  Fort St. Clair: A-286
  Fort Washington: A-8, A-147
  Gallipolis: A-70
  Glendale: B-285
  Greenville: A-147
  Greenville, Treaty of: A-286
  Hamilton County: A-8, A-342
  Harveysburg: B-22
  Highland County: A-342, B-64
  Jefferson County: A-109
  Knox County: A-245
  Lancaster: A-75, A-408
  Laura: A-342
  Lebanon: A-302, B-328
  Logan County: A-342
  McConnelsville: A-169
  Madisonville: A-8
  Miami County: A-342
  Miami University: A-236, A-361, B-285
  Middletown: B-299
  Montgomery County: A-214
  Morrow County: A-342
  Mt. Carmel: A-10
  Oberlin: B-58
  Oxford: A-88, A-123, B-245, B-285
  Piqua: A-307
  Preble County: A-342, B-126
  Ravenna: B-69
  Ross County: B-88
  St. Mary's, Treaty of: A-187
  Salem: A-291, B-206
  Toledo: B-75
  Troy: B-223
  Truro: B-27
  Urbana: A-111, A-243, A-266, A-376
  Warren County: A-342, B-204
    Waynesville: A-209
  Wilmington: A-342
  Wyandotte County: B-64

INDEX

Ohio and Mississippi Railway Company: A-276
Ohio Company: A-286
Ohio country
 American Revolution: A-287
Ohio County
 Rising Sun: A-150, A-236, A-237, B-92, B-286, B-291
Ohio Medical College (Cincinnati): A-174
Ohio River: A-125, A-250, A-280, B-48, B-49, B-219
Ohio Wesleyan University: B-365
Oil Dealers, Inc. (Lake Co.): B-12
Okinawa: B-166
Oklahoma: B-110, B-356
 Tulsa: A-390
Old Oak Grange: B-185
"The Old Seminary Boys": B-48
Olds, Frank A.: B-266
OLDS, WILLIAM C.: *B-266*
Olds Wagon Works (Fort Wayne): B-137
O'Leary, Helen Griffin: B-285
Oleomargarine Act: B-251
OLIN, FRANK W.: *B-267*
Oliver, Kenneth A.: B-268
OLIVER, REECE A.: *B-268*
Oliver P. Morton Monument: A-260
Oliver Typewriter Company: A-337
Olmsted, David: B-119
Olney, Richard: B-345
Ontario, LaGrange Co.: A-203
Orange County: A-104, A-342, B-325
 French Lick: B-102, B-343, B-365
 Lick Creek: A-342
 Orangeville: A-160
 Paoli: A-48, A-218, B-319, B-330, B-352
Orangeville, Dekalb Co.: A-149
Orangeville, Orange Co.: A-160
Ordine Figli d'Italia in America: A-239
Oregon: A-9, A-101, B-313
 Antelope Valley: A-201
 Jacksonville: B-87, B-135
 Monmouth: A-201
 Portland: A-129
 Sparta: B-394
 Trout Creek: A-201
Organizations
 charitable: A-7, A-12, A-31, A-49, A-64, A-103, A-105, A-112, A-156, A-188, A-194, A-196, A-204, A-268, A-279, A-300, A-309, A-404, B-56, B-147, B-173, B-177, B-181, B-222, B-237, B-267, B-330, B-360, B-361
 fraternal: A-15, A-101, A-102, A-228, A-230, A-235, A-239, A-292, A-298, A-300, A-336, B-2, B-28, B-47, B-48, B-147, B-185, B-187, B-202, B-236, B-258, B-275, B-285, B-308, B-310, B-351, B-353, B-359, B-398
 health: A-6, A-7, A-172, A-183, A-194, B-5, B-145, B-147, B-173, B-241, B-268
 labor unions: B-46, B-96, B-110, B-115, B-193, B-293
 literary: A-11, A-314, A-315, A-351, B-66, B-176, B-191, B-355, B-371, B-379
 political: A-15, A-42, A-51, A-55, A-166, A-225, A-226, A-259, A-357, B-115, B-120, B-149, B-180, B-277, B-334, B-360, B-393
 professional: A-66, A-157, A-178, A-185, A-186, A-190, A-268, A-298, A-350, A-405, A-406, B-56, B-95, B-172, B-178, B-179, B-184, B-196, B-253, B-275, B-276, B-346, B-368, B-396
 religious: A-20, A-31, A-49, A-83, A-128, A-162, A-181, A-188, A-199, A-204, B-233, B-303
 service: A-12, A-112, A-190, A-192, A-195, A-199, A-268, A-300, A-313, A-336, A-395, A-404, A-406, B-65, B-127, B-142, B-175, B-176, B-177, B-182, B-186, B-192, B-194, B-257, B-289, B-333, B-347
 veterans: A-58, A-101, A-112, A-126, A-133, A-216, A-377, B-40, B-49, B-83, B-113, B-133, B-240, B-301, B-350, B-359, B-360, B-376, B-389
 vigilante: A-15, A-225, A-226, A-352,

INDEX

Organizations—*Continued*
  B-115, B-120, B-163, B-283, B-334
  women's: A-31, A-83, A-102, A-128, A-162, A-194, A-204, A-235, A-259, A-279, A-288, A-298, A-403, A-404, A-405, A-406, B-17, B-46, B-65, B-76, B-78, B-176, B-188, B-190, B-191, B-192, B-216, B-281, B-323
Orleans, Territory of: A-272
Orr, Helen — see English, Helen Orr
Orr, W. W.: A-23
Orr family: B-23
ORTH, GODLOVE: *B-269*, A-15, A-145, A-229, A-232, A-272, B-124, B-254, B-284, B-286, B-348
Osborn, Charles: B-117
Osbourn, Alexander: B-273
Osbourn, Jennie Kellogg: B-273
OSGATHARP, HARLAND L.: *B-270*
OSGOOD, HOWARD G.: *B-271*
OSTROM, SUSAN MCWHIRTER: *A-288*
Ott, L. W. — see L. W. Ott Company
OTT, JOHN: *B-272*
Otter Creek, Vigo Co.: A-257
Otwell, Pike Co.: A-127, B-270
Ouiatenon (fur trade): A-286
Overstreet, James: B-44
Overstreet, Jesse: A-260, A-337
Owen, David Dale: A-15, A-272, A-282, A-302, B-263, B-394
Owen, Lottie Kellogg: B-273
Owen, Richard: A-15, A-282, B-284
Owen, Robert: A-237, A-250, A-272, A-282, B-114, B-273
OWEN, ROBERT DALE: *B-273*, A-15, A-101, A-136, A-229, A-232, A-272, A-282, A-381, A-391, B-114, B-249, B-254, B-263
Owen, Rosamond: B-273
Owen, William: A-282, B-114, B-273
Owen County: B-351
  Gosport: A-133, B-129, B-271
  Spencer: A-27

Oxford (Ohio) Female College: B-285

Paddock, A. S.: A-145
Page, Walter H.: B-342
Paine, Daniel L.: B-62, B-276
Paine, Robert Treat: A-302
Painter, Jacob: B-102
Palestine
  tours: A-402, B-167, B-324
PALMER, JOHN R.: *A-289*
Palmer, Thomas R.: A-91
PALMER HOUSE (Indianapolis): *B-274*
Palmerston, Lord: A-272
Panama: A-98, A-134, B-227, B-288
Panama Canal: B-44, B-348
Panama-Pacific Exposition: B-339
PANTZER, KURT: *B-275*, B-261
Paoli, Orange Co.: A-48, A-218, B-319, B-330, B-352
The Papacy and the Civil Power: B-348
Paraguay: A-249
Parke, Benjamin: A-8, A-101, A-136, A-147, A-187, A-223, A-237, A-302, A-303, A-381, A-384, B-212, B-351
Parke County: A-23, A-81, A-290, A-342
  Bethany: A-88
  Montezuma: A-75, B-88
  Rockville: A-88, A-332, B-394
  Rosedale: B-29
PARKE COUNTY. CIRCUIT COURT RECORDS, 1833-1848: *A-290*
PARKER, BENJAMIN STRATTAN: *B-276*, B-76, B-85, B-345, B-371
Parker, George F.: B-47
Parker, Isaac: B-276
Parker, Samuel W.: B-205, B-263, B-276
Parry, Samuel: B-212
PARSONS, GEORGE W.: *A-291*
Parvin, Dr. Theophilus: A-52, A-150, A-293
Pathology of Labor, Puerperium, and the Newborn: A-246
Patoka Township, Crawford Co.: B-102
Patrons of Husbandry-see Grange

PATRONS OF HUSBANDRY.
OLIVE GRANGE #189:
A-292
PATTERSON, AMOS: *A-293*
Patterson, J. M.: A-46
PATTON, WILLIAM C.: *A-294*
PAUGH, IONE SWAN: *A-295*
Paul, John: A-237
Paul Dresser Memorial Association: B-217
PAUL V. MCNUTT FOR PRESIDENT IN 1940 CLUB, INC.: *B-277*
Paulsen, Paul: B-110
Paxson, Frederick L.: A-176
Paxton, Elizabeth Luse: A-243
Paxton, James: A-111, A-243
Payne, Henry B.: B-335
Payne, Henry C.: B-259
Payne, Mary Elizabeth Riley: A-233
Payson, L. E.: B-393
Peabody, George F.: A-346, B-345
PECK, SARAH CAROLINE: *B-278*, A-157
Peck, William J.: B-278
Peckinpaugh, Harrison & Company (Alton, Ind.): B-108
Peel, Sir Robert: A-272
Peelle, Stanton J.: A-52
Pegg, John: A-296
PEGG, LYDIA J.: *A-296*
Pegler, Westbrook: A-172
Peirce, Robert B. F.: A-52
Pelham, Columbine: A-120
Peltz, Margaret: A-145
Pendleton, Madison Co.: B-279, B-318, B-360
PENDLETON UNIVERSALIST CHURCH: *B-279*
Pennell, Francis W.: B-95
Pennsylvania: A-125, A-349, B-110
 American Revolution: A-287
 Civil War: A-380, B-31
 Bedford County: A-374
 Carlisle: A-98, A-287, B-152, B-166
 Carmichaels: B-123
 Chambersburg: B-152
 Conneaut Lake: A-324
 Dickinson College: A-98
 Easton: A-312
 Evansburg: A-324
 Fort Pitt: A-8
 Gettysburg: A-253
 Gettysburg battlefield memorial: A-58
 Harrisburg: A-98
 Lafayette College: A-312
 Lebanon County: B-247
 Mount Airy: B-372
 New Berlin: A-266, A-275
 Philadelphia: A-23, A-54, A-63, A-130, A-131, A-198, A-253, A-287, B-36, B-165, B-252, B-273, B-280
 Pittsburgh: A-120, A-174, A-286, A-287, B-248, B-252, B-357
 Ransom: B-209
 Schuylkill County: B-53
 Scranton: B-209
 Uniontown: A-109
 West Chester: A-52
 Westtown Boarding School (Chester Co.): A-277
Pennsylvania Railroad Company: A-369
Pennybacker, Anna (Mrs. P. V.): B-76
Pennybacker, Samuel: B-111
Peoples Light and Heat Company: A-309
Peoria-French Dictionary: B-107
Pepper, Abel C.: B-119, B-137, B-351
Pering, Alfred: B-280
Pering, Cornelius: B-280
PERING FAMILY: *B-280*
Perkins, Justin: A-271
PERKINS, SAMUEL ELLIOTT: *A-297*
Perkins and Winslow — see Winslow and Perkins
Perrault, Joseph Francis: A-8
Perry, Oliver Hazard: A-147, A-272
Perry County: A-397
 Cannelton: A-180, B-365
 Poison Creek: B-71
 Troy: A-47, B-49
Perryman, William: B-73
Perryville, Vermillion Co.: A-318
Pershing, John J.: A-46, B-236
Persia: A-271
 Tabriz: A-162
Peru: B-227

Peru, Miami Co.: A-25, A-51, A-403, B-26, B-119, B-212
Pestalozzi, Heinrich: A-237
Petersburg, Pike Co.: A-382
Pettingill, Samuel B.: A-172
Pettit, John: A-81, A-101, A-229, B-119
Pettit, John U.: A-15, B-119, B-212, B-286, B-351
Pfaffenberger, Frank: B-52
Pfrimmer, W. W.: B-276
Phelps, John S.: B-119
Phi Delta Theta: B-147
Philanthropy: A-337, A-390
Philippine Islands: B-33, B-124, B-166, B-268, B-295
  insurrection: A-134, A-224
  World War II: B-268
Phillips, Charles: B-114
Phillips, William B.: A-101
Phillips Academy (Andover, Mass.): A-108, A-210
Phipps, George A.: B-360
Phipps, Henry M.: B-360
Phipps, J. N.: A-369
Photography: A-217
PI LAMBDA THETA. INDIANAPOLIS CHAPTER: *A-298*
Piatt, John H.: A-147
Piatt, John J.: B-276
Pickering, Timothy: A-272, A-286
PICKETT, PHINEAS: *A-299*
Pickford, Mary: B-147
Pickney, Henry L.: A-91
Pierce, Douglas: B-281
Pierce, Edward L.: B-205
Pierce, Elizabeth Vinton: B-281
Pierce, Franklin: A-272
Pierce, Gilbert A.: B-286, B-393
Pierce, Henry Douglas: B-281
Pierce, Theresa — see Krull, Theresa Pierce
Pierce, Winslow S.: B-153, B-281
PIERCE-KRULL FAMILY PAPERS: *B-281*
Pierre Chouteau & Company: B-119
Pierrepont, Edwards: A-69
Pigeon Roost Massacre: B-258
Pike, Zebulon: A-147, A-286, A-381

Pike County: A-127, A-397
  Otwell: A-127, B-270
  Petersburg: A-382
Pinchot, Amos: B-110
Pinchot, Gifford: B-124, B-219
Pine Hills, Montgomery Co.: A-15
Pine Hills Nature Preserve, Montgomery Co.: B-79
Pittsboro, Hendricks Co.: B-367
Pittsburg, Carroll Co.: B-360
Plainfield, Hendricks Co.: A-299, A-342, A-357, B-159
Platt, Thomas C.: A-164
Playfair, William: A-70
Pleasant Run (Indianapolis): B-48
PLEASANT RUN CHILDREN'S HOME (Indianapolis): *A-300*
Pleasonton, Alfred: B-225
Plumb, Preston: B-393
Pocahontas: B-273
Poets and Poetry of Indiana: B-276
POGUE, GEORGE: *A-301*
Poison Creek, Perry Co.: B-71
Pokagon, Simon: B-293
Political Recollections: B-205
Politics — See also individual political parties
  -1815: A-147, A-302, A-381
  1816-1849: A-8, A-25, A-69, A-71, A-75, A-78, A-91, A-111, A-125, A-136, A-138, A-147, A-155, A-216, A-219, A-229, A-230, A-237, A-266, A-282, A-302, A-361, A-369, A-381, A-408, B-58, B-84, B-114, B-131, B-137, B-204, B-205, B-212, B-240, B-252, B-263, B-269, B-276, B-285, B-286, B-328, B-348, B-394, B-395
  1850-1879: A-5, A-15, A-23, A-25, A-47, A-52, A-57, A-59, A-69, A-81, A-83, A-89, A-91, A-95, A-101, A-102, A-111, A-119, A-136, A-154, A-155, A-156, A-164, A-165, A-215, A-216, A-219, A-221, A-229, A-230, A-237, A-254, A-260, A-282, A-283, A-302, A-311, A-337, A-341, A-351, A-361, A-383, A-391, A-395, A-407, B-43,

Politics — *Continued*
  1850–1879 — *cont.*
    B-56, B-58, B-80, B-84, B-86,
    B-105, B-114, B-131, B-137,
    B-153, B-155, B-156, B-161,
    B-204, B-205, B-212, B-215,
    B-240, B-249, B-252, B-254,
    B-262, B-269, B-276, B-281,
    B-284, B-285, B-286, B-335,
    B-348, B-387, B-393, B-394,
    B-395
  1880-1909: A-15, A-23, A-52, A-55,
    A-60, A-69, A-89, A-95, A-101,
    A-102, A-145, A-146, A-154,
    A-164, A-165, A-173, A-237,
    A-247, A-254, A-260, A-302,
    A-312, A-337, A-341, A-395,
    B-19, B-26, B-33, B-44, B-56,
    B-58, B-69, B-76, B-80, B-96,
    B-124, B-138, B-154, B-156,
    B-161, B-180, B-205, B-222,
    B-236, B-240, B-267, B-276,
    B-284, B-335, B-339, B-342,
    B-343, B-345, B-348, B-393
  1910-1945: A-23, A-51, A-60, A-68,
    A-76, A-95, A-128, A-167,
    A-172, A-225, A-231, A-237,
    A-249, A-285, A-317, A-352,
    A-365, A-407, B-17, B-20, B-61,
    B-79, B-96, B-110, B-120,
    B-124, B-130, B-143, B-147,
    B-149, B-155, B-156, B-180,
    B-196, B-200, B-203, B-216,
    B-218, B-219, B-226, B-236,
    B-256, B-259, B-261, B-267,
    B-275, B-277, B-285, B-289,
    B-334, B-335, B-339, B-342,
    B-343, B-345, B-352, B-361,
    B-381
  1946- : A-76, A-167, A-231, A-288,
    B-2, B-12, B-24, B-50, B-61,
    B-89, B-98, B-99, B-130, B-143,
    B-147, B-168, B-180, B-198,
    B-200, B-203, B-216, B-251,
    B-256, B-275, B-289, B-301,
    B-369, B-381, B-399
Polk, James K.: A-272
Polk, Trusten: B-119
POLK SANITARY MILK COMPANY
  (Indianapolis): *B-282*

Polke, William: B-351
Pollard and Wilson (Logansport): B-384
Polley, Frederick: B-149
Pond, James B.: A-391
Pope, Elijah: A-37
Pope, John: A-80, B-94
POPLAR RIDGE HORSE THIEF
  AND DETECTIVE COM-
  PANY (Carmel): *B-283*
PORTER, ALBERT GALLATIN:
  A-302, B-284, A-111, A-164,
  A-232, A-272, A-311, A-383,
  A-391, B-153, B-240, B-286
Porter, Aurelia: B-285
Porter, David: A-272
Porter, Gene Stratton: B-95
Porter, Helen — see Griffin, Helen
  Porter
Porter, William A.: B-285
Porter County: B-11, B-167
  Indiana Dunes State Park: B-174
  Valparaiso: A-18, B-211, B-309,
    B-330
PORTER-GRIFFIN FAMILY
  PAPERS: *B-285*
Portland, Jay Co.: A-86, B-9
POSEY, THOMAS: *A-303*, A-57,
  A-101, A-147, A-272, A-286,
  A-302, B-212, B-351
Posey County: A-397
  Mt. Vernon: B-208, B-365
  New Harmony: A-120, A-237, A-250,
    A-282, B-17, B-142, B-273,
    B-284
  St. Wendel: B-305
Post, C. C.: B-293
Post, Martin M.: B-384
Potts, William: B-342
Powell, Adam Clayton: B-301, B-399
Power, T. C.: A-146
PRAIRIE TREK EXPEDITIONS:
  A-304
Prairieton, Vigo Co.: A-128
Pratt, Charles D.: B-286
PRATT, DANIEL D.: *B-286*, A-15,
  A-83, A-111, A-229, A-232,
  A-272, A-302, A-383, B-84,
  B-119, B-137, B-212, B-263,
  B-345, B-348, B-351, B-384,
  B-395

Pratt, James P.: B-286
Presbyterian Board for Ministerial
    Relief: B-147
Preston, Margaret: B-287
PRESTON, NATHANIEL: *B-287*
Preston, William: B-287
PRICHETT, JOHN: *B-288*
PRICKETT, THOMAS: *A-305*
Prince, George W.: B-339
Prince, William: A-223, B-114, B-212
Princeton, Gibson Co.: A-35, A-136,
    A-137, A-278, A-354, B-16,
    B-114, B-285
Princeton University (N.J.): A-111,
    B-281
PROCTOR, JOHN: *A-306*
Proctor, Redfield: B-345
Proffit, George H.: B-137
Progressive Party: B-124, B-342
Prohibition Party: B-155, B-289
PROHIBITION PARTY OF
    INDIANA: *B-289*
Pro-League Independents: B-76
Prussia: B-394
Public Service Company of Indiana:
    B-20
Publishing: A-145, A-221, A-391,
    A-400, B-51, B-65, B-85, B-276,
    B-342, B-348
Pueblo Incident: B-211
Pueblo Land Board (Santa Fe, N.Mex.):
    B-114
Pulaski County
    Winamac: B-18
Pulitzer, Joseph: A-341
Pulliam, Eugene: B-20, B-193
Pullman Strike (Lake Co.): B-240
Purcell, John Baptist: A-391
Purdue University: A-15, A-231, B-255,
    B-285 — see also Lafayette, Tippecanoe County
Puritan Republic: A-170
Putnam, George P.: A-346
Putnam, Rufus: A-272, A-286
Putnam County: A-153, A-231, A-270
    Bainbridge: A-72, A-231
    Eel River District Association: B-71
    Greencastle: A-144, B-122, B-346,
        B-365 — see also DePauw
        University

Putnamville: B-146, B-214
Russellville: B-229
Washington Township: B-32
Putnamville, Putnam Co.: B-146, B-214

Quaife, Milo M.: A-176
Quincy (Elwood), Madison Co.: A-340

R. W. Heth & Brothers (Corydon):
    B-285
Rabb, Kate Milner: A-336, B-62, B-218,
    B-257, B-265
Rafinesque, Constantine: A-393
RAISBECK, SAMUEL M.: *A-307*
Ralston, Samuel M.: A-358, B-76,
    B-114, B-124, B-216, B-335,
    B-343
Ramsey, Alexander: B-160, B-348
RANDOLPH, CATHERINE LAWRENCE: *A-308*
Randolph, John: A-272
Randolph County: A-28, A-208, A-237,
    A-342
    Bloomingsport: A-296
    Harrisville: A-292
    Huntsville: B-68
    Losantville: A-28
    Ridgeville: A-13
    White River: A-342
    Winchester: A-62, A-126, B-68
Rankin, Oliver Smith: B-323
Ransom, Freeman B.: A-390
Ransom, Willard B.: B-6
Rapp, Frederick: A-54, A-57, A-250,
    B-212
Rariden, James: A-111, B-119, B-137,
    B-351
Rauh, Charles S.: A-189, A-309
Rauh, Henry: A-309
Rauh, Leopold: A-309
RAUH, SAMUEL E.: *A-309*, A-189
Rauh family: A-189, A-309
Ray, James Brown: A-101, A-302,
    B-212, B-351
Ray, James M.: A-111, A-267, A-275,
    A-302, B-119, B-299
RAY, JOHN W.: *A-310*
Raysville, Henry Co.: A-45, A-109,
    B-139

Read, Daniel G.: B-263, B-394
REAGAN, CHARLES M.: *B-290*
Recollections of Thomas R. Marshall: B-236
Reconstruction: A-254, A-335, B-273
RECORDS, WILLIAM H.: *B-291*
REDDING, THOMAS B.: *B-292,* A-156, B-260
Reed, George W.: A-402
Reed, Isaac: A-402, B-146
Reed, Thomas B.: B-393
Reed, Walter — see Walter Reed Hospital
Rees, Hulda: A-296
Rees, Samuel: B-384
Rees, Seth: A-296
Reese, Alexander: A-125
Reese family: A-125
Reeves Pulley Company (Columbus, Ind.): B-142
Reid, Whitelaw: A-164, A-302, A-341, A-346, A-391, B-84
Reifel, Theodore: B-56
Religion: A-181, B-211, B-233
  Baptist: A-18, A-20, A-36, A-37, A-375, B-71, B-379
  Dunkard: B-35
  Episcopalian: B-70, B-116, B-357
  Jewish: A-204
  Mennonite: B-35
  Methodist: A-77, A-397, A-400, B-152, B-242, B-324, B-365
  Methodist Episcopal: A-310, A-344, B-385
  Moravian: A-393
  Presbyterian: A-34, A-95, A-117, A-156, A-162, A-236, A-253, A-402, B-146, B-147, B-285, B-302, B-303, B-374, B-384
  Quaker (Society of Friends): A-31, A-43, A-49, A-83, A-129, A-188, A-237, A-296, A-299, A-314, A-342, A-357, A-363, B-28, B-64, B-78, B-117, B-139, B-276, B-290, B-356
  Roman Catholic: B-63, B-167, B-212, B-213
  Universalist: B-279
  anti-Catholic: B-348
  anti-Semitism: A-204
  education: A-18, A-36, A-49, A-129, A-181, A-310, A-314, B-242, B-303, B-356
  interfaith: A-181, A-199, B-233
  ministers/clergy: A-18, A-34, A-37, A-77, A-117, A-181, A-236, A-253, A-271, A-344, A-397, A-402, B-146, B-213, B-302, B-324, B-357, B-365, B-373, B-384, B-385
  missionaries: A-111, A-152, A-162, A-393, B-146, B-267
  spiritualist: A-9, B-223, B-273
Remington, Frederic: B-111
Remy, William H.: A-352
Rensselaer, Jasper Co.: A-167, B-63
Republican Finance Committee: B-275
Republican National Committee: B-130, B-147, B-301
Republican Party:
  1850-79: A-5, A-15, A-25, A-47, A-52, A-59, A-69, A-83, A-102, A-111, A-136, A-150, A-164, A-219, A-221, A-229, A-230, A-237, A-302, A-337, A-341, A-351, A-361, A-383, A-391, B-56, B-80, B-84, B-105, B-114, B-131, B-155, B-205, B-254, B-269, B-276, B-284, B-286, B-345, B-348, B-393, B-394, B-395
  1880-1909: A-52, A-55, A-60, A-69, A-102, A-145, A-164, A-237, A-247, A-302, A-337, A-341, A-383, A-395, B-56, B-80, B-84, B-113, B-124, B-138, B-155, B-180, B-222, B-254, B-267, B-276, B-284, B-339, B-342, B-345
  1910-1945: A-52, A-60, A-68, A-102, A-167, A-172, A-231, A-317, A-352, B-110, B-113, B-124, B-147, B-149, B-180, B-218, B-219, B-226, B-259, B-267, B-285, B-339, B-342, B-352, B-361, B-381
  1946-: A-167, B-2, B-24, B-50, B-61, B-89, B-98, B-130, B-143, B-147, B-168, B-180, B-211, B-251, B-259, B-275, B-301, B-352, B-381, B-399

INDEX

Revels, W. R.: A-111
Revolution—When? Where? How?: A-172
REYNOLDS, JAMES MADISON: *A-311*
Reynolds, Joseph Jones: A-311
REYNOLDS, STEPHEN MARION: *A-312*, B-149
Reynolds, William: B-56
Rhea, James: A-187
Rhode Island: A-52, B-117, B-169
   Brown University: A-22, A-111, A-210
   Newport County: B-37
   Providence: B-107
Rhodes, James Ford: B-76
Rhue, Sarah: A-114
Rhue, Ward: A-114
Rhue-Fry family — see FRY-RHUE FAMILY
Rhyan, Arminda: B-314
Rice, Alexander Hamilton: A-346
RICE, MARY: *B-293*
Rich, John G.: B-240
RICHARDSON, IDA FRANCES: *A-313*
Richardson, Joel F.: A-313
RICHARDSON, LEWIS BRADFORD: *B-294*
RICHARDSON, MILDRED KNIGHT: *B-295*
Richardville, John B.: B-351
Richardville, Joseph: B-137, B-351
Richmond, Wayne Co.: A-14, A-129, A-146, A-164, A-221, A-226, A-237, A-239, A-269, A-336, A-349, A-357, A-388, A-396, B-28, B-98, B-124, B-139, B-230, B-356, B-368 — see also Earlham College
Richmond Enterprise: B-28
RICHSQUARE ACADEMY (Lewisville): *A-314*, A-132
Richsquare Literary Society (Lewisville): A-314
Ridgeville, Randolph Co.: A-13
Ridgeway, Robert: B-95
Ridpath, John Clark: B-348, B-371
RIGG, MARY: *B-296* — See also MARY RIGG CENTER

RILEY, JAMES WHITCOMB: *A-315*, B-297, A-112, A-233, A-322, A-407, B-62, B-76, B-111, B-124, B-259, B-261, B-276
Riley, Mary Elizabeth — see Payne, Mary Elizabeth Riley
Ripley County: A-138, A-379
   Batesville: B-370
   Milan: A-142
   Sunman: A-265
   Versailles: A-138, A-142, B-123, B-196
Ripley County Bar Association: B-196
Rising Sun, Ohio Co.: A-150, A-236, A-237, B-92, B-286, B-291
Ristine, Richard O.: B-24
Ritchie, Albert C.: B-236
Rivers, Walter: A-101
Rivet, John Francis: B-212
Roachdale, Montgomery Co.: B-15
Roache, Addison: A-81, B-394
Roanoke, Huntington Co.: A-241
Robb, David: B-114
Robbins, Grant: B-79
ROBERTS, ELIJAH: *A-316*
Roberts, G. B.: A-369
Roberts, Kenneth A.: B-24
Roberts, Lizzie: A-296
Roberts Settlement, Hamilton Co.: A-316
ROBERTSON, CARRIE FRANCIS: *A-317*
Robertson, James: A-272, A-286
Robinson, A'Lelia Walker: A-390
Robinson, Andrew L.: A-176, B-205
Robinson, Arthur R.: A-68, A-358, B-149, B-381
Robinson, James C.: A-81
Robinson, James M.: B-348
Robinson, John L.: A-237
Robinson, John M.: A-303
Robinson, Solon: B-119, B-351
ROBINSON, WILLIAM H.: *B-298*
Robinson, Woodfin D.: B-114
Roby, Elizabeth J.: B-150
Rochester, Fulton Co.: B-19, B-20
Rochester Sentinel: B-19, B-20
Rochester Telephone Company: B-19, B-20
Rockefeller, Nelson A.: B-369

Rockhill, William: B-137, B-204, B-351
Rockport, Spencer Co.: A-217, A-306, A-382, A-383, B-49
Rockport Democrat: B-49
Rockville, Parke Co.: A-88, A-332, B-394
ROCKWOOD, WILLIAM: *B-299*
Rockwood, William O.: A-123
Rocky Mountain News: A-358
Rocky Mountains: B-55
Rodzinski, Artur: A-327
Rogers, Bruce: B-85
Rogers, John: B-341
Rogers, Will: B-147
Rogers, William K.: A-341, B-348
Romney, George: B-369
Roosevelt, Edith Kermit: B-342
Roosevelt, Eleanor: B-200
Roosevelt, Franklin Delano: A-272, A-302, A-407, B-200, B-256, B-343
Roosevelt, Theodore: A-52, A-95, A-272, B-124, B-147, B-342 — See also Theodore Roosevelt Memorial Association
Root, Elihu: B-84, B-236, B-259
Root, Erastus: A-83, A-237
Root, Oren, Jr.: A-172
Rose, John C.: B-342
Rose Marie Cruzan Parliamentary Club (Indianapolis): B-182
Rose Polytechnic Institute (Terre Haute): B-58
Rosecrans, William S.: A-15, A-173, A-391, B-94, B-254
Rosedale, Parke Co.: B-29
ROSS MEAT MARKET (Ambia): *B-300*
Rothschild Brothers (Paris, France): A-410
ROUDEBUSH, RICHARD: *B-301*, B-369
Rous, Linda — see Shaw, Linda Rous
Roush, J. Edward: B-99, B-369
Ruger, Thomas H.: A-402
Ruggles, Samuel B.: A-387
RULE, LUCIEN V.: *B-302*
Rumely, Edward A.: B-334
Rupp family: B-285
Rush, Benjamin: A-272

Rush, Richard: A-272, A-302, **B-394**
Rush County: A-3, A-181, A-342, A-397, B-247, B-248
Carthage: B-385
Homer: B-52
Melrose: A-2
Milroy: B-47, B-52
Rushville: B-157
Rushville, Rush Co.: B-157
Russell, Alexander W.: B-47
Russell, John: A-272
Russell, William: A-147, B-212
Russellville, Putnam Co.: B-229
Russia: A-162 — See also Soviet Union
Petrograd: A-116
Russian Revolution: A-116
Russiaville, Howard Co.: A-49
Russo-Japanese War: A-116
Ryan, Thomas J.: B-285

S. S. Kresge Company: B-209
SABBATH SCHOOL UNION SOCIETY (Indianapolis): *B-303*
Sagamore of the Wabash: B-275
Sage, Anna: B-129
Sage, Russell: A-102
Sage, Suydam & Company — see Suydam, Sage & Company
St. Ange, Louis: A-223, A-302, B-212
St. Clair, Arthur (1736-1818): A-8, A-101, A-237, A-272, A-286, A-302, A-308, A-341
St. Clair, Arthur (1803-1841): A-237
St. Clair, Arthur Jr.: A-381
St. Elizabeth's School (Flora, S.D.): A-175
St. Francis Xavier Church (Vincennes): B-212
St. Joseph County: B-354
Liberty Township Teachers' Institute: B-109
Mishawaka: B-23
Notre Dame: B-213
South Bend: A-69, A-270, A-347, B-44, B-84, B-89, B-101, B-109, B-335, B-354, B-391
St. Josephs (fur trade): A-286
St. Joseph's College (Ind.): B-63
St. Martin, Adhemar: B-212

INDEX

St. Mary-of-the-Woods Academy (Vigo Co.): B-167
St. Mary-of-the-Woods College (Vigo Co.): A-91, A-313, B-47
St. Mary's College (Wilmington, Del.): A-91
St. Mary's Institute — see St. Mary-of-the-Woods College
St. Paul, Decatur Co.: A-380, B-52
St. Wendel, Posey Co.: B-305
Salem, Washington Co.: A-52, A-117, A-273, A-277, B-150, B-280
Sales Executive Council (Indianapolis): A-192
Sallee, A. C.: B-343
Salvation Army: B-330
Sample, Samuel C.: A-408, B-137, B-212, B-351
Samuel Moore & Company (Mooresville): B-252
Sandburg, Carl: A-176
SANDERS, F. E.: *A-318*
Sanders family: B-238
Sargeant, Carrie — see Carr, Carrie Sargeant
Sargent, L. S.: B-95
Sargent, Winthrop: A-8, A-147, A-237, A-272, A-286, A-302
Saunders family: B-248
Saundersville (now Inglefield), Vanderburgh Co.: A-198
Say, Thomas: A-282
Scammon, J. Young: B-167
Schenck, Peter: A-132
SCHERRER, ADOLPH: *A-319*
SCHERRER, ANTON: *A-320*
SCHLICHTE, EDWARD J.: *B-304*
Schliemann, Heinrich: B-153
SCHNEIDER, WILLIAM: *B-305*
Schools of New Castle, Indiana: A-156
Schortemeier, Frederick C.: B-259
SCHRADER, CHRISTIAN: *B-306*
Schramm, Anna: A-321
Schramm, Gustave: A-321
SCHRAMM, WILHELM AUGUST: *A-321*
Schricker, Henry F.: B-20, B-219
Schroeder family: B-238
SCHUMACHER, GEORGE A.: *A-322*
Schurz, Carl: A-341, A-391, B-342

Science: A-109, A-156, A-304, B-56, B-95, B-257, B-292, B-372
  Botany: A-109, B-95, B-218, B-219, B-257
  Horticulture: A-313, B-127
  Ichthyology: B-118, B-121
  Inventions: B-292, B-345
  Meteorology: B-151, B-212
  Ornithology: B-56, B-118
Scioto Company — see Compagnie du Scioto
Scotland: B-170, B-312
Scott, Agnes: B-150
Scott, Almira Maria — see HARRAH, ALMIRA MARIA (Scott)
Scott, Caroline — see Harrison, Caroline Scott
Scott, Charles: A-272, A-286, A-303
Scott, Harvey D.: A-144, B-348
SCOTT, JOHN (fl. 1841-1884): *A-323*
Scott, John: B-307
SCOTT, MARGARET M.: *B-307*, A-315
SCOTT, RANSOM D.: *A-324*
Scott, William: B-150
Scott, Winfield: A-272, A-387, A-391, B-84, B-94
Scott County: A-101, A-397
  Lexington: A-77, A-101, A-174
  Woosterstown: A-323
Scott family: A-144
Scott Masonic Lodge (Lexington): A-101
Scott Township, Vanderburgh Co.: A-33
SCOTUS, GAUL PICTI: *B-308*
SCRIBNER, BENJAMIN FRANKLIN: *A-325*
Sears, Ella Springer: B-330
Sears, Jesse M.: B-330
SEBASTIAN, BENJAMIN: *A-326*, A-8, B-212
Sebree, Shubert: B-96
Securities Corporation Limited: A-337
SEEHAUSEN, PAUL: *B-309*
Seligman, Jesse: B-348
Seligman, Joseph: B-348
Selma, Delaware Co.: A-274
Senate Hotel (Indianapolis): B-112
Sennett, William T.: B-229

INDEX

Sergeant & Jenners — see Jenners & Sergeant
Severinghaus, Nora — see Walker, Nora Severinghaus
SEVITZKY, FABIEN: *A-327*, A-364
Sewall, May Wright: B-76, B-124, B-190, B-393
Seward, Frederick W.: B-348
Seward, Jennie Dalrymple: B-92
Seward, William H.: A-15, A-229, A-230, A-272, A-346, A-391, B-43, B-84, B-394
Seymour, Horatio W.: B-281, B-335
Seymour, Jackson Co.: B-52, B-146, B-365
Shackelford, Bessie Van Scyoc: B-310
SHACKELFORD, RALPH: *B-310*
SHADES INN (Montgomery Co.): *B-311*
Shaffer, John C.: B-33
Shank, Lew: A-161
Shanks, William F.: A-391
Shannondale, Montgomery Co.: A-409
Sharp, George: B-212
Sharpe, Robina — see TUCKER, ROBINA SHARPE
Sharpe, Thomas H.: A-111
Sharpsville, Tipton Co.: B-123
Shaw, Carpus N.: A-144
Shaw, Leslie W.: B-259
Shaw, Linda Rous: B-312
SHAW, WILLIAM: *B-312*
Shelby, Isaac: A-147, A-272, A-286
Shelby County: A-30, A-397, B-386
  Flat Rock: A-211
  Marietta: A-209
  Shelbyville: A-30, A-191, A-380, B-281, B-375
Shelbyville, Shelby Co.: A-30, A-191, A-380, B-281, B-375
Sheldon, Lionel A.: B-254
Shelley, Mary Wollstonecraft: B-273
Shepardson, Lorenzo Dow: B-313
Shepardson, Otis: B-313
Shepardson, Pliny: B-313
Shepardson, Samuel: B-313
Shepardson, Susan — see Freligh, Susan Shepardson
SHEPARDSON FAMILY: *B-313*

SHEPHERD, JAMES NELSON: *B-314*
Shepherd, Thomas E.: B-314
Sherman, Ellen B. E.: A-302
Sherman, John: A-101, A-164, A-272, A-302, A-341, A-391, B-84, B-345, B-348, B-395
Sherman, William Tecumseh: A-69, A-80, A-302, A-383, A-391, B-286
Shields, James: B-105
Shipman, Harry: A-125
Shipman family: A-125
Shipp, May Louise: B-76, B-261
SHIRK, ANDREW: *A-328*
Shirk, Mattie — see Goodwin, Mattie Shirk
Shirk, Samuel: A-123
Shively, Benjamin F.: A-101, B-19, B-114, B-335
SHOCKLEY, DAVID: *A-329*
Shockley, Susan — see Curts, Susan Shockley
SHOEMAKER, HERMAN: *A-330*
Sholts, Frederick: B-86
Short, J. H.: B-76
Short, John Cleves: A-381
SHORT, LUTHER: *B-315*
SHORTRIDGE, NORMAN H.: *B-316*
Shriver, R. Sargent: B-61, B-301
SHRYER, JOHN D.: *A-331*, *B-317*
Shryock, K. G.: B-138
Shurtleff College (Alton, Ill.): A-265
Sibelius, Jean — see Jean Sibelius Fund
Sibley, Henry: B-119
Sibley, John: A-272
Sibley, Solomon: A-381, B-212
Sicily
  World War II: A-362
Sick Children's Aid Society (Ft. Wayne): B-241
Sieg, Paul: B-285
Sigel, Franz: B-94
Silberman, Abris: A-364
Silberman Brothers (New York): B-344
SILVER, THOMAS: *B-318*
Silver, William: B-318
Silver Creek, Clark Co.: B-71
Simcoe, John Greaves: A-286
Simonton, James W.: A-341

SIMPSON, ELIZABETH: *A-332*
SIMPSON, JOHN R.: *B-319*
Sims, Fred E.: B-339
Sims, Grant Co.: A-23
Sinclair, Upton: A-172
SINKER-DAVIS COMPANY (Indianapolis): *B-320*
SINKS, DANIEL: *B-321*
"Sixteen Hundred and Seven": B-273
"Six Months in Saddle and Camp, or Roughing It in the Rockies in 1870": B-55
Sketches of My Own Time: B-355
SLACK, JAMES R.: *B-322*, B-335
Slade, William: A-111
Slater, Amanda — see Van Pelt, Amanda Slater
Slaughter, Thomas C.: A-229, B-124, B-286
Slavery: A-254, A-302, A-351, B-273
  in Indiana: A-302, B-212, B-284 — see also Blacks
Slawson, Delanson: A-333
Slawson, Simeon: A-333
SLAWSON-TARKINGTON FAMILY PAPERS: *A-333*
Smith, Abraham: B-223
Smith, Alfred E.: B-147, B-343
SMITH, BENJAMIN WILSON: *A-334, B-334*
Smith, Caleb B.: A-5, A-8, A-91, A-232, A-264, A-43, B-114, B-124, B-137, B-249, B-254, B-259, B-263, B-286
Smith, Charles: B-324
SMITH, CHARLES W.: *A-335*
SMITH, CLARENCE H.: *A-336*
SMITH, DELAVAN: *A-337*, A-46, A-102, A-237, B-147
SMITH, EDGAR: *A-338*
Smith, Edmund Kirby: A-391
SMITH, GEORGE R.: *A-339*
Smith, Gerrit: B-28
Smith, Jacob: A-336
SMITH, JOSEPH TAYLOR: *A-340*
Smith, Margaret: A-339
Smith, Morgan: A-335
Smith, Nicholas: B-73
Smith, Oliver H.: A-8, A-111, A-229, A-266, A-272, A-302, B-119, B-137, B-204, B-249, B-263, B-351
Smith, Richard: A-341
Smith, Robert (1802-1867): A-81
Smith, Robert Barclay (1835-1900): A-336
SMITH, RUTH BURGESS LEBO: *B-324*
SMITH, SAMUEL A.: *B-325*
Smith, Seth: A-336
Smith, Thomas: B-212
Smith, Truman: B-114
SMITH, WILLIAM HENRY (1830-1911): *B-326*
SMITH, WILLIAM HENRY (1833-1896): *A-341*, A-46, A-237, A-337
SMITH & COMPANY (Mooresville): *B-327*
Smithsonian Institute: B-372
Snedeker, Caroline Dale: B-85
Social Service Exchange (Indianapolis): A-103
Socialism: A-312, B-273
Socialist Party: A-128, A-312, B-96
Society of Friendly Visitors (Indianapolis): A-103
SOCIETY OF FRIENDS: *A-342* — see also Religion-Quaker
Society of Indiana Florists: A-350
Society of the Army of the Cumberland: B-113
Sociology: A-128, A-172
Soldiers Aid Society: B-40
Soldier's and Sailor's Monument (Indianapolis): A-319
Soldier's and Sailor's Rights and Service Pension Alliance: A-133
Sons of Italy in America: A-239
Sons of the American Revolution (S.A.R.): A-336
SOULE, JOSHUA: *B-328*
Soulé, Pierre: A-346
South America: A-54, A-285, B-95, B-143, B-261, B-281, B-287, B-339
South Bend, St. Joseph Co.: A-69, A-347, B-44, B-84, B-89, B-101, B-109, B-335, B-354, B-391
South Bend Housing Authority: B-101

South Bend Pad and Comb Company: B-109
South Bend Power Company: B-109
South Carolina: A-37
  Civil War: B-141, B-231, B-244
  Charlestown: A-250
  Newberry: A-131
  Port Royal (Civil War): A-242
South Dakota: A-175, B-356
South Pacific (World War II): B-166, B-213, B-364
South Sea Islands: A-317
Southall, Mrs. George A.: B-134
Southport, Marion Co.: B-393
Southport and Indianapolis Gravel Road Company: B-112
Southwest Social Center (Indianapolis): B-296
Southwest Social Club's Women's Auxiliary (Indianapolis): B-237
Southwestern Indiana Historical Society: A-176, B-114
Soviet Union: A-46, B-211 — See also Russia
Spain
  relations with Napoleonic France: A-32
  relations with United States: A-286, A-326
Spanish-American War: A-224, B-109
  158th Regiment: B-15
  13th Minnesota Regiment: B-295
  medical corps: B-295
  veterans: A-101
Spanish Conspiracy: A-326
Spann, John C. — see John C. Spann Company
SPANN AND RASSMAN (Indianapolis): *A-343*
SPARKS, JEREMIAH BURRIS: *A-344*
Spaulding, H. S.: B-84
Spearbeck, George W.: A-242
SPEED, EDWARD B.: *A-345*
Speed, James A.: A-229, A-302
Speed, John J.: A-391
Speed, Jonathan: A-229
Spencer, Owen Co.: A-27
Spencer County: A-6, A-176, A-181, A-383, B-13, B-323
  Dale: B-49

Gentryville: B-365
Grandview: B-13
Rockport: A-217, A-306, A-382, A-383, B-49
Spiceland, Henry Co.: A-259, B-117, B-356
Spiceland Academy (Henry Co.): A-259
Spooner, Benjamin: B-286
Spooner, John C.: B-393
SPRING MILL STATE PARK (Mitchell): *B-329*
Spring Valley Road Company (Marion Co.): B-27
Springer, Carrie — see Brayton, Carrie Springer
Springer, Ella — see Sears, Ella Springer
Springer, N. M.: B-330
Springer, Raymond S.: B-143
Springer, William H.: B-330
Springer, William N.: A-101
SPRINGER-BRAYTON FAMILY: *B-330*
Springfield, Franklin Co.: A-328
Springville, Lawrence Co.: B-315
SQUIER, EPHRAIM GEORGE: *A-346*
Stahr, Elvis, Jr.: B-6
Standing Commission on Structure of the National Church (Episcopal): B-116
Standish, Benjamin: B-329
STANFIELD, EDWARD P.: *A-347*
Stanford, Leland: A-302
Stanhope, Philip Henry: A-346
Stanton, Edwin M: A-272, A-391, B-43
Stanton, Elizabeth Cady: B-96
Stapp, Milton: B-263
STAR GROCERY (Broad Ripple): *B-331*
STAR MILL COMPANY (Huntingburg): *A-348*
Starling Medical College (Columbus, Ohio): A-243
STARR, WILLIAM C.: *A-349*
State Automobile Insurance Association: B-267
STATE FLORIST ASSOCIATION OF INDIANA: *A-350*
State Line City, Warren Co.: B-1

INDEX

STAUDT, CARL: *B-332*
Staudt, John M.: B-332
Steele, George W.: A-102
Steele, Helen McKay: A-351
STEELE, SELMA NEUBACHER: *B-333*, A-128, A-351
Steele, Theodore Clement: A-128, A-210, B-85, B-124, B-333
STEELE, THEODORE L.: *A-351*
Stephens, Alexander H.: A-272
STEPHENSON, DAVID CURTISS (D. C.): *A-352, B-334*, B-120
Stetson, Francis Lynde: B-342
Steuben, Baron Friedrich von: A-286
Steuben County: A-242, B-23
   Angola: B-381
   Flint: A-242
   Hamilton: A-26
Stevens, Thaddeus: A-267
Stevenson, Adlai E.: B-240
Stickney, Lyman: B-114
Stimson, Henry L.: B-259
Stock, Frederick: A-237
STOCKDALE, WILLIAM: *A-353*
STOCKWELL, ROBERT: *A-354*
Stockwell Collegiate Institute (Tippecanoe Co.): A-30
Stokes, Caroline — see Hunter, Caroline Stokes
STOLL, JOHN B.: *B-335*, A-173, B-19
Stone, David M.: A-341
Stone, Harlan F.: B-147
Stone, Henry Lane: A-229
Stone, Irving: A-172
Stone, Melville E.: A-341
STOOPS, HARRY M.: *B-336*
Storey, Moorfield: B-342
STOREY, THOMAS J.: *A-355*
Storey, W. W.: A-302
Stotsenburg, John H.: A-52
Stout, Elihu: A-57, B-114, B-212
STOUT, MARTHA: *A-356*
Stover, Daniel: B-337
Stover, Harney B.: B-337
Stover, Harney W.: B-337
STOVER, URBAN C.: *B-337*
Stowe, Harriet Beecher: B-273
Stowman, C. B.: B-338
STOWMAN, CHARLES W.: *B-338*

Strawn, Ida: see BAKER, IDA STRAWN
Streightoff, Frances Doan: A-357
STREIGHTOFF, FRANK HATCH: *A-357*
STUART, JAMES ARTHUR: *A-358*
STUCKEY, WILLIAM ROBERTS: *A-359*
Studebaker, Clement: B-345
Studebaker, J. M.: B-19
Studebaker, John: B-345
Studebaker, Peter: B-44
Studebaker Company (South Bend): B-354
Sturm, Herman: A-391
STUTESMAN, JAMES FLYNN: *B-339*
STYER, WILLIAM: *A-360*
Sugar Creek Township, Hancock Co.: A-321
Sugar Grove, Hendricks Co.: A-342
Sugar River, Montgomery Co.: A-342
Sulgrove, Berry R.: A-302
Sulgrove, James: B-321
SULGROVE, LESLIE: *B-340*
Sullivan, Algernon Sydney: A-361
SULLIVAN, JEREMIAH: *A-361*, A-8, A-302, B-263, B-348, B-361
Sullivan, Margaret Frances: A-341
Sullivan, Mark: B-342
Sullivan, Sullivan Co.: A-60, B-147
SULLIVAN, WILLIAM G.: *B-341*
Sullivan County: B-152
   Sullivan: A-60, B-147
"Sultana" (steamboat): B-314
Sulzer, William: B-345
Summer Mission for Sick Children (Indianapolis): A-103, B-173
SUMMERS, FRANK WALLACE: *A-362*
Sumner, Charles: A-346, B-84, B-205
Sumner, William Graham: A-52
Sunman, Ripley Co.: A-265
Sunnyside Sanatarium (Indianapolis): B-5
Suydam, Jackson & Company (New York): B-137
Suydam, Sage & Company (New York): B-119
Swan, Caleb: A-8, A-286, A-381

INDEX

Swan, Ione — see PAUGH, IONE SWAN
Swan, James: A-295
Swan, Noble Co.: B-23
Swan, Robert: A-295
Swan, William: A-295
Swayne, Wager: A-341
Swearingen family: B-123
Sweetser, Madison: B-119
Swift, Louis F.: A-337
SWIFT, LUCIUS BURRIE: *B-342*, A-52, B-76, B-124
The Swiss Settlement of Switzerland County: B-106
Switzerland: A-120, A-319, A-410, B-106, B-145
   Geneva: A-79
Switzerland County: A-302, A-333, A-396, A-397, B-31, B-106
   — See also *The Swiss Settlement of Switzerland County*
   Vevay: A-102, A-120, A-215, A-237, A-266, A-392, B-93, B-106, B-111, B-312
Symmes, John Cleves: A-8, A-272, A-286

Taber, Cyrus: B-119, B-137, B-351
Taber, John: B-24
Taft, Charles P.: A-341, B-342
Taft, Robert A.: A-172, B-24, B-275
Taft, William Howard: A-52, A-60, A-102, A-272, B-76, B-124, B-147, B-236, B-259, B-342, B-345
Taft-Hartley Act: B-251
Taggart, Samuel: B-204
Taggart, Thomas D.: B-343
TAGGART, THOMAS T.: *B-343*, A-319, B-76, B-147, B-219, B-335
TALBERT, MARTHA WHITE: *A-363*
Talleyrand, Prince Charles Maurice de: A-32
Tampico, Howard Co.: A-269
Tappan, Benjamin: A-282
Tarbell, Ida: A-176, A-210
Tardiveau, Bartholomei: A-384
Tardiveau, Pierre: A-8

TARKINGTON, BOOTH: *A-364*, *A-365*, *B-344*, A-210, A-249, A-285, A-327, A-358, A-366, B-76, B-85, B-147, B-261, B-281
Tarkington, John S.: A-333
Tarkington, Joseph: A-333
TARKINGTON, SUSANAH (Kiefer): *A-366*, A-68, A-365
Tarkington-Slawson family — see SLAWSON-TARKINGTON FAMILY PAPERS
Taussig, Frank William: B-342
Taylor, Catherine: A-156
Taylor, Harold: A-229
Taylor, Harriet — see Upton, Harriet Taylor
Taylor, James: A-8, A-272
Taylor, James H.: B-346
Taylor, John J.: A-81
TAYLOR, ROBERT S.: *B-345*, A-52, A-145, B-286
TAYLOR, TUCKER W.: *B-346*
Taylor, Waller: A-101, A-125, A-272, B-351
Taylor, Zachary: A-147, A-237, A-272, B-205, B-258
Tecumseh
   death of: A-272
Temperance and Prohibition: A-17, A-111, A-144, A-163, A-254, A-259, A-288, A-302, A-400, B-155, B-286, B-289, B-303
Tennery, Charles H.: B-109
Tennessee: A-175, A-259, A-288, B-92
   Civil War: A-21, A-24, A-29, A-35, A-47, A-59, A-80, A-96, A-97, A-113, A-129, A-140, A-143, A-145, A-160, A-168, A-205, A-206, A-208, A-209, A-213, A-220, A-228, A-234, A-241, A-244, A-252, A-259, A-269, A-291, A-294, A-305, A-325, A-339, A-340, A-345, A-347, A-359, A-368, A-373, A-381, A-402, B-21, B-94, B-136, B-141, B-144, B-170, B-197, B-199, B-221, B-223, B-228, B-231, B-235, B-244, B-265, B-266, B-285, B-293, B-298,

INDEX

Tennessee — *Continued*
  Civil War — *cont.*
    B-313, B-314, B-322, B-330, B-358, B-360, B-376, B-382
  Chattanooga (Civil War): B-230
  Dover: A-400
  Fort Pickering (Civil War): A-360
  Friendsville: A-129
  Gallatin (Civil War): A-216
  Jackson: A-302
  Knoxville: A-390
  Lebanon: A-26
  Memphis: A-210, B-92
    Civil War: A-383, B-322
  Murfreesboro: A-26
    Civil War: B-114, B-230
  Nashville: A-379, B-170, B-197, B-364
    Civil War: A-389
  Pelham (Civil War): B-230
  Rockwood: B-376
  Shiloh (Civil War): A-383
  Stone River (Civil War): B-199
  Tennessee Valley Authority: B-142
  Terre Haute, Vigo Co.: A-5, A-11, A-91, A-100, A-128, A-144, A-254, A-312, A-369, B-3, B-29, B-34, B-67, B-96, B-104, B-122, B-146, B-200, B-212, B-217, B-232, B-287, B-347, B-348, B-353
    Camp Thompson (Civil War): B-348
    Fort Harrison: B-212
Terre Haute Atalantian Literati: A-11
Terre Haute (land) Company: B-212
TERRE HAUTE SCHOOL SOCIETY: *B-347*
Terrell, William H. H.: A-5, A-15, A-52, A-150, A-302, B-85, B-160, B-212, B-225, B-284, B-348, B-376, B-393
Test, John: B-119, B-137, B-263, B-351
Texas: A-72, A-168, A-177, B-212, B-263, B-270
  annexation: B-273
  Civil War: A-41, A-106, A-143, A-259, B-322, B-353
  Mexican War: A-78, A-218
  Brownsville: B-354
  Galveston: B-77
  Goliad: A-175
  Weatherford: B-215
Thayer, Alexander W.: B-394
Thayer, John M.: A-391
Theodore Roosevelt Memorial Association: B-147
THOMAS, ANNE BUTLER: *A-367*
THOMAS, JAMES S.: *A-368*
Thompson, George Alfred: B-138
Thompson, John H.: B-132
Thompson, Maurice: A-322, A-391, B-85, B-276
THOMPSON, RICHARD WIGGINTON: *A-369, B-348*, A-5, A-8, A-15, A-81, A-144, A-145, A-229, A-232, A-266, A-272, A-311, A-395, B-114, B-119, B-137, B-160, B-249, B-286, B-393
Thompson, Will Henry: A-391
Thornton, Henry C.: B-286
THORNTON, HENRY P.: *A-370*, B-351
THORNTON, WILLIAM WHEELER: *B-349*
325th FIELD ARTILLERY ASSOCIATION: *B-350*
Thurman, Marion: B-49
Ticknor, Benjamin H.: A-391
Ticknor, George: A-346
Tiffin, Edward: A-125, A-147, B-351
Tilden, Samuel J.: B-205
Tippecanoe, Battle of: B-258, B-284, B-351
Tippecanoe Battlefield reunion: B-258
Tippecanoe County: A-181
  politics: B-79
  Americus: B-23
  Lafayette: A-73, A-75, A-79, A-151, A-169, A-209, A-311, A-334, A-388, B-339, B-357, B-372 — see also Purdue University
  Montmorency: B-291
  Ouiatenon: A-286
  Stockwell Collegiate Institute: A-30
Tippecanoe County Democratic Central Committee: B-79
Tipton, George T.: B-351

TIPTON, JOHN: *B-351*, A-111,
  A-125, A-136, A-147, A-237,
  A-267, A-272, A-302, A-391,
  A-408, B-119, B-137, B-212,
  B-263, B-286
Tipton, Matilda: B-351
Tipton, Spear S.: B-286, B-351
Tipton, Tipton Co.: B-278, B-324
Tipton County
  Hobbs: B-52
  Sharpsville: B-123
  Tipton: B-278, B-324
Todd, Charles N.: A-253
Todd, Charles S.: A-147, A-272
Todd, John: B-212
Todd, Margaret McLean: A-253
Todd, Robert: A-101
Tomlinson, George: B-393
Toucey, Isaac: A-101
Tourgee, Albion: A-260, B-138
Tousey, George: B-370
Tousey, Omer: A-302, B-263
Town, Ithiel: A-266
Towner, John H.: A-135
Towner-Hackleman family — see
  HACKLEMAN-TOWNER
  FAMILY
Townsend, M. Clifford: B-20, B-219
Trafalgar, Johnson Co.: B-294
Transportation
  air: B-168
  buses: A-197
  canals: A-91, A-123, A-132, A-157,
    A-158, A-229, A-264, A-387,
    A-394, A-407, B-1, B-104,
    B-119, B-137, B-234, B-263,
    B-286, B-348, B-370, B-395
  electric railways: A-79, A-101, A-146,
    A-164, A-200, B-110
  ferries: A-280
  railroads:
    1816-1849: A-8, A-111, A-156,
      A-264, A-266, A-267, A-302,
      A-381, B-36, B-137, B-204,
      B-252, B-263, B-281, B-285,
      B-286, B-394, B-395
    1850-1879: A-8, A-9, A-52, A-81,
      A-94, A-101, A-108, A-111,
      A-136, A-156, A-189, A-229,
      A-240, A-264, A-266, A-307,
      A-313, A-369, A-381, B-7, B-23,
      B-40, B-47, B-93, B-104,
      B-114, B-137, B-146, B-153,
      B-204, B-215, B-223, B-252,
      B-281, B-285, B-286, B-348,
      B-359, B-394, B-395
    1880-1909: A-9, A-52, A-94, A-102,
      A-146, A-156, A-164, A-179,
      A-189, A-237, A-240, A-276,
      A-369, A-371, B-23, B-114,
      B-223, B-240
    1910-1945: A-94, A-179, A-189,
      A-237, A-240, B-33, B-46,
      B-114, B-147, B-149
  roads and highways: A-72, A-92,
    A-123, A-125, A-132, A-171,
    A-231, A-313, B-27, B-28,
    B-137, B-158, B-234, B-263,
    B-395
  steamboats: A-125, B-49, B-93,
    B-314, B-387
TRASK, GEORGE KELLOGG:
  A-371
Traubel, Horace: A-312
Travel Accounts:
  -1815: A-8, A-253, A-286, B-106
  1816-1849: A-11, A-72, A-83, A-111,
    A-161, A-175, A-198, A-237,
    A-250, A-334, B-146, B-165,
    B-212, B-272, B-288, B-323,
    B-391
  1850-1879: A-29, A-52, A-69, A-72,
    A-198, A-219, A-339, A-391,
    A-407, B-55, B-131, B-286,
    B-288, B-364
  1880-1909: A-63, A-83, A-162,
    A-229, A-317, A-391, B-205,
    B-240, B-248
  1910-1945: A-123, A-134, A-216,
    A-317, A-334, A-367, B-145,
    B-248, B-324, B-361
  1946-: B-248
Treaty of Greenville (1794-95): A-286
Treaty of St. Mary's (1818): A-187
Trippett, William H.: B-114
Trist, Nicholas P.: B-273
Trittipo, Albert W.: B-155
Trotter family: B-336
Troy, Perry Co.: A-47, B-49

INDEX

Troy, Mass., Cotton and Woolen Mill Company: B-37
Trubner, Nicholas: A-346
True Indian Stories: B-107
Trumbull, Lyman: B-105
Tucker, Hannibal Smith: A-372
Tucker, Irwin St. John: B-96
TUCKER, JAMES M.: *B-352*
TUCKER, ROBINA SHARPE: *A-372*
Tudor Hall School (Indianapolis): B-275
Turkey: A-162, A-391
    Constantinople: A-162
Turley, Benjamin: B-353
Turley, Jennie: B-353
TURLEY, JONATHAN: *B-353*, B-329
Turley, Lida: B-353
TURNBULL, DAVID C.: *B-354*
Turner, Eli Barton: B-90
Turner, Frederick Jackson: A-176
Turner, Ora Cunningham: B-90
Turner, Roscoe: B-301
TURPIE, DAVID: *B-355*, A-5, A-52, A-101, A-102, A-232, A-272, B-1, B-119, B-124, B-212, B-286, B-335
TUTEWILER, HENRY W.: *A-373*
Tuttle, Joseph F.: B-284, B-286
Twigg, William A.: A-282, B-114
Twitchell, Marshall: A-335
Tyler, John: A-147, A-272
Tyler, Orpha — see Flanner, Orpha Tyler
Tyndall, Robert H.: A-193
Tyner, James N.: A-164, B-339

U.C.: B-115
U.S. INFANTRY. FIRST INFANTRY COMPANY, SECOND OFFICERS TRAINING CAMP: *A-377*
U.S.O.: B-177, B-194
U.S.S. *Independence:* A-325
U.S.S. *Pensacola:* B-227
U.S.S. *Peosta:* A-381
Udall, Stewart L.: B-99
Ulen, Anna — see Engleman, Anna Ulen
ULRICH, DANIEL: *A-374*
Ulrich, Daniel D.: A-374
Uniform Commercial Code: B-275

Union, Franklin Co.: A-328
Union County: A-270, A-342, B-215
    Liberty: A-227
Union Inn Hotel (Indianapolis): A-98
Union Labor Party: B-155
Union of Christian Endavors: B-139
Union Railway Transfer and Stock Yard Company (Indianapolis): A-189
Union Reduction Company (Cincinnati): A-189
UNION REGULAR BAPTIST CHURCH (Hendricks Co.): *A-375*
Union State Central Committee: B-393
United Episcopal Charities: B-116
United Hias Service: A-204
United Jewish Appeal: A-204
United Mine Workers: B-110
United Nations: B-50, B-143, B-216
United Negro College Fund: A-268
United States and British High Command for the Adjustment of Canadian Questions: A-102
United States Army: A-137, A-140, A-174, A-286, A-315, A-381, B-79, B-243, B-261, B-316
    41st Colored Infantry: A-177
    109th Colored Infantry: A-177
    Judge Advocate's Office: B-337
United States Army Reserve: B-243
United States Bureau of Fisheries: B-121
United States Circuit Court: B-250
United States Commission for Indian Affairs: B-119, B-137
United States Conference of Mayors: A-193
United States Government
    Executive: A-164, B-47
        Atomic Energy Committee: B-61
        Attorney General: A-283, B-250
        Census Bureau: B-1
        Civil Service Commission: B-342
        Civilian Conservation Corps (CCC): B-219, B-270, B-316
        Commerce Department: B-20
        Customs Collectors: A-341
        Defense Department: B-50, B-61, B-80, B-89, B-301 — see also United States Army, United

United States Government—*Continued*
  Executive—*cont.*
    Defense Dept.—*cont.*
      States Navy, and United States Marine Corps
    Department of Agriculture: B-61
    Environmental Protection Agency: B-168
    F.D.I.C.: B-61
    Farm Credit Administration: B-239
    Federal Power Commission: B-61
    H.E.W.: B-50, B-399
    Horse Claims Division: B-47
    Internal Revenue Service: A-383
    Interior Department: B-219
      Office of Indian Affairs: B-59
    Interstate Oil Compact Commission: B-369
    Job Corps: B-301, B-399
    National Archives: B-234
    National Park Service: B-219, B-243
    Office of Price Administration: B-61
    Post Office Department: A-75, B-147, B-256, B-259
    President: A-44, A-145, A-272, B-138
    Reconstruction Finance Corporation: B-61
    Secretary of the Navy: B-348
    Secretary of War: A-147, A-187
    Surveyor General of the Lands North-West of the Ohio River: A-400
    Treasury Department: B-61, B-144, B-161
    State Department/Foreign Service: A-249, A-285, A-302, A-346, A-391, B-2, B-50, B-61, B-131, B-138, B-143, B-205, B-261, B-267, B-284, B-339, B-394
    U.S.-Canadian International Joint Commission: B-369
    Veterans Administration: B-301
    Vice-President: A-102, B-84, B-236
    War Department: B-160, B-243
  Judicial: B-16, B-50, B-196
    Court of Appeals: B-275
    Supreme Court: B-275, B-301
    U.S. Marshal: A-264
  Legislative (House): A-60, A-81, A-101, A-283, A-302, B-2, B-19, B-24, B-44, B-50, B-80, B-84, B-89, B-98, B-99, B-114, B-131, B-137, B-143, B-161, B-168, B-198, B-200, B-204, B-211, B-249, B-251, B-263, B-301, B-348, B-361, B-399
  Legislative (Senate): A-102, A-146, A-164, B-43, B-61, B-254, B-286, B-343, B-351, B-381, B-394
  Legislative (biographies): A-232
  Legislative (Committees)
    Appropriations Committee: B-168
    Banking and Currency Committee (House): B-61, B-80
    Claims Committee: B-286
    Committee on Expenditures (House): B-143
    Congressional reapportionment: B-363
    Energy and Resource Task Force: B-399
    House Un-American Activities Committee: A-172, B-301
    impeachment proceedings: B-98, B-399
    Internal Security Committee (House): B-399
    International Trade Task Force: B-399
    Interstate and Foreign Commerce Committee: B-24, B-61
    Judiciary Committee: B-89, B-98
    Pension Committee: B-286
    Public Works Committee (House): B-399
    Securities and Exchange Commission: B-61
United States Independent Telephone Association: B-20
United States Indian Agency: A-91
United States Marine Corps: A-224
United States Military Academy (West Point, N.Y.): A-141
United States Naval Academy (Annapolis, Md.): A-54, A-378

INDEX

United States Naval School: B-47
United States Navy: A-54, A-283,
    A-378, B-47, B-152, B-227,
    B-287, B-348, B-369
United States Potash Company: B-147
University Canterbury Association
    (Danville): B-116
University of California-Berkeley:
    A-110
University of Chicago: A-231, B-113
University of Illinois: A-357
University of Iowa: B-261
University of Michigan: A-140
University of Notre Dame: B-213
UNTHANK, SUSAN B. (Hunt): *B-356*
UPFOLD, GEORGE: *B-357*, A-111,
    A-302, B-116
Upton, Harriet Taylor: A-145, B-76
Urban Center (Episcopal): B-116
URBANA (OHIO) BANKING COM-
    PANY: *A-376*
Urquijo, Chevalier: A-32
Usher, John P.: A-5, A-91, A-229,
    B-119, B-286, B-348
USHER, NATHANIEL P.: *A-378*
Utah: A-59, A-142, B-110
Utah Commission: A-145

Valley Exchange Telephone Company
    (Monroe Co.): B-129
Valparaiso, Porter Co.: A-18, B-211,
    B-309, B-330
Valparaiso University: B-309
Van Buren, Martin: A-272, A-387
VAN DYKE, AUGUSTUS M.: *A-379*
Van Dyke, Henry: B-236
VAN HOOK, JAMES M.: *B-359*
Van Nostrand, Albert D.: A-365
Van Nuys, Frederick: A-285, B-142
Van Pelt, Amanda Slater: B-360
Van Pelt, Edna: A-380
VAN PELT, FRANCIS MARION:
    B-360
VAN PELT, MATHIAS C.: *A-380*
Van Rensselaer, Stephen: A-272
Van Scyoc, Bessie — see Shackelford,
    Bessie Van Scyoc
Van Scyoc, John W.: B-310
Vance, George: A-381
Vance, Harvey: A-381

Vance, Laddie: A-381
Vance, Lawrence M.: A-381
Vance, Samuel: A-381
VANCE, SAMUEL C.: *A-381*, A-147
VANDERBILT, JAMES CORNE-
    LIUS: *B-358*
Vandenberg, Arthur H.: B-147, B-381
Vanderburgh, Henry: A-286, A-302,
    B-212
Vanderburgh County: A-6, A-382
    Evansville: A-4, A-15, A-33, A-57,
        A-176, A-382, B-99, B-114,
        B-146, B-166, B-210, B-232,
        B-246, B-251, B-330, B-353,
        B-364, B-365, B-399
    Inglefield: A-198
    Saundersville: A-198
    Scott Township: A-33
VANDERBURGH COUNTY MIS-
    CELLANEOUS PAPERS,
    1815-1910: *A-382*
Vannest, Charles G.: A-176
Vassar College (N.Y.): A-367, B-281
Vawter, John: B-40, B-348
Vawter Park, Kosciusko Co.: B-122
VEATCH, JAMES C.: *A-383*, A-136,
    B-94, B-254
Venable, William H.: B-371
Venezuela: A-249, B-138
Vermillion County: A-228, A-229,
    A-318
    Clinton: A-228, B-240
    Eugene: A-332
    Newport: B-252
    Perryville: A-318
Vermont: A-267, B-165
    Andover Seminary: B-165
    Brandon: B-287
    Ludlow: A-111
    Peacham: A-216, A-266, A-267
    Windham County: B-313
Vernon, Jennings Co.: B-69
Versailles, Ripley Co: A-138, A-142,
    B-123, B-196
VESTAL, ALBERT H.: *B-361*, B-147
Veteran Company of the Indiana
    Legion (Brown Co.): A-58
Vevay, Switzerland Co.: A-102, A-120,
    A-215, A-237, A-266, A-392,
    B-93, B-106, B-111, B-312

Vickery Brothers (Evansville): A-382
Viereck, George S.: B-96
Vietnam War: B-2, B-50, B-168, B-211, B-301, B-399
  My Lai: B-399
  opposition to: A-166
  prisoners: B-399
  servicemen: A-338, B-100
View from the Statehouse: B-369
VIGO, JOSEPH MARIA FRANCESCO (Francis): *A-384*, A-57, A-223, A-286, A-302, A-369, A-385, B-212
Vigo County: A-6, A-228, B-234
  Camp Vigo (Civil War): A-168
  New Goshen: A-228, B-314
  Otter Creek: A-257
  Prairieton: A-128
  St. Mary-of-the-Woods: A-91, A-313, B-47, B-167
  Terre Haute: A-11, A-91, A-128, A-144, A-254, A-312, A-369, B-3, B-29, B-34, B-67, B-96, B-104, B-122, B-146, B-200, B-212, B-217, B-232, B-287, B-347, B-348, B-353
Vigus, Cyrus: B-286, B-395
Vilas, William F.: B-47
Villard, Oswald Garrison: B-342
Vincennes, Francois Bissot sieur de: A-286
Vincennes, Knox Co.: A-54, A-57, A-70, A-108, A-124, A-210, A-223, A-230, A-237, A-283, A-286, A-302, A-308, A-322, A-378, A-379, A-382, A-384, A-385, B-105, B-156, B-210, B-212, B-262, B-269, B-284, B-287, B-382
  Fort Knox: A-286
  French Settlement of: A-101, A-286, A-302, A-384
  militia: A-302
Vincennes Baseball Association: A-385
VINCENNES MISCELLANEOUS PAPERS, 1769-1908: *A-385*
Vincennes Road: A-125
Vincennes University: A-322
Vincent family: B-336

Vinton, Elizabeth — see Pierce, Elizabeth Vinton
Vinton family: B-281
Virgin Islands
  St. Croix: B-84
Virginia: A-90, A-101, A-334, A-336, B-249, B-252, B-270, B-285, B-323
  American Revolution: A-16, A-101
  Civil War: A-21, A-27, A-58, A-97, A-140, A-168, A-216, A-228, A-259, A-264, A-329, A-379, A-402, B-31, B-135, B-223, B-231, B-295
  religion: B-64
  World War II: B-270
  Alexandria: A-70, A-174
  Augusta County: B-39
  Camp Lee (World War II): B-270
  Chancellorsville (Civil War): A-58
  Culpepper County: B-348
  Fredericksburgh (Civil War): A-58
  Lexington: B-249
  Loudon County: A-336
  Lynchburg: A-111
  Richmond (Civil War): A-111
  Shenandoah County: B-22
  Union: A-336
  Washington County: A-16
Virginia (West) — See also West Virginia
  Wheeling: A-75
Virginia Avenue Building and Loan Association (Indianapolis): B-112
VONNEGUT, CLEMENS: *A-386*
Vonnegut, Eleanor Goodall: A-110
Voorhees, Daniel W.: A-57, A-81, A-101, A-173, A-215, A-232, A-272, B-104, B-105, B-286, B-335, B-348, B-393

W. G. and G. W. Ewing Company (Fort Wayne): B-119, B-286
W. W. Frybarger & Company (Connersville): A-115
Wabash, Wabash Co.: B-24
WABASH AND ERIE CANAL: *A-387*, A-91, A-229, A-407, B-1, B-104, B-119, B-263, B-286, B-348

Wabash College (Crawfordsville): A-18, A-56, A-216, A-271, A-284, A-336, A-381, A-401, B-137, B-146, B-147, B-165, B-236, B-275, B-286, B-345, B-351, B-388 — see also Crawfordsville, Montgomery County
Wabash County: A-181, A-342, B-184, B-356
  North Manchester: A-163, B-53
  Wabash: B-24
Wabash Railroad: B-23
Wabash River: A-125, B-200, B-301
Wade, Aletha Heaton: B-299
Wade, Harrison Heaton: A-388
Wade, Isaac Ferris: A-388, B-299
Wade, Lucy: A-388
Wade, Margaret: A-388
WADE, WILLIAM H.: *B-362*
WADE FAMILY PAPERS: *A-388*
Wadsworth, Frank L. O.: B-345
Wadsworth, James W.: B-342
WAGGAMAN, JOHN STANLEY: *B-363*
Wagner, Farrel: A-327
Wahl, Donald: B-364
WAHL, HENRY E.: *B-364*
WAINWRIGHT, WILLIAM A: *A-389*
Walam Olum: A-393
Walker, Francis: B-365
Walker, John George: A-391
WALKER, JOHN MANN: *B-365*
WALKER, MADAM C.J.: *A-390*
Walker, Mary Graham: B-365
Walker, Nora Severinghaus: B-365
Walker, Robert J.: A-282, B-47
Walker, Ryan: A-312
Walker Beauty Schools: A-390
Walker Casino (Indianapolis): A-390
Walker Company Benevolent Association: A-390
Walker Drug Company (Indianapolis): A-390
Walker Manufacturing Company: A-390
Walker Realty Company (Indianapolis): A-390
Walker Theater (Indianapolis): A-390
Wallace, David: A-91, A-272, A-391, B-26, B-137, B-252, B-351

Wallace, George: B-369
Wallace, Henry Lane: A-391
WALLACE, LEW: *A-391, B-366*, A-15, A-95, A-102, A-111, A-134, A-164, A-230, A-266, A-272, A-322, A-383, B-43, B-84, B-94, B-254, B-259, B-345
Wallace, Susan Elston: A-210, A-229, A-391
Wallace, Tom: B-219
Wallace, Zerelda: B-76
Walling, William English: B-342
Walsh, Hugh S.: B-119
Walter, Bruno: A-327
Walter Reed Hospital: B-145
Wampler family: B-364
Wanamaker, John: A-145
War of 1812: A-101, A-147, A-272, B-84, B-86, B-212, B-258, B-290, B-351
  Battle of the Thames: A-272
  Hull's surrender of Detroit: A-272
  veterans: A-230, A-370, B-234
Ward, Julia — see Howe, Julia Ward
Warner, Charles Dudley: B-111
Warren, Eliza Bethell: A-33
Warren, Fred D.: A-312
Warren, Louis: A-176
Warren, William, Sr.: A-33
Warren, William, Jr.: A-33
Warren-Bethell family
  — see BETHELL-WARREN FAMILY
Warren County: A-224, B-22, B-380
  Little Pigeon Creek: B-71
  State Line City: B-1
  Williamsport: A-41, B-1, B-380
Warren Township, Marion Co: B-149, B-163
Warrick County: A-176, A-397
  Little Mt. Zion Church: B-71
  Lynnville: A-359
  Newburgh: A-4, A-33, B-365
Warsaw, Kosciusko Co.: B-162
Washburne, Elihu B.: A-69, A-260, B-281
Washington (state): B-313
Washington, D.C.: A-12, A-44, A-52, A-69, A-81, A-83, A-90, A-150,

Washington, D.C. — *Continued*
   A-161, A-253, A-302, A-390,
   A-391, A-407, B-81, B-118,
   B-131, B-138, B-145, B-165,
   B-205, B-212, B-223, B-225,
   B-243, B-287, B-361, B-372,
   B-384, B-394
Washington, Booker T.: B-147, B-345
Washington, Bushrod: A-272
Washington, Daviess Co.: B-146,
   B-185, B-330
Washington, George: A-272, A-286
Washington County: A-130, A-261,
   A-342, A-397, B-252
  Claysville: A-213
  Kossuth: A-85
  Livonia: B-329
  Martinsburg: A-34
  Salem: A-52, A-117, A-273, A-277,
    B-150, B-280
Washington Township, Putnam Co.:
   B-214
Watergate scandal: B-168, B-211
Waterloo, Fayette Co.: A-118
Waters, Isaac: B-367
WATERS, JOHN T.: *B-367*
Watson, James E.: A-60, A-68, A-102,
   A-167, A-176, A-249, A-336,
   A-352, B-76, B-114, B-124,
   B-147, B-218, B-259, B-345,
   B-381
Watson, Thomas: B-147
Watson, William: B-47
Watson, Macy, and Goodrich
   (Winchester): A-62
Watson and Cheney — see Cheney and
   Watson
Watterson, Henry: A-101, A-341, A-358
Watts, John: A-143
Watts, Joseph: A-143
Waveland, Montgomery Co.: A-88,
   B-15
Waycross Retreat Center: B-116
Wayne, Anthony: A-8, A-272, A-286,
   A-287, A-303, A-384
Wayne County: A-6, A-14, A-23, A-28,
   A-130, A-132, A-342, A-397,
   B-368
  Cambridge City: A-264

Centerville: A-9, A-220, A-263,
   A-397, B-205, B-287, B-324
Dalton: B-28
Dover: A-342
Dublin: A-92
Economy: A-259, B-82
Fountain City: A-226
Hagerstown: A-28, A-132, A-222,
   A-374, B-336
New Garden: A-342, B-64
Newport (Fountain City): A-130
Richmond: A-14, A-129, A-146,
   A-164, A-221, A-226, A-237,
   A-239, A-269, A-336, A-349,
   A-357, A-388, A-396, B-28,
   B-98, B-124, B-139, B-230,
   B-356, B-368
White Water: A-342
Williamsburg: B-68
WAYNE COUNTY MEDICAL
   SOCIETY: *B-368*
Weatherwax, Paul: B-95
WEAVER, JACOB: *A-392*
Webster, Daniel: A-272, A-387
Weddell, Alexander W.: A-285
Weed, Thurlow: A-272
Weeks, John W.: B-259
WEER, PAUL: *A-393*
Wehner, Marion: A-111
Wehr, Paul: A-178
Weik, Jesse: A-176, B-105
Weinstein, Mae Hunter: A-128
Weinstein, Thirza Belle: A-128
Weinstein family: A-128
Welfare and Correction:
  -1815: B-132
  1816-1849: A-123, A-125, B-132,
    B-173, B-263
  1850-1879: A-15, A-93, A-103,
    A-123, A-188, A-196, A-300,
    B-173, B-263
  1880-1909: A-93, A-103, A-123,
    A-128, A-188, A-196, A-204,
    A-279, A-300, B-173, B-176,
    B-241
  1910-1945: A-103, A-105, A-123,
    A-128, A-188, A-196, A-204,
    A-268, A-279, A-300, B-56,
    B-97, B-173, B-176, B-177,
    B-186, B-188, B-200, B-203,

Welfare and Correction—*Continued*
  1910–1945—*cont.*
    B-216, B-222, B-226, B-237,
    B-241, B-246, B-296, B-302,
    B-315, B-374
  1946-: A-64, A-103, A-105, A-204,
    A-268, A-279, A-300, B-101,
    B-173, B-176, B-177, B-186,
    B-188, B-203, B-216, B-226,
    B-237, B-241, B-246, B-296,
    B-301
Welles, Gideon: A-272, A-346
Wells, Harriet Eitel — see Johnson, Harriet Eitel
Wells, Herman B: A-112, B-20, B-333
Wells, William: A-8, A-147, A-286, A-381, A-384
Wells County: A-143, A-200
  Bluffton: B-95
WELSH, MATTHEW E.: *B-369*, A-358, B-203, B-256
Wendell Willkie Notification Committee: B-361
Wentworth, John: A-272
WESLER, CHARLES H.: *B-370*
West, George P.: B-110
West, Nathaniel: B-137
West, Roberta — see NICHOLSON, ROBERTA WEST
West, Roy: A-352
West, William H.: A-341
West family: B-157
West Indies: B-339
West Middleton, Howard Co.: A-49
West Union, Morgan Co.: A-342
West Virginia: B-110, B-248 — See also Virginia (West)
  Harrison County: B-323
  Parkersburg: B-22
  Sisterville: B-92
Westerfield, Samuel Z., Jr.: B-6
Western Associated Press: A-337, A-341
WESTERN ASSOCIATION OF WRITERS: *B-371*, B-85, B-276
Western Female Seminary (Oxford, Ohio): A-123
Western Methodist Book Concern (Cincinnati): A-400
Western Sun (Vincennes): A-57

Western Yearly Meeting of Friends: A-342
Westfield, Hamilton Co.: A-21, A-342, A-363
Westfield Academy (Mass.): B-319
Westinghouse Corporation: B-345
Westtown Boarding School (Chester Co., Pa.): A-277
WETHERILL, CHARLES MAYER: *B-372*
Wetherill, William: B-372
Wharton, William: B-373
WHARTON, WILLIAM L.: *B-373*
Wheatland, Knox Co.: B-54
Wheeler, Burton K.: A-258
Wheeler, Everett: B-342
Wheeler, H. Q.: A-176
Whig Party: A-8, A-25, A-71, A-91,
  A-111, A-136, A-147, A-219,
  A-237, A-270, A-302, A-361,
  A-369, A-408, B-84, B-105,
  B-114, B-131, B-137, B-205,
  B-252, B-263, B-268, B-276,
  B-285, B-286, B-348, B-395
Whistler, John: A-187, B-167
Whitcomb, Franklin Co.: A-356
Whitcomb, James: A-101, A-111,
  A-264, A-266, A-272, B-1, B-37,
  B-47, B-119, B-212, B-240,
  B-328, B-348, B-351
Whitcomb, Martha — see Matthews, Martha Whitcomb
White, Albert S.: A-8, A-81, A-91,
  A-267, A-272, A-311, A-391,
  A-402, B-26, B-119, B-137,
  B-212, B-286, B-348, B-351
White, Bertha Hale: B-96
White, Charles: B-137, B-165
White, Horace: B-342
White, Isaac: A-101, B-119
White, John P.: B-110
White, Martha — see TALBERT, MARTHA WHITE
White, Thomas J.: B-110
WHITE, THOMAS P.: *B-374*
White, Valette Miller — see MILLER, VALETTE
White, William Allen: A-358
White, Wright and Boleman Collection Agency (Indianapolis): B-310

White County: A-334, B-323
  Brookston: A-215
  Monticello: B-360
White River: B-200
White River, Randolph Co.: A-342
White Water, Wayne Co.: A-342
White Water Valley Canal Company: A-158
White Water Valley National Farm Loan Association: B-239
Whitehurst, Elsie — see Lightburn, Elsie Whitehurst
White's Indiana Manual Labor Institute (Wabash Co.): B-184, B-356
Whitewater Canal: A-123, A-157, A-394, B-263, B-370
WHITEWATER CANAL ASSOCIATION: *A-394*
Whitewater Female College (Centerville): A-397
Whitley County
  Columbia City: B-74, B-130, B-236
WHITMER, JACOB: *B-375*
Whitthorne, Washington C.: B-348
Whittlesey, Elisha: B-105
Wick, William W.: A-81, A-101, A-111, B-205, B-212, B-348, B-351
Wickard, Claude R.: B-256
Wicker, Joel H.: B-167
Wickliffe, Charles A.: A-147
Widney, Samuel: A-400
Widows and Orphans Friend Society of Indianapolis: A-196
WILDER, JOHN THOMAS: *B-376*, A-373, B-360
WILDMAN, JAMES A.: *A-395*
Wiley, Caroline — see O'Hair, Caroline Wiley
Wiley, James: A-396, B-377
WILEY, JAMES JEROME: *A-396*, B-377
WILEY FAMILY: *B-377*
WILKINSON, ASBURY: *A-397*
Wilkinson, James: A-8, A-101, A-147, A-272, A-286, A-287, A-303, A-381
Willard, Ashbel P.: A-101, A-215, A-272
Willard, Francis E.: B-111
Willard, William: A-177

William H. Clarke Company (Indianapolis): A-65
Williams, Charles R.: A-102, A-164, B-342
WILLIAMS, CHARLES T.: *B-378*
Williams, E. T.: A-400
Williams, Edwin: A-402
Williams, Ellen: A-398
Williams, Gertrude — see Williamson, Gertrude Williams
WILLIAMS, HERBERT: *A-398*
Williams, James D.: A-57, A-272, B-212
Williams, Jesse L.: B-137
Williams, John Sharp: B-114
Williams, Josiah C.: A-402
WILLIAMS, PETER W.: *A-399*
WILLIAMS, SAMUEL: *A-400*
WILLIAMS, SAMUEL PORTER: *A-401*
Williams, Thomas Hill: A-381
WILLIAMS, WORTHINGTON B.: *A-402*
Williams College (Adams Mass.): A-302
WILLIAMS CREEK BAPTIST CHURCH (Fayette Co.): *B-379*
Williams family (Franklin Co.): B-336
Williams family (Putnam Co.): A-402
Williamsburg, Wayne Co.: B-68
Williamson, Edwin: A-402
Williamson, Gertrude Williams: A-402
Williamsport, Warren Co.: A-41, B-1, B-380
WILLIAMSPORT DEBATING SOCIETY: *B-380*
Williamsport McClure Workingmen's Institute (Ind.): B-380
Willis, Frank B.: B-259
WILLIS, RAYMOND E.: *B-381*, B-147
Willkie, Wendell: A-172, B-147, B-350
  — See also Wendell Willkie Notification Committee
WILLOUGHBY, AURELIUS: *B-382*
Wilson, Earl: B-24, B-369
Wilson, Edith Bolling: B-236, B-343
Wilson, Henry K.: A-81
Wilson, Henry Lane: A-391, B-124, B-147
Wilson, James: A-229, A-230
Wilson, Miriam — see GREEN, MIRIAM WILSON

Wilson, Nathaniel: A-75
Wilson, Robert E.: B-24
Wilson, Thomas H.: B-384
WILSON, WILLIAM (d. 1920): *B-383*
WILSON, WILLIAM T. (1854-1943): *B-384*, B-286
Wilson, Woodrow: A-272, B-76, B-236, B-335
Wilson family: B-336
Winamac, Pulaski Co.: B-18
Winchester, James A.: A-147, A-272
WINCHESTER, JOHN S.: *B-385*
Winchester, Randolph Co.: A-62, A-126, B-68
Windom, William: A-302, B-119, B-138
Wines, Elizabeth: A-407
Wines, Marshall S.: A-407
Wines, Marshall W.: A-407
Wingate, Montgomery Co.: B-91
Winslow and Perkins (New York): A-267
Winter, George: A-237, B-212
WINTIN, GENDRON M.: *B-386*
Wirz, Henry: A-391
Wisconsin: B-292
  Indians: A-83, A-369, B-119
  Fond du Lac: B-209
  Janesville: B-169
  La Crosse: A-100
  Lake Winnebago: A-83
  Milwaukee: A-197
  Mineral Point: B-27
  Racine: A-333
  Waterville: A-242
  Waukesha: B-63
"Wisconsin" (steamboat): B-93
Wise, Henry A.: B-348
Wishard, Albert W.: B-114
Witt, Peter: B-96
WOLCOTT, ANSON: *B-387*, A-15
Wolcottville, Noble Co.: B-71
WOLFF, HERMAN CLARK: *B-388*
Wolverton, Charles A.: B-24
Wolves against the moon: B-4
Woman's Department Club of Indianapolis: A-288, B-188
Woman's Franchise League: B-76
WOMAN'S FRANCHISE LEAGUE OF INDIANA: *A-403*, B-216

WOMAN'S IMPROVEMENT CLUB (Indianapolis): *A-404*
WOMAN'S PRESS CLUB OF INDIANA: *A-405*
Woman's Relief Corps (G.A.R.): A-126, B-389
WOMAN'S RELIEF CORPS. INDIANA DEPARTMENT. GEORGE H. THOMAS POST #20: *B-389*
Women
  charitable work: A-84, A-279
  clubs: A-128, A-259, A-288, A-404, A-405, A-406, B-17, B-46, B-65, B-76, B-78, B-176, B-188, B-190, B-191, B-192, B-216, B-281, B-389
  professions
    in art: B-14, B-333
    in business: A-390, B-14, B-188
    in education: A-129, A-143, A-298, A-356, A-357, B-220, B-285, B-332, B-393
    in history: A-127
    in journalism: A-405, A-406
    in literature: A-134, A-150, A-210, A-233, A-391, B-4, B-44, B-76, B-78, B-145
    in medicine: A-22, A-163, A-186, A-194, A-216, B-145, B-166, B-281
    in military service: A-216, B-81, B-281
    in newspapers: A-127, A-288
    in politics: A-167, A-288, B-17, B-76, B-96, B-200, B-203, B-216
  religion: A-31, A-128, A-162, A-204, B-64
  rights and suffrage: A-22, A-144, A-211, A-288, A-357, A-403, A-406, B-19, B-76, B-124, B-147, B-205, B-216, B-273, B-281
Women Friends of Western Yearly Meeting: A-31
WOMEN IN COMMUNICATIONS, INC., INDIANAPOLIS CHAPTER: *A-406*

Women's Christian Temperance Union:
    A-163, A-288
Women's Hope Hospital Association
    (Fort Wayne): B-241
Women's Missionary Society: A-162
Wong Kai Kah: B-342
Wood, Leonard: A-260
Wood, Thomas: B-94
Wood, Will R.: B-339
Woodbridge, William: B-351
Woodburn, James A.: B-76, B-85, B-342
Woodbury, Levi: A-267, A-272, A-387
Woodbury, R. W.: B-84
WOODFILL, JAMES M.: *B-390*
Woodland (Mitchell), Lawrence Co.:
    B-329
Woodruff Place (Indianapolis): A-351,
    B-79
Woods, William A.: A-145
WOODWARD, WILLIAM: *B-391*
Wool, John E.: A-272
Woolf, Samuel J.: A-364
Woollen, Evans: A-52, B-219, B-343
Woollen, William Wesley: A-101, B-1,
    B-205, B-257, B-345
Woollen's Garden of Birds and Botany
    (Indianapolis): B-257
Woostertown, Scott Co.: A-323
Wooton, Daniel P.: A-129
WORDEN, CHARLES J.: *A-407*
WORKMAN, HAZEL: *B-392*
World Court: B-124
World War I: A-46, A-211, B-268,
    B-360
  army camps: A-114, A-167, B-14,
    B-287, B-337
  England: B-360
  France: A-12, A-49, A-114, B-287,
    B-332, B-337, B-360
  Germany: A-114
  home defense: B-147
  nurses: B-281
  opposition to: B-96
  politics: B-19, B-110, B-124
  relief and fund raising: A-12, A-49
  servicemen: A-46, A-114, A-123,
    A-167, B-20, B-63, B-99, B-102,
    B-129, B-134, B-145, B-157,
    B-243, B-270, B-275, B-285,
    B-287, B-330, B-332, B-337,
    B-361
  veterans: A-377, B-350
World War II: A-365, B-45, B-145,
    B-147, B-194
  5th Marine Division: B-213
  14th Air Force: B-79
  21st Photo Squadron: B-79
  England: A-127
  Italy: A-362, B-270
  medical corps: B-270
  North Africa: A-362, B-270
  Philippines: B-268
  relief work: A-84
  servicemen: A-127, A-288, A-362,
    B-79, B-99, B-102, B-110,
    B-166, B-213, B-270, B-285,
    B-296, B-364
  Sicily: A-362
  South Pacific: B-166, B-213, B-364
  women in service: B-81
Worth, Daniel: A-111, A-237, B-137
Worthington, Greene Co.: A-17
Worthington, Thomas: A-147, A-237,
    A-286, A-341
Wright, Albert J.: B-394
WRIGHT, ANNA W.: *B-393*
Wright, Frances: A-282, B-273
Wright, Jacob: B-393
Wright, John C.: B-394
WRIGHT, JOSEPH ALBERT: *B-394*,
    A-5, A-15, A-81, A-111, A-136,
    A-272, A-302, B-114, B-137,
    B-254, B-348
Wright, White, and Boleman Collection
    Agency — see White, Wright
    and Boleman Collection Agency
WRIGHT, WILLIAMSON: *A-408*,
    B-395
WYATT, ROBERT H.: *B-396*
Wylie, Andrew: A-302, A-381, B-146
Wyllys, John P.: A-8
Wyoming: A-59, A-311, B-356

Yale University: A-107, A-210, B-44
Yandes, Anne — see Hampson, Anne
    Yandes
YANDES, DANIEL: *B-397*
Yandes, Lafayette: B-397

Yandes, Margaret — see HOLLIDAY, MARGARET YANDES
Yandes, Simon: A-111, B-212, B-284, B-286
Yates, Richard: B-43, B-94
Yeoman, Carroll Co.: B-360
YMCA: A-12, A-268, B-177, B-267, B-360
Young, Bennett H.: A-52, B-114
Young, Merl: A-211
YOUNG, W. L.: *A-409*
Young Men's Literary Association (Williamsport): B-380

Yugoslavia: B-381

Zangwill, Israel: A-210
Zeisberger, David: A-286
ZIG ZAG CYCLE CLUB (Indianapolis): *B-398*
ZION, ROGER: *B-399*
Zionism: A-204
Zionsville, Boone Co.: A-368
Zulauf, Agnes Hutchings: A-174
ZULAUF, JOHN: *A-410*